Remapping Reality

97

Internationale Forschungen zur
Allgemeinen und
Vergleichenden Literaturwissenschaft

Remapping Reality
Chaos and Creativity in Science and Literature

(Goethe - Nietzsche - Grass)

John A. McCarthy

Rodopi

Amsterdam - New York, NY 2006

Le papier sur lequel le présent ouvrage est imprimé remplit les prescriptions de "ISO 9706:1994, Information et documentation - Papier pour documents - Prescriptions pour la permanence".

The paper on which this book is printed meets the requirements of " ISO 9706:1994, Information and documentation - Paper for documents - Requirements for permanence".

Die Reihe „Internationale Forschungen zur Allgemeinen und Vergleichenden Literaturwissenschaft" wird ab dem Jahr 2005 gemeinsam von Editions Rodopi, Amsterdam – New York und dem Weidler Buchverlag, Berlin herausgegeben. Die Veröffentlichungen in deutscher Sprache erscheinen im Weidler Buchverlag, alle anderen bei Editions Rodopi.

From 2005 onward, the series „Internationale Forschungen zur Allgemeinen und Vergleichenden Literaturwissenschaft" will appear as a joint publication by Editions Rodopi, Amsterdam – New York and Weidler Buchverlag, Berlin. The German editions will be published by Weidler Buchverlag, all other publications by Editions Rodopi.

ISBN: 90-420-1818-6

Printed in The Netherlands

CIP Data Page

Permission to reproduce copyrighted material is gratefully acknowledged. Portions of the Introduction were previously published as "Chaos: Motif, Theme, or Theory" in *Thematics Reconsidered. Essays in Honor of Horst S. Daemmrich*, ed. Frank Trommler (New York and Amsterdam: Rodopi, 1995), 133–43. Parts of chapter 2 are adapted from "Strategien der Schöpfung: Paradigmenwechsel in Natur und Kunst" in *Paragrana* 4.2 (1995): 261–79. Sections of chapter 5 are drawn from "'A Chain of Utmost Potency': On the Agon and the Creative Impulse" in *Agonistics: Arenas of Creative Contest*, ed. Janet Lungstrum and Elizabeth Sauer (Albany, NY: State University of New York Press, 1997), 199–225.

The artwork for the cover, "Cracking the Code" (2003),
was created specifically for this project
by Kristin Aileen McCarthy (1981-),
a Ph.D. candidate in behavioral neuroscience at the
Oregon Health Sciences University.

"Cracking the Code"

This image draws upon the mythical symbolism of the egg as an embryonic source of life in the broadest sense and of the serpent as both threat and stimulus. As symbol of genetic coding and promise of future development, the egg is embraced by the serpent as harbinger of change – an intrusion both feared and welcome. The promise of future development encapsulated in the egg is augmented by the ambiguous meaning of the serpent both as Biblical icon of forbidden knowledge and as malleable phallic symbol. Its ambiguity as fear-inspiring intruder and, simultaneously, as catalyst for change is mirrored in its encircling of the embryonic promise. If the serpent is viewed as voluntary movement, then the egg – which also plays upon the medulla oblongata, the egg-shaped enlargement at the lower center of the human brain – is representative of involuntary vial processes such as breathing and digestion (the medulla oblongata is involved in involuntary movement). Is the serpent protecting or thwarting that promise of change, that encoded movement? Do all principles of reality ultimately derive from the unity of opposites – convergence and divergence, inner and outer spaces, matter (egg) and mind (serpent = knowledge)? The agonistic, ambivalent quality of the essential tensions between serpent and egg, between environment and seed of life lies at the heart of *Remapping Reality*.

The most powerful of human faculties is the *power of thinking*.

It is the greatest remedy of the mind if a few thoughts can be found from which infinite others arise in order, just as from the assumption of a few numbers, from one to ten, all the other numbers can be derived in order.

Gottfried Wilhelm Leibniz, "Of an Organum or Ars Magna of Thinking" (c. 1679)

CONTENTS

List of Illustrations

Preface

This book derives from an enduring interest in the Age of the Enlightenment. I had long noted the frequent boundary crossings between humanistic and scientific concerns in the Enlightenment project and have previously sought to explore them in an expanded approach to the phenomenon with a special emphasis on literary production and consumption. I offer now an innovative approach not discernible in previous studies on the Enlightenment and its legacies. Research of late gravitates to such prescient developments as race and gender construction, physical anthropology, the disciplining of knowledge, the concept of sociability, the rise of historicism, the shape of the public sphere, Enlightenment science, and nascent consumerism. Some years ago, while exploring the open and questioning stance of eighteenth-century essayistic literature, I was struck by the compresence of instrumental reason and philosophical deconstruction that seemingly lies at the very heart of the Enlightenment proposition. Whereas instrumental reason is today associated with the precise and systemic thinking typical of technology and the natural sciences, deconstruction is aligned with an open-ended, antisystemic mode of humanistic questioning. Both attitudes share the skepticism of the inquiring mind, albeit to differing degrees. One thrust leads to the establishment of systems, whereas the other seems intent upon deconstructing ordered paradigms. Could there, I wondered, be a hidden connection between the linearity of instrumental reason and scientific inquiry, on the one hand, and the nonlinearity of radical skepticism, now associated with postmodernism, on the other? Both the scientific and the philosophic attitudes were (and are) motivated by the search for truth. Both represent an effort to get to the bottom of things, be it via foundationalism or hermeneutic universalism. Both are interested in truth and both suggest reasons why we are so interested in it.

A period of retooling was necessary to gain better insight into the modes of scientific inquiry. I am indebted to a number of organizations for their generous support of this project. A senior Fulbright research fellowship to Munich, Germany, enabled me to examine the nexus of chaos, Nietzsche, and creativity in the Bavarian State Library. Special thanks go to Dr. Merta and his cordial, helpful staff, who kept me supplied with materials and ample workspace. Interactions with members of the chaos research group at the Technical University there and an advanced seminar at the University of Munich helped to clarify the direction of this study. A sabbatical leave from Vanderbilt University made it possible for me to write some of the theoretical sections of this study; a grant from the University Research Council at Vanderbilt University allowed me to visit archives and to meet with colleagues in refining my arguments. A year as the Rebecca Webb Wilson Fellow and as co-director of an interdisciplinary faculty seminar on "Science and Culture" at the Robert Penn Warren Center for the Humanities of Vanderbilt University honed the focus and refined the argument even further. In dialogue with a geneticist, laser physicist, critical theorist, mathematician, psychologist, historian of science, historian of ecology, and two literary scholars, I delved more deeply into chaos and complexity theory, reflections on the limits and the unity of knowledge, the nature of creativity, and the role of the imagination in mapping reality. It was there, after experiencing how disciplines shape the way we see things, that I learned how important it is to develop a common language of discourse. These opportunities allowed me to map out new pathways in talking about the Enlightenment and its legacies.

I also wish to acknowledge contributions over the years by students at Penn, Vanderbilt, and Rutgers, who engaged in lively discussions in courses on Goethe, Nietzsche, Grass, chaos, and complexity. Four groups deserve special mention because of their extraordinary devotion to the theoretical premises proposed in the following pages. The students in comparative literature courses on "Beyond Good and Evil" at Vanderbilt University and the University of Munich helped me focus on the interconnections among chaos theory, Nietzsche's radical ethics, and the nature of evil in literature. Students in the Master of Liberal Arts Program at Vanderbilt eagerly delved with me into complexity and catastrophe theory in a course on creativity and metaphor in science and literature. Students in another course on complexity theory and postmodernism were instrumental in revealing similarities among science, philosophy, and literature. The stimulating discussions experienced in these settings, the insightful contributions, and especially the tenacious resistance of budding philosophers, mathematicians, and physicists to the "fuzzy logic" from which this project was born (and which still bears its marks) caused me to rethink certain premises. To all, I am deeply grateful.

Many individuals read and responded to various parts of the manuscript during its long genesis. In particular, I would like to thank John Briggs, Keith N. Clayton, David Ernst, Karl J. Fink, William Franke, Steffi Habermeier, Richard Haglund, Kate Hayles, John Lachs, Felicitas Munzel, Arcady Plotnitzky, Jaideep Prabhu, Julie Reahard, Herbert Rowland, Frank Trommler, and Arlene Tuchman for their interest and comments. Without Shawn Kendrick, my copy editor, many imperfections would have slipped through. To her a hearty thanks! She is a consummate professional with an eagle's eye for detail. For the outcome, however, I bear full responsibility. Ernst Grabovszki solved many a formatting difficulty, for which I am deeply grateful. Last, but not least, I wish to acknowledge Richard McCarty, Dean of the College of Arts and Science at Vanderbilt University, for his generous assistance with publication costs. I dedicate this book to my right hand, Mecki, and my daughters, Monika and Kristin, who put up with my shifting moods throughout its genesis. They let me do my work and make doing my work worthwhile. (My son, Brian, lucky lad, was spared everything.)

Brentwood TN, December, 2004

Introduction: Getting to the Bottom of Things

> Der Gründliche
> Ein Forscher ich? Oh spart diess Wort –
> Ich bin nur *schwer* – so manche Pfund!
> Ich falle, falle immerfort,
> Und endlich auf den Grund.
>
> – Nietzsche, *Die fröhliche Wissenschaft*, "Scherz, Lust und Rache," #44

1. Remapping the Terrain

From the beginning of time, human beings have engaged in map making as an aid in getting from one place to another. Maps help us to know where we have been and where we are going. Maps are even used to explain *why* we are where we are. Over time, mapping reality became a highly sophisticated endeavor, with maps becoming ever more minutely detailed and nonlinear. Today, global positioning systems (GPSs) can establish one's location with astonishing accuracy. On the extraterrestrial level, the Sloan Digital Sky Survey is charting distant galaxies with previously unimaginable clarity. Obviously, the more recent refinement in map making is directly related to increased information resulting from the extension of our senses since the advent of the original telescopes and microscopes. Maps also serve particular purposes. There are road maps, topographical maps, charts of distant novae, maps of the jet stream, sequences of DNA, guides to museums, outlines of metaphysical thought, etc. Because of changing information, maps are constantly being redrawn and new ones emerge. While some older cartographs provide too little detail, others prove to be too project specific and thus of little general use. This book is about important paradigm changes since the Enlightenment that have had and continue to have an impact upon our conceptions of reality and of our place in it, changes that affect how we see ourselves.

Central to the expansion of our knowledge about the world and the maps we make of it are factors such as our ethical and philosophical assumptions, the physical evidence produced by sense-extending instruments (e.g., the Hubble Space Telescope), and the creative power of the imagination itself. An essential ingredient in charting both the physical and metaphysical universe is the *agonistic relationship* between analytical reason and the desire for a totalizing vision of things. The former, so essential to map making, entails precise mathematical calculations, while the latter, crucial to the creative arts and humanities, employs a fuzzy logic, the kind we associate with Faust's pairing of magic and critical inquiry and with Nietzsche's exhortation to go beyond good and evil. "The map of the material world," biologist Edward O. Wilson suggests, "including human mental activity, can be thought [of as] a sprinkling of charted terrain separated by blank expanses that are of unknown extent yet [are] accessible to coherent interdisciplinary research."[1] In the following, both an appreciation of scientific rigor and border-crossing interdisciplinarity function as guides in an ambitious attempt to fill in some of the blank spaces in our map of reality. Unmistakable in it all is a wonderment for the autonomous complexity of nature itself that elicits an ethos of reverence for being, in Heidegger's sense of *Da-sein.* It is, moreover, in keeping with the European Enlightenment – the wellspring of this study – as an attitude of awe and curiosity, as if the acquisition of some knowledge merely underscores what has yet to be learned and how it is interconnected.

Thus, on the one hand this project is factual, on the other, speculative. Philosophical and ethical values play out within the fields of contest framed by science and literature. At the center of rumination is the creative act in both nature and the arts. The chief hypothesis is the belief that science and the arts are interrelated via deep structures. As a synthetic process, interpretation is viewed as conjoining history, biography, personal confession, and the facts of science. In other words, scientific reductionism and artistic holism go hand in glove, as strange as that might sound. The result is a reinvigorated understanding of the legacies of the Enlightenment and, in particular, of the creative genius as part and parcel of the naturally creative universe. At the heart of this undertaking is a concept of philosophy that pushes the envelope of inquiry to the extreme, one that begins to be genuine philosophy only when the inquirer insists upon an independent and thorough thinking through of the questions posed. It is a radical kind of thinking because its ultimate focus is on the root of things in the world of our experience. It is "prinzipielles Denken," as Werner Schneiders formulates the process in his assessment of how much philosophy humankind needs.[2] This approach drives to the fundamental issues and seeks a set of more or less universal principles by looking in different directions.

The aphorism from Nietzsche's *Die fröhliche Wissenschaft* (The Gay Science) cited at the masthead and entitled "Der Gründliche" (The Well-Grounded One) draws attention to this essential activity of knowledge extension through reductionism and expansion: "Me a researcher? Oh, please spare me this sound. / I am only *heavy* – by many a pound! / I am falling downward bound, / until I get to the ground!"[3] Just as a

1 Edward O. Wilson, *Consilience: The Unity of Knowledge* (New York: Alfred A. Knopf, 1998), 267.

2 Werner Schneiders, *Wieviel Philosophie braucht der Mensch? Eine Minimalphilosophie* (Munich: C. H. Beck, 2000), 35–39.

3 The German is cited according to Friedrich Nietzsche, *Sämtliche Werke: Kritische Studienausgabe*, ed. by Giorgio Colli and Mazzino Montinari, 15 vols., 2nd ed. (Munich and Berlin: Deutscher Taschenbuch Verlag & de Gruyter, 1988), hereafter cited as *KSA*. The newest English translation is

physical body is drawn to its basin of attraction by gravity, so is the seeking mind lured ever further into the recesses of the undiscovered, until, ultimately, it reaches the bottom; that is, until it uncovers the final cause or perhaps is forced to concede that the "bottom" keeps receding, and only approximations are possible. The heaviness of an object, as we know from science, can be measured in terms of chemical or atomic composition as well as simple corporeal weight: the higher the number of elements or molecules in an object, the more complex its inner dynamic, the more concentrated its energy, and the greater the attraction exerted. All that makes it even more difficult to get to the bottom of things, whether we are engaged in the search for the inner workings of quarks, or the first second of the universe, or in explaining the artistic merit of Goethe's *Faust*. The existence of the top quark was first felt indirectly through the appearance of such "heavy" (i.e., complex) phenomena as the hadron; the first second of the universe is approached indirectly through its cosmic afterglow and the wrinkles in time; and the inherent indeterminacy of the literary work permits only indirect access to its essential meaning. The reader's (or observer's) growing awareness of the great complexity of the phenomenon increases his or her burden of choice. In both the sciences and the arts, "all good things approach their goal crookedly," as Nietzsche avers in *Also Sprach Zarathustra* (Thus Spoke Zarathustra, 1883–85).[4] Complexity adds to this "heaviness" even as it stimulates optimal brain activity. Moreover, without theory we would not know what to do with the details. Theory is thus a necessary part of map making, for it points the way.

The phrase, "auf den Grund fallen" is pleasingly multivalent. While its literal meaning is "to fall to the ground," metaphorically it conveys the sense of getting to the bottom of things or of arriving at the final cause. "Grund" also signifies ground (as in earth). Thus, "auf den Grund fallen" indirectly recalls Adam and Eve's fall from grace. Seeking to know the final cause by becoming like God, Adam and Eve came to recognize the difference between good and evil. Their expulsion from Eden was tantamount to living in sin, to being subject to exertion, to the force of gravity, and to being earth bound. Adam's connection to the earth is explicit in his very name, for *adam,* Hebrew for "man," is etymologically related to *adamah*, Hebrew for "ground." Thus, Adam is thrust back upon himself and is forced to recognize the very basis of his existence from which he is to draw his sustenance and meaning. Eve's name complements Adam's, for it is derived from the Hebrew verb signifying "to live."

Friedrich Nietzsche, *The Gay Science*, ed. by Bernhard Williams, trans. by Josefine Nauckhoff, poems trans. by Adrian Del Caro (Cambridge: Cambridge University Press, 2001). Here I offer my own translation to draw out the connotations of "Grund" and "fallen." Otherwise, I will cite readily available translations, especially those in the Cambridge University Press texts in the History of Philosophy series.

4 Friedrich Nietzsche, *Thus Spoke Zarathustra*, trans. by Walter Kaufmann (New York: Random House, 1995), 294. The original quotation is found in *KSA* 4:365.

When taken together, the significance for these first humans is that their lives really began only after they had been returned to the "ground" to eke out their existence and give it meaning. Of course, this interpretation complicates the opposition between good and evil in the Biblical story of creation. All these issues figure prominently in the chapters that follow.

While the inquisitive spirit of the first mythic humans caused them to recognize their nakedness and their earth-boundedness, the modern "heavy" researcher is heir to their intellectual curiosity. In using scientific procedure to understand how nature works as a unit and how humankind fits into it all, the modern scientist, like the mythic Faust, seeks to be like God by knowing "all causes in heaven and on the earth."[5] This effort involves consciousness raising, even if the path to knowledge proves to be self-similar and involves a turning in on oneself as well as a turning away from oneself. In the following, I draw upon all of these meanings of "to fall" inherent in the phrase "auf den Grund fallen."

2. Chaos and Complexity

In recent years, a good deal of attention has been paid to the science of chaos and complexity, with books, articles, dissertations, and Web pages appearing in rapid succession. Inevitably, the tendency in the popular realm has been to detach the object of study from its scientific moorings and unleash it on a dizzying journey across the pages of tabloids, paperbacks, and journals. Popular periodicals and newspapers on both sides of the Atlantic, ranging from *Geo-Wissen*, *Der Spiegel*, and *Die Süddeutsche Zeitung* to *Omni*, *Nature, Time Magazine*, and the *New York Times*, have devoted extensive space to chaos, complexity, and "wild science," labeling it a "whole new universe of thought," which posits the delicate equilibrium of opposing forces as the essence of reality.[6] Exemplary of this popularizing effect – and of the dangers of misappropriation – are the national bestseller, *Chaos: Making a New Science* (1987) by James Gleick and the lengthy and detailed article by Peter Brügge continued over three issues of *Der Spiegel* in 1993, entitled: "Kult um das Chaos: Aberglaube oder Welterklärung?" (The Cult of Chaos: Superstition or Explanation of the World?). "Chaos breaks across the lines that separate scientific disciplines," Gleick writes in *Chaos*, adding that because its focus is on the global nature of systems, "it has brought together thinkers from fields that had been widely separated."[7] Brügge notes that the movement has its chaos fanatics, disciples, addicts, agitators, stars, and occasional

5 *Historia von D. Joh. Fausten*, repr. of the chapbook of 1587, ed. Hans Henning (Halle: Verlag Sprache und Literatur, 1963), 14: "alle Gründ am Himmel und Erde."

6 *Geo-Wissen: Chaos + Kreativität*, ed. by Günter Haaf (Hamburg: Gruner + Jahr AG and Co, 1990), 3, 48.

7 James Gleick, *Chaos: Making a New Science* (New York: Penguin, 1987), 5.

"chaos monster." Yet he concludes that no one really knows what chaos is.[8]

In the late 1990s, two German researchers, Peter Weingart and Sabine Massen, detailed the remarkable spread of the term "chaos" from its original scientific discourse across the spectrum of disciplines in the social sciences and humanities in a lengthy, scholarly essay entitled "The Order of Meaning: The Career of Chaos as a Metaphor." The authors note that while the term "chaos" or "chaotic" occurred in 23 publications listed in *Science Citation Index* in 1974, that number had risen to 1,008 by 1996. Add to that the fact that the *Social Sciences Citation Index* for the years 1974–96 lists 154 documents on chaos and complexity for the field of economics, 95 for psychology, 75 for political science, 63 for psychiatry, 50 for international relations, and 25 for environmental studies and history each, and the stage is set for excess. And these figures do not even include publications in the humanities.[9] The filming of Michael Crichton's *Jurassic Park* (1993) by Stephen Spielberg was just icing on the cake. Weingart and Maasen published their analysis of the metaphoric uses of chaos in *Configurations* (1997), a journal devoted to the study of science and literature.

In scientific circles, chaos is used to describe unpredictable nonlinear movement that is apparently devoid of any overriding structuring principle. This does not mean that there is no inherent order; it only suggests that the order is not discernible in ordinary terms. However, because chaos has been overused, even misappropriated, I have become more cautious about employing the term since I first began this project. This book, therefore, does not deal with contemporary popular manifestations of chaos or with the history of the myth since Hesiod's *Theogony*. On the other hand, it is not about mathematics or computer-generated images, nor does it simply equate chaos with fractal geometry. Rather, I wish to underscore the fact that the rise of chaos as a catch-all phrase has signaled a growing sense that we have discovered a new tool for remapping our image of reality. It is this latter function of the term "chaos" that continues to be attractive. It is reminiscent of Nietzsche's famous line in aphorism #109 of *The Gay Science* that the total character of the world is essentially chaos ("Der Gesamtcharakter der Welt ist dagegen in alle Ewigkeit Chaos"; *KSA* 3:468). Nietzsche's dictum is informed by the view that chaos is the key to creativity and that renewal is permanent in nature. Our world is what we would now call a periodic center,

8 Peter Brügge, "Kult um das Chaos: Aberglaube oder Welterklärung?" *Der Spiegel* 39 (1993): 156–64; 40 (1993): 232–41; 41 (1993): 240–52. Here 39:161 and 41:252.

9 Peter Weingart and Sabine Maasen, "The Order of Meaning: The Career of Chaos as a Metaphor," *Configurations* 5.3 (1997), provide a "bibliometric analysis of the *SCI* and the *SSCI*" (468–72). Weingart and Maasen are the only researchers I know of who cite Peter Brügge. Although Paul R. Gross and Norman Levitt, *Higher Superstition: The Academic Left and Its Quarrels with Science* (Baltimore and London: Johns Hopkins U P, 1998[2]), frequently use German terminology, they seem unaware of the relevant work done in German on the topic of "postmodern science." They are right, of course, to assert that chaos has frequently been understood in a superficial manner (95). Hereafter cited as *HS*.

an island of seemingly mechanistic order in a vortex. Nietzsche's goal in that celebrated passage is to demythologize the world while simultaneously portraying humankind much more like nature in its essential dynamics. Thus I wish to conjoin chaos and creativity in an effort to go beyond common conceptions and challenge established patterns. Indeed, I wish to get to the bottom of things. We might even speak of the "good" of chaos. In asking what good is chaos, I mean good to imply not only the immediate practical benefits of scientific knowledge, but more profoundly the ethical value of calling clearly ordered relationships into doubt by emphasizing the creation of the new. To know the good entails being creative. In breaking with fixed structures, however, we open ourselves up to what is often called "evil." Yet we need to acknowledge the benefits of altered states and newly perceived dimensions of reality resulting from the influx of new information.

Both the good and the chaotic are thus important to my undertaking, but not in any popular sense of the words. In an effort to avoid unnecessary confusion, I will, therefore, tend to speak more in terms of complexity theory, which, like the science of chaos, was born in the 1970s and rose to prominence following the establishment of the Sante Fe Institute in 1984. Unlike chaos, complexity has remained ethically value free. Yet complexity, too, has been heralded as a new paradigm in a slew of works mostly intended for a more limited audience, e.g., Jack Cohen and Ian Stewart's *The Collapse of Chaos: Discovering Simplicity in a Complex World* (1994), John L. Casti's examination of chaos and complexity in *Complexification: Explaining a Paradoxical World Through the Science of Surprise* (1994), Stuart Kauffman's search for the laws of self-organization in *At Home in the Universe* (1995), Edward O. Wilson's attempt at a unity of knowledge in *Consilience: The Unity of Knowledge* (1998), Paul Cilliers's application of complexity theory to postmodernism in *Complexity and Postmodernism: Understanding Complex Systems* (1998), and Brian Greene's lucid pursuit of the complexities of string theory in *The Elegant Universe* (1999). If chaos is the study of how simple deterministic systems can generate complicated behavior, then complexity is the study of how complex relational systems can generate simple behavior. While both are embedded in community dynamics and involve multiple levels of interaction, complexity is the more general of the two. Like chaos, it has its critics as well as advocates.

Ultimately, researchers wish to understand human nature itself. "The future of the liberal arts," Wilson avers, "lies [...] in addressing the fundamental questions of human existence head on" (*Consilience* 269). Humanists have of course always seen themselves in this role. Alexander Pope's axiom in his *Essay on Man* (1733–34) still rings true: "The proper study of mankind is man." This exhortation has lost none of its validity or urgency. In one of its major contributions over the past three hundred years, science has taught us that we learn almost as much about an object indirectly, through its reflections and reverberations, as we do directly, through dissection and analysis.

That indirectness underscores the value of metaphor in science and literature as a means of rendering truth, establishing facts, assessing the importance of the environment in shaping us, and, generally, of judging humanity's role in shaping the world. Today we are much more inclined to see humankind as part of a larger, complex ecosystem and to study humans in that wider context of immediate and more distant interconnections. Science has come to realize that we shape reality by our perceptions as much as our perceptions are shaped by reality. Our body, the means by which we gather sensory input, and our brain, the highly complex organ that interprets the input, are determined by genetic codes and chemical reactions. Human consciousness, although linked to genetic processes, seems to follow a dynamic of its own and is the seat of theory. Like the Russian doll, then, which contains yet another doll within it, humankind exists within a series of different frameworks, ranging from the inorganic to the organic, from the molecular to the mental.

Yet unlike the dolls, which are separate entities closed off from one another by their external shells, the walls separating humans from their environment are porous membranes. They are more like life-worlds (*Lebenswelten*), which mutually influence one another while maintaining their individuality. It is within and between these spaces separating and conjoining the life-worlds that we can hope to learn what it means to be human, what it means to be creative. Moreover, if we really want to get to the bottom of things, we should consider the crossover points between quantum and classical levels of reality in assessing the question. Obviously, human beings play a primary role in discovering (or perhaps even creating) the order of the universe. When we map reality, we cannot be entirely sure that the meaning we impart to the order discerned is inherent in external nature or originates with us. We are seemingly intimately interlocked with the object of our study. The question of creativity, then, must take this interconnection into account. We must be careful, however, about imparting purpose to natural processes. It may be a matter only of results, not of intention.

3. Defining Terms

A preliminary definition of terms such as theory, chaos, complexity, metaphor, motif, and theme is in order. In defining any key term there is an understandable urge to return to original meanings. While I will do this, I will not ignore Friedrich Schlegel's warning of 1798 that a return to etymological origins frequently leads to greater confusion rather than enhanced clarity.[10] Words change through usage; they show the wear and tear, the use and abuse of generations. They also change because our

10 Cf. Friedrich Schlegel, "Fragmente," in *Athenäum: eine Zeitschrift*, 3 vols., ed. by August Wilhelm and Friedrich Schlegel (Berlin: Heinrich Frölich, 1798–1800), vol.1, no. 2, 183.

knowledge of the world and of our place in it is constantly being redefined and extended. Yet beneath the overlays of meaning and semantic nuance, a core signifier remains. It is not as if words such as *θεωρία* (theory), *χάος* (chaos), and *μεταφορά* (metaphor) or *κόσμος* (cosmos) and *movere* (to move) are empty vessels whose significance is determined solely by what is put into them. Certain constants such as cosmic background radiation or metaphors such as that of the serpent remain despite all the changes in the foreground or the environment.

Theory in these pages is understood in two ways. First, the term designates a scientifically acceptable principle or set of principles used to explain phenomena, literary or material. In this first sense, theory can be general and abstract. Secondly, theory will be used in its etymologically original sense of consciously seeing, of looking at what occurs within one's field of vision. In this sense, theory connotes the analysis of a set of facts in their relationships to one another. In any event, theory refers to the act of going beyond the isolated artifact or event, even beyond the *visible* stuff of existence. Theory moves through reductionism back to a view of the whole. "Nothing in science," Wilson contends, "– nothing in life, for that matter – makes sense without theory" (*Consilience* 52). And the cosmologist George Smoot notes quite tellingly that what does not meet the eye is perhaps more critical than what does: "It is what you are *not* seeing that is of increasing importance to theorists."[11]

The common definition of chaos points to disordered formlessness and utter confusion inaccessible to the inquiring gaze. Mythologically, the formless anarchy of chaos reigned supreme over a horror of blank and boundless vacancy at the beginning of time. Yet, paradoxically, from this unbroken nothingness two offspring emerged: Night and Erebus. Together they represent the impenetrably deep darkness in which Death abides. Inexplicably, but apparently by virtue of their very fear of emptiness (*horror vacui*), Night and Erebus in turn gave birth to desire for the opposite of their beings: love, light, order, purposefulness.[12] Thus, chaos is ultimately, and ironically, the mother of all distinct forms. It is the endless potential for infinite realizations of matter and energy. A kind of Eve. The story of the fall from Eden mirrors these ancient pagan myths by picking up on the themes and motifs of finding one's way through the maze of unstructured existence outside the "perfect" order of Paradise back to a state of lost

11 George Smoot and Keay Davidson, *Wrinkles in Time* (New York: William Morrow and Co., 1993), 12.

12 Edith Hamilton, *Mythology: Timeless Tales of Gods and Heroes* (New York: NAL, 1963), 63–64. Cf. Walter Gebhard, "Erkennen und Entsetzen: zur Tradition der Chaos-Annahmen im Denken Nietzsches," *Friedrich Nietzsche: Strukturen der Negativität*, ed. by Walter Gebhard (Frankfurt a.M.: Peter Lang, 1984), 20–30. For other variations of the chaos theme in the Western tradition see also *Allgemeine Encyclopädie der Wissenschaften und Künste in alphabetischer Folge, 6. Teil: Cea bis Chiny*, ed. by J.S. Ersch and J.G. Gruber (Leipzig: Johann Friedrich Gleditsch, 1827), 142, and *Großes vollständiges Universal-Lexikon aller Wissenschaften und Künste, welche bißhero durch menschlichen Verstand und Witz erfunden und verbessert worden*, Bd. 5: C-Ch (Halle and Leipzig: Johann Heinrich Zedler, 1733), 1998–99.

innocence, of undividedness, of oneness. In the science of chaos, the term "chaos" refers to both of the above trends and to neither.

Chaos, as understood in the following, does not refer to the primordial mass from which our universe evolved. It is not the disordered, formless matter cited by Hesiod and portrayed in the Bible as the raw material of God's ordered creation. Nor does it connote in the science of chaos utter confusion and incomputability in the material or neurological realms. Rather, researchers in the natural sciences use "chaos" to designate a paradoxical state of deterministic randomness marked by a highly complex nonlinear dynamic with exceptional sensitivity to initial conditions, which themselves are in a state of flux. The exponential amplification of initially minuscule fluctuations in the conditions makes it impossible to track with utmost accuracy the trajectory of the interactive processes. Tiny fluctuations can lead to major alterations in the activity. While not *in*computable, chaos is not *easily* computable, thus prompting one to speak of indeterminacy as one of its chief traits. Scientifically speaking, however, chaos is only the appearance of randomness, not the real thing. Chaos is a system.[13] Hence the term "deterministic chaos." In terms of higher-dimensional computation, it is an ongoing struggle between stretching and folding. Favorite examples from nature of such a system are the weather and the demographics of animal populations in the wild.

Complexity or complexity theory is related to chaos but is more closely attuned to biological phenomena than chemical or nuclear interactions. Premised on the notion that deep laws account for the emergence of various kinds of systems, ranging from biological cells to ecosystems and the human mind itself, complexity theory is interested in discovering the laws or algorithms of nature that display common features across many levels of organization. The attraction of divining a few simple laws from which vast complexity emerges proves to be irresistible. "Complexity is what interests scientists in the end," Wilson muses, "not simplicity." Hence he believes that complexity theory needs more empirical information (*Consilience* 54, 90). However, Stuart Kauffman, a major proponent of complexity theory, considers robust and typical properties more important than details for the emergence of a new system.[14] Another chief advocate of complexity theory, the Technical University of Vienna mathematician John L. Casti, argues that complexity is a natural phenomenon that defies human efforts to compute the whys and ways of the world. It is not possible to get at it all by following a set of rules, because "system complexity is a subjective, not an objective, property of an isolated system. But it can become objective, once our formalism takes

---

13 Gregor Morfill and Herbert Scheingraber, *Chaos ist überall ... und es funktioniert: eine neue Weltsicht* (Frankfurt a.M.: Ullstein, 1991), 42–55; Edward Ott, *Chaos in Dynamical Systems* (Cambridge: Cambridge University Press, 1993); Ian Stewart, *Does God Play Dice? The Mathematics of Chaos* (Cambridge, MA: Basil Blackwell, 1989), 16–21.

14 Stewart Kauffman, *At Home in the Universe: The Search for Laws of Self-Organization and Complexity* (New York: Oxford University Press, 1995), 19.

into account the system with which our target system interacts."[15] Strikingly, the observer is one of those interacting systems one must factor into objective formalism. This highlights the role of the observer (or abstract theorist, as the case may be) in creating a theory of models in which intuition is (the unexpected) key. That is why Casti promotes complexity as the "science of surprise."[16]

For his part, literary theorist Paul Cilliers notes that the concept of complexity remains elusive at both the quantitative and qualitative levels; complexity is not simply the sum of its parts, but is also constituted by the sum of the intricate *relationships* among the components. By cutting up the system, we destroy the very relationships we are trying to understand. Thus, Cilliers sees a role for philosophy not so much as a "meta-description of that which happens in science and technology," but rather as "an integral part of scientific and technological practice" itself.[17] Schneiders sees philosophy as fundamentally interested in determining the relationship between chaos and order. Theoretically for him there are four possibilities, two extreme positions, two medial ones: (1) the universe is total chaos, (2) total order dominates, (3) the universe is essentially ordered but with spots of disorder, and (4) the universe is essentially chaotic with intermittent ordered spaces. The latter two are of relevance to this study and will pop up repeatedly. Schneiders labels the third possibility a kind of "Swiss-cheese theory of reality," the fourth, a "theory of the Happy Iles" ("eine Art Schweizer-Käse Theorie der Wirklichkeit," "eine Art Theorie der Seligen Inseln"; Schneiders 2000: 274). The metaphors are well chosen.

In this volume, the designations "chaos" and "complexity" should be largely understood as synonymous, although complexity is the larger concept. Complexity drives to the heart of what is so fascinating about chaos in terms of creativity and emergence; it is also less open to misappropriation. The science writer and frequent contributor to the journal *Science*, M. Mitchell Waldrop, who himself holds a doctorate in particle physics, draws specific attention to the connection between complexity and chaos in his story of exciting discoveries by such scientific luminaries as Murray Gell-Mann, Kenneth Arrow, and John H. Holland. The very title of Waldrop's book, *Complexity: The Emerging Science at the Edge of Order and Chaos* (1993), is revealing. Waldrop argues that complexity is concerned with so-called adaptive systems, which actually consist of various subsystems interlinked in intricate ways. This, in turn, allows them to store information based on past experiences while engaging in recombinations of information within each subsystem and among other

---

15 John L. Casti, *Complexification: Explaining a Paradoxical World Through the Science of Surprise* (New York: HarperCollins, 1994), 276; see also 170.

16 Casti creates with his argument an opening for border crossings between the formalism of the objective natural sciences and the intuitiveness of the subjective humanistic sciences.

17 Paul Cilliers, *Complexity and Postmodernism: Understanding Complex Systems* (London and New York: Routledge, 1998), 2.

subsystems. All the while they remain open to new input from outside the global system. The adaptations and innovative recombinations occur at the edges of the subsystems, at their interstices, where everything is in flux. This arrangement provides for a balance between stability and productive change because, on the one hand, the adaptive systems typically have many niches in which autocatalytic sets can operate and, on the other, because the adaptations ensure that the system can anticipate the future by reacting to a broader changing environment independent of its own inner workings. "At some deep, fundamental level," John H. Holland contends, "all these processes of learning, evolution, and adaptation are the same."[18] It all amounts to "perpetual novelty." It is also a matter of what I am calling "getting to the bottom of things."

Most nonscientists believe that metaphor plays no role in the doing of science, that reductionism is the guiding principle, and that the multivalent metaphor is confined to the arts and humanities. To many, then, science and the arts appear to be antithetical. Yet natural scientists rely almost as heavily on metaphor to achieve representation as do humanists. As an expression of the ability to find similarities in seemingly dissimilar things, metaphor is one of the tropes through which meaning is achieved. One proceeds from the known to the unknown, using the familiar to explain the unfamiliar. In this sense metaphors are an example of the so-called cultural matrix. In essence, a metaphor is an implied analogy between two objects, each of which is partially imbued with the traits and "emotional" content of the other, although they may only faintly resemble one another. When the metaphor extends meaning beyond the particular object itself to convey an otherwise incommunicable truth, it functions as a symbol. When the metaphor extends in an elaborate and consistently constructed manner, it becomes an allegory. Metaphors, then, can be considered the building blocks of creative thought, something Edward O. Wilson himself readily concedes (*Consilience* 218).[19] One could, I suppose, speak of a "humanizing" effect or of the "domestication" of scientific language via metaphors and other figures of speech.[20] Yet mathematics – the essential language of science – clearly retains its objectivity by comparison. The operative metaphor in complexity theory, for example, is that of plant morphology: a simple seed gives rise to a complex living organism. It is an unfolding from the bottom up or, if you will, a reversal of the reductive gaze to the holistic panorama. One of the most frequently cited paradigms of complexity theory is the "edge of chaos," where

18 As reported by Mitchell Waldrop, *Complexity: The Emerging Science at the Edge of Chaos* (New York: Simon and Schuster, 1993), 146.

19 Arthur I. Miller suggests a similar thesis for the critical role of metaphor and imagery in the scientific reasoning of Henri Poincaré, Albert Einstein, Niels Bohr, and Werner Heisenberg. See A. I. Miller, *Imagery in Scientific Thought: Creating 20th-Century Physics* (Boston: Birkhäuser, 1984).

20 Brian Ward, "The Literary Appropriation of Chaos Theory," Ph.D. diss., University of Western Australia, Nedlands, Western Australia, 1998, 9–12.

everything is in flux and agents are constantly forced to adapt to one another (Waldrop 327–30). Dominant metaphors for chaos are coastlines, storm fronts, and the so-called gingerbread man. Of course, chaos is itself a metaphor, a polysemous voice, so to speak, with layered sonority, ranging from the scientifically rigorous to the unserious and playful. In complexity theory, the references are to the living organism, ecosystems, the web of technology, the linkages between production and consumption, the earth as an open thermodynamic system. Without these tropes, theory would not get beyond the artifact itself.

Theory, chaos, and complexity, therefore, are all infused with metaphor. Indeed, the whole nature of language is highly metaphorical, as Immanuel Kant pointed out long ago in his *Critique of Judgment* (§59) of 1790.[21] Weingart and Maasen map the metaphor of chaos in its various applications across diverse disciplines, for their purpose is to seriously consider chaos a metaphor.[22] For his part, Kauffman draws liberally on metaphors in his "stories" of complexity, convinced that they are suggestive of ideas worthy of serious investigation (*At Home* 294). Specifically in regard to "replicators," which are invented, imitated, and varied in complex patterns of cultural transmission, he sees "self-sustaining and mutually defining sets of beliefs, behaviors, [and] roles" worthy of theoretical reflection, even though they might be only "the start of a real theory" (*At Home* 300). "Replicators" (or recurrent metaphors, themes, memes, motifs, archetypes) are already expressive of real theory. They echo Kant's symbolic conceptualization and inform the ensuing chapters.

A motif is an observable quality forming "the concrete nucleus of a narrative," which captures in striking manner a key element of human perception and valuation.[23]

---

21 *Critique of Judgment*: metaphorical (or symbolic) and schematic. Whereas schematic representation is a more direct form of representation, operating on the basis of demonstration, metaphorical or symbolic thinking is indirect, proceeding by analogy. In this latter sense, the act of expression is a symbol of our reflection upon the object of inquiry rather than an actual schemata of it. Since language is riddled with analogical expressions, it is difficult to avoid their use. Symbolic thinking, therefore, is already a matter of theory. See Immanuel Kant, *Kritik der ästhetischen Urteilskraft*, in *Werke in zehn Bänden*, ed. by Wilhelm Weischedel (Darmstadt: Wissenschaftliche Buchgesellschaft, 1983), 8:459–60, §59.

22 Weingart and Maasen, "The Order of Meaning," 473–84. Drawing upon Luhmanian and Foucaultian discourse theory to explain what literary critics have long known, they seek to disclose metaphors as "media and sites of knowledge transfer" (475). While I do not entirely agree that metaphors are "identifiable by their relative lack of familiarity" (477) – there are many well-known metaphors, chaos being one of them – I agree that meanings change, that the contemporary understanding of chaos theory amounts to "another kind of rationality" (483), and that the recent history of the chaos metaphor itself exemplifies the nonlinear, recursive processes associated with the natural phenomenon (520).

23 See Horst S. Daemmrich and Ingrid Daemmrich, *Themes & Motifs in Western Literature: A Handbook* (Tübingen: Francke, 1987), 187–90. See also Raymond Trousson, *Thèmes et mythes: questions de méthode* (Bruxelles: Éditions de l'Université de Bruxelles, 1981), 21–30; and Elizabeth Frenzel,

It can even have archetypical significance, such as the Fall, which can have either comical or tragic overtones. The indication of positionality is one of the motif's chief functions, Horst Daemmrich argues, for it facilitates "integrational relations with successively different planes of signification." When placed sequentially, motifs "contribute to the formation of a textual field of tension and re-enforce thereby the process of reflection" (Daemmrich 189). Elizabeth Frenzel emphasizes the particular importance of such linking of related motifs when she argues that a "cluster of motifs" can achieve a life of its own, appearing as a kind of "motif-biology" ("Erst der Motivkomplex kann ein Eigenleben führen, und an ihm läßt sich eine Art Motivbiologie ablesen"; Frenzel 30). This particular dimension of an "Eigenleben" (a life of its own) will be taken up in the literary analyses of the second half of this study. Perhaps the most notable characteristic of the motif, whether alone or in clusters, is the dynamic quality it lends to its community of (con)texts. But then motif derives from *movere*.[24]

Themes are generally recognized to be "central organizational units of texts," capable of standing alone but simultaneously of interacting on various levels with metaphors, similes, figures, and motifs (Daemmrich 241). As embodiments of a text's ideational content, they also represent a fundamental mode of thought marked by fields of tension. "The substance of a theme," Daemmrich remarks, "resides in qualitative (meaning) and quantitative (occurrences) properties" (240). However, there is no agreement among thematologists as to how abstract the ideational contact can become. Perhaps this is due to the disparate attributes of themes: concept, probability, delineation, function, recurrence, and individuation. The blurring of the boundary lines between theme (e.g., concept) and motif (e.g., individuation) is symptomatic of the close proximity of the two constitutive elements of meaning with which the reader is confronted. In his handbook of literary terms, for example, Hendrik van Gorp notes that the reader, by reflecting upon the recurring markers in the text, progressively and incrementally conjoins the individual instances into an essential overriding motif via a process of anticipation and retrospection.[25] Frenzel complicates the relationship even further by involving the notion of the symbol. She remarks that the theme (*Stoff*) can become highly energized in a motif, while the motif can be transformed into an abstraction at the level of a symbol (Frenzel 21). Finally, Ulrich Weisstein decides that

---

Stoff- Motiv- und Symbolforschung (Stuttgart: Metzler, 1963), 21–32.

24 Cf., e.g., Ulrich Weisstein, *Comparative Literature and Literary Theory: Survey and Introduction* (Bloomington: Indiana University Press, 1973), 145. See also G.P. Knapp, "Stoff – Motiv – Idee," *Grundzüge der Literatur- und Sprachwissenschaft*, ed. by Heinz Ludwig Arnold and Volker Sinemus, vol. 1: *Literaturwissenschaft* (Munich: Deutscher Taschenbuch Verlag, 1978), 201.

25 Hendrik van Gorp (ed.), *Lexicon van literaire Termen*, 2nd ed. (Leuven: Wolters, 1984): "Door te reflecteren op zulke recurrente tekstkenmerken verknoopft de lezer, via anticipatie en retroversie, die concrete gegenvens progressief tot ze a.h.w. uitmonden in een grondmotief [ook sluitmotief of kernmotief]" (202).

themes (generally) refer to characters, while motifs (generally) relate to situations (Weisstein 139).

Fundamental, however, as in the case of motifs, is the human content of both. Motifs and themes also have epistemic and hermeneutic functions, for they enable human beings to interpret and understand themselves within their (changing) environment. Recurring primary themes raise such questions as the limits of knowledge, the laws of the universe, the logic of the personality, and the relationship of the individual to society (Daemmrich 241). The implicit assumption is that the writer/artist invests her text with the motif selection best suited to the development of the theme and message. The number of motifs is relatively limited, and the themes to which they are attached recur in a cycle of ebb and flow throughout history. The tropic scaffolding inherent in literary, musical, and artistic texts betrays a set of meta-patterns, which strongly suggests the existence of near-universal themes, a kind of deep structure. The focus is on the individual as the center of measurement and meaning. Of course, the act of evaluation represents both the strength and the weakness of thematology. Part of my purpose – and that is the reason for the preceding detailed discussion – is to expand the traditional context for the study of themes and motifs beyond the parameters of the artistic text to include nature itself. By the same token, I wish to transfer the reflections of natural and social scientists beyond their disciplinary boundaries into the realm of the arts and humanities in more than a simplistic fashion. Science and the humanities are here intrinsically intertwined.

Observers have long noted a natural longing of humankind for nature. Researchers such as Wilson now hypothesize that the biological evolution of our species has equipped us with a genetic code that endows us with an emotional link to nature. Wilson espies in that link the source of human creative genius. According to that thesis, early survival depended upon our ancestors being able to prosper in a robust natural environment. Experience taught early humans to recognize threats to their well-being (snakes, enclosed spaces inhabited by predators) as well as benefits (e.g., partially open, livable spaces). Those emotions of fear and contentment have entered human genetic material; contacts with nature set off the ancient responses. The thesis, dubbed the "biophilia hypothesis," explains the recurrent need of modern urban humans to return to nature, be it in city parks, in the suburban back yard, or in the open countryside.[26]

In these pages the phenomenon of biophilia will serve as a sign of the interconnectedness of the so-called two cultures of science and the humanities. Throughout this study, the biological basis of behavior and of human consciousness – matter and mind – serves as a kind of Ariadne's thread to guide us through the labyrinth of life. Wilson adopts Ariadne's thread as a metaphor of consilience, that is, the linkage of

26 Edward O. Wilson and Stephen R. Kellert (eds.), *The Biophilia Hypothesis* (New York: Island Press/Shearwater Books, 1993). See also Wilson, *Biophilia* (Cambridge, MA: Harvard University Press, 1984), and *Consilience*, 78–81.

facts and theories across disciplines to create a common ground of understanding. He calls the biological origins of the arts a "working hypothesis" (*Consilience* 8, 67, 229). Wilson's book appeared after I had developed the theoretical portion of my study in reaction to the science of chaos, complexity theory, and Nietzsche's philosophy of the will to power. His argument confirms my essential thesis from a different perspective.

4. A Note On and For Readers

Even though modern civilization and the search for a unity of knowledge are products of the Enlightenment with its instrumental reason and enhanced human consciousness, the economy of world history cannot replace the greater economy of the history of the world. For Friedrich Hegel (the ultimate Enlightenment thinker), for example, the history of consciousness was decisive. In the history of the world, self-consciousness is but one of several dimensions of reality. The old hierarchies no longer prevail. Humankind has long since receded as the center of the universe. Now even the long-lived anthropocentrism that continued to dominate our thinking into the late twentieth century is itself beginning to wane as a result of the ravages of the Copernican Revolution.[27] There is more than human history, there is more than consciousness, there is more than the unconscious, as Arkady Plotnitzky remarks at the end of his long journey in the shadow of Hegel: "[T]here is always something else: something other than philosophy, something other than history, something other than the unconscious."[28] The current project represents one more attempt to get at that "something else," to get to the bottom of things, even if it proves to be a false bottom, even if the reach proves too short. To be successful, any attempt at consilience must master several different discourses and disciplinary languages. And, as we well know, interdisciplinarity is hard to do. The result might, indeed, be a book for all and for none (to play immodestly on the subtitle of Nietzsche's *Zarathustra*). Nonetheless, I hope that the disciplinary purist will look beyond the "accent" in the language I use and seek to understand the message that the remapping of reality extends across all disciplines.

---

27 Cf., e.g., Manon Andreas-Grisebach, *Eine Ethik für die Natur* (Zürich: Ammann Verlag, 1991), who argues against traditional anthropocentrism in favor of periodic centers independent of human beings: "Immer sollte im Bewußtsein verankert werden, daß die Zentrum-Position der Menschen überholt ist, daß alles Mitte sein kann, alles ebenso zum Mittel wie auch zum Selbstzweck werden kann, Das ist das Neue, das Entscheidende, lebensentscheidend. Erst die Anerkennung der Verschiebbarkeit von Mittelpunkten wird eine Ethik erzeugen helfen, die den Fortbestand des Lebens für alle und alles möglichst lange sichert" (51). See also Paul Davies, *The Cosmic Blueprint* (London: Unwin, 1987), 197–203.

28 Arkady Plotnitzky, *In the Shadow of Hegel: Complementarity, History, and the Unconscious* (Gainesville: University Press of Florida, 1993), 159–60. Plotnitzky offers an incisive reading of Hegel's influence. In Nietzsche's iconoclasm, Freud's the unconscious, and Bohr's complementarity principle he sees reactions to Hegel's economy of history.

The extent of that interdisciplinary reach is discernible in the numerous footnotes and parenthetical references to source materials contained in these and the following pages. Sources cited parenthetically in the text, which are not obvious references to footnote material, can be found in the bibliography. While the main text can be fruitfully read without perusing those references and commentaries, the latter are designed to provide illuminating sidelights and suggestions for further reading. Often they contain the original wording of the passage cited so that the reader can draw her own conclusions. Scholarly readers are always grateful for critical commentary on unfamiliar and even familiar material, if it offers new insights. The general reader is free to ignore it. In either case, the notes should be taken as a sign that although we live in the present, the past forms the ground upon which we stand.

Granted, my project is not only ambitious but perhaps even foolhardy, especially in light of the chastisements by Gross and Levitt (1994) and Alan Sokal (1996) concerning humanistic "intrusions" into the realm of science. Yet it is based on the widely accepted view that interaction between the cultures of the humanities and sciences is fertile ground for inquiry (Kellert 1996) and is to be encouraged (Wilson 1998). Nonetheless, some will no doubt question the wisdom of commingling the two fields, preferring to keep separate what seem to be distinct cultures.[29] Even recognizing the reciprocity of the human and natural sciences and the benefit of enhanced communication between them, some readers will still experience a nagging doubt that a layperson can adequately understand the intricacies of coding in the double helix, the nature of high-energy physics, the dynamics of entropy, the complexity of an adaptive system, or Nietzsche's radical re-evaluation of all values. If one is not a trained expert in the respective fields of specialization, cross-disciplinarity would prove to be more menacing than exhilarating. "A little learning," Jacques Barzun once remarked, "is dangerous in one who tries to teach or use that little in professional work; it is not a

29 See, for example Ronald Shusterman's review of Alan Sokal and the hostilities in the French debate between the two cultures: "Ravens and Writing-Desks: Sokal and the Two Cultures," *Philosophy and Literature* 22 (1998): 119–35. Specifically, he reacts to Sokal's attack on postmodernism in "Transgressing the Boundaries" (1996) and in *Impostures intellectuelles* (Paris: Odile Jacob, 1997), co-authored with Jean Bricmont. Sokal has had both a salutary and deleterious impact. On the one hand, Sokal (along with Gross and Levitt) has tended to hinder "illicit borrowings" from science (such as Lacan's use of mathematics) (Shusterman 128); on the other, he reinforces the simplistic view that each culture has of the other. Included in Shusterman's review is Isabelle Stengers, *Science et pouvoirs: la démocratie face à la technoscience* (Paris: La Décourverte, 1997). More judicious than Gross and Levitt (*Higher Superstition*) in assessing both sides of the argument, Shusterman suggests a way out of the "two cultures" controversy. In essence, he considers the two cultures of science and the humanities to be incommensurable: "[S]cience gives us descriptions of the 'external world' while literature, criticism, and speculative philosophy help formulate the inner world" (Shusterman 134). My view is that the two discourses are connected via deep structures and that the inquiring subject is the unavoidable point of mediation between the inner and outer worlds.

danger but a source of pleasure to the observer of life as a whole. Thus does a map, yielding a superficial knowledge of geography, add to the traveler's enjoyment even though he himself could not survey the ground and draw the map."[30] Using different maps of the same terrain from different eras and points of view and driven by mounting evidence of astonishing parallels, patterns, analogies, and metaphors across disciplinary boundaries, the traveler can, of course, connect the points in ways not anticipated by the map makers. It proves to be an irresistible lure. Themata or memes – around which "communities" of tropes establish themselves – reappear like so many strange attractors in science just as they do in literature. Their prominence or absence in the researcher's or writer's consciousness is dependent upon factors external to the particular project. All factor into map making and the reading of maps.

Of course, I am not aiming this analysis at recalcitrant readers. I see no need for scientists to defend what they do, nor for humanists to legitimize their own work through appeals to authorities external to humanistic studies. Although I am concerned with the way scientific discoveries alter our general sensibilities for the spaces and modes of reality and thus of the potential for creativity, I am equally cognizant of the impact that humanistic thinking has on the doing of science. I have no desire either to privilege science over the humanities or to minimalize the role of science in shaping human values. The ideal reader for this volume is in the middle ground between the expert and the general reader, inquisitive and open to different ways of understanding the same thing (here the nature of creativity). The reader envisioned is the kind who might be found perusing the science section of the *New York Times* or the pages of *Nature*. The joys of discovery – seeing what has not been seen or viewed in the same light as before – outweigh for me any concerns about the breadth of this interdisciplinary project. Seeing in new ways is, in itself, a critical dimension of creativity. Indeed, creativity is the phenomenon of the new. To recognize the unfamiliar is always a challenge.

A promising way of getting to the bottom of things is to consider the nature of creativity in terms of a common taproot of science and the humanities. Such an approach allows us to speak of the interaction of the two cultures as constituting a "third culture" as something more than just social history or discourse theory.[31] Theoretical science and philosophy (or literary theory), for example, can even be seen as branches of aesthetics, i.e., the tradition of the new. All disciplines study the same

30 Jacques Barzun, *Science: The Glorious Entertainment* (New York: Harper & Row, 1964), 27. Barzun mounts a defense of one culture, not two. He cites "specialism" as the culprit in causing the perceived rift between scientists and non-scientists, by which he means disciplinary territorialism. It has brought about the loss of a public culture, of the feeling of belonging to one community despite one's professional allegiance (26–29).

31 See Elinor S. Shaffer (ed.), *The Third Culture: Literature and Science* (Berlin and New York: Walter de Gruyter, 1998), 1–5.

ultimate subject matter (life), albeit from different angles, with different foci, and to different ends. An aim of the eighteenth-century European Enlightenment was to form a grand union of knowledge based on a set of universal laws in an effort to reconcile objectivity and subjectivity, empiricism and rationalism, body and spirit. My project could be seen as an attempt at a "new" Enlightenment, an effort to view synoptically what at first sight does not go together. A Grand Unified Theory of sorts? It could also be seen as offering a way out of the crisis in professing the humanities today, which in some quarters are considered to be without ethical value.[32] A foundationalist base of sorts will be offered to ground the hermeneutic circle that characterizes much of contemporary literary theory. Nonetheless, a number of openings, gaps, and non-closures are likely to be encountered in mapping resonances among science, ethics, and the creative imagination.

5. Organization

To illustrate the pervasiveness of innovative thought, I have selected representative cases from the realms of science, philosophy, and literature. The science of chaos and complexity represents the first and Nietzsche's ethical thought the second, while products of literary phantasy from Goethe's *Faust* to Nietzsche's *Thus Spoke Zarathustra* and Günter Grass's *The Tin Drum* offer classically innovative views from literature. Inevitably, some readers will view the selections as whimsical or idiosyncratic, considering the point of view alternately too narrow or too broad, and comparatists will bemoan the extreme selectivity. Yet I hope that all will recognize the necessity of restraint. My initial plan to be inclusive rather than exclusive quickly proved to be unwieldy. A detailed historical overview, including such writers as Fyodor Dostoevsky, Charles Baudelaire, Gerhard Rühm, William Faulkner, Joseph Roth, James Joyce, Salman Rushdie, Michael Crichton, Richard Powers, Nicholson Baker, Tom Stoppard, Dan Brown, Doris Lessing, and Toni Morrison, would account for diversity and fullness, but would be unfeasible. Even with the view restricted to just three works, it proved impossible to do justice to the voluminous scholarship on most of these authors.

The more deeply I inquired into the possible significance of the science of chaos and the theory of complexity for literature, the more parallels I discerned between science, philosophy, and literature, and the more complex the entire project became. Like geneticists, particle physicists, theoretical mathematicians, and neural scientists, who discover ever greater complexities the further they delve into their subject matter,

32 Peter Levine, *Nietzsche and the Modern Crisis of the Humanities* (Albany: State University of New York Press, 1995), mounts a defense of the modern humanities as an ethical enterprise (see esp. 206–12). Wilson's *Consilience* also presents itself as heralding a resurgence of the Enlightenment project.

the further I progressed, the more I recognized the richness of my material.[33] Undoubtedly, the impulse for this study to locate order in the dynamic of existence was itself the result of seeds implanted much earlier. Thus, I consciously tried to counteract the myopia of which Brügge accuses the "chaos-fanatics."[34] Still I had to press forward, for as Arthur Koestler pointed out: "Carrying bricks to Babel is neither a duty, nor a privilege; it seems to be a necessity built into the chromosomes of our species."[35] Although acutely aware of the gaps in my presentation, I trust that my efforts have not resulted in a new Tower of Babel.

The study is divided into two parts: "Theoretical Encirclements" and "Literary Iterations." Part 1 of the book, in which the scientific and philosophical implications of the topic are explored and mapped out, is an effort to encircle the thorny issues under study and thereby delineate the spaces of inquiry. The demise of dogmatic theory and unity of purpose, which has loosened canonical knowledge from its moorings and set humankind adrift in a sea of uncertainty, is recounted. I argue, however, that all this movement and dislocation in mind (postmodernism) and matter (complexity) are not negatively disjunctive but rather signs of the essential tension of the whole. A fitting metaphor for this essential tension is the seemingly chaotic yet regulated whirl of movement deep within the molecular structure and organization of our bodies and of the universe. My focus is on the mimetic and autocatalytic principles of nature and art – specifically, on their vectors of interaction. Central in this initial phase are the nature and role of mimesis across the disciplines. Throughout, however, I suggest that physical reality, ethics, and aesthetics surprisingly share common, deep structuring principles. The seeming universality of the relation-constant number phi (1.618) points in the same direction. Understanding these agonistic relationships is fundamental to finding a way out of the philosophical and aesthetic dead ends of the post-Enlightenment period. Central in this development is the nature and role of imitation: scientist and artist both set out to understand and – if at all possible – to imitate or clone nature.

Beginning with an introduction to the general problems involved in assessing how the two cultures of science and the humanities view things, Chapter 1 reviews the role played by revolutions in nature's movements and in reconfigurations of human thought. Perspectives range from the Copernican Revolution through the Big Bang and

---

33 For example, Katherine Hayles notes in reference to Stanislaw Lem how difficult it is to determine sequences in closed "topological spaces." While the number of possible forms within the space are limited, their actual configuration cannot be predicted with great accuracy because all forms are linked to each other within the space, impacting in imperceptible ways upon each other's "evolution." The great number of variables makes it impossible to know what will happen further on. Yet it is possible to argue for consistency within the topological space. See N. Katherine Hayles, *Chaos Bound: Orderly Disorder in Contemporary Literature and Science* (Ithaca: Cornell University Press, 1990), 185; hereafter cited as *CB*.

34 Peter Brügge, "Kult um das Chaos," *Der Spiegel*, 40 (1993), 239 et passim.

35 Arthur Koestler, *Bricks to Babel* (New York: Random House, 1980), 685.

molecular structure to an analysis of brain functions. The point of view is increasingly widened to embrace the wholeness of existence, which was supposedly lost when Adam and Eve were driven from Paradise. The growing differentiation of experience and knowledge, made possible by the fruit of knowledge, gave birth to disciplinarity and a bounded focus. At first, the disciplines grew apart as they became ever more specialized, but now seem to be growing closer together again. The ripples of insight emanating from each disciplinary center eventually encounter and partially merge with spheres of influence radiating from other centers of inquiry. In this sense, chapter 1 examines the essential unity of human inquiry that encompasses varying disciplines of knowledge. Whether scientist or artist, each seeker feels the allure of nature and is drawn to imitate it. It is important to elucidate which dimensions of nature each viewer endeavors to fathom and re-create. That is the purpose of the next chapter.

Chapter 2 zeros in on the age-old debate on mimetic theory, adding to it insights gained from the previous chapter and highlighting the function of perspective in the creative act. Communicative interaction and complex dynamics mark the creative impulse. More importantly, this chapter argues for the grounding of the creative impulse in the deep structures of reality that lead to a kind of "deep naturalism" in mimetic expression. This more profound notion of mimesis revitalizes our understanding of imitation; it is no longer concerned with mere surface play.

Chapter 3 continues the exploration of creativity by scrutinizing Friedrich Nietzsche's re-examination of values within the context of his response to an altered view of physical and biological reality. The chapter offers an innovative rereading of the philosopher's indebtedness to scientific paradigms. His vision of the new universe is central because it impacts directly on the issue of how objectivity and subjectivity interact. That query prompts one to question the place of received notions of good and evil in the grand scheme of things.

Chapter 4 takes up the same issue, seen this time through the lens of historical attempts in the Western canon to explain the nature of evil in religious and philosophical terms. Morality is inherent in the remapping of reality because each revolution in the theory of things has directly influenced conceptions of good and evil. Over time, humanity was forced to reposition itself within a widening context. Beginning with the Biblical narrative of the temptation of Adam and Eve in the mythical Garden of Eden, the chapter traces how the promise of becoming like God through partaking of the fruit of the tree of knowledge introduced evil into human consciousness and, paradoxically, firmly embedded Adam and Eve in the earth. This chapter rounds out the first part of the study by showing how evil was rethought at seminal points in time from Leibniz to Kant, Nietzsche, and Baudrillard. This initial section, then, seeks to ground humanity in the earth and its various revolutions.

Part 2 further investigates the ideas developed in part 1 through an analysis of seminal literary works from the eighteenth, nineteenth, and twentieth centuries. Three highly complex and canonical texts have been selected to illustrate monumental attempts at remapping reality in the wake of enhanced awareness of the working of nature from the Renaissance to the Nuclear Age. The works were chosen, to be sure, because of their monumental stature, but in particular because of their sensitivity to paradigm change and resistance to easy categorization. These literary texts have lost none of their original allure despite all attempts to explain that appeal. Taken together, they reveal an astonishing, autocatalytic behavior not unlike that of a strange attractor. Each reacts to major revolutionary events and insights. Each grapples with the nature of evil in an autopoietic universe that is marked by the phenomenon of emergence at the edge of chaos. Each re-evaluates values, while endeavoring to show how humankind is at home in the universe. Chaos and the Overman (*Übermensch*) act as explicit or implicit leitmotifs in each of the works.

Chapter 5 is offers a dramatic new reading of Goethe's *Faust* against the backdrop of chaos and complexity and Nietzsche's philosophy of eternal emergence. The protagonist of this self-styled "novel of the universe" emerges as the embodiment of the creative thinker, who is fully in tune with the deep structures of the eternally evolving universe. In combining scientific and humanistic concerns, *Faust* addresses the workings of both the macrocosm and the microcosm, thereby setting the tone for the ensuing analyses, since the thema "spirit of the earth" recurs in altered form throughout the remaining chapters.

Chapter 6 centers on Nietzsche's *Thus Spoke Zarathustra* as a late-nineteenth-century reworking of Goethe's commentary on the meaning of life on earth. Here, writing – or, more generally, interpreting – is revealed as a willful ordering of reality congruent with the laws of nature. The cult of the surface and the art of mastering life oppose as well as complement the Faustian theme and the laws of motion explored therein. Gravity and "anti-gravity" figure predominantly. *Zarathustra* is viewed both as a remaking of the myth of salvation and as a commentary on then contemporary science. The universe appears as the will to power.

Chapter 7 examines the mythological constructs inherent in Gunter Grass's *The Tin Drum*. It reverses the order of reality and myth by arguing that while the deep structures of reality are seemingly fixed, the way they play out on the surface is quite unpredictable. In other words, although the rules are fixed, the strategies are variable. On the one hand, DNA presents itself as the great organizer, while on the other hand, the space of interaction between the micro and macro worlds is capable of changing the rules.

In a final rounding out of the inquiry, the epilogue emphasizes the complexity of the feedback loops that simultaneously bind and liberate humankind within the world it inhabits. The horizons sketched in part 1 are recalled and compared to the literary reactions to perceived reality from Faust to Zarathustra to Oskar. The literary analyses reach back into the eighteenth century as a means of underscoring the intellectual continuity of the overarching epoch, despite the alleged failure of the Enlightenment project in the sociopolitical realm. In the scientific domain, on the other hand, with its attitude of awe and curiosity, the project proved to be astonishingly successful.

The feeling of standing at the threshold of new dimensions of understanding and creative power was dominant in almost all fields of knowledge then as it is now. If the sense of being in the vanguard of a total revolution of human experience is blatantly foregrounded in Goethe's *Faust* and Nietzsche's *Zarathustra*, the hidden manipulators of human fate are all the more backgrounded in Grass's *The Tin Drum*. Both extremes give evidence of what Katherine Hayles would call "a denaturing process" (*CB* 265). Reasons for these disjunctive reactions are the initial focus in the following pages.

Part One

Theoretical Encirclements

Chapter 1
From Matter to Mind: Revolutions Real and Conceptual

> Vielleicht würde eine ganz neue Epoche der Wissenschaften und Künste beginnen, wenn die Symphilosophie und Sympoesie so allgemein und so innig würde, daß es nichts seltnes mehr wäre, wenn mehrere sich gegenseitig ergänzende Naturen gemeinschaftliche Werke bildeten. Oft kann man sich des Gedankens nicht erwehren, zwey Geister möchten eigentlich zusammengehören, wie getrennte Hälften, und nur verbunden alles seyn, was sie könnten.
>
> – Friedrich Schlegel, "Athenäums-Fragmente" (1798)

1. Paradigm Change and Chaos: The Analysis of Position

The full consequences of the Copernican Revolution are now being realized. Copernicus's heliocentric change together with the diurnal motion of the earth provides for infinite multiplicity within the strictest unity.[1] Thinking through these multiple possibilities in a rigorous and ineluctable manner amounts to "consistent Copernicanism," which Hans Blumenberg defines as "the carrying out of the elementary insight that man's point of view and his optics, in relation to the universe, are arbitrarily eccentric, or, in the least favorable case, extremely unsuitable" (*Genesis* 549). Not surprisingly, then, perspective and vision – "vision" in the meaning of both sight and imagination – prove(d) crucial to advances in science (as well as in the arts). Chaos theory picks up on man's "arbitrarily eccentric" point of view, making it central to its own dizzying observations. The process de-emphasizes the position of the human in material creation. New trails are blazed.

In this chapter changes in the way we think about the world and its interactions are at center stage. At the heart of the matter is the concept of revolution. By that I mean both actual movement around a center and also altered ways of looking at things. I begin with the obvious and proceed through various stages of expanding complexity to the composition of matter and the structure of the mind, concluding with a suggestion that the world and our place in it are best viewed holistically: the whole is filled with essential tensions of divergent and convergent forces. This overview of the mappings of reality is necessary in order to set the stage for the ensuing inquiry into the nature of

---

1 Hans Blumenberg, *The Genesis of the Copernican World* (Cambridge, MA: MIT University Press, 1985), 609.

the relationship between imitation and creativity.

We really do not consider it as we go about our daily lives, but it is nonetheless true: we compute time, review history, organize our lives, and respond on numerous levels to the revolutions of the earth. While these revolutions are not "revolutionary" in a political or innovative sense of the word, the rotation of the earth on its axis every 23 hours, 52 minutes, 58seconds; the orbiting of the planet around the sun every 365.256 days; and the trajectory of the sun around the center of the Milky Way every 250 million years or so have a decided and important impact on everything we do. Only now are we generally becoming more aware of how interconnected our lives are with the revolutions of the earth, solar system, and galaxy we inhabit. Each rotation of the earth on its axis and around the sun is the same; then again, it is not. Similarly, each day of our lives is not merely a mechanical reiteration of the previous one. This chapter is about the significance of revolutionary insights borne of the iterative revolutions of the earth, the planets, and the sun itself.

Within the natural sciences there is an increasingly broad perception of a radical change in the way that the material world and its regulating principles are seen. Essentially an analysis of position and the distances between positions, it is a conceptual shift from reductionism to holism seldom encountered, and it extends throughout the disciplines. It is as profound a paradigm shift as any encountered in the history of science.[2] One even hears that the movement – frequently associated with but not limited to chaos theory – is not merely breaking new ground, but is in fact "an entirely new universe of thought."[3] Just how innovative the movement is, however, is open to question, for in one sense the alteration in perspective can be seen as the

2 Cf. N. Katherine Hayles, *The Cosmic Web* (Ithaca: Cornell University Press, 1984), 15; Ilya Prigogine and Isabelle Stengers, *Order Out of Chaos: Man's New Dialogue with Nature* (New York: Bantam, 1984), xxvii [originally: *La nouvelle alliance*, 1979]; Gregor Morfill and Herbert Scheingraber, *Chaos ist überall ... und es funktioniert: Eine neue Weltsicht* (Munich: Ullstein, 1992), 7–8; Paul Davies and John Gribbin, *The Matter Myth: Dramatic Discoveries That Challenge our Understanding of Physical Reality* (New York: Simon and Schuster, 1992), 29, 62.

3 *Geo-Wissen: Chaos und Kreativität*, ed. by Günter Haaf (Hamburg: Verlag Gruner und Jahr AG & Co, 1990), 3. The claim of a radically new way of seeing things is made specifically with regard to chaos research. In *Higher Superstition: The Academic Left and Its Quarrels with Science*, 2nd ed. (Baltimore: Johns Hopkins University Press, 1998), Paul R. Gross and Norman Levitt adamantly oppose the notion that chaos theory represents a radically new way of looking at the world, stating: "What we have in chaos theory is a recommitment to taking seriously some deep old issues, such as the 'structural stability problem'" (98). On the other hand, they do not by and large discuss the same works used in this present study. Regarding the two archetypes of cosmos and chaos, see G. Kepes, *The New Landscape* (Chicago: P. Theobold, 1956), 102, 286–87. See also George Smoot and Keay Davidson's discussion of WIMPs (weakly interacting massive particles) and GUTs (grand unification theories) in their *Wrinkles in Time* (New York: William Morrow Co., 1993), 167–79. While not concerned with the archetypes of order and disorder, the two theories are inclined to posit a unity of opposites.

cumulative result of historical advances over many years in our understanding of the cosmos and its workings.

In fact, the current perception of a revolution in science is a logical extension of humankind's preceding assessments of motion from the regular clockwork operation of Copernicus's universe in *De revolutionibus* (1534) to Kepler's explanation of the planets' elliptical orbits and changing velocities in *Astronomia nova* (1609) to the nonlinear excitations and accentuations at the atomic and even subnuclear levels which go under the name of solitons and waves (Davies and Gribbin 1992: 47–61). Ultimately, even the kinetic energy of human consciousness seems related to these kinds of nonlinear movement. Viewing matter in an analogous manner, Friedrich Nietzsche in *The Gay Science* (1882) declared human consciousness to be "the last and latest development of the organic."[4] Human beings are all like volcanoes: we will all experience our eruptions someday (GS 1, #9; KSA 3:381). In the 120 years since then, science has learned more about those suspected interconnections.

Nonetheless, the skeptical reader will surely raise an eyebrow at this grouping of dissimilar levels of exploration, even though we find ourselves at the dawn of an age of "integral culture," one in which the "I" no longer stands at the center of things, but is seen to be entrenched in all the other structures of existence.[5] Drawing on the essential tensions between the rational forces of discrete logic associated with the left hemisphere of the human brain and those of instinct emanating from the right hemisphere, Johannes von Buttlar and others posit a meta-unity of apparent contraries that is dubbed "metathinking." Metathinking is nonbinary, nonlinear, multidimensional, and paradoxical as it coordinates three different levels of perception: instinct, emotion, and reason (von Buttlar 81–111). Moreover, our current age of consilience is marked by an "interpretive turn," which – at least in the human sciences – has followed on the heels of an earlier "linguistic turn" and an even earlier "epistemol-

---

4 Friedrich Nietzsche, *The Gay Science*, trans. by Bernhard Williams (Cambridge: Cambridge University Press, 2001), Book 1, #11, p.37 (= *KSA* 3:382-83).

5 Johannes von Buttlar, *Gottes Würfel: Schicksal oder Zufall* (Munich: Herbig, 1992), 94–95. Robert G. Jahn and Brenda J. Dunne, *Margins of Reality: The Role of Consciousness in the Physical World* (San Diego, New York, London: Harcourt Brace Jovanovich, 1987), reach similar conclusions. Richard Maurice Bucke, *Kosmisches Bewußtsein: Zur Evolution des menschlichen Geistes* (Frankfurt a.M.: Insel Taschenbuch, 1993), designates the highest level of awareness "cosmic consciousness." For him it signifies the integration of all existence, not just of human mental capacities. Tracing the evolution of "cosmic consciousness" from Moses through Laotse, Mohammed, Böhme, Spinoza,, etc. to Ramakrishna and Walt Whitman, Bucke emphasizes that this highest level of consciousness is neither an anomaly nor transcendent. In his eyes, "cosmic consciousness" is the result of a natural genesis (24). Moreover, Bucke suspects, "daß der ich bewußte Mensch [...] den psychischen Keim nicht nur einer, sondern gleich mehrerer höherer Menschenarten in sich trägt" (211). Bucke's (1868–1899) work first appeared in 1901 as *Cosmic Consciousness*.

ogical turn."[6] The interpretive approach applied in this study is a form of hermeneutic contextualization, which states that meaning is established by an individual not in isolation but in communities of shared knowledge, values, and experience. Eschewing foundationalism without embracing universal hermeneutics, it distinguishes between "understanding" and "interpretation," whereby understanding does not require the linguistic formulations endemic to the conscious, problem-solving "translating [of] one meaningful expression into another one" involved in interpretation.[7]

The history of science locates the first modern fundamental revolution in the fifteenth and sixteenth centuries, the Renaissance era. It consisted of a transition from a predominately Ptolemaic to a Copernican world-view, a shift that was tantamount to a decentering of the earth and of homo sapiens. While Copernicus changed the model for explaining order in the universe by making the spectator revolve and the heavenly bodies remain at rest, he did not essentially alter the method for setting up and handling the new model. More precisely, he calculated the real movement of the planets by subtracting the observer's changing motions caused by the revolutions of the earth. Thus, despite all the (co-)motion, the universe remained stable. Competing cosmological theories in the eighteenth century involved Lambert's notion of a massive center in the universe with encapsulated galaxies and solar systems confined to their own circles within circles, all of which, in turn, was confined to a limited space. Kant, on the other hand posited an unlimited space within which solar systems and galaxies were created through the demise of other worlds (Blumenberg, *Genesis* 576). In this world of exact motion, there was no allowance for nonlinear fluctuation traceable to the system dynamic itself; comets and meteorites were considered to be manifestations of divine intervention. In the realm of physiology, the English court physician William Harvey was able to explain the human circulatory system, albeit in

6 See *The Interpretive Turn: Philosophy, Science, Culture*, ed. by David R. Hiley, James F. Bohman, and Richard Shusterman (Ithaca: Cornell University Press, 1991), 1–14. The volume addresses central issues of interpretation as they relate to the "two cultures" of science and the humanities in essays by prominent philosophical thinkers such as Thomas Kuhn, Hubert Dreyfus, Richard Rorty, David Couzens Hoy, Alexander Nehamas, and Charles Taylor. Challenges to positivism – Nietzsche plays a seminal role here – have raised awareness of the ubiquitous role of the interpretive act across the disciplines. Critical to my argument is the interdependency of theory and practice, for theory depends on feedback from the successes and failures of its application. My "interpretive turn" is different from the one that informs this valuable collection of essays in that the interpretive act is grounded as much in the workings of physical nature as in shared values of conceptual traditions. Thus, my approach is a modified version of "hermeneutic contextualism" rather than of "hermeneutic universalism," for it allows appeal to experience independent of interpretation (7). Positively, hermeneutic contextualism implies holism; negatively, it denies atomism. I do not wish to deny atomism, nor do I wish to understand contextualism as circular justification. Chaos and complexity theory allow me to tread where the authors of *The Interpretive Turn* could not go.

7 Richard Shusterman, "Beneath Interpretation," in *The Interpretive Turn* (1991), 102–28, here 126–27.

a mechanistic sense fully in keeping with the then dominant view of the universe as a clockwork and of God as the great clock maker. The universe came to be seen as one of many possible universes that the Deity could have created; gradually, the concept of multiplicity and vistas of new possibilities began to capture the popular imagination. Associated with the Golden Age of the Copernican turn are first and foremost Giordano Bruno, Galileo Galilei, Johannes Kepler, Christian Huygens, Isaac Newton (the "new Moses"of the Book of Nature), and the philosopher-mathematician Gottfried Wilhelm Leibniz.[8] Goethe's *Faust* plays on many of these ideas.

The second revolution – fueled by theories of thermodynamics, relativity, and quantum physics – commenced in the nineteenth and continued into the twentieth century. Advances in physics were augmented by tremendous strides in chemistry. Given the rising incidence of unpredictability, the amount of (co-)motion began to heat up. Mathematical calculations indicated that our ordered universe is stable only in a relative sense and is not permanently immutable. Researchers contributing to the new view that the world was in danger of turning turbulent include William Faraday, Hermann von Helmholtz, Henri Poincaré, Max Plank, Niels Bohr, Albert Einstein, and Werner Heisenberg. Their contributions were made directly through their basic research but also indirectly through the popularization (and distortion) of their ideas in the broader culture, which was fascinated more by the perception of disturbance than of an intricate order of complexity. All of their efforts can be seen in relation to the scientific positivism of the nineteenth century which accompanied the rise of modernism to a position of dominance.

This second turn in the art of seeing – which analyzed movement by focusing on a fixed point (*analysis situs*) – was, like the Copernican one, also evident in the human sciences. One need only recall the new mappings of humankind by Friedrich Nietzsche, Sigmund Freud, C. J. Jung, Georg Simmel, and Alfred North Whitehead. All of these developments amounted to an assault on the traditional view of the human being as a stable, self-directed creature. The upshot was a radical revision of an essentially static world to one of force fields and flux. Humankind was increasingly seen as part and parcel of the dynamic interplay discernible in the physical realm and subject to continued evolution.[9] *Steppenwolf* (1927) by the naturalized Swiss popular novelist Hermann Hesse, *Mann ohne Eigenschaften* (Man Without Qualities, 1930) by the Austrian writer-mathematician Robert Musil, and *Die Blechtrommel* (The Tin Drum, 1959) by the German poet-activist Günter Grass are examples of this transfer

---

8 Prigogine and Stengers, *Order Out of Chaos* (1984), 27. See also Karl S. Guthke, *The Last Frontier: Imagining Other Worlds from the Copernican Revolution to Modern Science Fiction*, trans. by Helen Atkins (Ithaca: Cornell University Press, 1990), chap. 2: "The Renaissance–Science Falls From Grace" (43–111).

9 On the foregoing, see, e.g., Alexandre Koyré, *From the Closed World to the Infinite Universe* (New York: Harper, 1958); Blumenberg, *Genesis* (1987); and Prigogine and Stengers, *Order Out of Chaos* (1984).

from the physical to the social and even mental dimension. Two of the authors received the Nobel Prize for literature.

A third revolution in our conception of the world and humankind's place in it has various roots but generally began in the 1960s, later crystallizing in part as the science of chaos (and subsequently succumbing to the diluting effect of popularization). Even before the term "chaos" came into use, however, there were signs of a fundamental paradigm change in some disciplines in the late 1950s. By the late 1960s, it had all the earmarks of a broad transformation of the first magnitude in our world-view. For example, in 1955 Rudolf Carnap published an influential essay on the "Logical Foundations of the Unity of Science."[10] His interest was in the languages of the disciplines and how they might contribute to a unity of science. Using the term "science" in its widest sense – that is, inclusive of the social sciences and humanities as well as of the natural sciences – it essentially connoted "merely a more systematic continuation" of everyday activities aimed at acquiring and validating knowledge of every kind. However, his intent was not to promote a unity of science in ontological terms (e.g., "Is the world one?"), but rather to question whether there was a unity of the "logical relationships between the terms and laws of the various branches of science" (397). While granting that the line separating the physical and biological branches of knowledge is not all that clear – for example, physics forms a sublanguage in the vocabulary of biology – Carnap nevertheless retained the distinction between the two branches because physics precedes biology as a discipline. Similarly, he saw no clear demarcation between psychology and the social sciences. Their languages of discourse are infused with concepts from the other fields of inquiry such that there is no way to determine which sublanguage is antecedent. Concerning the question of fundamental laws of logic transcending disciplinary lines, Carnap concluded that a future development in science would be the "construction of one homogeneous system of laws for the whole of science" ("Foundations" 403). His was a contribution to the then heated "two cultures" debate associated with C. P. Snow and F. R. Leavis.

Three years later, the biologists Paul Oppenheim and Hilary Putnam took up the same question.[11] In contrast to Carnap, however, they defined science in a more traditionally narrow fashion, placing maximum stress on the hard sciences. They

---

10 Rudolf Carnap, "Logical Foundations of the Unity of Science," *International Encyclopedia of Unified Science*, vol. 1, ed. O. Neurath, R. Carnap, and C. Morris (Chicago: University of Chicago Press, 1938–55), 42–62. The essay was reissued in *The Philosophy of Science*, ed. Richard Boyd, Philip Gasper, and J. D. Trout (Cambridge, MA: MIT University Press, 1991), 393–403. The reprint is cited.

11 Paul Oppenheim und Hilary Putnam, "Unity of Science as a Working Hypothesis," Minnesota Studies in the Philosophy of Science, vol. II, ed. H. Feigl, M. Scriven, and G. Maxwell (Minneapolis: University of Minnesota Press, 1958): 3–36; rpt. in *The Philosophy of Science*, ed. by Richard Boyd, Philip Gasper, and J. D. Trout (Cambridge, MA: MIT University Press, 1991), 405–27; the foregoing is based on 405–09.

argued that unity of science can be seen in three general ways:

- the reduction of all the terms of science to those of one discipline (unity of language);
- the reduction of the laws of science to those of one branch of science (unity of laws);
- the innate interconnectedness of that one set of laws.

The last was more the result of intuition than of empirical evidence. For them, the term "unity of science" denoted both an ideal state (= unitary science) as well as a palpable *trend* within science. Although they concurred with Carnap that *unitary* science (that is, commonality of language and laws) did not exist, they considered it to be a valuable working hypothesis. To achieve the ultimate objective of unitary science, they offered a six-step paradigm of "inclusion relations" which range upward from discrete units of matter to complex systems of interaction:

1. elementary particles,
2. atoms,
3. molecules,
4. cells,
5. multicellular living things,
6. social groups.

These levels are inclusive because "each level includes *all higher levels*" and "the highest level to which a thing belongs will be considered the 'proper' level of that thing" ("Hypothesis" 409; emphasis added). Given that the six fundamental categories roughly correspond to the sciences, the perhaps inadvertent impression arises of a hierarchical and teleological model. In any event, the paradigm seems biased toward communities of living beings. For instance, levels 1-3 fall within the realm of physics, 4-5 biology, and 6 (the most complex because the most inclusive) correlates to the social sciences ("Hypothesis" 421). The lines of division along the six levels are not clear; physics is the base from which biology and the social sciences emerge, and biology is present in levels 3 and 6 as well as in the core area of 4–5. This ordering anticipates the catchword of "community" in more contemporary scientific discourse. Giant polymers and multicellular organisms can be described as "communities"of individual molecules and cells, respectively.

It seems self-evident that primordial living substance evolved from inanimate molecules and gradually evolved into the unicellular ancestors of all living things. Because of the capacity for self-duplication and mutability, life is possible. That ability was not a single chance event, but a process requiring about two billion years and entailing the cooperation of protein and nucleic acid. "Borderline" living organisms such as viruses have been successfully synthesized out of nonliving highly complex macro-molecules. Protein taken from a virus has been joined with nucleic acid to obtain an active virus. Giant polymers with about 10,000 amino-acid residues had also been cultivated by the late 1950s ("Hypothesis" 420). More recently, these earlier, modest successes have led to the human genome project and to initial successes in the cloning of human stem cells; indeed, whole multicellular organisms (sheep, rats) have been synthesized. Although no one has yet created a virus out of atoms, the general facts of biology, geology, paleontology, biochemistry, and radiology suggest that organic and inorganic matter are related at some level. Consequently, Oppenheim and Putnam provide a scientifically detailed picture of the growing complexity of biological organisms derived from relatively simple inorganic matter.

Arthur Koestler's work on unitary science in the 1960s and 1970s emphasized the biological disciplines even more. In *The Act of Creation* (1964) Koestler displayed an enhanced awareness of the complexity of phenomena as innovative process. Yet Koestler approached the question of the creative act from a humanistic rather than a scientific perspective, a point highlighted by George Steiner in his review of Koestler's later *Beyond Reductionism* (1970), a compilation of the proceedings of the 1968 Alpach symposium. Steiner commented that the "codings" and "fields" advocated by Koestler and his group were part of a general revolution in perspective. The anti-reductionism of Alpach could be seen as "a polemic salvo in the early stages of a scientific revolution."[12] The stage was set for a momentous change in the way we see the relationship between humans and their environment. The next step followed logically and immediately.

The academic year 1970-71 marked another providential juncture in the evolution of a new paradigm and potential unity of language across the disciplines. That year David Ruelle spent as a fellow at the Institute for Advanced Study in Princeton where he elucidated his theory on the onset of turbulence and the role of strange attractors, which became known as the Ruelle-Takens thesis. Following subsequent experiments at Harvard and City College in New York, the controversial ideas evolved into interesting and ultimately well-known concepts. Retrospectively, Ruelle designated that period a turning point: "A new paradigm arose, and it received a name – *chaos* – from Jim Yorke, an applied mathematician working at the University of Maryland."[13] The perception of a radical break was, as had been the case with the Copernican turn, perhaps even more influential than the actual scientific discourse preceding and accompanying the realignment or the proliferation of new and intermediate disciplines in its wake. (Disciplinary studies in a modern sense began in the eighteenth century

---

12 George Steiner, "Life-Lines," in Steiner, *Extraterritorial. Papers on Literature and the Language Revolution*, 5th printing (New York: Atheneum, 1976), 176–77, 195–96.

13 David Ruelle, *Chance and Chaos* (Princeton: Princeton University Press, 1993), 67.

with the establishment of philosophy, mathematics, anthropology, aesthetics, psychology, and historiography as increasingly distinct domains.) Attention is ultimately directed at understanding the interconnectedness of the cosmos. And cosmos is derived from the Greek word for order: *κόσμος*.

Although a young science, chaos drew heavily upon long-known facts and myths of the past in outlining a new vision of order and reality. In the process, it liberated matter from its previous confines. By freely drawing upon other schools of thought, most notably the general and special theory of relativity and the laws of thermodynamics, chaos has attracted wider attention to the "unnoticed revolution" between 1900 and 1930 wrought by the radical questioning of classical physics. The first signs of mounting dissent were discernible even before the turn of the century. In fact, the rethinking of classical physics coincided with Friedrich Nietzsche's re-evaluation of values, a point to be pursued later in this study.

The father of deterministic chaos is generally seen to be Henri Poincaré (1854–1912), the first scientist to describe what is now known as a chaotic system. In 1887, King Oskar II of Sweden offered a prize of 2,500 Swedish crowns for the best response to the thorny question that had puzzled scientists for generations: Is the solar system stable? Although Poincaré did not completely answer the question, he did prove that Newtonian equations were inadequate to the task. Poincaré's 270-page response on the three-body dynamic, *Les méthodes nouvelles de la méchanique céleste*, contained so many new and unusual insights that it was awarded the prize.[14] In essence, he called for the creation of a new science to explain the complex dynamics regulating the interplay of the earth, moon, and sun. Among other advances, he invented a new brand of mathematics, topology, containing such archetypical properties as "connectedness" and "knottedness." Topology has also been dubbed "rubber-sheet geometry" because it is the mathematics of stretching, of continuity, and of infinitely mutable shapes.

Given the dimensions of the problem – the solar system consists of twenty larger and 4,000 smaller bodies – it is no wonder that the dynamics of interaction eluded quantifying systems of Poincaré's day. Today's picture is further complicated by the recognition that our sun is just one of about 100 billion stars circling the center of the galaxy. Troubling for Poincaré were the apparently random gyrations of a simple three-body system. Although he had no desire to break with classical physics, his analysis of position did not leave him much choice but to think in unusual ways. An essential point developed further in his later work is that chance and determinism are reconciled in long-term predictability. In this connection he deepened insight into the sensitive dependence on initial conditions that was later to become a hallmark of chaos theory. Yet his explanations, perhaps because they were mind-boggling, found no echo

14 Henri Poincaré, *Les méthodes nouvelles de la méchanique céleste* (Paris: Gauthiers-Villars, 1892).

among his contemporaries. Ruelle surmised that Poincaré's ideas simply came too early; neither the mathematics of measure theory nor the ergodic theorem nor computer technology yet existed to formulate Poincaré's intuitive insights. Besides quantum mechanics offered a ready explanation for chance and randomness (Ruelle 49–50). It was not until Edward Lorenz of the Massachusetts Institute of Technology rediscovered Poincaré's work in the 1970s that it was recognized as an early landmark in complex dynamics. Since then the full consequences of the paradigm shift from Euclidean geometry to fractals has been felt.[15]

Chaologists generally use the term "chaos" in the sense of deterministic chaos because they see it as a system in which everything is interconnected, even if the picture is turbulent and the outcome unpredictable in the "short" term. Accident plays no role; initial and intermediate values do. In his inimical manner, Ian Stewart laconically defines chaos as "lawless behaviour governed entirely by law" and sums up its curious properties as "sensitivity to initial conditions, existence of random itineraries, common occurrence of random itineraries, and cake-mix periodicity/aperiodicity" (Stewart 1989: 17, 124). This extreme sensitivity to change is captured in the metaphor of the famous "butterfly effect" so often invoked by chaologists. It refers to radical changes brought about by even the slightest change (e.g., the flapping of butterflies' wings off the coast of Jamaica can cause – or prevent – a typhoon in the Indian Ocean a month later). The black hole at the center of our galaxy, too, effects changes at the fringes thousands of light years away. (Of course, we will not be around to see the ultimate effect of that influence.) Yet even the butterfly and black-hole effects represent a brutal intrusion in atmospheric conditions compared to the gravitational pull of an electron at the edge of the known universe on distant objects that are closer to the center. Despite its minuscule force field and its distance of 10 billion light years, the electron exerts such a strong impact on the movement of an oxygen molecule that the latter's orbit becomes unpredictable after 56 iterations; the rate of interference is several billion per second. Thus, the correlation time is a mere nanosecond. But of course the oxygen molecule is subject to other influences as well.

All of this causes us to rethink the classical conception of equal force/equal reaction and to reconceptualize the Newtonian metaphor of the universe as a mechanistic clockwork. While physicists thought for some time that chaos does not occur on the nanoscale, more recent advances in measuring instruments (e.g., the electron microscope, but also the differential microwave radiometer and the Hubble Space Telescope) make it appear entirely likely "that the microworld is governed not by deterministic laws that precisely regulate the behavior of atoms and their

15 The foregoing discussion is based on Morfill and Scheingraber, *Chaos* (1992), 44–55; Ian Stewart, *Does God Play Dice? The Mathematics of Chaos* (Cambridge, MA: Blackwell, 1989), 59–72; Ruelle, *Chance*, 45–79; and Paul Davies, *Other Worlds: A Portrait of Nature in Rebellion – Space, Superspace and the Quantum Universe* (New York: Simon and Schuster, 1980), 11–15.

constituents, but by randomness and indeterminacy" (Davies, *Other Worlds* 75). True, quantum phenomena are so minuscule as to have no discernible effect on our daily lives, but that does not mean that the quantum "leap" is without its butterfly effect, even if the wavelength of quantum phenomena is a billion billion times smaller than an atomic nucleus (10^{-18}). Mounting evidence now indicates, for example, that the quantum-level events of the first fraction of a second following the creation of the universe probably produced the cosmic seeds from which we and our world evolved (Smoot and Davidson 1993: 1–18 and 272–97). Even before these latest discoveries, Prigogine concluded his investigation of paradigm shifts in the history of science with the remark: "At all levels, be it the level of macroscopic physics, the level of fluctuations, or the microscopic level, *nonequilibrium is the source of order. Nonequilibrium brings 'order out of chaos'*" (Prigogine and Stengers 286-87).

Several years later, the physicist Paul Davies reminded us that linearity and nonlinearity are not mutually exclusive within the same system (probably because linearity is in reality only a mathematical approximation, whereas in the popular mind it tends to be much more specific and absolute). On the minutest scale of measurement, analysis of the parts alone proves insufficient to understand the nature of their interplay because the whole is now greater than the sum of its individual parts.[16] The advantage of chaos as a theory is that it endeavors to understand the nonlinear system in its totality. That totality is beginning to extend to the quantum level. This is especially true in string theory.

String theory, as it has evolved over the past twenty years, suggests that the basic constituents of the universe are neither point nor wave-like particles, but rather tiny wriggling strings. Because string theory can mathematically explain the dynamics of the universe on both the nano and micro scales, submicroscopic and cosmic operations are increasingly viewed as being the same subject. Analogies to holograms are cited to explain how the inner and outer elements are interrelated (Davies and Gribbin 1992: 42; see also Smoot and Davidson 1993: 296). "Once you get down to strings," Brian Greene remarks in his best seller, *The Elegant Universe* (1999), "you can't go any further."[17] An essential difference between strings and discrete particles is that strings are extended objects; moreover, they oscillate and have the ability to curl up, to wrap

16 Davies and Gribbin, *Matter* (1992), 45-46. See also the concept of "hypnons" introduced by Prigogine and Stengers (1984): they are "sleepwalkers, since they ignore each other at equilibrium. Each of them may be as complex as you wish [...], but at equilibrium their complexity is turned 'inward.' Again, inside a molecule there is an intensive electric field, but this field in a dilute gas is negligible as far as other molecules are concerned" (287).

17 Brian Greene, *The Elegant Universe: Superstrings, Hidden Dimensions, and the Quest for the Ultimate Theory* (New York: Vintage Books, 2000), 233. See also the brief summary by Dennis Overbye, "String Theory, at 20, Explains It All (or Not)," *New York Times*, Tuesday, December 7, 2004, section D: "Science Times," pp. 1, 4.

themselves around a cylindrical universe. While Riemannian geometry (topology) based on space between points holds true at the greater distances involved in particle-point mapping in a flat universe, it proves inadequate to explain the distortions at the very short distances of quantum operations compounded by the vibrations of the strings in a winding mode of motion. (Perhaps the *ends* of the strings appear to us to be more or less discrete points?) Because of the strings' twisting and turning, distance takes on new meaning; it is made even more complex by ten (rather than four) space-time dimensions. A new quantum geometry is called for, one that sets a lower limit to physically accessible distance scales (Greene 231–41).

In any event, in the paradigm shift toward complexity, *force* (gravitational, electromagnetic, thermal, material), as the dominant concept in the natural and social sciences, is being challenged by *information communication* as the new ordering principle of systems, communication, not in the human sense of understanding but of "data transfer." Force is not simply discarded; it is participatory in the transmission of information.[18] Knottedness as a leitmotif in topography, by the way, implies the presence of more densely packed information in a space-time dimension. It bears resemblance to the energy knots and solitons observed in the physical world and is analogous to the clustering of celestial bodies in the universe. These diverse examples of "knottedness" in the topography of existence seem related to the oscillating "winding mode of motion" critical to superstring theory. In terms of force, string theory is not a theory of just the strong force but of all forces. Nonetheless, and despite the attractiveness of string theory in explaining how space-time is constructed, theorists readily grant that they are no closer to understanding the deep structure of strings (Overbye D4, col.2). Critical are the paths of information communication facilitated by the strings.

18 Steiner, "Life-Lines," 180. Jahn and Dunne, *Margins* (1987), emphasize the continued value of quantum energy in assessing the nature of reality and of human consciousness (see especially 195–287). On information transmission in the phenomenon of entropy, see 335-40, where entropy is defined as "the lowest information order," that is, the state of highest unpredictability (336). Davies and Gribbin, *Matter*, refer to work on "soliton ripples" in molecular biology (rather than chemical reactions) as the means of transmitting energy along the length of the DNA molecule (1992: 54).

2. THE GROUND OF IMMANENCE OR PARSING PARTICLES

More than two billion years ago, a new cell capable of breathing oxygen emerged and became the foundation of multicellular life on earth as we know it today. The geneticist Lynn Margulis theorizes that this innovative cell was the result not of genetic mutation but of a symbiosis of various bacteria. In other words, the cell necessary for life came about not through aggressive interaction with other forms competing for survival but through cooperation with them. For example, the cooperation of archaebacteria, respiring bacteria, and quick-moving spirochaete bacteria brought together their talents in a host cell. The combined cell learned to breathe oxygen and thus to thrive in an atmosphere "poisoned" by "fumes" resulting from climactic changes. The crisis caused by the production of oxygen led to the cooperative effort of several bacteria, which in turn laid the basis for our own culture. Recent work in biology tends to confirm the thesis of a shift from exclusionary dominance to cooperation and symbiotic relationships between originally alien organisms in eukaryotic cells that characterize carbon-based life forms on earth.[19] The cooperation is based on shared information and skills.

The Max Planck Institute for Biophysical Chemistry in Göttingen, under the direction of Manfred Eigen, interprets nucleotides as so many letters and ribbons of nucleic acid as so many words of a text to be translated by molecular "machinery" in the cells into another molecular language: that of amino acids which combine into protein. The simplest form of this cooperative chain of events – or "hypercycle" – is a "catalytic circle" of cooperating nucleic acids. Nucleic acid A catalyzes the reproduction of nucleic acid B without altering its own identifying characteristics; B helps C, C supports D and so on, until the chain makes its way back to A. On the accompanying graph (fig. 1.1) reproduced from *Geo-Wissen*, this potent chain of molecular information sharing is represented by the shift from catalytic molecule (Katalytischer Moleküle) K1 to K2, K3 etc., until the loop feeds back into K1. In each instance, the information-bearing molecule (I1, I2, etc.) is affected by the change while also affecting alterations in information. Two kinds of molecules (ribosomes and enzymes) function as catalysts in these open systems. This kind of hypercycle of cooperation can consist of two nucleic acids, but it can just as easily consist of several thousand. The human body, for example, is composed of about 100,000 different kinds of autocatalytic molecules, all bound together in an extraordinary, dissipative system

19 John Briggs and F. David Peat, *Turbulent Mirror. An Illustrated Guide to Chaos Theory and the Science of Wholeness* (New York: Harper and Row, 1989), 154-61. See Roger Penrose, *Shadows of the Mind* (Oxford: Oxford University Press, 1994), 361.

of grand cooperation.[20]

Figure 1.1: Hypercycles with Information Transfer Paths
(from Franz Mechsner, "Im Anfang war der Hyperzyklus," in *Geo-Wissen: Chaos + Kreativität*, 83)

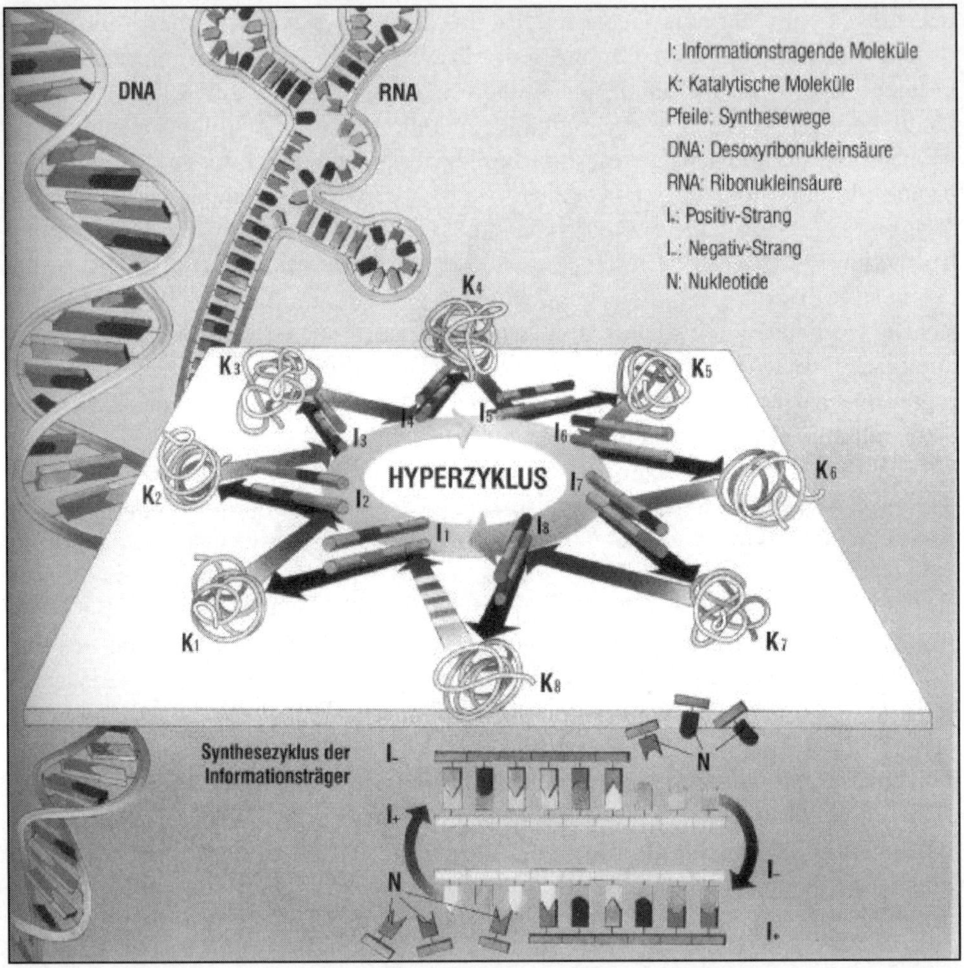

The feedback loops make of the catalytic circle a nonlinear system that proves to be more than the sum of its parts. Enzymes and ribosomes allow for the accurate reproduction of more than a hundred nucleotides in a string. And we know that superstrings of 10,000 or more nucleotides became possible only when the twisted

20 Stuart Kauffman, *At Home in the Universe* (New York: Oxford University Press, 1995), 52. Kauffman gives his version of the creation myth in describing how life arose from inanimate matter (54–69).

helix of DNA took over from the RNA virus. The complexity of DNA allows for the self-regulation of genetic information. Far from being errors, deviations in the copying of the complex information ensures the creativity that is the essence of life. Eigen's team concluded that there must have been nucleic acids from the very start that did not compete with one another, but rather cooperated in order to enhance mutual productivity.[21]

As the diversity of molecules in a system increases, the number of "edges" and "communication lines" increases. Eventually, the molecules take on the function of catalysts themselves, and, Kauffman opines, a giant catalyzed reaction web forms, snapping a "collectively autocatalytic system" into existence and causing life to emerge as a "phase transition" (*At Home* 62). Replacing evolution, coevolution now emerged as the key term. Single-cell and multi-cell organisms are reciprocal in their codetermination.[22] There is also mounting evidence that genes and culture in the broadest sense are coevolutionary (Wilson, *Consilience* 125-63).

Moreover, we can take an example from high-energy particle physics for the cooperative nature of the agon (popularly associated with antagonism rather than with coordination). For years, high-energy physicists have been colliding proton beams in an accelerator in the hope that the resultant decomposition of the particles will reveal the mysterious mechanism that gives mass to all matter (the so-called Higgs mechanism). While that goal has not (yet) been achieved – that is, while researchers have not yet gotten to the bottom of things – their experiments have led to a fuller picture of the smallest particles in the universe, or at least of what currently count as the smallest, indivisible particles in the universe. Of the several hundred types of subatomic particles identified thus far, the vast majority are unstable, that is, they decay after only fractions of a second of human time. Only a small number seem to be indivisible with no internal structure. The most familiar of the fundamental particles are leptons and quarks. All other subatomic particles, hadrons, fall into two categories: baryons and mesons. Leptons are particles of very low mass that are not affected by the strong nuclear force interactions in the nucleus. Quarks are the building blocks of

---

21 Franz Mechsner, "Im Anfang war der Hyperzyklus," in *Geo-Wissen: Chaos + Kreativität*, ed. by Günter Haaf (Hamburg: Gruner and Jahr AG, 1990), 72–86; here 80. See also the graphs in Kauffman, *At Home* (1995), 59, 61, 65. Arthur Koestler, *The Act of Creation* (New York: Macmillan, 1964), has also attached great importance to the open thermodynamic system – which he called "morphogenesis" – stressing the coding and recoding abilities of DNA (see esp. 416–29).

22 The dominant trend is to explain mind and spirit as a stage in coevolution from inanimate to animate and ultimately mental states, all of which exist within feedback loops. See, e.g., *The Ghost in the Atom: A Discussion of the Mysteries of Quantum Physics*, ed. by P. C. W. Davies and J. R. Brown (Cambridge: Cambridge University Press, 1986), esp. 31–34; Paul Davies, *The Cosmic Blueprint* (London: Unwin Hyman, 1989), 183–96; and David Bohm, *Wholeness and the Implicate Order* (Cambridge: Routledge and Kegan Paul, 1980), 196–213.

the subatomic universe; they are components of protons and neutrons.[23] Together with the indivisible electrons, protons and neutrons are the stuff of atoms (see fig. 1.2). Messenger particles (bosons) carry the four fundamental forces of the universe: photons carry the electromagnetic force, gluons convey the strong nuclear force, W^+/ W^-/ Z^o particles exchange the weak nuclear force, and theoretical gravitons, not yet observed, are thought to be responsible for transmitting the force of gravity between objects.

Figure 1.2
Sample Elementary Particles

baryons. Hadrons that consist of three quarks.

bosons. Particles that carry the basic physical forces.

electrons. The lightest letptons. They have a charge of -1. Electrons play important roles in electrical and chemical reactions.

fermions. All particles with an odd hald-integral spin, such as 1/2 or 2/2. Examples include leptons and baryons.

gluons. Bosons that carry the strong force between quarks

gravitons. Bosons that presumably carry the gravitational force. Gravitons have not actually been observed yet.

hadrons. All particles that are made up of quarks.

leptons. Particles that are found outside the nucleus. There are six types: electrons, muons, taus and their respective neutrinos.

mesons. Hadrons formed from one quark and its antiquark.

muons. Leptons that are slightly heavier than the electron. Although they existed in the early moments of the universe, they now exist only in cosmic rays and particle accelerators.

neutrinos. No electric charge, very little mass.

neutrons. Uncharged elementary particles that, along with photons, are constituents of atomic nuclei.

photons. Bosons which carry the electromagnetic force.

protons. Along with **neutrons** these positively charged particles constitute atomic nuclei.

quarks. Particles that make up neutrons and protons. They come in six types called flavors: up, down, charm, strange, top, and bottom.

taus. The heaviest leptons. Once abundant in the early universe, now found only in particle accelerators and cosmic rays.

vector mesons (also called $\mathbf{W^+}$, $\mathbf{W^-}$, **and** $\mathbf{Z^0}$). Bosons. Carry the weak force; responsible for some types of radioactive decay.

According to the accepted model there are currently twelve ordinary particles. Evidence for five of six suspected quarks was found in the 1970s (up, charm, top; down, strange, bottom), along with evidence for six leptons (electron, muon, tau; electron-neutrino, muon-neutrino, tau-neutrino). The quest for the superheavy top

23 The physicist Murray Gell-Mann proposed the quark model in the mid 1960s, lifting the term "quark" from James Joyce's *Finnegans Wake* to designate the basic building blocks of the universe.

quark, which was not detected until 1995, took another twenty years. Like the bottom and charm, the top quark can exist only at very high energies. Up and down quarks and electron and electron-neutrino leptons make up the world as we know it. The rest of the particles are associated with matter that existed in the infant universe when temperatures ranged from 10^{15} to 10^{27} degrees Kelvin; these temperatures are re-created in particle accelerators.[24] In their efforts to get to the bottom of things, researchers have noted that the collision of protons and antiprotons does not necessarily result in the fragmentation of the particles aimed at one another. For one thing, protons and antiprotons are actually conglomerates of three quarks whirling around each other, exchanging particles called gluons that serve to bind the quarks together in an interquark gluon force that seems to be a much stronger version of the force that binds neutrons and protons together.[25] Because of that extremely complex dynamic and the intervening spaces, the collisions are seldom clean, producing widely divergent results. But when a direct hit occurs, the results can be spectacular, as happened in 1992 at Fermilab in Illinois. A collision of two protons produced a highly energetic electron and a highly energetic muon, as well as two jets of hadron and a neutrino.[26] What is especially noteworthy in our context, however, is that the collisions produced new particles (pions, kaons, lambdas, sigmas, the xi-minus, xi-zero) more complicated (i.e., heavier) than the colliding proton and antiproton. "Instead of simplicity – a few smaller particles – physicists were facing complexity – hundreds of large particles," Teresi noted (*Omni* 16/4: 86). What occurs is expansion, not micro-reduction. The bottom of things just kept receding.

In 1911, Ernest Rutherford, who argued that matter was mostly empty space, estimated that if the nucleus of an atom were the size of a pea, then the electrons circling it would be 300 feet away. By comparison, the quark is infinitesimally smaller. Another way of looking at it is to say that if an atom were the size of a Great Pyramid of Egypt, then an electron would be the size of a peach in relation to it. The

---

24 See Smoot and Davidson, *Wrinkles* (1993), 92-112, 173-91; and Davies and Gribbin, *Matter* (1992), 150-73. Antimatter is a different matter again. For all elementary particles of matter there exist according to this theory exact counterparts, but not in the world as we know it, for when matter and antimatter collide they annihilate one another. It is suspected that matter and anti-matter annihilated each other almost at the instant of creation of the universe (1 second, 10^{10} degrees Kelvin), leaving however a slight residue of matter due to a tiny asymmetry in the rate of "decay" between the two. To be more precise: the excess of matter amounted to about one-in-a-billion. The amount of antimatter present in our galaxy is estimated at less than one part in a million.

25 Davies and Gribbin, *Matter* (1992), 240. For a readable account of some advances in particle physics, see Dick Teresi, "The Last Great Experiment of the 20th Century," *Omni*, vol. 16, no. 4 (1993): 39–47, 82–89; Paul Davies and John Gribbin, *Matter* (1992), 235–60; Greene, *The Elegant Universe* (2000). Greene includes a useful glossary of scientific terms.

26 Hadrons are narrow, energetic streams of particles. The term is derived from the Greek word for heavy. Hadrons consist of either two or three quarks.

suspected mass for the top quark was somewhere between 113-250 GeV (billion electron volts). When detected, the top quark weighed in at an enormous 176GeV (1.76×10^{11} electron volts). That high energy level ensured that it would be short-lived. Because it does not exist long enough to be measured accurately, researchers must rely upon circumstantial evidence (such as hadrons and neutrinos) to determine the top quark's "nonpresence." Given the difficulty of achieving a direct hit capable of producing the high energy level necessary to make the massive top quark, which statistically should happen every billion collisions or so, the search for it was indeed arduous.

Related to the above, and even more significant for my thesis of a common base for creativity in nature and humankind, is the inner tension of the atom. This field of tension seems driven by three of the four known forces of nature: the electromagnetic force, and the strong and weak nuclear forces. (Gravity is the fourth, which Newton had dubbed the single most important force at the beginning of the eighteenth century). The search is on for evidence of supersymmetry, which could relate these four forces to one another. It is known, for example, that a proton is strongly repelled by the electrical charges of its neighboring protons. However, the much stronger attraction of the nucleus prevents the proton from being propelled outside the nuclear surface. That binding nuclear force is qualitatively different from the electromagnetic fields within its environment. As mentioned, researchers suspect that the nuclear field is created by the exchange of virtual quanta (gluons) among the nuclear particles. Unlike virtual photons, virtual quanta possess mass. The inner tension is further evident in the fact that neutrons – which are themselves electrically neutral – are accompanied by a cloud of virtual particles, some of which are electrically charged.[27]

Virtual particles are exceedingly short-lived, fleeting entities that appear and disappear spontaneously. The closer they are to their particular center, the more energetic and more short-lived they are. Real particles, on the other hand, are long-lived and thus more familiar to us. (Of course, even celestial bodies, which are indeed real, are drawn like real particles to their "center" or dominant black hole.) Moreover, virtual photons fulfill an important role as messengers through empty space, binding particles of matter together like so much glue. Without them, divergence would be the order of the day:

> If it were not for the unending network of messenger traffic, particles of matter would be completely oblivious of one another; there would be no interactions at all. Every article would simply fly off along its own independent path through space, never deviating, and to all intents and purposes it would be alone in the Universe. (Davies and Gribbin, *Matter*, 239–40)

27 Davies, *Other Worlds* (1980), 80–90. See also Davies and Gribben, *Matter* (1992), 235–60.

From this description of particle behavior, divergent and convergent forces are obviously at work, even at the smallest level of existence. (One cannot help but wonder at the uncanny similarity, at least on a rudimentary level, between this view of particle physics and Leibniz's theory of the self-contained yet interconnected system of monads driven by an underlying symmetry. Except for the lines of communication, each monad would be isolated.) The grand unified force that coordinates all this movement is embodied in the messenger particle called "X" which has: a million billion times the mass of a proton. Extremely short-lived, it can travel only about a trillionth of the distance across a proton before disappearing again (= ca. 10^{-18}m); thus, it can even appear *inside* a proton. As infinitesimal as those distances seem, the spatial relationship would equate to that of three bees in an aircraft hangar measuring 10 million kilometers across (Davies and Gribbin, *Matter* 258–59).

The standard model of the nucleus, composed of protons and neutrons, is thus based on complementary and covalent forces in a cloud of probability (see fig. 1.3). To summarize, the standard model allows only two kinds of ordinary particles: quarks and leptons. Quarks form the nuclei of neutrons and protons, each of which consists of three quarks. The neutron has two down quarks (-1/3 charge) and one up (+2/3 charge), while the proton has two up quarks and one down. Leptons orbit the nucleus. Quarks and leptons are, in turn, classified into three families of particles. One inhabits the realm of low energy (= normal matter), the remaining two exist only in high-energy fields (e.g., cosmic radiation or a supercollider). All of these interacting forces – both within the nucleus and between it and its electron shell – bring about a covalent

Figure 1.3: Models of the Atom (from *Encarta Encyclopedia* 2002)

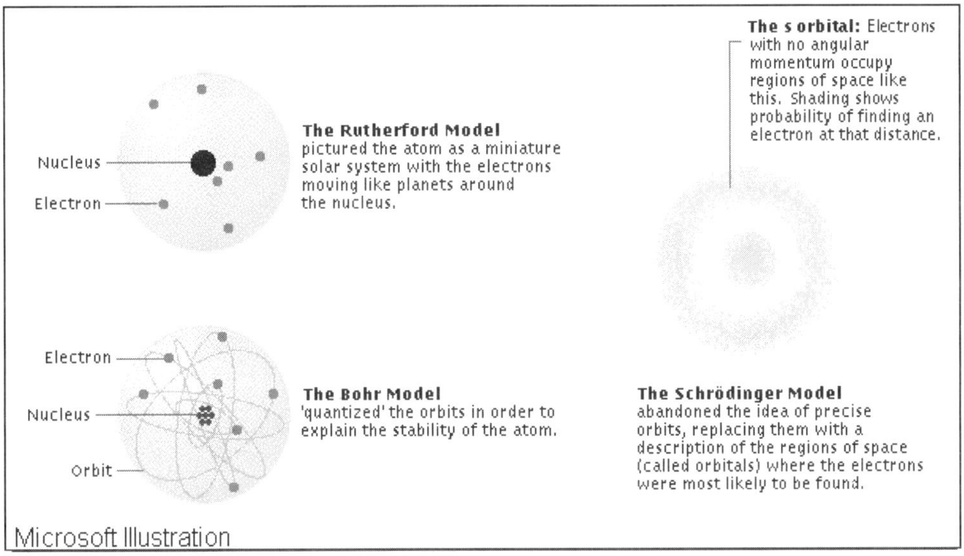

bond of the spinning protons and virtual particles with the nucleus, despite their individual differences. The three quarks in each proton and neutron are bound loosely together, for instance, by the rapid and continuous exchange of gluons.

A potentially philosophical significance of these observations arises with the top quark being nicknamed the "truth" quark (*Omni* 16/4: 89), while its partner, the bottom quark, is also known as the "beauty" quark. No doubt there is a strong incentive to see in all this symmetry an aesthetic experience as well. A broader philosophical dimension is suggested by the hypothesis of kinetic bonding that results from shared information. Robert Jahn and Brenda Dunne speak of "the surrender of *information*" that distinguishes "the identities of two interacting subsystems." For them, that "translates into an increment in the structural *energy* of the bonded system."[28] (The significance of this particular point will be seen most poignantly in the later discussion of the soliton and its relationship to creativity.) After some translation of terminology, we might see in the "surrender of information" among interacting subsystems, which brings about a closer bonding, a modern scientific explanation of Adam and Eve's sharing in the divine knowledge of good and evil. At first they seem to have experienced a loss. But their growing share of knowledge led them inexorably to a fuller appreciation of *what* they had lost. The amassing of information enhances the ability to differentiate, which in turn leads paradoxically to a stronger bond of the complex whole. Maybe the scientist's quest for the top quark is not unlike Plato's love of Truth or Augustine's yearning for God. Like the top quark, God and Truth do not form nicely packaged entities that can be grasped firmly and held fast. They seem more analogous to the atom as a cloud of probability. To accept this (radical) analogy, one must shift dimensions of thought.

These phenomena from cell biology and particle physics belie the usual connotations of the terms "agon," "dominance," and "antagonism." We need to think in new ways in order to comprehend what happens at the microchemical and particle levels. Some time ago, Werner Heisenberg called for a new, more open way of thinking.[29] That has led today, in the wake of ever clearer insights into the deep structure of reality, to the interconnectedness of different kinds of force fields and different kinds of matter. Our world after all, as researchers conjecture, resulted from the fundamental antagonism between primordial matter and antimatter, whose mutual annihilation at the beginning of time resulted in gamma radiation and left a small residue of matter from which our present-day solar system coevolved with other celestial constellations. Looking out into the universe, we detect no evidence of anti-atoms. All of the natural

28 Jahn and Dunne, *Margins of Reality* (1987), 223. If we add to this notion the model of particles as multidimensional strings with the ability to weave and bob rather than one-dimensional points, the dynamic repertoire is further enhanced. Cf. Davies and Gribbin, *Matter* (1992), 254.

29 Werner Heisenberg, *Physics and Beyond* (New York: Harper and Row, 1972), 324–25. On particle physics, see also Davies, *Other Worlds* (1980), 90; and Jahn and Dunne, *Margins* (1987), 253-55.

antimatter in the universe seems to have disappeared. Now scientists think that the all-pervasive neutrino, which they previously thought to have no mass, does indeed have mass – perhaps as much as 90 percent of that of the known universe. That could make the combined mass of all neutrinos equivalent to invisible "dark matter."[30] Then there are the wobble and shadow techniques astronomers use to determine indirectly whether an unseen planet is orbiting a star.[31] These are intriguing, perhaps even paradoxical, findings that underscore the interconnections between motion and revolutionary thought. The closer we get to the bottom of things, the more motion we discover.

3. Parsing the Brain: Cytoskeletons and the Limits of Computability

Another foray into new territories that forces us to think in altered ways is Roger Penrose's *Shadows of the Mind* (1994). Penrose, the Rouse Ball Professor of Mathematics at Oxford University, offers a rigorously scientific yet sensitive reading of recent developments in the physical and biological worlds as they appear to relate to the structure and operation of the human brain. Rather than putting "thinking aside" (Koestler), Penrose pushes scientific evidence and logical reasoning to the limits in his exploration of how thinking and reflective thought arise in physiological terms. In extending the envelope, he ferrets out the limits of computability. Expressly, he asks: "Is the phenomenon of human consciousness something that is beyond the scope of scientific enquiry, or may the power of scientific method one day resolve the problem of the very existence of our conscious selves?" (*Shadows* 7). In answering the question, Penrose details a more refined image of the deep structures of the brain that mirrors the complexity of quantum and chemical dynamics.

Penrose is persuaded that no physical theory is complete without an accounting of consciousness. He is driven to demonstrate that artificial intelligence (AI) cannot clone

---

30 It is difficult – and dangerous – to speak of these matters because of the rate of new discoveries in the physical sciences. In early 1996, for example, astronomers unveiled photographs from the Hubble Space Telescope. The revelation was mind-boggling. Overnight the number of known galaxies in the universe quintupled from 10 billion to 50 billion. Moreover, researchers now have evidence of the suspected dark matter, which is invisible because it can neither absorb nor emit light. Dark matter is an important theoretical part of the equation, for it would explain why the universe does not dissipate in all directions, but forms centers of attraction that give shape to visible matter. Truly, what one does *not* see is becoming more important than what one *does* see. For a brief introductory account, see George Johnson, "Dark Matter Lights the Void," *New York Times*, January 21, 1996, section 4: "The Week in Review," pp. 1, 4. See also George Johnson, "Cosmic Weight Gain: A Wispy Particle Bulks Up," *New York Times*, April 28, 2002, Section 4: "The Week in Review," p. 16.

31 Tim Appenzeller, "At Home in the Heavens," *U.S. News and World Report*, June 24, 2002, 64–66.

human consciousness (despite Kubick/Spielberg's *A.I.* or Alex Proyas's *I, Robot*), and confident that science will one day be able to map the physical foundations of consciousness. In pressing his point, he cites the very promising roles of nonlocality and counterfactuality and the phenomenon of quantum entanglement in explaining the rise of consciousness. His insistence on embedding the mental realm in the physical allows him to avoid an all too easy adaptation of chaos theory (*Shadows* 23, 178-79, 214-15). Moreover, it leads him away from using emergence – the phenomenon resulting from a high, critical level of complexity – as an explanation for the rise of consciousness (*Shadows* 216). But it does not spare him the need to talk in terms of a highly complex organization at the cellular level. In tacit compliance with the Kuhnian model of scientific revolutions, Penrose has tried everything to make the scientific evidence fit the old mold but concludes that he must break with the past. Thus, he suggests a more refined way of conceiving the role of neurons and their synapses. He is forced to argue for a fundamental change in our present quantum-mechanical world-view, concluding that we must accept the noncomputational character of natural and neural phenomena.

The brain, he surmises, "is geared to take advantage of non-computable action in physical laws" (216). That gearing he finds deep within the brain's neurons in what is called the cytoskeleton (*kytos* = hollow vessel + skeleton = framework). Each neuron is a single cell consisting of a cytoskeleton. It is an amazing structure that not only appears to give the cell shape but also seems to be the actual control mechanism for the cell itself. By analogy one can assert that the cytoskeleton is the combined unit of skeleton, circulatory system, muscle system, legs, and nervous system all rolled into one (*Shadows* 357–58). Of central importance to Penrose is the cytoskeleton's function as the nervous system.

Consisting of protein-like molecules arranged in various types of structures (actin, microtubules, intermediate filaments), the cytoskeleton is most intriguing because of the microtubules – minute substructures at the "borderline between the quantum and classical levels" of operation (*Shadows* 371). (Where else to look for the real action but at the margins?). Each microtubule is a protein polymer consisting of dimer subunits known as tubulin, which – as the designation "dimer" indicates – consist in turn of two distinct parts (α-tubulin and β-tubulin). Each of these, again in turn, is composed of about 450 amino acids. There are normally 13 columns of tubulin dimers forming the external walls of the hollow tube of each microtubule. The mass of each microtubule in absolute terms is of about 10^{-14}. An electron, strategically placed at the juncture of the α- and β-tubulin parts of the microtubule, can shift the dimer's electric polarization, thereby also affecting its shape.

While it is perhaps not entirely accurate to speak of a control center for the cyto-skeleton separate from the total interaction of the constituent parts, researchers have isolated two cylinders of nine triplets of microtubules, known as the "centriole," that seem to serve this function. "The centriole," Penrose explains, "forms the critical part of a structure called the *microtubules organizing centre* or *centrosome*" (*Shadows* 359). The two cylinders within the centriole have the ability to replicate themselves, to separate from their hosts, and to serve as the focal point around which microtubules assemble. Microtubule fibers somehow connect the new centriole to the separate DNA strands in the nucleus at center points known as centromeres. The centriole functions as a kind of strange attractor (in the language of chaos) within an autopoietic system. The cytoskeleton, within which the centriole is embedded, apparently controls the cell's movements and organization independently from the controlling function of the nucleus. This point bears emphasizing. What Penrose then proposes is that a second control system operates at the single-cell level in addition to the nucleus with its genetic coding. Therefore, there are two separate control centers that somehow work in concert. Microtubules may be "cellular automata" that can grow and shrink (*Shadows* 362). Neurons do not merely turn on and off, fire or do not fire. They are themselves not the basic units, but rather contain self-replicating mechanisms, an attribute that dramatically enhances their potential computing powers. If tubulin dimers are the basic computational units, then the computational ability of the neuron-alone model would have to be raised from 10^{14} to around 10^{24} basic operations per second (*Shadows* 366). The cytoskeleton nevertheless "communicates" with the nucleus via the microtubule fibers. The cells of all animals and almost all plants (but excluding bacteria, blue-green algae, and viruses) reveal this dual system. Obviously, we have here a highly complex yet fully integrated interactive system which redefines the inner workings of nature (that which Goethe's Faust was so keen on knowing).

While it appears that dimers can exist in two conformational states and can switch from one to the other, depending upon the electron charge at the juncture point, the state of each dimer is subject to the influence of its immediate six neighbors so that a kind of community of interaction is formed. This conformation, Penrose explains, "would allow all kinds of messages to be propagated and processed along the length of each microtubule. These propagating signals appear to be relevant to the way that microtubules transport various molecules alongside them, and to the various inter-connections between neighbouring microtubules" (*Shadows* 363–64). The micro-tubules share information via bridge-like connections known as microtubule associated proteins (MAPs). Although single microtubules apparently do not extend along the entire length of the neural axon to the presynaptic endings or the other way into the postsynaptic spines of the dendrites, they are present in interconnected fashion throughout the entire neuron via the bridges (see figs. 1.4, 1.5, 1.6).

The growth and degeneration of these spines, perhaps even on a time scale of less than a second, seems related to the phenomenon of brain plasticity (*Shadows* 353, 365). Moreover, microtubules seem to play a role in maintaining the strength of the synapses and in effecting alterations in strength as needed. Located in the presynaptic

Figure 1.4: Neuron Structure (from R. Penrose, *Shadows of the Mind*, 352)

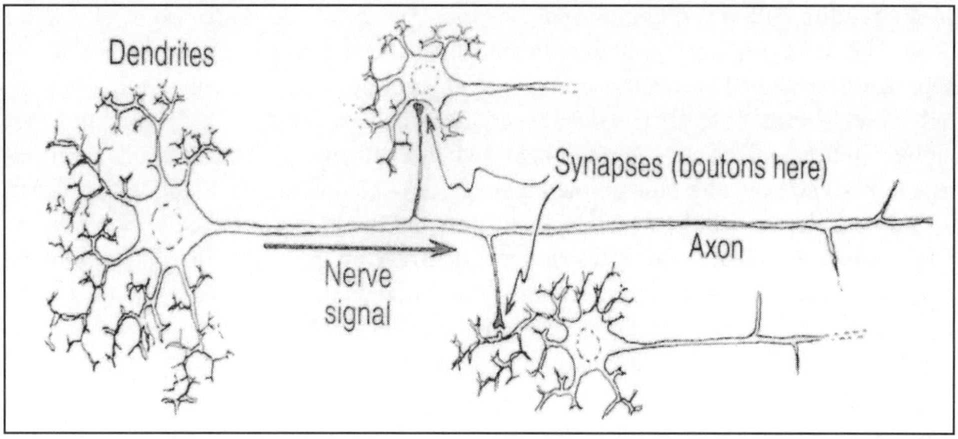

Figure 1.5: Microtubules (from R. Penrose, *Shadows of the Mind*, 364)

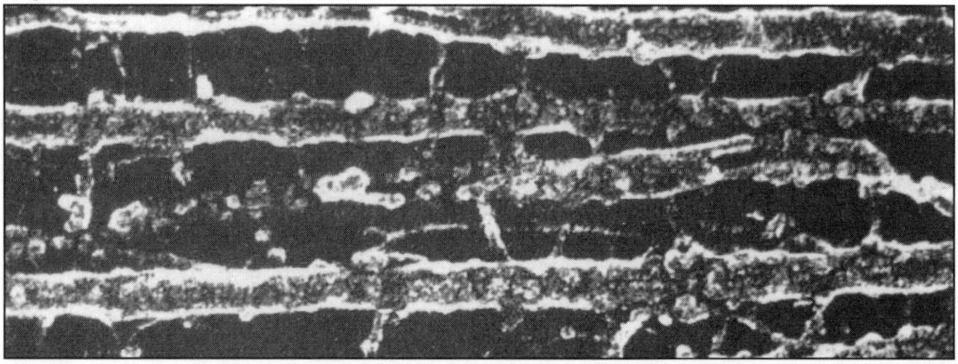

Figure 1.6: Photomicrograph of Multipolar Nerve Cells

The central cell body in each cell is visible with the dendrites here. Although not microtubules, the nerve cell composition shows by analogy their proposed structure (from Microsoft *Encarta Encyclopedia* 2002).

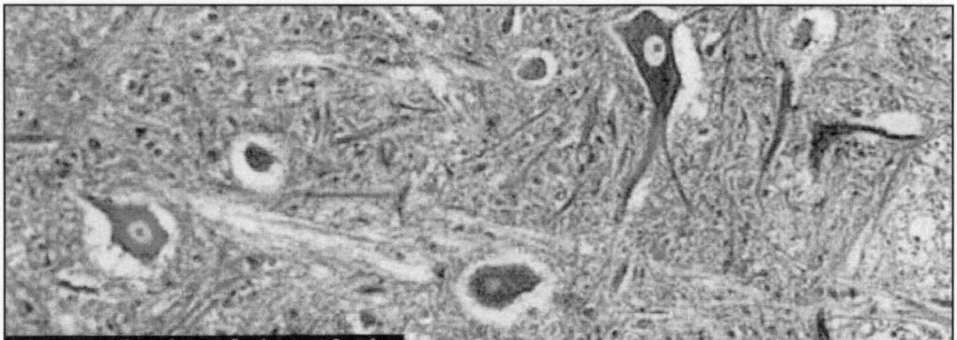

endings of axons are protein trimers known as clathrin triskelions that are important for the release of neurotransmitter chemicals (*Shadows* 364-65). Thus, through the interactive components of the cytoskeleton – more specifically, the "cytoskeletal control of synaptic connections"– consciousness seems to arise (*Shadows* 371). Penrose thereby provides a remapping of reality at the very foundations of reflective thought that forces us to put aside our normal thinking habits.[32]

The shift toward the intricate deep structure of neurons – the cytoskeleton and the incumbent microtubules – requires a quantum-mechanical explanation of how things work that is different from discussions of neurons for which classical terminology seems largely appropriate (*Shadows* 368–69). By following the lines of the molecular and microbiological structure, Penrose strongly suggests that we must abandon the analogy of neurons and their connecting synapses as fixed "printed circuits" or as a collection of transistors and wires. Instead, we should adopt an image of "large-scale quantum coherence" to preserve the chance for "the subtle quantum-level effects, such as non-locality, quantum parallelism [= superpositions] [...] or effects of counter-factuality at the classical level of brain activity" (*Shadows* 351). The adoption of a noncomputable, wavelike quantum-mechanical image is needed to describe what happens when consciousness arises. This move, Penrose suspects, will have profound consequences for our philosophical outlook in general. At the very least, his doing of science, while observing the rigorous logic invoked by Gross and Levitt, undermines the classical rendering of natural laws advocated by those critics. The realm of incomputability that Penrose exposes could provide support for the contention of "wild-eyed" postmodernists that multidimensional openness is key to understanding. If nothing else, multipolar conceptionality on the astrophysical, quantum-physical, cellular, and now neural scale should prompt a renewed look at what factors into creativity.

4. Getting It Together: Solitons, Wave Packets, and Brain

Extremely promising for understanding creative processes as the merging of complementary and contradictory impulses is the notion of the soliton or "wave packet."[33] The term "soliton" designates an amplification of impulses in a narrow, localized

32 For a concise overview of the structures and processes addressed by Penrose, see Karl R. Gegenfurtner, *Gehirn und Wahrnehmung*, 2nd ed. (Frankfurt a.M.: Fischer Taschenbuch Verlag, 2004), 15–20.

33 On the following see Briggs and Peat, *Turbulent Mirror* (1989), 84–87, 132–33; Davies, *Blueprint* (1987), 166–77; Davies and Gribbin, *Matter* (1992), 52–61; Jahn and Dunne, *Margins* (1987), 203–52; Davies, *Other Worlds* (1980), 107–27; F. David Peat, *The Philosopher's Stone: Chaos, Synchronicity, and the Hidden Order of the World* (New York: Bantam Books, 1992), 226–27.

region of space that retains a discrete profile despite its wavelike properties. A complex network of internal feedback loops coordinates the movement of wavelets (or pulses) of varying lengths and amplitudes into a solitary wave not susceptible to dispersion and dissipation. The word "soliton" was coined in the mid 1960s as a counterpart to protons and neutrons, which have both wavelike and particle properties in quantum mechanics. Hence, basic assumptions of quantum theory are indispensable for appreciating the concept of the wave packet. As is obvious in Penrose's vision of microtubules, quantum theory replaces the classic building-blocks conception of reality with one dominated by a universal flux of events and processes. "Nonlinearity," Davies and Gribbin state explicitly, "opens the way to the formation of solitons" (*Matter* 55).

Instead of thinking in terms of discrete and separate identities, we need to think in terms of fluid motions such as ripples, waves, and currents but which can nonetheless stand apart starkly profiled. Solitons appear everywhere on the micro and macro levels: in molecular biology as ripples of energy, in superconductors as fluxons tunneling their way quantum-mechanically through the insulating barrier between the sections of superconducting material, and as the electric-charge polarons (which can move through solid-state crystalline structures). Even more rarefied versions of the soliton have been proposed, such as the notion that elementary particles may themselves be considered as pulses of energy within the right force field. Four-dimensional, short-lived instantons, the reconceptualized inner dynamics of neurons, and winding mode of cosmic superstrings round out the new category. In whatever garb the soliton might appear, it always results from the correlation of a whole system of movement unlinked mechanically.

David Bohm suggests that we think of this open flux of wave forms "as vortex structures in a flowing stream." While we can abstract them and make them stand out in our thinking – perhaps prompted by the thought process itself – in actuality the flow patterns merge into one integrated movement of the flowing stream. "There is no sharp division," Bohm concludes, "nor are they to be regarded as separately or independently existent entities." Human beings and all their inventions are ultimately bound up in and a product of this incessant interplay of vortices (*Wholeness* 10–11). Within these vortices wave concentrations occur. But they are not entirely restricted to the "space" of the vortices. (The preponderance of water imagery in *Faust*, *Zarathustra*, and *The Tin Drum* will be related to this notion of wave function.)[34]

Because the soliton results from the nonlinear congruence of individual sine waves,

34 Wholly independently of the developments outlined in the preceding, Martin Buber proposed that we think in terms of a continuously swirling vortex of possibilities to discuss what happened after Adam and Eve acquired the knowledge of good and evil. This point will re-emerge in chapter 4. Martin Buber, *Images of Good and Evil*, trans. by Michael Bullock (London: Routledge & Kegan Paul, 1954), 66–68.

it can be seen as an example of self-organization, contradicting with its positive feedback loops the principle of the equipartition of energy; dispersion is a sign of negative feedback loops. Although a bundle or pulse (or quantum) of localized energy that takes on a clearly discernible form (e.g., a "standing" wave pattern), the wave packet can also be a mirror of chaos, especially when it occurs at sea as a tidal wave (Briggs and Peat, *Turbulent Mirror* 127). Harmless on the open sea, the tsunami rises to destructive potency as it clashes with the coast line, i.e., with firmly bounded areas that intensify its potency, for the constricting boundaries serve to enhance the energy of the standing wave as the collision becomes ever more imminent. The standing wave – a notion I would like to conjoin with wave packet – is really very complex. Jahn and Dunne explain how the standing wave comes about:

> When any wave train reaches a boundary or discontinuity in the medium in which it is propagating, some portion of it is reflected and some portion is transmitted. If all relevant boundaries of the medium are fixed in some fashion, the succession of incident, reflected, and re-reflected propagating waves compounds to establish a pattern of 'standing' waves, wherein the displacements of the medium wax and wane in a stationary, rather than propagating, configuration. (*Margins* 213–14)

By injecting Bohm's reality concept of vortices in a flowing stream into the wave pattern, we can give back to standing waves their "propagating" essence, that is, their essential movement. Standing waves, then, in our adaptation of the term, would not be stuck in one spot but would rather be on the move, like the tidal wave already mentioned. In fact, the synchronized energy characteristic of the standing wave occurs everywhere in the universe from pulsating stars to aftershocks to alpha rhythms and the minute electrical impulses needed to coordinate the nerve and muscle fibers in a body riding a bicycle.[35] Because of their characteristics, solitons are widely used in optical fiber cables to transmit information. Perhaps the apparent switching of electrical charge from negative to positive (and vice versa) in neutrinos is related?

Roger Penrose seems to suggest that solitons exist within the deep structure of the neuron as well when he conceives of the microtubules as "dielectric waveguides," adding saliently: "Perhaps the tubes themselves serve to provide the effective insulation that would enable the quantum state in the interior of the tube to remain unentangled with its environment for an appreciable time" (*Shadows* 368). The movement within the tube is wavelike. He then goes on to explain that Emilio del Giudice and his group at the University of Milan have argued that "a quantum self-

---

35 The coordination of competing impulses is especially evident in arrhythmia. In a normal state, the muscle fibers in the heart contract all together, controlled by an electric impulse that travels along the length of the fibers in wavelike fashion. Chaotic behavior can however evolve through periodic doubling of the rhythm, causing the heart to beat 200–300 times a minute and leading to instant death. (Charlotte Kerner, "Hab Chaos im Herzen...," in *Geo-Wissen: Chaos + Kreativität*, 139–42). Morfill and Scheingraber, *Chaos ist überall*, devote a lengthy chapter to the phenomenon (134–168).

focusing effect of electromagnetic waves within the cytoplasmic material in cells causes signals to be confined to a size that is just the internal diameter of microtubules" (*Shadows* 368). (The inside diameter of a microtubule is 14 nanometers; a nanometer is 10^{-9} meters.) The evidence is coincidental but invites serious reflection. It is unclear whether the microtubule is the cause or effect of the quantum state within it. In any event, the ubiquity of wave packets in nonlinear nature speaks volumes for the concept of holism, since wave packets are the result of coherence at both the quantum and macro levels. The characteristics of the high-profile wave packet would appear to be closely related to the high level of energy concentration needed to bring the creative act itself to fruition. Let me give a few examples.

While it might seem like backpeddling, it is nonetheless useful to take up the issue of the brain once again – this time in light of the soliton. Like the heart, the brain functions according to the principle of coherence and wave formation. The Belgian chemist Ilya Prigogine sees the chaotic activity of the neural network as an expression of such coordination. We should keep in mind that the human brain bears the marks of its 400+ million-year evolution, and that brain scientists do not know with certainty how the brain works. "What is lacking," Edward O. Wilson affirms, "is a sufficient grasp of the emerged holistic properties of the neuron circuits, and of cognition, the way the circuits process information to create perception and knowledge" (*Consilience* 109). In the absence of greater specificity, conjectures abound. Penrose has been cited for the micro level.

Systems scientist Paul LaViolette has developed a structural model in collaboration with psychiatrist William Gray to describe how the human brain transforms a feeling into a cognitive response. Their model is based on the tripartite brain theory of neuroanatomist Paul Maclean, which divides the traditional forebrain, midbrain, and hindbrain somewhat differently (see fig. 1.7 and 1.8). According to Maclean, the brain is composed of three layers or shells, developed during various stages of human genesis: (1) the reptilian brain (≃ hindbrain), (2) the old mammalian brain (≃ mid-brain), and (3) the new mammalian brain (≃ forebrain).[36] The innermost layer, or "reptilian" portion, is composed of the brain stem, cerebellum, and reticular activating system. The basic elements of consciousness and arousal are located here. The second layer, the limbic system or old mammalian brain, includes the amygdala (emotion), the hippocampus (memory, especially short-term), the hypothalamus (memory, temperature control, sex drive, hunger, thirst), the pituitary gland (hormone secretion), and the thalamus (control functions for hormone levels, digestive system, heart rate, and respiration). The hypothalamus is the seat of pleasure, while the amygdala is that of

---

36 This and the following are based on Briggs, *Fire* (1988), 50–61, and Gegenfurtner, *Gehirn* (2004), 11–15, 20-22. For very useful, interactive websites that allow one to highlight the different sectors of the brain and their functions, see http://www.msnbc.com–MSNBCInteractive–MicrosoftInternet, http://www.med.harvard.edu/AANLIB/home.html, and http://marymt.edu/~psychol/brain.html.

emotion. The hippocampus is particularly active during dreaming. In brief, the limbic system controls a complex mix of stimuli: emotions, sensations, and memories (see fig. 1.8).

Figure 1.7: The Human Brain
(from Microsoft *Encarta Encyclopedia* 2002)

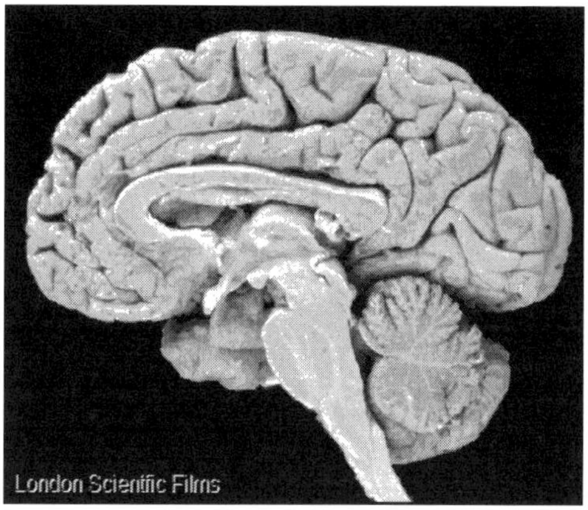

Figure 1.8: The Human Brain

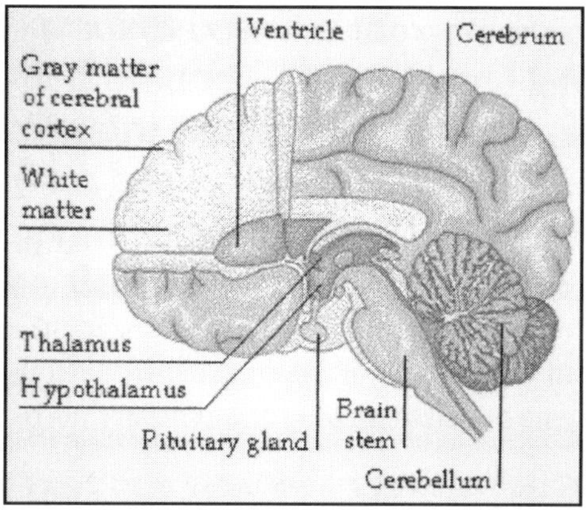

The new mammalian brain (cerebrum) has expanded to cover the rest of the brain; it is the outer shell of cells enfolding the inner two and consisting of gray and white matter.[37] The neocortex contains 100 billion cells, each with 1,000 to 10,000 synapses. The cerebral cortex – the surface layer of the cerebrum (about 4mm thick) – is the site of abstract thought. Its cells are arranged in six similar layers. Within them different regions carry out various aspects of cognition, ranging from sensory perception (parietal lobes) to vision (occipital lobes), language perception (temporal lobes), and volition (frontal lobes). The frontal lobes of the cortex, which also involve social judgment and a sense of self, are the object of intensive research. If the frontal lobes of the cortex are severed, it is known, loss of creativity and emotional capacity ensue. Injuries to the temporal lobes often cause personality and mood changes. Thus, there would appear to be a connection between intentionality and creativity. The attractiveness of the triune brain as a model for creativity resides in the fact that the cerebrum (or new mammalian brain) "enfolds" and interconnects with the older stages of neural evolution. There are, for example, 10 times as many feedback loops from the neocortex to the other layers of the brain as there are from them to the neocortex.

37 Wilson, *Consilience* (1998), 102–24. With a little openness to unexpected symmetry, one could conceivably see this arrangement of the new mammalian brain enfolding the inner two as a kind of parallel to the standard model of the atom with its inner dualism of neutrons and protons surrounded by the outer shell of electrons, compounded, of course, by the fractional distribution of the positive and negative charges within the nucleus itself, which add up to 1.

Hence, we are inclined to accept a continuity of development from motor coordination through sensations of feeling and desire to abstract, logical thought. Through intricate feedback loops, the tripartite brain acts as one.

In accepting the tripartite model of the brain, there is no need to discard the split-brain – or hemispheric model – for it too operates as a unit via innumerable feedback loops (see illustrations at http://encarta.msn.com/media). Thus, we can view both models as complementary rather than exclusionary, just as reductionism and chaos need not be irreconcilable. This is not a question of displacement, but rather of augmentation. Bohm proposed a similar model with his triangular relationships among energy, matter, and meaning, whereby each mediates between the other two. (With a shift in perspective, Bohm's model could be seen as analogous to the traditional concept of the triune Christian God in whom Father, Son, and Holy Spirit are in constant communication with one another.) Energy and matter are known to be aspects of the same thing; they enfold one another, giving rise to meaning as humans endeavor to expound their interconnections. Conversely, meaning enfolds energy and matter. The magnetic field of tension can thus be rendered as a three-point trajectory (fig. 1.9).

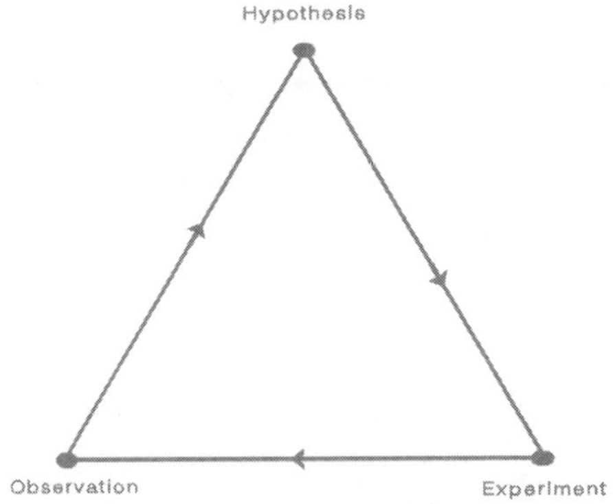

Figure 1.9: Matter-Meaning-Energy
(Source: John L. Casti, *Complexification* 14)

In LaViolette and Gray's model, external stimuli pass through the thalamus into the limbic system, reaching the brain via the wavelike electric responses of the nervous system. In the brain, they are transformed into biochemical reactions and begin to course around and between these three shells as so many "nuances" of raw sense data. Of particular note is the circulation around the so-called Papez circuit, a network of neurons in the (new) mammalian portion of the brain. It is here, LaViolette and Gray theorize, that the stimuli trigger "feeling-tone responses" and generate "themes" (see Briggs, *Fire* 52). Here we might think of Gerald Holton's use of the thema as an organizing principle of emotional directedness in the creative process. By way of analogy, we might also recall Edward O. Wilson's use of archetypes or Richard Dawkins's use of memes, or Daemmrich's citation of motifs as organizing principles. LaViolette even believes that these feeling tones become physically manifest as wave forms (Briggs, *Fire* 53). The wave forms take on a more distinct profile through a process of polarization, interface penetration, diffraction, and interference. Resonance among similar nuances or frequencies causes a transferral of "vibrations" to another tone feeling (object or person). Through resonance, more confining boundaries are established until the swirling feeling tones form a wave packet. That wave packet, I would suggest, is the more clearly defined thought, feeling, or sensation that rises like a standing wave. For his part, Wilson speaks of inferred pathways endemic in consciousness that lead in "circular" fashion "from the cerebral cortex to the amygdala and hippocampus, then to the thalamus, then to the prefrontal cortex ... and then back to the cortex for storage" (*Consilience* 107). Aside from the central conception of thought formation as a wave packet, important for my definition of creativity is the inherent connection between thought and emotion, body and mind. "Emotion," Wilson avers, "is not just a perturbation of reason but a vital part of it" (*Consilience* 106).

Nuance, resonance, and wave forms would thus appear to be related to one another. Briggs notes the resemblance among them metaphorically: "Nuance is the aura or nimbus that surrounds a thema or several thema, the energy that infuses thematic convictions. It is the vibrating field around thematic magnets" (*Fire* 47). In their examination of the nature of consciousness, Jahn and Dunne also replace particularity with a complex overlay of interlacing fields. Analogous to the space-time domains of the quantum world, they speak of consciousness in terms of "probability-of-experience waves," which freely traverse their own space-time coordinates if unchecked by environmental constraints. Jahn and Dunne even draw a comparison to the unrestricted ride of unbounded ocean waves. When the probability-of-experience wave becomes bounded by some kind of container or category – such as a thema – then something astonishing happens: "[C]haracteristic patterns of standing waves, or eigenfunctions, will be established that represent the experiences of that consciousness in that situation" (*Margins* 242). Next, Jahn and Dunne extend the wave function analogy to the interaction of various personalities and individual instances of consciousness. Each "wave-mechanical consciousness" is capable of interacting with the others; in fact, they form "communities." The individual human consciousness is thus not sharply localized and entirely discrete (see also Wilson, *Consilience* 113). Rather, each interconnects with several environments and other instances of consciousness with their own environments. "Any community of interacting personalities," they conjecture, "takes the form of a complex interplay of consciousness standing wave patterns, each centered in one of a corresponding myriad of mobile environmental containers" (*Margins* 243). The centering of wave packets in numerous, changing contexts might be construed as another form of the periodic center characteristic of the science of chaos.

The extension of such "inner vibrations" to the particular resonances in external reality beyond human consciousness is a logical step. The swing of a pendulum, the motion of the planets, the beating of the heart, the pulsations of tuning forks: all have their own special way of resonating. And if we recall Bohm's analogy of the inseparable vortices in the flowing stream, as well as Jahn and Dunne's centering of consciousness within a "myriad of mobile environmental containers" – we have little difficulty in appreciating how these economies of scale are alike despite being clearly different.

Could it be that human creativity is the ability to recognize feeling tones, as Gray and LaViolette suggest? Their concept of thinking as a highly complex process involving random bundles of sensations, nuances, and feeling tones introduced into an internal vortex of the cortex points to the same kind of turbulence cited by Bohm, Davies, and Buber as the essence of reality. The image of the brain as a circuit board consisting of some hundred billion neurons alternately turning on and off, with each neuron interacting sometimes randomly and sometimes systematically with about 100,000 other neurons, conveys a sense of the awesome complexity of the entire neural anatomy. However, when we add to that picture Penrose's imaging of the far more complex (and apparently autonomous) biological cytoskeleton, the result is truly mind-bending. To be sure, it is a fine example of deterministic chaos, which is capable of selectively amplifying small fluctuations, chosen randomly or preconditioned by deep-structure themata. The feedback loops lead to more distinct thoughts and awareness of sensations.[38] Whereas Descartes defined the Age of Rationalism pithily with his dictum "cogito ergo sum" (I think, therefore I am), more appropriate for our own contemporary era would appear to be the off-handed remark of the biologist S. J. Singer: "I link, therefore I am!" (cf. Wilson, *Consilience* 110).

5. Attitude and Positionality

Before we move on to the question of imitation and creativity, one final step is necessary. We must locate the observer in the order of things. All scientific research seeks to remain true to the ideal objectivity of the Newtonian method of inquiry which disallows as mere hypothesis any idea unsupported by material evidence. While the supposedly uninvolved stance of the observer has been increasingly called into question by natural scientists themselves, those researchers involved in the study of chaos, especially those in Europe, often cling to the notion of the absent subject in their observations. They prefer to speak of their field as chaos research or the science of chaos. By contrast, those researchers interested in quantum mechanics are less

38 Briggs and Peat, *Turbulent Mirror* (1989), 116, 132–34; see also Davies, *Blueprint*, 183–96.

squeamish about referring to their efforts as theory, maybe because positionality looms so large for them. A generation ago Karl R. Popper pointedly rejected the notion of science being a system of only clearly stated, verifiable assertions steadily advancing toward finality. "*We do not know*," Popper observes, "*we can only guess*.[39] In any event, theory is not seen here as a closed system but as a seeing beyond observed objects.

Given the predicament of the hermeneutic circle as being indeterminate and perspectival, humanists cannot easily measure the validity of their theories against empirical evidence in the manner of natural scientists. Whereas the former gravitate to transcendental arguments and ludic constructions, the latter insist upon an objective world against which to test their opinions and observations. Moreover, humanists lack the sophisticated technological instruments for measuring and quantifying the world they study. At least, that was the customary thinking on the difference between the two cultures before the interpretive turn. Mounting evidence from cosmology, physics, biology, chemistry, and neurology indicates, as we have seen, that the chasm between the efforts of artists and scientists is much smaller than customarily thought. In his book *Chaos and Order: The Complex Structure of Organic Matter* (1993), Friedrich Cramer speaks of the "departure from principles" (Abschied vom Prinzipiellen) in our postmodern era, even in physics and mathematics. Research methods based on completely objective standards are made impossible by the continuous feedback loops between humans and the things or theories they produce, as well as by interference from the measuring instruments themselves.[40] Because of the self-reference factor, we have arrived at the boundaries of science. Meaning is (once again) replacing

---

39 Karl R. Popper, *The Logic of Scientific Discovery* (New York: Basic Books, 1959), 279–80. Italics in the original. Much of Popper's writing was aimed at debunking scientific determinism. Most notable in this regard is his *The Open Universe: An Argument for Indeterminism* (1956; first American publication, Totowa, NJ: Rowman and Littlefield, 1982). See especially the addenda to the volume containing an essay entitled "Indeterminism Is not Enough: An Afterword," first published in 1973, and another work, "Scientific Reduction and the Essential Incompleteness of all Science," which first appeared in 1974 (= pages 113–30 and 131–62, respectively, of *The Open Universe*). Indeterministic physics, he argues, is insufficient to explain free will, and for that reason he (re-)introduces his three-world concept of the interconnectedness of the physical, subjective, and rational (114–22). See also his *Objective Knowledge: An Evolutionary Approach* (Oxford: Clarendon Press, 1972), chaps. 3–4.

40 Friedrich Cramer, *Chaos und Ordnung: Die komplexe Struktur des Lebendigen* (Frankfurt a.M: Insel, 1993): "Abschied vom Prinzipiellen," "Unmöglichkeit [...] prinzipielle[r] Lösungen," "auf sich selbst rückgekoppelt," "die Grenzen der Wissenschaft" (294, 296). In another vein, John Ziman argues that increased "market pull," changing professional roles, and alternative career paths have impacted upon the doing of pure science, which asks general questions. Science now shades off into other, practical activities, such as engineering and medicine, that ask specific questions. All this means that instrumental reason increasingly intrudes upon the realm of basic research and reflective thought. See John M. Ziman, *Prometheus Bound: Science in a Dynamic Steady State* (Cambridge: Cambridge University Press, 1994), 26–41, 67–92.

knowledge as the achievable goal. Cramer concludes: "Science is a product of the human spirit. This product can not extend beyond its originator. Philosophically, the point has been evident in principle since Kant. [...] Empirically, it is now accepted as a given in the biological and neurological realms since they possess the quality of fundamental complexity."[41] Consequently, we cannot wholly discard the anthropic principle in our renditions of the world and the self (Davies, *Web* 163). That principle in effect states that human consciousness itself is ultimately a product of the laws of nature and in turn acts creatively upon that which produced it.

Moreover, the structure of discrimination and association that constitutes human consciousness is itself perhaps the only access to reality available to us. Without consciousness we would not have been able to construct our contemporary existence out of the chaos of stimuli. "Only form," Friedrich Schlegel had argued in his Jena lectures around 1800, "comes into empirical consciousness" (Seyhan 1992, 29). Almost two hundred years later, David Bohm conjectured in a similar manner that thoughts and value formation are not separate from the physical realm (the soma). Thought itself is part of the one overall reality (or holomovement) so that any transformation of consciousness translates into a transformation of meaning. Consciousness *is* its content, is its meaning. In a way, we could say that we *are* the totality of our meanings (*UM* 93). The more heightened our self-awareness, the greater the content of meaning. And that content is capable of indefinite extension.[42] Like order, meaning is indefinitely variable and includes a teleological moment (e.g., purpose, directed attention). Perhaps the creative act alone is real. Perhaps all principles of reality are ultimately derivative of the one principle of creative convergence and divergence of inner and outer spaces, of matter and mind. However, this "perhaps" is not a sign of equivocation or indecision; rather, it is an affirmation of the personal opportunity for participation in the shaping and mapping of reality.[43]

The title of this chapter, "From Matter to Mind: Revolutions Real and Conceptual," is a reference to inevitable linkages. It acknowledges the participatory role of the

---

41 "Wissenschaft ist ein Produkt des menschlichen Geistes. Dieses Produkt kann nicht über seinen Urheber hinausgehen. Philosophisch war das im Prinzip spätestens seit Kant klar. [...] Materiell ist es nun gesichert für den Bereich der Biologie und die vom Zentralnervensystem gesteuerten Bereiche, da diese die Qualität der fundamentalen Komplexität besitzen" (Cramer, *Chaos und Ordnung*, 303).

42 David Bohm, *Unfolding Meaning: A Weekend of Dialogue with David Bohm* (London and New York: ARK Paperbacks, 1987), 93, 102. See Chap. 3: "Soma-Significance: A New Notion of the Relationship Between the Physical and the Mental" (72–120).

43 See Jahn and Dunne, *Margins* (1987), Chap. 10: "Perhaps Principles" (341–47). Their conclusion regarding the role of consciousness is quite similar to Cramer's. Michael Talbot, *The Holographic Universe* (New York: HarperCollins, 1992), draws upon Jahn and Dunne as well as David Bohm (139–40). Thus, "uncertainty is real," Davies and Gribbin remind us, while the "idealized mathematical line" is a fiction (*Matter* 38). The uncertainty Davies and Gribbin speak of is self-similar to Penrose's "noncomputability."

scientist engaged in basic research in the hope of gaining insight into the workings of reality. It recognizes popularizations of that research, which intentionally or inadvertently add their own conceptual perceptions in reconfiguring "real" revolutions in our way of thinking. And the title also connotes the efforts of philosophers and writers who dare to combine divergent modes of thought in rendering judgments about the nature of reality. Innovative approaches of this type fulfill Romantic philosopher-writer Friedrich Schlegel's advocacy – as noted in the citation in the masthead of this chapter – for a new era of cooperation between the sciences and the arts. When divergent disciplines combine their complementary forces, they will give rise to a unified system of thought, a "symphilosophy" (Symphilosophie), and of expression, a "sympoesy" (Sympoesie). Only in concert, Schlegel submits, can the sciences and arts realize their full potential. David Bohm, Paul Davies, Roger Penrose, and Michael Talbot are exemplary of modern extensions outward (from starting points in natural science) to be all inclusive. Finally, the chapter title includes a faint hint of the turns of interpretation that have followed upon growing insights into how matter and mind work in concert. Indeed, as Richard Shusterman puts it: "Our age is even more hermeneutic than it is postmodern" (1991: 102). The need to interpret seems rooted in a natural process.

The overriding significance of chaos theory in my context is that it is consciously opposed to a philosophy of alternatives that has traditionally dominated so much of our thinking in the sciences and humanities. Once we begin to distance ourselves from the binary mode and think complementarily – even holistically – we begin to notice linkages previously unsuspected. We also come to appreciate the fact that nonlinearity is actually the rule in the real world, whether in cloud formations, gypsy moth populations, particle physics, our heart rhythms and brain waves – or in enduring works of art. The convergence between the seer and the seen, occasioned by the seer's dependence on such irregularities within and without, is the topic of the next chapter. It will act as a bridge to further discussions of convergence between divergent disciplines.

Chapter 2
Imitating Nature – Gaining the Right Perspective

> Es gibt Dinge, die, ihrer Natur nach, dergestalt von unserer Willkür abhängen, daß sie sind oder nicht sind, sobald es uns beliebt, daß sie sein oder nicht sein sollen.
>
> – C. M. Wieland, "Gedanken [...] zu philosophieren" (1788)

> There are no fixtures in nature. The universe is fluid and volatile.
>
> – R. W. Emerson, "Circles" (1841)

> But true art is never fixed, but always flowing.
>
> – R. W. Emerson, "Art" (1841)

1. Thinking Aside and Creativity

The aesthetic experience associated with mimesis stands in close proximity to the epistemological issues and consequent remapping of reality considered in the preceding chapter. Aesthetics and epistemology are both inherent in the notion of creativity. Innovation has to do with seeing things differently, and the perception of difference is as characteristic of scientific research (which is naturally conservative) as it is of the arts (which willfully adds new perspectives) (cf., e.g., Guthke 1990). Thus, the innovative scientist and the creative artist are alternately iconoclastic and preservationist, albeit to differing degrees. Thomas Kuhn focused on just this element of innovation in science and art in his *The Essential Tension* (1977).[1] In that sense, the creative researcher is like the creative artist: Janusian. Janusian thinking is the special quality of being able to conceive of two or more contradictory ideas simultaneously and to negotiate between them.[2] This process Koestler designates as "bisociative

1 Thomas S. Kuhn, *The Essential Tension: Selected Studies in Scientific Tradition and Change* (Chicago: University of Chicago Press, 1977), 226–27, 342–43, 350.

2 Arthur Rothenberg, *The Creativity Question* (Durham: Duke University Press, 1976), 11. In *The Emerging Goddess: The Creative Process in Art, Science, and Other Fields* (Chicago: University of Chicago Press, 1979), 125–37, Rothenberg, who normally has only the subjective side of creative thinking in mind (125), raises the question of the agon with a reference to Janusian thinking (131–32). He thus moves in the same direction as Arthur Koestler in his essay "Janus" in the collection *Die Wurzeln des Zufalls* (Frankfurt a.M: Suhrkamp, 1972), 107–24. Janus is the two-faced being capable

thinking" and considers it to be a distinguishing mark of the creative act (*Act*, 656–60). The creative moment contains elements of both the old and the new.

"There are things," Christoph Martin Wieland (1733–1813), one of Europe's most celebrated authors of the last third of the eighteenth century, contended, "which by their very nature are so dependent upon human caprice that they either exist or do not exist as soon as we desire that they should or should not exist."[3] This comment, cited at the masthead of this chapter, is remarkable for at least two reasons. First, it implies the importance of perspective in determining what is and is not real to us. We are, at the very least, reminded that seeing is a talent that needs to be cultivated, as John Berger saliently argued in his popular *Ways of Seeing* (1972). In this latter sense, the statement is thoroughly representative of the highly charged debate on perception and the limits of knowledge in the Age of Enlightenment. Enlighteners began to understand, as Berger was later to put it, that "perspective makes the single eye the centre of the visible world."[4] That discussion was largely prompted by the Copernican Turn with its emphasis on the role that positionality has in our acts of seeing. In her 2001-2002 exhibition, *Devices of Wonder*, at the Getty Museum, art historian Barbara Stafford drew particular attention to the ways science and technology have augmented human (in)sight in the wake of the Copernican Turn. She traces those developments from the seventeenth through the twentieth century. Stafford labeled the installation an "exercise in analogical thinking" that was intended "to encourage inquisitive voyaging among associate assemblies."[5] That essentially describes Wieland's joy of discovery through the drawing of analogies.

Secondly, and somewhat astonishingly, is the explicit meaning of Wieland's assertion: there are aspects of reality that are *entirely* contingent upon the individual's attitude. In the wake of Pauli, Heisenberg, and Bohm, we might be tempted to rephrase Wieland's statement in terms of Pauli's uncertainty principle or of the soma's relationship to the implicate order (where thought itself is, for Bohm, part of one all-encompassing reality). Elsewhere Wieland remarks that we need to find the proper

---

of looking in opposite directions simultaneously. See also Koestler's *Janus: A Summing Up* (New York: Random House, 1978). As the title states, the book sums up his work on the life sciences spanning a quarter of a century.

3 Christoph Martin Wieland, "Gedanken von der Freiheit über Gegenstände des Glaubens zu philosophieren" (1788), *Werke*, ed. by Fritz Martini and Hans Werner Seiffert (Munich: Hanser, 1964–68): "Es gibt Dinge, die, ihrer Natur nach, dergestalt von unserer Willkür abhängen, daß sie sind oder nicht sind, sobald es uns beliebt, daß sie sein oder nicht sein sollen" (3:516). This edition is cited hereafter as Hanser.

4 John Berger, *Ways of Seeing* (London: Penguin Books, 1972), 16.

5 Barbara Maria Stafford, "Revealing Technologies / Magical Domains," in Barbara Maria Stafford and Frances Terpak, *Devices of Wonder: From the World in a Box to Images on a Screen*, Catalogue of an Exhibition held at the J. Paul Getty Museum from Nov. 13, 2001 through Feb. 3, 2002 (Los Angeles: Getty Research Institute, 2001), 2. Cited hereafter as Stafford.

perspective for judging what is real: "The true seer is the person who has located the right standpoint. And that is not at all easy!"[6] Achieving the right perspective entails a shift from representation and symbolism toward a rendering of pure structure. That is the topic of this present chapter: achieving the proper perspective.

In order to invent, it has been remarked, one must be able to "think aside." In his *The Act of Creation*, Arthur Koestler approvingly cites Ferdinand de Saussure's dictum "pour inventor il faut penser à côté. The phrase means that one must resist calculative thinking in order to be open to the unexpected. Koestler even titles his chapter on the limits of logic "Thinking Aside" (*Act* 145–77). In it he explores the "forerunners" of Freud's thinking on the role of the unconscious in directing our conscious awareness: Socrates, Kepler, Paracelsus, Descartes, Leibniz, Kant, Goethe, Wordsworth, William James, and Max Planck. Vision – sometimes very indistinct – plays a critical role in directing our attention and thus our discoveries. We never know at the outset whether the goal we have set for ourselves is the goal we will actually achieve (*Act* 145). Indeed, peripheral vision can prove more revealing than direct focusing, as we know from experience when trying to discern a point on the distant horizon. And, of course, we do have a blind spot at the rear of the retina where the optical nerves enter (conveniently offset in each eye so as not to overlap).

More recent contributions to our understanding of creativity include the case studies offered by the psychiatrist Albert Rothenberg in his interdisciplinary volume *The Creativity Question* (1976), the analysis of originality put forward by the literary critic John Briggs in *Fire in the Crucible* (1988), and the innovative thesis devised by the theoretical physicist David Bohm in *On Creativity* (1998). The studies by Rothenberg and Briggs are based on interviews with extraordinary individuals in the sciences and humanities, whereas Bohm draws upon his background in particle physics. Rothenberg summarizes his findings by observing that "creativity is determined and undetermined at the same time." Briggs concludes that genius is perhaps simply the effort to see things in a unified manner. And Bohm avers that "the creative state of mind [...] is always open to learning what is new, perceiving new differences and new similarities, leading to new orders and structures, rather than always tending to impose familiar orders and structures in the field of what is seen."[7]

At the conclusion of his lecture on "Soma-Significance," Bohm reflects upon the place of creativity in the new structure of things. He asserts that creativity involves the inclusion of the new and not yet manifest in the realm of known material existence, the

6 Wieland, *Schach Lolo*, Hanser 5:92, verses 125–26: "Der wahre Seher / Ist der sich auf den rechten Standpunkt stellt. Das hält oft schwer!"

7 Albert Rothenberg and Carl R. Hausman (eds.), *The Creativity Question* (Durham: Duke University Press, 1976), 23; John Briggs, *Fire in the Crucible: The Alchemy of Creative Genius* (New York: St. Martin's Press, 1988), 333; David Bohm, *On Creativity*, ed. by Lee Nichol (London and New York: Routledge, 1998), 17.

soma. The presence of the infinite and inexpressible within the finite acts as a guide for his deliberations: "For the present we can say that creativity is not only the fresh perception of new meanings, and the ultimate enfoldment of this perception within the manifest and the somatic, but I would say that it is ultimately the action of the *infinite* in the sphere of the finite – that is, this meaning goes to infinite depths."[8] This insight guides my own thinking on the nature of creativity. Indeed, it seems to me to be related to Kant's sense of awe at the sight of manifold nature. If we could find the right perspective, we might even consider the infinite depths of nature as conjoining such conceptions as the Kantian *Ding-an-sich*, the alchemist's philosopher's stone, and the fabled *prima materia*. For example, in *On Creativity* Bohm extolls the benefits of "thinking outside the box" for scientists and artists alike for its ability to demonstrate what they have in common. If each group familiarized itself with the way the other perceives and renders reality, each could experience a widening of its own horizon, liberating itself from preconceptions. Bohm's own contact with artists caused him to take a fresh look at the structures of reality as comprehended directly with the senses. "Vice versa," he continues saliently, "new scientific notions of structure may be significant to the artist, not so much because they suggest particular ideas to be translated into artistic form, but, rather, because if they are understood at a deep level they will change one's way of thinking about *everything*, including art" (*Creativity* 38–39). Increasingly, as Stafford's recent work shows, sensitivity to perceptual matters (structure, patterns, similarities) is shared equally by the two cultures of science and the arts. "Visual technologies," Stafford remarks, "expand human consciousness, allowing people to see their material connections to larger ideas, forces, and movements" (Stafford 112).

2. More on Mimesis or Making Motion

Long before the by major scientific discoveries of the nineteenth and twentieth centuries became known, intellectuals throughout Europe looked to the creative

8 David Bohm, *Unfolding Meaning: A Weekend of Dialogue with David Bohm* (London: Routledge and Kegan Paul, 1985), 99. Bohm defines creativity at the conclusion of *Wholeness and the Implicate Order* (London: Routledge and Kegan Paul, 1980) in a more contorted manner: "[B]y creativity one means just the inception of new content, which unfolds into a sequence of moments that is not completely derivable from what came earlier in this sequence or set of such sequences. What we are saying is, then, that movement is basically such a creative inception of new content as projected from the multidimensional ground. In contrast, what is mechanical is a relatively autonomous sub-totality that can be abstracted from that which is basically a creative moment of unfoldment" (212). The essential aspect to be noted here is the event-character of creativity. The creative act is itself, and also results from as well as leads to, movement. That, then, is the ultimate definition Bohm offers of creativity in his last work, *On Creativity* (1998), 77–78 et passim.

imagination – the single most important attribute of the genius – as the key to unlocking nature's secrets. William Duff captured that nigh universal belief of his era in the mimetic power of imagination in his *An Essay on Original Genius* (1767) when he wrote: "Imitation indeed, of every kind, except that of nature, has a tendency to cramp the inventive powers of the mind, which, if indulged in their excursions, might discover new mines of intellectual ore, that lie hid only from those who are incapable or unwilling to dive into the recesses in which it lies buried."[9] While Bohm emphasizes the creativeness of nature itself, Duff accentuates the popular belief in the role of the gifted individual. Their confluence occurs in the mixing of the two matrices of subject and object, that is, in the acts of discernment and imitation.

The problematization of epistemic questions and the belief in a special quality of aesthetic perception both arose in the eighteenth century. As the classical understanding of mimesis underwent major revision, aesthetics was established as a separate discipline. In essence, it was a shift away from imitating the *products* of nature to imitating its inner *processes*. In his *Beiträge zur geheimen Geschichte des menschlichen Verstandes und Herzens* (Contributions to the Secret History of Human Understanding and Sentiment 1770), for example, Wieland addresses the issue of art as imitation head on. He perceives two general stances: (1) art as the refinement of nature and (2) art as the bastardization of nature. The first is like the Homeric Venus who appears cleansed, clothed, and perfumed to enhance her natural beauty; the second is likened to the power of magic capable of transforming the Phorkyads into Helen of Troy. But Wieland cautions that the first group puts too little stock in art while the second too much. Yet, "both are wrong when they speak of nature and art as essentially different and heterogeneous since upon closer examination, it appears that what we call art [...] is essentially nothing other than nature itself." To be sure, the perfection of nature is latent in its very laws, but nature requires the ingenuity and industry of humanity to realize its full potential. Nature prods and cajoles humankind to intervene, alter, and nurture.[10]

Wieland thus poses the same questions as Koestler, Rothenberg, and Briggs: Who or what conveys to humankind the power of art? What nurtures this ability? What is

---

9 William Duff, *An Essay on Original Genius and Its Various Modes of Exertion in Philosophy and the Fine Arts, Particularly in Poetry*, ed. John L. Mahoney (London, 1767; rpt. Gainesville, FL: Scholars' Facsimiles and Reprints, 1964), 131–32.

10 Wieland, *Beiträge*: "Die ersten scheinen der Kunst zu wenig einzuräumen, die andern zuviel; beide aber sich zu irren, wenn sie von Natur und Kunst als wesentlich verschiedenen und heterogenen Dingen reden, da doch, bei näherer Untersuchung der Sache, sich zu ergeben scheint, daß dasjenige, was wir Kunst nennen [...] im Grunde nichts anders ist, als die Natur selbst, welche den Menschen [...] veranlaßt und antreibt, 'entweder ihre Werke nach seinen besondern Absichten umzuschaffen, oder sie durch Versetzung in einen andern Boden, durch besondere Wartung und befördernde Mittel zu einer Vollkommenheit zu bringen, wovon zwar die Anlage in ihnen schlummert, die Entwicklung derselben aber dem Witz und Fleiß des Menschen überlassen ist'" (Hanser 3:229–30).

the source and cause of the content of art? Who provides the models? Who sets the rules? Wieland's answer in each case is nature. Nature provides the material, the reason, the impulse, and the self-organizing principles. Emphatically he states: "The works of nature in this sublunar world [...] arrange themselves into organized and non-organized [groupings]" ("Die Werke der Natur, in dieser sublunarischen Welt [...] teilen sich von selbst in organisierte und unorganisierte"; *Beiträge* 3:230). Strikingly, Wieland sees these general classifications of nature as categories of self-regulation. Of course, this eighteenth-century poet assumes a teleological principle at work similar to the one operative since Plato and reformulated by Leibniz.

In the first general category one finds inanimate and animate objects, sentient beings, and self-aware ones. Of all these groups, humankind alone has the greatest potential and responsibility for development: "Humankind is almost pure potential as it emerges from the formative hand of nature," Wieland argues in concert with J. J. Rousseau. "Humans must develop that potential and complete their formation [...] in brief, humankind must [...] be its own second creator."[11] Nevertheless, nature continues to have a hand in things since the principles of self-development are derivative of nature itself (3:232). Art, then, *is* nature. What we call art, Wieland summarizes, is "the combined powers of experience, ingenuity, instruction, example, persuasion, and necessity."[12] Here he addresses the relation of art to human development and renders humankind as part and parcel of nature.

While Wieland does not speak further about man's relationship to "unorganized" natural phenomena, humankind would appear to partake of both the ordered and chaotic dimensions of reality in his view of things. Although he sensed the presence of deep structures within reality and the hidden dynamics of vortex and unpredictability (e.g., he refers to the dynamics of fire), he remained true to the spirit of the eighteenth century, more comfortable addressing the readily recognizable self-organizing principles evident in nature such as crystal formation, plant biology, metamorphosis of the caterpillar, the beaver's technological acumen, and the beehive.[13] The problem of

---

11 Wieland, *Beiträge*: "Der Mensch, so wie er der plastischen Hand der Natur entschlüpft, ist beinahe nichts als Fähigkeit. Er muß sich selbst entwickeln, sich selbst ausbilden [...] – kurz, der Menschen muß gewissermaßen sein eigener zweiter Schöpfer sein" (Hanser 3:231).

12 Wieland, *Beiträge*: "die vereinigten Kräfte von Erfahrung, Witz, Unterricht, Beispiel, Überredung und Zwang" (Hanser 3:233).

13 Wieland, *Beiträge*, writes, e.g.: "Wenn es die Natur ist, die im Feuer leuchtet, im Cristall sechseckicht anschießt, in der Pflanze vegetiert, im Wurme sich einspinnt, in der Biene Wachs und Honig in geometrisch gebaute Teller sammelt, im Biber mit anscheinender Vorsicht des Zukünftigen Wohnungen von etlichen Stockwerken an Seen und Flüsse baut, und in diesen sowohl als vielen andern Tierarten mit einer so zweckmäßigen und abgezirkelten Geschichtlichkeit würkt, daß sie den Instinct zu Kunst in ihnen zu erhöhen scheint; -Warum sollte es nicht auch die Natur sein, welche im Menschen, nach bestimmten und gleichförmigen Gesetzen diese Entwicklung und Ausbildung seiner Fähigkeiten veranstaltet?" (Hanser 3:231–32).

complex dynamics had to wait until the nineteenth century when more sophisticated, perception-extending measuring techniques became available. Striking, nonetheless, is the allusion in the title *Contributions to the Secret History of Human Understanding and Sentiment* to a deep structure of reality that impacts upon human action in subtle as well as more manifest ways. The point is underscored by his choice of subtitle: *Aus den Archiven der Natur gezogen* (Drawn from the Archives of Nature). Those archives were – and are – yet to be fully explored. It is widely believed to be a matter of finding the right key to unlock the doors of the inner vaults.

Within the tradition of aesthetics, Wieland's views represent a dramatic turn in the debate on the relationship between idea and reality. Almost from the start, art and reality, by contrast, were often seen as divergent. For instance, Plato devalued the phenomenal realm as a mere imperfect reflection of the higher reality of ideal forms, whereas Aristotle reinvested value in phenomena as the only reality available for study and imitation. The debate has continued ever since. In his richly detailed and informative essay "The Imitation of Nature: Concerning the Prehistory of the Idea of the Creative Individual" (1956), Hans Blumenberg reviews those sometimes divergent, sometimes convergent lines from Plato to Paul Klee.[14]

For Plato, mimesis signified the "negativity of difference between the idea [*Urbild*] and the copy [*Abbild*]"; art is thus derivative, and imitation falls short of the essence (Blumenberg, "Nachahmung" 64–65). Aristotle closed the gap by asserting that nature and art are self-same, since the cosmos consists of both the actual and all possible worlds. The purpose of art is consequently to be innovatively iterative, not monotonously repetitive. The creative person is merely a servant of nature without the capability for original input ("Nachahmung" 71–73). By introducing the element of contraries, Heraclitus provided greater leeway for the authenticity of the creative work. However, art remained bound to the laws of nature. Heraclitus saw in nature "a network of contraries" that exist in a superimposed state without canceling one another out. Examples of such agonistic forces are masculine-feminine, dry-damp, and warm-cold ("Nachahmung" 74).

A development with far-ranging consequences began when Poseidonios (135–51 BC), mentor of Pompejus and Cicero and chief representative of the middle Stoa, introduced the concepts of movement and energy as crucial characteristics of both nature and art. There was for him but a single ενέργεια (*enérgeia* = action, operation, energy) at work ("Nachahmung" 75). The root word "έργον" (ergon), which denotes work, connotes a "working within" when applied to the movement of life itself; that is to say, it refers to an internal movement and is not immediately perceptible to the

14 Hans Blumenberg, "'Nachahmung der Natur': Zur Vorgeschichte der Idee des schöpferischen Menschen," in H. Blumenberg, *Wirklichkeiten in denen wir leben* (Stuttgart: Reclam, 1981), 55–103. The essay first appeared in *Studium Generale* 10 (1957): 266–83, and was originally delivered as a lecture at the University of Munich in Nov. 1956.

unassisted senses, although nonetheless manifest (cf. Bohm, *Creativity* 79). Consequently, Poseidonios understood reason to be the logical outcome of nature, not a force to be superimposed upon it. Augustine applied the concept as potentiality in the Godhead: "omnia possibilia sund Deo" ("Nachahmung" 80). By suggesting that Divine potentiality is infinite, he reversed the customary derivation of the possible from the potential; now the potential was defined from the standpoint of the possible. Slight though the shift might appear, its consequences proved far-reaching. Potentiality loosened itself from empirical bondage, took on a life of its own, and far outdistanced the bounds of the possible, which had hitherto been defined by comparison to manifest reality. The result? Empirical reality ceased to be the sole point of orientation.

One of the first to pick up on the notion of *potentia infinitiva* was Nikolaus von Cues. Cues further developed the notion that the real world is the highest form of reality. By implication, however, it is not the only form of reality, since God has not only created the actual world, but also incorporates in His/Her being the *principle* of possibility. That principle states that the possible is infinite, that the possible – freed from its empirical moorings – is identical with the deity.[15] On the other hand, because the manifest world is but one of endless possibilities, God is not identical with the world realized and manifest before us even though the divine spirit infuses nature as an active force ("ein Wirkendsein"). For example, in an effort to explain divine nature, Cues defines the deity as an infinite triangle ("unendliches Dreieck"), an infinite circle ("unendlicher Kreis"), and an infinite sphere ("unendliche Kugel") (Cues 91). By transforming geometric shapes from angular ones to circles and ultimately to straight lines to underscore the infinity of God, Cues anticipated the topology of fractals. The longest, endless line, he argues, would logically have to be the one without any angles or bends (Cues 92). Angular, circular, and spherical shapes, are therefore analogies for the potential forms of reality. As the circumference of an infinite circle, the endless straight line contains all other possible forms. (This argument overlooked, of course, the possibilities of infolding in phase space.)

Interesting is Cues's remark that "formlessness is simultaneously the shape of the possible" ("die Formlosigkeit aber ist gleichsam die Form der Möglichkeit"; 140). The remark is of special interest because Cues immediately follows it up with a reference to chaos as the origin of the existing world and with the suggestion that chaos is also the mother of all beings and shapes. Precisely because the absolutely possible lacks manifest form and is adaptable to any shape, its proximity both to endless, formless chaos and to the infinite, amorphous deity is striking (Cues 140–41). Nevertheless,

---

15 Nikolaus von Cues, *Die Kunst der Vermutung: Auswahl aus den Schriften*, ed. by Hans Blumenberg (Bremen: Carl Schünemann, 1957), writes: "Daher ist die absolute Möglichkeit in Gott, und sie ist Gott selbst; außerhalb seiner ist sie aber nicht möglich" (142; cf. also 81, 139–40).

Nikolaus von Cues did not pursue the association of God with chaos. Given the mindset of the time, he did not see the full consequences of the infinite latitude created for possible worlds or for identifying God with chaos; it would surely have proven destabilizing (cf. Blumenberg, "Nachahmung" 86–88).

Leibniz elaborated further on the notion of possible worlds, contending that the existent one was the "best of all possible worlds" not because it was perfect but because it allowed for the greatest flexibility of chance and determination. To this notion of manifest and latent possibilities Leibniz also added a new dimension, one achieved by redefining the concept of substance. He begins his essay *Principes de la nature et de la grâce, fondés en raison* axiomatically: "La Substance est un être capable d'action." Thus essential to the concept of substance are motion, action, movement (i.e., *enérgeia*). In the *Monadologie*, the monads are seen as dynamic "systems" interacting in a larger framework with porous borders. The processes of growing consciousness are also linked dynamically by the "strange attractor"of inner logic.[16] No wonder, then, that Jill Anne Kowalik concludes in her assessment of Leibniz's impact on eighteenth-century poetics that the three qualities of the real, the potential, and movement must be conjoined in measuring Leibniz's significance: "In the context of Leibniz's metaphysics [...] 'possibility' and 'possible worlds' are given the status of dynamic potentiality. The possibles are those things that are realized as the world becomes more perfect, which it does ceaselessly. Indeed they are the precondition for the world's perfection."[17] In brief, the "best of all possible worlds" demands imaginative re-creations. The seed, planted by Nikolaus von Cues, bore first fruit here and led to even more radical conjectures on the infinite possibilities of manifest or potential reality in the twentieth century.

Through the mediation of Christian Wolff, these notions of reality and its imitation reached the Swiss theorists Johann Jakob Bodmer and Johann Jakob Breitinger, who, in their celebrated literary feud with the Saxon Johann Christoph Gottsched, firmly established in the public mind the pre-eminence of art as a participatory rather than merely iterative event. They included in their view of an almost infinitely variable world the recipient as well as the producer of the work of art. For that reason, Blumenberg (as do and literary historians in general) accords Bodmer and Breitinger a prominent position within the history of literary theory. The critical turn – related to the Copernican Turn remarked upon earlier – occurs in the encounter between

16 Gottfried Wilhelm Leibniz, *Monadologie*, trans. by Herrmann Glockner (Stuttgart: Reclam, 1954): "Die Tätigkeit des inneren Prinzips, welches den Wechsel oder den Übergang von einer Perzeption zur anderen bewirkt, kann als Begehren bezeichnet werden" (p. 14, #15).

17 Jill Anne Kowalik, *The Poetics of Historical Perspectivism* (Chapel Hill: University of North Carolina Press, 1992), 50. See also Nicholas Rescher's excellent edition and commentary: *G. W. Leibniz's* Monadology*: An Edition for Students* (Pittsburgh: University of Pittsburgh Press, 1991), 228–32, 265–66.

philosophy and critical theory in the first four decades of the eighteenth century.

After reaching this point in his review, Blumenberg telescopes his sketch of the ramifications of the possible-worlds theory to skip forward into the twentieth century, leaving out most of the nineteenth century with its scientific positivism. Only barely does he touch on twentieth-century developments and concludes his survey by wondering aloud whether the infinite worlds that Leibniz bequeathed to aestheticians were "merely infinite reflections of one basic configuration of existence"? He did not think that the question could be answered.[18] Actually, the same question had been posed by Breitinger; and the Swiss critic had already proffered an answer.

In the *Critische Dichtkunst* Breitinger contends that "humankind has been endowed by nature with an insatiable thirst for knowledge which extends equally to possible worlds as well as to the manifest one." Indeed, he continues, humans seem more interested in the potential and possible than they are in the *res natura* manifest before them.[19] Moreover, he cites approvingly Cicero's contention that the expansion of our knowledge is accompanied by an aesthetic experience of pleasure, adding that the greater the thirst for knowledge, the greater the aesthetic experience. The poet and artist are called upon to school their reason and broaden their knowledge in order to imitate nature more fully. Imitation of nature, as Breitinger repeatedly insists here, is aimed not at the products of nature but at its underlying energy, its processes, which bring about manifest forms.[20] Following Leibniz, he asserts that nothing in nature can be self-contradictory. That which appears nonsensical to our minds is unworthy of

18 Blumenberg, "Von der Nachahmung": "Sind die unendlichen Welten, die Leibniz der Ästhetik beschert hat, nur unendliche Spiegelungen *einer* Grundfigur des Seins? Wir wissen es nicht, und wir wissen auch nicht, ob wir es je wissen werden; aber es wird unendlich oft wieder die Probe darauf gemacht werden" (93–94).

19 Breitinger, *Critische Dichtkunst* (1740), in J. J. Bodmer and J. J. Breitinger, *Schriften zur Literatur*, ed. by Volker Meid (Stuttgart: Reclam, 1980), 89.

20 Breitinger, *Critische Dichtkunst*: "Alle diese möglichen Welten, ob sie gleich nicht würcklich und nicht sichtbar sind, haben dennoch eine eigentliche Wahrheit, die in ihrer Möglichkeit, so von allem Widerspruch frey ist, und in der allesvermögenden Kraft des Schöpfers der Natur gegründet ist. Nun stehen auch dieselben dem poetischen Mahler zum Gebrauche bereit und offen, und leihen ihm die Muster und die Materie zu seiner Nachahmung; und da er die Natur nicht alleine in dem Würcklichen, sondern auch in dem Möglichen nachzuahmen fähig ist, so erstrecket sich das Vermögen seiner Kunst eben so weit, als die Kräfte der Natur selbst; *folglich muß der Poet sich nicht alleine die Wercke der Natur, die durch die Kraft der Schöpfung ihre Würcklichkeit erlanget haben, bekannt machen, sondern auch, was in ihren Kräften annoch verborgen lieget, fleissig studieren, um so viel mehr da dieses leztere, nemlich die Nachahmung der Natur in dem Möglichen, das eigene und Haupt-Werck der Poesie ist*" (emphasis added) (*Schriften*, 86). The argument is repeated elsewhere in the *Critische Dichtkunst* (see *Schriften*, 88, 97, 140). In regard to expanding vision toward the possible see John A. McCarthy, "Enlightenment Today or Movement at the Borders," *Transactions of the Ninth International Congress on the Enlightenment,* ed. by Werner Schneiders, 3 vols. (Oxford: The Voltaire Foundation, 1996), 1:173–86 (= *Studies on Voltaire and the Eighteenth Century*, 346–348).

imitation, for it is a false appearance and as such is nothing but the result of blind, incomprehensible chance.[21]

The repeated reference to our not comprehending the phenomenon implies the limitations of reason and echoes Cues's assertion that reason can never apprehend the truth completely because reason is itself not truth.[22] Thus, Breitinger's exhortation to refocus our attention from the contradictions of appearance to the internal workings of nature is a clever move. Possible worlds have their own self-regulating principles. The only restriction is that the internal logic should not be self-contradictory. After that, anything goes. The free play of imagination, however, does come at a cost. The further the imaginary world moves away from the empirical realm of experience, the more wondrous it becomes. Conjoining the wondrous and the mundane in a tenuous tilting of tensions is the key to Breitinger's aesthetic theory, for that conjuncture affords the most intense aesthetic pleasure. Later he reiterates that "the more precisely the poet understands the laws and forces of nature and the essence of all things, the more successful he will be in accurately defining the probable and the more skilled he will be in delineating the adventurous and the wondrous" (*Schriften* 143). The discreteness of knowledge ensures the aesthetically most pleasing balance between the probable and the wondrous. "Poetic truth," he further states, "is the cornerstone of [aesthetic] pleasure," and since "novelty is the mother of the wondrous, it too is a source of pleasure" (*Schriften* 123).

The fountainhead of pleasure is twofold: the object of imitation ("die Materie der Nachahmung") and the manner of imitation ("die Kunst der Nachahmung"). Whereas the first is the touchstone for determining the character of the wondrous and its distance from the probable, the latter is strongly influenced by our understanding of the inner operations of nature. Because of the latter, the poet can bring new perspectives to bear, thereby accentuating qualities of experience otherwise lost in the mundaneness of life. Thus art amplifies nuances of existence until they assume a sharp profile in our awareness. In short, art imitates nature by making manifest what is hidden (cf. *Schriften* 96–97). Exposing the latent is a way of saying that the laws of nature are designed to bring nature to full fruition. Those laws are potently active and favorable to expansion, and adapt to changing environments. The creative person unleashes this inherent potential movement.

All this points to the dissolution of the traditional identification of art with manifest

---

21 Breitinger, *Schriften*: "ein Zero, ein Nichts, wovon der Verstand nichts begreiffen kann [...] es ist eine blosse Würkung des blinden und unverständigen Zufalles" (90).

22 Cues, *Vermutung*: "Die Vernunft, die nicht die Wahrheit ist, begreift daher die Wahrheit niemals so genau, daß sie nicht noch unendlich genauer begriffen werden könnte. Sie verhält sich zur Wahrheit wie das Vieleck zum Kreis: je mehr Ecken das Vieleck besitzt, um so ähnlicher wird es dem Kreis; aber selbst wenn die Zahl der Ecken ins Unendliche vermehrt wird, wird es dennoch nie dem Kreis gleich, es sei denn, es ginge in Wesenseinheit mit dem Kreis über" (78).

nature. Blumenberg calls this shift "the dissolution of the mimetic concept" ("Zersetzung der Mimesis-Idee"; "Nachahmung" 77). He cites it as the clear result of our enhanced knowledge of the inner workings of the world. Lamenting the conservative stance of poets who remained tethered to old concepts, Breitinger followed the lead of natural scientists, who broke new ground in the art of seeing (Kowalik, *Poetics* 41). We can construe his argument to mean that poets must become as perceptive and visionary as their counterparts in the sciences. One of Bodmer's and Breitinger's most successful students, Wieland, did just that with such early products of the new aesthetic as *Die Abenteuer des Don Sylvio von Rosalva* (1764), *Die Geschichte des Agathon* (1766–67), and *Die Dialogen des Diogenes* (1770). Undoubtedly, these developments in aesthetics, set in motion by Copernicus and Kepler, were part of the dynamic of modernity, which Sloterdijk dubbed "the abolition of the obvious,"[23] and which found apt expression in John Berger's study of perspective in art, *Ways of Seeing*. In a sense, then, Breitinger anticipated Kant's own Copernican Turn by half a century.

The new view does not limit artistic imitation to so many iterations of a sole fundamental structure of reality. Rather, it expands it radically to include all worlds conceivable by the human mind. Like the empirical world itself, the poetic process is in a constant state of flux; the processes in both lead to the continual creation of new forms. "The production of form," Kowalik noted, unconsciously echoing the concept of feeling-tone emergence in the neural network, "the merging of diffuse, numerous, unnoticed particulars of experience into a perception, is an act of focusing executed in the aesthetic insight. [...] it is a process occurring in nature."[24] And David Bohm emphasized that in the movement of existence, "things" do not exist as discrete elements but "are abstracted out of the movement in our perception and thought, and

23 Peter Sloterdijk, *Kopernikanische Mobilmachung und ptolemäische Abrüstung* (Frankfurt a.M.: Suhrkamp, 1987), 49: "die Abschaffung des Selbstverständlichen." He also speaks of the role of art as a liberator of energy ("Freisetzung") (16).

24 Kowalik, *Poetics*, 85. What Kowalik has to say about the concept of perception rejection in Leibniz's system obviously also applies to Breitinger's aesthetic conception: "Rejection means that 'petites perceptions' never 'rise' to that level of activity where they represent themselves in perception. They are not compossible and remain unrecognized. Following this, the wondrous in Breitinger's system comprises not those things we reject, but those things we may have never noticed but then eventually assimilate" (84). Kowalik's explicit reference to both Breitinger and the notion that nuances of meaning ("petites perceptions") rise in and out of consciousness, thus causing shifts in focus, underscores the nexus of reality and perception. Unfortunately, Kowalik argues in her concluding chapter that the interactive poetics advanced by Breitinger (also by Johann Martin Chladenius), and based on Leibniz, "was overlooked" in the years after publication of the *Critische Dichtkunst* (87). She loses sight of the direct impact Breitinger had on creative writers such as Klopstock and Wieland, both of whom had daily contact with Bodmer and Breitinger as guests in Bodmer's home. Klopstock and Wieland (whom she does not mention in her study) passed the banner of "poiesis as intellective activity" (87) on to subsequent generations of writers via their theoretical and poetic works.

any such abstraction fits the real movement only up to a point, and within limits. Some 'things' may last for a very long time and be fairly stable, while others are as ephemeral as the shapes abstracted in perceptions of clouds" (*Creativity* 78).

We can then without hesitation adopt Blumenberg's neologism of "*Vor*ahmung" to characterize genuine imitation of nature in place of the usual "*Nach*ahmung" ("Nachahmung" 93). A play on the German word for anticipation ("Vorahnung"), "Vorahmung" might be translated as a "making in advance" or "pre-imitation" instead of the "after making" or imitation inherent in "Nachahmung." Furthermore, we can align "Vorahmung" with Spinoza's notion of nature in flux (*natura naturans*), while "Nachahmung" is directed at the products of nature formed (Spinoza's *natura naturata*). "Vorahmung" is possible, we might conjecture, because human beings are part and parcel of self-organizing natural forces and therefore resonate with them. In this sense, the artwork is more than either a mere schematic representation ("Darstellung") of a phenomenon or a symbolic representation of an abstract concept in Kant's twofold meaning of "Darstellung."[25] Rather, it is a creative act, a reification of *enérgeia*, of energy and movement.

3. Mimesis as an Interdisciplinary Undertaking

Although Goethe did not provide a separate, definitive study of poetic imagination, he did comment widely in numerous publications on the aesthetic experience and its proximity to natural phenomena.[26] One of the most finely tuned is found in the introduction ("Einleitung") to his journal, *Die Propyläen* (1798), wherein he argues that attitude is key to the imitation of nature. Even more emphatically than the German Romantics writing at the same time, Goethe recognized the benefit of interdisciplinary

25 See Frederick C. Beiser, "Kant's Intellectual Development 1747–1781," *The Cambridge Companion to Kant*, ed. by Paul Guyer (New York: Cambridge University Press, 1992), 26–61, here 31–33. On representation, cf. Immanuel Kant, *Dialektik der ästhetischen Urteilskraft*, in *Werke in zehn Bänden*, ed. by Wilhelm Weischedel, 5th ed. (Darmstadt: Wissenschaftliche Buchgesellschaft, 1983), 8:459–60. In his early metaphysical phase, Kant was at pains to place Leibniz's concept of dynamic nature on a firm foundation in such works as *Thoughts on the True Estimation of Living Forces* (1746–47), *Universal Natural History and Theory of the Heavens* (1755), and *Physical Monadology* (1756). The dynamics of interaction and the notion of inner "living" forces are also part and parcel of Kant's later work.

26 Cf., e.g., Dorothea-Michaela Noé-Rumberg, *Naturgesetze als Dichtungsprinzipien: Goethes verborgene Poetik im Spiegel seiner Dichtungen* (Freiburg: Rombach Verlag 1993); Matthew Bell, *Goethe's Naturalistic Anthropology: Man and Other Plants* (Oxford: Clarendon Press, 1994); *Ein unteilbares Ganzes. Goethe: Kunst und Wissenschaft*, ed. by Günter Schnitzler and Gottfried Schramm (Freiburg i.B.: Rombach Verlag, 1997); Margrit Wyder, *Goethes Naturmodell: Die Scala Naturae und ihre Transformationen* (Weimar: Böhlau, 1998); and Astrida Orle Tantillo, *The Will to Create: Goethe's Philosophy of Nature* (Pittsburgh: University of Pittsburgh Press, 2002).

knowledge for the achievement of aesthetic goals.[27] His treatise, therefore, continues the discourse on perspectivism and attitude traced to the end of the eighteenth century. Moreover, the holographic conception of modern science is clearly prefigured here. The proximity of Goethe's art of envisioning to developments in twentieth-century science also becomes evident when one thinks of Werner Heisenberg's pioneering concept of *Anschaulichkeit* (visualizability) developed in the 1930s as a result of his work in nuclear physics and elementary particles. But first things first.

The purpose of Goethe's preamble was to introduce the reading public to this new journalistic undertaking and to explain the critical method envisioned for it. The latter proved to be subjective and relative. At the outset, Goethe asserts that "no one views the world exactly like the next person, and different people often apply the same agreed-upon principle in different ways." Indeed, individuals are not even consistent in their own judgments.[28] This stance clearly locates Goethe solidly within the context of the debate on perspectivism. New, however, is the exhortation for interdisciplinary expertise that follows. Like others before him, Goethe expected the artist to be a talented copyist, who was to study nature and create works in its image.[29] Despite some general similarities between Goethe's position and that of Gottsched (with the latter's more restrictive view of imaginative free play), and especially that of Breitinger (with its emphatic poetic license), Goethe accentuated the act of imitation somewhat differently. The call to imitate nature was for him a tremendous challenge ("ungeheure Aufgabe") that was accomplishable only through the gradual refinement of intellectual attunement ("fortschreitender Bildung"). He saw "such a large chasm

---

27 See Gerhart Baumann, "Goethe: Schriften zur Kunst – Vermittlungen einer Poetik," in *Ein unteilbares Ganzes* (1997), 89–116, here 99. John A. McCarthy, "The 'Pregnant Point': Goethe on Complexity, Interdisciplinarity, and Emergence," in *Goethe, Chaos, and Complexity*, ed. by Herbert Rowland (Amsterdam and Atlanta: Rodopi, 2002), 17–31. On the Romantic view of imitation and representation, see Azade Seyhan, *Representation and Its Discontents: The Critical Legacy of German Romanticism* (Berkeley: University of California Press, 1992); Helmut Müller-Sievers, *Self-Generation: Biology, Philosophy, and Literature Around 1800* (Stanford: Stanford University Press, 1997); Laurie Johnson, "Bringing Chaos into the System: The Aesthetic Authority of Disorder in Friedrich Schlegel's Philosophy," in *Disrupted Patterns: On Chaos and Order in the Enlightenment*, ed. by T. E. D. Braun and John A. McCarthy (Amsterdam: Rodopi, 2000), 119–33.

28 Johann Wolfgang von Goethe, "Einleitung zu den Propyläen" (1798), in *Sämtliche Werke*, Frankfurter Ausgabe, ed. by Friedmar Apel and Hendrik Birus et al, 40 vols. (Frankfurt a.M: Deutscher Klassiker Verlag, 1985–99), 18:460: "kein Mensch betrachtet die Welt ganz wie der andere, und verschiedene Charaktere werden oft Einen Grundsatz, den sie sämtlich anerkennen, verschieden anwenden. Ja der Mensch ist sich in seinen Anschauungen und Urteilen nicht immer selbst gleich." Hereafter this edition is cited as FA.

29 Goethe, "Einleitung" (FA 18:461): "Die vornehmste Forderung, die an den Künstler gemacht wird, bleibt immer die: daß er sich an die Natur halten, sie studieren, sie nachbilden, etwas, das ihren Erscheinungen ähnlich ist, hervorbringen solle."

between nature and art that even a genius cannot bridge it without external help."[30] The creative individual is thus placed before a seemingly unsolvable problem since his talent is so far removed from nature itself. Without external input, he has little hope of success in imitating nature. In other words, the genius is dependent upon the external object in order to realize his own potential.

But then again, the situation is not so simple. The creative person is not totally dependent upon external nature. "Everything we perceive," Goethe explains, "is only raw material" (FA 18:461), which must be refined by nature as well as by humankind. Goethe solves the dilemma of traversing the chasm separating art and nature by declaring humankind to be subsumed under the general laws of nature: "Humankind is the highest, nay the actual object of the creative arts" ("Der Mensch ist der höchste, ja der eigentliche Gegenstand bildender Kunst"; FA 18:462). In order to discover the inner workings of nature, the creative individual must delve into the depths of natural objects, must allow them to speak; she must delve equally deeply into her own being. Only by means of detailed insights into *natura naturata* and *natura naturans* will the artist be in a position to imitate nature fully and produce a "spiritually organic" product ("etwas geistig-organisches"; FA 18:462). When art operates on the level of natural laws, "crude naturalism" gives way to what Matthew Bell calls "deep naturalism."[31]

That is the only way to compete with nature, the only way to cross over the great divide between nature and art. Analysis and categorization of natural phenomena are a mere prelude to truly artistic endeavors. For creative work, a general knowledge of organic processes is indispensable ("unerläßlich"). *Active, participatory observation* is thus a sine qua non of the creative act. Goethe concludes that what one sees, one truly *sees* when the penetrating gaze of the creative individual pierces the surface phenomena and lays bare the inner workings of nature in humankind as well as in the external object. Only to this sort of piercing gaze does the "foundation of surface play" ("das Fundament der Erscheinung"; FA 18:462) reveal itself. (I translate "Erscheinung" as "surface play" rather than the customary "manifestation" or "appearance" in order to carry through with the concept of motion.) But Goethe does not stop there. The artist who would imitate nature must also possess knowledge of *inorganic* nature. Only via such encompassing interdisciplinary knowledge of deep structures is genuinely creative imitation viable.[32] Goethe cites physicists, chemists, botanists, and

---

30 Goethe, "Einleitung" (FA 18:461): "die Natur ist von der Kunst durch eine ungeheure Kluft getrennt, welche das Genie selbst, ohne äußere Hülfsmittel, zu überschreiten nicht vermag."

31 Bell, *Goethe's Naturalistic Anthropology* (1994), 189–205, esp. 190, 194. Bell does not cite the "Einleitung."

32 Goethe, "Einleitung" (FA 18:462).: "Auch von den unorganischen Körpern, so wie von allgemeinen Naturwirkungen, besonders, wenn sie, wie zum Beispiel Ton und Farbe, zum Kunstgebrauch anwendbar sind, sollte der Künstler sich theoretisch belehren."

biologists as important collaborators in the creative act.

Using light as an example for his thesis, Goethe conjectures that the phenomenon of color, as well as that of electric and magnetic fields, is rooted in an essential tension within a holistic dialectic of nature. Natural scientists, he believes, will one day shed more light on the secret functioning of artistic creation and its relationship to fundamental principles of nature. His goal is not to dissect the whole into its discrete parts but rather to recognize in the individual parts subwholes (i.e., "holons") of the totality (FA 18:463–64). Goethe not only utilizes here fundamental qualities of the Leibnizian world of organic integration, but also anticipates aspects of modern physics with its view of the physical realm as a giant puzzle. Analysts view the individual pieces of the puzzle not just as fitting mechanically together but as being essential to understanding the dynamics of the whole.[33] In particular we note an anticipation of Koestler's concept of the holon and Bohm's vision of the undivided universe. All are stages in "consequent Copernicanism."

By means of his own creative energy, the artist transforms external reality, not through aggressive intrusion but through sensitive attention to hidden nuances of meaning and movement inherent in nature. Goethe explains in a manner paralleling Ralph Waldo Emerson's notion of the transparent eye: "By the mere fact of his attention to any object of nature, the artist separates it from nature, recreating it in that very moment by abstracting from the object its significance, its special characteristics, its interesting aspects; or rather, he invests it with a higher value via this act of abstraction."[34] Hence for Goethe, the proper imitation of nature is premised on the artist's ability to acquire interdisciplinary knowledge and bring it to bear in the creative act. It is an energizing process. Interdisciplinary data enhance and enlarge the normal perspectives available to the creative person, enabling her to find "the right perspective" for accessing the secrets of nature. The right perspective is the one richest in nuance. The problem of attitude and positionality greatly complicate the search for the right perspective. Thus Goethe's warning about the immense challenge to the artist in closing the gap between imitation and nature. Convinced that the chasm indeed exists, he nevertheless was confident that the participatory efforts of the artist would succeed in narrowing the difference. With that he has moved into the gray area of that which cannot be easily quantified.[35] As creative artist and natural scientist, Goethe

---

33 See Anthony Zee, *Magische Symmetrie: Die Ästhetik in der modernen Physik* (Frankfurt a.M. and Leipzig: Insel Taschenbuch, 1993), 274. Herbert von Einem, *Beiträge zu Goethes Kunstauffassung* (Hamburg: Schröder, 1956), 64 et passim.

34 Goethe, "Einleitung" (FA 18:465): "Indem der Künstler irgendeinen Gegenstand der Natur ergreift, so gehört dieser schon nicht mehr der Natur an, ja man kann sagen, daß der Künstler ihn in diesem Augenblick erschaffe, indem er ihm das Bedeutende, Charakteristische, Interessante abgewinnt, oder vielmehr erst den höhern Wert hineinlegt."

35 On efforts in modern science to quantify the subjective, see Robert G. Jahn and Brenda J. Dunne, *The*

bridges the positions associated with modern physics and modern interactive aesthetics (*Wirkungsästhetik*).

Goethe's friend and confidant Friedrich Schiller also reflected upon these issues (evident in, e.g., from their common work on dilettantism; FA 18:739-86), presenting the reader with a variation on the central theme of eighteenth-century German epistemology and aesthetics. Like the Romantics, who argued that only discrete forms enter human consciousness, Schiller propounded the idea that the external world is something formless in itself; it is only consciousness that gives it structure. Myth proves to be a key to unlocking the mysteries of human understanding. Consequently, in the opening lines of his seminal essay of 1793 *Über Anmut und Würde* (On Grace and Dignity), Schiller alludes to the mythical belt of Aphrodite that inspires love in the onlooker by lending grace to the wearer's natural beauty. The extended metaphor underscores the role of symbolic imagination in conveying meanings that reason could not easily grasp. Schiller drew heavily upon Kantian epistemology in a whole series of essays in an attempt to delineate more closely the role of the imagination and of the aesthetic experience. He also diverged from Kant, for the latter's view seemed too static to Schiller. In reaction, Schiller assigned physical movement and spiritual energy to the sensation of grace and beauty.

As "the symbol of kinetic beauty" ("das Symbol der beweglichen Schönheit"), the belt of Aphrodite grants to the wearer an essential, objective quality. For this reason, beauty of movement is not an accidental or subjective quality that makes the self only *appear* to be graceful: the self *is* graceful beauty. In fact, only through movement can the essential identity of the hybrid human being, who partakes of body and spirit, come into view as a morally beautiful creature. The "bewegende Kraft," which Kant had designated as the essential characteristic of matter, Schiller here expands to include the immaterial, the soul.[36] It is all in the motion, we might say. The critical difference between *Anmut* (grace) and *Würde* (dignity) is the role that consciousness plays in satisfying both the laws of nature and the demands of humankind's moral character. As hybrid creatures of spirit and body, humans were for Schiller (and the whole Platonic tradition) symbolic of the apotheosis of nature. Yet they are drawn in opposing directions. Man's moral calling asks him to harmonize duty ("Pflicht") and

---

Margins of Reality: The Role of Consciousness in the Physical World (New York and London: Harcourt Brace Jovanovich, 1987). They present an elaborate argument for "consciousness coordinates" (227–241).

36 Friedrich Schiller, "Über Anmut und Würde," in *Werke*. Nationalausgabe, 43 vols., ed. by Julius Petersen, Benno von Wiese, and Helmut Koopmann et al. (Weimar: Hermann Böhlaus Nachfolger, 1940ff.), 20:251–54, 287. Kant had devoted his *Metaphysische Anfangsgründe der Naturwissenschaft* (1786) to examining matter as movement in space ("Materie ist das Bewegliche im Raume"). The work appeared just before Schiller began to develop his aesthetic theory in reaction to Kant's *Critique of Judgment*. See Kant, *Werke in zehn Bänden* 8:25, 35, 47, 73.

inclination ("Neigung"). The artist's calling requires him to reconcile these opposites. Because human beings combine both the sensual and the moral, they appeared to Schiller as the epitome of creation and thus the highest object of artistic rendering.

Later, in his lengthy essay *Über die ästhetische Erziehung des Menschen* (1795), Schiller defined this autonomous movement within a determined framework as the "play-drive" ("Spieltrieb"). Schiller designated its actualization as humankind's proper calling. In his scheme of things, play became the ontological ground of all meaningful experience. In it the conflict between the two determining "force fields" of human experience – the sense-drive ("Stofftrieb") and the form-drive ("Formtrieb") – was resolved in the beautiful (see Seyhan 1992: 53). This did not mean that the two contending fields of dependency/passivity (sense-drive) and self-activation/autonomy (form-drive) were negated. What it did mean was that they both functioned agonistically via the medium of the play-drive because the play-drive was capable of conjoining "process with absolute being, change with identity" ("Werden mit absolutem Sein, Veränderung mit Identität zu vereinbaren"; 20:353, see also 360). For this reason, the aesthetic realm was the appropriate sphere of activity for the play-drive. The guiding principle was activity; the individual was called upon to be proactive in the realization of the ultimate self. Schiller wrote emphatically: "Humans only play when they are in the fullest sense of the word human beings, and *they are only fully human when they play*" ("der Mensch spielt nur, wo er in voller Bedeutung des Worts Mensch ist, und *er ist nur da ganz Mensch, wo er spielt*"; 20:359).

Moreover, the object of the play-drive is a living form ("lebende Gestalt"; 20:355); it is neither sterile nor mechanical. The reason is quite simple: becoming is the essence of being, not the having-become something. Moreover, being is not some immutable substance called "I" or "self." "We are because we are," Schiller reasons here, "we feel and think and desire because there is something else outside of us" (20:342). And that which is external to us impacts upon us either directly or indirectly. We must contend with it in an active fashion. The "idea of one's humanity" ("die Idee seiner Menschheit"; 20:353) serves as the catalyst for and guiding principle in change, evolution, and the realization of the full potential of the self. (The continuity of tradition from Cues and Leibniz is manifest here.) "Only by experiencing change," Schiller asserts, "does [man] *exist*; only by remaining immutable, does he exist" (20:343). Schiller's chiasmic formulation emphasizes that man remains the same despite the changes wrought by each such encounter. This paradoxical assertion pays tribute to the two fundamental drives impacting upon humans ("Stoff" and "Form"), which are ideally played out in the exchange-force field Schiller labeled the "Spieltrieb." To accept the challenge of reifying the ideal-beautiful ("das Ideal-Schöne"; 20:361), there is a need for force ("Kraft"), for energy of resolve ("Energie des Muts"; 20:330–31), and for energy of feeling ("Energie der Gefühle"; 20:362). The intellect acquires content through deeds, and thus the very act of mapping the space-time coordinates lends meaning to our lives ("eine absolute Tathandlung des Geistes [...] diese Handlung des Gemüts heißt urteilen oder denken, und das Resultat derselben der *Gedanke*"; 20:369). From this he concludes that only "energetic beauty" ("die energische Schönheit"; 20: 361) is truly worth possessing. No wonder that Goethe and Schiller considered humankind the epitome of creation. In their view, only humans have the capacity for (re-)creating themselves in the image of the ideal-beautiful in a mode that transcends temporal categories of past, present, and future.

In yet another famous essay, *Über naive und sentimentalische Dichtung* (On Naive and Sentimental Poetry, 1793), Schiller's main point is the difference between the poet who consciously strives for harmony with nature (i.e., himself) and the writer who automatically resonates with nature (i.e., Goethe). Both approaches are equally legitimate, for Schiller was convinced that the work of both is really a matter of interpretation. And *interpretations* are as close as we can come to objectivity, a claim strikingly prescient of Nietzsche's later position. Imagination and intuition play the primary role in mapping (moral) reality; knowledge is revealed as a function of the way we sense the world ("Empfindungsweise"). Ultimately, as Harry Ritter concluded, "theoretical science and philosophy are branches of aesthetics, and not the other way around."[37] However we view the relationship, change, event, and motion represent key common elements. It is a legacy that found its way to Nietzsche and the postmodernists (cf. Seyhan 1992: 53).

4. Attitude and Aesthetic Experience

The foregoing provides the historical background to nineteenth- and twentieth-century theorizing on the nature of the aesthetic experience and how it relates to the attitude of the observer/artist. Goethe's kindred spirit in America and a connoisseur of German idealism, Ralph Waldo Emerson captured the progressive spirit of his own time and place, formulating the essence of poiesis in a pointedly contemporary manner: "How can we speak of the actions of the mind under any divisions, as of its knowledge, of its ethics, of its works, and so forth, since it melts will into perception, knowledge into act? Each becomes the other. Itself alone is. *Its vision is not like the vision of the eye, but is union with the things known*" (emphasis added).[38] The cohesion of perception,

37 Harry Ritter, "Science and the Imagination of Thought of Schiller and Marx," in *The Quest for the New Science: Language and Thought in Eighteenth-Century Science*, ed. by Karl J. Fink and James W. Marchand (Carbondale, IL: Southern Illinois University Press, 1979), 28–40, here 35. On the role of the imagination, see also Elizabeth F. Potter, "Synthesis and Consciousness," *Rice University Studies* 61.3 (Summer 1975): 59–66.

38 Ralph Waldo Emerson, "Intellect," in *Selected Writings*, ed. by Brooks Atkinson (New York: Random House, 1950), 292. On Emerson and German thought, see John A. McCarthy, "Emerson,

value, and action of which Emerson speaks is an example of theory in the original sense of *théoria*, that is, of deliberately observing. Such was also Goethe's understanding of seeing in the sense of "anschauen" (to look at) and of "betrachten" (to observe carefully). Seeing in this manner obviously entails more than just the effect of photons acting on nerve endings. That impact is just the beginning. The next, unavoidable step involves a value judgment – a conscious and almost instantaneous interpretation of what those stimuli might mean. The seer thus goes beyond a mere physiological reaction and engages in a higher level of discerning abstract connections among the stimuli. The intellect is the unifier of impressions. Emerson's concept "actions of the mind" echoes Schiller's understanding of the intellect as willed deed ("Tathandlung des Geistes"). Learning to see more than what meets the eye and to act on it is in itself already a creative strategy of the constructive intellect.[39] All this is an essential aspect of the anthropic principle that places humanity at the center of things in a delicately tuned universe. As the judging/assessing instance, the eye/I constantly re-emerges as the center of the visible world.

While humanistic scholarship and scientific inquiry seem to go about this task in different ways, their respective strategies of establishing the "full facts" and of engaging in "dynamic objectivity" appear to share a common taproot. To be sure, the one focuses on the subject, while the other zeros in on the object. They are, however, integrated even as they were for Emerson, Schiller, or Goethe. William James stressed the importance of the perceiving subject in his famous definition of a "full fact" as a "conscious field *plus* its object as felt or thought of *plus* an attitude toward the object *plus* the sense of self to whom the attitude belongs." All this together he called a *full* fact, even though the fact might be an insignificant one. Key was his insistence that "it is of the *kind* [of fact] to which all realities whatsoever must belong."[40] On the other hand is historian of science Evelyn Fox Keller's definition of "dynamic objectivity." Displaying an enhanced respect for the object being studied, Fox Keller defined dynamic objectivity as the cooperative effort between the subject and the object,

---

Goethe und die Deutschen," *Goethe Yearbook of North America* 8 (1994): 179–93.

39 Using the chemical table as an analogy, Emerson emphasizes the role of intellect as an independent force that contributes perspectives not inherent in phenomena themselves and thus stands at the apex of a hierarchy of natural "substances." He avers: "Every substance is negatively electric to that which stands above it in the chemical tables, positively to that which stands below it. Water dissolves wood and iron and salt; air dissolves water; electric fire dissolves air, but the intellect dissolves fire, gravity, laws, method, and the subtlest unnamed relations of nature in its resistless menstruum. Intellect lies behind genius, which is intellect constructive. Intellect is the simple power anterior to all action or construction. Gladly would I unfold in calm degrees a natural history of the intellect, but what man has yet been able to mark the steps and boundaries of that transparent essence?" ("Intellect" 292).

40 William James, *The Varieties of Religious Experience* (Cambridge, MA: Harvard University Press, 1985), 393.

having recognized in it "an opportunity for a deeper and more articulated kinship."[41] Similarly, Jahn and Dunne defined the comprehension of a deeper more articulated kinship as a soliton of consciousness resulting from the subject's attitude and disposition. As the critical factor in observation, consciousness was for them the actual medium for "the conceptualization and formulation of matter waves" (*Margins* 218). That sounds like the activity of a creative artist. But it does not simply happen. The "reality" or work of art is mediated by a point of view, which acts as a sort of polarizer. Critical in this stance is "the intensity, attitude, and orientation of the consciousness in its interaction with its personal environment" (*Margins* 251; see also 219).

In this regard, let us digress momentarily to recall Paul Davies' discussion of how photons behave when they pass through one or more polarizers, for it seems to be directly related to the role of the observer in the act of perception outlined here (*Other Worlds* 107–27). The filters represent an either/or situation because either parallel or perpendicular states are allowed to pass but not both. Moreover, the angle (or attitude) of the polarizer determines the direction of vibration to be passed. A photon passing through a series of polarizers, each twisted relative to one another, will emerge from each "twisted" in the prescribed direction. The Einstein-Rosen-Podolsky paradox complicates the matter in unexpected ways. It supposes that a decomposing atom sends two photons simultaneously off toward two parallel polarizers that are not equidistant apart. As required by the basic laws of mechanics, the photons travel in opposite directions and with correlated clockwise-anticlockwise spin. We expect that if photon A passes through polarizer A, then photon B would be blocked by polarizer B since photon B would have the counterspin while polarizer B is parallel to polarizer A (i.e., will admit only one spin direction). However, the unthinkable happens: if polarizer A passes its photon, so too will polarizer B, even though the photons do not pass through their respective polarizers at the same time and may even be millions of light years apart. If A blocks its photon, so does B. The question, how does B know what A will do? arises. Other questions follow: And why do they do the same thing? Why do the photons cooperate in their behavior although separated by space and time? How could the original atom that emitted the two photons know at which angle the polarizers were set?

The answer to these questions seems to be that it is neither a failure of the measuring instrument nor attributable to the ignorance of the observer. Rather, the notion that a photon would have a definite polarization direction is false. Davies concludes: "There is an inherent uncertainty in the *identity* of the photon itself, not just in our knowledge of it" (*Other Worlds* 121). Nor can we say that the photon is at this or that place in space. The uncertainty that troubles us extends to the very identity of

41 Evelyn Fox Keller, *Reflections on Gender and Science* (New Haven: Yale University Press, 1985), 117.

the "electron-at-a-place." In sum, the "either-or" notion attached to the two emitted photons is not a question of alternatives but of entanglement. They are in reality overlapping waves. We should assume by analogy that the observer/artist functions like the polarizer, giving identity to the direction and movement of the hybrid so that we too are part of quantum entanglement. By acting in the manner of A, we affirm one direction, while B acts at a distance in resonance with us. Or, of course, the line of entanglement could also be the reverse. In any event, as Davies explains, "Until we make a definite observation of the world, it is meaningless to ascribe to it a definite reality (or even various alternatives)" (*Other Worlds* 122).

The lesson to be drawn from the above "digression," is simple: the creative individual gives identity to "discrete identities" within the superspace of infinitely vast alternative worlds. The artist, like the observer in Davies' example, selects from the richness of existence that which he returns to the space of existence in articulated form with a well-defined value. "We seem to have a situation," Davies remarked, "in which the universe is in a sort of suspended state of schizophrenia until someone undertakes an observation, when it 'collapses' suddenly into reality."[42] Wieland had no way of knowing about the behavior of photons passing through filters, but he was right on with his assessment of our ability to create worlds by the powers of imaginative perception.

Bearing all this in mind, let us now consider the views of a more contemporary aesthetician, Jerome Stolnitz, which pull all the foregoing together into a succinct theory of how the aesthetic experience occurs. Four central moments within the aesthetic experience are foregrounded: interest, sympathetic reaction, attention (or contemplation), and awareness. Or in Stolnitz's formulation, the aesthetic experience is "disinterested and sympathetic attention to and contemplation of any object of awareness whatever, for its own sake."[43] The object of awareness itself is of little

---

42 Davies, *Other Worlds*, 124. Also of interest in this regard is Pauli's exclusion principle, according to which no two interacting electrons can exist in precisely the same space. Like the alternatives open to the two photons emitted from the decaying atom, each electron has either a clockwise or counter-clockwise spin around a given axis. The spin taken can be either plus or minus 1/2 unit of h/2pi. The opposing spin directions allow the two electrons to occupy the same space. In a sense, then, the opposite spin direction acts as a kind of bonding tendency. In the wave packet, that bonding tendency could conceivably appear as amplification of one wave direction through resonance with another occupying the same space. See Jahn and Dunne, *Margins* (1987), 223.

43 Jerome Stolnitz, "The Aesthetic Attitude," in *Aesthetics and the Philosophy of Art Criticism* (Boston: Houghton Mifflin, 1960), 29–42; rprt. *The Philosophy of the Visual Arts*, ed. Philip Alperson (New York: Oxford University Press, 1992), 7–14. See also R. G. Collingwood, "Consciousness and Attention in Art," in Albert Rothenberg and Carl R. Hausman (eds.), *The Creativity Question* (1976), 334–42. Stolnitz's argument is reminiscent of *Wirkungsästhetik* as forwarded by Breitinger and later by Wolfgang Iser and Umberto Eco. See Wolfgang Iser, *Der Akt des Lesens*. UTB636 (Munich: Fink, 1976); and Umberto Eco, *The Role of the Reader: Explorations in the Semiotics of Texts* (Bloomington: Indiana University Press, 1984).

consequence; disposition or attitude are paramount. Even as David Bohm's notion of the holomovement might be seen as the ultimate consequence of the Copernican Turn, so too can Stolnitz's scintillating analysis be considered a logical extension of the mimesis debate since Plato and Aristotle.

First of all, disinterested is not synonymous with uninterested because the experience cannot take place without the observer intensely identifying with the object itself. Thus, Stolnitz rightly emphasizes the participatory moment, that is, the sympathetic reaction of the observer herself. Sympathetic in this context means that one allows the perceived object to act upon the perceiver in its own individual way. It is not seen merely as an object to be exploited according to a preconceived plan. Stolnitz concludes that one must accept the object on its own terms ("Attitude" 10). Equally important for a proper understanding of the aesthetic moment is the third thrust of Stolnitz's definition: the observer's attention. Attention transforms the aesthetic moment from a passive event to active intervention. The aesthetic stance thus amounts to dynamic interaction with the perceived object. Only this dialectic of subject and object allows the full value of the object to evolve without the subject subjecting it to personal whim. Aspects of this activity include the physical response to external impulse, such as the rhythmic drumming of fingers during a musical concert, the emotional catharsis experienced in the theater, the rapid heart beat in moments of anxiety, and so on. Several impulses combine into an energy knot and explode from subliminal existence into conscious reality. In short, "Appreciation [...] is awareness, alertness, animation. Attention is always a matter of *degree*, and in different instances of aesthetic perception, attention is more or less intense" ("Attitude" 11).

The fourth marker of the aesthetic attitude is the degree of epistemic refinement. How many details are consciously assessed simultaneously? Perceptual discrimination results from the enhanced attention the observer brings to bear on the perceived object(s). As the consequence of an open stance toward the perceived object, discrimination has nothing to do with contemplation, that is, losing oneself in the object in the classical sense. Rather, it is a matter of actively and consciously engaging the object in a dialogue that allows both the object and subject to merge without loss of identity for either. Therefore, we are to understand attention in its broader connotation of awareness – or perhaps even more precisely of growing awareness – rather than as mere perception ("Attitude" 12–13). The operation of aesthetic attention would seem to be related to an early, conscious phase of Schiller's *Spieltrieb*, that is, before it becomes habit.

Logic suggests that any experience, regardless of whether purely imagined or actually encountered, can have an aesthetic dimension. The aesthetic element is independent of the object itself, being traceable to the viewer's open stance. Stolnitz concludes this line of reasoning by stating that "[a]nything at all, whether sensed or perceived, whether it is the product of imagination or conceptual thought, can become the object of aesthetic attention" ("Attitude" 13). The aesthetic attitude seems to me to be a useful complement to the notion of the creative act proposed by Koestler, Briggs, and chaos research or the notion of imitation expounded by Breitinger, Wieland, Goethe, and Schiller.

For instance, John Briggs concludes his book on chaos with a chapter on aesthetic experience that is astonishingly close to Stolnitz's theory. Briggs sees in the creative person someone who is extremely receptive to the boundary interfaces of feeling, perception, and cognition (*Mirror* 194). In fact, he argues with Ilya Prigogine that the mystery of creativity with its unpredictable outcome lies within the "creative chaos" of nuances and "feeling tones" circling within the highly complex neural networks of the brain (*Mirror* 150, 166). These nuances come to the fore especially in the gaps in communication or the spaces between the levels of interaction. Clearly inviting closure, these semiotically fertile "gaps" and "spaces," which seem to show up everywhere from literary semiotics to philosophical reasoning to scientific investigations, are ultimately discernible in mathematical constructs. Most notably expressed in fractals, they seem as richly nuanced as nature itself.

Umberto Eco, for example, analyzes "a new mechanics of aesthetic perception" in his "Poetics of the Open Work" (1984).[44] Recognizing openness as the fundamental possibility for both artist and consumer in an Einsteinian concept of the universe, he "installs a new relationship between the *contemplation* and the *utilization* of a work of art" (Eco 65). In doing so, Eco implicitly cites this move as a consequence of the Copernican Turn (Eco 57–61). The suggestiveness of the open spaces in a "work in movement" endows the various component parts of the text with equal value and dignity. While raising the value of the part and the role of the perceiver to that of performer, he does not intend to devalue the objective world. Rather, he senses a mutual value enhancement of both the subject and the object. In essence, the perceiver imitates the organizing role of the creator by allowing a "conditioning center of reference" to emerge from the multiple stimuli (Eco 61). Sounds like the polarizer function. While a "work in movement" may well deny a single prescribed point of view, Eco remarks,

> it does not mean complete chaos in its internal relations. What it does imply is an organizing rule which governs these relations. Therefore, to sum up, we can say that the *work in movement* is the possibility of numerous different personal interventions, but it is not an open invitation to indiscriminate participation. The invitation offers the performer the chance for an oriented insertion into something which always remains the world intended by the author. (Eco 62)

The guarantee of an external order in the Einsteinian universe is the belief that God does not play dice. Nor does S/he allow senseless gaps.

---

44 Umberto Eco, "The Poetics of the Open Work," *Reader* (1984): 47–66.

John Sallis addressed the importance of spacings, gaps, and openings in *Spacings*, his 1987 study of reason and imagination in Kant, Fichte, and Hegel.[45] *Spacings* speaks of the relationship between reason and imagination in marking the limits of absolute claim and enhancing the perspectives on the undefined whole. Sallis writes pointedly in his introduction: "[S]pacing is an operation of spreading something out, of inserting intervals into its interstices, of dispersing it so that it loses its compactness, its closedness. Thus spacing leaves difference open, dis(as)sembling the plane of truth so as to set its parts at various angles to one another, reintroducing depth, a new kind of depth" (xv). Sallis's notion of a new kind of depth resonates strongly with the scales of existence in the physical world, ranging from the nano through the meso to the supermacro. Spacings represent closures, therefore, as well as the opening up of new perspectives through suggestiveness and eccentricity. This dynamic allows one to judge the interactions of bodies (or meanings) interspersed throughout the open spaces. Even philosophical works, then, can be seen as "works in movement" in Eco's sense of the literary text (or in Smoot's sense of the interactive cosmos), expanding out beyond the limits of reason, engaging our imaginative powers, and deepening our perceptions all at the same time. Unlike Eco, however, Sallis seems unwilling to accord the object of our perceptions an inherent function in ordering our "willful" perceptions.

5. Spaces, Gaps, Openings, Tensions: Mapping Reality

The foregoing is central to the human ability to visualize what is only partially formed or perhaps not formed at all in our mapping of new and unexplored territory. An extraordinary example of this creative ability to conceive of the new is Werner Heisenberg's visualizing of the inner space of molecular physics. Working in the early 1930s to overcome the impasse reached in the traditional imaging of what was inaccessible to the inquiring eye, he hit upon an innovative approach. His breakthrough came with his suggestion of using the "metaphor of motion" to explain more accurately the actual phenomenon in the nucleus of the atom than was possible with the image of "exchange phenomenon in molecules."[46] He was led to the metaphor of motion by the abstract, unvisualizable mathematical description of the exchange force of molecular physics. Substituting for it the *Anschaulichkeit* (visualizability) of a migrating electron, he moved science forward in significant fashion.[47]

45 John Sallis, *Spacings – of Reason and Imagination in Texts of Kant, Fichte, Hegel* (Chicago: University of Chicago Press, 1987).

46 Arthur I. Miller, *Imagery in Scientific Thought: Creating 20th-Century Physics* (Boston: Birkhäuser, 1984), 255.

47 See Miller 127–27 for a definition of terms and esp. 143–73 and 253–59 for key moments in this

The shift in focus away from *Bild* (static image, picture) and even away from the Kantian *Anschauung* (which reflects more the beholder than the object) to *Anschaulichkeit* (which addresses more the action of the object) is essentially related to the displacement of *natura naturata* by *natura naturans*. In other words, mechanical relationships among fixed bodies are replaced by the concept of motion itself being the defining element in nuclear physics. This would appear to lead us back to the *enérgia* or *Kraft* or *lebendige Gestalt* or any of the other forms of dynamic interplay inherent in the operations of nature and of the mind.

In the 1970s both fractals and chaos were in their infancy. At first appearing unrelated, they eventually proved to be closely intertwined, for both are strategies for dealing with randomness or "gaps" in the structure of irregularity. Geometry is endemic to both, but in chaos, dynamics takes precedence over geometry, whil in fractals geometry dominates. To put it somewhat differently, fractals are the products of mathematics, and chaos is a natural phenomenon that we try to understand mathematically. Thus, fractals offer us a language for discussing the shape of chaos. Fractals such as the Cantor and Mandelbrot sets have assumed great significance within the science of chaos because they reveal a recursive symmetry, implying that chaos has a deep structure and that its apparently random divergences are somehow convergent after all, although not exactly so.[48]

The Cantor set is perhaps the most basic fractal of them all. Ian Stewart defines the Cantor set metaphorically as "an interval that has been got at by mice. Infinitely many vanishingly small mice, each taking tinier and tinier bites."[49] The Cantor set (Fig. 2.1) is created by removing the middle third of an interval of length 1 over and over again. When the middle third of the line *ab* is removed, the remaining two parts *ac-cb* are

---

revolutionary mode of thought. On the importance of visualizing in the creative act in humans and the role of metaphors, see also David Bohm and F. David Peat, *Science, Order, and Creativity: A Dramatic New Look at the Creative Roots of Science and Life* (Toronto: Bantam Books, 1987), 32–38.

48 Of the three models of the "geometry of space" – the Riemannian, the Euclidean, and the Gauss-Lobachevski hyperbolic – the last proves to be the most accurate description of how space appears to us: as an open universe in which parallel lines diverge rather than remain a constant distance apart (as in the Euclidean model) or converge (as in the Riemannian model). What determines the geometric shape of the universe is the density of matter distributed in it, of which less than 1 percent is visible. Smoot's investigations lead him to describe the universe as an open one, but one structured nonetheless by attractors great and small. See George Smoot and Keay Davidson, *Wrinkles in Time* (New York: William Morrow and Co., 1993), 160–62, 169, 184.

49 Ian Stewart, *Does God Play Dice? The Mathematics of Chaos* (Cambridge, MA: Basil Blackwell, 1989), 121–24, here 121. On fractals, see Benoît Mandelbrot, *The Fractal Geometry of Nature* (San Francisco: W. H. Freeman, 1982); Heinz-Otto Peitgen and P. H. Richter, *The Beauty of Fractals* (Berlin: Springer-Verlag, 1982); Heinz-Otto Peitgen, Hartmut Jürgens, and Dietmar Saupe (eds.), *Bausteine des Chaos: Fraktale* (Berlin and Stuttgart: Springer-Verlag / Klett-Cotta, 1992); Herbert Zeitler and Wolfgang Neidhardt, *Fraktale und Chaos. Ein Einführung*, 2nd ed. (Darmstadt: Wissenschaftliche Buchgesellschaft, 1994).

fractals of the original line *ab*. The process can continue ad infinitum (for example: *ad-dc*, *ce-eb*). By multiplying either *ac* or *cb* (or *ad*, *dc*, *ce*, *eb*) by 3, the

Figure 2.1: Cantor Set

```
a__________________________________________________________b
a__________________c                    c__________________b
a______d     d_____c                    c______e     e_____b
d_ff_d       d_g g_c                    c_h h_e      e_i i_b
```

original line can be reconstituted, i.e., the gap closed. Despite endlessly iterating the removal of the middle-third set, the relations among the remaining parts are constant. Each segment of each newly broken line is one-third the size of the segment from which it was created. Ultimately, the Cantor set will consist mostly of holes or gaps; more accurately, it *does* consist mostly of missing parts, and that is why it is often referred to as "Cantor dust" (Fig. 2.2). The missing parts act like signifiers, telling us

Figure 2.2: Cantor Set on Its Way to Cantor Dust (see Stewart, *Does God Play Dice?*, 122)

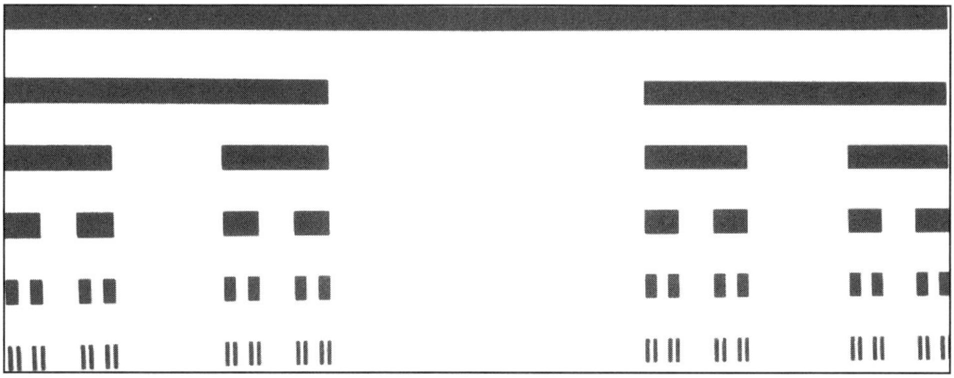

something about that which is absent. These openings seem related to the gaps Wolfgang Iser has identified as key to activating the reader's (or viewer's) productive imagination in interpreting a text.[50] The essence of the Cantor set is, in other words, the spaces separating what is left of the original interval. They might be seen as the threshold areas that connect even as they disconnect. The smoothness of our skin, for instance, is revealed under magnification and scaling to be a mountainous surface full of chasms (figs. 2.3, 2.4). Our reality is really a matter of perspective. The latter "wanders," Iser remarks, as the reader negotiates foreground and background information and becomes aware of the gaps (Iser 177). In his work *Nonlinear Systems*,

50 Wolfgang Iser, *Der Akt des Lesens* (Munich: Wilhelm Fink, 1976), 175–93.

P. G. Drazin explains how the Cantor set is related to fractals and how they are different from Euclidean geometry. Drazin points out that fractals are instrumental in mapping topographical variations using factors of dimension.[51] They are thus logical extensions of Euclidean concepts of point, line, surface, and solid, as well as of Cartesian coordinate geometry. Henri Poincaré, whom we encountered earlier, formalized the modern mathematics of topology. Poincaré suggested letting a point have a zero dimension, that is, neither positive nor negative value. His idea was to correlate space dimensionally so that it could be divided by boundaries and become open to mathematical calculation. Cuts of zero dimension sever a curving line into constituent points with but one dimension; surfaces can be charted via one-dimensional cuts producing two-dimensional figures (e.g., curves), and so on. Cantor's middle-third sets have a topological value of 0.[52]

Figure 2.3: Human Hand Viewed at 1 cm (http://www.powersoften.com)

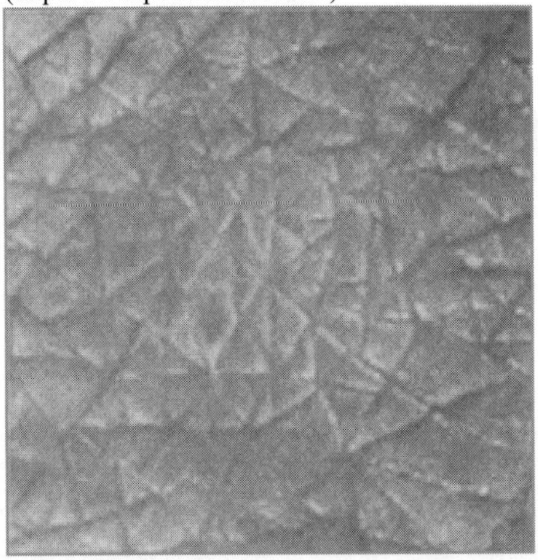

Figure 2.4: Human Hand Viewed at 1 mm (http://www.powersoften.com)

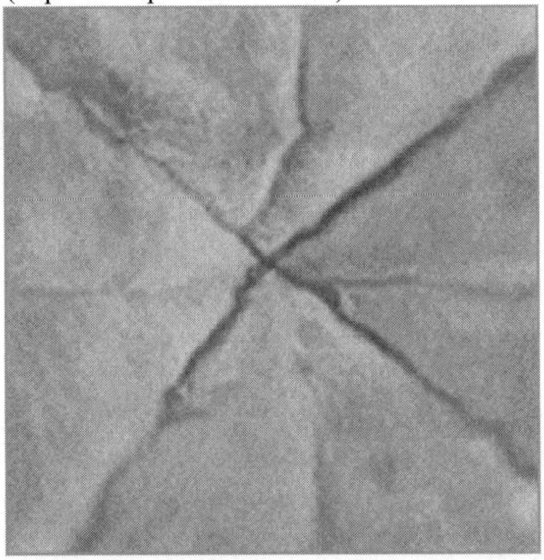

The Cantor middle-third set is of significance in our context because on the one hand it functions a strange attractor in chaos theory, and on the other, it is fundamentally related to the gaps and nonclosures of poststructuralism. The latter correspond to "various dimensions of infolding," which force the beholder to complete the hint of the missing parts. These infoldings are thus essential to the aesthetic experience (see, e.g., Koestler, *Act* 398). Strange attractors – which are mapped by using an

51 P. G. Drazin, *Nonlinear Systems* (Cambridge: Cambridge University Press, 1992), 127.

52 Henri Poincaré, *La Valeur de la Science* (Paris: Ernest Flammarion, 1905), chap. 3, para. 3. Drazin, *Nonlinear Systems*, writes that Cantor's third set has a "topological dimension d = 0 because it is a subset of R with zero length (and so has neither breadth nor length)" (127).

(arbitrarily) fixed point to trace their flow and then analyzed by scaling their movement into minimalistic units of phase space – are analogous to the coming-into-being of meaning in the quantum universe. Of course, strange attractors also disappear, although not permanently for they can reappear somewhere else. (Thus, they act like Holton's themata.) Derivative of the measurement technique used in the Cantor middle-third set, the fractal scaling of strange attractors cycles into minimum components.

A fractal then, Drazin explains further, is a "set whose dimension is strictly greater than its topological dimension, i.e., D > d." Is this a mathematician's way of describing a "subwhole"? Like the strange attractor, the fractal is easier to spot than to define. It is clear that the fractal's structure is infinitely variable on very small-length scales, as for example in the fixed-point Cantor middle-third set. Cantor sets are therefore definable as strange attractors.[53]

Figure 2.5: Gingerbread Man (http://en.wikipedia.org/wiki/Mandelbrot_set)

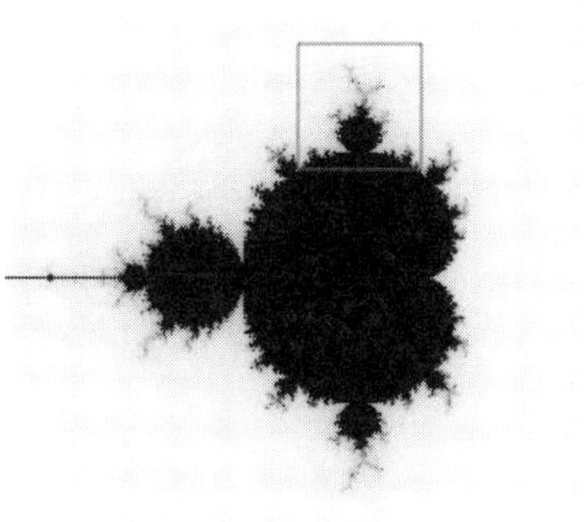

The Mandelbrot set – more popularly known as the gingerbread man (Fig. 2.5) – is, by comparison, a most complex fractal, which retains its highly complicated structure despite the level of magnification. And inside the gingerbread man, other infinitesimally small gingerbread men occasionally turn up. The iterative quality is a startling discovery, given the fact that the orthodox shapes of geometry (triangles, circles, spheres, cylinders) lose their structure upon magnification (Stewart, *Dice?* 217). Thus, they verify Cues's conjectures of several centuries ago. Complex, by the way, means having several components (e.g., $z = x + y\sqrt{-1}$). Complex numbers have their own arithmetic (algebra) and analysis (as, e.g., the complex mappings of $z \rightarrow z^2 + c$ where c is a constant). "The idea," Stewart tells us, "is to fix a value of *c*, and ask what happens to any given initial value *z* as this formula is iterated" (*Dice?* 235).

Surprisingly, some starting values of *z* rapidly go off into infinity while others do not. By coloring the iterations black or white depending upon whether they move off into infinity or not, we can come up with another surprise. Inside the Mandelbrot set

53 Drazin, *Nonlinear Dynamics*, 125, 131. Poincaré defines the strange attractor in the following way: "Let us seek to visualize the pattern formed by the two curves and their infinite number of intersections [...] The intersections form a kind of grid [...] with an infinitely tight mesh; each curve never intersects itself, but must fold upon itself in a very complicated way in order to intersect infinitely often the vertices of the grid" (1899, para. 397; cited by Drazin, 254–55). This pattern is now called a *homoclinic tangle*. See also N. Katherine Hayles, *Chaos Bound* (Ithaca: Cornell University Press, 1990), 154–60.

Figure 2.6: Julia Set
(http://en.wikipedia.org/wiki/Fractals)

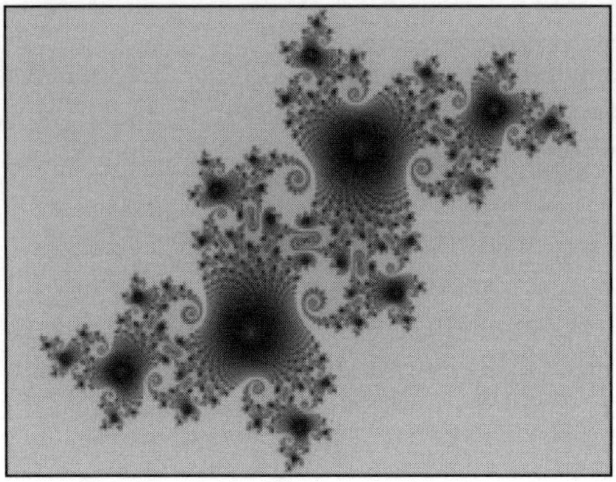

are all possible Julia sets with their successive approximations, iterations, and mappings of self-similarity. The Julia sets prove to be the boundary of "the basin of attraction of the point of infinity" (*Dice?* 236). Even more remarkably, the Julia sets are either open or closed. (According to the actual terminology, we would have to say "connected" and "disconnected.") Nonetheless, the Julia sets would appear to mirror the "spacings" uncovered in aesthetics, philosophy, and science. Fractals, then, prove valuable by revealing patterns in what otherwise looks to be formless and chaotic. They capture the "texture of reality."[54] Similar to Novalis's crooked line ("krumme Linie") as nature's way (Seyhan 1992: 29), fractals may, in fact, provide the "proper" perspective from which to view reality. In the ensuing literary analyses, the Julia sets will be a useful analytical tool, especially with regard to Günter Grass's *The Tin Drum*.

Feedback loops on various scales give rise to individual characteristics, that is, to the "texture" of the work of art just as much as to the artifacts of reality. Tracing the iterations and bifurcations leads the observer to an appreciation of special characteristics within the varied webbing of the reality created. Paradoxically, the spacings between them unite rather than separate them. An autopoietic process or deep structure seems to be at work independently of the performer/observer. The strategy of creation, in short, would appear to be precisely the self-regulation of the material itself in dialectical interplay with its environment. That, in turn, leads to mutations and variations of the starting point in much less direct a manner than in the Cantor set. A component of that interactive environment is the creative imagination of the onlooker who sees more than meets the eye.

The variations (i.e., bifurcations) occur strangely enough when the curving line reaches the critical point where the coordinate $a = 3$ (three seems to be a magical number). This first period doubling (x) can now take two values and oscillates between them (= binary dialectic). The rate of bifurcations increases further down the tree until another critical value of a is reached (= 3.5699...). This value marks the onset of chaotic behavior. The closer the branches approach the critical point, the closer together they get. The gap between the period doublings has been measured at

54 Stewart labels chapter 11 in *Dice?* "The Texture of Reality" (215–42). The foregoing is based on Stewart's analysis.

approximately 1/4 of the previous one (1/4.669201...) (four also proves to be fundamental). Mitchell Feigenbaum calculated the rate of shrinkage between the prongs of the bifurcations to be 1/2.5029.... In other words, as the onset of chaos is approached, the vertical gap between the bifurcation prongs is about 2/5 of the previous one (and the numeral five will later appear to be "magically" significant).[55] It all sounds rather complex. And, indeed, it is. Sort of like the aesthetic experience itself.

We might adapt the above idea of complicated relationships between order and chaos and apply it to our review of the debate on mimesis. We have seen that the work of art seeks harmony with nature in a manner analogous to the artist's need to be in tune with the creative energy of the universe in order himself to be creative. Viewed thusly, it is not simply a bifurcation of reality into subject and object, but a fusion whereby the point of fusion itself becomes a kind of third player in the creative process. Fusion is simply the reversal of the direction of the period doubling, that is, the point where the curving lines come together into one. The original starting point is of course uncertain. We sort of start in midstream. Being does not precede becoming; becoming precedes becoming.

Let us shift focus to the field of genetics for a related example of how creativity works in terms of deterministic chaos. Barbara McClintock explained to a young assistant how she could work for years on the breakage-fusion-bridge cycle in maize genetics (to the untrained eye the color variations present themselves as a veritable, impenetrable maze). Mapping a genetic marker is a relatively straightforward undertaking, for it consists of following the passage of traits from one generation to the next. McClintock's task was to map the genetic sequence in the chromosomes of young corn seedlings. To achieve the objective she had to cross pairs of "parents" of different genetic makeup and then note the genetic exchange in the offspring. Not only did she not know what the outcome would be, as a cytogeneticist she was dealing with the visible manifestations of genes (phenotypes) and the invisible operations of genes. In order to "see" those very discrete alterations (genotypes), she had to employ her inner eye to envision what the connection might be. Her assumption was that genes are distributed in a linear fashion along the chromosome. Any crossover of two chromosomes carrying differing traits would probably show up at regular intervals in the new fusion of genetic material. She reasoned that the greater the distance between the markers, the more likely it was that a break had occurred along that stretch of the chromosome. Thus, the space between markers would indicate whether a crossover of chromosomes had taken place. The frequency of offspring combining the genetic traits of both chromosomes would determine the relative location of the genetic factors.

Following these alterations through phenotypes is complicated enough, but

55 See Paul Davies, *The Cosmic Blueprint* (London: Unwin Paperbacks, 1989), 42–43.

McClintock's task was even more complex. She was trying to track a genetic factor that would be expressed *negatively* in terms of the *loss* of a phenotype rather than positively in terms of a gain in visible genetic factors. In other words, she was trying to map mutations that did not meet the eye, that became manifest only through the opening of "gaps" in the original genetic alignment. Later McClintock would have to map the changes at even greater distances without the benefit of any visible indicators (*Feeling* 129). We might call this task of tracking "dissociations" the mapping of "negative presences" to distinguish it from the normal tracking of actual, observable presences.[56] The similarity of McClintock's work and reasoning with that of a postmodernist literary critic in search of "traces" as well as with the rearranging of the Cantor set, would seem self-evident.

After much work, McClintock was able to pinpoint the factor apparently responsible for the dissociation. She located it on the short arm of chromosome 9 and was able to determine that the breakage kept occurring at the same point, which she designated *Ds*. Later she was forced to recognize that there were two different loci, one on the long arm of chromosome 9 and one on the short arm. While she still did not know what caused the dissociation, she did discover that the *Ds* locus undergoes dissociation "only when a particular dominant factor is present" (*Feeling* 131). She called this factor *Ac* since it *ac*tivates dissociation. Moreover, she determined that the *Ds* could show up elsewhere in the chromosome. She suspected that something in *Ds* triggers breakage and that something in *Ac* triggers *Ds*. Strangely enough, that triggering occurred over distances, since the *Ac* was found on the long arm of chromosome 9, not even close to *Ds*. Mutable loci, all related to *Ac*, kept cropping up. She identified four such loci on chromosome 9 alone. She surmised, that *Ac* was exerting some kind of control over these changes of state.

Unfortunately, *Ac* was not directly observable. It was only indirectly, through the plotting of *Ds*, that *Ac*'s presence was revealed. Ultimately, McClintock learned that there was a causal relationship between the dosage of *Ac* and the frequency of transposition, loss of chromosome fragments, or changes of state: the higher the dose, the later the occurrence of *Ds*. *Ds* could change its location to "any other part of the chromosome complement where a concurrent break might have occurred" (*Feeling* 133). Because *Ds* is a covert expression of *Ac*, McClintock could conclude that the feedback between *Ds* and *Ac* is symptomatic of an autocatalytic mechanism.

56 In an article in 1947 entitled "Cytogenetic Studies of Maize and *Neurospora*" (*Carnegie Institution of Washington Yearbook* 46 [1947]), McClintock explicitly wrote: "In this one case, mutability is expressed not bv a visible phenotypic change in the action of a gene, but rather by dissociation of the bonds that normally would maintain a linear cohesiveness of the locus with an adjacent locus in the chromosome. As an ultimate consequence of the mutation, the chromosome is dissociated into two completely detached segments" (147). On the broader subject of "presences," realized and potential, see George Steiner, *Real Presences* (Chicago: University of Chicago Press, 1989).

Moreover, the environment of the cell, that is, its developmental stage, impacts upon the particular change in *Ac* (*Feeling* 135). That environment is external to the cell as well as internal. The interaction of these "fields of tension" appears to account for the great deal of variation in the patterns of mutability.

McClintock was led to this astonishing conclusion not by any desire to break radically with traditional paradigms of mutation, but by the evidence that presented itself to her. She was guided in her creative insights, in other words, by the material itself. When asked by an assistant how she knew what to look for, McClintock responded that she didn't. Rather, she worked together with her material, allowing it to direct her attention and determine the next step in the experiment: "You let the material tell you where to go, and it tells you at every step what the next has to be because you're integrating with an overall brand new pattern in mind. You're not following an old one; you are convinced of a new one. And you let everything you do focus on that. You can't help it, because it all integrates" (*Feeling* 125). There is an echo here of Goethe's insistence that the object be allowed to "speak" for itself and that the observer must be attuned to it.

It is a participatory process quite analogous to the sculptor's response to the stone, the photographer's sensitivity to light conditions, and the writer's feeling for language. In each case, the medium of expression is allowed to speak for itself. At the risk of sounding heretical, let me suggest that the artist/scientist seems to be a facilitator rather than a maker. To be sure, the creative artist must be able to open herself to the process of helping the material to realize its potential. It is an act of pro-creation.

Forty years after McClintock's insight, John Briggs argued in a similar vein, albeit in the language of chaos. Normal thought patterns are like repetitive limit cycles. When asked to create form from a formless, complex offering of material, we usually respond by reducing the material's richness of nuance and variety to pedestrian simplicity. That is to say, we impose preconceived notions of order upon the material from without. Briggs suggested, however, that we allow the fractal dimensions of the material to organize themselves in the observer's consciousness. It is a matter of coordinating an essential link between individual will and natural forces, much as the poet must work in tandem with the natural tendencies within language itself (Briggs and Peat, *Mirror* 195).

To designate this essential tension as a fundamental trait of artistic creativity, Briggs coined the term "reflectaphor." Reflectaphors produce in the reader, listener, or observer an "*unresolvable tension* between the similarities and the differences" within a piece of artwork. The individual parts of the piece mirror the work as a whole; that is, the work is simultaneously convergent and divergent (*Mirror* 196). In a *Festschrift* for the physicist David Bohm, Briggs explains in greater detail the meaning of the term. It is a composite of the Greek *μέτα* (*meta*), the Aryan *medhi*, and the Greek *φόρος* (*phoros*), which when put together convey the sense of "having the quality of carrying between and beyond by a constant bending back."[57] Thus, reflectaphors, which appear as geometric shapes in the graphic arts or as irony, metaphor, punning, paradox, and synecdoche in literature, have a global function by revealing the interaction of the various parts with the whole, thereby making manifest the hidden order of the artistic work ("Reflectaphors" 414). They are "hinges" (434), points pregnant with allusions to dimensions accessible from them by moving out in different directions. They are themselves only markers of virtual reality, that which is not yet present but which is always opening up on the horizon. A work characterized by reflectaphors is therefore always turning away from closure while simultaneously holding the whole together ("Reflectaphors" 424).

In the completed artwork, the charged atmosphere is not resolved but rather continues to exist just below the surface in an uneasy, potent, but nonetheless stable union.[58] Aesthetics is grounded in ambivalent rules that challenge the artist and poet to mirror a reality only partially sensed. What the artist renders in a successful work is a subwhole of the intuited totality that is similar to but also different from observed or experienced reality. The artist, moreover, is creative in those moments of crisis caused by the confrontation of conflicting forces, ideas, sentiments, and so forth. Their consolidation or "resolution" in the completed art form equates to so many periodic centers in the alternating process of fusion and dispersion. The resolution of tension is essentially intermittent. That temporariness is also highly dependent upon the work being received by an appreciative viewer. The creative moment, in short, is most evident in situations that occur as a result of some deep crisis or heightened tensions.

Yet a balance between severe mental burden and the absence of any conflict-laden mentality is the actual arena of the creative process. While severe psychic stress can inhibit creativity, as empirical studies of creative artists at Lund University in Sweden have demonstrated, the lack of deep and troubling experiences can result in "tame art products." Consequently, creativity is advanced by "tendencies toward repression and sensitivity," but is inhibited by "tendencies toward depression and compulsive isolation." Repression here involves a transformation of the troubling stimulus from a distance, while sensitivity is to be understood as openness to marginal cues. Repression and sensitivity are essentially aligned with receptivity toward conflict and

57 John Briggs, "Reflectaphors: The (Implicate) Universe as a Work of Art," in *Quantum Implications*, ed. David Peat and Basil Hiley (London: Routledge & Kegan Paul, 1987), 414–36, here 421. See also Briggs's *Fire in the Crucible*.

58 Here I disagree with Briggs's implication that the artist's completed work is "perfected vision," is the philosopher's stone itself (*Fire* 89 et passim). While the completed artwork is the (partial) result of the artist's vision, it does not exhaust the possibilities. It merely *hints* at the fullness – it is not itself the fullness. Even granting that the *prima materia* is equatable with "vision" (*Fire* 20), the distiller is not the thing distilled. Complete identity between the artist/visionary and the *prima materia*/philosopher's stone/perfected vision is difficult to accept.

anxiety in the face of the new. Thus, the key to the creative process – and this is in total agreement with A. Rothenberg's findings – is an agonistic state of contending forces that are resolved into a steady state of tension. It has, in the view of Smith and Carlsson, "as a constituent quality the ability to transgress a conventional conception of reality" (191).[59]

6. Creative Strategies

The trick picture of the young, attractive woman wearing a luxurious fur coat, with a dainty necklace around her neck and a saucy feather stuck in her hair is a well-known example of the importance of openness toward the viewed object and the tensions inherent in it (fig. 2.7). The viewer soon learns to let the image direct his attention to other structures and patterns imbedded in the image. With some surprise the viewer determines that the picture is really that of an old woman with a large, hawk-like nose, drooping eyes, toothless mouth, and pointed chin, wearing a fur draped around her shoulders. Because there are no clear indicators as to which of the two renditions – the young woman or the older one – is the "right" perception, the picture can be called a trick or ambivalent. With practice the viewer can alternate with ease between the two "presences." With even more refined practice in bisociative seeing, the viewer learns that there is a point of juncture where the two images merge and are present simultaneously in the viewer's consciousness. (Some see the convergence at the point of the eye. How prophetic.) Aesthetic experience, consequently, is closely bound to "shifts of attention" (Koestler, *Act* 233). These shifts are directed partly by the material being studied and partly by the investigator/artist.

Figure 2.7: Shifts of Attention

Another example of the importance of shifts of attention is the so-called "Duncker Puzzle" (after its originator, the psychologist Carl Duncker). A brain teaser, it goes like this:

59 On this notion of "steady-state tension," see Gudmund J. W. Smith and Ingegerd M. Carlsson, *The Creative Process: A Functional Model Based on Empirical Studies from Early Childhood to Middle Age* (Madison, CT: International Universities Press, 1990), 190–227. Passages cited are found on pages 199 and 210. The empirical studies are based on 32 artists, none of whom is considered a celebrity.

> Two trains are traveling along the same track toward one another. Each train is moving at 20 mph. The starting distance between them is 100 miles. Frightened by the movement of one of the trains, a stupid bird abruptly changes direction and flies at 30 mph along the tracks in the direction of the oncoming train until it encounters the second train, is frightened once again, again turns abruptly and returns along the previous path at 30 mph until it encounters the first train, turns abruptly, etc., etc. The bird flies back and forth in this manner until the two trains collide. The question is, how many miles does the bird fly before the two trains collide?

The solution to the problem is simple once one shifts attention from the spatial to the temporal dimension. It takes the trains two and one-half hours to reach the midpoint of their collision path. Consequently, the bird, flying at 30 mph, covers a total of 75 miles (30 mph x 2.5 hours).

My own reflections on the nature and role of the creative impulse in humans go beyond the traditional aspects of perspective and attitude outlined in this chapter. They are expanded by the bisociative theory advanced by Koestler and the phenomena of bifurcation and period doubling, which lead to chaos. My own thoughts, then, should be considered within the context of the morphogenetic dynamic of a creative universe in a state of constant flux that bends and alters the space around it. Since we are constituent parts of the universe, it seems to me that the divergent and convergent dimensions of the creative act should not be situated exclusively in the (creative) individual, as is the tendency in the psychologically oriented sciences.[60] Our place within the self-regulating cosmos itself must be factored in. "The creativity of the universe," George Smoot writes in the conclusion to *Wrinkles in Time*, "is its most potent force, forming through time the matter and structures of stars and galaxies, and, ultimately, us" (1993: 295).

Increasingly, as we have seen, natural scientists such as Smoot, Bohm,and Davies; the science writer Johannes von Buttlar; and the philosopher Bernulf Kanitscheider are focusing on the creative powers of the universe.[61] Their thinking is an extension of Heisenberg's wondering about the role of "intention" in what makes a bacteriophage enter a bacterium for purposes of multiplying (*Physics* 242). Then, too, it is nature that has produced life and creative humans such that creativity in no way contradicts the laws of physics. As Popper notes at the conclusion of *The Open Universe* (1982):

---

60 In addition to Smith and Carlsson, cf. Rothenberg, *The Emerging Goddess* (1979), 125–37 (= chap. 6: "The Creative Process"); and *Theories of Creativity*, ed. Mark A. Runco and Robert S. Albert (Newbury Park: Sage Publications, 1990). Their findings lend weight to the conclusions drawn by Smith and Carlsson regarding the agonistic quality of the creative process.

61 David Bohm and F. David Peat, *Science, Order, and Creativity* 229–71 (= chap. 6: "Creativity in the Whole of Life"); Paul Davies, *Blueprint*, 138–51 (= chap. 10: "The Source of Creation"); Johannes von Buttlar, *Gottes Würfel: Schicksal oder Zufall* (Munich: Herbig, 1992); Bernulf Kanitscheider, *Von der mechanistischen Welt zum kreativen Universum: Zu einem neuen philosophischen Verständnis der Natur* (Darmstadt: Wissenschaftliche Buchgesellschaft, 1993).

> Whether or not we look at the universe as a physical machine, we should face the fact that it has produced life and creative men; that it is open to their creative thoughts, and has been physically changed by them. We must not close our eyes to this fact or permit our appreciation of the successes wrought by reductionist programmes to blind us to the fact that the universe that harbours life is creative in the best sense: creative in the sense in which the great poets, the great artists, the great musicians have been creative, as well as the great mathematicians, the great scientists, and the great inventors. (*Open Universe* 174)

Similarly, John Briggs suggests that creativity is nothing more than the passive act of *allowing* the feedback loops in the self-structuring process of complex systems to produce whatever they produce. In that sense, creativity is not spontaneous but a way of life; it is an unfolding, in David Bohm's meaning of the word in *Wholeness and the Implicate Order* (1981). Truly creative individuals learn to let unfold what is enfolded in their physical and mental being, while most of us let the creative impulse whither and die on the vine, preferring instead the comfort of homeostasis to the discomfit of turbulence. We lose our unique perspective, our uncommon way of seeing – we become ever more beholden to a homogenized cultural perspective, and thus become mechanical in our sensitivities and responses.[62]

In this vein I wish to see the creative individual as a product of the laws of nature and as being deeply rooted in natural processes that alter the spaces of existence. The genius in the traditional sense, with her usual characteristics of autonomy, intuition, feminine sensibility, subjective orientation, flexibility, self-confidence, or psychological openness to complexity, is no longer the only defining moment in the creative process.[63] She is one of a number of factors. In this system, spontaneity is not as central as it is in the Newtonian and thermodynamic models of the world (see Davies, *Blueprint* 199–200). The "deification of the world" ("Vergottung der Welt") as the calming of the growth process in the world ("Beruhigung der Weltwerdung"), according to Alfred Whitehead, is also not my meaning, for this approach proves too static.[64] The symptoms of apparent spontaneity nevertheless turn up in the course of this inquiry. And

62 Briggs, *Fire*, 332–33. Given the thrust of his own argument, it is remarkable that Briggs pays such scant attention to Koestler, who anticipated his work in so many ways. Briggs cites Koestler's tome of 750 pages a mere five times in his own work of 370 pages. The dulling effect of civilization was, of course, noted by Rousseau and his contemporaries, such as William Duff and Johann Gottfried Herder.

63 Albert Rothenberg, "Introduction: The Creativity Question," in A. Rothenberg (ed.), *The Creativity Question* (Durham: Duke University Press, 1976), 3–26; here 12. Bell, *Goethe's Naturalistic Anthropology* (1994), 193. In his preface to Koestler's *Act of Creation* Sir Cyril Burt offers a similar assessment and characterization of the creative individual (*Act* 14–16). See also William Duff, *An Essay on Original Genius* (1767; rpt. 1964) with its emphasis on "a more vivid and more comprehensive Imagination" (89) "and depending in its excursion wholly on its own strength" (179). For a historical overview of the traditional concept of genius, see Jochen Schmidt, *Die Geschichte des Genie-Gedanken*, 2 vols. (Darmstadt: Wissenschaftliche Buchgesellschaft, 1985); and Penelope Murray (ed.), *Genius: The History of an Idea* (Oxford: Blackwell, 1989).

64 Cf. Peter Böhm, "Energie - Kreativität - Gott," *Perspektiven der Philosophie* 17 (1991): 37–75; here 75.

creativity nonetheless continues to appear as problem solving in the traditional sense.[65]

Creativity, I suggest, is the perception of the unexpectedly expected and is conditioned by a healthy respect for uncertainty and wholeness. It requires going with the flow. But it also employs a prism to "polarize" the vibrations in the environment, filtering out only self-similar wave lengths, spins, or charges. We might argue analogous to Bohr's contention that photons are not truly real until their encounter with the polarizers. In our context, I suggest that the act of creation functions as a filter to give life to certain dimensions of vibrations that are omnipresent. The filter can be likened to the attitude of the artist, to his particular position within the matrix. Fusions occur via the filter of polarization. Without human situatedness, inventiveness in the arts (or in science) lacks context and direction (cf. Stafford 115).

What this means, then, is that deterministic chaos provides the grid and the impulse to creativity. The creative mind is a combination of physical determinism and moral free will. Briggs cautioned us to de-emphasize "the myth of inspiration, the myth of the lone creator, the myth that creators are motivated by the desire to make something new, the myth that creativity is primarily an unconscious process, the new myth that it's primarily a conscious one, and finally, the growing myth that intelligence and creativity may one day be duplicated by a machine" (*Fire* 13–14). Human beings are neither insentient automata nor playthings of cosmic forces.[66] I have intentionally cited works by such diverse writers as Bohm, Breitinger, Goethe, Popper, Koestler, Briggs, Fox Keller, Smith and Carlsson, and Morfill and Scheingraber in order to underscore the unity within the manifold. "Every property of matter," Ralph Waldo Emerson had determined long ago, "is a school for the understanding – its solidity or resistance, its inertia, its extension, its figure, its divisibility. The understanding adds, divides, combines, measures, and finds nutrient and room for activity in this worthy scene. Meantime, Reason transfers all these lessons into its own world of thought, by perceiving the analogy that marries Matter to Mind."[67] Multiple attunements are required to gain the right perspective in imitating nature. The many concepts outlined in the foregoing pages provide the framework for assessing the nature of the creative act as matter and mind interact in *Faust*, *Zarathustra*, and *The Tin Drum*. The next step in encircling the topic of mind and matter is to examine the ground of creativity as formulated by Nietzsche, a pivotal figure in this investigation.

---

65 Rothenberg, *Emerging Goddess* 130.

66 Gregor Morfill and Herbert Scheingraber, *Chaos ist überall ... und es funktioniert: Eine neue Weltsicht* (Frankfurt a.M. and Berlin: Ullstein, 1991): "Wir sind *keine* willenlosen Automaten im Ablauf eines Uhrwerks, und wir sind auch nicht Spielbälle des Zufalls, sondern gestaltet und gestaltende Teilnehmer eines offenen dynamischen Systems: der Welt; unserer Welt, dem kompliziertesten System, das wir kennen" (55).

67 Ralph Waldo Emerson, "Nature," in *Selected Writings*, ed. by Brooks Atkinson (New York: Random House, 1950), 20.

Chapter 3
Grounding Creativity – Nietzsche and the New Universe

> Die chemischen Verwandlungen in der unorganischen Natur sind vielleicht auch künstlerische Prozesse.
>
> – Nietzsche, *Nachlaß I*

> Der siegreiche Begriff "Kraft," mit dem unsere Physiker Gott und die Welt geschaffen haben, bedarf noch einer Ergänzung: es muß ihm eine innere Welt zugesprochen werden, welche ich bezeichne als "Willen zur Macht."
>
> – Nietzsche, *Wille zur Macht* (#619)

1. It's All in the Motion

Nietzsche can be seen as an important link in the revolutionary thinking associated with Copernicus's *De revolutionibus* (1534) and continuing into modern complexity theory. For example, in a fragment from summer 1885, published posthumously in *Will to Power*, he remarked that the concept of energy, which was being used widely in scientific debates of the era, needed to be extended to include an interior realm in order for it to be complete. All movement, all phenomena, and all so-called "laws," he averred, harking back to Heraclitus, are in reality just "symptoms of an inner event."[1]

1 Friedrich Nietzsche, *The Will to Power*, trans. by Walter Kaufmann and R. J. Hollingdale (New York: Random House, 1967), 333, aphorism #619. Hereafter cited as *WP* by aphorism number. The German version cited is Friedrich Nietzsche, *Sämtliche Werke: Kritische Studienausgabe*, ed. by Giorgio Colli and Mazzino Montinari, 2nd ed., 15 vols. (Munich: Deutscher Taschenbuch Verlag and de Gruyter, 1988), 11:563. The German edition is cited hereafter as *KSA* by volume and page number. *Will to Power* consists of 1,067 aphorisms, of which Nietzsche had designated only 372 for inclusion. His friend Peter Gast and his sister Elisabeth Förster-Nietzsche made the additional selections. Nonetheless, the work is widely considered to be Nietzsche's most important as the final sum of his thought. In their preface to the unpublished fragments dating from fall 1887 to March 1888, *Nachgelassene Fragmente: Herbst 1887 bis März 1888* (Berlin: Walter de Gruyter, 1970), the editors Giorgio Colli und Mazzino Montinari note that *Will to Power* surfaced as the main title for a volume on the transvaluation of all values ("Umwertung aller Werte") for the first time in late summer 1885. But by early September 1888, Nietzsche had decided against doing a volume under the title *Wille zur Macht*. Instead, he pressed ahead with a multipart project with the tentative main title of *Der Anti-Christ* and subtitle of *Umwertung aller Werte* (Part 8, vol. 2, pp. v–vi; 8.3: v–vi). Not only did Nietzsche, therefore, not complete *Will to Power*, he also did not intend the aphorisms for a reading

Seen in this light, everything from start to finish is a matter of dynamics: it's all in the motion. To ground creativity, then, we must look at the whole picture. We must take an ontological approach. Nietzsche's medial position – between the external and the internal, between science and literature, between myth and reality – is the topic of this chapter. As such, his vantage point serves as a link between the foregoing considerations of scientific explanations of reality and creativity and the literary mappings in the ensuing chapters. Consequently, this chapter should be viewed as a further installment on revolutions real and imagined. It should also be considered within the context of the aesthetics of seeing.

In *Order Out of Chaos*, Prigogine and Stengers date the birth of the science of complexity to the year 1811, when Baron Jean-Joseph Fourier's mathematical description of the propagation of heat in solids won the prize of the French Academy of Sciences.[2] His solution revealed that heat flow was proportional to the gradient of temperature regardless of the state of matter, whether solid, liquid, or gaseous. Furthermore, it was independent of the chemical composition of the body. Because the universal character of Fourier's law departed from the dominant Laplacean and Newtonian views of energetic interactions, Prigogine and Stengers feel justified in seeing in his insight the beginning of a new science. Heat and gravity came to be viewed as two contrasting universals coexistent in physics. Not long after that, other new discoveries helped to revolutionize thinking about how the material world functions. For example, with his discovery of the hydrocarbon benzene in 1825, Michael Faraday founded an entire new branch of organic chemistry. Then, too, his laws of electrolysis, formulated in 1833, linked chemistry and electricity in exciting new ways. In 1847 Hermann von Helmholtz provided convincing evidence of the principle of conservation of energy and proposed the notion of potential energy. Three years later, Rudolf Clausius formulated the second law of thermodynamics, which states that entropy increases at the expense of the available energy. In 1859, Charles Darwin, the British theoretical evolutionist, published his celebrated *The Origin of Species* in which he provided empirical evidence supporting his thesis that all living things are related through the common bond of evolution. In 1864 – just five years before Nietzsche moved to Basel, Switzerland, as professor of classical philology – the British astronomer William Huggins helped to establish the new discipline of astrophysics with his discovery that some nebulae are gaseous. In 1865 the Austrian monk Gregor Mendel discovered the laws of heredity on which the modern science of

public (see his letter to Peter Gast dated 26 Feb. 1888; 8.2: vi, n3). Yet, one can agree that a critic can scarcely ignore Nietzsche's notes on will to power in any critical discussion of his philosophy. See Alexander Nehemas, *Nietzsche: Life as Literature* (Cambridge, MA: Harvard University Press, 1991), 25–26.

2 Ilya Prigogine and Isabelle Stengers, *Order Out of Chaos: Man's New Dialogue with Nature* (New York: Bantam Books, 1984), 104.

genetics is based. Also in 1865 the British physicist James Clerk Maxwell first presented his theory of electromagnetism, which laid the groundwork for twentieth-century quantum theory and a more sophisticated understanding of molecular structure. Five years later, in 1869, the Russian chemist Dmitry Mendeleyev published the first periodic table of chemical elements. And that same year witnessed the birth of ecology, a term coined by the German zoologist Ernst Haeckel in Jena.

These developments foreshadowed the rapid rise of various branches of the natural sciences to positions of dominance in the final quarter of the nineteenth century. Obviously, the epoch was rife with excitement about scientific discoveries, an excitement that reached the University of Basel itself. Yet only an occasional study centers attention on Friedrich Nietzsche's (1844–1900) dialogue with these scientific discourses, even though his interest in them is distinctly documented. Had he not been offered the professorship in Basel for classical philology at the age of 25 in 1869, he planned, for instance, to travel to Paris to study chemistry. In any event, Nietzsche continued to pursue a personal interest in the natural sciences throughout his life, as evidenced by the books he borrowed and bought. In fact, some of his most famous concepts were developed in response to scientific ideas of the times. For example, the "overman" he conceptualized as "evolutionary biology" (a term he coined); "eternal recurrence" he anchored in the phenomenon of heat and energy transfer; perspectivism he grounded in physiology (i.e., in the organs of the body, in nerve stimulation); and the "will to power" Nietzsche envisioned as energy distributed throughout the whole of creation. Thus, it is somewhat puzzling that the pivotal role played by natural science in the germination of his own philosophy has garnered so little attention.[3]

In view of his radical break with systematic philosophy and traditional ethics, Nietzsche fits very nicely into the scheme of increasing complexity and innovation. If we were to speak metaphorically about his world-view, we might say that it reveals traits characteristic of heat transfer and thermodynamics. Consequently, it is transformative and decidedly non-Euclidean, even as it retains the classic law of gravity. Specifically rejecting mechanistic linearity and science's claim to objectivity

3 Robert C. Holub, *Friedrich Nietzsche*, TWAS 857 (New York: Twayne Publishers, 1995), has provided an impulse to correct this deficiency. See esp. his chap. 4, "The Scientific Dilettante" (55–78). Brian Ward, "The Literary Appropriation of Chaos Theory," Ph.D. diss. University of Western Australia (1998), 103–9, notes Nietzsche's interest in the scientific thought of his day. Friedrich Ulfers and Mark Daniel Cohen, "Friedrich Nietzsche as Bridge from Nineteenth-Century Atomistic Science to Process Philosophy in Twentieth-Century Physics, Literature, and Ethics," West Virginia University Philological Papers (fall 2002) deliver less than they promise. How could it be otherwise in a nine-page paper? But the authors do recognize that Nietzsche was an ontologist, who based his philosophy on then current scientific insights and anticipated essential aspects of contemporary, "postmodern" science. See http://web3.infotrac.galegroup.com/itw/infomark/850/433/ 65217938w3/ purl=rcl_EAIM_O (user authentication required).

(although not rejecting science),[4] Nietzsche adopts an essentially nonlinear and literary attitude toward rendering the operations of reality and self. Suspicious of the one-dimensionality of the straight line and the unidirectional course associated with it, he asks bluntly: Why must you go straight in? Why must you straighten out what is crooked?[5] Nature is naturally crooked; growth is never linear. Rather, natural processes are essentially fractal so that we can speak of the "universal turbulence of growth."[6] That is why he preferred the inchoateness and tentativeness of the pithy aphorism and the open fragment as apt expressions of his philosophic thought. For Nietzsche, the closed finality of the straight-forward narrative and rigorous systematization of analytic philosophy led away from reality.[7]

The need to interpret the fundamental nature of growth in a world of immense energy led Nietzsche to adopt philosophical vitalism. Nothing in the chemical world is inalterable, nor does stasis occur in nature; energy/force is inherent in all movement, he noted.[8] Consequently, the individual is called upon to develop all of her potential, to

4 Friedrich Nietzsche, *The Gay Science*, trans. by Bernhard Williams, Josefine Nauckhoff, and Adrian Del Caro (Cambridge: Cambridge University Press, 2001), 238–39 (aphorism #373). Hereafter cited as *GS* by section or aphorism number. As a rule, I will cite Nietzsche in translation in order to reach the widest possible audience. Only if the original wording is especially noteworthy, do I provide the original German. To provide the German and the English in all cases would prove cumbersome.

5 Friedrich Nietzsche, *Beyond Good and Evil: Prelude to a Philosophy of the Future*, trans. by R. J. Hollingdale (Baltimore: Penguin, 1990), aphorism #208. Hereafter cited in the text as *BGE* and aphorism number. See also Fr. Nietzsche, *Human, All Too Human: A Book For Free Spirits,* trans. by R. J. Hollingdale, intro. by Richard Schacht (Cambridge: Cambridge University Press, 1996), I #270.

6 Alfred Döblin, "Zu Nietzsches Morallehre" (1903), in *Nietzsche und die deutsche Literatur*, ed. by Bruno Hillebrand, 2 vols. (Munich: Deutscher Taschenbuch Verlag, 1978), 1:331–58 : "allgemeine[r] Wirbel des Werdens" (338, 340).

7 Alexander Nehamas grounds Nietzsche's stylistic richness in his fundamental perspectivism, which holds that there are no independent facts to verify any particular interpretation as having universal validity. He thus views Nietzsche's philosophic project and self-presentation as being informed by an essentially literary model or representation. Nehamas contends: "Nietzsche's efforts to create an artwork out of himself, a literary character who is a philosopher, is then also his effort to offer a positive view without falling back into the dogmatic tradition he so distrusted [...]. His aestheticism is, therefore, the other side of his perspectivism." See A. Nehamas, *Nietzsche* (1985), 1–10, here 8. See also his chap. 2, "Untruth as a Condition of Life" (42–73), which treats Nietzsche's perspectivism. Also adopting an essentially literary approach to Nietzsche are Sarah Kofman, *Nietzsche and Metaphor*, trans. by Duncan Large (Stanford: Stanford University Press, 1993); Gary Shapiro, *Nietzschean Narratives* (Bloomington and Indianapolis: Indiana University Press, 1989); and Kathleen M. Higgins, *Nietzsche's Zarathustra* (Philadelphia: Temple University Press, 1987). I have found their readings instructive.

8 "Es giebt nichts Unveränderliches in der Chemie" (*KSA* 13:374; nachgelassene Fragmente). See also Friedrich Nietzsche, *Gesammelte Werke*, Musarionausgabe, 23 vols. (Munich: Musarion, 1933–42): "In der Natur kommt kein Stillstand der Kraft vor" (Musarion 11:175 = *Nachlaß II*) [= Kröner 83:466]; "Kraft ist Trieb, Wille, Wirken" (Musarion 15:304 = *BGE*) [= Kröner 76:272]. Hereafter references to this edition are cited in the text as Musarion.

increase the energy by participating in it, by struggling with it, by ordering it, by mapping it, by acting more randomly. Indeed, according to Nietzsche, the individual human being is ultimately supposed to encourage an "anarchy" of energy pulses, to go down in a frenzied crash. To perish. To disappear into the frenetic flow. The German formulation for the latter is quite telling in the context of "getting to the bottom of things" ("auf den Grund kommen"), for Nietzsche uses the formulation: "Gehe zugrunde!" (literally: Go to the ground!).[9] The notion of chaotic energy knots runs through Nietzsche's thinking like a leitmotif. I interpret this as a sign that he was getting to the bottom of things.

Nietzsche's biological conception is consciously based on the principles of energy conservation in the universe. Julius Robert Mayer and Hermann Helmholtz had formulated that principle in 1842 and 1847, respectively, that is, around the time of Nietzsche's birth in 1844. But Nietzsche saw not just the creative potential of the principle; he also saw the destructive capacity. Energy conversion is not simply the dissipation of difference in temperature and energy levels; it is also the creation of new differences. Thus, difference proved to be a seminal characteristic of physical existence. And difference became a cornerstone of Nietzsche's philosophical conceptions of life.

Early on, the German writer Alfred Döblin recognized that Nietzsche had grounded his philosophic thought in the earth itself. In an essay dating from 1902, Döblin baptized Nietzsche (somewhat awkwardly) "the will to the natural sciences in philosophy made man," suggesting that Nietzsche represented the spirit of nature itself.[10] The tendency to apply the positivistic methods of science to all spheres of life had increasingly come to typify the intellectual climate of Nietzsche's day. Yet it would be erroneous to see Nietzsche merely as the voice of protest against the dominance of rationalistic thought. In a very real sense, Nietzsche was as much a product of his times as he was a rebel against them. On the one hand, defining logic as "the quintessence of

---

9 Nietzsche, "Entwickele alle deine Kräfte – aber das heißt: entwickele die Anarchie! Gehe zugrunde!" (Musarion 10:437 = *Nachlaß II*) [= Kröner 83:155].

10 Alfred Döblin, "Der Wille zur Macht als Erkenntnis bei Friedrich Nietzsche" (1902), in *Nietzsche und die deutsche Literatur*, ed. by Bruno Hillebrand, 2 vols. (Munich: Deutscher Taschenbuch Verlag, 1978), 1:315-30: "Daß die Naturwissenschaft, in der Person Nietzsches, den Geist aus der Natur konstruiert" (326) and "der fleischgewordene Wille zur Naturwissenschaft in der Philosophie" (323). In general, Döblin characterizes Nietzsche's philosophy as a "Metaphysik der Kraft." Döblin's essay was first published by Hillebrand in this two-volume work. Essentially, Döblin is interested in demonstrating that the modeling of philosophy on scientific positivism revealed the "bankrupt" state of natural science based on philosophy, which to him seemed to be a straightjacket ("Zwangsjacke"): if everything is false, then anything goes (329). Paradoxically, however, Nietzsche simultaneously proved to be an *advocatus diaboli sive dei* (advocate of both the devil and of God) in disguise, for the anything-goes principle simultaneously reopened the doors for faith and religion (330).

the most important survival needs in the abstract form of humankind,"[11] he recognized that we cannot live "without a continual falsification of the world by means of numbers" (*BGE* #4) or without a "*narrowing of perspective*," which is "a condition of life and growth" (*BGE* #188). On the other hand, he acknowledged that there is a different kind of logic, one not dominated by linearity, precision, and commonality but by differences in movement: the way the Ganges flows, the tortoise walks, or the frog hops (*BGE* #27). Survival often requires a different way of moving and demands a circuitous path. In redefining logic as rules regulating the human urge to survive and thrive, Nietzsche sought to provide a biological basis of behavior.[12] Life for Nietzsche, Döblin thus concluded, translated into survival, even dominance. In essence, that view was cast in terms of an increase or a decrease in energy level ("Kraftsteigerung" vs. "Kraftverminderung"; Döblin 319). As a result, he suggests in another essay dubbing Nietzsche the "philosopher of the concept of growth."[13]

Given his abiding interest in natural science, Nietzsche's bonding of the natural sciences with moral philosophy via the concepts of biological differentiation and growth is not surprising. As a philologist, Nietzsche surely knew that chemistry is etymologically related to alchemy, which in turn is derived from the Arabic for the art of changing one thing into another. Thus, we might regard Nietzsche as a modern alchemist of the spirit, for he did indeed change things. Both the progressive discipline of chemistry (it was *the* science in the late nineteenth century) and the canonical field of philology were constructed to get to the bottom of things in a positivistic manner. To establish meaning, he felt he had to ground philosophy in the earth itself.[14] He meant more than just the soil.

2. The Total Economy of Life and the Nature of Genius

With his long and varied reception, Nietzsche has proven to be one of the most influential thinkers of the Western world. Indeed, without him our intellectual landscape would look much different. Initially understood by few, then heralded as the prophet of the avant-garde, usurped by the politics of National Socialism, fêted as the

11 Döblin, "Wille zur Macht": "der Inbegriff der wichtigsten menschlichen Erhaltungsbedingungen in abstrakter Form des Menschen" (318).

12 Terry Eagleton, *The Ideology of the Aesthetic* (Oxford: Basil Blackwell, 1990), cautions us not to overlook the agonal character of Nietzsche's discourse with the world and with himself (235, 258).

13 Döblin, "Morallehre," *Nietzsche und die deutsche Literatur*, 1:331–58: "Man kann ja Nietzsche geradezu, wie Spinoza den Philosophen der Substanz, den Philosophen des Entwicklungsbegriffs nennen" (336). Döblin's essay on Nietzsche's moral doctrine was also first published by Hillebrand in this volume.

14 See Kathleen Higgins, "Reading *Zarathustra*," *Reading Nietzsche*, ed. by Robert C. Solomon and Kathleen Higgins (New York and Oxford: Oxford University Press, 1988), 132–51, here 142.

epitome of existentialism, revered by semioticians, and, most recently, claimed as the inspiration for French postmodernism, Nietzsche has continually been seen in an ever-changing light. Every attempt to schematize his philosophy or to reduce it to a single fundamental concept has failed.[15] Considering his skepticism regarding all dogmatic thinkers (*KSA* 13:189), it is little wonder that the effort to reduce his thought to compact understanding has been unsuccessful. The suggestion to view Nietzsche's "antinomian thought" itself as his methodological principle and the primary purpose of his philosophy is useful, but not truly innovative, for it is ultimately rooted in his famous concept of the will to power.[16] On the other hand, Peter Pütz's claim that Nietzsche's legacy remains a largely untapped source "for the building of an intellectually radical, but also freer, world" is still useful for plotting the course of this present study, despite progress since that assessment (Pütz 1988: 28).

My main purpose is to demonstrate Nietzsche's close ties to modern chaos and complexity theory as they relate to creativity and to the nature of genius. The Nietzsche I wish to highlight is the "lord of the dance" within the total economy of life, the demythologizer of myth, the prophet of the lie. While these foci do not in themselves constitute entirely new perspectives, their grounding in chaos theory does.[17] Chaos

15 Peter Pütz, *Friedrich Nietzsche* (Stuttgart: Meztler, 1967); Peter Pütz, "Nietzsche: Art and Intellectual Inquiry," in *Nietzsche: Imagery and Thought*, ed. by Malcolm Pasley (Berkeley: University of California Press, 1978), 1–32; and, more recently, Robert Holub, *Nietzsche* (1995), offers concise, readable accounts of the main tendencies in Nietzschean scholarship. For example, (1) scholars have given up the attempt to seek overall harmony in Nietzsche's "system" (Bertram, Löwith, Jaspers, Horkheimer, Adorno, Heidegger); (2) scholars have reduced Nietzsche's complex views to a simplified dimension (e.g., for Alfred Baeumler, it is will to power; for Georg Lukaçs, it was the destruction of reason); (3) others have emphasized the unity of Nietzsche's thought in the pathology of his mind, sketching in biographical studies early signs of his pending insanity before 1889; (4) some have endeavored to render Nietzsche's life and work as a harmoniously integrated succession of historiographical and philological stages of development; (5) and, most recently, yet others have traced the origins of postmodernism and deconstruction to Nietzsche's theory of life as a fundamental act of interpretation. On the exploiting of Nietzsche by French postmodernists (Lyotard, Derrida, Deleuze, Irigaray), see Keith Ansell-Pearson and Howard Caygill (eds.), *The Fate of the New Nietzsche* (Aldershot: Avebury, 1993); *Looking After Nietzsche*, ed. by Laurence A. Rickels (Albany: State University of New York Press, 1990); and Peter Levine, *Nietzsche and the Modern Crisis of the Humanities* (Albany: State University of New York Press, 1995), esp. chap. 8, "Nietzsche Today" (151–86), and chap. 9, "The Postmodern Paradigm" (187–214).

16 Peter Pütz, "The Problem of Force in Nietzsche and His Critics," in *Nietzsche: Literature and Values*, ed. by Volker Dürr, Reinhold Grimm, and Kathy Harms, *Monatshefte* Occasional Volumes, No. 6. (Madison, WI: University of Wisconsin Press, 1988), 14–28, argues that the antinomian approach is a new attempt at a "Gesamtschau" (encompassing view) of Nietzsche's philosophical content and methodology (23).

17 I know of three studies that approach Nietzsche explicitly from the perspective of chaos. Useful is the Munich dissertation by Thomas Busch, *The Affirmation des Chaos: Zur Überwindung des Nihilismus in der Metaphysik Friedrich Nietzsches* (Erzabtei St. Ottilien: EOS Verlag, 1989). Busch's use of the

theory might very well help us to determine the purpose of Nietzsche's sketches on cosmology (especially in *Will to Power*) by providing the empirical evidence Nehamas finds lacking in Nietzsche's ambiguous theory of eternal recurrence (Nehamas 1985: 143). Although Stanley Rosen foregrounds chaos in Nietzsche's concept of the will to power, he does not make reference to contemporary chaos theory.[18]

In his analysis of Nietzsche's art of interpretation, Henrik Birus rightly emphasizes Nietzsche's dictum that one must ask new questions if one would hear new answers.[19] By asking what connection might exist between modern chaos and complexity theory in the natural sciences and Nietzsche's critical project in ethics and philology, I am asking a new kind of question. I proceed in the same manner of Nietzsche's own skeptical questioning, which he associated with looking behind the stage scenery, peering through the mask of presentation, and delving below the surface. Of interest is not only what empirical data *reveal* but also what they *conceal* (*Daybreak* #523; *KSA* 3:301). In other words, we need to read better or at least differently (Birus 1988: 68–69). It is not only that which reaches the eye that requires attention.

As a new kind of prophet, Nietzsche was substantially different from other seers such as Socrates or Christ, yet they were the primary foils of his own thought. Far from constituting a unified doctrine, his message essentially demythologized the prophet. Central to the argument in this chapter are interrelated works from the 1880s: *The Gay Science* (1882), *Thus Spoke Zarathustra* (1884–86), and *Beyond Good and Evil* (1886). However, the focus here will be primarily on *Beyond Good and Evil*, Nietzsche's

---

science of chaos, however, is limited; he is more interested in the overcoming of nihilism through the affirmation of an essentially "chaotic" world, one which resists efforts to reduce it to a common denominator through the instrumentalization of reason. Modern chaos theory itself appears more like an afterthought than as the hermeneutical key to interpretation. Nonetheless, Busch's study does represent a new approach to Nietzsche's use of the metaphors of chaos and of play. Walter Gebhard, "Erkennen und Entsetzen: Zur Tradition der Chaos-Annahmen im Denken Nietzsches," *Friedrich Nietzsche. Strukturen der Negativität*, ed. by Walter Gebhard, *Bayreuther Beiträge zur Literaturwissenschaft* 5 (Frankfurt a.M.: Peter Lang, 1984), 13–47, is unaware of the modern science of chaos. His analysis focuses primarily on *The Birth of Tragedy* and is traditional with its emphasis on possible etymological derivations of the term "chaos," Nietzsche's indebtedness to Schopenhauer's understanding of chaos as fear inspiring, and finally the impetus for Nietzsche's creative energy in his endeavors to overcome negativity. The last issue is dealt with more thoroughly and competently by Busch. See also P. Köster, "Nietzsches Beschwörung des Chaos," *Tübinger Theologische Quartalschrift* 153 (1973): 132–63.

18 Stanley Rosen, *The Mask of Enlightenment: Nietzsche's Zarathustra* (New York: Cambridge University Press, 1995). Although Rosen highlights Nietzsche's own understanding of chaos as it relates to *Thus Spoke Zarathustra*, he is unaware of contemporary science debates and is primarily interested in the relationship between philosophy and politics (xv).

19 Musarion 3:338: "Man muß neue Fragen formulieren können, wenn man neue Antworten erhalten möchte." See Henrik Birus, "Nietzsche's Hermeneutical Considerations," in *Nietzsche: Literature and Values* 66–80.

attempt at writing a "natural history of the higher man" (his favorite designation for this project in those years). *Zarathustra* is accorded more detailed analysis in a later chapter as the monumental modern myth-making event of the late nineteenth century, analogous to the myth-making power of *Faust* in the late eighteenth century and of *The Tin Drum* in the twentieth century. In fact, a critique of science is prominent in all of these works. Since truly innovative developments that challenge preconceived notions often do not take root for some time, it is not surprising that Nietzsche's revolutionary thought did not immediately enter general consciousness. Although he was avidly read in some circles around 1900 and in the 1920s, he was not broadly received (in and outside Germany) until the second half of the twentieth century. Then he rapidly emerged as a modern classic, which fulfilled his own prophecy that the Germans might someday read him.[20] What he wrote in the 1880s was too new, too multivalent, too passionate for the general reader's taste (*KSA* 6:167; 13:540–45).

The delay in his broader reception was due no doubt in part to the reading modes then dominant. But then Nietzsche must bear some responsibility for the delay, for he insisted that he was not driven simply by a wish to be understood broadly; on the contrary, he also desired *not* to be understood.[21] The desire for limited comprehensibility and his break with traditional narrative form is coupled with notions of chaotic movement and periodic ordering on a grander scale. That interconnection explains why he would even consider writing "a book for all and for none," as he subtitled *Thus Spoke Zarathustra*. "Books for everybody," he stated laconically, "are always malodorous books" (*BGE* #29). To write for everyone is to write for no one. His reader must be like himself: a rugged individualist in intellectual matters. Besides writing and reading are not the same thing as living. Nietzsche much preferred life to idle reading. In *Zarathustra*, he suggested that the spread of literacy is subversive because it eventually corrupts not only writing but also thinking: "Another century of readers – and the spirit itself will [begin to] stink"(*Za* 40). Nonetheless, he took pen to hand, unable to deny his own inherent drive to master his environment. Above all, he wanted to animate. Since he considered thinking itself to be action (*KSA* 12:17-19; *WP* #458) and because he saw writing to be an extension of thinking, writing proved to be an essential part of living for him. In any event, the fact that he did not write easy books can be seen as an

20 *KSA* 13:538: "Was macht es mir, wenn die Deutschen mich nicht lesen? Um so mehr bemühe ich mich noch darum, ihnen gerecht zu sein. – Und, wer weiß? Vielleicht lesen sie mich übermorgen." See John A. McCarthy, "Nietzsche-Rezeption in der Literatur 1890–1918," in *Hansers Sozialgeschichte der deutschen Literatur*, vol. 7, *Naturalismus, Fin de siècle, Expressionismus (1890-1918)*, ed. York-Gothart Mix (Munich: Hanser, 2000), 192–206. Volker Gerhardt, *Friedrich Nietzsche* (Munich: C. H. Beck, 1992), 211–24, sketches Nietzsche's reception across the disciplines in the twentieth century.

21 *GS* #381; see also *BGE* #27, #44, #290.

attempt to animate rather than to persuade his reader.[22] The best interpreter, therefore, is the one who suffers a thousand burdens and struggles to gain insight.[23] *Zarathustra* (1882-85) and *Beyond Good and Evil* (1886) force us by their very style to see things in an unaccustomed way. It is not simply a matter of adopting a perspective proffered by Nietzsche, but rather of finding a medial perspective between the positions of author and reader. That in-between-space is the site of innovation. And that space is constantly shifting. Such was Nietzsche's intent throughout.

For Nietzsche, life was literature and philosophy was life. In view of the role that the genius has traditionally played in the history of the world, it is strange that the concept of genius is rarely encountered in his writings. Perhaps the presumed avoidance of the designation "genius," as Michael Tanner argues, is due to his unpleasant break with the one great personality he truly knew well: Richard Wagner.[24] Yet it is more fundamental and more logical to conclude that Nietzsche's essential attitude toward life is the real reason why he shied away from using the word "genius" in his pronouncements. The overarching theme of his opus – especially that of the 1880s, following the death of Wagner in spring 1883 – is the "total economy of life" that embraces the full range of human emotion and instinct (*BGE* #23). That outlook on life was rooted in a biological understanding of the relationship between body and spirit, between the creative individual and his various life-worlds. After spring 1885, the reorientation of Nietzsche's thinking became even more pronounced with an expansion into the inorganic realm and the incorporation of the physical concept of force/energy ("Kraft") in the initial formulation of "will to power" ("Wille zur Macht") (cf. Giorgio Colli, *KSA* 11:722–25). In a fragment from June/July 1885, Nietzsche specified that the will to power is manifest in "every combination of force" ("in jeder Kraft-Kombination"; *KSA* 11:560). In fact, the essence of being is equated with process itself ("Die Prozesse als 'Wesen'"; *KSA* 11:560). Three years later, in another fragment, he spoke of the "will to accumulation of force" and wondered whether this will to energy increase should be hypothesized for chemical reactions and cosmic order as well ("Der Wille zur Accumulation von Kraft." *KSA* 13:261). Thus, he was thinking in terms not only of a constant level of energy, but also of energy fluctuation with periodic knots of energy vying with one another for superiority. He labels the concept "maximizing an economy of energy

22 Nehemas, *Life*, 41. In an unpublished preface to a planned study entitled "Der Wille zur Macht: Versuch einer Umwerthung aller Werthe," Nietzsche called *Zarathustra* his most profound book. *Will to Power* was to be his "most independent" (*KSA* 13:194). See also *Götzen-Dämmerung* (*KSA* 6:153).

23 In the prelude to *The Gay Science* (#23), he cautions: "Leg ich mich aus, so leg ich mich hinein; / Ich kann nicht selbst mein Interprete sein. / Doch wer nur steigt auf seiner eignen Bahn, / Trägt auch mein Bild zu hellerm Licht hinan" (*KSA* 3:357).

24 Michael Tanner, "Nietzsche on Genius," in *Genius: The History of an Idea*, ed. by Penelope Murray (Oxford: Basil Blackwell, 1989), 128–40, argues that the term "genius" is infrequently encountered in Nietzsche's writings. However, Richard Oehler fills four columns with citations relating to "Genius" and "Genie." See Richard Oehler, *Nietzsche-Register* (Stuttgart: Alfred Kröner Verlag, 1965), 136–38.

use" ("Maximal-Ökonomie des Verbrauchs"; *KSA* 13:261).[25] The genius was simply one of these energy knots ("Kraftzentren").

In the preface to the second edition of *Gay Science,* Nietzsche conjectured that "behind the loftiest estimates of value by which the history of thought has hitherto been governed, misunderstandings of the bodily constitution, either of individuals, classes, or entire races are concealed" (*GS*, #2). His purpose in *Beyond Good and Evil* and elsewhere is to confront "the terrible basic text *homo natura*" in a rigorously scientific manner, the way that the rest of nature was confronted in the age of positivism (*BGE* #230). His purpose is to get back to the text that has "*disappeared beneath the interpretation*" (*BGE* #38), to ground existence in the "reality of our instincts" (*BGE* #36), and to disclose the essence of every living thing as "a fundamental organic function" (*BGE* #259). After all, he did claim that the genius is a being who impregnates or gives birth (*BGE* #206) and who is perhaps not so rare that he would deserve special notice (*BGE,* #274). Then too, life itself was for him at its very core nothing but "appropriation, injury, overpowering of the strange and weaker, suppression, severity, imposition of one's forms, incorporation, and at the least and mildest, exploitation." Translated to the body politic, he continues, this life-drive "will want to grow, expand, draw to itself, gain ascendancy – not out of any morality or immorality, but because it *lives*, and because it *is* will to power" (*BGE* #259). Genius is part and parcel of this general compulsion for emergence.

The individual human being he defines as being "a delicate, empty, elegant, flexible mold which has to wait for some content so as 'to form' itself by"; man is "without content" and without a prescribed "self" (*BGE* #207). This definition is later adopted by Robert Musil in *Man Without Characteristics* (1930). Portrayed thusly, man is a mere vehicle for giving shape and form to experience and sensation. Speaking paradoxically (and in direct opposition to Kant), Nietzsche asserts that the human being is neither an end and ultimate purpose of "the *rest* of existence" nor is s/he even "a beginning, a begetting and first cause" (*BGE* #207). The paradox will be explained later.

On the other hand, the human being appears to be something much more than a vessel. The most alive individual is a creator of values, a commander and lawgiver, whose "knowing" is "*creating*" and whose will to truth is "*will to power*" (*BGE* #211). Such a human being lives life unphilosophically, unwisely, and imprudently "and bears the burden and duty of a hundred attempts and temptations of life" (*BGE* #205). (This is all very reminiscent of Goethe's Faust.) This individual is Nietzsche's philosopher of the future. The paradoxical description offered is, then, the terrible basic text *homo natura*: the will to power in its agonistic wholeness. The human being is both reactive

25 The passage reads in its entirety: "nicht bloß Constanz der Energie: sondern Maximal-Ökonomie des Verbrauchs: so daß das *Stärker-werden-wollen von jedem Kraftzentrum* aus die einzige Realität ist – nicht Selbstbewahrung, sondern Aneignung, Herr-werden-, Mehr-werden-, Stärker-werden-wollen" (*KSA* 13:261; emphasis in original).

and proactive, a mere mold and vessel but also a creator and builder of molds. Hermann Hesse in *Steppenwolf* and Günter Grass in *The Tin Drum* later explore this basic text. They are preceded in their efforts by Dostoevsky in *Notes from Underground*.[26]

If we accept Nietzsche's definition of the genius as a twofold being that is fundamentally driven to create but is also open to being impregnated with new life from without, we can easily draw an analogy between the genius and the fluctuating "Kraftzentrum" (energy knot), a phenomenon found throughout the universe. Such an individual lives life fully, embracing its contradictory forces of contraction and expansion as the essential tensions of his own existence. Like Nietzsche's vision of the genuine philosopher, this creative individual is capable of imagining and experiencing extraordinary things nonstop. She would be analogous to the summer storm, pregnant with ever new lightning bolts and resounding with rolling claps of thunder that extend in all directions.[27] "This shall be called greatness," Nietzsche asserts, "the ability to be as manifold as whole as vast as full" as life itself (*BGE* #212). "Manifold" implies an enhanced energy state. Obviously, the genius is part and parcel of the general will to power. In external nature, genius expresses itself as the venting of energy; in human nature it appears as the ordering and appropriating of life-worlds through the act of interpretation, whether the interpretation is in the realm of physics, ethics, or literature.

The interpretive act amounts for Nietzsche to a lie by means of which humanity derives meaning from the surface play of the earth. He calls this ability "the creative talent par excellence of humankind," discerning its source in the very operations of nature. The true artist imitates nature by acting out the dynamic forces of nature, not by copying its artifacts. The mere copyists Nietzsche labels "false free spirits," those "tirelessly scribbling slaves of the democratic taste" (*BGE* #44). The creative artist himself, however, partakes of "the genius of the lie" ("er selbst ist auch ein Stück Genie der Lüge"; *KSA* 13:193). The "lie" is any interpretation of the world or of humanity. In other words, while a matter of the will, the genius is not wholly dependent upon *human* will. Nietzsche's explanation of the "origin of genius" drives to the heart of the matter:

> The way in which a prisoner uses his wits in the search for a means of escape, the most cold-blooded and tedious employment of every little advantage, *can teach us what instrument nature sometimes makes use of to bring genius into existence* – a word I ask to be understood without any flavor of the mythological or religious: *it takes it and shuts it in a prison* and excites in it the greatest possible desire to free itself. – Or to employ a different image: someone who has completely lost his way in a forest but strives with uncommon energy to get out of it again sometimes discovers a new path which no one knows: *that is how those geniuses come about who are famed for originality*. – It has already been remarked that *a mutilation, crippling, a serious deficiency* in an organ offers the occasion for an uncommonly successful development of another organ, the reason being that it has to discharge not only its own function but another as well. In this way one can suppose many a glittering talent to have originated.[28]

---

26 In fact, Nietzsche admitted to the strong influence of *Notes* on his own thinking.

27 Cf. *BGE* #292. Cf. also Eagleton, *Ideology*, 259.

28 Nietzsche, *Human, All Too Human,* trans. by R. J. Hollingdale (1996), I, #231, pp. 110–11. My emphasis.

The three images invoked – the metaphor of the imprisoned freedom-seeker, the soul hopelessly lost in the forest, and the crippled organ – draw attention to the agonistic principle involved: nature orchestrates matters to ensure creative results. One organ, one talent – or a concert of talents – is stimulated by external circumstances to compensate in agonistic fashion for the absence of something else. Genius is born of necessity, of absence.

In spring 1888, in an unpublished note on the "real world" of physicists, Nietzsche argued that the interpretation of the world offered by physicists is essentially the same as that offered by philologists; they just do it in a more refined manner. However, he insists that physicists "have unwittingly omitted something from the constellation: namely, the necessary perspectivism, by means of which *every energy knot – and not just the human being* – constructs the rest of the world from within itself (i.e., measures, handles, and forms it according to its own energy)."[29] Genius, then, is not essentially different from other energy impulses in the universe. This interpretation of genius is as much a general characteristic of how things become manifest or emerge as are the interactions of cold and warm fronts, of planets, molecules, and chemical reactions: "Planets and atoms are different only in magnitude; they obey the same laws" ("Weltkörper und Atome nur größenverschieden, aber gleiche Gesetze"; *KSA* 11:702).[30] "Chemical changes in inorganic nature," Nietzsche conjectures, "are perhaps

29 Nietzsche: "Und zuletzt haben sie in der Constellation etwas ausgelassen, ohne es zu wissen: eben den nothwendigen Perspektivismus, vermöge dessen jedes Kraftcentrum – und nicht nur der Mensch – von sich aus die ganze übrige Welt construiert d. h. an seiner Kraft mißt, betastet, gestaltet" (*KSA* 13:373; my translation and emphasis).

30 Joseph Rouse, "Interpretation in Natural and Human Science," in *The Interpretive Turn: Philosophy, Science, Culture,* ed. David R. Hiley, James F. Bohman, and Richard Shusterman (Ithaca and London: Cornell University Press, 1991), 42–56, addresses this question of whether there is a philosophically interesting difference between the natural and human sciences by examining the positions of Charles Taylor and Thomas Kuhn. Taylor adopts a realist approach, ascribing to the human sciences a doubly interpretive quality (doubly, because human sciences for him are inescapably hermeneutical, and humans are essentially self-interpreting agents). On the other hand, the natural sciences deal with objects that are not considered self-interpreting. Rouse rejects this line of demarcation between the human and natural science in favor of a position closer to Kuhn's insistence that our knowledge of nature is conditioned by the successes and failures of prior knowledge, that is, by paradigms or by shared communities of knowledge. Yet despite the clear difference in the stances taken by Taylor and Kuhn, they are not in practice incommensurate. When combined, they yield the insight that there is no epistemologically distinctive domain or activity of interpretation. It is a conclusion Rouse "happily" endorses (43–46) because the difference between humans as self-interpreting agents and themselves as physical objects proves inconsequential for him (49–50). The interpretive act for Rouse, then, is characterized by the hermeneutic circle, by the entanglement of understanding and self-understanding: it "is a general characteristic of how things become manifest" (55). Rouse nonetheless cautions the reader not to mistakenly assume that there is only one kind of science, now modeled on the human sciences rather than on physics (56). Rouse's position comes very close to Nietzsche's argument as I render it here. What is different, however, is

artistic processes too." Elsewhere he notes laconically that aesthetics makes sense only as a natural science, "like the Apollonian and Dionysian."[31] Although Nietzsche expressly rejected the teleological foundation typical of the thinking expressed in Leibniz's *Monadology*, the autopoietic energy knots represented by the monads proved nonetheless central to his philosophy of life and of art.[32] The citations at the masthead of this chapter focus our attention on the main points of this present attempt at a theoretical encirclement: the earth as the ground of physical and mental existence, nature as an aesthetic process, and originality as grounded in nature. They provide a new way of seeing.

It is not by accident, then, that Nietzsche dedicates the last aphorism in *Beyond Good and Evil* to the tempter god Dionysus, the patron of wine, song, exuberance, and dance – the celebrator of life on earth. Strikingly, Nietzsche labels Dionysus "the genius of the heart" (*BGE* #295), lauding him as the great ambiguous tempter and rendering himself as Dionysus's last devotee. The conflation of the forces of life and philosophy in the myth of Dionysus is perfectly clear. Dionysus involves much that is secret, new, strange, and unnerving (in other words, all that which Nietzsche valued most and encapsulated in the images of the serpent and tiger; see *BGE* #239).[33] Precisely for that reason anyone who comes into contact with him and his philosophy leaves richer (more manifold) for the experience. Nietzsche explained the results of the encounter with Dionysus: "richer in himself, newer to himself than before, broken open, blown upon and sounded out by a thawing wind, more uncertain perhaps, more delicate, more fragile, more broken, but full of hopes that have as yet no names, full of new will and flowing [Strömens], full of new ill will and counter-flowing [Zurückströmens]" (*BGE* #295). Elsewhere Nietzsche designated the genius as dynamite (*Götzen Dämmerung* #44). Actually, the explosive effect is the inherent

---

Nietzsche's insistence that the interpretive activity is similar to the "negotiations" of matter and energy in chemistry, physics, and biology.

31 Friedrich Nietzsche, *Nachlaß I* (Musarion): "Die chemischen Verwandlungen in der unorganischen Natur sind vielleicht auch künstlerische Prozesse" [= Kröner Bd. 82, S.56]; "Aesthetik hat nur Sinn als Naturwissenschaft: wie das Apollinische und das Dionysische."(*KSA* 7:395, *Nachgelassene Fragmente 1869–74*). My translations.

32 Julian Young, *Nietzsche's Philosophy of Art* (Cambridge: Cambridge University Press, 1992), 66–70, demonstrates Nietzsche's demythologizing of the genius as a divinely inspired individual, concluding that aesthetic activity for Nietzsche was of the same order of other, more mundane human activities (70). I do not think Young, whose book bills itself as the first comprehensive treatment of Nietzsche's philosophy of art, goes far enough. Genius is anchored in the wider and more fundamental operations of nature.

33 Nehamas notes that Dionysianism is "a religion that emphasizes the infinite repetition of the cycles of nature," "even the phases that consist in degeneration and decay" (*Life* 1985: 146). See also Adrian Del Caro, *Dionysian Aesthetics: The Role of Destruction in Creation as Reflected in the Life and Works of Friedrich Nietzsche* (Frankfurt a.M: Peter Lang, 1981), 86–-87 et passim.

design of his own writing in the 1880s. Logically, then, Dionysus, the god of the dance who deconstructs ordered worlds, serves as the culmination of Nietzsche's overall argument that grounds human life ontologically in the economy of the earth with its organic and inorganic interconnections.

Nietzsche specifically notes that the message of *Beyond Good and Evil* might arrive too late or not at the right time to ensure a positive reception among his readers, for they no longer believe in God or in the gods. (This is an echo of the parable of the madman in *Gay Science* #125, who points out to his noncomprehending listeners that they have killed God through the advances of science and their loss of faith; now they lack a transcendental anchor for human activity.) Ultimately, Nietzsche refers to the passage in which Dionysus is alluded to as "my story" ("meine Erzählung"). By extension, we can label the entire opus of *Beyond Good and Evil* a highly nuanced narrative, since it prepares the reader for the entrance of Dionysus the tempter-god, the god of change and intoxication. A detailed analysis of the individual sections of *Beyond Good and Evil* would reveal how intricately interwoven the thematics of the text actually are. A "story line" unfolds incrementally in the nine parts of *Beyond Good and Evil*, reaching a crescendo in the rendition of Dionysus as the genius of the heart. But that narrative structure is not our primary concern here.

Having culminated his general argument on the nature of the will to power and the philosopher of the future in the figure of Dionysus, Nietzsche adds a final aphorism (*BGE* #296) in which he reflects upon his entire undertaking in *Beyond Good and Evil* as if from without. What is striking about this final aphorism is its dialogic tone. Indeed, that engaging voice encapsulates Nietzsche's style throughout the book and marks *The Gay Science* and *Zarathustra* as well. We do well to recall in this regard that David Bohm and F. David Peat cite the dynamic repartee of dialogue as a prerequisite for the new kind of innovation they celebrate in their book on science, order, and creativity. While they make no reference to Nietzsche, their purpose resonates with his clear intent in *Beyond Good and Evil* to open up the fertile in-between-space where new ideas can emerge through dialogue and critical inquiry.[34] That point is underscored when Nietzsche eulogizes his just completed work as his "written and painted thoughts." Once fresh, strange, and disconcerting, the shimmering ideas captured in the preceding pages have already begun to take on a familiar and fixed air simply because they have been inscribed and displayed like so many butterflies pressed behind glass. However, what had fascinated Nietzsche throughout was not the idea of capturing "trophies" to immortalize his efforts but rather the *attempt* to latch onto the ephemeral movement inherent in the associations themselves. "Alas," he laments, "only that which is about to wither and is beginning to lose its fragrance! Alas, only storms departing

34 David Bohm and F. David Peat, *Science, Order, and Creativity: A Dramatic New Look at the Creative Roots of Science and Life* (Toronto and New York: Bantam Books, 1987), 240–48.

exhausted and feelings grown old and yellow! Alas, only birds strayed and grown weary in flight who now let themselves be caught in the hand – in *our* hand. We immortalize that which cannot live and fly much longer" (*BGE* #296). The task of nailing down, holding fast, or grounding proves frustrating because Nietzsche sensed that what was truly valuable was constantly beyond his grasp. He had to make do with what has slowed down sufficiently for him to comprehend and "name." Yet his task *is* to name, is to *create* by "naming."

Perhaps this process is analogous to the particle physicist's search for the fast-moving, short-lived top quark, which has a lifetime of only about 10^{-24} seconds, or even smaller objects within quarks? Yet she mostly ends up discerning more mundane particles such as protons.[35] In this manner, Nietzsche drove home his overarching theme: the *venting* of energy is the essential thing, not the *having vented* energy. Living fully is the key, not having lived but partially. "Only he who changes remains akin to me," Nietzsche thus affirmed in the lyric epode to *Beyond Good and Evil*. Unpublished notes dating from spring 1873 on Heraclitus, Anaxagoras, Empedocles, Parmenides, and others evince his long-standing fascination with the phenomenon of motion and the essentiality of change ("Werden") (*KSA* 7:571–72), both of which figure prominently, by the way, as the centerfold of Leibniz's map of reality, as will become clear in the ensuing chapter. In those notes Nietzsche also first reduced the objective categories of time and space – by means of which we perceive and measure motion – to sensations of the observing subject (*KSA* 7:577–79). In this light we are to understand Alexander Nehamas's claim that the traditional distinction between *being* and *becoming* dissolved for Nietzsche (Nehamas 1985: 172). Being *is* becoming.[36] So too was it for Leibniz, his Saxon compatriot and for Goethe, his poet kin.[37]

---

35 Now that they have captured the top quark, particle physicists are currently endeavoring to determine whether there are even smaller objects within quarks and to test the supersymmetry theory (supersymmetry assigns as yet undiscovered partners to every particle in the Standard Model). The revamped accelerator and detector upgrades at Fermilab – which will allow investigators to find top quarks thirty times faster than before – and the Large Hadron Collider at CERN (going on line in 2006), capable of generating almost one top-antitop pair per second, will facilitate that search immensely. See Tony M. Liss and Paul L. Tipton, "The Discovery of the Top Quark," *Scientific American* (Sept. 1997): 54–59.

36 Busch, *Affirmation des Chaos* (1989), includes a detailed analysis of Nietzsche's reception of Heraclitus's concept of becoming (270–80). Heraclitus did not have a concept of a fixed and static being.

37 In addition to the *Monadology*, see also Leibniz's reflections "On the Principle of Indiscernibles" (c.1696), "On the Ultimate Origination of Things" (3 Dec. 1697), and "A Résumé of Metaphysics" (c. 1697). Without wishing to belittle the major differences between these two very contrastive thinkers, their apparent agreement on certain major points – that "the predicate is in the subject," that the universe is of one piece despite its diversity, that "necessary being is existence-creating," and that "everything possible demands existence" – should nonetheless not be ignored. The key for both Leibniz and Nietzsche was the creative thrust, the affirmation of being as becoming. See Gottfried Wilhelm Leibniz, *Philosophical Writings*, ed. by G. H. R. Parkinson, trans. by Mary Morris and G. H.

3. Quanta of Energy

The problem with nineteenth-century science, Nietzsche complained in Book 3 of *Will to Power*, wherein he specifically criticized the scientific community, was that the scientific *method* had triumphed over science itself (*WP* #466). By this he meant that science had ceased to be self-critical, had applied universally the unquestioned belief in linear cause and effect and in the reducibility of all phenomena to mathematical or chemical formulae. He did not question the objective world of science per se, but wondered whether one could be confident of seeing everything, catching everything. Is a piece of music understood, he asked by analogy, "if all that were calculable in it and capable of being expressed in formulae were reckoned up?" (*WP* #624). For him there was no difference between the phenomenalworld and the noumenal world since everything proceeds from the body, which is far richer than the spirit anyway (*WP* #492, #532). Furthermore, there is no single subject; everything is already multiple and complex (*WP* #491). Already in *Beyond Good and Evil* he had emphatically argued that physics itself offered only interpretations of the world, and explanations (*BGE* #14, #34). In *Will to Power* he pushed that view even further.

For this reason he was attracted by the nonlinear flow and flux in the complex interactions of thermodynamics. In aphorism #634, labeled "A Criticism of Materialism," Nietzsche offered a succinct explanation of his view of the physical world. Decisive is his notion of will to power as the venting of life-giving, life-enhancing energy: "'Things' do not act regularly, they follow no *rule*: there are no things (that is our fiction); neither do they act in accordance with any necessity" (*WP* #634, 15:117; cf. *KSA* 13:373). Reality consists of the interplay of actions and interactions; what we call the "world" is simply the totality of these interconnections (*KSA* 13:371). The claim that there are "no things," just our perceptions of movements and relations, resonates with Bohm's statement that there is "NO THING."[38] Thus, Nietzsche criticized natural scientists for not looking at things the right way, for not asking the right questions, declaring that they need instead to focus on the dynamics of interaction: "The degree of resistance and the degree of superior power – this is the question around which all phenomena turn: if we, for our own purposes and calculations, know how to express this in formulae and 'laws,' all the better for us!" (*WP* #634, 15:117). Even then the formulae would not actually reveal anything about the operations of the physical world itself, he implies. Rather, the "laws" merely reflect our need to impose discreet order.

Instead of pursing the normal path of deducing calculability, Nietzsche suggested a

---

R. Parkinson, The Everyman Library (London: J. M. Dent, 1997), 133–47, here 135, 136, 145. Such coincidences justify an overarching view that encompasses late-seventeenth- and late-nineteenth-century philosophical thought. Both were influenced by the science of their day.

38 David Bohm, *On Creativity*, ed. by Lee Nichol (London and New York: Routledge, 1998), 78.

new way of thinking about the physical universe, one that predated Niels Bohr by a quarter century. His proposal was to raise quantum physics to a new level of significance for everyday life by insisting that all movement, all phenomena are grounded in inner, invisible operations of matter (*KSA* 11:563). Thus he spoke of "molecular operations" ("Molekül-Arbeit"; *KSA* 13:374) and "quanta of power" ("Machtquanta") as seminal to understanding the operation of the whole. These energy centers – which he believed include humans as well as stars and atoms – produce effects and resist influences in incessant fashion (*WP* #634; *KSA* 13:373). The "Machtquantum" was "essentially a will to violate and to defend oneself against violation. Not self-preservation." In the latter he departed from the Darwinian model of the survival of the fittest. "Every atom," he goes on to say, "affects the whole of being – it is thought away if one thinks away this radiation of will-power. That is why I call it a quantum of 'will to power'; it expresses the characteristic that cannot be thought out of the mechanistic order without thinking away this order itself" (*WP* 338, #634). Nietzsche's argument is tantamount to linking the internal mental and the external empirical realms of reality inextricably together. The "will" is expressed equally in both.

The visible world, Nietzsche surmises, we take to be the effect of some deep structure. By force of habit we posit the causal connection. This visible world is "a world for the eyes," and we discern it essentially because of movement. We suppose, then, he reasons, that something has moved, "whether as the fiction of a little clump of atom or even as the abstraction of this, the dynamic atom, a thing that produces effects" (*WP* 338, #634). This movement is the link to thermodynamics beyond the range of a mechanistic theory of causation. It also points in the direction of the concept of becoming. When you get to the very bottom of everything by eliminating such concepts as subject/object and cause/effect, Nietzsche concludes, nothing remains but dynamic quanta and their essential tensions: "[T]heir essence lies in their relation to all other quanta, in their 'effect' upon the same. The will to power is not a being, not a becoming, but a *pathos* – the most elemental fact from which a becoming and effecting first emerge –"(*WP* 339, #635; cf. also #581, #617). The focus on *pathos*, a reductionist move, is important because it highlights the inchoative moment in a more salient fashion than is achieved by stopping at the notion of becoming. Becoming itself is already a kind of existence, whereas the Greek *pathos* signifies more precisely "event," "occasion," and "passion." Each in its own way addresses the birthing state, so to speak: the space or state from which becoming emerges. Clearly, Nietzsche took motion to be essential, for it is not broken up into discrete, easily quantifiable entities or units appearing over time.[39] The quantum of energy coexistent with other quanta of

39 As early as spring 1873, Nietzsche had begun to reflect on the nature of time as being no continuum at all, since motion is discontinuous over time: "Die Zeit ist aber gar kein Continuum, sondern es giebt nur total verschiedene Zeitpunkte, keine Linie." And further: "Keine Bewegung in der Zeit ist stetig" (*KSA* 7:579).

energy in a field of tension represents, therefore, the quintessence of his philosophy. He took the "triumphant concept of '*energy*,' with which our physicists created God and the world," and developed the notion further, imparting to it an inner will that he characterized as the will to power. (Hence, I have placed the citation in the masthead of this chapter.) This will to power he defines as "an insatiable desire to manifest power; or the application and exercise of power as a creative instinct" (*WP* #619; *KSA* 11:563).[40] The will to power, then, is the inner working of all movements. Sarah Kofman asserts that the will to power "*designates* every force which acts." More specifically, it expresses "the plurality and the greater or lesser differentiation in the relations between the forces" (Kofman, 1993: 94; similarly Rosen 1995: 57).

Chemistry is a more fitting model for Nietzsche than "a firm *systematizing of atoms* in necessary motion" (*WP* 339, #636) because "there is nothing unchanging in chemistry." Molecular changes (i.e., movements) from one form to another are actions that "we cannot see or weigh" (*WP* 334, #623; *KSA* 13:374). If we remove our eye and our psychology from the concept of numbers, the idea of the subject, the notion of causality, and the concept of movement, nothing remains but the dynamic quanta themselves in their relation to all other dynamic quanta. This medley of agonistic interactions stands in contrast to the "perspective-setting force" of the physicist's approach (*WP* 339, #636; *KSA* 13:373).[41] To ensure that he was understood, Nietzsche added:

> My idea is that every specific body strives to become master of all space, and to extend its force (–its will to power), and to thrust back all that resists its extension. But it continually encounters similar efforts on the part of other bodies and ends by coming to an arrangement ('union') with those of them that are sufficiently related to it; *thus they then conspire together for power*. And the process goes on – (*WP* 340, #636; *KSA* 13:373–74)

---

40 Here I use Anthony M. Ludovici's translation (15:110) rather than Kaufmann's (see bibliography). Generally, Ludovici's wording often seems more archaic. By the same token, however, he is truer at times to the original than Kaufmann. Kaufmann chooses to translate "Kraft" as "force" rather than "energy." The latter, however, is more accurate in the current context. Cf., e.g., Nietzsche's use of the term *dynamis* as the final word in the preceding aphorism in *WP* #618. *Dynamis* means power, energy, potency, a point Kaufmann himself makes but does not utilize. This is important to note because it parallels Faust's translation of John 1:1, with its progression "Wort-Sinn-Kraft-Tat." "Sinn" (mind) and "Kraft" connoted for Goethe bundles of inner and outer energy, whereas "Wort" (logos) seemed static. Similarly, Goethe moves on to "Tat" (deed) even as Nietzsche was to move on from "becoming" to "*pathos*" (event). Both men aimed at the moment of emergence from which everything else comes.

41 Nietzsche had formulated this notion in *Beyond Good and Evil* to cover all sorts of "objective" reasoning when he remarked: "It is *we* alone who have fabricated causes, succession, reciprocity, relativity, compulsion, number, law, freedom, motive, purpose." When humankind imputes such criteria to the external world, he insists, it behaves "mythologically" and introduces a false "world of symbols" (*BGE* #21). Gleick notes how critical narrowed vision is to scientific progress (*Chaos* 194).

Nietzsche further underscored the interconnectedness of the components, whose sum total is greater than the individual parts, when he introduced the concept of environment into his calculations, that is, when he averred that an energy knot ("atom of energy") in the inorganic world is concerned only with its immediate region ("neighborhood"), whereas distant forces ("*actio in distans*") balance each other out. This concern with the immediate environment anchors perspective in the local economy. It is the reason why "a living organism is 'egoistic' to the core" (Ludovici's trans., *WP* #637). Perspective, moreover, is much more than a relativizing moment; it is actually "a complex form of specificity" (*WP* 340, #636) that helps the subject to better understand the whole. Perspective draws attention to the shifts in energy concentrations and movement within the complex whole and allows the viewer to recognize the thermodynamic, nonsequential quality of the interactions: "[A]ny transposition of force to any place would affect the whole system – thus, together with sequential causality there would be a contiguous and concurrent dependence" (*WP* 340, #638). The transference of energy from one part of the body to the other (whether human body, body politic, rain forest, or universe) is thus nonlinear. The motion was not simply mechanistic, as was the prevailing view in late nineteenth century.

With regard to the dispersal of energy, Nietzsche rejected the notion that the universe is headed toward a state of absolute equilibrium, arguing instead that the quantum of energy present has from the outset experienced phases of increased and decreased intensity, depending on the local economies within the overall system and on the venting of energy of individual beings: "The same amount of energy means different things at different stages of evolution" (*WP* 340, #639). What *is* important for growth, then, is the economy or efficiency with which the energy is used to achieve the sensation or actuality of growth. "That the world is not striving toward a stable condition is the only thing that has been proved" (*WP* 341, #639). The general and the specific development is toward enhanced complexity and sharper differentiation (*WP* 342, #644). This plurality of interactive forces bound by a mutually supportive process is what Nietzsche called life (*WP* 341, #641). The narrative of that life is not a simple linear one with a fixed beginning, middle, and end. It is all a becoming without becoming something entirely discrete.

4. Vision of the New Universe and Eternal Recurrence

Peter Gast and Elisabeth Förster-Nietzsche arranged the unpublished fragments of *Will to Power* in such a way that they culminate in a vision of a new universe in aphorisms #1066 and #1067 (= *KSA* 13:374–76). Reference has already been made to the chief point of aphorism #1066, namely, that the universe can be conceived of as a finite number of centers of energy that go through an infinite number of recombinations in the great game of chance. The result is a continuous cycle of movement of absolutely identical series, which constitutes its existence (*WP* #1066; *KSA* 13:376). The subject of much inquiry, this concept has been variously interpreted. On the basis of a careful analysis of critical moments in this discourse, Alexander Nehamas offers his own interpretation of Nietzsche's meaning, introducing an implicit, if not explicit, dimension of Nietzsche's formulation: "(C) If anything in the world recurred, including an individual life or even a single moment within it, then everything in the world would recur in exactly identical fashion."[42] The introduction of the conditional "if" is important because it implies that the identical repetition of the cycle is not very likely, given the dynamics of the whole. Nehamas bases his view primarily on psychological reactions and on the principle of will to power. Key is not the actual repetition, but rather the willingness to affirm life in all its vagaries. In this context, the final aphorism in the opus is especially forceful and nuanced, and thus deserving of citation in full, something Nehamas did not do:

> And do you know what 'the universe' is to my mind? Shall I show it to you in my mirror? This world: a monster of energy, without beginning, without end; a fixed quantum of energy that does not grow bigger or smaller, that does not expend itself but only transforms itself; as a whole, of unalterable size, a self-sufficient economy without either loss or gain, but likewise without increase and new sources of revenue; surrounded by nonentity as by a frontier. It is nothing vague or wasteful, not something endlessly extended, but is a definite quantum of energy located in limited space, and not in space that would be "empty" here or there. It is rather energy everywhere, the play of forces and force-waves, at the same time one and many, increasing here and diminishing there, a sea of forces storming and raging in itself, forever changing, forever rolling back over incalculable ages to recurrence, with an ebb and flow of its forms, producing the most complicated things out of the most simple structures; producing the hottest, the most turbulent, and most contradictory things out of the quietest, most rigid, and most frozen material, and then again from the play of contradiction moving back into the delight of consonance, still affirming itself in this uniformity of its courses and its years, blessing itself as that which must return eternally, as a becoming that knows no satiety, no disgust, no weariness: this, my *Dionysian* world of the eternally self-creating, eternally self-destroying, this mysterious world of twofold voluptuous delight; this, my "beyond good and evil," without aim, unless there is an aim in the bliss of the circle, without will, unless a ring feels goodwill to itself [...] – This world is the will to power – *and nothing else!* And you yourselves are also this will to power – and nothing besides! (*WP* 549–50, #1067)

The above translation adopts the most felicitous formulations from both the Ludovici and Kaufmann renditions of the text. Special care has been given to ensure accuracy. The key elements traced in the foregoing are all present here in cogent and logical manner. To wit, they are in order of reference:

---

42 Nehamas, *Life*, 141–69, here 156.

- a monster of energy
- only transforms itself
- a self-sufficient economy without either loss or gain
- surrounded by nonentity as by a frontier
- energy everywhere, the play of forces and force-waves
- a sea of forces storming and raging in itself, forever changing
- producing the hottest, the most turbulent, and most contradictory things out of the quietest, most rigid, and most frozen material
- from the play of contradiction moving back into the delight of consonance
- my *Dionysian* world of the eternally self-creating, eternally self-destroying

Each element underscores the dynamic and unquantifiable quality of existence as order emerges from chaos and leads back to chaos. What Nietzsche describes here is what meteorologists currently know about the formation of weather patterns in the earth's atmosphere. Thermodynamic change can cause extreme, violent turbulence or pristine clarity. The totality of energy envisioned by Nietzsche is thus the agonistic sum of all individual actions and reactions of energy knots ("Kraftzentren") interacting via positive and negative feedback loops with one another. In a fragment from spring 1888, Nietzsche defined the function of energy quanta ("Kraft-Quanta") as consisting in influencing all other energy quanta (*KSA* 13:261). "Since the energy mass is constant in the universe," Döblin noted in his early reaction to the vision, "that is, mathematically quantifiable, whereas only the concentrations (or centers) of this quantum are in continual flux, the constant shifts in concentrations of energy are what constitutes the world process."[43] That which makes the sum of the parts greater than the parts is the key to the entire process. While the total energy mass might be quantifiable – and thus subject to a tidy narrative – the fluctuations of the "Kraftzentren" (also "Kraftatome"; *KSA* 11:560) at the local level provide only "petits récits."

A monster of energy is not easily harnessed. Without a predetermined telos and surrounded by nonentity, the energy mass can only engage in surface play, constantly surging toward new and unforseen combinations (because without teleological aim). An intermingling of contradiction and consonance, the world Nietzsche envisions here is one of eternal self-creation and deconstruction. The notion of a definite number of finite recombinations of identical, exactly calculable "little stories" with known beginnings, middles, and conclusions finds no real legitimation in the metaphors chosen to express the dynamic complexity of the overall enormous energy source, which actually consists of a whole, changing series of identifiable "Macht-Centren." That image, by the way, is already apparent in notes Nietzsche penned in summer and

43 Döblin, "Wille zur Macht": "Da nun die Energiemenge konstant im Weltall, also quantitativ zahlenmäßig bestimmbar ist, während nur die Centration dieses Quantums beständig wechselt, – der beständige Centrationswechsel macht eben den Weltprozeß aus" (1:321).

fall 1881 in connection with the conception of *Thus Spoke Zarathustra*. Although the measure of all force is determined and finite ("Das Maaß der *All-Kraft* ist *bestimmt*"), its recombinatory potential is so great as to prove incalculable and certainly not precisely reiterable (*KSA* 9:523). Indeed, Nietzsche rejects the concept of concentricity, that is, of self-sameness on the basis of the multiplicity obvious in natural phenomena themselves.[44] If we think of the volatility within our own atmosphere, we can more readily comprehend his point.

Moreover, Nietzsche's own insistence that the higher man he envisions eschews the straight and narrow adds a factor of indeterminacy hitherto missing in the calculation. While the energy mass remains the same, the human participants in that play of force change with every birth and death. Nietzsche's own stress on individuality (*my* judgment, *my* thoughts, *my* way) and on the importance of attitude as the chief characteristics of the coming philosophers of the future ensures the introduction of variables, which would make an identical repetition of movement highly unlikely. Indeed, the situation in which man finds himself vis-à-vis other humans and nature itself is analogous to that of molecules interacting in the physical world. That state of interaction determines the *conditio humaine* in essential fashion (*KSA* 9:524). "The inorganic determines us completely," Nietzsche averred, underscoring the connection among humans as physical objects despite their self-awareness (*KSA* 9:525). Key in both the animate and inanimate versions of nature is the principle of a finite yet eternally re-creative force ("die Kraft ist ewig gleich und ewig thätig"; *KSA* 9:523). "Gleich" is here used in the meaning of self-similar, I propose, rather than self-same. Thus, the eternal recurrence would at best be self-similar, for a change in attitude (angle, junction, will) would make exact replication impossible.[45] Such changes are all too frequent.

Even though Nietzsche's vision of a spatially limited universe has not been borne out by contemporary astrophysics, he intuitively anticipated some general aspects of the contemporary view of the creative universe, which has grown extremely complex through continuous and experimental recombinations of the basic subatomic building blocks. "In molecules," he noted in 1881, "there are explosions and changes in the

---

44 *KSA* 9:560–62. Cf. Holub, *Nietzsche*, 68.

45 Higgins, *Nietzsche's Zarathustra*, 164-65. Holub, *Nietzsche*, argues that because Nietzsche's theory of eternal recurrence does not agree with the second law of thermodynamics and its hypothesis of entropy, he runs into problems (65). Yet Nietzsche's concepts of changing energy knots and action in time explain why entropy does not occur: the system, while finite, is not closed. Levine, *Nietzsche*, remains unconvinced that Nietzsche intended his theory of eternal recurrence to be scientifically based in the modern sense of the word. Rather, he suggests that Nietzsche was influenced by the concept of eternal return so common among the ancients. "Scientific" ("wissenschaftlich") was thus intended in the meaning of "scholarly" (122–25). It is not an implausible explanation, given the widespread efforts to establish philological standards of inquiry in the nineteenth century to rival (imitate) those of natural science. Yet there is compelling evidence to take Nietzsche at his word.

orbits of all atoms, also sudden eruptions of energy. Our entire solar system could react in an instant to a stimulus quite like the nerve's signal to the muscles. There is no way of proving that this has never happened or might not ever happen" (*KSA* 9:535).[46] When we add to this picture the psychological dimension, we see that it is not just a question of continuity, of rote iteration or self-sameness, but of "discontinuity" through sensitivity to slight deviations from established patterns in self-similarity. The latter are, of course, recurrent features of complexity theory and the science of chaos. From supersymmetry to superstrings, from cosmic radiation to the origins of organic matter in inorganic structures, from the alternating medley of turbulence and fixed forms to the intertwining of simplicity and complexity, much of what Nietzsche imagined, whether in his clear moments in 1881 or in his half-crazed state years later, is still with us today.

Based on these "new" grounds of existence, the affirmation of the world as it is, the transcendence of the traditional binary values of good and evil, and the view of humankind as rooted in the operations of the universe it calls home provide an apt transition from the purely scientific to the philosophic and literary. The creative individual mirrors the creative universe. Nothing more, nothing less. At least for Nietzsche. Taken together, the whole represents a total economy of life, what Döblin labeled Nietzsche's "metaphysics of energy" (Döblin 1:323). Maybe the justification for Nietzsche's concept of eternal recurrence is to be found in his physics after all, contrary to what Nehamas thinks (*Life* 154). While saliently formulated in *Will to Power*, these ideas are everywhere evident in Nietzsche's most famous work and self-proclaimed best book, *Thus Spoke Zarathustra*. We can read that work as an original hybrid of literature, philosophy, and science. And we will do so in chapter 6. First, however, we need to explore the extension of process science and process philosophy to the moral worlds we construct for ourselves as a way of ordering our existence. Nietzsche had defined originality as the ability "to *see* something that does not yet bear a name, that cannot yet be named, although it is before everybody's eyes. As people are usually constituted, it is the name that first makes a thing generally visible to them. – Creative persons have also for the most part been the namers of things" (*Gay Science*, Book 3, #261). The process of naming things is the next step in remapping reality according to the principles of emergence and autopoiesis. The first great namer was of course Adam. Together with Eve, he performed the first acts of seeing and initiated the expansion of knowledge. With their expulsion from the Garden of Eden, the movement of spiritual existence accelerated rapidly. Seeing and mapping in their relationships to ethics are the topic of the next chapter.

---

46 Nietzsche, *Nachgelassene Fragmente*, *KSA* 9:535: "Es giebt im Moleküle Explosionen und Veränderungen der Bahn aller Atome, und plötzliche Auslösungen von Kraft. Es könnte auch mit Einem Moment unser ganzes Sonnensystem einen solchen Reiz erfahren, wie ihn der Nerv auf den Muskel ausübt. Daß dies *nie* geschehen sei oder geschehen werde, ist nicht zu beweisen."

Chapter 4
Eden's Aftermath – The Nature of Evil

So gut das *Böse* betrachtet werden kann als Übertreibung, Disharmonie, Disproportion, so gut kann das *Gute* eine *Schutzdiät* gegen die Gefahr der Übertreibung, Disharmonie und Disproportion sein.

– Nietzsche, *Nachgelassene Fragmente* 1888

1. RETHINKING EVIL

Evil is a hot topic. It is a hot topic because you can find it everywhere: in history, in movies, in cults, in those who dissent from your views. The study of evil has been approached from psychological, theological, philosophical, social, political, and populist vantage points. My approach is philosophical. Moreover, my topic is neither radical evil nor the banality of evil evident in the Shoa or other genocidal acts such as in Cambodia, Rwanda, Bosnia, or the events of 9/11. My intent is to shift the focus in asking after the nature of evil from the simple to the complex. Thus, though evils of scale are important in the remapping of the moral terrain, a fixed Manichaean or Thomistic dualism is not my point of orientation. Key to my project is the elusive periodic centers derivative from contemporary chaos and complexity theory. The latter perspective is inherent in the adage: "Evil spelled backwards is live." Yet previous attempts at defining evil largely ignore the connection between evil/live and chaos/complexity.[1] While I will highlight that nexus, I must be selective regarding whom I can discuss within the given space limitations. Hence, even major contributors such as Arthur Schopenhauer and Friedrich Hegel are missing here.

In particular, I am interested in efforts since the Copernican Turn to situate evil ontologically in a world filled with motion. What place does evil occupy in a

---

1 See, for example, Hannah Arendt, *Eichmann in Jerusalem: A Report on the Banality of Evil* (New York: Viking Press, 1965); C. Fred Alford, *What Evil Means to Us* (Ithaca and London: Cornell University Press, 1997); *The Problem of Evil: An Intercultural Exploration*, ed. by Sandra A. Wawrytko (Amsterdam and Atlanta: Rodopi, 2000); Joseph F. Kelly, *The Problem of Evil in the Western Tradition: From the Book of Job to Modern Genetics* (Collegeville, MN: The Liturgical Press, 2002); Erich Joseph Maier, *Phänomenologie des Bösen. Von der Banalität zur Brutalität* (Puchheim: IDEA Verlag, 2002); and Karl Heinz Bohrer, *Imaginationen des Bösen. Zur Begründung einer ästhetischen Kategorie* (Munich: Hanser Verlag, 2004). A notable exception is Sjoerd L. Bonting, *Chaos Theology: A Revised Creation Theology*, St. Paul University Research Series: Faith and Science (Toronto: Novalis, 2002).

scheme of the universe uniquely revised by scientific inquiry since the seventeenth century? Our view of the cosmos and of the earth has progressed from a static, mechanistic model to an open-ended view of the world caught up in constant flux at both the cosmic and quantum levels and even at the middle range of our everyday experiences. In every age theology, philosophy, science, and literature have resonated with one another in various ways. They have reflected knowledge gains and knowledge losses. They have also reflected upon the consequences of empirical observations for assumptions about their a priori basis in fact. For instance, the philosopher of science Karl Popper recognized some time ago that materialism has transcended itself through modern physics.[2] In commenting on the debate regarding the role of the deity as creative cause, conserving cause, or concurrent cause, the theologian Elizabeth A. Johnson has argued for reconciling twentieth-century evolutionary science (e.g., R. Sheldrake, Edward O. Wilson) with medieval Thomism in what is called process theology.[3] She sees in Aquinas's thought "an economy of superabundance" (14) where "chance is not an alternative to law, but the very means whereby law is creative" (9). Chance actualizes the unrealized potential of the universe as God had created it from the start so that God appears as the *esse* or "livingness of Being" (12). "In this system of thought," Johnson contends, "it is incoherent to think of God as working in the world apart from secondary causes, or beside them, or in addition to them, or even in competition with them" (10). Sjoerd Bonting does not go quite as far as Johnson does here. In proposing his chaos theology, which has numerous affinities with process theology, Bonting continues to insist that God battles "remaining chaos till the final victory on the last day" (25–26). Although teleological with his slant toward ultimate order, Bonting does grant God and evil central roles in *creatio continua* here on earth (48–51, 76). Maier perceives a rudimentary connection between the *materia prima* and chaos, whereby chance plays a pivotal role. That unpredictable interaction brings about a "contrastive harmony" (Kontrastharmonie) within the overall teleology of existence (50–51). For his part, Rolston succinctly

---

2 Cf. Matthew Fox and Rupert Sheldrake, *Natural Grace: Dialogues on Creation, Darkness, and the Soul in Spirituality and Science* (New York: Doubleday, 1996), 18.

3 E. A. Johnson, "Does God Play Dice? Divine Providence and Chance,"*Theological Studies* 57.1 (March 1996): 3–16. Bonting, *Chaos Theology*, places his discussion of evil squarely within the context of scientific insights into the operations of nature (66-88). Holmes Rolston, III, *Genes, Genesis, and God: Values and Their Origins in Natural and Human History* (Cambridge: Cambridge University Press, 1999) makes biological complexity and evolutionary diversity the cornerstone of his thesis about the holistic nature of what constitutes good and evil (see esp. 1–53, 347–63). See also Owen Thomas (ed.), *God's Activity in the World: The Contemporary Problem* (Chico, CA: Scholars, 1983) and O. Thomas, "Recent Thoughts on Divine Agency,"*Divine Action*, ed. by Brian Hebblethwaite and Edward Henderson (Edinburgh: T. and T. Clark, 1991), 35–50.

notes that nature "produces matter and energy, then objective life, then subjective life, then mind and culture." Seen from the human standpoint, this "evolutionary epic" is "the story of good and evil" (302). Nonetheless, evil is not a primary concern of his. I suggest we see Johnson, Bonting, Maier, and Rolston as responses to Pope John Paul II's 1987 recommendation to see whether an evolutionary perspective in science could shed any light on theological anthropology, that is, on the human person as an *imago dei*.[4] The time was definitely ripe for a serious rethinking of evil.

With the exception of Bonting, evil itself did not figure explicitly in any of these reactions to the so-called contemporary problem of redefining divine agency. For the comparatist Joan Copjec, who edited eight critical essays for a volume titled *Radical Evil* (1996), however, it clearly was central. Copjec's collection foregrounds philosophic and psychoanalytic analyses of radical evil expressed in twentieth-century atrocities. In her introduction, Copjec sketches attempts since the eighteenth century to redefine evil as a positive rather than a negative act, to reconceptualize evil as a conscious choice rather than a defect.[5] She does so by focusing on Immanuel Kant's vision of evil in *Die Religion innerhalb der Grenzen der bloßen Vernunft* (Religion within the Limits of Reason Alone, 1793), where it is characterized as "the foul taint [of sheer egoism] in our nature" (Kant cited by Copjec xii). In this light, evil is the product of a free humanity. The battle between good and evil takes place, so the argument goes, between two possible types of rules: good or bad. Whereas the one is essentially disinterested because it is based on moral law, the other is fundamentally self-interested because it is based on self-regard (Copjec xi). Copjec's ultimate objective is to restore Kant's reformulation of evil to its proper political power in contemporary poststructuralist debate, reclaiming him from the backwaters of universalism. She considers Kant's move to be revolutionary because evil is placed squarely within human volition; humans now bear full responsibility for their actions. This kind of approach to analyzing evil relies on a thoroughly anthropocentric theory of existence.

Quite a different tack was taken by the evolutionary biologist Lyall Watson, who would dislodge the human person from center stage. In place of the self-centered humanoid acting as if she were the end of all creation, he installs nature itself. In his *Dark Nature: A Natural History of Evil* (1995), published almost simultaneously with the Copjec volume, Watson remarks almost in Hobbesean terms: "It is a jungle out there, a war very often of all against all, in which ten percent of all known species are parasites, whose job it is to harass, weaken, and

---

4 "Papal Message," in Robert Russell et al. (eds.), *John Paul II on Science and Religion: Reflections on the New View from Rome* (Vatican City: Vatican Observatory, 1990), M 1–14; here M 11.

5 Joan Copjec (ed.), *Radical Evil* (London and New York: Verso, 1996), vi–xxviii, esp. vii–xiii.

disfigure the others."[6] If 10 percent of all species are parasites, existing at the cost of others, should we be surprised at the depraved and radical evil within our own species? In talking about evil, "we are in murky territory," Watson tells us, when it comes to deviant or aberrant behavior glorified in movies and novels about serial killers such as *The Bone Collector* (1999) and *In Cold Blood* (1967) (xi). Deviant from what? Nature? Human nature? The film critic John Oppenheimer offers a theory of evil as a "specific form of physical and mental behavior rather than as a religious and ethical problem only," yet he still insists that any definition of evil must begin with criminality. And he remains convinced that evil occupies a special world, clearly relating the phenomenon to John Milton's notion of Satan and "confounded Chaos," the enemies of humankind.[7] But then Oppenheimer does readily grant that his diagnosis is limited in character. To others he leaves the task of elucidating the why of evil in a "system of cosmic energy that refuses to explain itself"; theirs will be the task of situating evil, as he formulates it rather poetically, "before the radiant colourful edges of the universe, embedded in blackness, that quiver beyond the galaxies" (Oppenheimer 171). Perhaps there is an actual law involved in the conservation of memory, he muses, a law analogous to the laws of thermodynamics (Oppenheimer 176). Perhaps there is.

"What is Man?" Georg Büchner asked in *Woyzeck* and showed us a half-crazed, undernourished and exploited automaton in response. Seventy years later and six thousand miles removed, Mark Twain asked the same question in an essay entitled "What Is Man?" (1906). In his novel *The Mysterious Stranger* (published posthumously in 1916), Twain framed the question in terms of the relationship between good and evil, featuring Satan in the lead role. Robert Louis Stevenson examined that very relationship in his tale *Dr. Jekyll and Mr. Hyde* (1886). By raising the contest between good and evil to the metaphysical level, Goethe's *Faust* is, of course, one of the most enduring attempts to fathom the question, what is man? Watson addresses the issues raised in these works indirectly when he states: "We need to know a great deal more about [evil's] biological roots and its organic history before dismissing it as 'psychopathic' and therefore beyond ordinary understanding" (Watson xi). We definitely need to rethink the Manichaean approach to good and evil.

Perhaps it is time to reconceptualize these qualities in ecological terms; an

---

6 Lyall Watson, *Dark Nature: A Natural History of Evil* (New York: HarperCollins, 1995), 249. Rolston, *Genes*, does not know Watson, Johnson, Bonting, or Maier. Instead, he draws heavily on Edward O. Wilson's theories of biophilia and sociobiology and augments that are filled with key references to Richard Dawkins (gene theory), Ernst Mayer (theory of evolution), and Max Delbrück (derivation of mind from matter) in presenting his own "fertility hypothesis" (296).

7 John Oppenheimer, *Evil and the Demonic: A New Theory of Monstrous Behavior* (New York: New York University Press, 1995), 1–5.

ecological view of nature positions humankind within natural processes and assumes a relationship of mutual participation.[8] To explain how the interconnections impact upon the parts of the whole system, the British theoretical physicist David Bohm drew an analogy between this participatory relationship and the hologram. The hologram is a phenomenon in which the part stands for and is mired in the whole. There is no fragmentation but rather complex interactions in a state of constant flux. Movement therefore assumes a primary value in the new scheme of things. And the skill we observers must cultivate is the "art of perceiving movement."[9] Bohm perceives in natural phenomena "a movement in which everything, any particular element of space, may have a field which unfolds into the whole, and the whole enfolds it [the field] in it" (Bohm xx). In his recent study, *Good and Evil*, the philosopher Richard Taylor strikingly states with regard to a new inclusive ecology: "Man is not the measure of *all* things, because he is not the measure of himself. That we are the kind of beings we are is a fact of nature, and it is from that fact that good and evil arise."[10] All this would seem to point in the direction of Friedrich Nietzsche's laconic aphorism in his *Beyond Good and Evil* (1886): "There are no moral phenomena at all, only a moral interpretation of phenomena."[11] Semiotics is the thing.

Part of what I want to accomplish in the following is to place the concept of evil squarely within the new paradigm of an open, inventive universe. I question how accurate it is to attribute a revolutionary new kind of ethical thinking to Kant, as Copjec is inclined to do, or to speak of attempts to redefine evil as a "contemporary problem," as Johnson explicitly does. I have problems with Bonting's assumption that evil is "the remaining element of chaos" and that the end of creation is ultimate order (87 et passim). I wish to point out a revolutionary rethinking of evil by Benedictus de Spinoza and Gottfried Wilhelm Leibniz, who prefigured a multidimensional way of looking at things. In so doing they anticipated Nietzsche's re-evaluation of values. They were the first to reconceptualize the universe as an emergent system, rather than seeing it simply as fixed and mechanistic. Yet neither

8 For an orientation to this new paradigm in literary studies, see Glen A. Love, "Ecocriticism and Science: Toward Consilience?" *New Literary History* 30 (1999): 561–576; and Dana Phillips, "Ecocriticism, Literary Theory, and the Truth of Ecology,"*New Literary History* 30 (1999): 577–602. Rolston, *Genes*, conceives of his project precisely in terms of ecosystems (e.g., 53–54, 93–96, 174–75, 301–302).

9 David Bohm, *On Creativity* (London and New York: Routledge,1998), 62–65.

10 Richard Taylor, *Good and Evil* (Amherst, NY: Prometheus Books, 1999), 191.

11 Friedrich Nietzsche, *Jenseits von Gut und Böse*, Kritische Studienausgabe, ed. by Giorgio Colli and Mazzino Montinari, 15 vols., 2nd ed. (Munich: Deutscher Taschenbuch Verlag and de Gruyter, 1988), 5:92. Hereafter cited as *KSA* by volume and page number. English translation cited according to Friedrich Nietzsche, *Beyond Good and Evil*, trans. with an introduction and commentary by R. J. Hollingdale (New York: Penguin, 1990), 96.

of them is cited by any of the authors mentioned thus far, even though they also came to grips with the "contemporary problem" of where to place evil within a new world system. In any age, gains in the natural sciences force theologists and philosophers to reassess their own thinking. While the catchwords today are the margins of chaos, complexity theory, emergence, and coevolution, the origins of such complex relationships occurred much earlier. Let's start by going back to the beginning: to the fall.

2. The Fall from Harmonious Order

This look at the interconnectedness of creation, creativity, and evil is premised on the notion inherent in the phrase "auf den Grund fallen" sounded in the introduction. While literally it means to fall to the ground, figuratively it hints at the desire to get to the bottom of things. Ground is thus simultaneously a root cause and a material substance. In order to fall, we must of course start at some kind of elevation, for the law of gravity draws us toward the center of the mass. Put differently, in a fall we move from the space of lighter elements to that of heavier ones. Conversely, we rise from heavier elements to lighter ones. On the other hand, if we move with sufficient velocity we can maintain a balance between falling and rising, as does, for example, the moon in orbiting the earth or the earth in orbiting the sun. The moon is always falling toward the earth even as the earth is always falling toward the sun. Yet the momentum of the moon's physical mass maintains its orbit around the earth and the earth's mass maintains its orbit around the sun. Since we move with the earth, we are, as it were, always falling. It is all very natural.[12]

The Old Testament tells of the origin of humankind and its fall from grace. God created Adam because She felt the world She had just created was incomplete without a sentient participant. God created Eve as a companion to Adam because She felt his species was incomplete without a partner of opposite sensibility. Both were placed in the verdant Garden of Eden, surrounded by all kinds of vegetation, and were given dominion over all creatures (see fig. 4.1). In the middle of the garden stood two dominant trees: the Tree of Life and the Tree of the Knowledge of Good and Evil. Adam and Eve were told that all trees were available to them except for the Tree of the Knowledge of Good and Evil; its fruit was poison and would cause death.

---

12 Cf. Jack Cohen and Ian Stewart, *The Collapse of Chaos: Discovering Simplicity in a Complex World* (New York: Penguin, 1994): 13-14.

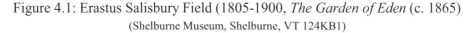

Figure 4.1: Erastus Salisbury Field (1805-1900, *The Garden of Eden* (c. 1865)
(Shelburne Museum, Shelburne, VT 124KB1)

Of all the creatures God had created, the snake was the most cunning. It seduced Eve – and indirectly Adam – to eat of the forbidden fruit, having persuaded her that she would become like God rather than be poisoned and die. The fruit of the tree, the snake suggested, would open her eyes, making her as knowledgeable and insightful as the deity ("sicut erit deus"). She would be able to distinguish between good and evil. Having eaten of the fruit, Eve convinced Adam to follow suit. And sure enough, so Holy Writ tells us, when both had partaken of the fruit, they saw that they were naked. God's wrath was swift in coming: the couple was banished from the well-ordered Garden of Eden and exiled to the barren spaces untouched by peace and harmony.

The tale is straightforward and lucid, the message clear: humankind sinned against the will of God and is condemned to a life of toil and discord as a result. However, upon a closer look the Myth of the Expulsion contains several interesting levels of meaning, which have been fascinatingly elucidated by Martin Buber in his slim volume, *Images of Good and Evil*.[13] Ostensibly metaphors, the Tree of Life

13 Martin Buber, *Images of Good and Evil*, trans. by Michael Bullock (London: Routledge and

and the Tree of Knowledge, which dominate the Garden, might symbolize self-regulatory biological processes on the one hand and moral and mental development on the other. Curiously, they exist side by side as if to say that they are co-evolutionary, that the dualism is complementary, much like Adam and Eve themselves complement one another. The crowns of the trees above the surface are as complex as the root systems below. The forbidden fruit of the Tree of Knowledge causes the founders of the human race to become aware of the fact that they, too, partake of the subsurface and suprasurface dimensions of existence. Of course, the fruit is also poisonous in the sense that it alters the steady state in which they had hitherto existed. The knowledge gained leads to *self*-awareness and disequilibrium. They are seduced by a snake that was at home outside the walls of Paradise rather than within, thus representing a fallen angel. The snake offers a different perspective, that of an outsider, over whom Adam and Eve have no dominion. The result of the action is Adam and Eve's loss of innocence and of their oneness with their environment, a loss prompted by the introduction of the ability to see a reality different from the one they lived. With the further development of life beyond the walls of the Garden of Eden, that initial bifurcation multiplied rapidly and repeatedly, leading to the Tower of Babel. That single act of disobedience made diversity possible. And diversity breeds diversity. Within the Garden of Eden – a subcritical state, to adopt Stuart Kauffman's terminology – the serpent, also functioning as a phallic symbol, is not the object of aversion for Eve that it would become for her in her fallen state.[14] Ignorance *is* bliss. The catalyst of movement in the realm of knowledge and discernment brought on by the forbidden fruit transforms the subcritical state of Eden into the supracritical state of life beyond the garden walls.

Thus, from the very start we have a fusion in human perception of sexuality, growing self-consciousness, the desire to be godlike, and the onset of chaos. The overall sequence of states of being is striking: chaos – the paradise of ordered relations – return to chaos. One cannot help but wonder whether the Garden of Eden, which seems to be situated at the edge of chaos, is a symbol of intermittence,

---

Kegan Paul, 1952), esp. chaps 1 and 2.

14 Stuart Kauffman, *At Home in the Universe* (New York: Oxford University Press, 1995), 114–16; Edward O. Wilson, *Consilience: The Unity of Knowledge* (New York: Alfred E. Knopf, 1998), argues that human beings possess an innate aversion to snakes (79–80). Snake aversion in Christian mythology apparently begins only after the expulsion. Christ associated not only the serpent but also the scorpion with evil. St. Luke tells us: "Now the seventy-two returned with joy, saying, 'Lord, even the devils are subject to us in thy name.' But he said to them, 'I was watching Satan fall as lightning from heaven. Behold I have given you power to tread upon serpents and scorpions, and over all the might of the enemy; and nothing shall hurt you" (Luke 10:17–19). Serpents and scorpions play a major role in literary works.

of the state of nonbirth. Is Eden the womb of the first stirring of individuation, the prerequisite for self-awareness, rather than the goal finally achieved? (This question will return in our later discussion of *The Tin Drum*.) The amorphous state of original chaos is interrupted by the nurturing Garden of Eden. But the Garden also contains the seed of individuated consciousness, which ultimately bears full fruit with the eating of the Tree of Knowledge of Good and Evil and the expulsion back into uncultivated territories. The cunning snake of primordial urges penetrates the host cell of willing accommodation and brings about a symbiotic relationship between originally alien organisms (see chapter 1). It thereby enables a new mode of existence, one that lends fullness to human nature. That nature is marked in particular by consciousness. Expelled from Paradise, Adam and Eve's destiny is to struggle through the multivalent possibilities for development outside Eden in an effort presumed to lead back to the well-tempered life in the wholeness of God. That way, however, is blocked. The path leads forward to ever greater complexity. The chaotic bifurcations of the roots and branches of both The Tree of Life and the Tree of Knowledge resonate with one another in telling fashion from the outset. In order to know the good, it must be contrasted with something to set it apart. In antiquity God was conceived of in terms of an immense mass distributed throughout the universe. In late antiquity Augustine initially adopted this notion of the Divine, but opposed evil to it as a similarly autonomous substance, albeit entirely inferior to the Divine substance. If we cannot conceive of nothing, how can we define evil as nothingness and God as something? (Goethe had problems with this particular contrast, as we will see in *Faust*.) A way out of the dilemma is to speak in terms of relationships, community, and positionality. Crawling with its belly on the earth, the lowly snake would appear to be thoroughly "grounded." As such it would suggest an appropriate contrast to the loftiness of God.

Consequently, if by evil we mean opposition to the divine, the serpent appears as a symbol of evil. Although the phallic function remains central, the snake is also more than a signifier of sexual urges so natural in the real world, indeed, without which humankind could not propagate.[15] As an extremely flexible, even graceful creature, capable of assuming various nonangular geometric shapes, it might even be a stand-in for the topology of nature itself. Especially salient is the serpent's ability to fold into itself. From the straight line of extension, it can transform itself into the wavy line of motion, and ultimately enfold itself in the tightest of spaces. This malleability and movement represent important, added dimensions of evil. In this scheme of things the serpent signifies not only sexuality but, more importantly, the disequilibrious state of the material realm; its essential tension is radically

15 Sexuality is so pervasive in nature because it provides for diversity and is linked to a survival strategy (Rolston, *Genes* 96–100).

different from the state of divine balance. In this sense, the serpent-theme connotes not only a threat (as in Wilson's view) but also an irresistible lure. The dynamic interplay of bifurcation and period doubling of life in nature make it almost impossible to fulfill the divine exhortation to return to undividedness. Hence, eating the forbidden fruit marks the beginning of self-awareness, diversity, and ultimately also potentiality. From simplicity complexity arises. The process is godly. To speak with Holmes Rolston, "God created Earth as the home (the ecosystem) that could produce all those myriad kinds. [...] There is nothing ungodly about a world in which every living thing defends its intrinsic value, those brought forth from its own perspective, at the same time that it shares, or distributes, these to offspring, to others, in the ongoing evolutionary narrative" (Rolston 52–53). In human terms, the evolutionary narrative began with Adam and Eve's mythical fall to the ground.

3. Evil According to Leibniz and Spinoza

Defining evil in the modern world is every bit as problematic as defining chaos. According to Gottfried Wilhelm Leibniz (1646–1716), who is best known for his concepts of plenitude and the compossible, there is, in fact, no absolute principle of evil *(principium maleficum)*. Standing in the tradition of St. Augustine, Leibniz sees in evil rather the absence of the good. However, he differs in defining absence as the nonpresence or nonmanifestation of the good. For instance, shade is the absence of light, cold the absence of heat. The presence of evil in the "best of all possible" worlds is essentially the absence of the discernible good. The greatest good is God, and God for Leibniz is the *Urmonade* of pure, goalless activity. Evil denotes distance from the active principle of the all-inclusive spirit; it possesses none of the encumbrances of corporeal substance or of the urge inherent in the monads toward self-preservation (= *prima materia*). Like so many energy pulses, all monads are related to the *Urmonade* or original "Strahlkraft."[16] Moreover, Leibniz's view that the universe allows for no empty space intuitively anticipates the notion in contemporary elementary particle theory that invisible neutrinos constitute 90 percent of the mass of the universe and are found everywhere. Placed in this context, evil is then not something in and of itself, although it is associated

16 Gottfried Wilhelm Leibniz, *Monadologie*, translated with an introduction and commentary by Hermann Glockner (Stuttgart: Reclam, 1963): "Man kann sich die Monaden als *Strahlkräfte* vorstellen, welche von einem immateriellen und schlechterdings einfachen Kern ausgehen und deren Wirkung sich – dem Kontinuitätsprinzip entsprechend – allenthalben durch den ganzen Kosmos erstreckt. Überall im Kosmos ist ein solcher Kern oder Weltmittelpunkt; denn es ist alles lückenlos mit einfachen Substanzen 'angefüllt'" (56).

with the bonds of physical being and identified with distance from the perfect inclusive activity of the *Urmonade*. Evil is the nonpresence of the actual whole in the individual part, even though the single phenomenon might give evidence of the whole. But that is not the same as saying that the world is evil. It is actually a matter of folds, "an infinity of converging series, capable of being extended into each other, around unique points."[17]

In another respect Leibniz seems to suggest that the principles of activity and passivity assume the roles of good and evil. Evil denotes for him above all the divergent force of stasis and the lack of convergent dynamic interplay as when, e.g., a monad in a more passive phase is overshadowed by another, more active one. God as perfect activity sees only the active modes.[18] For this reason Leibniz contends that there is no need for a principle of evil; it is all a matter of relationships.[19] In the *Théodicée* (1710) he writes, for instance: "Evil requires it [*a principium maleficum*] just as little as, nay even less than, cold and darkness: there is no primal coldness and no principle of darkness. Evil derives from privation alone."[20] Loss of energy equates to loss of the good. Enhancement of power translates into greater perfection. To be sure, Leibniz was not thinking in terms of what Nietzsche was later to label will to power, for Leibniz upheld the integrative

---

17 Gilles Deleuze, *The Fold: Leibniz and the Baroque*, trans. by Tom Conley (Minneapolis: University of Minnesota Press, 1993), 60. By emphasizing the folds of space, time, and movement inherent in Leibniz's monadology, Deleuze recaptures the theory of monads as a model for expression in twentieth-century aesthetics. Ernst Cassirer, *The Philosophy of the Enlightenment*, trans. by Fritz C. A. Koelln and James P. Pettegrove (Boston: Beacon P, 1955), and Arthur O. Lovejoy, *The Great Chain of Being: A Study in the History of an Idea* (New York: Harper and Row, 1960), long ago reviewed in detail the progressive quality of Leibniz's ideas on form and function in terms of science and aesthetics. These works were originally published in 1932 and 1936, respectively.

18 See Glockner's commentary, *Monadologie*, 40–42 and 56-57. In both passages (to "Lehrsätze" #8 and #49) Glockner discusses the principles of activity and passivity. While the focus of the first is on the qualitative qualities of the monads, which are marked by *vis inertiae* ("natürliche Trägheit") and "Selbst*erhaltung*" (= *prima materia*), the focus of the second is on the source of the "Strahlkräfte" immanent in the imperfect monads. God is the source of this active principle: "Gott, der ohne Schranken das Ganze der unendlichen Monadenwelt übersieht und durchstrahlt, vermag [...] im Grunde nur Vollkommenes zu erblicken" (57). Thus, the divine is discernible in the dynamic drive but absent in passive states, which are consequently imperfect.

19 Leibniz would have been pleased to learn that modern science is emphasizing the importance of relations in determining reality; see, e.g., Prigogine and Stengers, *Order out of Chaos* (1984) and Smoot and Davidson, *Wrinkles of Time* (1993).

20 *Théodicée* # 153: "Das Übel bedarf dessen [*principium maleficum*] ebensowenig, ja noch weniger als Kälte und Finsternis: es gibt kein primum frigidum und kein Prinzip der Finsternis. *Das Übel stammt allein aus Privation* (= *Kraftberaubung*). See Glockner, *Monadologie*, 53, note 41. The original French has "privation" for "Kraftberaubung" to connote loss of energy.

or convergent tendency within the agonal mix of life. Rather, he was drawing upon Thomistic traditions with roots in the fourth century AD. But the Saxon can nevertheless be seen as emphasizing a dimension of existence that proved useful to his later compatriot. Lovejoy, following in the footsteps of Leibniz, acknowledged the principle of plenitude as being propitious because it maximized diversity (*Chain* 180–81). Rolston, coming from a different tradition and unaware of either Leibniz or Lovejoy, similarly highlights the importance of "possibility spaces" and of relationships for "interaction phenomena" (*Genes* 350, 354). For our present purposes, let it suffice to suggest that Adam and Eve's fall entailed more good than evil. In exile, where the agon dominates, they are energized by the constant quest for resolution, whereas in Paradise the resolution of tension translated into stasis at worst, a steady state at best. Either way, absolutely ordered conditions are not good. (For that reason, I cannot agree with Bonting's essential thesis in his *Chaos Theology*.)

Benedictus de Spinoza (1632–77) had addressed this very concept of dynamic tension by aligning the essence of evil with inadequacy, incompleteness, and all that which we lack as individual beings. Obviously, without consciousness we – like Adam and Eve – would not know that we are (metaphorically speaking) naked. Spinoza's clearest formulation of the nature of evil is found in his correspondence with the Dutch merchant Willem van Blyenbergh, written between December 1664 and June 1665. Blyenbergh had initiated the exchange by inquiring after the philosopher's thoughts on the nature of evil. Spinoza developed his notion of evil in counterpoint to the concept of the whole, seeing evil not as an essence but as an attribute of relationships. Thus, Spinoza refused to interpret evil as a matter of the will. Especially important in this regard is his letter of January 5, 1665, in which he defines the evil ("das Böse") inherent in Adam and Eve's fall from Paradise as the loss of a state of greater perfection.[21]

Obviously, this definition is premised on our notion of what constitutes perfection. It is noteworthy that Spinoza writes "more perfect" ("vollkommeneren") because the comparative form implies a series of *relative* states of perfection. In fact, we develop a sense of perfection via comparisons and ever more refined differentiations. Ultimately, then, even our idea of perfection is relative. Thus, Spinoza concludes that evil, that is, sin, is merely a sign of imperfection and "does not constitute something which expresses a [concrete] reality."[22] Enhanced con-

21 Benedictus de Spinoza, *Briefwechsel, Sämtliche Werke*, in seven volumes and one supplemental volume, ed. by Manfred Walther, trans. by Carl Gebhardt (Hamburg: Meiner, 1989), 6:81 (letter # 19): "denn das Böse, das darin lag [in his decision to partake of the fruit], war ja nur das Beraubtsein eines vollkommeneren Zustandes, den Adam wegen jener Handlung verlieren mußte."

22 Spinoza, *Briefwechsel*: "so folgt klar daraus, daß die Sünden, da sie nur Unvollkommenheiten anzeigen, nicht in etwas bestehen können, was eine Realität ausdrückt" (6:80).

sciousness is the path toward unfolding the potential reality. Placed in this light, evil would seem to connote a nonexistence or a state of not yet realized actuality. Adam's (and Eve's) eating of the forbidden fruit could then be seen, Spinoza suggests, as being neither evil nor contrary to the will of God. Partaking of the apple was ultimately an expression of what was yet to come. According to Spinoza, the consciousness of inadequacy appears as such only to the mind of man not to that of God (6:82). To God all things are perfect and full

In other ways, Spinoza's argument seems to anticipate the fundamental notion of the holographic universe in modern science. To be sure, he ascribes beauty and order, ugliness and chaos to functions of human perception rather than to operations of nature.[23] Yet while granting that he cannot judge the exact mechanism which unites the parts of nature into a harmonious whole, he thinks (here in agreement with Leibniz) that they result from agonal coordination of conflicting forces "so that they will exist as little as possible in contradiction to one another" ("daß sie so wenig wie möglich im Gegensatz zueinander stehen"; 6:146).

To illustrate his point, Spinoza cites the example of the human circulatory system ("das Blut"). If a tiny virus ("Würmchen") living in the circulatory system were endowed with the powers of sight and discernment, it would be able to observe how the individual corpuscles interact in the turbulent flow coursing through our veins. Living within this closed system without knowledge of any external forces impacting upon the movement within the veins, the microbe would consider each blood cell encountered to be a whole unto itself, without connection to anything else except to its own movement. Each opposing force, each resistant body would appear always to be a self-sufficient unit. We know, however, that the circulatory system is enclosed in a larger, more complex interactive system. In just the same way, the part of the universe that humans inhabit and chart is only a part of a larger context.[24] Its modifications ("Veränderungen"), moreover, are limitless

---

23 Spinoza, *Briefwechsel*: "Doch will ich Sie zuvor darauf aufmerksam machen, daß ich der Natur keine Schönheit und Häßlichkeit, Ordnung und Verwirrung zuschreibe. Denn die Dinge können nur im Hinblick auf unser Vorstellungsvermögen schön oder häßlich, geordnet oder verwirrt genannt werden" (6:146).

24 Spinoza, *Briefwechsel*: "Da wir nun alle natürlichen Körper ebenso begreifen können und sollen, wie wir hier das Blut begriffen haben – alle Körper sind ja von anderen umgeben und werden von ihnen wechselseitig auf gewisse und bestimmte Art zum Existieren und Wirken bestimmt, unter ständiger Beibehaltung desselben Verhältnisses von Bewegung und Ruhe in allem zugleich, d.h. im ganzen Universum – so folgt daraus, daß jeder Körper, sofern er als durch einen bestimmten Modus modificiert existiert, als ein Teil des gesamten Universums betrachtet werden muß, daß er mit seinem Ganzen in Übereinstimmung und mit den übrigen Teilen im Zusammenhang steht" (6:147–48). [Because we can comprehend all natural bodies in the same manner as we have here understood the circulatory system ("das Blut") – all bodies are surrounded by others and are determined alternately by them to exist and interact in a certain and definite manner without loss

(6:148). And because the nature of the divine essence is infinite, each of the individual parts is integrated in the wholeness of that one undivided presence. It, in turn, could not be what it is without them.

Then, too, the intellect is part and parcel of nature. The human mind, limitless in its capacity for thought, can bring about change in the physical realm.[25] Consequently, there appears to be no hard and fast distinction between mind and matter for Spinoza. Because of these limitless possibilities of thought and matter, the proper perspective for attaining the level of perfection is the most inclusive perspective possible: not only horizontally, that is, outward in all directions, but also vertically along the scale from the very small to the very large.

Particularly striking about Spinoza's relational explanation of the nature of evil is just how modern his ideas were. Drawing upon the scientific advances of his day and encouraged by his own practical experiences as a lens maker, Spinoza assigned perspective a central role in his practical philosophy. Because of perspectivism he argued for the relativity of such fundamental valuations as good and evil, order and chaos in an age otherwise known for its dogmatism. Such value pairs were not oppositional by nature; they were actually complementary. In short, Spinoza emphasized very early on "a new feeling for proportion of compatibilities at any given time, of that which is balanced, that which is appropriate for us and everything else."[26] The traditional virtue of modesty gave way to propriety, that is, the hegemony of social decorum was challenged by a new consciousness of ecological appropriateness.

Obviously, Spinoza proposed some heretical ideas in his time.[27] Primary among them is that there is but a single substance with an infinite number of attributes and

---

of their own alternation of movement and rest in all things simultaneously; that is, throughout the entire universe – it follows therefrom that every body must be seen as part of the total universe inasmuch as it exists in a definite modified state. It follows, moreover, that it is unified in itself and is interconnected with the other parts as well.]

25 Spinoza, *Briefwechsel*: "Was aber den menschlichen Geist angeht, so halte ich ihn ebenfalls für einen Teil der Natur. Ich nehme nämlich an, daß es in der Natur auch eine unendliche Möglichkeit des Denkens gibt" (6:148).

26 Manon Andreas-Grisebach, *Eine Ethik für die Natur* (Zurich: Ammann Verlag, 1991), 218. Andreas-Grisebach draws the ultimate consequences of the ethical relativism initiated by Spinoza. In her study the author emphasizes throughout the "rightful" place of humankind within the total context of existence, thereby decentering the previously anthropocentric universe. In this "ethic of nature" at large, the virtue of modesty required initially by God gives way to the virtue of propriety ("Angemessenheit") as required by the system (219).

27 Because of his radical views, Spinoza was excommunicated in 1656. For an evaluation of his life and times, see Wilhelm Schmidt-Biggemann, *Baruch de Spinoza 1677–1977. Werk und Wirkung*, Ausstellungskataloge der Herzog August Bibliothek, Nr. 19 (Wolfenbüttel: Felix Meiner, 1977), and Gilles Deleuze, *Spinoza: Philosophie pratique*, 2nd expanded ed. (Paris: les Éditions de Minuit, 1981).

that all creatures are modifications of this substance, that is, they are modes of its existence. All of these concepts are summed up in the now famous formulation *deus sive natura*. Because of this identification of nature with divine self-regulation, so asserted by Spinoza in the twenty-ninth proposition of the *Ethik*, nature determines the manner in which all things exist and function; there is no room for accident.[28] By grounding ethics in social practice rather than in a transcendent essence, the *Ethik* opens up new territory. Whereas morality represents a judgmental system based on God's pronouncement to Adam and Eve to obey His command, ethics marks a reversal of that judgmental system. Adam and Eve elect to know things on their own, that is, to make their own judgments. It thus signifies a re-evaluation of values usually associated with Friedrich Nietzsche (Deleuze, *Spinoza* 27–43).

Key in all this is Spinoza's dualistic view of nature: it has a created and a creative side, a passive and an active dimension. Active nature ("naturende Natur") reveals "attributes of substance which express an eternal and infinite essence" ("Attribute der Substanz, die ewige und unendliche Wesenheit ausdrücken" (*Ethik* 2:32). Nature as process is self-regulative, by virtue of which the modi of existence are made possible. Nature as product ("genaturte Natur") designates for Spinoza, on the other hand, "the total sum of the modes of Divine attributes" ("die gesamten Modi der Attribute Gottes"; *Ethik* 2:32). Attributes, by the way, are those qualities that we comprehend rationally through differentiation (2:3). The manner of existence is dependent upon the immanence of God.

Because of their link via the intellect with the deity, rational beings are, therefore, simultaneously finite and infinite. However, the more a thinking being is able to use its powers of discernment to recognize more and more of the attributes of God and of nature, the more complete and therefore the more real it is.[29] Earlier Spinoza had declared that "the more reality or being a thing possesses, the more attributes it will have."[30] In other words, heightened consciousness leads to heightened reality; combined, they would seem to translate into a supracritical state of more concentrated perfection. Thus, God did not err in giving Adam and Eve an

---

28 Baruch de Spinoza, *Die Ethik nach geometrischer Methode dargestellt, Sämtliche Werke* in seven volumes and one supplemental volume, translation, notes, and index by Otto Baensch, introduction by Rudolf Schottlaender, vol. 2 (Hamburg: Felix Meiner, 1989): "In der Natur der Dinge gibt es nicht Zufälliges, sondern alles ist kraft der Notwendigkeit der göttlichen Natur bestimmt, auf gewisse Weise zu existieren und zu wirken" (2:31). Hereafter the *Ethik* is cited by volume and page number.

29 Spinoza, *Ethik*: "je mehreres ein denkendes Wesen denken kann, desto mehr Realität oder Vollkommenheit enthält es" (2:51).

30 Spinoza, *Ethik*: "Je mehr Realität oder Sein jedes Ding hat, um so mehr Attribute kommen ihm zu" (2:10).

imperfect will, for humankind's nature is to seek to know the mind of God, not actually to divine it. Within the overall scheme of things, the human will is thus exactly as it should be. Spinoza draws an analogy to the difference between a circle and a sphere to underscore his point: they are two different things, somewhat similar in kind, but not self-same (6:83). It would be ludicrous to blame the circle for being something it is not. Each rung of enhanced consciousness marks greater perfection.

In part 4 of the *Ethik*, Spinoza explicates the pleasure principle of good and evil. More accurately, Spinoza specifically speaks of good and bad ("gut und schlecht") rather than good and evil ("gut und böse") in keeping with his shift in focus away from transcendentally grounded morality to social practice. The good is defined more specifically as that which affords pleasure and advances humankind toward the ideal model of human nature ("das Musterbild der menschlichen Natur"; 2:189). Humankind, he specifically notes, is part and parcel of nature in general; humans do not function according to a separate set of laws (2:194). As active beings, their ultimate purpose is to be active (2:118). He thus "Begierde" with the essence of being human. "Begierde" can be translated as longing or desire, which in turn is related to instinct and the general impulse to movement (cf. Leibniz, *Monadologie*, end).[31] In short, longing is the impulse to act and to be active. Any action that enhances that basic desire for movement might be construed as being good, that is, as long as it does not lead to a sapping of one's life energies (as Leibniz comments). Consequently, Spinoza concludes that good is that which enhances our range of activity ("Wirkungskraft"), while bad is that which inhibits or restricts this field of tension. Coupled with the feelings of pleasure and displeasure – which are individually determined (*Ethik* 2:206–09) – this notion of good and bad seems to prefigure Nietzsche's concept of the will to power.[32]

In Spinoza's system of ethics, we should emphasize that no act is ipso facto good or bad. Depending upon the circumstances, it can be either. Priority is always accorded the active principle in nature and in humankind. Deleuze remarks

31 Spinoza, *Ethik*: "Hier verstehe ich also unter dem Wort Begierde jedes Streben, jeden Drang, jeden Trieb, jede Wollung, die ja nach dem verschiedenen Zustand desselben Menschen verschieden und nicht selten einander dergestalt entgegengesetzt sind, daß der Mensch nach verschiedenen Richtungen hingezogen wird und nicht weiß, wohin er sich wenden soll" (2:168).

32 Spinoza, *Ethik*: "Wir nennen [...] gut oder schlecht das, was der Erhaltung unseres Seins nützt oder zuwider ist, das heißt [...] das, was unsere Wirkungskraft vermehrt oder vermindert, fördert oder hemmt" (2:197). Deleuze comments: "Tout ce qui est mauvais se mesure donc à la diminution de la puissance d'agir (tristesse-haine), tout ce qui est bon, à l'augmentation de cette même puissance (joie-amour)" (*Spinoza* 75–76). For his part, Deleuze considers Spinoza to have anticipated three main concerns of Nietzsche: the role of consciousness, the relativity of value, and the role of the instincts or passions (Deleuze, *Spinoza* 27; cf. also 32–33, 40, 59–60).

insightfully that being good is "a matter of dynamics, of capacity, of the constitution of power" ("Car la bonté est affaire de dynamisme, de puissance, et de composition de puissance"; Deleuze 35). Practical philosophy for Spinoza, then, as it was later for Nietzsche, amounted to a way of life, a "mode d'existence." The more intensively one is capable of living, the higher the quality of one's existence and thus the more perfect the existence.[33] Life is then a test and experiment of the limits of one's capacity for life rather than a preliminary state of existence intended to purify the individual, making her worthy of eternal reward for a life well lived. Life is its own reward. In light of all this, Adam and Eve's fall from grace actually represents an opening up of the possibility for real perfection because they were enabled to recover in a conscious way that which they felt they had lost. Before their fall from grace, they could not fully appreciate what they had because it had been passively endowed. Not having been consciously earned, the perfection of Eden was not a real presence in the first couple's minds. It was a false perfection. Perfection in the total economy of things depends upon challenge, hard work, and diversification.

4. Kant on Moral Character

Like his predecessors, Immanuel Kant (1724–1804) reflected upon the origin of the universe and humankind's place in it. Of central concern here are his notions of evil, chaos, order, and the implied agonistic relationship among them. These ideas occupied his attention from early on in his career to its very end. Heavily indebted to binary thinking, he nevertheless pushed dialectical reason to its limits, arriving at an essentially holistic world-view. While he still privileged an anthropomorphic perspective, an unmistakable tension between his view of the operations of physical nature and his interpretation of the role of evil in the world became evident. Particularly modern is his vision of the ceaseless regenerative powers of a complex universe that exists on the edge of chaos. It is marked by movement caused by the powers of attraction and repulsion at every level from planetary interactions to particle physics, with humankind being embedded in all this movement. While he could not possibly have known about strong and weak electromagnetic forces, they are prefigured in his conception of the self-organization of the universe.

In her study of Kant's moral character and radical evil, G. Felicitas Munzel

---

33 Deleuze, *Spinoza*, avers: "Telle est donc la différence finale de l'homme bon et de l'homme mauvais: l'homme bon, ou fort, est celui qui existe si pleinement ou si intensément qu'il a conquis de son vivant l'éternité, et que la mort, toujours extensive, toujours extérieure, est peu de chose pour lui (59).

departs from a deontological view of Kant's formalism as rule driven. In doing so, she establishes several principles regarding Kant's endeavor to define moral character in relation to freedom, predetermination, and history:

- the centrality of action,
- virtue as adaptability,
- good and evil as complementary and
- progress as a collective movement toward the complete development of all human propensities.[34]

Munzel rightly underscores Kant's own differentiation between moral evil in the sense of "das Böse" and evil in the sense of "das Übel" as the ills of the human condition. While the former is squarely situated within the framework of human autonomy, the latter is located in physical nature. However, by foregrounding the self-regulatory forces of nature and focusing more intently on Kant's view of the interconnection between human nature and external nature, as well as on the agonistic context of that relationship, I think that I can tease out of Munzel's many illuminating insights an even more radicalized notion of evil. Key is the notion that progress is not as linear as Munzel sometimes seems to suggest, even when she states that regression is a constant companion to any progression (Munzel 138, 140, 167–68.). She is still thinking in terms of the straight line, which can be traced genealogically backward as well as forward into the future (171–72). Nor is there a simple binary struggle that promotes or hinders the development of human potential, as tempting as that conception is (143). Even the "hindering" can be promotion. The tension, rather, is agonistic. Thus, a nonlinear, serpentine movement seems more appropriate to describe progress in Kantian philosophy than the straight line. Munzel's foregrounding of the anthropocentric principle explains the difference in our accounts of evil. For example, she is not concerned with chaos or the complex workings of matter. Actually, neither is Kant. But he does juxtapose his views on evil and his thoughts on chaos, and that encounter is what I wish to explore.

In "Über das Misslingen aller philosophischen Versuche in der Theodizee" (On the Failure of All Philosophical Attempts at Theodicy, 1775), Kant defines evil in the sense of sin ("das Böse") as that which is at moral cross-purposes with the overall development of human nature ("das moralische Zweckwidrige"), whereas evil in the sense of physical harm ("das Übel") is characterized as pain. In this latter sense, evil is deleterious to optimal activity and adaptability. A third kind of evil, which we will not discuss here, is labeled the incongruity ("Mißverhältnis")

---

34 G. Felicitas Munzel, *Kant's Conception of Moral Character: The 'Critical' Link of Morality, Anthropology and Reflective Judgment* (Chicago: University of Chicago Press, 1999), chap. 3: "Character and Radical Evil," esp. 179–83.

between crime and punishment in the world.[35] Moral evil, he later explained in "Zum ewigen Frieden" (Perpetual Peace, 1795), is by nature negative and self-destructive so that eventually it will make way for the good that is innate in the unfolding of humankind and that equates to the actual purpose of coevolutionary forces in the physical and moral worlds.[36]

This is also the central topic of his treatise *Die Religion innerhalb der Grenzen der* bloßen *Vernunft* (Religion Within the Limits of Mere Reason, 1793). To be sure, this development is by no means linear. In his *Anthropologie in pragmatischer Hinsicht* (Anthropology from a Pragmatic Point of View, 1798), Kant spoke of the human being's constant deviation from his destiny ("beständiger Abweichung von seiner Bestimmung") and of the fragmentary nature of humankind's progress in the sciences.[37] Since nature intends for humankind to evolve into an ever more perfect state and since evil is transitory, admitting of no substance ("Charakter"), evil has no chance of ultimate predominance in Kant's conception of an emergent universe.[38] Good and evil are nonetheless coexistent in humankind.[39] On an even deeper level, evil seems to be the negative source from which the good is to arise. Toward the end of his *Anthropology*, Kant argued that nature in its wisdom has ordained that the human species (not the individual human) would one day "through its own activity bring about the development of the good *from evil*."[40] In *Religion within the Limits of Mere Reason*, Kant had explicitly stated that evil is inherently aligned with the moral autonomy of human beings, not with their physical natures (7:678–79), calling it the "actual" evil ("das eigentlich Böse"; 7:676). There is no propensity for evil ("Hang zum Bösen") in physical nature, only in the moral realm. Perpetuating the notion of a binary opposition between body and spirit, Kant posited a struggle between these two entities for dominance. (For him they are apparently distinct and separate.) The development from evil to good in the moral sphere is marked by a shift in perspective from the private and

35 Immanuel Kant, "Über das Misslingen aller philosophischen Versuche in der Theodizee," in *Werke in zehn Bänden*, ed. by Wilhelm Weischedel (Darmstadt: Wissenschaftliche Buchgesellschaft, 1983), 9:106–7.

36 Kant, "Zum ewigen Frieden. Anhang," in *Werke*, 9:242.

37 Kant, *Anthropologie in pragmatischer Hinsicht*, in *Werke*, 10:678, 680.

38 Munzel describes character in the absolute Kantian sense as being a rare occurrence. The realization of character is linked to a "state of comportment of mind" ("Denkungsart"), which is in turn linked to the concept of virtue. Virtue, etymologically related to "fitness" and "aptitude," is essentially a dynamic principle. In effect, it is "self-control characterizing the human processes of thinking, specifically of choice-making or the subjectively practical use of reason in human moral life." Moreover, character is moral fortitude in fulfilling one's duty (*Character* 163–66).

39 Kant, *Der Streit der Fakultäten*, *Werke* 9:354.

40 Kant, *Anthropologie*: "durch ihre eigene Tätigkeit die Entwickelung des Guten *aus dem Bösen* dereinst zu Stande zu bringen" (*Werke* 10:684; my emphasis).

individual ("Privatsinn") to the collective ("Gemeinsinn"). This shift can of course be cited, as Joan Copjek does, to explain current notions of radical evil as rooted in human volition. However, the shift could also translate into the contemporary insistence upon the wider concept of community and coevolution in scientific paradigms – wider in the sense of embedding the human person in her physical and biological environment. To be sure, Kant himself did not envision a coevolutionary process between the laws of nature and moral law.

For that reason, evil arose for him only after the fall from Paradise. In *Religion* Kant claimed that humankind has a natural aptitude for the good ("Keim des Guten," "Anlage zum Guten") that had never been lost, indeed, could not be lost (7:687, 695–96). However, this predisposition is present only in embryonic form. Like the higher-order monads in Leibniz's system, it must be nurtured to achieve full realization. Since there is no basis for evil in the physical dimension of human nature itself, its cause is subsequent to moral life. Yet Friedrich Theodor Rink, who transcribed Kant's lectures on pedagogy, suggests that evil is associated with the disordered or "chaotic" state of nature (which Kant labeled "zweckfrei" or "purposeless"). In the introduction to *On Pedagogy* (1803), Rink writes: "The aptitudes ("Keime"), which lie in humankind, must be cultivated more and more. The causes of evil, then, are not located in human aptitudes. The real source of evil is when nature is not ordered by laws. In humankind we find only aptitudes for the good."[41] While acknowledging that Kant is being interpreted here by a former student, we have some justification for associating evil not only in the sense of "das Übel" but also in the meaning of "das Böse" with chaos in Kant's thinking. If one focuses on Kant's use of the term "Hang" to refer specifically to "das Böse," there would not seem to be much justification for linking his thoughts on external and human nature.

Yet in his famous essay "What Is Enlightenment?" Kant clearly used "Hang" in connection with the good. The conclusion of that piece is emphatic in its insistence that the human being is more than a mere machine. Rather she is endowed with an innate "aptitude" for unencumbered, critical thinking ("Hang und Beruf zum freien Denken"). In fact, the development of that calling is both an individual and a collective process. No monarch, no other human being need fear adverse cones-quences for himself or the state. Kant opined:

---

41 Kant, "*Über Pädagogik*: "Die Keime, die im Menschen liegen, müssen immer mehr entwickelt werden. Denn die Gründe zum Bösen findet man nicht in den Naturanlagen des Menschen. Das nur ist die Ursache des Bösen, daß die Natur nicht unter Regeln gebracht wird. Im Menschen liegen nur Keime zum Guten" (*Werke* 10:705). I translate "Keime" as aptitudes rather than as germs or nuclei in order to underscore the potential for the development of innate predispositions.

When nature has developed the seed under this hard shell for which she cares most attentively – namely, the inclination and the calling to *think freely* – this gradually influences the thinking of the people (who thereby become more and more capable of *acting freely*) and, finally, it will even affect the principles of government, which finds it advantageous to treat the human being, who is now *more than a machine*, according to its inherent dignity.

[Wenn denn die Natur unter dieser harten Hülle den Keim, für den sie am zärtlichsten sorgt, nämlich den Hang und Beruf zum freien Denken, ausgewickelt hat: so wirkt dieser allmählich zurück auf die Sinnesart des Volks (wodurch dieses der Freiheit zu handeln nach und nach fähiger wird), endlich auch sogar auf die Grundsätze der Regierung, die es ihr selbst zuträglich findet, den Menschen, der nun mehr als Maschine ist, seiner Würde gemäß zu behandeln.][42]

It could be that Kant was using a biological metaphor merely to explain moral and intellectual development. Yet the reference to the fundamental quality of the aptitude for the good of critical thinking is firmly rooted in the ways of external nature. The connection between human consciousness and internal biological developments appears to be manifestly present.

A half century earlier, in his "Universal Natural History and Theory of the Heavens" (1755), Kant had envisioned chaos as the disordered state of things at the beginning of the time before the self-organizational forces of attraction and repulsion began to draw matter and energy toward unseen centers to form and regulate interactively our solar system, the Milky Way, and countless other stellar systems.[43] In the wake of Newton, this conception is based on the distribution of matter throughout the whole of space and a tension of the whole held together by the underlying force of gravity. While one might be tempted to see in Kant's vision an anticipation of the late-twentieth-century notion of shaping forces at the edge of chaos, Kant's primordial state lacked the wrinkles of time. He averred:

Gravity is doubtless as universal a quality of matter as is the coexistence of substances in space bound together via mutual dependency. Or, to speak more clearly, attraction is just this universal connectivity, which conjoins the parts of nature in space. Consequently, the power of attraction extends throughout the whole projection of space, right down to the vast expanses of its own infinity.

[Die Anziehung ist ohne Zweifel eine eben so weit ausgedehnte Eigenschaft der Materie, als die Koexistenz, welche den Raum macht, indem sie die Substanzen durch gegenseitige Abhängigkeiten verbindet, oder, eigentlicher zu reden, die Anziehung ist eben diese allgemeine Beziehung, welche die Teile der Natur in einem Raume vereinigt: sie erstreckt sich also auf die ganze Ausdehnung desselben, bis in alle Weiten ihrer Unendlichkeit.][44]

---

42 Kant, "Beantwortung der Frage: was ist Aufklärung?" *Werke* 9:61). My translation.

43 Kant, "Allgemeine Naturgeschichte und Theorie des Himmels," *Werke* 1:232, 276–79, 328.

44 Kant, "Allgemeine Naturgeschichte," *Werke* 1:328. My translation.

At the beginning of time, this elementary attribute of existence was found throughout the universe and was without a predetermined design ("auch ohne Absicht auf ein System"; 1:275). Today, theoretical physicists speak of muons, which are involved in the exchange of energy between two or more elements, as the bonding agents in nuclei. In keeping with scientific thinking since Copernicus, Kant – the so-called Copernicus of philosophy – saw as the key to this development the energy inherent in matter, which causes movement and is itself a source of life ("eine Quelle des Lebens"; *Allgemeine Naturgeschichte* 1:276). The emergence of the universe is ongoing and without end in time or space, he argued (1:335). Periodic centers (as we would call them today) are formed and dissolved through forces of attraction and dispersion in an endless array of activity caused by the tension between chaos and order (1:341–42). We might want to see a corollary between Kant's concept of chaos and Spinoza's notion of *natura naturans*, between Kant's order and Spinoza's *natura naturata*, between Kant's conception of interconnectivity and Leibniz's view of monads as so many irreducible *centres* all related to the *Urmonade* or absolute *centre*.

The impetus for all this evolutionary movement was present within chaos itself before the self-organizational propensities of the universe became apparent. That is the only way Kant (like Leibniz before him) could explain a creative universe without interference from a Divine Being. To be sure, he did still retain the conception of an ultimate telos, God, as the creator of chaos from nothingness (1:275, 337). The Big Bang or the spontaneous emergence of something from nothing was as yet inconceivable. Nonetheless, the step from seeing God as external to nature to being internal in its dynamic, creative forces themselves had already been taken by Spinoza. The universe Kant described could do very nicely without a traditional concept of the Creator, if God were identified with the creative forces evident in nature itself.

Clear from all this is the complex interweaving of good and evil in the evolution of the universe and of humankind. Their opposition is only superficially binary. Activity is good; passivity is evil. And as Munzel and others have demonstrated, activity is at the core of Kant's anthropological conception. Indeed, "intense purposive activity" is just one side of the coin. The other is its open-endedness, despite its being teleologically directed. Because the goals of virtue-as-fitness for both the individual and the community are essentially utopian, moral striving requires an ever renewed "*active commitment* to moral ends for the development of individual virtue."[45] We would seem to have a reversal of good and evil as expressed in the

45 Thomas Auxter, *Kant's Moral Teleology* (Macon, GA: Mercer University Press, 1982), 169–72. J. B. Schneewind, *The Invention of Autonomy: A History of Modern Moral Philosophy* (Cambridge: Cambridge University Press, 1998), places Kant's moral thinking within its historical context

myth of Adam and Eve in Eden, where equilibrium was desirable, disequilibrium anathema. Strikingly, Kant defines the ideal of virtue precisely as a continuously creative, never mechanical enterprise: "[V]irtue is moral fortitude in the fulfilling of one's duty, which should never degrade to habit but rather emerge ever new and original from the conduct of thought" ("Denkungsart").[46] The view of the virtuous individual as being continuously wakeful and alert, always creating anew, never slipping into soporific habits, points forward to Nietzsche's reconceptualization at the end of the nineteenth century of the genuine free spirit, to his definition of energy quanta, and to his rendering of innovation as evil.

5. Nietzsche, Consciousness, and the Centrality of Design

In fact, Friedrich Nietzsche completes the redefinition of good and evil initiated in the seventeenth century. At the same time, he complicates it anew. Noteworthy first of all is his association of evil with abruptness and newness. "What is evil?" he once asked bluntly and responded just as bluntly: "accident, uncertainty, spontaneity."[47] Elsewhere he stated emphatically: "Innovation is in all cases evil" ("Das Neue ist unter allen Umständen das Böse"; Musarion 12:41). The self-assured, self-conscious individual he designated "the most evil of all" ("Der mächtigste Mensch, der Schaffende müßte der böseste sein"; Musarion 19:350). All three formulations revolve around the same point: newness is decisive, whether it is a matter of chance or of self-directed acts. In either case, it amounts to a drawing-into-life of latent potentialities or of making discernible virtual reality. In his literary estate is a reflection dating from spring 1888 upon the nature of good, bad, and happiness: "What is good? – Everything which enhances the feeling of power, the will to power, the power even in the human individual. What is bad? – Everything which comes from weakness. What is happiness? – The feeling that power has increased, that resistance has again been overcome."[48] The sentiment is

(which includes Spinoza and Leibniz). That is the clear strength of his study. However, Schneewind does not include the dimension of chaos in tracing notions of moral autonomy. See esp. 508–530.

46 Kant, *Anthropologie*: "Tugend ist die moralische Stärke in Befolgung seiner Pflicht, die niemals zur Gewohnheit werden, sondern immer ganz neu und ursprünglich aus der Denkungsart hervorgehen soll" (*Werke* 10:437).

47 Nietzsche, *Gesammelte Werke*, Musarionausgabe, 23 vols. (Munich: Musarion Verlag, 1920–29): "Was ist das Böse? Dreierlei: der Zufall, das Ungewisse, das Plötzliche" (19:344).

48 Nietzsche, "Nachgelassene Fragmente": "Was ist gut? – Alles, was das Gefühl der Macht, den Willen zur Macht, die Macht selbst im Menschen steigert. Was ist schlecht? – Alles, was aus der Schwäche stammt. Was ist Glück? – das Gefühl davon, daß wieder die Macht gewachsen, – daß wieder ein Widerstand überwunden ward" (*KSA* 13:481–82).

echoed in many different versions over the years. Then there are the famous lines from his *Beyond Good and Evil* (1886) that recall the connection between the seductive snake in the Garden of Eden, the primitive life beyond its protective walls, and the nature of evil: "[E]verything evil, dreadful, tyrannical, beast of prey and serpent in man serves to enhance the species 'man' just as much as does its opposite."[49] Again in spring 1888, in a section of his literary estate labeled "My Own View," he contends that the evolution of Homo sapiens is not a singular event but rather coevolutionary with the entire animal and plant worlds. Thus, evil, anxiety, fear can be good when viewed as a counterforce to debilitating entropy in a world marked by emergence. Not a matter of hierarchical structure, the dynamic is agonistic and nonlinear.[50] Adopting this integrative view of evolution would move us out of the purely anthropological realm. Indeed, Nietzsche declared in yet another fragment from spring 1888 that evil could be seen as that which is excessive, disharmonious, and disproportionate, whereas good is the effort to maintain balance. That is why the passage is cited at the masthead of this chapter.[51] Moreover, it seems to have inspired Deleuze and Baudrillard in their reflections on the nature of evil.

At least implicitly present in the foregoing discussion of the nature of evil is the role of human consciousness in the remapping of the moral terrain. In fact, consciousness is a central aspect of the re-evaluation process within the total scheme of things, from Adam and Eve's initial desire for greater awareness to our own expanded consciousness of the universe and our role in it resultant of modern science.[52] In many respects, consciousness has replaced earlier notions of what

---

49 Nietzsche, *Jenseits von Gut und Böse*: "Alles Böse, Furchtbare, Tyrannische, Raubtier- und Schlangenhafte am Menschen dient so gut zur Erhöhung der species 'Mensch' als sein Gegensatz" (*KSA* 5:61–62, #44). English translation cited according to Nietzsche, *BGE*, trans. by R. J. Hollingdale (1990), 54 (#44). See also *Die Fröhliche Wissenschaft* #4, #19 (*KSA* 3:376–77, 390). Hereafter cited as *FW*.

50 *KSA* 13:316–17. Deleuze, *Spinoza*, remarks in this regard: "All evil can be traced back to the bad, and everything that is bad bears the mark of poison, incompatibility, contamination. Even the evil I do (bad = evil) only consists in my associating my concept of an act with the concept of an object which cannot measure up to this act without losing its constitutive relationship." ["Tout mal se réduit au mauvais, et tout ce qui est mauvait est du type poison, indigestion, intoxication. Même le mal que je fais (mauvais = méchant) consiste seulement en ceci, que j'associe l'image d'une action à l'image d'un objet qui ne peut pas supporter cette action sans perdre son rapport constitutif."] (103).

51 Nietzsche, *Nachgelassene Fragmente*: "So gut das *Böse* betrachtet werden kann als Übertreibung, Disharmonie, Disproportion, so gut kann das *Gute* eine *Schutzdiät* gegen die Gefahr der Übertreibung, Disharmonie und Disproportion sein" (*KSA* 13:250).

52 Regarding the increased attention to consciousness – which is frequently tied in with quantum mechanics – see, e.g., Robert G. Jahn and Brenda J. Dunne, *Margins of Reality: The Role of Consciousness in the Physical World* (San Diego: Harcourt Brace Jovanovich, 1987); Paul Davies

constitutes evil. The growing awareness of the interconnectedness of mind and matter has led to a relativizing of once dogmatic concepts. For this reason, the concept of consciousness deserves a closer look.

In his *The Gay Science* Nietzsche explicated his notion of consciousness as an end-phase-phenomenon in the material world. For him it was a sign of growing debilitation that makes humankind less capable of living life in an ever new, spontaneous, and risk-taking manner. The evil of the "poisonous" fruit of the Tree of Knowledge reemerged with Nietzsche as the worst poison of all because of its ability to sap humankind of its taste for life. Nietzsche concluded: "Consciousness is the last and most recent development in organic nature and consequently also the most unfinished and least vital dimension of it."[53] Innumerable errors and false judgments arising from consciousness prove extremely debilitating because they tame one's natural instincts. One of the chief misinterpretations regards the rational ordering capacity of consciousness as the very essence of human nature. But by considering self-awareness to be a thing unto itself – self-contained, autonomous, and unchanging – humankind has actually prevented the natural evolution of human consciousness from developing into the force nature actually intended it to be.[54] Ultimately, Nietzsche suggested, the overvaluation of human consciousness will lead to the demise of humankind.

The affirmation of life was his ultimate concern. And primitive existence with its chaotic uncertainty paradoxically gives rise to enhanced awareness. Nietzsche emphatically affirmed chaotic processes because he saw them as the essence of life forces themselves. He even likened the human being to a dormant volcano for whom violent eruptions are merely a matter of time, although the exact timing of the eruptions is not predictable (*FW* #9; *KSA* 3:381). In fact, we might even see chaos as the central concept of his world-view, not just as a consequence of but also as the precondition for his own critical project.[55] The resultant dance around

---

and John Gribbin, *The Matter Myth: Dramatic Discoveries That Challenge Our Understanding of Physical Reality* (New York: Simon & Schuster, 1992); Michael Talbot, *The Holographic Universe* (New York: HarperPerennial, 1992); Roger Penrose, *Shadows of the Mind: A Search for the Missing Science of Consciousness* (New York: Oxford University Press, 1994); and Edward O. Wilson, *Consilience: The Unity of Knowledge* (New York: Alfred A. Knopf, 1998).

53 My translation. Nietzsche, *FW* #11: "Die Bewusstheit ist die letzte und späteste Entwicklung des Organischen und folglich auch das Unfertigste und Unkräftigste daran" (*KSA* 3:382).

54 Cf. Nietzsche, *FW* #11: "Man denkt, hier sei *der Kern* des Menschen; sein Bleibendes, Ewiges, Letztes, Ursprünglichstes! Man hält die Bewusstheit für eine feste gegebne Grösse! Leugnet ihr Wachstum, ihre Intermittenzen! Nimmt sie als 'Einheit des Organismus'! – Diese lächerliche Überschätzung und Verkennung des Bewusstseins hat die grosse Nützlichkeit zur Folge, dass damit eine allzuschnelle Ausbildung desselben *verhindert* worden ist" (*KSA* 3:382-83).

55 Thomas Busch, *Die Affirmation des Chaos. Zur Überwindung des Nihilismus in der Metaphysik Friedrich Nietzsches*, Dissertationen: Philosophische Reihe, 6 (St. Ottilien: EOS Verlag Erzabtei

the edges of deep-seated, volatile forces bubbling to the surface (of consciousness) is invigorating *and* threatening. It also has concomitant aesthetic and ethical dimensions. Appropriately, Nietzsche considered chaos to be the source of evil in a destabilized world. In the *Gay Science* he avers that the world is essentially chaos for all time. Not in the sense of there being no necessity to it but rather by the "lack of order, structure, form, beauty, wisdom, and all other forms of our aesthetic anthropomorphism."[56] Consequently, chaos does not signify for him the lack of necessity. Chaos is not mere chance without any kind of pattern. Instead it represents the opportunity, indeed, the need for creative solutions. Humankind must find its own way through the field of lava, altering direction and setting a new course as necessity demands. Virtue as fitness and adaptability ensures not only survival but also self-enhancement.

Genuine consciousness is open to both myth and fact, the art of association and that of rigorous mathematical calculation. Yet it follows its own, sometimes circuitous, path and enters unchartered territories. A few individuals have begun to suspect that what has been inculcated into them as conscious and valuable knowledge is really based on prejudice and false judgments.[57] Liberating consciousness from the mechanistic paradigm of the past three hundred years and allowing it to revert to a primordial state were, for Nietzsche, the most urgent of tasks. Human awareness must once again reflect upon its instinctual character, its oneness with the chemical and biological bases of existence. That vision is a far cry from those critics who ignore the omnidirectional thrust of Nietzsche's remapping of the moral terrain and vulgarize his moral views by reducing them either to a simple insistence on the ideal of the *Übermensch* or to a one-sided emphasis on suffering. One must always bear in mind the context of Nietzsche's own re-evaluation of values and not forget his embrace of joyful science.[58]

St. Ottilien, 1989), 220. Busch's dissertation represents the first full-dress rehearsal of the meaning of chaos in Nietzsche's opus. He argues convincingly that chaos plays a dominant role in the philosopher's thinking, somewhat comparable to the notion of will to power. While Nietzsche uses the term at times rigorously to designate an essential concept and at other times loosely as a rhetorical figure, Busch compiles enough evidence to show that its main connotation is to denote the nature of reality itself (cf. esp. 217–42). David Goiccoiccea, "The Bad and the Evil in Augustine and Nietzsche," in *The Problem of Evil: An Intercultural Exploration*, ed. by Sandra A. Wawrytko (Amsterdam and Atlanta: Rodopi, 2000), 53–60, acknowledges chaos as a source of evil for Nietzsche.

56 Nietzsche, *FW* #109: "Der Gesammt-Charakter der Welt ist dagegen in alle Ewigkeit Chaos, nicht im Sinne der fehlenden Notwendigkeit, sondern der fehlenden Ordnung, Gliederung, Form, Schönheit, Weisheit, und wie alle unsere ästhetischen Menschlichkeiten heissen" (*KSA* 3:468).

57 Nietzsche, *FW* #11: "Es ist immer noch eine ganz neue und eben erst dem menschlichen Auge aufdämmernde, kaum noch deutlich erkennbare *Aufgabe, das Wissen sich einzuverleiben und instinctiv zu machen*" (*KSA* 3:383).

58 C. Fred Alford, for example, does not do justice to Nietzsche. See his *What Evil Means to Us*

6. EVIL IN THE NEW SCHEME OF THINGS

In May 1993, the Cologne philosopher Florian Rötzer published an article in the *Süddeutsche Zeitung* on the all-pervasiveness of evil.[59] At the center of his argument is the decentralization of life on all levels. In our current epoch of "systems destabilization," he intones, the role of evil requires a renewed look. Rötzer espies a remarkable convergence of science, economics, technology, art, and everyday experience in this connection. With its principle of unpredictability in complex dynamic systems, chaos research has contributed significantly to the new world order.

Little wonder that the traditional concept of evil once again appeared inadequate to Rötzer. Its customary opposition to the good, the beautiful, and the true seems to have outlived its usefulness in a world of ever-changing shapes and forms. Traditionally, good and evil did not merely happen; they were most often willed. The Kantian imperative, Rötzer thus suggests, stood for the steady balance of tensions in humankind's struggle to maintain accepted norms against the forces of change. Placed in this light, the good was always conservative in nature, whereas evil appeared as opposition to received values. Innovation, as Nietzsche remarked (and Spinoza had implied), is always evil (*FW* #35; *KSA* 3:404).

What happens, however, when the firm structures of the world are rattled, when received values unravel into mere subjective prejudices, when the seeker no longer knows what is up and what is down, when there is no absolute center to the universe? Rötzer remarks that it is becoming ever more apparent that everything, from the expansion of the universe to the evolution of life on earth, and even to our social systems, results from "'creative' catastrophes, chance events, imbalances or evolutionary process."[60] They have produced the very circumstances that shape our views of them. Given this clear shift of emphasis from foreground to background, from center to periphery, the normally autonomous human protagonist on the stage of life is overshadowed by the stage itself. The background actions move to center stage, replacing the highly profiled individual protagonist in the lead role on the

(Ithaca and London: Cornell University Press, 1997), esp. 121–29.

59 Florian Rötzer, "Das Böse ist überall," feuilleton section, *Süddeutschen Zeitung,* May 11, 1993, no. 107, p. 11.

60 Rötzer, "Das Böse ist überall": "Das Gute ist, wie beispielhaft der Kantische Imperativ, mit der Schwäche behaftet, stets konservativ, auf Gleichgewicht bedacht sein zu müssen. Andererseits beruht offenbar nicht nur unser Gesellschaftssystem, sondern auch die Evolution des Kosmos und des Lebens auf der Erde auf 'kreativen' Katastrophen, Zufällen, Ungleichgewichten oder Entwicklungen, die überhaupt erst den Zustand geschaffen haben, dem wir uns mitsamt dem Weltbild, das wir haben, verdanken" (*SZ*, no. 17, May 11, 1993, p. 11). For a judicious review of recent publications on science and evil in English, see Joseph F. Kelly, *The Problem of Evil* (2002), esp. chap. 15: "Some Scientific Theories of Evil" (200–212).

stage of life. In this reconfiguration, the old definition of evil cuts a sorry figure. Rötzer is aware of the historical attempts at relativizing the notion of evil and formulates a definition of it that goes beyond Spinoza, which avoids Bonting's paradoxical pairing of evil with "morally neutral" chaos (Bonting 76), and which seems more encompassing than Nietzsche's view. Evil for Rötzer is nothing less and nothing more than the principle of discontinuity. He writes:

> If one defines it [the concept of evil] in accord with the new world-view now on the rise so that it encompasses not only human interaction – a seemingly inescapable conclusion in light of ecology and technical developments ranging from gene technology to robotics and artificial life – *then evil can be defined as the impairment of the autonomy and the integrity of an organism, an object, a state, or of a process*. Such a definition would retain the objective dimension of ethical action, while the intentionality of the acting subject is suspended. Evil, understood in this way, impairs or destroys ordered states, initiating the disequilibrium that can cause catastrophic consequences.
> [Wenn man ihn [den Begriff des Bösen] im Sinne des entstehenden neuen Weltbildes weit genug faßt, so daß er nicht nur das Handeln von Menschen gegenüber Menschen faßt, was angesichts der Ökologie und der technischen Entwicklung von der Gentechnologie über die künstliche Intelligenz und die Robotik bis hin zum künstlichen Leben notwendig erscheint, *so ließe sich das Böse als Verletzung der Autonomie und Integrität eines Organismus, eines Objekts, eines Zustandes oder eines Prozesses fassen*. In dieser Definition wäre die Objektdimension des Ethischen enthalten, während die Intentionalität des verursachenden Subjekt suspendiert ist. Das Böse, so verstanden, verletzt oder zerstört Ordnungen und ruft Ungleichgewichte hervor, woraus katastrophale Folgen entstehen können.] (Rötzer, "Das Böse ist überall," 11; emphasis added)

Rötzer's definition contains several important moments: (1) evil is a universal phenomenon within creation and is not limited to humankind; (2) evil is determined by objective, not subjective criteria; (3) evil is equated with motion, the flux of time and space, and dynamic processes. Thus, not surprisingly, Rötzer wonders: "Is evolution evil? Is evil precisely that which generates new things?" ("Ist die Evolution böse? Ist das Böse gerade der Generator des Neuen?"; 11). The question is not rhetorical. Yet Rötzer has no ready answer. Upon further reflection, how can there be ready answers to highly complex phenomena?

Writing three years before Rötzer and equally sensitive to the shifting paradigms in modern scientific inquiry, Jean Baudrillard unintentionally provided a fitting response to the detection of a common plan of immanence that Deleuze had discerned in Spinoza and Leibniz. In his *La Transparence du Mal* (1990), Baudrillard focuses on extreme phenomena and the role they play in contemporary science and society. He sees these "phénomènes extrêmes" by and large as expressions of turbulence whose effect is to make evil transparent in the modern world.[61] Like Rötzer, therefore, he directs attention away from the human to the

61 Jean Baudrillard, *La Transparence du Mal. Essai sur les phénomènes extrêmes* (Paris: Galilée, 1990). The following is based especially on pp. 11–27 and 105–15.

operations of nature itself. Decentralization and destabilization result from an "orgy" of emancipation (9) and initiate an "escalation" of mutation (26) in all areas of existence, from the moral to the molecular. For this reason Baudrillard readily speaks of an "epidemic of values" and of "universal metastasis" (11), terms that seem to echo Nietzsche's view of change and movement as the essence of existence at all levels. These interactions and transformations reveal the transparency of existence, rendering a transcendental plane obsolete. "There is no longer a revolution," he declares unequivocally, "there is only circumvolution, involution of values" (10). Revolution would seem to connote a movement to a more differentiated or evolved state (the kind Bonting prefers), while circumvolution implies a principle of self-regulation trapped in the repetitive vortex of its own (com)motion. That is why Baudrillard claims that we have entered a "fractal stage" of existence (11), one which would appear to be a "catastrophic development," albeit stripped of value judgments (115). All this is a result of the natural process of energy release, a process that has, in turn, elevated humankind to chief engineer in devising and accelerating dissipative systems (115). This escalation is self-renewing, Baudrillard speculates, by virtue of its very activity so that entropy does not occur.

Clearly identifying this out-of-balance system with the notion of evil, Baudrillard asserts that the *principium maleficum* is neither a moral issue nor a matter of death or entropy but rather involves a principle of natural vitality and strength. Specifically, he defines evil as a principle of seduction, disequilibrium, antagonism, complexity, nonreducibility, alterity, and incontrovertibility.[62] Any attempt to cleanse the system of unwanted components in the hope of establishing a state of equilibrium weakens the overall structure or organism and ultimately leads to its demise. "Energy is everywhere present," he concludes, "where things have gotten out of balance, are viral, accelerated, and compounded."[63]

Evil, in other words, is now identified precisely with those transformations first made possible by the expulsion of Adam and Eve out of a false state of perfection. That means, of course, that evil has been redefined from indicating opposition to the divine will to an acting out of the compossible structures of reality. It is not merely an absence of the good or an empty nonpresence, but the unrealized

---

62 Baudrillard, *La Transparence* (1990): "Le principe du Mal n'est pas moral, c'est un principe de déséquilibre et de vertige, un principe de complexité et d'étrangeté, un principe de séduction, un principe d'incompatibilité, d'antagonisme et d'irréductibilité. Ce n'est pas un principe de mort, tout au contraire, c'est un principe vital de déliaison" (112). By utilizing images of chaotic movement and dynamic vortices, by foregrounding the concept of "the plenitude of possibility," Martin Buber anticipates a complexity-based definition of good and evil long before the term "complexity theory" was coined. See Buber, *Images*, 66–67.

63 Baudrillard, *La Transparence* (1990): "son énergie inverse partout à l'oeuvre dans le dérèglement des choses, dans la viralité, dans l'accélération, dans l'emballement des effets" (111).

potential of what Leibniz had designated the infinitude of worlds, Buber had characterized as "the plenitude of possibility" (*Images* 66), and Deleuze had dubbed areas of "interindividual, interactive clustering" (*Fold* 115). Yet it would be wrong to equate "unrealized potential" with "imperfection." The latter is premised on movement toward a universal state of divine perfection. But God now resides in the parts.

The spirit of evil, Baudrillard conjectures – in a manner echoing Spinoza and Leibniz – dwells in the system itself rather than in people. Like Rötzer, he too discerns an "*objective* energy" of evil (124). Moreover, since the release of energy impacts equally on good as well as on evil, good and evil are holograms of one another. Each contains the other; each is inseparably bound to the other, even when the presence of the one seems to preclude the presence of the other. All kinds of events occur, Baudrillard writes, of which we take no notice or which have long since ceased to be by the time we sense their existence. Thus, the world of virtual reality ("ce monde virtuel"; 115) is much more complex than the world we actually perceive and give structure to via our measurements and theories. We become aware of only those facets of reality that present themselves to us. Heightened awareness can capture more of those fleeting events, but acute awareness increases the presence of evil by highlighting the constant threat of destabilization to our intermittent steady states. With that shift, evil essentially moves from a predictable single site to multiple sites of periodic predictability. The center has been lost. That proves unnerving.

While Rötzer seems to suspend the individual's responsibility for his actions, Baudrillard (and Kant) allows for a sphere of influence still subject to human volition and thus responsibility (cf. E. A. Johnson on Thomism). We can also draw upon Lyall Watson's conclusion that human consciousness and culture have developed via complex evolutionary processes into a semi-autonomous state such that humankind is no longer blindly subject to the dictates of biochemical changes and genetic codes. Critical in the new scheme of things is the "how" of communal interaction rather than the "what" of genes (Watson, *Dark Nature* 253–57). Despite the inroads that chaos research has made into all areas of thought, intentionality thus remains a viable notion.[64] While humankind is undoubtedly embedded in the evolutionary processes of existence, humans are capable of acting *as if* they were autonomous agents. Since evil is inherent in the iterations of life, we, as part of that system, have some control over its consequences. We can, in fact, alter the direction of the flow through the many feedback loops we create between ourselves and our environment(s).

---

64 The influence of chaos theory is omnipresent in Baudrillard's argument. See esp. his use of feedback loops, strange attractors, and nonlinear dynamics. For his part, Deleuze adopts concepts of periodicity, nonlinearity, and clustering.

Subsequently, the human being is not merely a roofing tile that comes loose and strikes a passer-by on the head. She is no comet incapable of altering its course, nor a rock slide that cascades down the mountainside simply because something dislodged it from above. On the contrary, human beings can alter their courses, can allow events to turn out differently, despite being entangled in the interconnecting networks of existence. The threat to our environment is a prime example of what impact human beings do have, for good and for bad, on their contexts and despite those contexts. Via self-awareness, the individual creates a different kind of feedback loop within the environment that would appear to augment the biological and physical realms. Johann Gottlieb Fichte's remark around 1800 seems fitting: "I have and enfold reality; it is in me; it is at home within me."[65] These multivalent feedback loops that mark continuing creation through its phases of order and disorder are the logical extension of Bonting's chaos theology. They are also indicative of Rolston's theory of the fecund Earth with its kaleidoscopic variations on geophysical, geochemical, and biological scales. Because of this fecundity of possibilities, the secular Earth becomes sacred ground, where human beings can realize their latent potential. "If there is any holy ground, any land of promise," Rolston opines, this promising Earth is it" (Rolston, *Genes* 362).

The preceding might be an explanation for the self-willed literary protagonists who explore the nature of human responsibility in a radically altered and decentered universe. That is the topic of the concluding chapters in this study. The reconfigurations of our changing understanding of the nature of evil is at the heart of the ensuing analyses of *Faust*, *Zarathustra*, and *The Tin Drum*. What follows are so many encirclements of the problem, so many iterations.

A word of caution before we proceed. We must guard against trivializing the questions posed here. The current and ensuing reflections on the need for re-evaluating our values, on the deconstructive method, or on radical relativism are not just mind games, or, as Rötzer puts it, not just mental "exercises in skepticism or pluralism" (11). While it might appear that we have lost our footing in the postmodern era, it would be premature to conclude that no new signposts guiding

---

65 Johann Gottlieb Fichte, *Die Bestimmung des Menschen*, ed. by Theodor Ballauff and Ignaz Klein (Berlin: Vossische Buchhandlung, 1800; rprt. Stuttgart: Reclam, 1981), 108: "Realität habe ich, und fasse ich: sie liegt in mir, und ist in mir selbst einheimisch." Fichte devotes the entire first part of his *Bestimmung* to demonstrating how integrally intertwined man and nature are, making claims that resonate with Leibniz's theory of monads and others that seemingly anticipate Nietzsche's vitalism. The collective consciousness of all individuals constitutes, Fichte argues, the perfect consciousness of the universe itself (28–29). Apt of Nietzsche's own claim that man does not think but rather that nature thinks in man is Fichte's statement: "ich oder die denkende Natur in mir, denkt Gedanken" (27). Fichte characterizes consciousness as discursive and progressive ("dieses discursiv fortschreitendes Bewußtsein"; 174).

our movement through life are forthcoming. To fend off evil, we must be aware of manipulation by selfish individuals, cognizant of the pressures exerted by self-serving institutions, mindful of the impulses of our own selfish genes, and willing to steer our own course between the rival forces of genetic and cultural evolution. Whatever upsets the ecology and disrupts the equilibrium is evil. By the very nature of things, then, evil is inevitable because change is inevitable. Based on his study of the natural world, Lyall Watson arrived at a similar conclusion (see his *Dark Nature* 1995: 271, 276, 282). The question, then, is how do we react? At the very least, we need to be always alert, to be as independent in our actions as the circumstances allow, and to reject what is not absolutely necessary. What *is* absolutely necessary, however, for life to be lived meaningfully is activity itself. Thus, "to die in the midst of energy is not to die at all."[66] If we accept the thesis that chaos in this real rather than mythological sense is the final word in Nietzsche's positive "metaphysics," then his presumed nihilism quickly fades as a viable hypothesis.[67] Reality is somethingness, not nothingness. Goethe's *Faust* gravitates to that very point. We turn to it now as the first of three major literary iterations of themes and motifs encountered in science and philosophy.

66 Cf. John Lachs, *In Love with Life* (Nashville, TN: Vanderbilt University Press, 1998), 123.

67 Busch, *Affirmation des Chaos*, 339. See also Walter Gebhard, "Erkenne und Entsetzen: Zur Tradition der Chaos-Annahmen im Denken Nietzsches," in *Friedrich Nietzsche: Strukturen der Negativität*, ed. by Walter Gebhard (Frankfurt a.M.: Peter Lang, 1984), 13–47. I cannot agree with Gebhard's implication that chaos amounts to an "entrance into the general worthlessness of life in the world" for Nietzsche (19) – apparently the result of his having adopted Schopenhauer's "negative ontology of things" (30). I endorse the notion that chaos had for Nietzsche both a theoretical and a highly practical component (17). Yet we must guard against assuming that chaos for Nietzsche represented "teleological frustration" (19). Margot Fleischer, *Der 'Sinn der Erde' und die Entzauberung des Übermenschen: Eine Auseinandersetzung mit Nietzsche* (Darmstadt: Wissenschaftliche Buchgesellschaft, 1993), scarcely touches upon the topic of chaos. The central passage #109 from Book 3 of *Die fröhliche Wissenschaft* is relegated to a brief comment in a footnote. Busch and Gebhard are missing from her bibliography, as is Alexander Nehamas.

PART TWO

LITERARY ITERATIONS

Chapter 5
"A Highly Complex Matter": The Spirit of the Earth, Evil, and Creativity in *Faust*

> Willst du ins Unendliche schreiten,
> Geh nur im Endlichen nach allen Seiten.
>
> – Johann Wolfgang Goethe, *Sprüche I*

> Goethe ist der letzte Deutsche, vor dem ich Ehrfurcht habe.
>
> – Fr. Nietzsche, *Götzen-Dämmerung*

1. INTERPRETING *FAUST*: CONNECTIONISM

In an attempt to get at its underlying, ontological meaning, critics have interpreted Goethe's *Faust* innumerable times and from differing vantage points. Early on, Anne Luise Germaine de Stael (1766–1817) drew attention to the difficulty of deciphering the text; she characterized it as a product of the wildest fantasy, calling it an "intellectual chaos" ("ein geistiges Chaos").[1] "It is impossible," she further remarked in her travel memoirs *De l'Allemagne* (1810), "to read *Faust* without being animated in a thousand different ways [...] to reflect on everything and then some more. [...] Yet *Faust* is by no means a good example. One might well see the work as the result of a confused mind or of saturated reason."[2] And this she observed without the advantage of knowing Part II of the opus or of having access to the hundreds of studies penned in an effort to clarify the text's messages and explore its many pathways. To be sure, in the Prologue in the Theater, one of the two prefaces to the play, the theater director openly announces that the audience can expect a heterogeneous piece, something for everyone's taste, a "ragout."[3] To

1 Madame de Stael, *De l'Allemagne* (Frankfurt a.M.: Insel Verlag, 1985), 350. She devotes an entire chapter to *Faust* (350–385).

2 De Stael, *De l'Allemagne* 385: "Es ist unmöglich, *Faust* zu lesen, ohne daß er das Denken auf tausenderlei Weise anrege [...] nachzudenken über alles, und *über alles noch etwas mehr*. [...] Übrigens ist *Faust* keineswegs ein gutes Vorbild. Man mag das Werk als das Resultat der Verwirrung des Verstandes oder der Sättigung der Vernunft ansehen [...]."

3 Johann Wolfgang von Goethe, *Faust: Texte*, ed. by Albrecht Schöne (Darmstadt: Wissenschaftliche Buchgesellschaft, 1999), lines 95–100. This edition is identical to J. W. von Goethe, *Sämtliche Werke*, ed. by Friedmar Apel et al., 40 vols. (Frankfurt a.M.: Deutscher Klassiker Verlag, 1985–99), vol. 7/1 (1994). Hereafter cited as FA (Frankfurter Ausgabe).

review the subsequent voluminous and often excellent scholarship devoted to this example of "intellectual chaos" would take us too far afield. Let it suffice to state that none of the more recent book-length analyses of the work adopts my chaos and complexity approach.[4] In the following I cast a wide net over different kinds of writing by Goethe and then pull the statements and attitudes captured into a tighter bundle as a prelude to analyzing similar conceptions and tropes in *Faust* itself. I start with Goethe's general intent and then move to connections between him and the doing of science before concluding with a renewed reading of *Faust*.[5]

---

4 Thomas Metscher, *Welttheather und Geschichtsprozeß: Zu Goethes Faust* (Frankfurt a.M.: Peter Lang, 2003), 189–95, sketches some of the older critical positions adopted by *Faust* scholars, in particular those of Wilhelm Emrich (1943), K. Kerényi (1941), D. Lohmeyer (1940), and H. Schlaffer (1981). His own focus, informed by Spinoza, is on the relationship between history and nature in Part II, Act II (196–221). Jochen Schmidt, *Goethes Faust I und II : Grundlagen – Werk – Wirkung* (Munich: C. H. Beck, 2001), is an excellent introduction to the entire opus; Karl Eibl, *Das monumentale Ich – Wege zu Goethes Faust* (Frankfurt a.M. and Leipzig: Insel Verlag, 2000); Willi Jasper, *Faust und die Deutschen* (Berlin: Rowohlt, 1998); Albrecht Schöne, *Kommentare: Johann Wolfgang von Goethe – Faust*, 4th printing, authorized for the Wissenschaftliche Buchgesellschaft Darmstadt (Frankfurt a.M.: Deutscher Klassiker Verlag, 1999). This is identical to FA 7/2 (1994). Metscher attempts to debunk the widespread impression that Schöne's commentary is "postideologically" exemplary, arguing that other text commentaries remain indispensable (317–31). Theodor Friedrich and Lothar J. Scheithauer, *Kommentar zu Goethes Faust*, 3rd edition (Stuttgart: Reclam, 1994); Ulrich Gaier, *Goethes Faust-Dichtungen: Ein Kommentar. Urfaust*, 2nd edition (Stuttgart: Reclam, 1990). Only Erwin von Löw, *Strukturen in Goethes Faust: Graphische Darstellungen* (Augsburg: Guido Pressler, 1982), comes close to my attempt to chart the complexity of the entire text, albeit using primarily traditional astrological, cabalistic, and alchemistic paradigms. Researchers have taken little note of von Löw's ingenious mapping of the text as captured in his various diagrams. See especially "das Geheimnis der Natur" (41), "Kulturzonenkreis im Faust-Ganzen" (72), "Farbenkreis im Faust-Ganzen" (112), "Kreis der Weltalter der Wissenschaften" (145), "Schema Werkstruktur" (167), "Kurzwellige Erfahrung – langwellige Idee" (225), and above all the "Hauptchiffre" (336) as the structural design of the entire work. The series of fourteen diagrams is rounded out by "Der astrologische Zwölf-Häuser-Kreis" (459).

5 On the connections between Goethe's science and his creative writing, see Dorothea-Michaela Noé-Rumberg, *Naturgesetze als Dichtungs-Prinzipien: Goethes verborgene Poetik im Spiegel seiner Dichtungen* (Freiburg: Rombach, 1993), considers the import of science for the poetic structure of *Faust* (204–13). *Goethe's Way of Science: A Phenomenology of Nature*, ed. by David Seamon and Arthur Zajonc (Albany, NY: State University of New York Press, 1998), contains only one essay on *Faust*; the emphasis is on seeing. Margrit Wyder, *Goethes Naturmodell: Die Scala Naturae und ihre Transformationen* (Cologne, Weimar, and Vienna: Böhlau, 1998), elucidates Goethe's evolutionary thinking. Herbert Rowland (ed.), *Goethe, Chaos, and Complexity* (Amsterdam and New York: Rodopi, 2001), squarely focuses on the topic at hand. It contains a number of relevant essays, especially those by Haglund on visualization and emergence, Kirchoff on complexity and holism, van der Laan on chaos and *Faust*, and Martinson on chaos as an organizing principle. Astrida Orle Tantillo, *The Will to Create: Goethe's Philosophy of Nature* (Pittsburgh, PA: University of Pittsburgh Press, 2002), talks about the phenomenon of

It has become fashionable in postmodernist critique to devalue authorial intent, to insist that the text can speak for itself. Yet we know that Goethe pursued several objectives in penning his masterpiece of 12,111 verses over the sixty years of its gestation. Those objectives range from social criticism to discourse on the tragedy of human limitation, reflections upon political upheaval,[6] visions of utopia, concepts of artificial life, theories of evolution, ideas on the formation of the earth, and philosophical musings on the nature of truth. Above all *Faust* is about the creative act. A multilayered work of global proportions, it utilizes rich Hellenic and Judeo-Christian traditions in innovative fashion and, as a result, has fascinated and puzzled readers from the start. In a famous letter of 17 March 1832 to Wilhelm von Humboldt, penned shortly before his death on 22 March and after having completed *Faust II*, Goethe characterized his opus as "these very serious jests" ("diese sehr ernsten Scherze") and as "this strange edifice" ("dieses seltsame Gebäu"). The serious jests have been interpreted as a reference to his own preoccupation with the humanities at a time of fundamental political and social change, while the "Gebäu" is seen as an allusion to the multiple literary figures, mythologems, traditions, forms, rhythms, and metrical variations used to choreograph the movement of *Faust I* and *II*.[7] Asserting that the conception of the entire complex project had been clear to him since the 1770s, he nonetheless granted that the individual stages of Faust's course became apparent to him only gradually (FA 38:550). The Faust theme accompanied him through life like an "inner fairy tale" (letter to Sulpiz Boisserée, 8 September 1831; FA 38:460). And we know that fairy tales have a logic all their own. They are playful and serious. And they are both at the same time.

It is this inner process that figures dominantly in the following. Little noted by Goethe scholarship, the process Goethe meant – and which to my mind is constitutive of the famed serious jests – is the agonal confluence of autopoietic

complexity, but not about complexity theory. Matthew Bell, *Goethe's Naturalistic Anthropology: Man and Other Plants* (Oxford: Clarendon Press, 1994), applies Goethe's knowledge of science as a hermeneutic matrix for discerning deep structures in *Werther* and *Wilhelm Meister*. On alchemy and Goethe's poetic verve, see Nabil Mesh-hadi, *Die Einschätzung der Alchemie in Faust-Deutungen* (Frankfurt a.M.: Peter Lang, 1979). The extent of Goethe's presence in the history of science from 1776–1990 is evident in the two-volume bibliography *Goethe in the History of Science*, ed. Frederick Amrine, 2 vols. (New York: Peter Lang, 1996).

6 The span is great from the Fall of Troy in1200 BC through the Battle of Pharsalus in 48 BC, the crusades around 1200 AD, the French Revolution and its aftermath from 1789 to 1793 AD, to the Battle of Missolunghi in 1824 AD, when Lord Byron died during the struggle for Greek independence. To be sure, Goethe does not refer to the events in chronological order.

7 Herman Meyer, *Diese sehr ernsten Scherze. Eine Studie zu Faust II* (Heidelberg: Lothar Stiehm Verlag, 1970), turns the oxymoron inherent in the phrase "diese sehr ernsten Scherze" into a commentary on the very essence of life, which is simultaneously serious and playful (20, 39–40).

movement inherent in the Faust-idea and in Goethe's willful act in drawing upon Hebrew, Christian, and pagan traditions to structure the material to fit his own design. In his last comment on *Faust* in the letter to Wilhelm von Humboldt just cited, Goethe reiterates his characterization of *Faust* as being "ernst gemeinte Scherze." Introducing the comment with a remark about the essential tension between his effort to manipulate material and nature's own autopoietic drive in forming matter, he writes: "Of course, the greatest difficulty arose at this point, namely, to achieve purposefully and resolutely the goal which nature alone should be allowed to bring about freely and actively" ("Hier trat nun freilich die große Schwierigkeit ein, dasjenige durch Vorsatz und Charakter zu erreichen, was eigentlich der freiwilligen tätigen Natur allein zu kommen sollte").[8] Nature and reason need to be attuned to one another, but in this case reason and will forced themselves on nature a bit more than Goethe desired. Actually, the stronger of the two are the inner workings of nature itself. Even when we violate nature, Goethe had asserted in an essay on nature in 1783, we still act in accordance with natural laws (FA 25:13). Thus, the idea of *Faust* was for Goethe rooted in natural processes, while his own efforts to manipulate the "mass" were a kind of counter-force, exerting formative influence from a position of conscious design. Moreover, in a conversation concerning *Faust* with a French visitor one month before his death, Goethe described his work as a "collective effort," since it owed so much to the ideas and inspirations of others; he "merely" reaped the fruit of the seeds planted earlier.[9] Quite obviously, however, Faust's "Geist" stood in opposition to the merely political "Zeitgeist" of the period in which Part II was penned. Because he feared that the general reading public would not understand the complex mixture of content, form, and style, Goethe sealed and locked away the completed

---

8 Letter to Wilhelm von Humboldt, 17 March 1832 (FA 38:550). This view is encountered repeatedly in Goethe's writing on art and the doing of science.

9 "Mon œvre est celle d'un être collectif et elle porte le nom de Goethe." Conversation with Fréderic Soret on 17 February 1832, cited by Schöne, *Faust: Kommentare,* FA 7.2:27 (cf. the entire report in FA 38:520-23). Schöne considers Goethe's letter of 27 September 1827 to Carl Jacob Ludwig Iken to contain the heart of the poet's compositional strategy. It is there that Goethe speaks of his technique of mixing seemingly contradictory elements together as a way of leading the attentive reader circuitously to a deeper understanding of the play's hidden meaning (FA 7.2:50; the letter is reproduced in FA 14:1034 and 37:546–49). The different logic of poetry is also the topic of a conversation with Eckermann on 6 May 1827 (FA 39:615–16). Goethe's conception is fully congruent with my chaos-based thesis. It also resonates with Johann Gottfried Fichte's view of the collaborative cast of the relationship between conscious humans and unconscious natural processes cited in chap. 4. See his *Bestimmung des Menschen*, 27–29, 109, et passim. Nicholas Boyle, *Goethe: The Poet and his Age*, 2 vols. (Oxford: Clarendon P, 1991, 1997) represents the best more recent study of the author. Eibl, *Das monumentale Ich* (2000) offers a lively, informative, if sometimes quixotic, interpretation of the play.

manuscript with instructions that it not be opened until after his death.

Nor was he of a mind to explain its meaning to those who queried him. His advice to the curious was to give themselves over to the text and let it work its magic (conversation with Eckermann, 6 May 1827; FA 39:615). Nonetheless, Goethe did envision an ideal, educated reader ("ein gebildeter Geist"), who was capable of understanding innuendo and subtle inference and who was not simply attuned to reading a straightforward narrative and not merely expecting rational logic (letter to Boisserée, FA 38:460). To get at the bottom of things in *Faust*, we will have to be attentive to innuendo and allusion and let the work speak for itself. However, we will also pursue the meaning of *Faust* by examining some of Goethe's scientific and aesthetic writings penned in conjunction with the opus. In analyzing *Faust I* and *II*, I will not proceed in a strictly linear fashion, but will map the labyrinthian pathways as they present themselves, especially in the form of themes, motifs, and symbols, moving freely between the two parts of the work. This approach is justified by the recognition that relationships between and among the constituent parts form the science of structure. Moreover, the memes of significance in an artistic work are the tropes, motifs, themes, and symbols that dot the textual landscape.[10] Whereas Part I is more the product of emotion and genius, Part II more clearly bears the mark of scholarly and scientific inquiry. The hybridity of art and science opens up unusual perspectives.

The main difference between Parts I and II of *Faust* has to do with the focus on the subject (in I) versus a focus on the situation (in II). Part I leads the reader through various attempts of Faust-Mephisto to expand the notion of the "I," to enhance the sense of individual consciousness within its various interconnections (social, theological, psychological, philosophical). Part II, on the other hand, is concerned with the "larger world" of settings and events worthy of the striving of an overman. Based on relationships, the latter offers a connectionist approach. Thus, the first word in Part I is the "I" in "I've read, alas, through philosophy, / medicine and jurisprudence too, / and, to my grief, theology / With ardent labor studied through" (lines 354–56).[11] By contrast, Part II begins with a clear reference

10 Cf. Bernd-Olaf Küppers, "Wenn das Ganze mehr ist als die Summe seiner Teile," *GeoWissen: Chaos + Kreativität* (Hamburg: Gruner + Jahr AG and Co., 1990), 28–31. This is also von Löw's methodology in *Strukturen*..

11 The English is cited according to Johann Wolfgang von Goethe, *Faust, Part One & Part Two*, trans. with an introduction and notes by Charles E. Passage, 14th printing (New York: MacMillan Publishing Co., 1987). To my mind, this is still the most felicitous translation, faithful to the original in form and function. In the German, the "I" is implicit: "Habe nun ach Philosophie [...]." In order to ensure accessibility to a wide range of readers, the American translation is cited throughout. The original German wording is included when the textual nuance absolutely demands it. To quote the German in every case would tend to make my text less readable. I cite

to a situation ("When the blossoms of the spring"; line 4613). This shift from the subject to the environment, which Goethe himself noted in conversation with Eckermann (17 February 1831), is mirrored as well in a quantitative analysis of Faust's speaking role in both parts of the poem. In Part I he has 30 percent of the dialogue; in Part II he has only 13 percent (Schöne, FA 7.2:387–89). In Part II the events are more significant than the willful acts of the subject, although Faust still acts willfully. Consequently, each of the five acts in Part II – indeed, even scenes within those acts – appear to be independent units. To be sure, how such dominant scenes as Spacious Hall of Act I, At the Upper Peneus of Act II, Inner Courtyard of a Castle of Act III, High Mountains of Act IV, or Mountain Gorges of Act V interrelate is not immediately clear. Yet Goethe was undoubtedly following a deep structure. Symbolism and imagery prove to be the major mapping devices in this work. Since Goethe had the denouement of the work clearly in mind from the outset, he composed everything else backward from the final scene, Mountain Gorges. Hence, the play's conclusion orchestrates the seemingly divergent movement of the entire opus in a convergent, unifying manner. Mountain Gorges is, then, analogous to the "inner fairy tale" Goethe spoke of. In his letter of 8 September 1831 to Sulpiz Boisserée, Goethe added that Part II should not and could not be as fragmented as Part I. There is a paradox in this explanation, as any first reader of *Faust* quickly notes. What did Goethe mean, when he stated that Part II is not as fragmented as Part I? The impression we gain, however, is that Part II lacks the clear linear narrative that is quite evident in the plot of Part I. Goethe must have been referring to something other than the plot. The new "narrative" amounts to a kind of novel of the universe, one marked by large-scale, nonlinear interaction in the mapping of reality.

2. Revolutions: Goethe, Science, and the Novel of the Universe

The first major turning point in the story comes when Faust decides against committing suicide. A decisive factor is the tolling of the Easter bells, announcing that Christ has risen to new life. Noteworthy is Faust's remark that is it the earth and not God that reasserts its claims on him: "[T]he earth has me again" (line 784). Having toyed with the idea of expanding his horizons by crossing over from life to death, Faust gives in to his childhood feelings, embracing life on earth once again. Whatever knowledge humankind is capable of, he reasons, is attainable in the here and now, in the microcosm. All knowledge must come from within the study of the

---

Faust by line number so that the reader can locate the quotation in any edition of the work.

hic et nunc in a coordinated effort. By consciously resolving to recommit himself to an earthly existence, Faust opens the way for the subsequent pact/wager with Mephistopheles. The intent of Mephisto's offer, as Goethe scholars well know, is to sate Faust's yearning for ultimate knowledge of how everything interconnects. Of course, Mephisto interprets that yearning as the desire for food, drink, sex, song, and fame. Frequently, he satirizes the quest for knowledge, pointing out its pitfalls. Nonetheless, he follows in the tradition of the serpent portrayed in the Garden of Eden. Faust's actual quest, however, is for a theory of everything (TOE).

Not surprisingly, Goethe's masterpiece is frequently quoted in scientific circles. For instance, Paul R. Gross cites the following lines spoken by Mephisto in the introduction to his volume, *The Flight from Science and Reason* (1996), in defense of the hard physical and biological sciences:

Scoff at all knowledge and despise	[Verachte nur Vernunft und Wissenschaft
Reason and Science, those flowers of mankind.	Des Menschen höchste Kraft,
Let the father of all lies	Laß nur in Blend- und Zauberwerken
With dazzling necromancy make you blind,	Dich von dem Lügengeist bestärken,
Then I'll have you unconditionally –	So hab' ich dich schon unbedingt –]
(lines 1851–55)	

Gross would have done better to cite Faust's own words: "[T]he earth has me again." Neither a literary nor Goethe scholar, Gross quite understandably misconstrues the lines, taking them out of context. What is at stake here is Faust's dismay at the limits of scientific knowledge, which has proved inept at grasping the inner workings of nature, at grasping what holds the whole of the universe together. Mephisto is incapable of comprehending the true nature of Faust's quest. Therefore, he cannot succeed in dazzling Faust with his black magic, nor can he win him over unconditionally.

By missing the point, Gross perpetuates the misconception that Goethe was opposed to rigorous scientific investigation rooted in mathematics, concluding that the poet rejected "the very reasoning that allowed science to escape the straightjacket of *naturphilosophie* [*sic*]."[12] Misguided in assuming that he can win Faust's soul by leading him down the path of necromancy, the Prince of Lies actually contributes to a more complex argument regarding the pursuit of scientific, philosophical, and religious truth. These truths are not reducible to a binary opposition, nor are they adequately rendered without including the subjective element of Faust's indistinct inner drive, his daimon. Consequently, Gross's

12 Paul R. Gross, Norman Levitt, and Martin W. Lewis (eds.), *The Flight from Science and Reason* (New York: The New York Academy of Sciences distributed by Johns Hopkins University Press, 1996), 1.

comment about the "straightjacket" of *Naturphilosophie* is a non sequitur. Inflexibility was rather a mark of the self-referentiality of mathematics as practiced in some quarters in Goethe's day.[13] Contemporary scholarship is in agreement that a facile assumption of a linear relationship between cause and effect leads to errors in judgment. For this very reason Goethe argued that the art of seeing and estimating is a highly complex act of symbolic ideation that necessarily involves the psychology of the seeing subject. Observation is conscious seeing, not just the registering of photons on the retina. It is what Fichte meant when he wrote: "I am animate seeing. I see – consciousness – I see my own seeing – a conscious seeing."[14]

By urging Faust to abandon his single-minded rationality in the pursuit of truth, Mephisto paradoxically succeeds in leading Faust to a full integration of objective experimentation, rational logic, and the creative impulse. Just a few lines earlier in the same scene, Study Room II, Mephisto had exhorted Faust to break out of the green pastures of contentment, to leave off his brooding circular speculation, and to explore the wider connections (lines 1828–33). We need therefore to understand the lines cited by Gross differently from his use of them. The path to be taken leads to fuller experience, not to greener pastures of fulfillment. While the message does not quite presage Nietzsche's diatribe against the bourgeois preference for limited and familiar space, Goethe was moving toward the later philosopher's exhortation to broaden one's sphere of experience.

Despite the differences between the poet's scientific method and that of modern times, Goethe and contemporary science share common ground. Twentieth- and twenty-first-century scientists frequently cite Goethe, a practice that underscores the poet's continuing influence and interdisciplinary appeal. The German physicist Carl Friedrich von Weizsäcker summarized this common ground by showing how both poet and scientists turned to Plato's concept of idea. But whereas for Goethe the Platonic idea became an individualistic form or "Gestalt," his modern counterparts saw a universal concept in the natural sciences.[15] The British mathematician Ian Stewart reports that Mitchell Feigenbaum was reading Goethe at the time of his insight into the mathematics and mapping ratio of periodic cycles. The scaling ratio he came up with (4.6692016090) subsequently came to be known as the Feigenvalue (analogue to "Eigenvalue"; that is "Eigenwert" or own value) for certain

---

13 See John A. McCarthy, "'The Pregnant Point': Goethe on Complexity, Interdisciplinarity, and Emergence," in Rowland, *Goethe, Chaos, Complexity*, 17–31.

14 Johann Gottlieb Fichte, *Die Bestimmung des Menschen* (Stuttgart: Reclam, 1981), 81: "Ich bin ein lebendiges Sehen. Ich sehe – Bewußtsein – sehe mein Sehen – bewußtes."

15 Carl Friedrich von Weizsäcker, "Einige Begriffe aus Goethes Naturwissenschaft," in Johann Wolfgang von Goethe, *Werke*, Hamburger Ausgabe, 14 vols., 14th ed., ed. by Erich Trunz (Munich: Deutscher Taschenbuch Verlag, 1989), 13:539–55; here 540. This edition is cited hereafter as HA.

kinds of mappings. While there are various classes of nonlinear mappings, each class proves to have its own universally valid scaling. The implication here is that a connection exists between Goethe's emphasis on the uniqueness of "Gestalt" and the particularity of periodic cycles. Important for our present purposes is the realization that any mapping is a dynamical enterprise with a relative value, but one that can nonetheless make universal claims.[16] Similarly, James Gleick noted Feigenbaum's fondness for Goethe's *Faust* and *Theory of Color*. Interestingly, Feigenbaum concluded that Goethe's ideas on color were essentially a function of perception and had "more true science in them" than Newton's efforts to correlate the sensation of color to a mathematical scheme for all physics. This led Feigenbaum to consider the mathematics of human perception, how he might schematize the way that the mind sorts through the chaos of perception.[17] In *Complexification* (1994), John L. Casti, also a mathematician, cites Goethe's 1826 judgment that the language of mathematics was becoming ever more particularized and thus increasingly inaccessible: "Mathematicians are a species of Frenchman; if you say something to them, they translate it into their own language and presto! it is something entirely different."[18] Lawrence Leshan and Henry Margenau approvingly cite Goethe in their *Einstein's Space and Van Gogh's Sky* (1982) in conjunction with the dominant view within scientific circles that "no domain of experience is more 'real' than any other."[19] Arthur Koestler frequently quotes Goethe's holistic approach to science in his *The Act of Creation* (1964) and in his follow-up volume, *Janus* (1970), in which he scorns the fragmentation of research into discontinuous parts as a reductionist fallacy.[20]

Of course, the eighteenth and nineteenth centuries were in general agreement with the Pythagorean notion of God as the supreme mathematician of the universe and of geometry as co-eternal with the mind of God. These ideas resonate in Kepler and Leibniz, for whom God was the chief mathematician, and also reverberate in the debate between Max Born and Albert Einstein over whether God played with numbers in quantum mechanics.[21] Eighteenth- and nineteenth-century science was steeped in a mathematical way of thinking that represented both a narrowly sol-

16 Cited by Ian Stewart, *Does God Play Dice? The Mathematics of Chaos* (Cambridge, MA: Basel Blackwell 1989), 204–7.

17 James Gleick, *Chaos: Making a New Science* (New York: Penguin Books, 1988), 163–66.

18 John L. Casti, *Complexification: Explaining a Paradoxical World Through the Science of Surprise* (New York: HarperCollins, 1994), 43.

19 Lawrence Leshan and Henry Margenau, *Einstein's Space and Van Gogh's Sky: Physical Reality and Beyond* (New York: Macmillan, 1982), 35.

20 Arthur Koestler, *Janus: A Summing Up* (New York: Random House, 1978), 23–24.

21 See Stewart, *Dice?* 293. For a general introduction, see *The World of Mathematics*, ed. by James R. Newman (New York: Simon and Schuster, 1956), 4–72 et passim.

ipsistic viewpoint as well as a new and potentially broader way of conceptualizing when compared to the medieval world-view (even as non-Euclidean geometry represents a radical expansion of thinking beyond classical Euclidean geometry). The growing empirical trend within the Enlightenment led to a certain skepticism toward the metaphysical quality of mathematical calculations. Many wanted a distinction between pure and applied mathematics. The result of these developments in the Enlightenment led to what Panajotis Kondylis has labeled the "epistemological devaluing of mathematics and the ontological enhancement of the material world."[22] These debates and developments form the backdrop for Goethe's own criticism of the "new guild of mathematicians" that earned him the (undeserved) reputation of being antipathetic toward the science of mathematics. In a letter to Boisserée dated 3 November 1826, he described himself as an ethical-aesthetic mathematician due to his deep-seated need to contrive universal formulas for explaining the world.[23] Goethe's thinking on these matters places him in the camp of Leibniz, with his emphasis on dynamic systems, rather than on the side of LaPlace, with his emphasis on mechanical causality.

The notion of dynamic interplay lies at the heart of Goethe's theoretical musings, which contribute to the rich texture of *Faust*. In the introduction to his *Materialien zur Geschichte der Farbenlehre* (Materials for the History of the Theory of Color, 1808), Goethe flatly states in reference to both the evolution of humankind and of the sciences: "Nothing is static" (FA 23.1:515). He later reiterates that view in *Zur Morphologie* (On Morphology, 1817) when defining the concepts of "Gestalt" and "Bildung" in the organic world: "[N]othing is unchanging, nothing is at rest" ("nirgend ein Bestehendes, nirgend ein Ruhendes"; FA 2:392). In his poem "Metamorphosis of Animals" (1820), he speaks in fact of "the law of dynamic order."[24] That very point, however, had already been made twenty-two years earlier in his didactic poem "Metamorphosis of Plants" (1798), in which he concludes that every plant announces universal laws of change and self-

22 Panajotis Kondylis, *Die Aufklärung im Rahmen des neuzeitlichen Rationalismus* (Munich: Deutscher Taschenbuch Verlag, 1986), 291–98 et passim.

23 Goethe: "als ethisch-ästhetischer Mathematiker muß ich in meinen hohen Jahren immer auf die letzten Formeln hindringen, durch welche ganz allein mir die Welt noch faßlich und erträglich wird" (FA 37:427). Albrecht Schöne, "... wie Teufel die Natur betrachten," *Goethe-Jahrbuch* 111 (1994): 141–50, points out Goethe's need for mathematical clarity, ascribing to it the extraordinary structural modernity of *Faust* (146). Jost Schieren, *Anschauende Urteilskraft: Methodische und philosophische Grundlagen von Goethes naturwissenschaftlichem Erkennen* (Düsseldorf and Bonn: Parerga Verlag, 1998), 115–19, outlines the contemporary debate. See also Gleick, *Chaos*, 165.

24 Johann Wolfgang von Goethe, *Werke*, Sophienausgabe, 6 divisions, 133 vols. in 143 parts (Weimar: Hermann Böhlau, 1887–1919), sect. I, vol. 3, 91. Hereafter cited as WA when the texts were unavailable to me in FA or HA.

similarity (FA 1:640–1). Inherently related to geological as well as morphological formations in nature, this self-similarity is tantamount to repeated mirrorings or "wiederholte Spiegelungen," as Goethe called the phenomenon. Those mirrorings evolved into a major aesthetic ordering strategy that is particularly evident in *Faust*.[25] In contemporary terms, they are reflectaphors (see Briggs) that act together with the narrative to produce a strong and vital work similar to the living organism, which draws equally on the spiral and the vertical tendencies obvious in plant life. In his last contributions to morphology in 1831, when he was putting the finishing touches on *Faust*, Goethe explained that these two separate tendencies function in conjunction to ensure perfection in the plant. The spiral drive is the structuring, nurturing, and progressive function, while the vertical drive is the spiritual one ("ein geistiger Stab"), the basis (or entelechy) of existence which ensures longevity. When not in harmony, monstrosities arise (FA 24:787–88). The manifestation of these two drives is the "Gestalt." In sum, "Gestalt" for Goethe is a dynamical and evolutionary event. The doctrine of forms is equivalent to a doctrine of metamorphosis, and metamorphosis is "the key to all natural signs" (FA 13:205; #2.70.3). A balance of these agonal forces is the prerequisite for success.[26]

A major factor in the evolution of Goethe's thoughts on the agonistic interplay of forces in nature was his acknowledgment of the Copernican Revolution, which had displaced the earth as the center of the universe, thereby leading to the unraveling of a slew of traditional conceptions.[27] Just as the positionality of the

---

25 See Wilfried Secker, *"Wiederholte Spiegelungen": Die klassische Kunstauffassung Goethes und Wilhelm von Humboldts* (Frankfurt a.M.: Peter Lang, 1985), esp.117–61; Peter Salm, *The Poem as Plant: A Biological View of Goethe's Faust* (Cleveland and London: The Press of Case Western Reserve University, 1971); and Noé-Rumberg, *Naturgesetze als Dichtungsprinzipien*, esp. 196–213 (chap. 10: "Wiederholte Spiegelungen"). Through his sensitive reading of the multivalent motifs and themes, von Löw concludes that nothing can be read outside the inner dynamic created by the contending forces of Daimon (individual character), Tyche (accident, the unpredictable), Eros (love. bonding force), Ananke (necessity, restricting force), and Elpis (hope, liberating force). These five functions orchestrate movement in Goethe's world-view, releasing the energy potential inherent in man and his world. See especially von Löw's argument regarding Goethe's late poem "Urworte. Orphisch" for its broader significance in Goethe's thinking (*Strukturen*, 247–63). The poem coincided with the poet's morphological studies. Goethe himself defined the terms cited above. See HA 1:403–7, 721

26 The spiral is cousin to the helix, which is essentially a curve that lies on a cylinder or cone and makes a constant angle with the line segments making up the surface of the cylinder or cone. (Of course, the cylinder is also twisted.) Many large natural molecules (proteins, nucleic acids) are helical in shape. A spiral is one of several plane curves in which a point winds about a fixed central point at ever increasing distances from it. We might see Goethe's emphasis on a spiral theory of growth in plant life, which Peter Salm and Dorothea-Michaela Noé-Rumberg have applied to *Faust*, as a prelude to the much more sophisticated helispheric shapes that geneticists employ.

27 Goethe, *Materialien zur Geschichte der Farbenlehre*: "Vielleicht ist noch nie eine größere For-

observer proved momentous for Copernicus, so did it too for Goethe and his scientific methodology. The observer became an active participant in fathoming the movements of nature; experiments and detailed observations brought about a kind of meditation that transformed the motion of representation into reflections of an intuited dynamic whole. That totality included the inner movement of the subject (also known as the entelechy). In an aphoristic addendum to *On Morphology,* Goethe contended that "the highest good we have received from God and nature is life, the rotating movement of the monad around itself which is never at rest." This inborn drive toward life no man may fathom.[28] Consequently, the inner dynamic of the perceiving subject with her ideal content resonates with the essential idea encapsulated within the object studied.[29]

In coming to grips with that dialectic, Goethe differentiated between two essential methods of inquiry usually associated with the Aristotelian and Platonic schools of thought. In his "Der Versuch als Vermittler zwischen Subjekt und Objekt" (Experiment as Mediator between Subject and Object; 1792, published in 1823), he labels one method mathematical and qualifies it as system building; it seems derivative of the Aristotelian mode of thought and is driven by the desire to prove a point. For the other mode of inquiry – roughly corresponding to the Platonic school of thought – Goethe had no clear label. Yet his description of it suggests that it is "aphoristic" or, better, " *essayistic*," for it records all observations without the benefit of a filtering grid to transform the isolated facts into a rigid system resistant to further questioning. This second method of inquiry he characterizes as being "of a higher art." It requires a different way of thinking, one that is open and closely attentive to natural processes in the empirical realm. While the "essayistic" system is also rooted in the subject-object relationship, the attitude of the subject toward the object is fundamentally different. The subject is no longer confident that the relationship between subject and object is binary, value free, quantifiable, or verifiable. The "essayistic" mode of inquiry is thus premised on the assumption of a mutable, holistic system in which the subject is an interactive

---

derung an die Menschheit geschehen: denn was ging nicht alles durch diese Anerkennung [die Lehre des Kopernikus] in Dunst und Rauch auf: ein zweites Paradies, eine Welt der Unschuld, Dichtkunst und Frömmigkeit, das Zeugnis der Sinne, die Überzeugung eines poetisch-religiösen Glaubens" (FA 23.1:666–7. On the concept of dynamism, see also Harold Jantz, *The Mothers in Faust: The Myth of Time and Creativity* (Baltimore: Johns Hopkins University Press, 1968), 59–62.

28 "Das Höchste was wir von Gott und der Natur erhalten haben ist das Leben, die rotierende Bewegung der Monas um sich selbst, welche weder Rast noch Ruhe kennt; der Trieb das Leben zu hegen und zu pflegen ist einem jeden unverwüstlich eingeboren, die Eigentümlichkeit desselben jedoch bleibt uns und anderen ein Geheimnis." *Zur Morphologie*, vol. 1., "Aphoristisch", FA 24:531.

29 Herbert Witzenmann, "Goethes Idee des Experiments und die moderne Naturwissenschaft," in *Goethes universalästhetischer Impuls: Die Vereinigung der platonischen und aristotelischen Geistesströmung* (Dornach 1987), 45–69; here 63–64.

participant and over which he does not exercise total control. Every individual investigation or experiment ("Versuch") is a tentative endeavor to identify the nature of the connections not just between each individual experiment but also between subject and object (HA 13:10–12). This tentativeness Harold Jantz interprets as the reflection of an underlying "principle of indeterminacy in the sciences" (*Mothers* 60). Drawing upon a later piece, "Bedeutendes Fördernis durch ein einziges geistreiches Wort" ("Significant Advancement through a Single Ingenious Word"), Alan P. Cottrell depicts this "essayistic" method of thinking as "organic and participatory" – a process that "comes alive in nature" and causes nature to come "alive in the activity of thinking."[30] Goethe's "bildende Kraft des Geistes" thus has its counterpart in "der lebendigen Natur" itself (FA 25:32–33). Goethe later labeled this new way of thinking "concrete thinking" ("gegenständliches Denken"). Inasmuch as this mode of thinking is dependent upon the productive input of human imagination and leads to changes in the observer's sense of self, Schieren characterizes it as being ethical.[31] From all this it becomes evident that Goethe was not constrained by the traditional philosophical binary encapsulated in the Platonic and Aristotelian methods of inquiry. Goethe moved beyond a philosophy of alternatives.

In *Materials For the History of the Theory of Color*, Goethe notes the human penchant for going into minute detail in classifying and dissecting nature but cautions us about focusing exclusively on those minutiae. The danger is that the researcher tends to pile up facts, no longer differentiates between more and less worthy insights, and loses sight of the whole. The proper place of humanity, Goethe states, lies in the middle space between the very large and the very small. That medial position makes it possible for humans to grasp and understand only the middle ground, although our striving toward both extremes leads to many an

---

30 Alan P. Cottrell, "The Resurrection of Thinking and the Redemption of Faust: Goethe's New Scientific Attitude," in Seamon and Zajonc, *Goethe's Way of Science*, 255–75; here 259. Richard F. Haglund, Jr., "Visualization and Emergence in Contemporary Physics," in Rowland, *Goethe, Chaos, and Complexity*, 57-68, argues that Goethe would have found the "contemporary physics of complex quantum systems more congenial to his thinking than the Newtonian science of his day" (57). Central to this thesis is Goethe's discomfort with the substitution of mathematical modeling for direct, animated experience (61).

31 Schieren, *Anschauende Urteilskraft*, 124. See also Wyder, *Goethes Naturmodell*, passim. Douglas Miller translates "gegenständlich" as "intuitive." I prefer the more literal "concrete." See D. Miller (ed. and trans.), *Johann Wolfgang von Goethe: Scientific Studies* (New York: Suhrkamp Publishers, 1988), 315 (= vol. 12 of the Suhrkamp Edition). Exemplary of "older" Goethe scholarship on productive rather than merely reproductive seeing is Ernst Cassirer, *Philosophie der symbolischen Formen*, Part III: *Phänomenologie der Erkenntnis*, 10th ed. (Darmstadt: Wissenschaftliche Buchgesellschaft, 1994), 153–56; and Rudolf Steiner, *Geisteswissenschaftliche Erläuterungen zu Goethes Faust, vol. 1: Faust der strebende Mensch* (Freiburg i.Br.: Novalis Verlag, 1955).

unsuspected insight.[32] By placing humankind in this middle position, Goethe favored images of gates, gateways, and passages, along with symbols of threshold states. We find here a cult of the surface as well as a philosophical probing of the depths.

Goethe readily admitted that his own method is deductive, but claimed that he was constantly in search of the "pregnant point" ("prägnanter Punkt"), from which he could derive numerous insights, or, better yet, a position that was capable of presenting to him, as if of its own accord, numerous insights (FA 24:598). Behind this conception lie both the alchemistic thought of Paracelsus and the feedback loops inherent in the forces of expansion and contraction favored by Goethe. Through various stages of metamorphosis in which expansion and contraction alternate with one another, Goethe conjectured, the seed evolves into the stem leaf, calyx, petal, stamen/pistil, fruit, and back to the seed.[33] Metaphorically speaking, the inquiring mind thus functions like sun, water, and nutrients to assist in bringing the object to fruition. We can also see in these bifurcation cycles the autopoietic interactions typical of chaos and complexity theory that extend to human consciousness itself.

In a letter to Frau von Stein dated 7 December 1781, at a time when his interest in geology and botany began to grow, Goethe mentions a plan to write a novel about the origins and development of the universe (FA 29:388). Although that plan was never carried out, essays such as "Über den Granit," ("On Granite," 1784) laid the groundwork. Drawing upon his own geological studies, the poet envisioned granite as the "fundament of our earth" ("Grundfeste unserer Erde"). Its origins are not traceable to the basic elements of fire and water and it constitutes the oldest, most noble monuments of time. Ancient altars of commemoration, granite slabs reach down into the innermost depths of creation itself while rising majestically upward into the thin atmosphere on the periphery. Standing on a mountain peak, Goethe is inspired to profound thoughts about the confluence of the primordial movements in the depths of the earth with those of the lofty heavens and their impact on him, positioned between the two on the solid granite (FA 25:313–15). Throughout the history of change and destruction wrought on the fertile plains, the

---

32 Goethe, *Materialien zur Geschichte der Farbenlehre*: "Was die praktischen Forderungen betrifft, so mögen unnütze Bemühungen noch eher hingehen [beim Hang "ins Minutiose zu gehen"], denn es springt zuletzt doch manchmal etwas Unerwartetes hervor. Aber der, dem es ernst um die Sache ist, bedenke doch ja, daß der Mensch in einen Mittelzustand gesetzt ist und daß ihm nur erlaubt ist, das Mittlere zu erkennen und zu ergreifen" (FA 23.1:967). Similarly, Goethe wrote in the essay on aesthetics, "Einleitung in die Propyläen": "Stufe, Tor, Eingang, Vorhalle, der Raum zwischen dem Innern und Äußern, zwischen dem Heiligen und Gemeinen kann nur die Stelle sein, auf der wir uns mit unseren Freuden gewöhnlich aufhalten werden" (FA 18:457).

33 Cf. Schieren, *Anschauende Urteilskraft*, 191. See also Cottrell, "Resurrection of Thinking," 266–67.

granite cliffs remain unchanged, a tribute to the permanence of creation (FA 25:314). The essay concludes with a review of common historical explanations of the origins of the earth and of granite, whether it happened all at once and in one piece or incrementally through evolution, or whether its origins reach back to chaos ("hier ist alles Trümmer, Unordnung und Zerstörung" FA 25:316). Goethe himself leaves the question open, wondering how he might reconcile the conflicting views.

A kind of belated answer to this question is given forty years later in an essay titled "Versuch einer Witterungslehre" ("Essay on Meteorology" 1825).[34] However, in contrast to the earlier piece in which the static, enduring quality of granite is emphasized, Goethe here applies the principles of dynamic interplay elaborated upon in his organic studies to inorganic matter with its binding and releasing of elements. To this alternation of opposing movement, he adds a certain pulsating rhythm without which vitality would be unthinkable ("ein gewisses Pulsieren," "Bändigen und Entlassen der Elemente," FA 25:292, 295). In both pieces, however, he stresses that humankind is an integral part of its physical environment and that we must be cautious about jumping to conclusions, must be patient in studying nature. The four elements of nature – earth, water, air, fire – he asserts, reveal their own inner drive and laws as they follow their often wild and raucous paths. Earthquakes appear to be the releasing of "telluric electricity," while volcanic eruptions are likened to aroused elemental fire. Both impact upon the atmosphere (FA 25: 297). The four elements seem to be colossal antagonists with which humans must contend. Through force of will ("die höchste Kraft des Geistes"), courage and cunning we can gain mastery over them, but only in some cases. The agonal struggle for dominance in nature, therefore, extends into the human sphere of the spirit as well.

Although Goethe never wrote that novel of the universe, his views are easily discernible in Faust's land acquisition project at the end of his long life in which the struggle to claim land mass from the sea becomes a metaphor for all human existence in a volatile world (the scene dates from 1825–26). Moreover, Goethe explains that the complex interactions of the earth's atmosphere are affected by the attraction of the earth ("Anziehungskraft") through its concomitant quality of gravity ("Schwere") and in cooperation with its opposing force, heat ("Erwärmungskraft"), which causes expansion ("Ausdehnung"). These two force fields – incipient formulations of the gravitational force between the earth and a body on its surface and of thermodynamics – interact through the medium of the atmosphere

34 Goethe, "Versuch einer Witterungslehre," FA, 25:274–300. An excerpt from this essay has been translated as "Toward a Theory of Weather" and included in the Suhrkamp Edition (12:145–50). Albrecht Schöne applies Goethe's views on cloud formation as an interpretive tool in analyzing the scene Mountain Gorges but does not go into the broader interpretation I offer here. See Schöne, *Faust: Kommentare*, FA 7/2:792–95.

itself. They are, quite definitely, one package. Goethe draws an analogy here between the forces of contraction and expansion in atmospheric pressure to the interaction of the opposites of light and darkness in the physical world. Each is contingent on its respective medium for its realization (FA 25:297). Add to this the fact that we humans become aware of atmospheric change through the effect on our bodies – which register the four elemental sensations of heat, cold, moisture, and dryness (FA 25:274) – and the ecological whole is unmistakable.

Furthermore, the alternation of night and day results from the inner, pulsating rotation of the earth around its own axis (FA 25:292). This is clearly a mirroring of the archangels' cosmic view in the Prologue in Heaven, which was penned much earlier around 1800. Thus, the entire opus of *Faust* is framed by telluric explanations. For Goethe, too, the essence of existence is all in the motion, which he variously describes as "a diastolic/systolic movement from the center to the periphery," a "living spiral," and a "living helix without end." We are part of this atmosphere and this surface interplay, existing as it were at the sea's edge. From the shores we move steadily into the interior of the land mass, climb the highest mountains, and even dare to rise higher with our thoughts to the moon, the planets, and the distant stars. We see ourselves as a part of the cosmos and cannot help but assume that it all has a noticeable effect on us and our lives.[35] (The positioning of the reflective observer on the mountaintop echoes the same strategy used in "On Granite.") Consequently, phenomena do not occur in isolation. They are interconnected in complex ways, and harmonize, but also conflict, with one another. Goethe labels this interaction a "highly complex matter" ("höchst komplizierte Sache"; FA 25:298). We would call it an ecological system. It is precisely this complex matter that Goethe expresses in *Faust* as symbol and allegory by interspersing myth, historical fact, and quantifiable reality. The first two – myth and history – originate in quantifiable reality as compensation for that which is not (easily) quantifiable.

Strikingly, Goethe introduces his argument in the essay on meteorology and cloud formation in a manner clearly reminiscent of the concluding lines in *Faust*: "Truth, identical with the Divine, never allows itself to be discerned directly; we perceive it only in a reflection, in an analogy, a symbol" ("Das Wahre, mit dem

35 The various passages referred to are formulated as follows: "Ein- und Ausatmen vom Mittelpunkt gegen die Peripherie," "lebendige Spirale," "belebte Schraube ohne Ende" (FA 25:294–295); "Wir leben darin [in the atmosphere] als Bewohner der Meeresufer [...] wir steigen nach und nach hinauf bis auf die höchsten Gebirge, wo es zu leben schwer wird; allein mit Gedanken steigen wir weiter, wir wagten den Mond, die Mitplaneten und ihre Monde, zuletzt die gegeneinander unbeweglichen Gestirne als mitwirkend zu betrachten, und der Mensch, der alles notwendig auf sich bezieht, unterläßt nicht, sich mit dem Wahne zu schmeicheln, daß wirklich das All, dessen Teil er freilich ausmacht, auch einen besonderen merklichen Einfluß auf ihn ausübe" (FA 25:275–76).

Göttlichen identisch, läßt sich niemals von uns direkt erkennen, wir schauen es nur im Abglanz, im Beispiel, Symbol"; my trans.; FA 25:274). The appropriate symbol of ultimate truth is the process of atmospheric change itself. Telluric movement rises and falls constantly through complex interactions of gravitational pull and caloric energy. Thus, the wisps of fog in low-lying meadows are interactive with higher-flying clouds, ranging from the stratus to the cumulus on up to cirrus formations (FA 25:232). And of course humanity cannot live without the atmosphere. These ideas are inherent in *Faust*, and not just in the final scene, Mountain Gorges, the conception of which dates back to 1800.

Of course, we should be wary of quick analogies. Goethe himself warned against the danger of precipitous judgments, suggesting that the similarities among phenomena will present themselves of their own accord, once we have taken the trouble to distinguish the differences carefully. That shift in attitude constitutes the decisive turn in Goethe's thinking during his Italian sojourn (1786–88). He confessed in the conclusion to his *Materialien zur Geschichte der Farbenlehre* (1810) that by re-examining truth in its "simplest elements" he was forced to re-envision much of what he had previously held dear (FA 23/1:971). He found those simplest elements in nature through his morphological studies. Proposing a "topographical" model to replace the traditional "Stufenleiter" of nature, Goethe argued for sharp, scientific observation and differentiation in contrast to an all too facile inclination to see analogies everywhere. Complexly fractal forms in nature (he speaks of crystallization) were the immediate impulse for this cautionary move. Thus, if we draw considered distinctions, the similarities will present themselves automatically (*Auszüge aus einem Reisejournal*; FA 18:234–35).

In a letter of 9 July 1790 to Ludwig von Knebel, Goethe announced that he was sending him two manuscripts, *Faust* and "Metamorphose der Pflanzen: Zweiter Versuch." They represent, Goethe noted, a shift in his orientation. *Faust* concludes a period of "genial creativity," whereas the "Metamorphosis of Plants" signals the beginning of a new career. His natural inclination to the natural sciences was becoming ever more pronounced (FA 24:938). The modal shift from art to science allowed him to see both activities in a new way. And seeing things in a new way is of course at the heart of creativity. Consequently, Goethe was keenly aware of the need for scientific rigor in registering observations. What one has to do, he realized, is to observe and describe the kind of order each thing actually has. Or, as the physicist David Bohm put it two hundred years later: "One has to be sensitive to the eternally changing differences that are actually to be observed within each thing, and to the unceasing emergence of new similarities and relationships across the boundaries of various things."[36] Any similarities will present themselves

36 David Bohm, *On Creativity*, ed. by Lee Nichol (London & New York: Routledge, 1998), 101.

naturally from physical manifestations or, to use Goethe's preferred term, "Gestalt." Goethe offered with this assessment an early example of the science of emergence that is closely related to chaos and complexity theory. Additionally, in his aphorisms on science Goethe warned the would-be researcher of two things. First, restricting one's view to one's discipline alone runs the risk of inflexibility ("Starrsinn"). Secondly, in moving beyond disciplinary borders, one quickly senses one's inadequacy ("Unzulänglichkeit").[37] One must, therefore, move cautiously. But one must move.

Animated by this drive to be scientifically exact in discerning differences, Goethe preferred to downplay the underlying commonalities. The chief objective in his modeling of nature was thus not to search for missing links in the model but rather to study nature scrupulously (Wyder 206). However, Goethe's insistence on understanding the nature of evolution ("Werden") within its particular contexts also convinced him of the complexity of nature and the need to account for the movement of organizing energy within nature.[38] Nature is so complex, so marked by singularities, he argued in his travel diary from Naples, that no one model of movement could do justice to it. Thus, while Goethe allowed that mineral, plant, and animal were three distinct categories with their own internal laws of continuity, and although he advocated disciplinary rigor, he rejected absolute reductionism in the analysis of natural phenomena. These three categories rose like three mountain peaks from a common valley floor. To be sure, Goethe's morphological interests were directed at the mountain peaks, not at the valley floor which they share in common. Nevertheless, he sought to learn as much about those medial spaces as possible, according special attention to those regions where mineral, plant, and animal seem to collude (FA 18:235). *Faust* reflects those mountain peaks and reveals their common grounding in the earth. While the tragedy does not offer a story of the universe, it does give an account of the deep structures of reality and explains the "similar differences" of the planet we inhabit (Bohm, *Creativity* 9).

---

37 "Vor zwei Dingen kann man sich nicht genug in Acht nehmen: beschränkt man sich in seinem Fache, vor Starrsinn; tritt man heraus, vor Unzulänglichkeit!" (undated; FA 13:104).

38 Tantillo, *Will to Create*, 120–32, argues, therefore, that Goethe was not a precursor of the Darwinian theory of the survival of the fittest. While nature was every bit as aggressive for Goethe as it was later for Darwin, it contained for Goethe aesthetic and compensatory features. See also Tantillo's essay, "Goethe's Evolutionary Thinking," in Rowland, *Goethe, Chaos, and Complexity* , 47–56.

3. Chaos and Creativity I: Spirits of the Earth

Goethe was well acquainted with the various connotations of the concept "chaos" contained in the diverse sources he used, such as Hesiod, the Old Testament, Milton's *Paradise Lost* (1667), and Georgius von Welling's *Opus Mago-Cabbalisticum et Theosophicum* (1735). He intermingled pagan, Christian, and quasi-scientific explanations, whose impact on *Faust* has not been ignored.[39] In the following I will expand those connotations to include contemporary chaos theory with a special focus on the creative moment. *Faust* contains some of Goethe's most famous literary metaphors for the creative impulse: the Spirit of the Earth (or Earth Spirit), Mephistopheles, the Mothers, and Homunculus. These four conceits will be discussed in terms of self-similarity or "similar differences," as advocated by Bohm, a designation he suggests as a replacement for the inaccurate term "dis-order." In chaos theory there is, of course, no binary opposition between order and disorder, just a poorly understood deep structure of relationships. While each of the mythological figures bears the mark of Goethe's own shaping and molding, each has a prehistory that is transformed by the poet's ingenious infusion of new meaning. In the following they will be interpreted as self-similar iterations of Goethe's search for a theory of everything. Taken together with the other products of Goethe's fertile imagination and scientific insight, they constitute a kind of " metaphysics of energy" and help to redefine the concepts of place and space. While Döblin coined the phrase "metaphysics of energy" to describe Nietzsche's will to power, it fits Goethe's notion of energy ("Kraft") as well. Moreover, the Earth Spirit, Mephisto, the Mothers, and Homunculus can all be seen as expressions of that which twentieth-century readers know as the will to power. Their sequence of appearance is noteworthy because it sheds light on the interconnections between each metaphor. I see those interconnections as emanating not from a rigid structuring principle, but from a random pattern of association that reinforces a general intuition of an inner organization, constituting their common ground. It is connectionism *avant la lettre* and offers another way of understanding Rolston's contention that the "Earth is a kind of providing ground, where the life epic is lived on in the midst of perpetual perishing, life arriving and struggling through to something higher."[40] After examining these figures and their spaces, I will consider whether Faust meets the criteria of Nietzsche's genuinely creative free spirit. Reflections on the strange attractor that holds all of these parts together will wrap up the discussion.

39 Friedrich and Scheithauer, *Kommentar zu Goethes Faust*, 182, 292. Gerhard Schulz, "Chaos und Ordnung in Goethes Verständnis von Kunst und Geschichte," *Goethe-Jahrbuch* 110 (1993): 173–83, closes with a nod toward chaos theory.

40 Holmes Rolston, III, *Genes, Genesis, and God: Values and their Origins in Natural and Human History* (Cambridge: Cambridge University Press, 1999), 362.

3.1. The Spirit of the Earth

Faust begins his adventure by contemplating the intricately complex yet mathematically ordered and calculative "pure signs" of the Macrocosm (line 440), an early theory of everything. Yet he rejects it as being a mere sign, that is, a rational construct rather than the vital core. Yearning to grasp the essence of existence – the alchemistic *encheiresin naturae* (line 1940) – he strikes upon the "more potent energy" of the mythical Spirit of the Earth (line 462). " Earth" refers, of course, to the planet as well as the element, the ground upon which we stand. It is thus larger than the connotations of the chemical term, *encheiresin naturae*, the force that bonds the individual molecules in a living organism into a whole. Yet the Earth Spirit defines itself in terms of water imagery, thereby evolving into a symbol of something more than mere earth: it takes on connotations of the even running, ever constant energy that pervades both organic and inorganic matter. Ironically addressing Faust as an *Übermensch*, the Earth Spirit defines itself in the telling lines:

In tides of life, in action's storm	[In Lebensfluten, im Tatensturm
I surge as a wave,	Wall' ich auf und ab,
Swaying ceaselessly;	Webe hin und her!
Birth and the grave,	Geburt und Grab,
An endless sea,	Ein ewiges Meer,
A changeful flowing,	Ein wechselnd Weben,
A life all glowing:	Ein glühend Leben,
I work in the hum of the loom of time	So schaff' ich am sausenden Webstuhl der Zeit
Weaving the living raiment of godhead sublime. (lines 501–09)	Und wirke der Gottheit lebendiges Kleid.]

The strong allusions to flowing water are traceable to (among other sources) the influence of Pietism in which the image signaled the origination of life and the passage of time in a grand design. The Spirit of the Earth expresses that which Nietzsche will later designate the "river of becoming" (*Zarathustra* 113). Intriguing with regard to the water motif is the contemporary scientific insight that ordinary ocean water is composed of randomly moving molecules and that quantum-coherent oscillations are unlikely to occur in such an environment.[41] Water imagery for Goethe, then, seems synonymous with the amorphous stuff of creation: chaos. If Goethe were alive today, however, he might very well refer to the Earth Spirit as the fine-structure constant (or alpha), which is defined in relation to the speed of light and the strength of the attraction between electrically charged particles within

41 Roger Penrose, *Shadows of the Mind: A Search for the Missing Science of Consciousness* (Oxford: Oxford University Press, 1994), 368.

atoms. Of course, those phenomena have wavelike qualities. Even if the alpha proves not to be an immutable law of nature, it has remained constant and even running for several billion years. In human time, that is forever.

Furthermore, there are clear echoes here of the archangels' view in the Prologue in Heaven of the chain of utmost agonistic potency everywhere operative in the cosmos. That agonism is manifest in the two elemental forces associated with the Earth Spirit, fire and water, as well as in its fundamental undulating modes of movement ("Lebensfluten," "Tatensturm"; line 501). In Goethean terms, fire is associated with Vulcanism, while water is the hallmark of Neptunism. Thus we have a conflation of several elements in the one Spirit of the Earth: earth, fire, and water. The fourth element, air, is implied by the fact that the countenance of the Earth Spirit hovers freely in the atmosphere and ultimately vanishes into thin air. But the connection to the atmosphere goes even deeper.

Concepts of the Earth Spirit as *Archaeus terrae* (Paracelsus) and *Anima terrae* (Giordano Bruno) were common in sixteenth-century nature philosophy to explain the inner workings of the animal, plant, and mineral worlds. Goethe added to them Welling's notion of the atmosphere as the "great progenetrix" from the latter's *Opus Mago-Cabbalisticum et Theosophicum.* Welling extended the common notions of creativity to include the spiritual realm alongside the mineral, plant, and animal kingdoms. His work was the inspiration for the early version of the Earth Spirit as "Welt und Thatengenius."[42] Given the Earth Spirit's association with the atmosphere as the mother of all living things, the atmosphere assumes the highest significance as the indispensable source of life for human beings. Furthermore, Welling placed the world spirit in proximity to Beelzebub, who has influence over human actions (Friedrich and Scheithauer 297–98).

While much has been made of the eighteenth-century spirit master Emmanuel Swedenborg and his influence on Goethe in the late 1760s, more important for the shaping of Goethe's thought was Benjamin Hederich's *Gründliches mythologisches Lexicon*. Goethe owned and used both the first (1724) and third (1770) editions of this encyclopedic work. It is a rich source for determining what the Earth Spirit represents and how it relates to Mephisto, a connection that has been the focus of much debate in *Faust* scholarship.[43] The linear sequence in the text is as follows: the sign of the Macrocosm gives way to the Earth Spirit, which makes way for Mephisto, who leads Faust to the Mothers and has a hand in the making of

42 Ernst Grumach, "Prolog und Epilog im Faustplan von 1797" (1952/53), reprinted in *Aufsätze zu Goethes "Faust I,"* ed. by Werner Keller (Darmstadt: Wissenschaftliche Buchgesellschaft, 1974), 310–26; here 317.

43 Cf., e.g., Eudo C. Mason, *Goethe's Faust: Its Genesis and Purport* (Berkeley and Los Angeles: University of California Press, 1967), 110–178, esp. 164–75; Grumach sees a linear connection between the Macrocosm, the Earth Spirit, and the planned Lucifer scene (325).

Homunculus, a miniature Faust. The stumbling block in this sequence has traditionally been the role that good and evil play in defining the figures, particularly whether the Spirit of the Earth is good and Mephisto is evil (a devil). In the following, I draw upon an understanding of good and evil as previously outlined to imply their common grounding: evil spelled backwards is live. And devil read in reverse is [to have] lived.

In his commentary, Erich Trunz speaks of the Earth Spirit as being mysterious, placing it in line with Mephisto, the chorus of spirits (lines 1259ff., 1447ff., 1607ff.), the creatures in the Witch's Kitchen, the figures in the Walpurgis Night, and Ariel and his fellow spirits in the scene Pleasant Regions of Act I, Part II (HA 3:519). These associations blur the line between good and evil. More emphatically than Trunz, Albrecht Schöne stresses the grounding of the Earth Spirit in the earth by citing Hederich's original explanation of the Daemogorgon as an elemental efficient source of energy rather than as a beneficent or malevolent daemon. The Daemogorgon

> essentially signifies the Earth Spirit and is used to designate the first and original essence which is the source of our threefold world; namely, the heavens, the earth, the oceans, and everything contained in them. Still, one ought not even name the thing. Daemogorgon was also the father of all the gods, although he was himself without origin. One should think of him as a pale, misshapen old man covered with dirt and moss and dwelling in the bowels of the earth and as a companion to Eternity and Chaos. [...] One attributes to Daemogorgon many offspring such as Discord, Pan, the three Parces, Erebus. [...] To be sure, however, this primary being was nothing other than what one calls nature.
>
> [soll so viel als der Erdgeist heißen und wird für das erste und ursprüngliche Wesen aller Dinge angegeben, welches die dreyfache Welt, nämlich den Himmel, die Erde und das Meer und alles, was darinnen ist, hervorgebracht hat, dessen Namen man aber eigentlich nicht nennen durfte. Er war auch der Vater aller Götter, hatte aber selbst keinen Ursprung. Man stelle ihn als einen kothigen, mit Mooße bedeckten, blassen und ungestalten Greis vor, der in dem Innern der Erde wohnete und die Ewigkeit und das Chaos zu Gefährten hatte. [...] Man giebt dem Daemogorgon sonst noch viele Kinder, als die Zwietracht, den Pan, die drey Parcen, den Erebus u.a. An sich aber war dieses Grundwesen nichts anders, als was man die Natur nennet.][44]

Moreover, in a perverted variation of *Genesis* 1, Daemogorgon created the atmosphere and sun out of sheer boredom, joining to them the earth, which produced Tartarus and Night. Key for my purposes is the clear prefiguring of Goethe's own use of the four elements to characterize the Earth Spirit in *Faust*. From the outset its function was much more encompassing than that of a metaphor for *an* element

44 Benjamin Hederich, *Gründliches mythologisches Lexicon*, ed. by Johann Joachim Schwabe, Leipzig 1770, Photomechanical reproduction (Darmstadt: Wissenschaftliche Buchgesellschaft, 1986), 858; cited in part by Schöne, FA 7.2:216.

of nature. Rather, the Earth Spirit is a kind of cosmic seed coexistent with Chaos, born of Erebus (Darkness) at the beginning of time.[45] Thus, we find the allusions in the Earth Spirit's self-definition to the functions of the Moirai – Atropos, Klotho, and Lachesis – in determining historical events:. The three fates spin the thread of life, measure it, and cut it into varying lengths (lines 142–47, 5305–44). These broader implications, albeit on a different scale, are also evident in the fine-structure constant in contemporary astrophysics: any variation in that constant impacts directly on our notions of time and space.

Moreover, the Earth Spirit also entails a religious dimension. Since it manifests itself in tongues of fire, one can see in it an allusion to the descent of the Holy Spirit upon the Twelve Apostles at Pentecost, imparting to them the gift of tongues. The ability to speak foreign languages enabled them to reach out and make new connections. As the expression of the bonding element between the Father and the Son in the Holy Trinity, the Holy Spirit is thus the original "connectionist" from the beginning of time. Transferred to the Earth Spirit, the subliminal allusion to the Holy Spirit might be construed to be an expression of the fifth element, the quintessence of existence that binds all things together. That would make it an emblem for more than the exchange of energy that bonds (gluons).

3.2 Mephistopheles

The Spirit of the Earth rejects Faust as incapable of understanding its essence, asserting: "You are like the spirit you comprehend, / Not me!" (lines 512–13). The spirit whom Faust does resemble is Mephistopheles. They are alike in being bound somewhat differently to the earth than the Earth Spirit. Because of their limited view, confusion arises. Misunderstanding is characteristic of both Faust and Mephisto. Whereas Faust mistakenly assumes that the Earth Spirit is "restless" and frustrated like himself, Mephisto believes that Faust is driven to seek contentment. Faust does not comprehend that the Earth Spirit encompasses the entire cycle of creation and destruction, of order and disorder. Coexistent with Chaos and Erebus from the beginning of time, according to Hederich, the Earth Spirit is thus related to Chaos. However, Mephisto, too, is part and parcel of Chaos and Night. He introduces himself to Faust as

45 Gerhard Gönner speaks of "eine kraftbeseelte Urmaterie." *Metzler Goethe Lexikon*, with 150 illustrations, ed. by Benedikt Jeßing, Bernd Lutz, and Inge Wild (Stuttgart and Weimar: J. B. Metzler, 1999), 121.

part of the part which once was absolute,
part of the Darkness which gave birth to Light,
The haughty Light, which now seeks to dispute
The ancient rank and range of Mother Night.

[Ich bin ein Teil des Teils, der anfangs alles war,
Ein Teil der Finsternis, die sich das Licht gebar
Das stolze Licht, das nun der Mutter Nacht
Den alten Rang, den Raum ihr streitig macht.] (lines 1349–52)

The indebtedness to traditional concepts of the pagan myth of creation according to Hesiod's *Theogony* is self-evident).[46] But Goethe injects a religious and philosophic element into the equation when he has Mephisto explain that the agonal struggle between Night and Light is a conflict between the light of the soul or the light of reason and the body or the material world. While ensuring the survival of the (inner) light, the body also hinders its development. Thus, Mephisto is hopeful that he and the forces of Night might still prevail (lines 1353–58). His mistake is to think in such binaries. It should be noted that in Mephistopheles' definition, the Absolute was originally Darkness, but it became divided when it gave birth to Light. That light, however, is still bound to the body. In fact, light does not become visible until it interacts with a material presence. Thus, in his version of the first nanosecond of creation, a binary opposition clearly obtains, an approach that distances him from the unifying Earth Spirit.

In his binary mode, Mephisto easily constructs himself monodimensionally as the consummate nihilist (lines 1338, 11550), who adamantly opposes "Somethingness" – "this stupid earth" (line 1364). Yet his opposition is to no avail, for "In spite of tempest, earthquake, flood, and flame / The earth and ocean calmly stay the same" (lines 1367–68). As a consciously oppositional force, Mephisto is unlike the connectionist Earth Spirit. The latter is more like the wave function of elemental particles (the even hum of existence); it gives no particular value to any individual physical manifestation but ensures that energy can be vented throughout the scales of existence. In opposing Faust's affirmation of life, Mephisto proves to be a complementary force, what has been called "a reality principle." By defining and completing one another, Faust and Mephisto guarantee continuity in change. The dialectic of creation/destruction, day/night, and affirmation/denial is autopoietic.

46 E.g., Ulrich Hoffmann, "Mephisto[phe]les: 'Ich bin ein Teil des Teils, der anfangs alles war,'" *Goethe-Jahrbuch* 109 (1992): 57–60. Various etymological attempts have been made to trace the name "Mephistopheles" back to Greek and Hebrew origins. Not always persuasive from a philological point of view, the conclusions are nonetheless useful. Accordingly, Mephistopheles connotes "one who shies from light" or "destroyer of the good." He also connotes the decay and decomposition of a physical presence. See Friedrich and Scheithauer (323) and Schöne FA 7.2:167.

Mephisto's efforts are in vain because he is part of that which once was whole, as the agonal, complementary force, he keeps the cycle going, functioning much like the negative pole to Faust's positive one. Without that opposition – as in an electric motor or an electromagnetic force field – there is no movement, no balance, no life. Consequently, he would "Do evil ever yet forever works the good" (line 1336). That in itself places him (and Faust) beyond traditional concepts of good and evil.[47]

Despite his differences, Mephisto shares much of the same territory with the Earth Spirit. This point is underscored when he specifically draws attention to the four elements (earth, water, air, fire) and the four sensations (dryness, wetness, warmth, cold) that constitute the earth and its life cycles. He himself is associated with the flame; that is, he is part of the whole set of basic elements of life as we know it. The four elements are even present in the forces of havoc: tempest, earthquake, flood, and flame (line 1367). Despite their assaults, earth and ocean remain undisturbed. The duality of firmament and formless sea signifies the opposite poles of attraction and dissolution inherent in form and formlessness. The imagery invoked by Mephisto in his lament reminds the reader of the cosmic view of the archangels, who can see the contesting forces in operative nature but who cannot comprehend them. The archangels prefigure Mephisto in this regard, for like them, he too does not comprehends neither the whole nor the positive function that he plays in what Nietzsche will later call the total economy of life (lines 4, 5, 1274ff., 1374). On the other hand, Faust could not conjure Mephisto by appealing individually to the four elements, because Mephisto is not a *minor* spirit bound to just *one* element. His association with fire transcends earthly (or hellish) flame to embrace the tongues of fire, designating both the Earth and the Holy Spirit, the latter connection being made on a deep, unconscious level.[48]

In his role as a devil, Mephisto is related to Lucifer, the original angel of light, who was cast down from majestic order into darkness and confusion for his sin of sheer egoism, that is, for believing himself to be a self-sufficient force. This story Goethe recounts at the end of Book 8 of his autobiographical *Dichtung und Wahrheit* (Poetry and Truth; FA 14:382–85). Read from the vantage point of chaos theory, Goethe essentially recounts the principle of iteration in the never ending decay of order *into* chaos and the rise of order *out of* chaos, in cycles of contraction and expansion. The young Goethe invested Lucifer with creative energies: every

47 Excellent, older interpretations of Mephisto include Albert Fuchs, "Mephistopheles" (1968), *Aufsätze zu Goethes "Faust I,"* 348–61; and Oskar Seidlin, "Das Etwas und das Nichts: Versuch einer Neuinterpretation" (1944), in *Aufsätze zu Goethes "Faust I,"* 362–68. Jane K. Brown, *Goethe's Faust: The German Tragedy* (Ithaca, NY: Cornell University Press, 1986), 85–96, designates Mephisto "a reality principle" that reveals "a spark of the higher world of spirit" (92–93).

48 For Dieter Breuer, "Mephisto als Theologe," *Goethe-Jahrbuch* 109 (1992): 91–100, the level is not all that deep. He interprets Mephisto as representative of a "theology of spurned love" (100).

material object, everything with qualities of weight, firmness, and darkness belongs to him. Even more, he created all of the angels in his own likeness. The paradox of the archangel of light being transformed into the arch-advocate of annihilation is rooted in the dialectic of the Deity itself. The essence of that dialectic Goethe identified as the impulse to (re)produce itself for all eternity ("ein Produktionstrieb"; FA 14:383). The first product of that impulse was the Son; together Father and Son brought forth the third being in the Trinity, the Holy Spirit. The Trinity was complete in itself and could not engage in mere repetitive action. Thus, the Trinity produced a slight variation of itself, changing the initial conditions so that it could take charge of every other creative act outside the perfection of the Trinity. That slight variation was Lucifer, Divine like his progenitors, but essentially aligned with everything the Trinity was not: matter. Yet matter ("die Materie"), Goethe argued, is as eternal and divine as the Trinity itself, since it emanates from the spirit/energy. By expressing itself as matter rather than pure energy, the Trinity could avoid simple replication. However, the self-similar rather than self-same replication of itself embodies a paradox: iteration contains the seed of potential disorder. And this paradox pertains "in all categories of existence" (FA 14:384). This perception dovetails with that of contemporary chaos theory, which argues that every particle, every manifestation of matter and energy contains an encrypted image of the totality.

As the consequence of thc principle of concentration/contraction, matter is the opposite of the principle of dissolution/expansion. Lucifer's fall was prompted by his single-minded orientation toward concentration. Indeed, had creation continued according to the Luciferean principle, it would have self-destructed and lost all claim to being equal to God. Thus, the Elohim simply willed to matter the ability to expand and to move against them, thus preserving the original dynamic. That marked the beginning of creation proper, with the birth of light, the re-establishment of the pulse of life, and the eventual creation of humankind as the one being capable of reconnecting with the godhead (FA 14:384). (Is there a parallel here to Goethe's view that humankind acts according to the laws of nature even when ostensibly contradicting nature?) Yet like Lucifer, humanity was/is simultaneously marked by a dialectic of expansion and contraction ("unbedingt und beschränkt") and soon assumed the role formerly played by Lucifer. "All of creation," Goethe contended, "is and was nothing other than a falling away from and a returning to the original state" ("obgleich die ganze Schöpfung nichts ist und nichts war, als ein Abfallen und Zurückkehren zum Ursprünglichen"; FA 14:384).[49] This, as we know,

49 Some readers might appreciate having Goethe's own formulations in this intriguing passage: "Ich möchte mir wohl eine Gottheit vorstellen, die sich von Ewigkeit her selbst produziert [...] . Da jedoch der Produktionstrieb immer fortging, so erschufen sie [Vater – Sohn – Heiliger Geist] ein

happened to Adam and Eve. Their offspring are still trying to return to the original state.

Given Mephisto's own explanation of the Fall, there is no consistent binary opposition even here. Instead, there is a complex interweaving of layered meaning – not concentric circles tracing one another's orbits indistinguishably, but slightly unfocused remappings that give rise to repeated mirrorings. Perhaps for this reason Faust calls Mephisto "Chaos' own fantastic son!" (line 1384). "The creative, living, and benign" (line 1382) cannot be undone by Mephisto. Those are qualities of the fifth element, which Mephisto does not understand or partake of and over which he has no control (cf. lines 11689–92, 11780–86). In fact, the pentagram prevents his departure (line 1395). Each point of the star represents a letter in the name of the Savior: J-E-S-U-S. And Jesus came to preach that love can make the world whole again. The vacillation in Mephisto's identity underscores the point that Goethe had conceived of a world beyond the traditional dualism of good and evil, rejecting it in favor of a dialectic between these mutually defining poles of attraction. Critical to their understanding is Goethe's fundamental emphasis in the play on mediation rather than on separation.[50]

Strikingly, the immediate precedent to Mephisto's manifestation is Faust's

Viertes, das aber schon in sich einen Widerspruch hegte, indem es, wie sie, unbedingt und doch zugleich in ihnen enthalten und durch sie begrenzt sein sollte. Dieses war nun Lucifer, welchem von nun an die ganze Schöpfungskraft übertragen war, und von dem alles übrige Sein ausgehen sollte. [...] Und so ereignete sich das, was uns unter der Form des Abfalls der Engel bezeichnet wird. Ein Teil derselben konzentrierte sich mit Lucifer, der andere wendete sich wieder gegen seinen Ursprung. Aus dieser Konzentration der ganzen Schöpfung, denn sie war von Lucifer ausgegangen und mußte ihm folgen, entsprangen nun alles das, was wir unter der Gestalt der Materie gewahr werden, was wir uns als schwer, fest und finster vorstellen [...]. Da nun das ganze Unheil, wenn wir es so nennen dürfen, bloß durch die einseitige Richtung Lucifers entstand; so fehlte freilich dieser Schöpfung die bessere Hälfte: denn alles was durch Konzentration gewonnen wird, besaß sie, aber es fehlte ihr alles was durch Expansion allein bewirkt werden kann; und so hätte die sämtliche Schöpfung durch immerwährende Konzentration sich selbst aufreiben, sich mit ihrem Vater Lucifer vernichten und alle ihre Ansprüche an eine gleiche Ewigkeit mit der Gottheit verlieren können [in der sie ja ihren Ursprung hat] [...]. Sie [die Elohim] gaben dem unendlichen Sein die Fähigkeit sich auszudehnen, sich gegen sie zu bewegen; der eigentliche Puls des Lebens war wieder hergestellt und Lucifer selbst konnte sich dieser Entwicklung nicht entziehen. [...] Es währte nicht lange, so spielte er [der Mensch] auch völlig die Rolle des Lucifer. [...] Man sieht leicht, wie hier die Erlösung nicht allein von Ewigkeit her beschlossen, sondern als ewig notwendig gedacht wird, ja daß sie durch die ganze Zeit des Werdens und Seins sich immer wieder erneuern muß. Nichts ist in diesem Sinne natürlicher, als daß die Gottheit selbst die Gestalt des Menschen annimmt" (FA 14:382–85).

50 Thomas Zabka, "Dialektik des Bösen: Warum es in Goethes 'Walpurgisnacht' keinen Satan gibt," *Deutsche Vierteljahresschrift für Literaturwissenschaft und Geistesgeschichte* 72.2 (1998): 201–26; here 207.

translation of the gospel according to John. Rejecting the translation of "logos" as "word" in the line "In the beginning was the word" ("Wort") as being too conceptual, he moves to "mind" ("Sinn") because of its connotations of putative power ("Denkkraft"). Dissatisfied that "mind" adequately captures the essence of "making and shaping" ("wirken und schaffen"), he decides upon "power" ("Kraft"). But then something (he specifically cites the Earth Spirit) warns him that this will not do either, and thus he ultimately chooses "deed" ("Tat") (lines 1229-37). Without deed there is, to Faust's egotistical mind, no making and shaping. Traditionally, this falsifying of the Biblical text has been viewed as signifying Faust's inherent willfulness. While it does do that, its significance is more profound because it confirms the concept of motion as fundamental to existence, something we have seen repeatedly in the wake of the Copernican Revolution.

At this point in the novel of the universe, Faust is not yet fully aware that nature functions independently of individual willful acts; he does not yet understand that volition and natural processes must cooperate in the manner of the vertical and spiral tendencies of the plant world or of the young Goethe's cosmogony. The vertical drive represented by Faust "in his dark drive" must be augmented in the earthly realm of growth and change by the spiral tendency, which extends to Mephisto himself. The dynamic is not simply that of opposing souls, one drawing Faust upward, the other binding him to the earth, but also that of a "wobble" of irregularity at the periphery caused by centrifugal and convergent forces. The nonlinear dynamics give the "system" (constitution) of the human being strength and stability as he grows upward, driven by his own internal seed, monad, or entelechy, that is, his own individual spiritual essence (for a possible schematic, see Fig. 5.1). The mistranslation of "logos" as "deed," therefore, confirms Faust's inability to comprehend the Earth Spirit as the even running energy of these essential tensions. His translation of the Biblical verse, on the other hand, is an affirmation of motion as seminal. At

Figure 5.1: Structure of *Faust*
(Erwin von Löw, *Goethes Faust* 336)

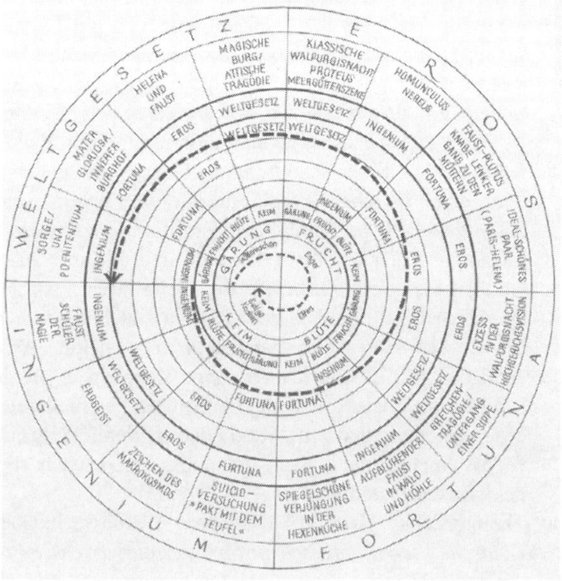

this very point in the narrative, Faust's alter ego, Mephisto, manifests himself to goad Faust to further action. From the Prologue in Heaven, we know that the Lord sent Mephisto (*actio in distans*?) before totally disappearing from the opus as a separate entity. The translation scene might at first appear to be an inadvertent incantation of the occult, but it proves to be entirely natural.

Magic clearly plays a major role in the history of the Faust theme. Faust states almost immediately that he has devoted himself to magic because reason has failed him in his pursuit of knowledge (line 377). In general, magic was aimed at gaining insight into the mysteries of nature and was thus known as *magia naturalis*.[51] The sources Goethe used – Paracelsus's *Philosophia sagax* (1537–38), Morhof's *Polyhistor* (1688), Bacon's *De dignitate et augmentis scientiarum* (1623), and Welling's *Opus Mago-Cabbalisticum et Theosophicum* – speak of two kinds of magic. One was aimed at the spiritual and at knowledge (*magia bona*) and was tolerated by the Church, while the other was aimed at the occult and at sensual pleasure (*magia mala*) and was disallowed. The first became known as white magic, the latter as black magic. Theories of magic are based on the belief that spirits inhabit all of nature and the universe. As a microcosm of the world, the human being mirrors the larger macrocosm in which she is integrated. It is easy to see in the Spirit of the Earth white magic, in Mephisto black magic. In fact, the following dichotomy of manifestations seems plausible:

magia bona	*magia mala*
Spirit of the Earth	Mephistopheles
Faust's thirst for knowledge	Witch's Kitchen
Homunculus	Walpurgis Night
Classical Walpurgis Night	Evil Spirit (3775–3832)
Helena	The Three Mighty Men
Euphorion	
The Mothers	
Mountain Gorges	

When Mephisto first appears, for example, it is as a black dog. The color black Goethe associated with evil, white with good (*Theory of Color* FA 23.1:291). Moreover, darkness connotes the material world, the world of sexuality, gold, sensual pleasure, power, social status. Everything in Mephisto's column is associated with these values; everything in the Earth Spirit's column is associated with creative potential and development through a balancing of conflicting forces.

51 See Trunz, "Kommentar," HA 3:513-16; Norbert Heinrichs, "Scientia Magica" (1970), in *Aufsätze zu Goethes "Faust I,"* 607–24; Gaier, *Goethes Faust-Dichtungen*, 1:103–19; and Ulrich Gaier, *Magie: Goethes Analyse moderner Verhaltensformen in Faust* (Konstanz: Universitätsverlag, 1999).

Yet as we have seen, it is not so simple to distinguish between white and black magic. They shade over into one another, even as the divine in Faust – this "image of the godhead" (line 516) – shades over into the animal. Mephisto states that his true element is what we call sin, destruction, and evil. He does not assert that he is identical to these forces, but that he is at home where they dominate; and they dominate at the edge of order. In Christian doctrine, only God is wholly consistent and enduring. And humankind designates that which has no consistency as related to evil. Hence, evil equates to incompleteness and imperfection. These are transitional states, with a tilt toward either expansion (more perfection) or contraction (less perfection). Whereas Faust tilts toward the former, Mephisto tends toward the latter. Since these attitudes arose with the dualism of Night and Light, they, like Mephisto, have been present from the beginning of time. It is their natural, hybrid element. Evil, then, is tantamount to the disequilibrious or destabilizing moments of existence, perhaps appearing as the focus on the self as realized matter. The devil can be associated with the force of gravity because it restrains humankind's impulse to soar. In terms of Goethean morphology, Faust is tantamount to the vertical tendency, Mephisto the horizontal one. The horizontal conditions and strengthens the vertical, causing the spiral dynamic. Furthermore, contemporary chaos theory underscores the natural alteration between positive and negative feedback. Order arises from positive feedback and declines through negative feedback. Mephisto can be associated with negative feedback. As the fantastic son of Chaos, he is also associated with productivity and growth. Hence, defining evil is a complex matter.

In the Classical Walpurgis Night, Mephisto naturally takes on the form ("Gestalt") of the mythological Graeae (Pemphredo, Enyo, Deino), who represent consummate ugliness. I say "naturally" not simply because ugliness is the only appropriate form for him to assume in his role as the opposing force in Greek antiquity. (The Greeks had no concept comparable to the Christian devil. Their ideal of perfection was related to beauty; ugliness connoted lack of perfection.) The Phorkyads are the appropriate shape because the three sisters – who share one eye and one tooth – are related to Night, Solitude, and Chaos. Mephisto claims to be their distant cousin (line 7987). According to Hederich's dictionary of mythology, they were the daughters of Phorkys and dwelled in a place where neither sun nor moon ever shone. Night was their mother, Chaos their father (lines 7985–8011). To be sure, Mephisto thinks they are the sisters of the Fates and of Chaos, while the Graeae identify themselves as Chaos's daughters (line 8028). After he has assumed their shape, Mephisto proudly proclaims: "And here I stand: / Chaos' well beloved son!" (lines 8026–27). The inherent productivity of nihilism and nothingness is revealed when he immediately notes that he is hermaphroditic, that is, autopoietically life producing (line 8029).

His hermaphroditism establishes a connection to Seismos, who is active within the bowels of the earth. Through the latter's powerful deeds, the mountains were thrust up from below the earth's surface, creating by this violent act space for life to germinate and contributing to the beauty of creation: "And had I not so shattered and so strewn, / Would this world not be beautiless?" (lines 7552–53). Specifically, Seismos notes that his show of strength occurred "under my great parents' eye – Chaos and Night" (lines 7558–59). Mount Olympus itself he raised to its heights, creating "new life for all dwellers here" (line 7573). The connection between Mephisto and Seismos is strengthened in the opening scene of Act IV, which is among other things a mirroring of Christ's temptation by Satan. While Faust, perched high on the rocky cliff, is conceiving his plan to create land and life at the edge of firmament (ordered molecules) and ocean water (random dynamic molecules), Mephisto seeks to draw his attention back to the land already created, endeavoring to tempt him with its surface play of "tumult, violence, and nonsense" ("Tumult, Gewalt und Unsinn"; line 10127). Arguing the Plutonic view of earth's cataclysmic formation in counterpoint to Faust's Neptunian perspective of evolution, Mephisto emphatically states:

... All is clear as the sun's glory;	[... Das scheint euch sonnenklar.
One who was there can tell a different story.	Doch weiß es anders der zugegen war.
And I was there when, seething down below,	Ich war dabei, als noch da drunten, siedend,
The abyss came flooding up in fiery tide,	Der Abgrund schwoll und strömend Flammen trug,
When Moloch's hammer forged cliffs at a blow	Als Molochs Hammer, Fels an Felsen schmiedend
and scattered mountain fragments far and wide.	Gebirges-Trümmer in die Ferne schlug.]
(lines 10105-10)	

Mephisto repeats his claim for added emphasis (line 10125).

Thus, despite his own focus on the moment of dissipation, Mephisto nonetheless induces new life and new order through the advancement of knowledge. As Nietzsche was to note: "The devil has the widest perspectives for God, and that is why he keeps so far away from him – the devil being the oldest friend of knowledge" (*BGE* #129). Mephisto's binary function requires his distance from God so that the Absolute can be put into proper perspective.

4. Chaos and Creativity II: Places and Spaces

4.1 Prologue in Heaven

Opening with dominant metaphors of movement, light, and sound in reference to the workings of creation, the Prologue in Heaven provides the metaphysical framework for Faust's subsequent deeds. The initial image is of the sun and planets interacting "in rival sound" and "in thunderous motion" according to their appointed rounds. The archangels draw strength from the sight, although they are incapable of comprehending its deep structure. Yet all is grand and new as on Creation Day (lines 243–50). Most likely, the reference is to both the *Book of Job* (38:7) – upon which *Faust* is partially based – and the spheric harmonies of the Pythagoreans.[52] The revolutions of the sun and its kindred spheres (i.e., here the planets) create a din as the orbs contend with one another for dominance while circling around a common center of fire, as the Pythagoreans envisioned the universe. The competitive movement is repeated continuously (as seen from the earthly perspective), as if each day were a new beginning. In other words, the periodic rotations of the sun, earth, and brother planets – while apparently mirroring the previous day's rounds – might be seen as a code for agonistic creativity itself, since the movement is caused by contending force fields emanating from the celestial bodies acting at a distance. The latter give rise to a din of sounds rather than to harmonies. Humans cannot hear the sounds. Angels hear discords. Only the Supreme Being is capable of hearing the harmonies. From reiterative movement a whole cacophony of divergences result. Those divergences become most notable in the clash between land and water on the earth's surface. Seen from the cosmic perspective, however, there is a unity of forces within this diversity. Operative throughout the system is gravity. This universal gravity smacked of the *anima mundi* of the ancients, which Copernicus, Kepler, and Galileo had sought to reject in favor of a mechanistic explanation of a clockwork universe. Yet the image projected in the Prologue in Heaven suggests that "the universe was held together by a mysterious force which, like the Holy Ghost, was acting at a distance, in defiance of all the laws of mechanics."[53] Hence, Goethe and his contemporaries

---

52 See Schöne, "Erläuterungen," FA 7.2:165–66 and Passage, *Faust* (12, n2). Albrecht Schöne, *Goethes Farbentheologie* (Munich: C.H. Beck, 1987), 84–93, discusses the significance of the sun and light as divine and life-giving. For another approach to this imagery, see John A. McCarthy, "'A Chain of Utmost Potency': On the Agon and the Creative Impulse," in *Agonistics: Arenas of Creative Contest*, ed. by Janet Lungstrum and Elizabeth Sauer (Albany, NY: State University of New York Press, 1997), 199–225; esp.202–8.

53 Arthur Koestler, *Bricks to Babel* (New York: Random House, 1980), 403. Koestler retraces the innovativeness of the early debate on gravity in chap. 34, "Gravity and the Holy Ghost" (394–403).

were living in a world far less solid and rational than was generally presumed. Contemporary models of infinite variety and agonistic balance are manifest in the self-duplication of desoxyribonucleic acid in living organisms and in the interactions of elementary particles in inorganic matter (see chap. 1).

The connotation of agonistic motion on the grand scale of things is brought out clearly in the ensuing lines, which emphasize the swiftness of movement and binaries on the surface of the earth such as light and dark, land and sea. The ordered motions of the sun and planets are transformed on earth into destructive oppositions. The archangels Gabriel and Michael describe what they see:

And swift beyond conception flies	[Und schnell und unbegreiflich schnelle
The turning earth, now dark, now bright,	Dreht sich umher der Erde Pracht;
With clarity of paradise	Es wechselt Paradieseshelle
Succeeding deep and dreadful night.	Mit tiefer, schauervoller Nacht;
The sea in foam from its broad source	Es schäumt das Meer in breiten Flüssen
Against the base of cliffs is hurled,	Am tiefen Grund der Felsen auf,
And down the sphere's eternal course	Und Fels und Meer wird fortgerissen
Both cliff and sea are onward whirled.	In ewig schnellem Sphärenlauf.
And storms a roaring battle wage	Und Stürme brausen um die Wette,
From sea to land, from land to sea,	Vom Meer auf Land, vom Land aufs Meer,
And forge a chain amid their rage,	Und bilden wütend eine Kette
A chain of utmost potency. (lines 251–62)	Der tiefsten Wirkung rings umher.]

These binaries are created by the earth turning on its axis and hurtling around a "common eternal grounding" with the sun and its brother planets.[54] Brilliant light alternates with deepest night, the raging sea thrusts itself incessantly on the brazen cliffs impeding its path. These potent images are bundled together as the entire scene is rendered as a projectile hurtling through endless space caught up in eternal combat with the elements. The extraterrestrial as well as the terrestrial mirror and condition one another involuntarily in a process of mutual (re-)creation. They constitute, as the final line summarizes, "A chain of utmost potency," an image later mirrored in Nietzsche's *Will to Power*. The potency emphasizes the interconnectedness of the cosmic and the human; each isolated movement is integrated in an evolutionary whole. Despite all the evidence of struggle, it would be a mistake, therefore, to define agonistic creativity solely in terms of prevailing and mastering, even though the wager between the Lord and Mephisto predisposes us to think in these terms. Here it is helpful to note Goethe's assessment in his 1783 essay, "Die Natur": "One abides by her [nature's] laws even when one resists them;

54 Schöne argues convincingly that the "allgemeiner ewiger Grund," the discovery of which was the goal of the *Theory of Color*, was synonymous for Goethe with the whole (*Goethes Farbentheologie* 94). See also Koestler, *Bricks*, 397–98.

one cooperates with her, even when one desires to act contrary to her" ("Man gehorcht ihren Gesetzen, auch wenn man ihnen widerstrebt, man wirkt mit ihr auch wenn man gegen sie wirken will"; FA 25:13). Consequently, although "agonist" denotes a competitive or divergent individual, it also connotes cooperation or convergence of forces. The agonistic movement of the image provides an example of the common, universal grounding of existence.

4.2 The Witch's Kitchen

The Witch's Kitchen (*Hexenküche*) appears to mirror the dialectic of the continual re-creation thematized in the opening passage of the Prologue in Heaven. Repulsed by the "stark raving rookery" (line 2339), Faust is ill at ease, while Mephisto basks in his true element of fire, heat, and chaotic movement, surrounded by creatures representing the lower instincts. The image of the earth is evoked in the large globe that the monkeys play with, emphasizing how endlessly turning, gleaming, and yet hollow and vain it is, and ultimately how easily it shatters into a thousand pieces. The significance of the symbol is efficiently summed up in the first and last lines of their characterization: "That is the world [...] Alive am I" (lines 2402–10). Playing the role of King of Chaos, Mephisto sits on a throne, scepter in hand, and holds court over the tumultuous activities of the monkeys. They break the crown intended for his head, speak nonsensically, and let the pot boil over as the Witch comes down the chimney, burning herself in the process. When she scoops flames out of the pot and casts them at Faust, Mephisto, and the apes, Mephisto rises from his throne, smashing the glasses and pots with his scepter.

While Mephisto thus reigns over the destructive side of chaos, Faust is fascinated by the image of "a woman of utmost grace" in a mirror (line 2436). Traditionally, the disconnection has been interpreted as Faust's alienation in the Witch's Kitchen; the reclining female nude is viewed as the expression of his inner nobler strivings, a foreshadowing of Gretchen and of Helena. However, the dynamics of the agon and the interconnections of chaos teach us to see Faust's apparent detachment from the chaotics of Mephisto's world as complementary to that commotion, coordinated in complex ways. Contemplation of the beauty in the magic mirror awakens in him sensual longing and initiates an inner chaos of emotions. Reluctantly, he is drawn away from the mirror and placed in a circle inscribed by the Witch. An ironic allusion to the harmonic spheres becomes evident when the glasses begin to ring and the kettle to boom in the making of music, after the Witch has placed strange objects inside the circle. With Faust as its center and focus, it is tempting to see the circle with the objects and human figure as a substitute for the sign of the Macrocosm, a reinterpretation of the universe, as it were, from the perspective of black magic and the devil. "Now tell me," Faust whispers to Mephisto, "what is all this leading to? / These frantic motions and this wild ado?" (lines 2532–33). We know by now that it all leads to new life, new horizons, and a new way of thinking.

This new way of thinking is reflected in the "nonsense" of the Witch's "one-times-one." It amounts to putting "thinking aside" (Koestler), a breaking away from the self-referentiality of traditional logic. Although Mephisto ridicules the role of numbers in the *Hexenküche* when it is a matter of the divine 3 (lines 2560–62; cf. lines 8015, 9700–2) and designates the Witch's one-times-one as a "total paradox" (line 2557), numbers are central to the meaning of *Faust*, with its intertwining of the macrocosm and microcosm (whereby the microcosm denotes the human being; line 1802). Albrecht Schöne sees the Witch's one-times-one as a parody of magic spells and utter nonsense (FA 7.2:286). His is one of the more recent judgments of the mathematical paradigm in a long series of analyses.[55] Mephisto considers it to be fun. With Nietzsche, I would argue that we need to learn to laugh, not to take things so seriously. At the same time, the golden track of laughter does have a deeper philosophical meaning. I lend my voice to those who argue for meaning in the paradox of numbers. Here's the Witch's one-times-one:

This must ye ken!	[Du mußt verstehn!
From one take ten;	Aus Eins mach Zehn,
Skip the two; and then	Und Zwei laß gehn,
Even up three,	Und Drei mach gleich,
And rich you'll be.	So bist du reich.
Leave out the four.	Verlier die Vier!
From five and six,	Aus Fünf und Sechs,
Thus says the witch,	So sagt die Hex',
Make seven and eight,	Mach Sieben und Acht,
And all is straight.	So ist's vollbracht:
And nine is one,	Und Neun ist Eins,
And ten is none.	Und Zehn ist keins.
This is the witch's one-times-one!	Das ist das Hexen-Einmal-eins.]
(lines 2540-52)	

55 Wolfgang Neubauer, *Das tragische Prisma des Irrtums: Überlegungen zur Lösung des 'Hexen-Einmal-Eins' und zu Mephistos 'Vaterschaft' in Goethes 'Faust'* (Konstanz: Hartung-Gorre Verlag, 1986), presents the provocative thesis of a connection between the mathematical one-times-one and the symbolism of sexuality in other scenes (27). In doing so, he draws upon Goethe's own understanding of mathematics as a symbolic system. He also offers an overview of the relevant research on the one-times-one. Neubauer goes too far, however, in suggesting that Mephisto impregnates Gretchen. The title of Sabine Prokhoris's *The Witch's Kitchen: Freud, Faust, and the Transference*, trans. from the French by G. M. Goshgarian (Ithaca and London: Cornell University Press, 1995), is somewhat misleading, for Prokhoris's focus is not really on the troubling scene in *Faust* but rather on Goethe's impact on Freud's theory of psychoanalysis.

Such mathematical wizardry has puzzled readers for centuries, causing many to respond with Faust: "I think the hag's in fever and delirium" (line 2553). Faust, of course, assumes that words uttered are framed by referentiality. Mephisto refers to this human penchant when he remarks: "Man has a way of thinking, when he hears a word, / That certainly behind lies some thought or other" (lines 2565–66). Yet Faust fails to grasp the Witch's meaning because he discerns no frame of reference. If one exists, it is radically different from his accustomed one. His is a language of human self-consciousness (a recent innovation in the total history of the universe), whereas hers seems primordial in its lack of discernible referentiality. The Witch's chaotic world transcends the linear logic of Faust's thinking up to that point.

Her spell resonates with the image of the ever agonistic struggle along the irregular seacoast; metaphorically anticipates the creative agonism of the rejuvenation scene with its turbulent bubbling of heated fluids, wild activity, and smashed globes and crown (symbols of order); and mirrors Faust's emergent inner turmoil in the spectral image of a seductive woman. Each symbol externalizes the transformation Faust undergoes in the scene, which marks a significant paradigm shift in his conception of the world. It is the temporal and spatial point at which he begins to live life fully in a decentered universe. The convulsive cataclysms of the Witch's Kitchen constitute a remapping and repositioning of the harmonic cosmic view presented in the Prologue in Heaven. It can be seen as a self-contained poem on the creative process with a refocusing on chaotic and sensual elements (lines 2448–80). Significantly, the Witch's Kitchen dates from Goethe's Italian sojourn, during which he underwent a personal rejuvenation and was led to embrace a new way of conceptualizing the world and humankind's place in it.

With the withdrawal of a ready frame of reference, disciplinary logic is transformed into gibberish for the conservative or divergent thinker. The Witch says to Faust, who is as much perplexed by the various actions in the room as by her words:

The lofty force	[Die hohe Kraft
Of wisdom's source	Der Wissenschaft,
Is from the whole world hidden.	Der ganzen Welt verborgen!
Once give up thinking,	Und wer nicht denkt,
And in a twinkling	Dem wird sie geschenkt,
It's granted you unbidden.	Er hat sie ohne Sorgen.]
(lines 2567–72)	

These lines express the core of Faust's incipient conversion from mechanistic Newtonian science to a new metathinking. The straight flow of mechanical energy through pulleys, ropes, and gears is replaced by gravitational force fields and the untidy thermal turbulence of eros and heated ambition. Faust's previously methodical inquiry becomes free flowing, seemingly random.[56] In his subsequent experiences, he realizes ever more the need to reorient his thinking radically. Instead of laboring further under the delusion that he can achieve ultimate knowledge through orderly, self-directed microreduction, he must allow himself to be moved by the deep structures of existence, i.e., by the impulses common to the internal and external worlds. While Faust earlier sensed the limitations of traditional means of scientific inquiry, his mental reorientation begins in earnest only with the deconstructive events of the Witch's Kitchen; it proves to be a powerful metaphor for creativity. To be sure, the process, although advanced by his encounter with the Mothers, is not completed until much later when he swears off all magic in the scene Midnight of Act V, Part II. Turning from the yonder and reaffirming his commitment to the earth, he proclaims:

A fool is he who that way blinks his eyes	[Tor, wer dorthin die Augen blitzelnd richtet,
And fancies kindred beings in the skies.	Sich über Wolken seinesgleichen dichtet!
Let him stand firm here and here look around:	Er stehe fest und sehe hier sich um;
This world is not mute if the man is sound.	Dem Tüchtigen ist diese Welt nicht stumm.
Why need he stray off to eternity!	Was braucht er in die Ewigkeit zu schweifen!
What he knows here is certainty.	Was er erkennt, läßt sich ergreifen.]
(lines 11443-48)	

The earth has him again. Then he dies. The Witch's Kitchen is a necessary prelude to the dangerous game that the Lord and Mephistopheles had earlier agreed would be played out. While the Lord functions as a kind of agonarch (that is, a judge or overseer), Mephisto assumes the role of an agonothete (a supervisor in the games of contest). Not simple binary logic, but the complex agonistic forces beyond the conventional polarity of good (the Lord) and evil (Mephisto), subject and object, mind and body become the key factors in Faust's development. Of course, Faust is unaware of these contending impulses and their wager as he undergoes the creative process of deconstructing and reconstructing his being for new days on new shores.

4.3 Sun and Cataract

The original image of new days and new shores is enriched in the opening scene of Part II, Pleasant Regions, in which Faust undergoes a second rejuvenation process following Gretchen's tragic end. The scene is marked by the gradual transition

56 Martin Esslin considers *Faust* generally to be "a brilliant example of a self-deconstructing text." See his "Goethe's *Faust*: Pre-Modern, Post-Modern, Proto-Postmodern," in *Interpreting Goethe's Faust Today*, ed. by Jane K. Brown, Meredith Lee, and Thomas P. Saine (Columbus, SC: Camden House, 1994), 219–227, here 225.

from dark to light at the earliest break of day and gives rise to successive shades of color at the edge of darkness and the edge of light as the rays of the sun encounter matter. Life is revealed, of course, through a mixture of these elements and is keenly associated with green, the "lower" end of the transition scale. In Goethe's color scheme, the state of the greatest absence of light – darkness – is equivalent to blue; the state of the greatest presence of light is equivalent to yellow. These are the two foundational colors. The transition from dark to light is marked by the color purple, whereas the movement from light to dark gives rise to green as the intermediate state. Purple is preceded by reddish blue, green by yellowish red. This cycle from blue via shades of red to yellow and back again to blue via green, which is at the heart of Goethe's *Theory of Color*, also functions dominantly in *Faust*. The theme, first sounded in Pleasant Regions, may indeed be associated with a shift in philosophical perspective from a focus on the idea or the thing-in-itself in Part I to the representation of the *idea phenomena* in Part II, as Géza von Molnár has argued.[57]

Faust notes how the rising sun gradually descends from the mountain peaks onto the valley floor where he is lying. New radiance and clarity extend "step by step," renewing "life's pulse" and engulfing Faust. As the light descends, Faust's eye is directed upwards toward the source. Complementary to the descending rays of the sun is the cataract, cascading down the mountainside, crashing into rugged rocks and breaking into tiny droplets of water. The resultant mist, caught by an updraft, rises back upward to catch the falling light and break it into the colors of the rainbow. In the scene Forest and Cavern, Goethe used the cataract motif as a metaphor for the modern "fugitive, the homeless, / The monster without rest or repose" who destroys all in its path ("der Flüchtling [...] der Unbehaus'te / Der Unmensch ohne Zweck und Ruh"; lines 3348–50); here he varies the theme. The cascading water at the conclusion of Pleasant Regions with its incumbent play of color ("des bunten Bogens Wechseldauer") symbolizes the recursive cycles of nature with its complex feedback loops. The water and light imagery conclude with the oft cited statement: "Man's effort is there mirrored in that strife. / Reflect and by reflection comprehend: There in that rainbow's radiance *is* our life" ("Der spiegelt ab das menschliche Bestreben. / Ihm sinne nach, und du begreiftst genauer: / Am farbigen Abglanz haben wir das Leben"; lines 4725–28).

Thus, the beginning of Part II of the tragedy mirrors the beginning of Part I, with reflections upon the rhythms of life, the proper element of humankind, and the interconnections of human life-worlds. "Newborn day" ("der neue Tag geboren";

57 Géza von Molnár, "Hidden in Plain View: Another Look at Goethe's *Faust*," *Eighteenth-Century Studies* 35.3 (2002): 469–96. Von Löw offers a persuasive interpretation of Goethe's color theory as it is mirrored throughout Faust (von Löw 1982: 105–22).

line 4668) is the major theme from the Prologue in Heaven (line 270) to Mountain Gorges (line 12093). The Easter celebration of Part I shades over into the rejuvenating powers of nature itself (Outside the City Gate ⇒ Pleasant Regions) and returns in the concluding scene of the two-part opus to the theme of resurrection (Mountain Gorges). These mirrorings of rejuvenation and transformations bond individual scenes through both parts of *Faust* together in an uneasy balance of the whole. Let us examine some of those repeated mirrorings.

4.4 The Mothers

Regeneration is, of course, a calling back to life, a calling into renewed existence, and that is precisely the theme of the Mothers, who represent chaotic, potential creativity in the scene Dark Gallery at the end of Act I, Part II.[58] Faust is in distress because he has promised the Emperor to conjure up the spirits of Helene and Paris for the court's delight. The challenge is one of the toughest for Mephisto. For one thing, Faust is here moving into an "alien sphere" ("fremdestes Bereich"; line 6195); for another, Mephisto is reluctant to reveal "high secrets to the light of day" (line 6213). Paradoxically, the nihilist shows the vitalist the way to the Mothers! The phrase "light of day" could, of course, refer to the light of reason and the ways of logic, for the Mothers are "strange and rare / [...] unknown to men, / Reluctantly acknowledged in *our* ken" (lines 6217–19). They are "reluctantly acknowledged" ("von uns nicht gern genannt") by Mephisto and his kind because they seem to be sheer nothingness, yet therein Faust finds "the All" (line 6256). The paradox of nothingness and of all is a prefiguration of Bohm's holomovement, the deep structure of existence and "fundamental ground of all matter."[59] It is awkward to say anything definite about the Mothers because they reign in sublime solitude, reside in a total void, exist beyond the coordinates of time and space. No road leads to them, no locks or bolts bar the way. There is no up, no down, no sound, no solid ground (lines 6214–28, 6246–48). As inhabitants of a realm of pure potential, "from forms set free" (line 6277), the Mothers are "Eternal Mind's eternal recreation" ("Des ewigen Sinnes ewige Unterhaltung"; line 6288). In darkness some stand, some sit, some wander about, "while round them float the forms of all creatures," shadows of all that ever was or will be (lines 6285–90).

Although the positions the Mothers assume – standing, sitting, wandering about

---

58 Harold Jantz's illuminating study, *The Mothers in Faust: The Myth of Time and Creativity* (Baltimore: Johns Hopkins University Press, 1969), is often overlooked in research.

59 David Bohm and F. David Peat, *Science, Order, and Creativity: A Dramatic New Look at the Creative Roots of Science and Life* (Toronto and New York: Bantam Books, 2000), 180. See also Talbot, *The Holographic Universe*, 47–49.

– can and have been associated with the three classifications of nature (sitting = mineral, standing = plant, wandering about = animal),[60] the realm Mephisto describes extends beyond the pale of quotidian reality. That point is underscored by reference to the free-floating forms all around them. Rather, their realm is related to that of enfolded frequency ranges where all manifestations and events are one and undivided and thus beyond traditional space and time coordinates. There is no such thing as pure energy or pure matter, for they enfold one another. All is the result of energy fluctuations; everything is interconnected as in a hologram (but without the latter's static quality). Time does not exist within this holomovement model as linear progression; rather, it can move multidimensionally in different directions simultaneously (as, in fact, happens throughout Part II of the play). Past, present, and future are all one. To comprehend the Mothers as representing the holomovement, a new way of thinking, a metathinking is required.[61] In answer to the question "Whence cometh all this bubbling activity and complexity?" we ultimately must conclude that it is "a natural expression of a universe that is not in equilibrium," that it is a question of the "differences [and] potentials that drive the formation of complexity."[62] Indeed, as part of this holomovement Mephisto mirrors the whole even when he denies it as being whole. He, too, was present from the beginning of time, although he is hardly the father of the Mothers.[63] To a generation of readers accustomed to cyberspace, the frequencies in which the Mothers exist are less an alien concept than they were for Faust, who was "scared by a new word" (line 6267). It is hard to hear something new, Nietzsche later correctly

60 Eibl, *Das monumentale Ich*, 381n31; Schöne, *Kommentare*, FA 7/2:471–72.

61 Johannes von Buttlar summarizes the chaos-theory-oriented arguments of the physicist David Bohm, the psychologist Karl Pribram, and the cybergeneticist David Forster in arguing the holographic nature of the universe: *Gottes Würfel: Schicksal oder Zufall?* (Munich: F. A. Herbig, 1992), 81–95. Cf. also Weingart and Maasen, "The Order of Meaning," *Configurations* 5.3 (1997): 463-520, who cite Schelling's view of chaos as untapped potential: "A more active account of chaos was advanced by F. W. J. Schelling, who took chaos to be an ensemble of mental/spiritual potentials still waiting to be developed by differentiation" (480).

62 Stuart Kauffman, *At Home in the Universe* (New York: Oxford University Press, 1995), 19, cf. also 208–9. Kauffman does not refer to *Faust*.

63 Albert Fuchs, "Die 'Mütter': Eine Mephistopheles-Phantasmagorie," in A. Fuchs, *Goethe-Studien* (Berlin: de Gruyter, 1968), 64-81, here 64. Schöne (*Kommentare*, 466–71, 476–78) emphasizes Mephisto's charlatanism and the technological side of the visual imagery as hallucination, thereby intimating that Mephisto "sires" the Mothers. If one chooses not to look beyond the entertainment value of such illusory techniques around 1800 and, moreover, plays down the serious ontological implications of the Mothers-mythologem, as both Schöne and Eibl do (also by suggesting that the sexual implications somehow denigrate the whole episode), one could of course conclude that Faust's "Gang zu den Müttern" is more "Scherz" (joke) than "Ernst" (seriousness). Obviously, I argue that it is not a question of alternatives but rather of an agonistic whole. I think that is the way Goethe intended it.

diagnosed. No wonder that Faust is skeptical.

Thus, just as Act I of Part II begins with an example of rejuvenation via natural fluctuations in energy levels, it also concludes with an act of calling into existence. Despite their differences, these two actions are both rooted in a *magia naturalis*, to which we might now want to add chaos and complexity theory. The complexity of their interconnectedness is underlined by Mephisto's central role in arranging Faust's descent to the Mothers. Sandwiched in between these positive acts of creation, by the way, are examples of false creativity: masquerade, paper money, artificial flowers, self-serving politics, courtly manners. The Mothers, I would further argue, are related in mysterious (holographic) ways to the Witch's one-times-one. I take seriously Faust's comment in reply to Mephisto's explanation of the Mothers:

Best skip such speeches! I can tell	[Du spartest, dächt' ich, solche Sprüche;
From time long past there is a smell	Hier wittert's nach der Hexenküche,
Of witch's kitchen in the air	Nach einer längst vergangnen Zeit.
Did I not have the world forced onto me?	Mußt' ich nicht mit der Welt verkehren?
Did I not learn – and teach – vacuity?	Das Leere lernen, Leeres lehren?
When I talked reason as I knew it,	Sprach ich vernünftig, wie ich's angeschaut,
The paradoxes lent a double echo to it.	Erklang der Widerspruch gedoppelt laut.]
(lines 6228–34)	

In terms now recognized as a mark of modern theories of complexity, Faust here draws particular attention to the logic of paradox, as is already evident in the so-called nonsensical scene, the Witch's Kitchen. In fact, paradoxically, upon his return from the Mothers, Faust proves to be their ardent admirer. In terms worthy of an advocate of the contemporary logic of paradox, Faust exclaims that "moving forms of life" swarm around the Mothers, "yet are devoid of life." These the Mothers dispatch to "the vaults of night or to the tent of day" to fuel both "life's lively course" and "the bold magician's quest" (lines 6427–36). He even recalls for the reader the magic mirror of the Witch's Kitchen, which revealed to him the lovely female form prefiguring Helena (line 6596). Actually, the key to the Mothers was provided in the Witch's Kitchen, for it was there that Faust was restored to sexual prowess. In both instances growth results, but in unanticipated ways.

The key to the Mothers is none other than the phallus. "That little thing" begins to grow in Faust's hand, and Faust is seized by enthusiasm: "It glows! It gleams!" (lines 6259–61). All Faust must do is let the key (phallus) do its work. There is no need for a road map; its mapping abilities are inherent, for it is attuned to what chaologists call a strange attractor. "The key will scent the right place," Mephisto explains, "Follow it down, it takes you to the Mothers" ("Der Schlüssel wird die rechte Stelle wittern, / Folg ihm hinab, er führt dich zu den Müttern"; lines 6263–64). Holding it upright away from his body (= erect phallus?), Faust is instructed to insert it into the burning tripod around which the Mothers are gathered (lines 6292–93). Traditionally, the burning tripod is interpreted to be the common feature in ancient sanctuaries, suggestive of oracular and spirit-summoning powers. We can see it, however, as related to the fundamental significance for Goethe of flame and light as symbolic of divine and life-giving qualities. Given the clearly phallic symbolism of the key that naturally seeks out the "right place," the argument for viewing the burning tripod as the aroused female genitals is more compelling. The triangular form of the tripod supporting the flaming bowl is reminiscent of the triangular shape of the gateway to the female reproductive organs. Once the tripod comes into contact with the key, we read, it will follow Faust "like a slave" ("als treuer Knecht"). Once drawn to the earth's surface, it accords Faust "the might / To call up hero and heroine from night" (lines 6294–98). The tripod and the key in combination manifestly refer to the creative potential of the sexual drive and the resultant manifestations of new periodic energy knots centered in bodies. As the spirit reigning over earthly pleasures and bodily functions (line 1355), Mephisto obviously represents sexuality. Indeed, he misses no opportunity to reduce all aspirations to the sexual instinct (cf. Gretchen as sex object, the Walpurgis Night lewdness, his homoeroticizing of the cherubim). Without the original procreative act, however, the nobler forms of yearning could not evolve through coevolution with the spirit.[64]

The Mothers, then, represent a seminal moment in *Faust*. With them – as with the Witch's Kitchen and the introduction of Gretchen – Faust reaches a turning point in his life that alters the bifurcation movement and changes the frequency. Following the encounter with the Mothers, he takes delight in his new "priesthood," which has opened the world to him as never before (lines 6490–91). Waxing enthusiastic at the sight of Helena, "passion's very fountainhead," he attributes to her his renewed strength: "All love, all adoration – madness too" (lines 6498–500). Ironically, Mephisto reminds him at this point to stay in character. But then Faust *is* in character. The realms of the real and ideal, of material manifestation and virtual reality, of the inorganic and organic become commingled. In the ensuing acts of Part II the dimensions of time and space do not obtain. The demarcations between reality, consciousness, the unconscious, dream, and fantasy disappear. Both the Witch's Kitchen and the Mothers – each a center of magic, the first black, the second white – lead Faust to a woman with whom he has a child and

64 Cottrell, "Resurrection of Thinking," argues unconvincingly that the key actually symbolizes thinking rather than sexuality. To press his point, he must ignore Mephisto's primary role as advocate of carnality and materiality (265–66).

whom he loses. With its linear polarity and crass sensuality, the Walpurgis Night on the Blocksberg of Part I is tied directly to the atmosphere of the Witch's Kitchen, whereas the Classical Walpurgis Night of Part II, with its balancing of diversity in various transformations from the inorganic to the organic, emanates from the domain of the Mothers. We might see this contrast as a progression toward an openly thermodynamic system. To adopt Cottrell's terminology, the complementarity of opposites comprises the seminal "pregnant point of the Mother-ground of existence" (272). And the pregnant point is the "threshold to a phase of creative expansion."[65]

4.5 HOMUNCULUS

The expansion of creativity is precisely the subject of the Homunculus mythologem, an early example of prebiological experimentation that points the way to modern artificial intelligence and gene technology.[66] A late addition to the Faust project, first appearing in Goethe's plan of 9 November 1826, Homunculus initially mirrors ideas of germination drawn from such alchemists as Paracelsus and Praetorius. In other words, the introduction of Homunculus coincides with the poet's criticism of the rigidity of self-referential, mathematical systems. Having been alchemically conceived in Wagner's laboratory (inherited from Faust) in a test tube, Homunculus symbolizes pure consciousness. He is even referred to as just a brain (lines 6869, 8249). Consequently, he is represented by a glowing light that can shine into the subconscious, even into the collective mythic past still present in human consciousness. While Paracelsus attributed parapsychological precognition to homunculi, the luminosity that characterizes Homunculus goes beyond that of the light of consciousness or reason. It also includes the biological.

In summer 1828 Goethe learned of the Göttinger chemist Friedrich Wöhler's (1800–82) famous experiments with ureal synthesis (*Harnstoffsynthese*), which made history by bridging the gap between inorganic and organic matter. Fascinated, Goethe recast his initial alchemistic characterization of Homunculus.

---

65 Nigel Hoffmann, "The Unity of Science and Art: Goethean Phenomenology as a New Ecological Discipline," in *Goethe's Way of Science* (1998), ed. by F. Amrine, 129–75, here 165.

66 Volker Zimmermann, "'Den Menschenstoff gemächlich komponieren': Vom Homunkulus zur Gentechnik," in *Faust: Annäherung an einen Mythos*, ed. by Frank Möbus, Friederike Schmidt-Möbus, and Gerd Unverfehrt (Göttingen: Wallstein Verlag, 1995), 343–56, addresses the connections. Manfred Osten, "Die evolutionäre Reise – Zur Modernität des Goetheschen Homunculus," *Goethe-Jahrbuch* 120 (2003): 216–27, is more interested in cultural than in technical aspects of modernity in this somewhat unfocused essay. Kauffman, *At Home*, 48–52, and Edward O. Wilson, *Consilience* (New York: Knopf, 1998), 97–98, discuss the contemporary situation.

Then, in fall 1830 Goethe learned of scientific advances in the study of luminous microorganisms ("Infusorien"). With this new knowledge in hand, he composed the ending of the act that celebrates the Vulcanian-Neptunian union of fire and water (lines 8347–74) .[67] Despite Goethe's shift in focus from medieval to contemporary science, his rendering of Homunculus is consistently marked by light and luminosity. At the beginning of the scene, the reader senses overtones of consciousness, while the final depiction associates the light with the fiery eruptions of creation. Noteworthy is the fact that Homunculus emerges into existence at the very moment Mephisto arrives on the scene. Surprisingly addressing Mephisto as his cousin and seeing in him an accomplice (line 6885), the clairvoyant dwarf immediately sets about his purpose: to help Faust realize his fondest dreams by leading the love-struck seeker back in space and time to antiquity in an effort to recall Helena to a more substantial existence than in her previous, holographic appearance.

By interpreting the sleeping Faust's dream, Homunculus displays more than telepathic powers. Himself the product of reflective creativity, Homunculus is able to interpret Faust's subconscious creativity while the latter dreams of Helena's moment of conception: Leda's seduction by Zeus, who appears to her in the form of a swan. In order to locate him in his proper element, Homunculus orders that Faust be borne off to the Classical Walpurgis Night (lines 6942–43). Although related to Homunculus, Mephisto is incapable of seeing what Homunculus sees or of comprehending the significance of the Classical Walpurgis Night; Hellenic traditions are alien to the Christian devil. Dependent this time on others to fulfill his pact with Faust, Mephisto dares not spurn his cousin's aid (line 7002) and follows him into the mythological and historical past. There Faust awakes from his dream and seeks his own way to bring Helena to conscious life, a way that leads through various allegorical stages of time and space from the Sphinxes to Chiron to Manto. Ultimately, Faust's journey was to end with his descent into the netherworld to Persephone, where he was to retrieve Helena. The action is a "wiederholte Spiegelung" of his "descent" to the Mothers. But the Persephone scene is missing. While the entire second act of *Faust II* is a multilayered metaphor of creative transformations involving Faust, Mephisto, and Homunculus, we will focus here only on Homunculus's experience.

On fire to break free from his steady energy state within his glass cage, Homunculus seeks the naturally unsteady state of nature, which will allow him to evolve freely. Unsure as to which form to assume and how to go about it, he seeks the advice of the two theorists of evolution, the nature philosophers Anaxagoras and Thales (lines 7831–41). Anaxagoras espouses Plutonic views (fire), whereas Thales is the spokesperson for Neptunism (water). Homunculus chooses the latter.

67 Cf. Schöne, *Kommentare*, FA 7/2:504–08, 530–32.

Thales hands him over to Proteus, the master of "shifting shapes" (line 8244), who is astonished at "a dwarf that lights" (line 8245) and comments: "You are, before you were supposed to be" (8254). Noting that Homunculus is hermaphroditic (line 8256) (like his cousin, Mephisto-Phorkyad), Proteus recommends that Homunculus begin the coevolutionary process in the far-flung sea, beginning small and allowing nature to determine autopoietically which corporal shape he will assume. In fact, Homunculus can expect to pass through innumerable forms; for the ultimate shape – that of a human being – there is plenty of time (lines 8324–26). What later constitutes scaling and reiteration in the construction of nature is here circumscribed in the lines "The first beginnings must be small, / Minutest things make up the diet, / Ensuing growth is gradual" ("Da fängt man erst im Kleinen an / Und freut sich Kleinste zu verschlingen, / Man wächst so nach und nach heran"; lines 8261–63). Proteus carries him on his back to wed him to the everlasting ocean (lines 8319–20). Homunculus shatters the artificial restraint of his glass receptacle at the feet of the beautiful Galatea, daughter of Nereus and stand-in for Venus genetrix, who surfs endlessly the boundless seas in her chariot-shell. When Homunculus merges with the elements of nature at great Eros's gate, his pulsating consciousness explodes in a frenzy of light, bathing the turbulently undulating waves in a radiant glow (lines 8478–79). The final lines of Act II are a litany of praise to the life-advancing forces of nature:

Hail to the sea! Hail to the waves	[Heil dem Meere! Heil den Wogen,
Which sacred fire in brilliance laves!	Von dem heiligen Feuer umzogen!
Hail to water! To fire, all hail! [...]	Heil dem Wasser! Heil dem Feuer! [...]
Hail to earth's mysterious lairs!	Heil geheimnisreichen Grüften!
Honor be forevermore	Hochgefeiert seid allhier,
To you elements all four!	Element' ihr alle vier!]
(lines 8480-87)	

This glorious finale in praise of the four elements is mirrored in Act III, which culminates in a similar litany as Helena and Euphorion return not to Hades but to eternally resurgent nature ("ewig lebendige Natur"; line 9989).

Galatea's allegorical rise from the sea, which coincides with Homunculus's conjoining with the water, can be seen as a reflectaphor of Faust's pursuit of Helena beneath the surface. Like Faust, Homunculus is called to an active life of striving (line 6888). Eros draws both to absolute beauty, with which human consciousness cooperates to bring about new life. The dream is realized in and through the scheme of nature. Saliently, Act III begins with Helena's figure rising from the sea onto the shore. That silhouetting of her form is repeated at the beginning of Act IV in the cloud formations (lines 10039–66). While the resonance of the concept of the Eternal Feminine with Galatea at the end of Act II is subtle, its expression at the beginning of Act IV is explicit when the feminine form (reminiscent of both Gretchen and Helena) "Does not dissolve, ascends aloft into the aether, / And draws the best part of my inner self to follow" ("das Beste meines Inneren"; 10065–66). The parallel to the final lines of the play are unmistakable, as are, for example, the interconnections with the realm of potential creativity and its manifestations, whether with the Mothers in their virtual realm or with Galatea in her nonlinear ocean:

All transitory	[Alles Vergängliche
Things represent;	Ist nur ein Gleichnis;
Inadequate here	Das Unzulängliche,
Become event,	Hier wird's Ereignis;
Ineffable here,	Das Unbeschreibliche,
Accomplishment;	Hier ist's getan;
The Eternal Feminine	Das Ewig-Weibliche
Draws us onward.	Zieht uns hinan.] (lines 12104–111)

The final scene of the play, Mountain Gorges, is likewise dominated by the elements of earth, fire, water, and air, here in the form of clouds and mountain slopes. The upward movement of Faust's immortal soul (that is, his entelechy) reverses the gradual downward movement of the sun in the first scene of Part II, Pleasant Regions, from the mountain peaks to the valley floor back upwards from mountain gorges into the stratosphere. Granite, which Goethe considered to be the fundamental type of rock, was thrust in great slabs from deep within the earth up through the earth's outer shell and into the sky, while the sky reached down into the valleys. Gretchen remarks on this dynamic of exchange in the final scene:

See how he wrests himself out free	[Sieh! wie er jedem Erdenbande
Of his integument of earth,	Der alten Hülle sich entrafft,
How in ethereal raiment he	Und aus ätherischem Gewande
Shows youthful vigor in new birth.	Hervortritt erste Jugendkraft.
Vouchsafe to me to be his guide,	Vergönne mir ihn zu belehren,
His eyes still dazzle with new day.	Noch blendet ihn der neue Tag.]
(lines 12088–93)	

The ground of creativity is located not merely in the earth (dirt) underfoot but in the total ecosystem of the planet Earth: earth, fire, water, air. Moreover, in this particular instance Goethe modeled Faust's final transformations on the biology of insect development, which he had studied assiduously in the 1790s.

Thessaly is the appropriate place to prefigure this allegorical, procreative act because it was formed by the joining of earth and water accompanied by volcanic eruptions (lines 7851–7935). In a sense, Thessaly served to conjoin metaphorically the two schools of thought on geological formation at the time: Vulcanism (Anaxagoras) and Neptunism (Thales). Vulcanists believed that volcanic eruptions shaped the surface of the earth, whereas Neptunists explained its formation through the flowing water and receding seas. Goethe had become familiar with geology and mineralogy during the 1780s when he was minister of mines. Then and in later years, he kept abreast of developments through his contacts with men of science such as the Weimar geologist and mineralogist Johann Carl Wilhelm Voigt (1752–1821), the Jena chemistry professor Johann Wolfgang Döbereiner (1780–1849), and the Jena natural philosopher Lorenz Oken (1779–1851), editor of the science journal *Isis* (1816–48). Moreover, he was a founding member of the Jena Mineralogical Society, established in 1798.[68] His background in geology notwithstanding, however, Goethe was essentially a Neptunist. He saw the sea as the source of all life. Not coincidentally, then, Goethe concludes Act II, with its debates on the formative force of flowing rivers and granite slabs, as a grand cultic celebration of the sea (Proteus, Neptune, Nereus). The high point of the description is the commingling of the antagonistic elements of fire (Homunculus's flame) and the life-giving water at Galatea's feet: an impassioned self-immolation on the altar of love.

Thessaly, the land of nurturing moisture and movement, is the path leading to the Corinthian isthmus – or gateway – to Arcadia. And Arcadia lies protected in the interior of the Peloponnesian peninsula. Surrounded by water and connected to the mainland by a sliver of land, its shape acts as a metaphoric womb. Euphorion realizes this when, defying the wishes of his parents, he climbs high up for a panoramic view of his home: "Now I see where I stand, / Midmost in island free, / Midmost in Pelops' land, / Kin to both earth and sea" ("Weiß ich nun, wo ich bin! / Mitten der Insel drin, / Mitten in Pelops' Land, / Erde- wie seeverwandt"; lines 9823–26). But of course, given his Faustian spirit, he must climb ever higher, gaze ever further, attempt to fly. In the process, he leaves the safety of the women and loses his grounding. On the other hand, he is naturally forced out of the "womb," much like the insect is compelled to leave its cocoon and take flight. In fact, all

68 A. G. Steer, "Goethe and Science," in *Approaches to Teaching Goethe's Faust*, ed. by Douglas J. McMillan (New York: The Modern Language Association of America, 1987), 55–65, provides a concise summary of Goethe's knowledge of the natural sciences, which ranged from alchemy to comparative anatomy, geology, chemistry, and insectology. See also Helmut Hölder, "Goethe als Geologe," *Goethe-Jahrbuch* 111 (1994): 231–45; Susanne Horn, "Bergrat Johann Carl Wilhelm Voigt (1752–1821): Beiträge zur Geognosie und Mineralogie," in *"Der teutsche Merkur" – die erste deutsche Kulturzeitschrift?* ed. by Andrea Heinz (Heidelberg: Universitätsverlag Winter, 2003), 199–214; Günther Martin, "Goethes Wolkenlehre im Atomzeitalter," *Goethe-Jahrbuch* 109 (1992): 199–206; and Sebastian Donat and Hendrik Birus, *Goethe: Ein letztes Universalgenie?* (Göttingen: Wallstein, 1999), 78–105.

humans must leave the womb of the Mothers in order to become what they are supposed to be, a topic that will be covered further in Grass's *The Tin Drum*.

5. Willful Acts, Natural Acts, Essential Tensions

Up to this point, I have essentially argued that the earth itself is the dominant force in this novel of the universe. A traditional reading of the critical scene Forest and Cavern (Wald und Höhle) in *Faust I* as symbolic of the bosom of nature embracing Faust serves to underscore that dominance. A more radical, metaphorical reading of the scene as symbolic of the female reproductive genitalia and as a nodal point for both parts of the drama highlights the scene's importance even more dramatically (cf. Neubauer, *Prisma* 30–49). Still to be evaluated within this broader context, however, is the role Faust himself plays within the total economy of life. Even though Nietzsche himself rejected the comparison, I wish to view Faust as a forerunner of the Nietzschean overman because Faust willfully engages in "the game" of contesting the forces eternally renewed in nature (line 10199). The contraction ("Bändigen") and dissipation ("Entlassen") of energy fluctuations characterize all of existence, so that the traditional understanding of Faustian striving must be subsumed under the totality of existence.

For many readers, the connection between Nietzsche and Goethe's *Faust* is not immediately obvious, although some have recognized it.[69] We do know that Nietzsche was an admirer of Goethe, even asserting that he was the last German for whom he had any respect (cited at the masthead of this chapter). In fact, Goethe seemed to him to be an exception ("ein Zwischenfall"), not only for Germany but also for Europe. What set him apart was his drive for and acceptance of the whole, of the totality. Goethe, Nietzsche claims in *Götzen-Dämmerung*, did not separate himself from life; rather, he thrust himself into it with enthusiasm, rejecting the pigeon-holing of reason, sensuality, passion, and will. Indeed, he re-created himself by affirming life ever anew. Dionysian in Nietzsche's meaning of the term, Goethe seemed to him to be a genuine free spirit: "ein *freigewordener* Geist" (*KSA* 6:151–53). An avid reader of Goethe, Nietzsche made numerous references to him in his own opus.[70] The first work he read was *Novelle*, and it left a lasting impression.

69 Cf., e.g., Avital Ronell, "Namely, Eckermann," in *Looking after Nietzsche*, ed. by Laurence A. Rickels (Albany: State University of New York Press, 1990), 233–57; and Nicholas Rennie, "Between Pascal and Mallarmé: Faust's Speculative Moment," *Comparative Literature* 52.4 (fall 2000): 269–90.

70 Richard Oehler, *Nietzsche Register: Alphabetisch-systematische Übersicht* (Stuttgart: Alfred Kröner Verlag, 1965), lists seven columns of references in Nietzsche's opus to Goethe's works. Of course, not all are laudatory. See, e.g., "Das Weib, das ewig Weibliche: ein bloß imaginärer

With *Zarathustra* in mind, he declared *Faust* to be "a pleasure without equal," most of all because of its earthiness (*KSA* 13:634). In *Jenseits von Gut und Böse* (#244, 246, 215, 260), he explicitly plays upon the two-souls theory and the concept of the eternal feminine. There they form a central thesis concerning human nature. Furthermore, *Also sprach Zarathustra* is arguably modeled, at least in part, on *Faust*, for both play upon the message of Christian salvation. Yet perhaps the most famous connection between Nietzsche and Goethe's *Faust* has been the popularization of the verse referring to Faust as an overman ("Übermensch," line 490). It was long thought that Goethe had coined the term, but it turns out that he had forebears in theologians of the sixteenth century. Moreover, Goethe could very well have learned of the term through Herder (Schöne 7.2:218).

A ready parallel between the two giants of German intellectual thought is their creative use of myth and scientific knowledge in creating models of a life beyond the usual polarities of good and evil. To be sure, Goethe's interest in science was much more sustained than Nietzsche's. Of course, the connections between the two men as well as their connections with myth and science or with science and humanity have not gone unnoticed. However, the role of myth, the grounding of existence in the telluric, the concept of cosmic seeds, the Nietzschean ideal of the overman, the phenomenon of feedback loops, chaos, and autopoiesis have not been previously conjoined in analyzing Goethe's masterpiece.

The very first description of the protagonist himself as driven by an inner ferment and half aware that he is mad (lines 302–3) characterizes Faust as a forerunner of Nietzsche's free spirit, who is willful and imprudent – and those turn out to be the very qualities that earn him redemption. The closing frame of Part II, Mountain Gorges (Bergschluchten), clearly states that the key to Faust's salvation despite his transgressions is his will to power: "Who strives forever with a will, / By us can be redeemed" ("Wer immer strebend sich bemüht / Den können wir erlösen"; lines 11936–38; see also 11965–68; cf. also Goethe's comment to Eckermann of 6 June 1831). The striving referred to is related to the inherent operations of nature. Seen from the perspective of Nature, which itself obviously knows nothing of good and evil (line 4619), Faust's striving cannot lead to condemnation. Viewed from a theological perspective, that will must, of course, be aided by divine grace in order to warrant salvation. Faust himself, however, is explicitly unconcerned with an afterlife, caring in Nietzschean fashion only for the present moment, as reflected in the wager-pact: "If I to any moment say:/ Linger on, you are so fair!" ("Werd' ich zum Augenblicke sagen: / Verweile doch! Du bist so schön!"; lines 1699–1700). Yet Faust's inner drive is but a mirroring of nature's own will to create. Goethe saw himself as a Lucretian; that is, he ascribed even to inanimate

Werth, an den allein der Mann glaubt" (*KSA* 13:477).

nature a striving will (cf. Tantillo 134). Consequently, Faust's redemption can be attributed solely to the autocatalytic nature of the universe, not to the intervening hand of God. God (or the Lord, as per the *Book of Job*) can disappear as a character after the Prologue in Heaven because God is in the parts, in operative nature, as Jakob Böhme and Spinoza had earlier proposed and as Heisenberg and others were later to suggest.

The only thing of value, Faust declares in the opening scene of Part I, is that which comes from within, that which "surges up from your own soul" (line 569). On the one hand, Faust's inflated sense of self-worth causes him to equate himself with the Deity, and his inner drive – his presumptuous will (cf. line 710) – induces him to want to flow in the manner of the Earth Spirit (lines 619–20). On the other hand, he also feels worthless and cringes like a worm when rejected by the Spirit of the Earth. Such fluctuations in energy level (demigod / worm) are not uncommon in Nietzsche's free spirit, who must both command and obey, surge and cringe. It is, however, entirely explainable in terms of Goethe's principle of compensation, which tracks the weaknesses as well as the strengths of an organism or a phenomenon. This principle, in fact, makes creativity in nature possible and, according to Goethe, holds the key to understanding "the relationship between natural beauty and human freedom" (Tantillo 110). Thus, Goethe also anticipates Nietzsche in regard to the nexus of humanity and natural processes.

With reference to the rising sun, Faust feels that he is ready "to rise to new paths unto aether's wide dominions, / To newer spheres of pure activity" (lines 704–5). This impetus marks him further as a philosopher of the future. Yearning for new experiences and new spheres of activity, he avows: "To open seas I am shown forth by signs, / Before my feet the mirror-water shines, / And I am lured to new shores by new day (lines 699–701).[71] Paradoxically, Faust mistakenly thinks that the path to new shores and new day leads through the portal of death when in actuality the gateway leads back into life in its various forms. (This insight is echoed at the end of each of the five acts in Part II.) With its celebration of rebirth and renewal, Easter recalls Faust from the brink of suicide and returns him to life, to the *hic et nunc* (lines 680–85). But it is an uneasy return, as the Chorus of Disciples points out, for it pairs the various (Nietzschean) masks of existence that Care assumes (house and home, child and wife, poison, dagger, flood, fire; lines 647–49) with the "creative joy" (line 790) of becoming and striving. These are serious jests.

The symbolism of new day and new shores is repeated in the scene Outside the

71 The entire passage reads: "Ins hohe Meer werd' ich hinausgewiesen, / Die Spiegelflut erglänzt zu meinen Füßen, / Zu neuen Ufern lockt ein neuer Tag, / Ein Feuerwagen schwebt, auf leichten Schwingen, / An mich heran! Ich fühle mich bereit / Auf neuer Bahn den Äther zu durchdringen, / Zu neuen Sphären reiner Tätigkeit." *Faust*, lines 699–705.

City Gate, which culminates in Faust's famous two-souls commentary on the essential tension of human existence, wherein one soul is drawn creatively onward and upward into light and space, while the other is bound destructively to the Earth and the flesh (lines 1112–17). Yet more important than these famous lines for our present concerns is the continuance of the regeneration theme. Saved from suicide by childhood memories of Easter renewal, Faust has left his musty study for an Easter Sunday stroll in the open countryside. Enthralled by the change of season, accompanied by the release of energy in thawing ice, greening meadows, blooming blossoms, and radiant sunlight, Faust lauds the chromatic display of creative nature (lines 911–13). The scene anticipates Nietzsche's vitalism with its emphasis on transitory states ("Grenzzustände") and the prioritizing of elastic bodies over solid states (cf. *BGE* #296). The thought that humans are capable of grasping hold of nature's flux only in its tired state is foreshadowed in Faust's recognition that lasting contentment is always just beyond humankind's reach, that ultimate knowledge exceeds our scope. Implicit in Outside the City Gate (lines 1066–67), the sentiment is explicit in Faust's litany of complaints in Study Room II when he curses all worldly attachments, rising to a crescendo of resignation and anger. One after another those dependencies are: lofty self-opinion, the attraction of experimental science, public opinion, reputation, worldly goods, family, adventurous deeds, leisure, inebriation, and enchanting love. The list culminates with the traditional virtues of hope, faith, and patience (1590–1606).

The effect of the curses is to unmake his former existence. He severs all previous connections that prevent the free spirit from experiencing the fullness of vitality. Without this destruction of the old, no new beginning is possible. The upshot is the conferring of the magic mantle wished for earlier to bear him off to a "new life of many hues" (line 1121) and of active doing (lines 1237, 10198). Adopting the function of the chorus in Greek tragedy, invisible spirits comment on Faust's deconstructive litany, the prelude to his many deeds:

Woe! Woe!	[Weh! weh!
You have destroyed	Du hast sie zerstört,
The beauteous world	Die schöne Welt,
With mighty fist;	Mit mächtiger Faust;
It crumbles, it collapses!	Sie stürzt, sie zerfällt!
A demigod has shattered it!	Ein Halbgott hat sie zerschlagen!
We carry	Wir tragen
The fragments to the void,	Die Trümmern ins Nichts hinüber,
We grieve	Und klagen
For beauty so destroyed.	Über die verlorne Schöne.
More mightily,	Mächtiger
Son of earth,	Der Erdensöhne,
More splendidly	Prächtiger

Bring it to birth,	Baue sie wieder,
Rebuild it in the heart of you!	In deinem Busen baue sie auf!
Begin a new	Neuen Lebenslauf
Life course	Beginne,
With senses clear	Mit hellem Sinne
And may new songs	Und neue Lieder
Hail it with cheer!	Tönen darauf!]
(lines 1607-26)	

These lines – which could easily be drawn from Nietzsche's *Zarathustra* – anticipate much of what is to come in Goethe's tragedy: violent acts, demigod-like behavior, the shattering of the whole into fragments, rebirth from the ashes, and eventual recapitulation of the cycle. Each part of the song is dominated by its own dynamic; the first half emphasizes destruction, whereas the second addresses the potential for new growth. Conjoined, they underscore the recurring cycle of destruction and creation or of chaos and order. The fragments of everything Faust had previously considered beautiful are transmitted by the spirits to the void ("das Nichts"). At the same time, they prompt Faust to reconstruct the beautiful in stronger, more luxurious fashion by reaching back down into the depths of his own being and bringing forth new day. Thus, these verses concisely express the complementary nature of agonistic force fields and the human will in creating the beautiful. While the chorus of spirits speaks of the aesthetically beautiful, Faust himself had mentioned only ordinary matters. Yet the quotidian inscribes human life with meaning. We might wish to see here an indirect reference to the belief that life is bigger than the individual, that it is an autopoietic process of decomposition and reconfiguration. The individual instance of expanding life is subordinate to the total process, yet the individual acts as if she does not know it.

The seemingly innocuous spirit song proves to have multiple layers of signification. The deeper one digs, the more manifold the view. For example, the customary values Faust rejects in his litany are carried away into the void. Yet Faust is instructed to build them anew from within his own inner depths. Consequently, the void and his inner being must be related. Moreover, Faust's deconstructive act opens the way for the wager/pact with Mephisto. Without the renunciation of everything that he (and humankind in general) holds dear and that makes him part of a community, Faust would not be ready for Mephisto's companionship and the magic mantle he provides (and which takes them off to faraway places in Part II). Nor would he be ready for the Witch's Kitchen, with its own deconstructive and rejuvenation processes. Having reassessed all of his values, Faust cares neither about the hereafter nor about "a new beneath and a new above" (line 1670). Cured of the will to gain knowledge, his sole goal is to engage in "a game that none may win who play" (line 1681). This comment resonates strongly with Nietzsche's notion of life as a "dangerous game" ("ein schlimmes Spiel"). The nature of the dangerous game – and of the person capable of playing it – is brought out in Faust's desire to

Plunge in the flood of time and chance,	[Stürzen wir uns in das Rauschen der Zeit
Into the tide of circumstance!	Ins Rollen der Begebenheit!
Let grief and gratification,	Da mag denn Schmerz und Genuß,
Success and frustration	Gelingen und Verdruß
Spell one another as they can;	Mit einander wechseln, wie es kann;
Restless doing is the only way for man.	Denn rastlos betätigt sich der Mann.]
(lines 1754–59)	

The proximity of this resolve to Nietzsche's later concept of the new philosopher and genuine free spirit is self-evident. Like Nietzsche's overman, Goethe's *Übermensch* pledges himself to a frenzied existence with its "agonies of gratification" and "quickening frustration" (lines 1766–67). He commits himself to willful act even over Mephisto's objection: "But I am set on it!" ("Allein, ich will!"; line 1785). The theme resonates through the whole of *Faust I* and *II* when Faust retorts that he does not wish to be cured of this will (cf. lines 7459) or when his son Euphorion rejects all caution and vows to fly ever higher (line 9899). Of course, there is no way that Mephisto can win his wager with Faust.

The spirit song thus mirrors Faust's transition from what Nietzsche was later to call the shift from a false free spirit to a genuine free spirit. The false free spirit is dependent upon good name, wealth, status, and recognition; the genuine free spirit endeavors to free herself from all dependencies, even of the will to be independent (*BGE* #41, 205, 211).

By endeavoring to force his forming will on the formless and wily sea in the final act of Part II, Faust constructs his coastal empire along the interface of that which is (formed) and that which is not yet (formed). Ultimately, he comprehends the nature of that chain of utmost potency. To master the elements he enlists thousands of workers under his despotic rule, who – thus bonded together in ceaseless struggle against the relentless onslaught of the waves – appear to him to be free, that is, free to do his supreme will. The vision of such orchestrated movement under his command, if it could be achieved, is enough for him to express contentment with the moment at the thought of an eternally recurring struggle that bonds individuals in community effort. The conditionality of the remark escapes Mephisto, who believes their individual contract now concluded.

The attentive reader, however, does not overlook the ambivalence inherent in the prospect of a race of people (free or not) seeking to exert control over the controlling forces of nature in endless reiteration of coordinated action and reaction ("Wirkung" and "Gegenwirkung"). The agonistic forces evident in creation (see, e.g., Davies, Kauffman, Smoot) would appear to be identical to the agonistic creativity prerequisite to the land reclamation project envisioned by Faust.

The final scenes of *Faust II* continue the imagery of this dynamic interplay through the adaption of cloud formation as a poetical structuring principle. Their mystical flavor has long fascinated Goethe scholars, who have wondered how Faust's heaven could ever be a state of rest. Goethe's God would have to be the eternal self-realization of the fundamental energy of the universe in localized time and space – what Whitehead called the "eternal accident of creativity."[72] The Deity at the end of Faust's journey into the inner realm would thus appear to be a self-creative "actual entity" and simultaneously a self-creative "actual event" (Böhm 46) or a "monster of energy" (Nietzsche), that is, both individuated instance and process. Faust's deeds are the natural consequence of the divine pronouncement "Let there be light!" His search for that light is the objective of his knowledge quest, which leads him to experience the endless cycle of chromatic shifts from blue to blueish-red, from yellow to yellowish-red in the dialectic evolution of dark/light to the green of life as well as, in the other direction, to the purple of noble power. It is his own acting out of Adam and Eve's quest for Paradise Lost, his own need to be an active agent in constituting the world. The grounding of that quest is right under his feet. It is life as we know it.

Maybe Goethe's allusion at the beginning of the play to the Pythagorean and neo-Platonic models of the universe is meant to express some deep structure not evident in visible matter, that is, matter made visible only through the introduction of light. In any event, the Faustian element is essentially realigned here with auto-poietic processes, and, what is most surprising, given the intervening sixty years of study and experience, it is fully in keeping with young Goethe's "strange confession of faith" ("wunderliches Glaubensbekenntnis") from the earliest stage of his interest in alchemical and chemical phenomena, as noted previously (FA 14:965). Goethe inserted that "Glaubensbekenntnis" as the conclusion to Book 8 in his *Dichtung und Wahrheit*, in which he recounts the events in Leipzig and Frankfurt in the years 1768–70. He even speaks of his efforts to formulate in mathematical terms those ideas about the origin of the relationship between perfection and imperfection, good and evil, action and reaction, light and darkness from a single source. This he achieves by designating God the Father (= 1) as the self-productive drive that leads to the bifurcated Son as an Other (= 2). Together they engage in continual creation ("den Akt des Hervorbringens fortsetzen"), thus constituting the whole of the Deity in the Holy Spirit (= 3). But because the Trinity is perfectly contained, it required a fourth element to continue the external productivity of the

72 Peter Böhm, "Energie – Kreativität – Gott: Anmerkungen zur Metaphysik Alfred North Whiteheads," *Perspektiven der Philosophie: Neues Jahrbuch* 17 (1991): 37–75; here 38–39, 59.

material world, that is, everything we associate with "schwer, fest und finster." This fourth element is Lucifer (= 4), who was relegated entirely to the material realm after his fall from grace (FA 14:382–83). Although Goethe does later endeavor to distance himself from that youthful exuberance, the similarity of Faust's redemption and future prospects in the hereafter to that early vision of reconciliation of opposites is indeed cause for wonder. According to both the young and the mature Goethe, Faust's redemption was preordained from the beginning of time and conditioned by the dynamics of renewal inherent in the eternally emergent universe of which he is a part. While repeating the hubris and fall of Lucifer, humankind is simultaneously the being in this designer universe best equipped to assume the role of reunifier by acting out "the pulse of life" ("der eigentliche Puls des Lebens), that is, the alternation between concentration ("Konzentration" but also "verselbsten") and expansion ("Expansion" but also "entselbstigen"). Promoting and losing the self are thus two dimensions of one event horizon (FA 14:383–85). It fell to humankind's lot to play a central role by assuming Lucifer's original function as master of creative energy and as the host for the Deity. But then, what is the motor that engages these two fundamental drives of contraction and expansion?

6. The Fifth Element

We have seen that Goethe likened his masterpiece to a fairy tale with its own logic of paradox and with its conflation of myth and reality. The logic of paradox, we recall, has been recognized as being endemic to complex systems. Fairy tales take liberties with chronological and logical linearity, with levels of reality and dream, favoring instead symbolic feedback loops, which play upon deeper intuitions. Likewise, fairy tales focus largely on the contesting forces of good and evil, frequently using love as the missing key to solve a mystery and ensure a fruitful existence. Although ostensibly a retelling of the trials of Job at the hands of the Lord, *Faust* is manifestly more a tale about love than about steadfastness and loyalty. It cogently illustrates Nietzsche's aphorism that whatever "is done out of love always takes place beyond good and evil" (*BGE* #153). And if the God of the New Testament is love, then we can apply another of Nietzsche's adages to *Faust*: "Around the hero everything becomes a tragedy, around the demi-god a satyr play; and around God everything becomes – what? Perhaps a 'world'? –" (*BGE* # 150). Faust as "hero" is a tragic figure; as a deunculus (little god, demigod) he is involved in a satyr at various times; as the loyal servant of the Lord, he takes on Lord-like functions in Part II. There he is instrumental in constructing the world to suit his needs. All this contributes to the perceived density of the text.

Since God is also the supreme mathematician, we should not be surprised at the use of numbers in *Faust* (as well as in fairy tales). The number of greatest concern to us in the present context, however, is five. In theories of the magic of numbers, five represents the midpoint on a scale from one to nine.[73] Zero is not counted because it signifies nonmanifestation in contrast to the One, which denotes undivided manifestation. One thus contains all potential manifestations, already thought of or not. It is like a cosmic seed or the original monad in Leibnizian terminology. As such, One is associated with light, marks the beginning of all things, and symbolizes universal interconnection. In a Christian context, One is synonymous with the undivided Father.

Two reflects the dialectical principle (dyade), the measurement of all things. According to Plato, the dynamic between the One and the Two gives rise to individuated manifestations. The Two's function is thus polarization and differenttiation in the process of making the unity of the One comprehensible. The principle of the Two, therefore, makes the fullness of the One manifest (cf. *Faust*, line 8016). The Two coincides in Christian thought with God the Son. The Three signifies the unity of opposites, that is, of manifestation (One) and nonmanifestation (Zero). Moreover, the Three (triade) is strongly associated with the creative act, for it has a bonding, healing, and reconciling function (cf. *Faust,* lines 9700–2). All events and constructed matter obey the principle of the Three, exemplified in the developmental process of beginning, middle, and end.[74] This linear development reveals that all existence devolves from the One, Two, and Three. The role of the Trinity, the unity of the Three in the One, the resolution of dialectical opposition – all are equally manifest in the designation of the Christian Deity as the alpha ('Υ) und omega (˚).

73 The following is based on Robert Zeller, *Astrologie und Zahlenmystik: Die arabischen Punkte im Horoskop* (Munich: Hugendubel, 1989), 40–74 (= translation of R. Zeller, *The Lost Key of Prediction: Inner Traditions* [1980]).

74 The principle of the number three also turns up in the physiological structure of the brain in the form of clathrin triskelions. Upon this remarkable curiosity Roger Penrose remarks: "As an apparent curiosity, it may also be mentioned that in the presynaptic endings of axons there are certain substances associated with microtubules which are fascinating from the geometrical point of view, and which are important in connection with the release of neurotransmitter chemicals. These substances – called *clathrins* – are built from protein trimers known as clathrin triskelions, which form three-pronged (polypeptide) structures. The clathrin triskelions fit together to make beautiful mathematical configurations that are identical in general organization to the carbon molecules known as 'fullereines' (or 'bucky balls') owing to their similarity with the famous geodesic domes constructed by the American architect Buckminster Fuller. [...] The particular clathrins that are concerned with the release of neurotransmitter chemicals at synapses seem mainly to have the structure of a truncated icosahedron – which is familiar as the polyhedron demonstrated in the modern soccer ball" (Penrose, *Shadows* 365). A polyhedron is many sided (more than four), whereas the icosahedron is twenty-sided (much more than four).

The number four (quadrate) stands for the earthly realm. In addition to the usual associations of the four elements (earth, fire, water, air), four geographical directions, and four primary sensations (hot, cold, dry, wet), we can think here of the alchemistic identification of the four "worlds" of emanation (jod), causation (he), formation (waw), and matter (he). Modern gene research has identified four nitrogenous bases that combine to constitute nucleotides: A (adenine), C (cytosine), G (quanine), and T (thymine). These are the basic elements of chromosomes, which consist of deoxyribonuleic acid (DNA), which in turn transmits the genetic code. The sequence of three of these four bases constitutes a unit of the genetic code; each sequence of three bases is a code for one of the twenty different amino acids that make up the proteins that control the characteristics of a cell. Consequently, we could say that at the basic level of existence the Divine Three combines with the Earthly Four to constitute life. This would seem to be a much more refined way of restating Goethe's strange confession of faith, which assigns Lucifer the number four.

In numerology, adding the Three and the Four together achieves their point of coincidence in the number Seven. Thus, Seven marks the unity of the Deity and the earth, their return to the monad. If we multiply three by itself, the result is nine, and Nine signifies the totality of manifestations or the totality of the One in individuated form. Three times four, on the other hand, results in Twelve. In Biblical terms the number twelve frequently stands for the totality (e.g., the twelve tribes of Israel, the twelve disciples, twelve times twelve). The Twelve, therefore, is seen to be inherently related to the Seven.

Against the background of numerology, we can better understand the significance of the Principle of Five. As mentioned, the Five indicates the midpoint between unindividuated unity (One) and the resolution of that undivided unity into its constituent "parts" (Nine). Like the Three, the Five also serves as the return to the point of origin. As the sum of the Three and the Two, it represents the unity of the principles of reconciliation and of division. Thus, the Five came to symbolize the human being as a hybrid of spiritual energy (Three – Trinity) and matter (Two – the principle of manifestation). As a hybrid of spirit and body, with four limbs and five senses to explore the world, the human being also stands for the conjoining of light and darkness. As the center of the quadrate (◙), the Five points to the distinguishing quality of humankind: the heart as a metaphor for the quintessence of what it means to be human – love. This connotation is present in the five-lettered name (Jesus), of the Savior, who came to redeem humankind by assuming human form and by preaching love for one another. It has also been suggested that the Five is related to Faust's *enceirisin naturae* (line 1940) and to that which holds the world together at its core (line 383). Magically, the lines of the pentagram naturally divide themselves into segments according to the relation constant phi (1.618), which seems ubiquitous throughout the scales of size in the universe.[75] Then too, as the polyhedral angle formed by four planes passing through a point, five is the geometric equivalent of 360°, that is, the circumference of a circle. No wonder that the number five is considered both magical and divine.

Scholarship has repeatedly noted that love as rendered in Mountain Gorges, the final scene of the opus, is the fifth element – the *quint*essential one that bonds the other four together and brings about much purposive movement.[76] Having undergone the transformations of the Witch's Kitchen and his encounter with the Mothers, Faust recognizes in love the strange attractor that causes his own movement between contraction and expansion, whether violent or tranquil, productive or destructive (line 6500). We should thus be alert to the role that the number four plays in framing Faust's telluric existence: four elements, four seasons, four sensations, four directions. If we conceive of these as indicating the rectangular coordinates of any given stage of Faust's journey, the very center of the frame would be the site of the fifth element. Thus, Faust must repeatedly reach down into his own inner being for renewal and strength. What he finds there is essentially related to the binding force in the world at large. (This point was not lost on the late-twentieth-century Hollywood film industry, which produced such science fiction movies as *The Fifth Element* [1996].) The geometric implications will return in chapter 7.

The scene Mountain Gorges is analogous to the Prologue in Heaven. It is the fitting closure to the entire opus, rendering unnecessary the "Epilogue in Chaos," which Goethe planned but never composed. The epilogue would have shifted the focus back to Mephisto (who is incapable of understanding love) and away from the unifying function of love – in its two forms of eros and agape – as the quintessential force of reconciliation and redemption. Eros is the driving impetus from below toward a higher station, while agape is the graceful gesture from above, drawing the object of attraction to a higher elevation. (Might we see here a mirroring of the dialectic between dark and light / light and dark?) As seen by the

---

75 Phi plays an essential role in Dan Brown's *The Da Vinci Code: A Novel* (New York: Doubleday, 2003). See esp. 93–98.

76 See, e.g., Jacob Steiner, "Die letzte Szene von Goethes *Faust*," *Études Germaniques* 38.1 (1983): 147-55; and Albrecht Schöne, *Fausts Himmelfahrt. Zur letzten Szene der Tragödie* (Munich: Carl Friedrich von Siemens Stiftung, 1994). Less compelling is Benjamin Bennett's interpretation in *Goethe's Theory of Poetry: Faust and the Regeneration of Language* (Ithaca and London: Cornell University Press, 1986), 305–29. He wants to see Mountain Gorges as the missing "Epilogue in Chaos on the Way to Hell" in disguise. Because his essential premise is language based, Bennett does not seriously engage Goethe's scientific views of nature and creation, nor does he explore the deeper connotations of chaos. Thus, Bennett considers Mountain Gorges to be an "inadequate," "antipoetic," "confused," and "contradictory" conclusion to the tragedy (310, 322).

striving subject, the first is active, the second passive. Eros and agape complement one another by earning and giving. Pater Profundus remarks revealingly: "Just so, it is almighty Love / That forms all things and all sustains" ("So ist es die allmächtige Liebe, / Die alles bildet, alles hegt"; lines 11872–73). This dynamic interplay is represented by the movement of the clouds and moisture and the bolts of lightning up and down the tree-girt gorge's slopes (lines 11874–81). All of these elements, Pater Profundus concludes, "All are Love's messengers proclaiming / Creation's ceaseless workings multifold" ("Sind Liebesboten, sie verkünden, / Was ewig schaffend uns umwallt"; lines 11883–84). Shortly before, Pater Ecstaticus (who is floating up and down) had spoken of "love's bond of hot desire" (line 11855). By focusing on the gleaming sun, the "essence of endless love" ("Ewiger Liebe Kern"; line 11865), one can overcome all pain and tribulation caused by nihilistic actions. Love (here symbolized by the blazing light) draws the soul upward, even as the physical elements of the plant grow upward toward the warmth and energy of the sun. Combined with the nurturing waters descending into the gorge where Faust's remains lie, the duality of sun and earth converge in a renewed unity capable of vanquishing the "nullity" of material decomposition (line 11863). This dynamic adds complexity to the simple geometric rendering of the mathematical relationship between the Four of earthly existence and the quintessentially transcending, bonding element of Five. New spaces are created.

The entire process turns "flames of love" (line 11801), be they "only" eros, "toward clarity" (line 11802). The "self-damned" are saved by the genuineness of their inferior love and are "self-redeemed" by virtue of their embedment in the totality (lines 11803–8). This assessment by the chorus of angels could not be a more apt expression of the holographic nature of the earth. In conversation with Eckermann, Goethe explained that the conflation of eros and agape was key to understanding the famous lines: "Who strives forever with a will, / By us can be redeemed" (lines 119436–37; to Eckermann 6 June 1831). The more perfected angels later address this unity as "the quintessence / of dual self made one" (lines 11961–62). The identification of the life-giving sun as the source of love and salvation is a clear expression of Goethe's theology.[77]

---

77 Goethe's explanation of the origin of the eye resonates with the essential tensions inherent in the relationship between eros, agape, and the sun, as discussed here. The physical organ, Goethe argued, is the result of the coordinated efforts of external light and an internal striving for the light. Light and spirit collaborate to shape the body: "Das Auge hat sein Dasein dem Licht zu danken. Aus gleichgültigen tierischen Hülfsorganen ruft sich das Licht ein Organ hervor, das seines Gleichen werde, und so bildet sich das Auge am Lichte fürs Licht, damit das innere Licht dem äußeren entgegentrete" ("Entwurf einer Farbenlehre"; FA 23.1:24). In a sketch dating from about 1806 on the nature of the eye for the *Farbenlehre*, Goethe noted in similar fashion: "In ihm [dem Auge] spiegelt sich von außen die Welt, von innen der Mensch" (FA 23.2:269).

Only after this identification does the focus shift to the chorus of female figures: Magna Peccatrix (the woman who washed Christ's feet with her hair), Mulier Samaritana (the Samaritan woman Christ meets at the well), Maria Aegytica (St. Mary of Egypt), Una Poenitentium (Gretchen), and ultimately the Mater Gloriosa (Virgin Mary). While the Virgin Mother is the highest of the highest, it falls to Gretchen to lead Faust's drifting, immortal remains farther up the slopes and into the upper atmosphere. The Mater Gloriosa instructs Gretchen to "rise, and in higher spheres abide; / He will sense you and find the way" ("Komm! hebe dich zu höhern Sphären! / Wenn er dich ahnet, folgt er nach"; lines 12094–95). These instructions resonate with Mephisto's advice to Faust to follow the key confidently, for it will sense the way to the Mothers. The Eternal Feminine draws us up and onward (line12111), it also draws us down and all around (one does not rise or descend to the Mothers, and the movement in the final scene is regenerative). Thus, the Eternal Feminine, as Harold Jantz has convincingly argued, connotes "the great creative continuity of life, birth, and rebirth in constantly renewed forms, the ultimate resolution of death, destruction, and tragedy in new cycles of life" (Jantz, *Mothers* 45; see also 56–58). The Eternal Feminine, then, encompasses not only positive figures such as Gretchen, the Virgin Mary, the Mothers, Galatea, Aurora, and Helena but also negative ones such as the witches in the kitchen and on the Brocken, Martha, the Graeae, Lilith, and the Sirens (cf. Mesh-hadi 168; Jantz *Mothers* 37–39). The path to perfection is a nonlinear, endlessly turning, living screw drawn between the positive and the negative. The Eternal Feminine is the ultimate strange attractor, for it is not only the point of attraction in a dynamic system but also the impulse to change the vacillations to a new frequency. It assures that Faust will not go astray. As a monad, Faust is connected to the *Urmonade*, and every monad, Goethe contended, is an entelechy, which may or may not become manifest.[78] Its realization is codependent on environmental conditions. Goethe thus saw in morphological studies a means of unlocking nature's innermost secrets.

Equally important along with the forward, evolutionary movement is the recursive motion around the quintessence of existence, whether in the form of energy or of matter. The central idea of "Bildung" in the Goethean sense applies equally to spirit and body. If we are willing to consider the soul as a metaphor for the genetic nucleus, we can see the body as forming around that center. Depending upon the environmental circumstances, that genetic code will play out somewhat differently. Slight variations in the initial conditions can, of course, lead to egregious

78 Goethe: "Jede Monas ist eine Entelechie, die unter gewissen Bedingungen zur Erscheinung kommt. Ein gründliches Studium des Organismus läßt in die Geheimnisse [schauen?]" (FA 13:403; aphorism. 6.36.4).

deviations from the expected path further down the line. But the strange attractor re-emerges to restructure and reorient. The scenes and acts of *Faust I* and *II* are fractal rather than fragmented. They are intended to provide more than just test cases for Faust's coevolution in his drive to know what holds the universe together – they are designed to verify a thesis. They are also examples of how that coevolutionary process functions. The earth has Faust again, even as his immortal soul rises to the stratosphere.[79] The cycle will begin again. While not self-same, it will be self-similar. The entire opus is a commentary on a highly complex matter. It represents, without resolving, the essential tensions. In his *Maximen und Reflexionen* from the 1820s, Goethe describes the fundamental characteristic of a living organism – the actual topic of *Faust* – as consisting in the contrary tendencies

> to divide, to unite, to merge into the universal, to abide in the particular, to transform itself, to define itself, and, as living things tend to appear under a thousand conditions, to arise and vanish, to solidify and melt, to freeze and flow to expand and contract. Since these effects occur together, any or all may occur at the same moment. Genesis and decay, creation and destruction, birth and death, joy and pain, all are interwoven with equal effect and weight; thus even the most isolated event always presents itself as an image and metaphor for the most universal. (trans. by D. Miller, Goethe's *Scientific Studies* 305)

> [Grundeigenschaft der lebendigen Einheit: sich zu trennen, sich zu vereinen, sich in's Allgemeine zu ergehen, im Besondern zu verharren, sich zu verwandeln, sich zu specificiren und, wie das Lebendige unter tausend Bedingungen sich dartun mag, hervorzutreten und zu verschwinden, zu solidesciren und zu schmelzen, zu erstarren und zu fließen, sich auszudehnen und sich zusammen zu ziehen. Weil nun alle diese Wirkungen im gleichen Zeitmoment zugleich vorgehen, so kann alles und jedes zu gleicher Zeit eintreten. Entstehen und Vergehen, Schaffen und Vernichten, Geburt und Tod, Freud und Leid, alles wirkt durch einander, in gleichem Sinn und gleicher Maße; deßwegen denn auch das Besonderste, das sich ereignet, immer als Bild und Gleichniß des Allgemeinsten auftritt.] (FA 13:48, #1.304)

The phrasing and conceptualization of this assessment saliently foreshadow Nietzsche's world-view.

Through the interactive process of the multifaceted unity described, supreme artistic expression becomes possible. Emergence, the process of manifestation, is the thing-in-itself. In a later, frequently cited maxim, the poet-scientist avers: "That is genuine symbolism, where the particular represents the general, not as dream or shadow but as a living revelation of the impenetrable in the moment."[80] In essence,

---

79 Here I disagree with Wyder, who contends that the earth has lost its attraction (*Goethes Naturmodell* 305). (Although she does not speak specifically of emergence, Tantillo's assessment of the centrality of the (earth's) atmosphere to the phenomenon of emergence is more judicious): (*Will to Create* 141-42).

80 My translation (not included in Miller's selection). Goethe: "Das ist die wahre Symbolik, wo das

the symbol alters the manifestation into an idea, and the idea assumes the form of an image so that the idea is always present, if never totally expressed. Hence, Goethe's last major work shares much in common with both his ideas of nature and his early conception of a dialectical universe that reconciles good and evil, expansion and contraction. Two of the major structuring symbols in *Faust* are the coastline and the life-sustaining atmosphere. "We dwell in it [the atmosphere] as inhabitants of the seashore," Goethe had opined in his commentary on Luke Howard's theory of weather, adding: "We gradually ascend to the highest peak where it is difficult to live, but in thought we climb further."[81] That is what I have aimed to do here.

Besondere das Allgemeinere repräsentiert, nicht als Traum und Schatten, sondern als lebendig-augenblickliche Offenbarung des Unerforschlichen" (FA 13:33, #1.196).

81 Miller, Goethe's *Scientific Studies*, 146: "Wir leben darin [in der Atmosphäre] als Bewohner der Meeresufer, wir steigen nach und nach hinauf bis auf die höchsten Gebirge, wo es zu leben schwer wird; allein mit Gedanken steigen wir weiter" (FA 25:275).

Chapter 6
Zarathustra – Life on Earth

Wann werden wir die Natur ganz entgöttlicht haben! Wann werden wir anfangen dürfen, uns Menschen mit der reinen, neu gefundenen, neu erlösten Natur zu *vernatürlichen*!

– Friedrich Nietzsche, *Fröhliche Wissenschaft*, #109

Einst war der Frevel an Gott der grösste Frevel, aber Gott starb, und damit starben auch diese Frevelhaften. An der Erde zu freveln ist jetzt das Furchtbarste und die Eingeweide des Unerforschlichen höher zu achten, als den Sinn der Erde!

– Friedrich Nietzsche, "Zarathustra's Vorrede," #3

1. A Philosophical Novel – Philosophy as Dance

Although Nietzsche himself regarded *Also Sprach Zarathustra* (Thus Spoke Zarathustra, 1883–85) as his most important work, critics have not always been in agreement. In general, two broad schools of thought on the issue have emerged. One opines that the work is a loose collection of aphorisms held together by a unity of concern but without poetic harmony, its abstractness and use of metaphors so daunting that Nietzsche required other works to comment on it (Kaufmann, Stern). The prophet Zarathustra is framed by the first (1882) and second (1887) editions of *Fröhliche Wissenschaft* (The Gay Science), into which Nietzsche injected parts of *Zarathustra* under the rubric "Incipit tragoedia," and by *Jenseits von Gut und Böse* (Beyond Good and Evil), which is generally seen as a glossary of *Zarathustra* and whose origins go back to long before *The Gay Science*.[1] Literarily, *Zarathustra* is considered to be a failure.[2] The other major school of thought (seminally represented by Martin Heidegger) sees in the work the quintessence of Nietzsche's most genuine and

1 Friedrich Nietzsche, *Sämtliche Werke: Kritische Studienausgabe*, ed. by Giorgio Colli and Mazzino Montinari, 15 vols. (Munich: Deutscher Taschenbuch Verlag, 1988), 14:345–46. Hereafter cited as *KSA* by volume and page number. Thematically, *Beyond Good and Evil* reaches back into Nietzsche's school years, when he authored an essay (1858) on the concept of "gut und schlecht" ("good and bad") in Theognis's thought. Chronologically, the first version of *BGE* predates the publication of *The Gay Science*. In order to enhance the readability and accessibility of my text, I will cite Nietzsche's works in translation and provide the original German when it adds important nuance.

2 See, e.g., J. P. Stern, *A Study of Nietzsche* (New York: Cambridge University Press, 1979), 157–59.

important philosophical teaching. This second school of thought accords more weight to the author's characterization of Zarathustra as his audacious, intellectual "son."[3]

An evidently essential tension exists between these two (extreme) attitudes toward Nietzsche as littérateur on the one hand and as analytical thinker on the other. In *Thus Spoke Zarathustra*, literature and philosophy converge to such an extent that we can legitimately speak of the work as philosophical fiction, a descendant of eighteenth-century versions of the genre, though definitely not a satire in the vein of Voltaire's *Candide*. (Nietzsche himself calls it "legendary.") While it does tell a story, character portraiture and narrative plot are clearly not its forte; the development of ideas through parable and metaphor, however, is. In this more rarified sense, *Zarathustra* is a philosophical anti-novel like Dostoyevsky's *Notes from Underground* (1864), which Nietzsche had read in French translation and much admired.[4] As such, it is closer to the immediacy of life than to the abstractions of philosophy (especially analytical philosophy). Its aphoristic style makes visible connections among energy knots of insight, creating an effect not unlike that of the human observer peering with eye and imagination into the night sky and discerning constellations of bright lights rather than a mere jumble of luminous points.

Despite its underdeveloped analytic structure and syncopated style, *Zarathustra* quickly emerged as one of Nietzsche's most enduring works, achieving the status of a cult book and serving as a kind of "handbook of revolution" for many readers (Rosen, *Mask* xiv). Its topic is life on earth and how most appropriately to live that life. To be sure, the novel does address various kinds of circular motion associated with earthly existence: circumlocutions, orbiting material bodies, and revolutions of thought. Both movements of mass and of thought prove to be symptoms of an unseen event.[5] In fact, some see the concept of the cyclical eternal return as the works's internal structuring principle.[6] *Zarathustra* found its way (along with Goethe's *Faust*) into the trenches as

3 Stern, *Nietzsche* , 21. Stanley Rosen, *The Mask of Enlightenment: Nietzsche's* Zarathustra (New York: Cambridge University Press, 1995), xv. In a letter to the publisher E. W. Fritsch, Nietzsche refers to his "verwegenen Sohn Zarathustra" (cited by Colli and Montinari, *Chronik zu Nietzsches Leben*, *KSA* 15:160).

4 On 23 February 1887, Nietzsche wrote to Franz Overbeck in passionate praise of *Notes from Underground*. (Translated as *L'esprit souterrain*, the novel evokes associations with the Earth Spirit.) Nietzsche remarked upon an "Instinkt der Verwandtschaft" between himself and Dostoyevsky and characterized the work as a hybrid of two novellas: "die erste eigentlich ein Stück Musik, sehr fremder, sehr undeutscher Musik; die zweite ein Geniestreich der Psychologie, eine Selbstverhöhnung des γνῶθι σεαυτόν." Cited in Colli and Montinari, *Chronik zu Nietzsches Leben*, *KSA* 15:163.

5 In a fragment from winter 1885/86, Nietzsche mused: "– alle Bewegungen sind *Zeichen* eines inneren Geschehens; und jedes innere Geschehen drückt sich aus in solchen Veränderungen der Formen. Das Denken ist noch nicht das innere Geschehen selber, sondern ebenfalls nur eine Zeichensprache für den Machtausgleich von Affekten" (*KSA* 12:17; see also 25).

6 John Carson Pettey, *Nietzsche's Philosophical and Narrative Styles* (New York: Peter Lang, 1992),

military issue to German troops in World War I and carried Nietzsche's fame into the late twentieth century, even if its concepts were frequently misunderstood or taken out of context.[7] Stanley Kubick's adaptation of Richard Strauss's symphonic poem, *Thus Spoke Zarathustra* (1896), in his classic science-fiction movie, *Space Odyssey 2001,* contributed to the book's popularity beyond the walls of academe. The novel itself continues to be read voraciously in both philosophy and literature classes at colleges across the United States. Perhaps precisely because of its (disputed) literary quality, *Zarathustra* did not attract the attention of philosophers until the late twentieth century.[8]

Thus Spoke Zarathustra is an elaborate parody of the Bible (cf. Pettey 113–21). Zarathustra appears as the modern Messiah who descends the mountain at age thirty to gather disciples and to teach them about the new man and the new vision of life. While ostentatiously aimed at deconstructing myth, the work paradoxically contributed to the making of a new myth, fulfilling its author's prophecy that the book would be read as widely as the Bible. Indeed, Nietzsche saw himself as heralding a new style and a new era ("Zeitrechnung") (*KSA* 15:187–88). Utilizing myth in this way underscored his belief that we cannot live without legends. The paradoxical quality of the novel is readily apparent in the fact that Zarathustra desires only disciples who are independent thinkers and who will resist following slavishly in his footsteps. His followers must be creators of values, makers of new paths, and strong-backed individuals who can bear the burden of a thousand lives and suffer constant disappointment.

Key issues raised here include the will to power, the nature of being human, the new man (overman), the need for balance, and the eternal return. These are, of course, qualities and themes already encountered in Goethe's *Faust*. Nietzsche commented in fall 1887 that Goethe had already achieved what the nineteenth century had vainly

---

124–32; Pettey cites Bernard Pautrat, *Versions du Soleil: Figures et système de Nietzsche* (Paris: Éditions du Seuil, 1971), 357.

7 Wolfgang G. Natter, *Literature at War: Representing the "Time of Greatness" in Germany* (New Haven and London: Yale University Press, 1999), 96, 126, 144–45. Stephen R. Aschheim, *The Nietzsche Legacy in Germany, 1890–1990* (Berkeley: University of California Press, 1992).

8 Kathleen Marie Higgins, *Nietzsche's Zarathustra* (Philadelphia: Temple University Press, 1987), broke with the main tendency in Nietzsche scholarship to dismiss *Zarathustra* as a peculiar work largely devoid of conceptual content and argumentative sequence, insisting that the work be taken seriously in its own right. She stressed above all its experimental and literary qualities. Pettey (1998) took a similar approach, placing Zarathustra within the context of Nietzsche's earlier writing and contrasting it with the dominant literary styles of the era (realism, naturalism, neoromanticism). Utilizing more conventional (H. Weinrich, J. Stenzel) and less conventional theories of narrative (J. Derrida, H. White), he illuminated Nietzsche's distinctive diegetic and mimetic style (45–71; 73–100). This allowed Pettey to explore briefly Nietzsche's early reception (1–21). As late as 1995, Stanley Rosen presented his own study of the philosophical content of the novel, *The Mask of Enlightenment*, as distinctive because of its exclusive focus on the work.

striven for: universal understanding, an openness to the possible, a respect for things (*KSA* 12:444). In a sense, Nietzsche picks up where Goethe left off, albeit with his own agenda, for Nietzsche rejected Faust in early 1886 as indecisive, lame, and not at all like the genuine free spirit *(KSA* 12:27). In playful allusion to the turning point in *Faust*, Nietzsche composed the one-liner in 1875: "Wer den höchsten Augenblick geniesst, *erblindet*" ("Whoever experiences the highest moment of pleasure will go blind"; *KSA* 8:186). Yet in an unpublished aphorism originally intended for the autobiographical *Ecce Homo* (1888–89), which appeared posthumously in 1908, Nietzsche described *Faust* as a kind of *Gesamtkunstwerk* of vibrant immediacy.[9] Reasons for the ambivalent stance of acceptance and rejection will be explained in the following.

Composed in the early 1880s, this novel out of step with its time ("ein unzeitgemäßer Roman"; Pettey 140) consists of four parts and narrates the oracular pronouncements of the prophet Zarathustra organized around a few episodes from his life. Similar to Goethe's effort in *Faust*, Nietzsche sought here to create a new mythology as advocated at the end of *Die Geburt der Tragödie* (The Birth of Tragedy, 1872). A sketch from 1881 indicates the intended structure, tone, and content. Taken together, they provide a salient expression of Nietzsche's philosophy and warrant our considering the novel an alternative to conventional philosophy. Indeed, the general title of the sketch is "outline of a new way of living" ("Fingerzeige zu einem neuen Leben"; *KSA* 9:519). Essentially, it represents an anti-philosophical attitude. Nietzsche states that Part I was to be composed in the style of the first movement of Beethoven's *Ninth Symphony*, probably to imply both the contemplative crescendo marked by a counterpoint of lyrical fluidity and explosive outburst of punctuated energy, in short, an emphatic announcement.

Moreover, the topic is announced as "Chaos sive natura," a manifest response to Spinoza's "deus sive natura." Apparently, chaos was to replace God as the creative principle in the new order of things. Equally revealing is the subtitle: "On the Dehumanization of Nature" ("Von der Entmenschlichung der Natur"). What Nietzsche urges is the repositioning of humanity within the total economy of nature as a constituent part, not as its teleological end. In an unpublished fragment from winter 1882–83, he likened the human being to a collection of atoms totally dependent upon the energy fluctuations around it, yet, like every individual atom, incalculable in its movements, a thing unto itself.[10] Far from being the telos of natural processes, as it was

---

9 Nietzsche, "Nachgelassene Fragmente, Oktober-November 1888": "Faust – das ist für den, der den Erdgeruch der deutschen Sprache aus Instinkt kennt, für den Dichter des Zarathustra, ein Genuß ohne Gleichen" (*KSA* 13:634). In the next lines Nietzsche explains that Faust – and Goethe – are rarely enjoyed; they have been reduced to objects of study. That is one reason for Nietzesche's ambivalence toward the Olympian.

10 Nietzsche: "Der Mensch eine Atomgruppe vollständig in seinen Bewegungen abhängig von allen Kräfte-Vertheilungen und -Veränderungen des Alls – und andererseits wie jedes Atom unberechen-

for the eighteenth century, humanity is now simply one of nature's accidents (cf. *KSA* 9:522, 525). In reflections on the conservation of energy dating even earlier from summer 1875, Nietzsche had already emphasized the agonistic quality of the complex intertwining of humankind with various life forms. He likened that nexus to the nervous dynamic of inorganic molecular structure. Little was known about those inner workings of nature, he volunteered, nor did he expect that we would ever get to the bottom of things. Yet cooperation clearly occurs among the parts, and nothing stands still ("es [das Grundatom] sitzt nicht still"; *KSA* 8:182–83). That appears to be the background for *Zarathustra*. In its final version, Part I of the novel describes the prophet's preparation for his descent from the mountain to spread the word. Himself still inexperienced and idealistic, Zarathustra sings the praises of self-overcoming.

Part II narrates the protagonist's encounters in real life among men. A radical shift of focus occurs away from putative enthusiasm toward the corporeality of experiencing the world. That would explain the choice of title for this section: "On the Corporealizing of Experience" ("Von der Einverleibung der Erfahrungen"). And Nietzsche means "corporealizing" (or "incorporation") literally as an enfolding in the body. If thought is paramount in Part I in which Zarathustra reverses the message of Christ shedding his blood and denying his body to redeem humanity, then *performing* the thought rises to the fore in Part II. Prophetically, Zarathustra declares his fundamental message unequivocally: "Of all that is written I love only what a man has written with his blood. Write with blood, and you will experience that blood is spirit."[11] Even earlier he had proclaimed: "[B]ody am I entirely, and nothing else; and soul is only a word for something about the body" (*Za* 34; "Leib bin ich ganz und gar, und Nichts ausserdem; und Seele ist nur ein Wort für ein Etwas am Leibe"; *KSA* 4:39). The body thereby definitely displaces the spirit at center stage, a move widely considered to be pioneering.[12] With it, Nietzsche saw himself as picking up where Leibniz had left off with

---

bar, ein An-und-für-sich" (*KSA* 10:150). Rosen suggests that the complex operations of nature replace God in Nietzsche's new scheme of things (*Mask* 19). Margot Fleischer, *Der "Sinn der Erde" und die Entzauberung des Übermenschen: Eine Auseinandersetzung mit Nietzsche* (Darmstadt: Wissenschaftliche Buchgesellschaft, 1993), 120, also discerns this trend from creative God to creative chaos. However, she rejects the extension of the will to power to inorganic and organic nature as unconvincing (250–54). Alastair Moses, *Nietzsche's Philosophy of Nature and Cosmology* (New York: Peter Lang, 1990), posits a link between the central concept of the eternal return and the natural pulsations of contraction and expansion in the universe (295).

11 The English translation cited Friedrich Nietzsche, *Thus Spoke Zarathustra: A Book for All and None*, trans. by Walter Kaufmann (New York: Viking Penguin, 1995), 40, "Prologue," #7. Hereafter this edition is cited as Za" by page number. The body of the text contains numbered subsections in addition to the main ones, thus the decision to cite by page number to avoid confusion. The German reads: "Von allem Geschriebenen liebe ich nur Das, was Einer mit seinem Blute schreibt. Schreibe mit Blut: und du wirst erfahren, dass Blut Geist ist" (*KSA* 4:48).

12 Cf. Fleischer *"Sinn der Erde,"* 53–56, 259. Gregory Moore, *Nietzsche, Biology and Metaphor*

his suspicion that we have perceptions of which we are not yet aware.[13] A little later he opines that human consciousness is an inessential property, an a posteriori "accident." "Our inner world," he concludes, reminiscent of Leibniz, "is much richer, more comprehensive, more hidden" than previously suspected (*GS* 218; "'Unsre innre Welt ist viel reicher, umfänglicher, verborgener,' so empfinden wir mit Leibnitz"; *KSA* 3:599). The tenor of Part II was appropriately to be "fleeting-skeptical-Mephistophelian" ("Flüchtig-skeptisch-mephistophelisch"; *KSA* 9:520). Manifest in this formulation is the logical progression from the belief that everything is transitory, to the skeptical attitude toward things in general, and finally to Mephisto's denial of anything external to the body.

Part III is the most "interior" of the sections, for it is here that the "final bliss of the solitary" ("vom letzten Glück des Einsamen": *KSA* 9:520) is celebrated. Instead of experiencing release and happiness, Zarathustra sinks into a deep melancholy because he senses that he is locked into the physiology of being (cf. letter of 3 September 1883 to Heinrich Köselitz, i.e., Peter Gast). The central theme here is eternal recurrence, which represents a kind of revocation of the initial optimism of Parts I and II that humanity can progress, that death can be overcome, that happiness and tranquility can be achieved. Seminal is the section labeled "The Convalescent" ("Der Genesende"), for it is there that Zarathustra – the "godless" one, "the advocate of the circle" – formulates his "most abysmal thought" (cf. *Za* 215–21; *KSA* 4:270–77). In a sense, Zarathustra replaces God in Part III in that he has come not to announce and prepare the way as the Messiah did for a better world but rather to teach a new way of living on earth that is without hope of an afterlife or of eternal bliss. His message dispenses with the transcendent and distant Deity. He counsels that "eternally the ring of being remains faithful to itself," that it requires nothing outside itself and is governed by the cycle of generation and degeneration (*Za* 217). This abysmal thought of nontranscendence is the cause of his despondency. The new mythology of eternal recurrence comprises a kind of "God-less theology" (Stern 169). Humanity must manage without the concept of transcendence or the belief in redemption from solitariness, sadness, suffering, and corporeality. Zarathustra's own self-overcoming thus proves to be a model for all humankind. Because of the primary directive to overcome self, it proves difficult to

(Cambridge: Cambridge University Press, 2002), seeks to locate Nietzsche's biologism within the context of nineteenth-century scientific debates. His focus is on the health of the body, with special interest in evolution and degeneration. By doing so he is able to demonstrate that Nietzsche's physiology of art and humankind is backed up by the (pseudo)science of his day. Although Nietzsche was not alone in mirroring that debate metaphorically and analogically, his use of the language and conceptions of science "was more wide-ranging, more total than that of his immediate successors" (e.g., Max Scheler, Oswald Spengler, Georg Simmel, Theodor Lessing, Ludwig Klages) (211).

13 Friedrich Nietzsche, *The Gay Science*, ed. by Bernhard Williams, trans. by Josefine Nauckhoff and Adrian del Caro (Cambridge: Cambridge University Press, 2001), 212; *KSA* 3:590.

state precisely who or what Zarathustra is or represents (cf. Fleischer 61–62). This echoes Nietzsche's puzzlement over the fact that his readers find him eccentric. How can he be "ex-centric," he wonders, if he has no center (*KSA* 15:168)?

Part IV essentially summarizes the content and intent of the preceding three parts. In doing so, it re-emphasizes Zarathustra's dedication to his own self-overcoming after the momentary despondency toward the end of Part III. Its tone, dithyrambic-enfolding ("dithyrambisch-umfassend"), underscores the overarching topic: "Anulus aeternitatis," or ring of eternity (*KSA* 9:520).

We can distinguish, then, three purposes underlying the novel: (1) to announce the new order; (2) to destroy the old order; and (3) to prepare the transition from the old to the new, "but without the divine tablets vouchsafed to Moses" (Rosen 73). Each phase corresponds to the three parts of the novel's original conception. However, I would emphasize more emphatically than Rosen that phase three is based on the fundamental principle of emergence known to us from chaos and complexity theory (Fleischer is simply unaware of this aspect). It signifies more than a transition from the old to the new; it is already the thing-in-itself ("thing" understood in Bohmian rather than Kantian terms, that is, "wave function," not discrete particle). At the heart of Part III, then, is creation – eternal re-creation. If there is an air of circularity about this movement, then surely it is because the arrow of time is not linear. As Zarathustra asserts in his initial oracular pronouncements, "In every Now, being begins; round every Here rolls the sphere There. The center is everywhere. Bent is the path of eternity" (*Za* 218; "In jedem Nu beginnt das Sein; um jedes Hier rollt sich die Kugel Dort. Die Mitte ist überall. Krumm ist der Pfad der Ewigkeit"; *KSA* 4:273). Nietzsche concludes his self-assessment of *Zarathustra* in *Ecce homo* by redefining the will to power as the will to create ("Wille zur Zeugung"; *KSA* 6:349).

During the composition of *Zarathustra*, various models presented themselves to Nietzsche so that one could conclude from the literary intertexuality that the novel is a mythopoetic work with multivalent voices. The most obvious source of inspiration, albeit a negative one, is the Bible, especially Christ's message of transcendence. Other models identified include Plato's *Phaedrus* (Rosen 60), *Thousand and One Nights* (Rosen 6), Dante's *Inferno*, and Apuleius's satirical *Golden Ass* (especially for Part IV of *Zarathustra*; see Higgins ix–xviii, 206–32, 233). To the above I would add Goethe's *Faust*, an affinity widely overlooked in research. The sketch to Part II suggests this affinity, as do Zarathustra's primary traits: his search for "truth," his willfulness yet final acceptance of the ever changeful in nature, his solitariness, his ceaseless doing. In each instance of imitation, a literary map of reality is charted, sometimes irreverent of tradition, sometimes in response to modern scientific knowledge, such as planetary movements (Copernicus), cloud formation (Howard), thermodynamics (Lord Kelvin), atomistic theory (Boscovich), or evolutionary biology (Darwin). This is not to say that models and theories were adopted wholesale. Rather, it was a matter of taking the

Enlightenment project seriously: critical inquiry is pursued to its logical extreme. It is possible to see in *Zarathustra* the ultimate outcome of the project of the eighteenth-century Enlightenment, a point I would stress much more than Rosen, who only hints at the connection (cf. Rosen, xiii, xv, 4 et passim).

Negotiating different disciplines and conceptions requires a style that enfolds difference while simultaneously preserving its distinctness. "My style," Nietzsche wrote to Erwin Rohde on 22 February 1884, "is a *dance*" (cf. Stern 20). The new prophet, the higher man, must be first and foremost a dancer. The *Übermensch* or overman is the complex individual who most fully represents the oppositional forces of expansion and appropriation and contraction and shutting out that are characteristic of the will to power. He is contrasted to the "last man" and the false free spirits who are small and small-minded (*Za* 17, 219). In an essay on Nietzsche from the year 1903, Döblin correctly identified Nietzsche's *Übermensch* as being marked by a heightened intensity of living ("erhöhte Lebensintensität") and of power ("Macht"), together with an enhanced sense of differentiation ("gesteigerte Differenzierung").[14] Enhanced intensity via diversification is, of course, a sign of complexity itself. Indeed, Nietzsche equates "higher" with "more complex."

The arguments presented in *Beyond Good and Evil* and in the *Will to Power* (see chapter 3) are in essence a commentary on the person and character of Zarathustra, the prophet of the overman and harbinger of the new. Indeed, as a prophet who paradoxically seeks disciples who are not willing to be followers in the traditional sense, he is already an example of the overman. A parody of the Biblical story of salvation and a reversal of Platonic idealism rather than a philosophical argument in the conventional sense, *Thus Spoke Zarathustra* turns much previous thought on its head. Perhaps even philosophy is turned upside down. When Zarathustra descends the mountain as the new law-giver, he proclaims: "Human existence is uncanny and still without meaning, a jester can become man's fatality. I will teach men the meaning of their existence – the overman, the lightning out of the dark cloud of man" (*Za* 20; "Unheimlich ist das menschliche Dasein und immer noch ohne Sinn: ein Possenreisser kann ihm zum Verhängnis werden. Ich will die Menschen den Sinn ihres Seins lehren: welcher ist der Übermensch, der Blitz aus der dunklen Wolke Mensch"; *KSA* 4:23). The metaphor is reminiscent of Erwin Schrödinger's later characterization of the atom as a cloud of interacting particles. The lightning might be likened to the crystallization of energy knots. Of course, you never know where the lightning will strike. Zarathustra's coming is mandated by the state of humanity, by the metaphorical turbulence and raging of the seas rendered in Nietzsche's view of the universe and resonant with modern science. Zarathustra finds nothing whole – no human beings –

14 Alfred Döblin, "Zu Nietzsches Morallehre" (1903), in *Nietzsche und die deutsche Literatur*, ed. by Bruno Hillebrand, 2 vols. (Munich: Deutscher Taschenbuch Verlag, 1978), 1: 331–58; here 348.

only "fragments and limbs of men." He finds humans "in ruins and scattered as over a battlefield or a butcher-field" (*Za* 138). His coming is aimed at making them whole again, but not whole in the transcendental sense of the soul taking precedence over the maimed body, fleeing it for a Utopian Eden. Zarathustra's purpose is to reconstruct the fragments and limbs into whole individuals through a delicate balance of weight and lightness.

But what does *that* mean? It means that Zarathustra is a complex individual who unites within his person agonal forces of instinct, conscious will, and unwill. He is a "seer, a willer, a creator, a future himself and a bridge to the future – and, alas, also, as it were, a cripple at this bridge: all this is Zarathustra" (*Za* 139). Moreover, he unifies into a whole all that which is "fragment and riddle and dreadful accident" by transforming fragments into coherent structures, by solving riddles, and by recasting that which is outside his power into an object of his will (*Za*, 141). Above all, Zarathustra is a creator, as are all "higher men" (*Za* 291). Through the act of willing, Zarathustra teaches humanity that it can master the past, control the present, and codetermine the future. This amounts to mastering human destiny, to transforming forces and events outside of human control into products of human will. In other words, Zarathustra teaches that humankind needs to negate determinism and nihilism by embracing the eternal return of events as a paradoxical means of "progressing" toward the ideal of the overman. Since it stands in contrast to the progressive, temporal-sequential view of history characteristic of modernism, the concept of eternal return, with its reversal of temporality, appears as a postmodern proposal.[15] The goal of the

---

15 I take exception to Nehamas's contention that eternal recurrence "has little if anything to do with the nature of the universe." He asserts that its model "is not to be found in Nietzsche's superficial reflections on thermodynamics," and that the psychological use of it "is quite independent of any theory of the physical universe." See Alexander Nehamas, *Nietzsche: Life as Literature* (Cambridge: Harvard University Press, 1985), 6, 142, 167. I argue with the majority of critics that the phrase does indeed designate a quality of external reality and is not simply a strategy for developing a more psychologically nuanced view of the self (150). Even if it is true, as Nehamas asserts, that Nietzsche never worked out his cosmology in scientific proofs, Nietzsche left little doubt about the anchoring of his philosophy in the earth. See Robert C. Holub, *Friedrich Nietzsche*. TWAS 857 (New York: Twayne Publishers, 1995), 64–67. The context in which Nietzsche is currently being discussed might be viewed as strong circumstantial evidence (if not scientific proof) of the theory Nietzsche proposed. While Nehamas argues against a mechanistic operation of recurrence because each human being is constituted by every act and experience, he takes into account neither the complexity of interactions in the realm of matter and energy nor the fact that humans are part of that external realm. On the other hand, Nehamas does want to claim individual freedom from any mechanical return because of the human being's ability to decide differently. Nehamas does not draw the logical consequences from his own argument, or so it seems to me. Higgins (1987) does, although (unlike Moses 1990, Fleischer 1993, and Moore 2002) she does not reflect upon Nietzsche's cosmology. The complexity of movement and the possibility of change involve both the physical and the mental. Then again, Nehamas rightly argues that the life of the overman is an *ideal*. By their very nature, ideals are unreal-

overman is achieved by going over the common herd man, under modern man (that is, those reduced to fragments and limbs), and deeper into man – thus the need for an overview ("Überblick"), a panoramic view ("Umblick"), and a penetrating gaze ("Tiefblick"). Ultimately, it is a question of embracing what it means to be human in the fullest possible sense and not being selectively drawn to that which is only pleasant and contented. And it means that one cannot submissively follow the lead of another, even Zarathustra's lead. Consequently, his disciples are independent thinkers who resist following slavishly in his footsteps, are makers of new paths, and can bear the burden of a thousand lives.

The key to success, for those who heed Zarathustra's call, lies in achieving a tenuous balance between reaching too far and not reaching far enough. Thus, filled with a "double will" of over- and underextension, Zarathustra (and with him the overman in general) remains a torn individual. One part of his being strives like Goethe's Faust upwards to the heights, and another throws him down into the abyss. Or, as Zarathustra expresses himself paradoxically; his glance "plunges" into the heavens, while his hand would "grasp and hold onto the depths" (*Za* 142, also 276). (Notable is Nietzsche's reversal of rising and falling movement, as if to emphasize their complementarity.) But then the unexpected happens: the opposing motions of falling and rising are combined into an agonistic and reciprocal movement. The original fall from grace is transformed in *Zarathustra* into a rising to the demands of the earth. Whereas the greatest sin for the archangels and for Adam and Eve was to sin against God, now the "most dreadful thing" is "to sin against the earth," the ground of all things (*Za*, "Prologue" #3). The driving force in life is twofold: the force of gravity and the desire to resist it. "I would believe only in a god who could dance," Zarathustra confides to his listeners (*Za* 41). One can no longer believe in the traditional God because modern science has dismantled the foundations of belief in a God of the ordered universe. This development led the madman in *The Gay Science* (#125) to proclaim that modern man has killed God; he foreshadows the views of the anti-prophet Zarathustra.

In *Human, All Too Human I* (1878), Nietzsche had already argued that science ("die Wissenschaft") no longer seeks knowledge for its own sake, instead directing its critical gaze at the wrong objects: the constructs of metaphysics, religion, and art. In seeking first and foremost to discredit these humanistic disciplines ("die Nicht-Wissenschaft"), scientific inquiry, Nietzsche avers, has impoverished the wellspring of humanity itself. To initiate a reinvigoration of science and promote the rise of a higher culture, a "double-brain, as it were two brain-ventricles" ("ein Doppelgehirn, gleichsam zwei

---

izable. They can only be approximated ever more closely. Perhaps the eternal recurrence is designed to underscore the natural process of ceaselessly refining rather than to propose a strict duplication. Thus, unlike others, I argue for interpreting eternal recurrence as self similar, not selfsame.

Hirnkammern"), is required. Lying side by side – each separable and capable of being individually shut off – they would work in concert. One he likens to the power source ("Kraftquelle"), the other to a regulator ("Regulator"). The first is designed for the humanities, the second for science. The heat and power of the former ("Illusionen, Einseitigkeiten, Leidenschaften") must be regulated by the "aid of knowledge furnished by science" ("mit Hilfe der erkennenen Wissenschaft"). If the two brains do not work in concert, the nonscience one would overheat, and the science one would not be stimulated to seek innovative approaches and ask penetrating questions. The truths of science would gradually become commonplace and provide no source of joy, Nietzsche remarks, even as "we have long since ceased to take pleasure in learning the admirable two-times-table." The health of humankind depends upon the complementarity of these two brains.[16]

The dance, then, is introduced as an appropriate simile to express the character of the higher man and of the higher culture Nietzsche envisions. In aphorism #278 of *Human, All Too Human I*, Nietzsche explained early on the meaning of the dance:

> Nowadays it is to be regarded as the decisive sign of greater culture when anyone possesses sufficient strength and flexibility to be as clear and rigorous in the domain of knowledge as at other times he is capable of as it were of giving poetry, religion and metaphysics a hundred paces advantage and entering into their power and beauty. Such a situation between two so different demands is very hard to maintain, for science presses for the absolute dominance of its methods, and if this pressure is not relaxed there arises the other danger of a feeble vacillation back and forth between different drives. To indicate the way towards a resolution of this difficulty, however, if only by means of a parable, one might recall that the *dance* is not the same thing as a languid reeling back and forth between different drives. High culture will resemble an audacious dance; as aforesaid, why one only needs a great deal of strength and suppleness. (*HA I*, #278)

---

16 Friedrich Nietzsche, *Human, All Too Human*, trans. by R. J. Hollingdale with an intro. by Richard Schacht (Cambridge: Cambridge University Press, 1996), I, #251 (p. 119). Hereafter cited as *HA I*. The entire passage reads: "Die Wissenschaft giebt Dem, welcher in ihr arbeitet und sucht, viel Vergnügen, Dem, welcher ihre Ergebnisse l e r n t, sehr wenig. Da allmählich aber alle wichtigen Wahrheiten der Wissenschaft alltäglich und gemein werden müssen, so hört auch dieses wenige Vergnügen auf: so wie wir beim Lernen des so bewunderungswürdigen Einmaleins längst aufgehört haben, uns zu freuen. Wenn nun die Wissenschaft immer weniger Freude durch sich macht und immer mehr Freude durch Verdächtigung der tröstlichen Metaphysik, Religion und Kunst, nimmt: so verarmt jene grösste Quelle der Lust, welcher der Menschheit fast ihr gesammtes Menschentum verdankt. Desshalb muss eine höhere Cultur dem Menschen ein Doppelgehirn, gleichsam zwei Hirnkammern geben, einmal um Wissenschaft, sodann um Nicht-Wissenschaft zu empfinden: neben einander liegend, ohne Verwirrung, trennbar, abschliessbar; es ist diess eine Forderung der Gesundheit. Im einen Bereiche liegt die Kraftquelle, im anderen der Regulator: mit Illusionen, Einseitigkeiten, Leidenschaften muss geheizt werden, mit Hülfe der erkennenden Wissenschaft muss den bösartigen und gefährlichen Folgen einer Ueberheizung vorgebeugt werden" (*KSA* 2: 208–209).

> [Jetzt ist es als das entscheidende Zeichen grosser Cultur zu betrachten, wenn Jemand jene Kraft und Biegsamkeit besitzt, um ebenso rein und streng im Erkennen zu sein als, in anderen Momenten, auch befähigt, der Poesie, der Religion und Metaphysik gleichsam hundert Schritte vorzugeben und ihre Gewalt und Schönheit nachzuempfinden. Eine solche Stellung zwischen zwei so verschiedenen Ansprüchen ist sehr schwierig, denn die Wissenschaft drängt zur absoluten Herrschaft der Methode, und wird diesem Drängen nicht nachgegeben, so entsteht die andere Gefahr eines schwächlichen Auf- und Niederschwankens zwischen verschiedenen Antrieben. Indessen: um wenigstens mit einem Gleichniss einen Blick auf die Lösung dieser Schwierigkeit zu eröffnen, möge man sich doch daran erinnern, dass der Tanz nicht das Selbe wie ein mattes Hin- und Hertaumeln zwischen vershiedenen Antrieben ist. Die hohe Cultur wird einem kühnen Tanze ähnlich sehen: weshalb, wie gesagt, viel Kraft und Geschmeidigkeit noth thut.] (*KSA* 2:228–29)

An advocate of high culture, a teacher of parables, and a master of this dance is Zarathustra. To follow him requires physical strength and flexibility as well as the attitude of self-distancing. Attitude continues to matter. Matter is subject to mind, and mind is a result of matter.

2. Life on the High Wire – Gravity as the Devil

The metaphor of man as a rope strung over an abyss is an apt image of the dangerous task that humanity must perform – rather, a task that humankind *is*. That is surely the reason why it is so frequently cited in Nietzsche scholarship. I am no exception, but I wish to frame this metaphor in conjunction with the parable of the dance and against the backdrop of chaos theory:

> Man is a rope, tied between beast and overman – a rope over an abyss. A dangerous across, a dangerous on-the-way, a dangerous looking-back, a dangerous stopping. What is great in man is that he is a bridge and not an end: what can be loved in man is that he is an *overture* and a *going under*. (*Za*, Prologue #4)
>
> [Der Mensch ist ein Seil, geknüpft zwischen Thier und Übermensch, – ein Seil über einem Abgrunde. Ein gefährliches Hinüber, ein gefährliches Auf-dem-Wege, ein gefährliches Zurückblicken, ein gefährliches Schaudern und Stehenbleiben.] (*KSA* 4:16)

The dangerous game referred to at critical junctions in *Beyond Good and Evil* (#41, #205, #224) is given poignant expression here by defining human existence essentially as emergence: a transitory moment, an unstable crossing over gaping space. Critics are understandably drawn to the fundamental symbolism of man as a rope, a bridge, an overture, and a going under ("ein Übergang und ein Untergang"). Less attention has been accorded the chasm and the anchoring points, although they are indispensable to defining the mode of human existence. All that really exists is the materiality of the rope, the bridge, and the human body moving through space. The key to suspension over the void – in the void – is the art of balancing the forces that act on and within the

llslip Request 10/17/2019 4:51:38 PM

Richard Albert Dionne

Richard Albert Dionne
300172955
Student

Call Number: PT 148 .S3 M33 2006
Author: McCarthy, John A. (John Aloysius), 1942-
Title: Remapping reality : chaos and creativity in science and literature (Goethe, Nietzsche, Grass) / John A. McCarthy.

Item ID: 03469079
Location: Vernon Circulating
Enum: c.1

User Comment:

Request date: 10/17/2019 04:20 PM
Pickup Location: Kelowna Circulation Desk

Reassignment History:
None

Reply to Reader: Item is not available.
__Item type not available for request
__Not Found
__Other problem with item
__The item you requested is on its way to you.

(Request number)

body to enable the performer to cross over despite the fear of falling. There is no reality beyond the "energy center" and its movement in space. "Body am I entirely," Zarathustra insists,

> and nothing else; and soul is only a word for something about the body. The body is a great reason, a plurality with one sense, a war and a peace, a herd and a shepherd. (*Za* 34; cf. *WP* #659)
>
> [Leib bin ich ganz und gar, und Nichts ausserdem; und Seele ist nur ein Wort für ein Etwas am Leibe. Der Leib ist eine grosse Vernunft, eine Vielheit mit Einem Sinne, ein Krieg und ein Frieden, eine Herde und ein Hirt.] (*KSA* 2:39)

The multiple parts must cooperate in agonistic unison to accomplish the "dance" of life in opposition to the pull of the earth as the "dancer" moves from one anchor point to the other, from birth to death. Zarathustra urges his listeners to remain true to the earth and to learn to walk like him, that is, like a dancer (*Za*, Prologue, #2).

One of the earliest parables in the work is that of the tightrope walker who entertains the crowds below by venturing to cross slowly and deliberately between two towers, tenuously balanced on a rope. It is a dangerous undertaking, requiring strength and suppleness, a task the walker had undertaken many times before. Yet the tightrope walker's walk is hardly a dance. This time a dreadful accident occurs when a jester emerges from one of the towers and sprightly approaches the tightrope walker from behind, calling out the whole time to him to make way, for he, the jester, wishes to pass. Unnerved by such impudence and the taunting of the motley-dressed individual, who veritably dances across the rope, the artist loses his balance when the jester suddenly jumps over him and continues on his merry way across the abyss. In the meanwhile, the artist plunges into the depths to his death, landing at Zarathustra's feet. Before the man expires, Zarathustra assures him that the jester is no devil and that there is no hell. Rather, life is its own reward. Admiring the tightrope walker's courage for having practiced his dangerous balancing act and for perishing in his vocation, Zarathustra decides that the artist deserves an honorable burial and carries him off on his back.

Obviously, the truth of Zarathustra's message is narrated in parables and riddles, which necessitate interpretation of the signs. As we have seen, Nietzsche made no secret of the fact that the fundamental act of the will to power was precisely to interpret, for "it defines limits, determines degrees, variations of power" (*WP* #643). The will enhances its power through interpretation, which Nietzsche variously defines at several different points as confrontation, subjugation, assimilation in an organic sense. Hence, the reader is called upon to interpret the meaning of the tightrope walker. One might say that the tightrope walker symbolizes the would-be overman who pulls up, stops short, hesitates, and loses heart at a critical moment. Proving to be too tentative, too serious, he succumbs to the force of gravity.

While the artist forgets to "dance," the jester blithely forges ahead with a self-confident and death-defying leap over the tightrope walker, who is blocking his forward movement. Even though the latter does not succeed in the dance, his lifetime of attempts and temptations warrants Zarathustra's admiration. After carrying the corpse for days in search of an appropriate burial site, Zarathustra finally awakens to a recognition of his own folly: his mission is not to serve the dead but to aid the living. It is wrong to want to enshrine the deceased and immortalize the done deed. It is right, on the other hand, to affirm the creative dance and the delicate balance of life, for "only where there is life is there also will [...] to power" ("Nur, wo Leben ist, da ist auch Wille: aber nicht Wille zum Leben, sondern – so lehre ich's dich – Wille zur Macht!"; *Za* 115; *KSA* 4:149). To his fellow man, therefore, Zarathustra appears to be "the mean between a fool and a corpse" ("Eine Mitte bin ich noch den Menschen zwischen einem Narren und einem Leichnam"; *Za*, Prologue #7; *KSA* 4: 23). That in-between state is his proper state as "prophet of the dance."

The jester is not the devil, as the tightrope walker suspects; rather, the devil is the force of gravity itself. This thought runs like a leitmotif through *Zarathustra*. Opposed to this devil are the young maidens, with their light-footed, joyous, "godlike dances," whom Zarathustra encounters in the forest clearing (*Za* 107–9). Related to gravity is the spirit of melancholy. Thus, melancholy is "the devil of the dusk" and the prophet's adversary (*Za* 296–97). Moreover, the devil is associated with skin, that is, with the body (*Za* 274). Yet the clearest association is with gravity as formulated at the beginning of Part III of *Zarathustra* where the phrase "beyond good and evil" is introduced in a section entitled "Vom Gesicht und Räthsel" ("On the Vision and the Riddle," *Za* 155–60; *KSA* 4:197–202). The vision is that of Zarathustra's encounter with the dwarf, whereas the riddle is that of a young shepherd into whose mouth a black snake has crawled. Before attempting to interpret the vision and solve the riddle, however, we need first to establish the context of Zarathustra's narrative, for it provides the fertile environment for both the vision and the riddle.

In Part III the prophet, having left his friends, is alone and depressed, and is about to embark on a journey over the sea. From his vantage point high on a hilltop, Zarathustra sees a ship dancing precariously on the rolling sea, suspended between two distant shorelines, between the ocean depths and the sky above. The scene recalls the opening image of the tightrope walker balanced on an unstable element between two anchoring points. Moreover, Zarathustra characterizes the seafarers as bold searchers and researchers ("Sucher, Versucher"), underscoring the ties to the attempts and temptations of the doomed artist. The night before boarding the ship – on which the actual narration of the vision and the riddle takes place – Zarathustra climbs a steep mountain and gains a view of the expansive ocean. The act of climbing the mountain is likened to an overcoming of the self, for Zarathustra must struggle against the gravity that draws him back down the mountainside. The view from the mountain peak, however, opens his eyes to the fundamental sameness of the opposing mountain peak and ocean depth, for the highest mountains have come from the sea: "Peak and abyss – they are now joined together" (*Za* 152). The next day he is to begin the dangerous sea voyage, which, as suggested, is akin to the perilous act of the tightrope artist balanced between the depth of the abyss and the expansiveness of the heavens. Success will require looking resolutely ahead with only occasional glances downward and upward. The vision and the riddle are part and parcel of this context.

But back to the mountain ascent. The strenuous struggle to ascend the mountain peak is made more difficult by the weight of a dwarf who has attached himself to Zarathustra's back. "Half dwarf, half mole, lame, making lame, dripping lead into my ear, leaden thoughts into my brain" ("halb Zwerg, halb Maulwurf; lahm; lähmend; Blei durch mein Ohr, Bleitropfen-Gedanken in mein Hirn träufelnd"), this creature, the exact opposite of the overman, is Zarathustra's "devil and archenemy" (*KSA* 4:198; *Za* 156; see also *Za* 192, 310). Like a lead weight, the dwarf's body drains Zarathustra's strength and will to continue the ascent in defiance of the forces of gravity and the dwarf's discouraging babble. The gnome mocks the prophet by comparing his philosophy to a stone thrown into the air. No matter how far up Zarathustra throws the stone, it always falls back to the earth. Such is the philosopher's stone that it is made of earth and returns to the earth. No amount of alchemy can change its earthly composition, no amount of transformation from ordinary matter to gold can overcome the pull of the earth. Yet one continually seeks that stone and heaves it into flight, knowing full well that success will always be ephemeral. There is, then, no release from the Sisyphean lure of achieving something higher from something lower. Zarathustra responds that the courage to persist leads the way to self-overcoming as well as the overcoming of all other obstacles: "Courage also slays dizziness at the edge of abysses" (*Za* 157). His reply recalls Faust's insistence vis-à-vis *his* devil. "Allein, ich will!" Faust insists in counterpoint to Mephisto's mocking depiction of humankind's striving as the ungainly, short-lived flight of the grasshopper that constantly falls back to the earth. Via contrasting images of agonistic interaction, the reader is reminded of the tightrope walker's lapse of courage, which led to his fatal plunge. Courage, then, is the best slayer of indecision and reluctance; it leads in Dionysian manner to an affirmation of life despite its pains and failures.[17]

17 Cf. Thomas Busch, *Die Affirmation des Chaos: Zur Überwindung des Nihilismus in der Metaphysik Friedrich Nietzsches*, Dissertationen. Philosophische Reihe, vol. 6 (St. Ottilien: EOS Verlag Erzabteil St. Ottilien, 1989), 85–88, 248–50.

3. The Gateway

The next narrative thread weaving separate phenomena into a comprehensible whole is Zarathustra's vision of a gateway that suddenly opens directly in front of him. At the gateway two paths meet: one stretches back to the past; the other leads into a future eternity. "They contradict each other," Zarathustra explains, but "it is here at this gateway that they come together" (*Za* 157–58). All that ever was, was necessary to reach the present moment of the open gateway. Everything that could happen *did* happen to bring about the present moment. The gateway symbolizes the present moment and acts as a stimulus for further action, as an affirmation of all that has led to the opening: "[A]re not all things knotted together so firmly that this moment draws after it *all* that is to come?" ("Und sind nicht solchermaassen fest alle Dinge verknotet, dass dieser Augenblick *alle* kommenden Dinge nach sich zieht?" *Za* 158; *KSA* 4:200). The two paths converging at the gateway represent the cycle of eternal return. Yet it is not a mechanical process by which exactly the same events will occur for all eternity like a broken record that plays the same melody over and over again, as we are frequently led to conclude from this passage.

To be sure, the prophet's animal friends do later assert that Zarathustra would probably say that he would return to "this same, selfsame life, in what is greatest and in what is smallest" ("zu diesem gleichen und selbigen Leben, im Grössten auch im Kleinsten" (*Za* 221; *KSA* 4:276). But this assertion is itself an interpretation. Moreover, the animals act out of fear that Zarathustra is dying. They express here their heartfelt desire to have him come back in just the same way, preaching about the overman and arguing for a life on the earth and of the earth. Thus, the emphasis is on an exact replication of Zarathustra's life. His life, of course, is a revisionist parody of Christ's teaching of eternal salvation. Zarathustra affirmed life in all its vagaries and erratic movements. He advocated wakeful resistence to the force of gravity, to the pressure of conformism, and to mechanical, unthinking repetition. In the meantime, we know that iterations in nature never duplicate exactly over large-scale time dimensions; they are always approximations. Even the self-duplication of the double helix is not inalterable. Exact and precise reinscription is not key here. Saying yes to life despite everything discouraging about it is. The affirmation is of the eternal return of the same smallness and greatness inherent in the Sisyphean task of humanity as envisioned by Zarathustra. The jester will not always jump out and disturb the balancing act in exactly the same way. Hence, the eternal return should be seen as a metaphor for the affirmation of life with its self-similarity rather than being viewed as an inalterable law of physics.

The oft analyzed gateway can gain in significance through new interpretive approaches. One method is to view the gateway as an analogy to geographical point zero, that is, a point that is neither north nor south. This approach has to do with the agon. Another perspective is offered by the double helix. Let's begin with point zero and the agon. Although on one level the modern term "agonist" designates an aggressive or divergent attitude, on another, more fundamental level it denotes cooperation and convergence. For example, in medical terminology the agon is used to describe a reflex that involves two muscles acting together to prevent an "antagonistic" intrusion from outside. The coordination of muscle reflexes in this manner has a counterpart in the synchronization of team members in a hockey game; the coexistence of the interquark gluon force with the strong, weak, and electromagnetic covalent forces; or the interaction of multiple systems in the body of a hiker climbing a mountain lugging a weight on his back. Each of those coordinated acts will return again and again, but never in a selfsame manner.

Moreover, the word "agonist" is etymologically related to *ά-γωνία* (agonia), which means nonangular. *Agonos* (*ά-γονος*) signifies a wavy line without angular shifts caused by colliding lines; it does not refer to an absolutely straight line without any deviations from a norm. Because *agonos* is etymologically related to *γονος* (*gonos*), which designates the offspring of humans and animals, the fruit of plants, race or even the act of begetting, *agonos* also recalls the potentiality of that which has not yet achieved perceptible existence in the material world (the "*ά*" means without). (Here we are reminded of Leibniz's concept of the compossible explored in chapter 4.). Equally striking with regard to the gateway in *Zarathustra* is the connotation of *agonos* to indicate the coordinates on the earth's surface where the geographical directions of north and south are united, that is, at zero latitude. The exact center between opposing directions is itself neither north nor south, just as the integer 0 has neither a negative nor a positive value. Similarly, good and evil also converge at a zero point. Applying the concept of *agonos* as the designation of unified opposites in the original state of nondifferentiation, we can see Nietzsche's gateway as representing the common space of opposing forces. The gateway thus symbolizes the common taproot of past and future in the present moment of recurring choice. Face to face, they contradict and offend each other; yet at their meeting in the gateway, in the present moment, they are complementary in Janusian fashion.[18] The gateway is even inscribed in Delphic manner as "Augenblick" (present moment).

Similarly, we need to keep separate the struggle for knowledge (or dominance), on the one hand, and surrender to ignorance, on the other. Consequently, the term "agonistic" signals an intellectual attitude that is not simply oppositional in the meaning of antagonistic. I use the term, therefore, to mark a mirror effect, one conducive to amplification and leading to a convergence of several refractions or movements without reducing the inherent pluralism to a mechanistic monism. The goal of the agonistic dynamic is not dominance over other movements, not displacement or usurpation, but rather cooperation and coordination of effort at any given moment in time or space. The

---

18 Cf. Arthur Koestler, *Janus: A Summing Up* (New York: Random House, 1978).

result is an effect similar to the function of the soliton. Any dominance manifests itself at the local level; complex interaction is the norm at the global level. This new reading of the gateway as agonistic corresponds to Edward O. Wilson's "principle of universal rational consilience across the natural sciences."[19]

The second innovative approach derives from the model of the double helix. The splitting of the double helix allows the DNA strand to reproduce previous combinations while also responding to new input from the broader environment. When the hydrogen bonds holding the two strands of the double helix together are broken, the two enfolded ribbons unfold. From the surrounding fluid, each nitrogenous base attracts its complementary partner to form a new strand: adenine (A) always pairs with thymine (T), while guanine (G) bonds with cytosine (C), so that the base sequence of the two new strands remains complementary (albeit in opposite sequence). Hydrogen bonds form between the old strand and the new one to produce two new double helixes; the unfolded is folded once again. This type of semi-conservative replication ensures that the "past" continues into the "future." While this explanation of DNA replication does not detail the complexities of the actual process, it is accurate enough for my purposes. Slight variations or mutations are possible and likely, despite the built-in corrective mechanism to catch "errors." If reinforced through feedback loops, the mutant iterations will eventually disrupt any exact pattern. Thus, while "fixed" in a local sense, the genetic code is not immutable on a universal plane.

When compared to a modern understanding of the genetic code, Zarathustra's gateway could be seen as symbolizing the continuity of past and future through eternally present recombinations and redistributions of force. Like the gateway, DNA semiconservative replication is always open. In the tale of Zarathustra, the vision of the gateway is explained as the need to affirm one's commitment to active participation in the ebb and flow of existence. Drawing upon a metaphor derived from Heraclitus (cf. Busch 274-75), Nietzsche has Zarathustra describe the task of accepting life as "the river of becoming" ("Fluss des Werdens"; *Za* 113; *KSA* 4:146). Each meeting at the gateway itself of what is upstream and of what follows downstream is like a Poincaré section of the flow cycle. Nonetheless, we cannot know what might slip into the stream farther down the river of life. Because Nietzsche himself had spoken of chaotic movement and periodic ordering on a grander scale in his views on life and the universe and exhorted his readers to study physics to know themselves (cf. *FW* #355; *KSA* 3:563), these associations are justified. But first the snake and the shepherd, as promised.

---

19 Edward O. Wilson, *Consilience: The Unity of Knowledge* (New York: Alfred A. Knopf, 1998), 125. Consilience connotes a literal "jumping together" of fact and theory (8).

4. The Snake and the Shepherd

This riddle involves a shepherd boy whom Zarathustra finds choking on a heavy black snake. To save himself, the boy follows the prophet's spontaneous advice to bite off the snake's head, since no amount of pulling has succeeded in extricating it from the boy's throat. This the youth does and immediately is transformed by the act. No longer shepherd, no longer human, he breaks out in radiant laughter (*Za* 160). The laughter exerts such a powerful draw on Zarathustra that we can assume it functions like a strange attractor. In *Beyond Good and Evil* laughter is hailed as the counterforce to gravity of spirit. It is the prerogative of the immortals, for they are the ones with the necessary detachment from the turbulence of existence.

To guess the meaning of the riddle is not difficult. Familiar from the story of Eden, the phallic snake represents the earth and earthly longings, which surprise the innocent shepherd sleeping quietly on the ground in the peaceful meadow. The unconscious state opens the gateway to the young shepherd's conscious being, but the suddenness of the intrusion so startles him that he begins to gag. Only when he awakens from his "stupor" and affirms his "fallen" state – that is, his being grounded in the earth and in instinct rather than in spirit – is he capable of rising above a narrowly protective life. He gains the "height" necessary for the golden laughter of the immortals. Both the vision of the gateway – a "foreseeing" (*Za* 160) – and the snake-shepherd riddle point in the same direction. Zarathustra's offer of salvation leads deeper into the organic functions of life; it leads back to the earth. "We have no wish whatever," Zarathustra explains, "to enter into the kingdom of heaven: we have become men – *so we want the earth*" (*Za* 316). The shepherd boy, then, represents Zarathustra himself as he was before he affirmed the active life. Past, present, and future all come together in the gateway. While change occurs, continuity is preserved. Thus, the gateway – reinforced by the riddle of the shepherd boy – is a metaphor for the ecological becoming of the earth as a living organism.

The ultimate lessons of *Thus Spoke Zarathustra* are, first, to learn to laugh at oneself "as one must laugh" (*Za* 292) and, second, to learn to dance (*Za* 295). These two go together, as we know from Nietzsche's unpublished fragments on *Zarathustra* (*KSA* 10:596). The gateway with the incumbent mountain climbing is related to the dance. In the section "On the Spirit of Gravity" in Part III, Zarathustra expressly states his belief that humanity must learn to fly. Yet one cannot immediately start flying. Intermediate steps are mandatory, "[H]e who would learn to fly one day must first learn to stand and walk and run and climb and dance: one cannot fly into flying" ("Das ist aber meine Lehre: wer einst fliegen lernen will, der muss erst stehn und gehn und laufen und klettern und tanzen lernen: – man erfliegt das Fliegen nicht!" *Za* 195; *KSA* 4:244). Each movement is a step further removed from the prone position of the serpent lying on the ground (as, e.g., was also the recumbent shepherd boy). Progress from standing upright to walking, running, climbing, and ultimately dancing requires hard work, concentration, and self-overcoming. The gracefulness of flight-like dance comes only after the arduous resistance to the pull of gravity lessens. Each individual must travel this path alone. And each path is different.

Biting off the head of the snake is comparable to grabbing the bull by the horns and accepting one's state. The riddle is later elucidated indirectly in the section in Part III entitled "On the Three Evils"(*Za* 186–91) that immediately precedes the discussion of gravity. The three so-called evils, which weigh heavily on humans as the inherited burdens of tradition, are sex, the lust to rule, and selfishness. Each of these natural instincts is deemed evil by despisers of the body and detractors of strong individuals who break out of the herd mentality of conformity and equality. After conquering the serpent by making it his own through the act of decapitation, the young shepherd is no longer young and innocent. Nor is he a shepherd, the guardian of universal notions of good and evil in Christian mythology (cf. *WP* #902). Overcoming fear of the snake allows laughter to occur. And laughter is possible only with the courage to counteract prejudice and accept inherent limitations.

In a melancholy mood that renders him incapable of such detachment, Zarathustra later associates the serpent with the evilness of humankind's smallness as earth-bound creatures. The thought that the dominant type of small-minded, unimaginative human being will return eternally and remain incorrigible initially nauseates him.

> "*This* great disgust with man," Zarathustra complains, "this choked me and had crawled into my throat [...] knowledge chokes. [...] And the eternal return even of the smallest – that was my disgust with all existence. Alas! Nausea! Nausea! Nausea!" (*Za* 219)

> ["Der grosse Überdruss am Menschen – *der* würgte mich und war mir in den Schlund gekrochen ... Wissen würgt. ... Und ewige Wiederkunft auch des Kleinsten [= Menschen]! – Das war mein Überdruss an allem Dasein! Ach, Ekel! Ekel! Ekel!"] (*KSA* 4:274–75)

A symbol of earth-boundedness, the serpent recurs throughout the novel as a counterpart to the flight of the eagle (*Za* 221, 303, 325). It is a dangerous game and a dangerous life that the former shepherd embarks upon as a higher man (*Za* 287, 302–3). "A trying and questioning was my every move" ("Ein Versuchen und Fragen war all mein Gehen"), Zarathustra reminisces at the end of "On the Spirit of Gravity" (*Za* 195; *KSA* 4:245). Given the strong emphasis on movement ("gehen"), the statement invites us to think of other motions (those of celestial bodies, electrons, protons) and interactive combinations (the delicate balance of the double helix). Of course, the act of learning how to dance gracefully and gayly must be practiced assiduously. The dance – not the flight of the eagle, which remains an unattainable ideal – is the desired and achievable goal of human self-control.

Immediately following the narration of Zarathustra's melancholiness in the later section, "The Convalescent," we find a reversal of moods in a section labeled "On the Great Longing." Here the prophet recounts how he has just redefined the soul not as something independent of the ground of existence but as its very spirit. Tellingly, he remarks in implied reference to the shepherd's tale: "I have even strangled the strangler that is called 'sin'" (*Za* 222; *KSA* 4:278). The strangler is, of course, the serpent that was choking the boy. By rejecting sin in its normal serpent-linked connotations, Zarathustra is able to reinstate the freedom over both the created and the uncreated. He reformulates the concept of soul as "destiny" ("Schicksal"), the "circumference of circumferences" ("Umfang der Umfänge"), and the "umbilical cord of time" ("Nabelschnur der Zeit") (*Za* 222; *KSA* 4:279). Man's destiny is to be earth-bound while experiencing an upward impulse. That destiny reaches to the widest of wide circumferences, thus, encompassing everything. Finally, the umbilical cord of time, like a superstring, is never severed. It extends continuously, uniting all that was with all that will be. Zarathustra has taught his followers to acknowledge the phases of time but also to transcend with light foot both time (past, present, future) and space (here, there, yonder) in a continuous *hic et nunc* (*Za* 221). The dancing away of the soul is further linked to a bark floating over "longing seas" in search of the "golden wonder around whose gold all good, bad, wondrous things leap." The boat is driven by wind and current, yet it does have a master ("the voluntary bark and its master"; *Za* 223). Understandably, the ship's (soul's) master seeks to give direction, while never ceasing to be dependent on the environment. The message of the shepherd and the snake is here restated as a sailing on the surface to wondrous destinations. The lesson taught is once again to learn to laugh. In this instance, however, Zarathustra writes that he bade his own soul to sing. Indeed, that was the last thing he had to give. The singing is tantamount to embracing life as it is. The last thing he had to give was his willing it to be as it is (*Za* 224).[20] Then again, it may simply be a matter of autopoiesis: the master of the bark *is* part of the environment, too.

---

20 When he does this, he is able to experience oneness with everything else as a comfort and not as a disturbance. Such is the meaning of the concluding section of the novel, "The Sign" ("das Zeichen"). Zarathustra emerges from his cave, espies an eagle on the hunt, is surrounded by flocks of birds "embracing" him from all sides, and finds the lion lying subserviently at his feet, even peacefully interacting with doves. The sign is, of course, that the soaring eagle is a beast of prey (such is the way of the world) and one must have heart (lion) to defy gravity through light-limbed flight (the flocks of birds). By taking heart and embracing life, one can see beast of prey and docile dove to be complementary (see *Za* 324–27; *KSA* 4:405–407).

5. Chaos and Autopoiesis

In one of the few explicit examinations of the connotations of chaos in Nietzsche's opus, Thomas Busch argues that chaos is seminal to Nietzsche's philosophy. Not simply the consequence of thwarted epistemological objectivity, it is the precondition of Nietzsche's entire critical project. In fact, Busch argues, chaos for Nietzsche is the nature of reality itself. As such, it denies any logically ordered ground. Moreover, the fundamental characteristic of chaos in Nietzsche's view is its dynamic self-organization (Busch, 217–42). Busch concludes that one must understand Nietzsche's exhortation to live a life of Dionysian creativity as the embracing of turbulence, in which the creative individual merges with chaos completely. In contrast to Busch's interpretation of this merger as a loss of the creative self (252), I wish to emphasize that the innovative individual is an extension of the principles of chaos. That is why Zarathustra states that he has given back to the soul "the freedom over the created and uncreated" (*Za* 222). Moreover, Busch chooses to follow up his reflections on chaos and creativity by examining the metaphor of the child at play (Busch 281–302). However, I focus more on Nietzsche's dance metaphor to express his new ideal. Granted, the lightness of the dance is not unrelated to the natural levity of the child, even though the child lacks suppleness of movement.

Central to Nietzsche's undertaking is the concept of perception as creative act. Equally indispensable is the notion that humanity is its own art object ("Kunstprodukt"). Terry Eagleton, Alexander Nehamas, and others emphasize this Dionysian moment of self-formation in the authentic artwork.[21] Viewed in this way, art teaches us the wisdom of living life on the surface (Eagleton 258). This autopoietic play is simultaneously creative and dangerous because humans lack the art of getting to the bottom of things, what Nietzsche calls true philology (*BGE* #47).[22] In essence, the artist is merely the "nurturing soil of art" ("Nährboden der Kunst"), that is, its precondition, not its cause. Nietzsche sees the artist as the "womb" of art, a kind of Gaia figure. Yet the artist is not the earth mother; she is just one of many different centers of energy that configures the world according to its own power (*KSA* 13:373). The animals loyal to Zarathustra during his solitary despondency at the end of Part III of the novel interpret the master's view of eternal recurrence in telling fashion:

---

21 Terry Eagleton, *The Ideology of the Aesthetic* (Oxford: Basil Blackwell, 1990), 238; Nehamas, *Life*, 194–95; del Caro, *Dionysian Aesthetics*, 52–54. Julian Young, *Nietzsche's Philosophy of Art* (Cambridge: Cambridge University Press, 1992), 136–39.

22 Nietzsche delineates specific features of organic functions in *BGE* #36: "self-regulation, assimilation, nourishment, excretion, metabolism," which are all "synthetically bound together" ("Selbst-Regulirung, Assimilation, Ernährung, Ausscheidung, Stoffwechsel" and "synthetische Gebundenheit"; *KSA* 5:55).

> But the knot of causes in which I am entangled recurs and will create me again. I myself belong to the causes of the eternal recurrence. I come again, with this sun, with this earth, with this eagle, with this serpent – not to a new life or a better life or a similar life: I come back eternally to this same, selfsame life. (*Za* 221).

> [Aber der Knoten von Ursachen kehrt wieder, in den ich verschlungen bin, – der wird mich wieder schaffen! Ich selber gehöre zu den Ursachen der ewigen Wiederkunft. Ich komme wieder, mit dieser Sonne, mit dieser Erde, mit diesem Adler, mit dieser Schlange – *nicht* zu einem neuen Leben oder besseren Leben oder ähnlichen Leben: – ich komme ewig wieder zu diesem gleichen und selbigen Leben.] (*KSA* 4:276)

Whoever wishes to understand art, therefore, must be a physiologist and a "vivisectionist of the spirit" ("Vivisectionist des Geistes").[23]

"We are ourselves a kind of chaos," Nietzsche remarks, meaning the commingling of past forms and cultures in the modern "soul" of man (*BGE* #224). As hybrids, we are constrained to negotiate the relationship between the authority of received values and the sway of the shaping forces of the present. When we accept that task willingly, we are what Nietzsche calls real philosophers and higher men, whose insights are creative and legislative, whose will to truth is will to power (*BGE* #211). And – as we have seen – the will to power is the will to life (*BGE* #13, #36).

In the preface to *Zarathustra*, Nietzsche formulates the oft quoted metaphor of the dancing star to symbolize the intense jumble of convergent and divergent forces that we know create stars and super novae: "[O]ne must still have chaos in oneself to be able to give birth to a dancing star" (*Za* #5). The connotation seems to be that we are like a turbulent energy knot that explodes into a fiery presence, a presence that dances luminously across the sky, providing a spectacle or even a guide to distant viewers. The star feeds off its own energy in frenzied yet controlled movement until the ultimate implosion and explosion. The idea resonates with Zarathustra's explanation of the gateway as the present moment in which all past forms, events, and impulses are united to create something new from something old. In humans, chaos is constantly present, for each moment is a new instance of a previous opportunity that challenges and seduces one to act out a new order. That is perhaps why Nietzsche further believed that in the human being "*creature* and *creator* are united: in man there is matter, fragment, excess, clay, mud, madness, chaos; but in man there is also creator, sculptor, the hardness of the hammer, the divine spectator and the seventh day" ("Im Menschen ist *Geschöpf* und *Schöpfer* vereint: im Menschen ist Stoff, Bruchstück, Überfluss, Lehm, Koth, Unsinn, Chaos; aber im Menschen ist auch Schöpfer, Bildner, Hammer-Härte,

23 Henrik Birus, "Nietzsche's Hermeneutical Considerations." in *Nietzsche: Literature and Values*, ed. by Volker Dürr, Reinhold Grimm, and Kathy Harms, *Monatshefte,* Occasional Volumes No. 6 (Madison, WI: University of Wisconsin Press, 1988), 66–80; here 78. See Nietzsche's "Der Fall Wagner," *KSA* 5:341.

Zuschaer – Göttlichkeit und siebenter Tag" (*BGE* #225; *KSA* 5:161). Both passive and active forces coalesce; that which is formed is not irresolutely formed but is always capable of further transformation, of "going over" and "going under."

Aphorism #109 of *The Gay Science* contains a clear indication of the grounding of each individual part within the complex whole. In this text, which seems aimed against Plato's *Timaios* (Busch 235n), Nietzsche exhorts his readers to avoid uncritical acceptance of the conclusions of science, with its emphasis on order, linear causality, and the universality of laws. Our perspective on these matters, he cautions, is conditioned by our geographical and biological place within the surface play of life, that is, our existence on the crust of the earth between deep structure and extended space. Our perceptions of order and regularity in the movement of the stars, he continues, is also superficial, because our dominant binary manner of thinking leads us to conclude that order and chaos must be in opposition to one another. We see the world as either organic or mechanical, and in both cases we think of it as being orderly. Yet neither interpretation by itself, Nietzsche suggests, is entirely accurate. The universe is not subject to our will. Essentially, it follows its own autopoietic operations. What humans perceive as harmonious, mathematically precise, and quantifiably ordered is our own interpretation and an exception to the normal state. The stellar system we inhabit, he asserts, is an exeption that, in turn, has allowed biological evolution as we know it. "The general character of the world," Nietzsche avers, "is to all eternity chaos; not by the absence of necessity, but in the sense of the absence of order, structure, form, beauty, wisdom, and whatever elsc our aesthetic humanities are called" (*GS* #109, 10:152).[24] Nietzsche finds the evidence for his conclusion in the heavens themselves, which seem equally marked by calculable and not-so-easily calculable interactions of heavenly bodies.

His observations echo Poincaré's mathematical formulae, which reinforce the accuracy of his intuitive judgment:

---

24 The full passage reads: "Die astrale Ordnung, in der wir leben, ist eine Ausnahme; diese Ordnung und die ziemliche Dauer, welche durch sie bedingt ist, hat wieder die Ausnahme der Ausnahmen ermöglicht: die Bildung des Organischen. Der Gesammt-Charakter der Welt ist dagegen in alle Ewigkeit Chaos, nicht im Sinne der fehlenden Nothwendigkeit, sondern der fehlenden Ordnung, Gliederung, Form, Schönheit, Weisheit, und wie alle unsere ästhetischen Menschlichkeiten heissen" (*KSA* 3:467–69). Like so much else in Nietzsche's argumentation, aphorism #109 from *The Gay Science* sounds like a play on Goethe's *Faust*. Specifically, it echoes Faust's litany of curses in "Study Room II" aimed at all that holds the soul enchanted (lines 1587–1606). The swearing-off of dependencies opens Faust up to the attempts and temptations that follow. With Nietzsche, to be sure, there is a reversal of mood. Whereas Faust casts off caution to embrace the All, Zarathustra warns against making universalizing statements. When, he asks, will we be allowed to apply the same principles of inquiry to the human sciences that we do to the natural sciences? It is here that the word "vernatürlichen" applies: "Wann werden wir anfangen dürfen, uns Menschen mit der reinen, neu gefundenen, neu erlösten Natur zu *vernatürlichen*!" (*KSA* 3:469).

> Let us beware of assuming that anything so methodical as the cyclic movements of our neighbouring stars obtains generally and throughout the universe; a mere glance at the Milky Way induces doubt as to whether there are not many cruder and more contradictory motions there, even stars with continuous, rectilinearly gravitating orbits, and the like. (*GS* #109)
>
> [Hüten wir uns, etwas so Formvolles, wie die kyklischen Bewegungen unserer Nachbar-Sterne überhaupt und überall vorauszusetzen; schon ein Blick in die Milchstrasse lässt Zweifel auftauchen, ob es dort nicht viel rohere und widersprechendere Bewegungen giebt, ebenfalls Sterne mit ewigen geradlinigen Fallbahnen und dergleichen.] (*KSA* 3:467–68).[25]

Fanciful though the vision of "continuous, rectilinearly gravitating orbits" might be, Nietzsche's essential objection to neat orbital movement indicates his rejection of the harmony of the spheres (another allusion to *Faust*) and reveals an openness to an anti-reductionist attitude (*KSA* 3:468). Nor are there any eternally enduring substances in Nietzsche's world-view. Inherently unstable, the world and the universe are eternally re-creating themselves. And so are human beings. This regenerative process entails the rise of ordered states from stochastic ones, as well as the disintegration of order into chaos. The laws governing such transformations were for Nietzsche not yet evident in the scientific world, resulting in his objection to the doing of science in the late nineteenth century, which he saw as resulting from the intellect's aversion to chaos ("aus dem Widerwillen des Intellekts an dem Chaos"; *KSA* 10:656). He was convinced that we create the world through our alignments of sense impressions (*GS* #110; see also his fragments from winter 1883–84: *KSA* 10:651). That is surely why he turned to psychology for an explanation of why humans see the world as they do.

6. The Cult of the Surface and the Need to Interpret

It is safe to say that human beings are creatures of the surface, the word "surface" being variously understood. In fact, Nietzsche insists that "the world of which we can become conscious is only a superficial and symbolic world" (*GS* #354). Defining the wisdom of the "superficial man" as focused on quantification, he even speaks of a "cult of the surface" (*BGE* #59). Without falsification via numbers, he argues (*BGE* #4), without a restriction of the horizon and a narrowing of perspective (*BGE* #188), humankind could not contend with the richness of phenomena. Indeed, he believes – in contrast to what most of us believe – that for humankind there are "no *eternal* horizons or perspectives" (*GS* #143). (The postmodern roots of absolute relativism are evident here.) While natural scientists are bound by empirical reality, Nietzsche's genuine philosophers and

---

25 I have altered the Cambridge University Press translation to reflect more accurately Nietzsche's text.

artists are not.[26] But then, the genuine free spirit is not marked by traditional wisdom. Whoever has looked profoundly into the world recognizes what wisdom there is in human beings who live superficially. "It is their instinct for preservation which teaches them to be fickle, light, and false," Nietzsche affirms (*BGE* #59). He has no doubt that there are philosophers and artists who have readily returned to the surface after having looked deeply into things. But that does not relieve them of the need to interpret. The agonal contradictions inherent in life cry out for explanation. In this connection, Peter Pütz argues that we must "go beyond the contradictions and look for indications, not of a reconciliation of those opposites, but of opposition to the principle of opposition."[27] The focus on oppositional relationships underlies Zarathustra's ideal of the dance as just such a mastering of agonal forces.

Alan Schrift convincingly argues that interpretation amounts to an ordering of a chaotic aggregate of differing viewpoints into a meaningful unified whole (1990: 159). However, when he suggests that by universalizing the interpretive process,we can establish *the* "'foundational' presupposition" of Nietzsche's philosophy, he pulls up short in his own explanation (182). Or so it seems to me. Schrift displays no awareness that the foundational view propounded by Nietzsche was not the surface play of the interpretive act *itself* but rather the underlying chaotic movement of the universe which produces the surface play and thereby invites, even mandates, interpretation. Even though Schrift acknowledges, for example, that the text and its re-inscriptions (via the interpretative acts to which it is subjected) exist "only in a relationship of *reciprocal* creation," he concludes that a text "*is* nothing other than a product of interpretive activity"(196).[28] Such relativistic-sounding pronouncements have raised so many doubts about the value of postmodern inquiry that we need to stress an important, if subtle, point: the interpretive process is not merely a matter of language games; it is not a closed hermeneutic circle. If we assume with Schrift (and others) that there is no

26 Nietzsche criticizes the natural scientists who naively believe that their "laws of nature" actually explain reality: "It is perhaps just dawning on five or six minds that physics too is only an interpretation and arrangement of the world (according to our own requirements, if I may say so!) and *not* an explanation" (*BGE* #14).

27 Peter Pütz, "The Problem of Force in Nietzsche and His Critics," in *Nietzsche: Literature and Values*, ed. by Volker Dürr, Reinhold Grimm, and Kathy Harms (Madison and London: University of Wisconsin Press, 1988), 14–28; here 24.

28 Alan D. Schrift, *Nietzsche and the Question of Interpretation: Between Hermeneutics and Deconstruction* (New York: Routledge, 1990), 159, 182, 196. The need to look for an underlying impetus for the act of interpretation outside interpretation itself is recognized by Richard Shusterman, "Beneath Interpretation," *The Interpretive Turn: Philosophy, Science, Culture*, ed. by David R. Hiley, James F. Bohman, and Richard Shusterman (Ithaca NY: Cornell U P, 1991), 102-28. Despite his efforts to ground "hermeneutic universalism" in something other than language games, however, Shusterman still remains within the traditional framework of discourse on Nietzsche's philosophical perspectivism. The centrality of complexity in the physical world goes unheeded.

world against which humans measure their perceptions, human interpretation must have been multiple from the outset, for otherwise there would be no relational modes between anything. Without introducing the notion of the universe, which was multiple from the first nanosecond, Shrift is caught in a non sequitur from which he is unable to escape. He loses sight of the fact that the world, too, was a "text" for Nietzsche and that the act of interpretation was mandated by the need for humans to negotiate the realities of physical and biological existence. Our bodies exist independently of the way we see them: too fat, too thin, too angular, etc. Nietzsche knew that. He was not the post-modern that postmodernists make him out to be (cf. Holub 1995: 68).

By highlighting the autopoietic nature of the interpretative process, however, I seek to anchor more firmly in the earth the traditional grounding of interpretation that has centered either on the subject or on the object. Unlike Schrift, however, I do not ground the interpretative act simply as "in the *between*, in the space which separates" subject and object (Schrift 191), thereby essentially freeing it from the object being interpreted. That in-between space, for example, is not empty, and it does not separate. It conjoins in the manner of the gateway. Thus, the grounding I propose is analogous to the bonding that occurs in high-energy physics or in chemical compounds. It is a working of the relational forces not dissimilar to the effect of gluons that are ultimately responsible for the stability of atomic nuclei or to hydrogen bonding in forming the double helical structure of DNA. This perspective on a dialogue between text and interpreter derivative of modern science and of complexity theory is new in my interpretation of Nietzsche's much heralded (and reviled) call for a pluralistic approach to interpretation. While the text may disappear under the hermeneutic inscriptions it occasions, it does not cease to exist.

That which rises to the surface and presents itself as visible and tactile phenomena constitutes the essence of existence in the only way humans can experience it; namely, through the sensory organs. How the surface play comes about and what lies beneath the visible surface fascinated Nietzsche just as much as the surface play itself. If that subsurface domain is accessible at all, he averred, it would be reachable through the new and most promising science of the late nineteenth century – psychology (not physics or chemistry, as Nietzsche understood them). "My problems are new," Nietzsche wrote to Carl Fuchs in December 1888, adding, "My psychological horizon is vast to a terrifying degree" (*KSA* 15:169). The carefully orchestrated movement of Part I of *Beyond Good and Evil* culminates in unbounded praise of psychology as "the queen of sciences, to serve and prepare for which the other sciences exist. For psychology is now once again the road to the fundamental problems" (*BGE* #23). That pathway leads into the labyrinthian interior of the basic text of biological drives hidden beneath all of the interpretive inscriptions scribbled in multiple layers on the surface. That scribbling and ordering – a natural and necessary enough process – conceals as much as it reveals about the foundations. We can read this assertion as resulting from

Nietzsche's rejection of the conscientious man of science, the humorless quantifier, who acts out of fear of the unknown and the chaotically unpredictable (*Za* 301–2). But that would be only half the story. The other half is Nietzsche's desire to get to the bottom of things by exploring the fundamental problems of human existence, by interpreting (thus shaping, creating) the terrible basic text *homo natura*. Thus, he notes, "Interpretation," understood as negotiating, "is the first principle of the organic process" (*WP* #643).

7. Writing as Ordering

But why, then, do you write? Nietzsche asks himself in *The Gay Science*. He answers his own question by insisting that he *must* write: he has found no other means "of *getting rid of*" his thoughts (*GS* #93). The formulation is telling because it recalls the intrinsic necessity of volcanic eruptions and earthquakes as a way for the earth to vent its pent-up energies. Like such chaotic ruptures and tremors, writing is tantamount to a rearranging of powerful forces. Writing is ordering. Books are what G. E. Lessing had called *fermenta cognitionis*, mental energy spewed out and setting other minds on fire. In *Menschliches, Allzumenschliches* (Human All Too Human, 1878) Nietzsche characterized the book as itself being almost human, for, once released from its author, it takes on a life of its own, encounters other minds through the readers it finds, and engenders in them new, maybe even fiery thoughts. This is what makes the interpretive process an extension of the energy knots of physical reality. Arguing in concert with Ralph Waldo Emerson, the American essayist he so admired, Nietzsche speaks of the life and energy that the written thoughts, sentiments, and deeds continue to nurture long after the author himself has turned to ashes. The written word is like a molecule, interacting with other molecules through strong and weak magnetic forces, succumbing to gravity, and exerting influence throughout the entire network of interacting particles.[29] Nietzsche asserted saliently:

> If one now goes on to consider that, not only a book, but every action performed by a human being becomes in some way the cause of other actions, decisions, thoughts, that everything that happens is inextricably knotted to everything that will happen, one comes to recognize the existence of an actual *immortality*, that of motion: what was once moved is enclosed and eternalized in the total union of all being like an insect in amber. (*HA I*, #208)

---

29 This is exactly the impact that Nietzsche himself had beyond his own death through his life and his thought. See the monumental study by Geoff Waite, *Nietzsche's Corps/e: Aesthetics, Politics, Prophecy, or, The Spectacular Technoculture of Everyday Life* (Durham and London: Duke University Press, 1996). Waite traces the readings of Nietzsche's own readings in impressive fashion. He notes sardonically that many critics who write about the philosopher's reception have apparently not actually read his work.

[Erwägt man nun gar, dass jede Handlung eines Menschen, nicht nur ein Buch, auf irgend eine Art Anlass zu anderen Handlungen, Entschlüssen, Gedanken wird, dass Alles, was geschieht, unlösbar fest sich mit Allem, was geschehen wird, verknotet, so erkennt man die wirklichke *Unsterblichkeit*, die es giebt, die der Bewegung: was einmal bewegt hat, ist in dem Gesammtverbande alles Seienden, wie in einem Bernstein ein Insect, eingeschlossen und verewigt.] (*KSA* 2:171)

It is, once again, all in the motion.

Nietzsche's goal was not to write more compactly in a closely defined space in enclosed, classical fashion but to open up the margins and cross borders. His art takes aim at the future, while drawing upon the past. Thus, the book, the act of writing, is itself a kind of gateway where everything meets in the present written word. Systematic logic or rigorous reasoning is not the proper pathway. Rather, "Many images have to be there, according to which one can live!" ("Viele Bilder müssen da sein, nach denen gelebt werden kann!" "Nachgelassene Fragmente," *KSA* 10:183; my translation). It is a question of ever new ludic constructions that force the reader to ponder ever emergent new meaning.

The way to achieve this ultimate goal is to change the perspective on the surface play that meets the eye and ear and tongue. The frequent changing of perspective, the play upon images old and new, the innumerable metaphors, all symbolize the multiple points of view with which one who seeks knowledge must contend. "It *is* this play," Sara Kofman contends, "which coincides with *'amor fati,'* the affirmation of life in all its forms." This she calls "the will to a total art form" (Kofman 1993: 102). Thus, even in a supposedly "fixed," written text, the subtext is always the same. It is grounded in motion. The basic terrible text of *homo natura* is life in all its forms; it is will to power (Kofman 1993, 92–94). At the conclusion of the preface to his planned volume on will to power, Nietzsche wrote that everything is art, that art is a great seduction *to* life and the great enabler *of* life. Art, then, is a "Versuch" and a "Versuchung."[30] In this world of circumscribed human perception, metaphor proves to be a useful analytical tool. Writing emerges as the path to self-realization and to a mapping of reality.

8. On the Creative Attitude

The guiding principle in these reflections on the nature of chaos and creativity is the importance of perspective, of gaining the *right* perspective. If we wish to experience something new, we must learn to see things in a new way. Attitude is the key to changing how we see things. Of course, perspectivism did not arrive first with Nietzsche. Long before him it motivated Cusanus, Galileo, Leibniz, Spinoza, Kant,

---

30 The full passage reads: "Die Kunst und nichts als die Kunst. Sie is die große Ermöglicherin des Lebens, die große Verführerin zum Leben, das große Stimulans zum Leben" (*KSA* 13:194).

Goethe, and Wieland. Such was also the case with those who came after him: Koestler, Heisenberg, Kuhn, Prigogine, Wilson, Penrose, and Kauffman, to name just a few, none of whom is/or was a Nietzschean. In each instance, the new perspective led to a critical insight and/or resulted in a creative act. David Bohm and F. David Peat conclude their reflections on the interrelationships among science, order, and creativity with a call for creativity to involve "the whole of life"; creativity is to be general and pervasive rather than limited and discrete. They foresee "a rich new field for creativity" between the two extremes "of simple regular orders and chaos."[31] "It is clear," they assert, "that a proper appreciation of the artistic attitude should not be left solely to those who specialize in art. An artistic attitude is needed by all, in every phase of life" (Bohm and Peat 262).

In his 1968 essay on the relationships of science and art, republished in 1998, Bohm drew particular attention to the creative moment in the move away from the mimetic representation of nature in the sciences to a tracing of pure structure. In mathematics this amounted to an "axiomatic approach" expressed as purely abstract mathematical operations, an alteration that paralleled the rise of metaphoric paradigms to denote scientific theories (Thomas Kuhn). No longer restricted to mere passive understanding of known facts, this shift in perspective provided the opportunity to create theories of new relationships. The similar refocusing on structural self-referentiality in art was captured in the work of Monet and Cézanne. From all of these developments, Bohm concluded that "a mode of experiencing, perceiving, and thinking in terms of *pure structure*" has evolved in science, art, and mathematics, one which is no longer merely associative.[32] The "pure structure" of which Bohm here speaks proves to be a common foundational baseline for different mappings of reality. Yet, paradoxically, as he reasoned in the later essay, "The Art of Perceiving Movement" (1971), this baseline is not to be conceived of as unchanging. Each "thing" has its origin and eventual dissolution "in a broader whole, extending ultimately to the universal field movement from which even the atomic particles are abstracted." Consequently, we must be attentive to the "unceasing emergence of new similarities and relationships across boundaries of the various things" (Bohm, *Creativity* 100–1).

At the end of the nineteenth century, contemporaneous with major developments in the natural and mathematical sciences, Nietzsche defined originality as the capacity for envisioning the new in the field of essential tension between the extremes of linear order and turbulent chaos. Science, art, and morality were for him all a matter of constructing meaning and artifice where there was only autopoietic natural process.

31 Bohm and Peat, *Science, Order, and Creativity*, 268–69. Specifically on Nietzsche and creativity, see Adrian Del Caro, *Nietzsche contra Nietzsche: Creativity and the Anti-Romantic* (Baton Rouge: Louisiana State University Press, 1989); Del Caro, *Dionysian Aesthetics: The Role of Destruction in Creation as Reflected in the Life and Works of Friedrich Nietzsche* (Frankfurt a.M: Peter Lang, 1981).

32 David Bohm, *On Creativity*, ed. by Lee Nichols (London and New York: Routledge, 1998), 34–35.

Humankind itself appeared to him an expression of the in-between state, rich in creative potential, formed yet unformed, being but also becoming. In *The Gay Science* he clearly contends that originality is the ability to "*see* something that does not yet bear a name, that cannot yet be named, although it is before everybody's eyes. As people are usually constituted, it is the name that first makes a thing generally visible to them. – Creative persons have also for the most part been the namers of things" (*GS* #261).[33] Naming things is to discern form and structure amidst turbulent movement and complex interactions. It is the ability to see points of distant light in the night sky invisible to less capable seers. Such seeing might be aligned with the concept of *natura naturans* itself. The construct or artifact resulting from naming corresponds, of course, to the products of nature or *natura naturata*. Those stars may have existed for thousands of light years. But not for us. We "create" them by discerning them. Because Nietzsche views the human being as both creature and creator, it is not surprising that he blurs the distinction between becoming and being (as did Bohm).

Similarly, Nietzsche laments the leveling tendencies of the modern age, which has transformed philosophy and the act of living into mechanical, sedate busy work with no real sense of striving or contention. Dynamic thrust and continual renewal as antidotes to intellectual and emotional lethargy are at the heart of *Zarathustra* and *Beyond Good and Evil* wherein Nietzsche emphatically formulates his concept of the philosopher of the future, a concept that remained with him to the end. Nietzsche envisions these philosophers not necessarily as those who will come in the future, but as those who offer hope for a better future through their efforts at rejuvenation and the reinvigoration of value in the present. He writes in *Will to Power*, published posthumously in 1909 but dating from the 1880s:

> But where may I look with any kind of hope for my kind of philosopher himself, at least my need of new philosophers? In that direction alone [...] where a *creative* mode of thought dominates that does not posit the happiness of repose [...] as a goal for the world, and honors even in peace the means which lead to new wars; a mode of thought that prescribes laws for the future, that for the sake of the future is harsh and tyrannical towards itself and all things of the present; a reckless, "immoral" mode of thought, which wants to develop both the good and the bad qualities in man to their fullest extent, because it feels it has the strength to put both in the right place – in the place where each needs the other. (*WP II*, #464)

In a note to this translation, Kaufmann rightly points out that most of the ideas in aphorism #464 were developed in *Zarathustra* and *Beyond Good and Evil* (*WP II*, 256n). (Mode of thought is, of course, synonymous with attitude of mind.) In ever so

---

33 Nietzsche: "*Originalität.* – Was ist Originalität? Etwas *sehen*, das noch keinen Namen trägt, noch nicht genannt werden kann, ob es gleich vor Aller Augen liegt. Wie die Menschen gewöhnlich sind, macht ihnen erst der Name ein Ding überhaupt sichtbar. – Die Originalen sind zumeist auch die Namengeber gewesen" (*KSA* 3:517; #261).

succinct a manner, Nietzsche collapses into this one passage the chief tendencies of the creative spirit as they have evolved in the preceding pages. In summary fashion they are:

- attitude as the determining factor in achieving movement in a new direction;
- the complementarity of opposites (i.e., good and evil);
- the essentially agonistic quality of life and creativity;
- life as the full development of all qualities, not just for survival, but for dominance; and
- complex, interactive dynamics as the hallmark of organic and intellectual life.

These qualities are essential to Nietzsche's overarching concept of ordering as fundamental to existence: ordering as tyranny, ordering as mastery, ordering as creating meaning out of chaos. All of the action takes place in the turbulent stream of life. The philosophers of and for the future are creative individuals who embrace change as the essence of earthly existence.[34] The genuine artist, like the genuine philosopher, is the person who imitates the processes rather than the products of nature. While these qualities of action and reaction should also function as reinvigorating impulses within humanistic studies, they have paradoxically led to a modern crisis of the humanities in some quarters.[35] This circumstance may be due to a misunderstanding or misappropriation by some critics of Nietzsche's principles of perspectivism and vitalism. Nonetheless, we have lived with a sense of crisis consciousness since the Enlightenment.[36] Formulated metaphorically as "the tense bow," with arrow armed and aimed but not released (*BGE* #262, "Epode"), crisis consciousness has largely proved to be productive and invigorating rather than debilitating. Progress comes from living on the edge, not from grazing contentedly in protected pastures. Nietzsche's particular narrative of this state – most notably in *Zarathustra* – resists the tendency to evolve into a meta-narrative favored by traditionalists because it relies on consistency, principles of causality, and discreteness of meaning. Rather, for Nietzsche the story of humankind and its world is a question of quanta of energy, of *petits récits*, of periodic centers of

34 See Alexander Nehamas, "Who Are the 'Philosophers of the Future'? A Reading of *Beyond Good and Evil*," in *Reading Nietzsche*, ed. by Robert C. Solomon and Kathleen M. Higgins (New York and Oxford: Oxford University Press, 1988), 46–67.

35 See, e.g., Levine, *Nietzsche and the Modern Crisis of the Humanities*, who believes that Nietzsche was fundamentally mistaken in his understanding of culture and the value of relativism. Unfortunately, Levine does not consistently differentiate between Nietzsche and so-called Nietzscheans in the way that Geoff Waite (1996) does.

36 John A. McCarthy, "Crisis Consciousness: An Enlightenment Legacy from Kant to Bloom," in *Crisis and Culture in Post-Enlightenment Germany: Essays in Honor of Peter Heller*, ed. by Hans Schulte and David Richards (New York: Lanham, 1993), 42–72.

meaning that come into and fade out of focus, drawn together by some strange attractor that occasions a number of gaps, indeterminancy, and double codings.[37] This represents the quintessence of his philosophy. It requires attention to those shapes not determined by metaphysical thought alone (cf. Bohm, *Creativity* 101).

To this vision of an endless cycle of opportunity and missed opportunity, of alternating suffering and joy in eternal recurrence, of the continuously re-emergent selfsame ground of existence, Nietzsche too could speak his "Verweile doch, du bist so schön!" Naturally, Nietzsche's version of the Faustian climax is different. In Part IV of the novel, Zarathustra asks his listeners:

> Have you ever said Yes to a single joy? O my friends, then you said Yes too to *all* woe. All things are entangled, ensnared, enamored; if ever you wanted one thing twice, if ever you said, "You please me, happiness! Abide, moment!" then you wanted *all* back. All anew, all eternally, all entangled, ensnared, enamored – oh, then you *loved* the world. (*Za* 323)
> [Sagtet ihr jemals Ja zu Einer Lust? Oh, meine Freunde, so sagtet ihr Ja auch zu *allem* Wehe. Alle Dinge sind verkettet, verfädelt, verliebt, – – wolltet ihr jemals Ein Mal Zwei Mal, spracht ihr jemals "du gefällst mir, Glück! Husch! Augenblick!" so wolltet ihr *Alles* zurück! – Alles von neuem, Alles ewig, Alles verkettet, verfädelt, verliebt, oh so *liebtet* ihr die Welt, –] (*KSA* 4:402)

At the outset of his trials, Faust had declared that he cared nothing for an afterlife; his place was here on the earth. Even as Care weighs his body down with old age, he rejects her rule by emphasizing the spirit. If we can interpret Faust's own "Verweile doch!" as a yes to the constant struggle in this world to extend the formed landmass against the relentless onslaughts of the formless sea and despite the burden of time, how much easier is it to accept the youthful Zarathustra's yes to the spirit of the earth without any transcendental overlay at all? Despite all its mythological finery, Faust's heaven is, by all indications, essentially full of the same motion as is Zarathustra's earth with its caves, rocky mountain peaks, and gateways. Nietzsche, by contrast, has stripped his vision of all other worldly qualities.

The tree that offers Zarathustra respite from the noonday sun in "At Noon" of Part IV is described as old, crooked, and knotty – almost barren, were it not for the luscious

37 In the opening chapter, entitled "How Philosophical Truth Finally Became a Fable," to his *Nietzschean Narratives* (Bloomington and Indianapolis: Indiana University Press, 1989), Gary Shapiro argues against the dominant Derridian view of Nietzsche, which denies his works a narrative strategy. Shapiro emphasizes: "Now while the aphoristic books are not large-scale narratives, and while they do contain a critical narratology, it would be a mistake to suppose that all of Nietzsche's works are aphoristic, or that individual aphorisms themselves cannot have a narrative form" (22). The actual topic of the Nietzschean narrative is "the experienced nature of change, process or transformation" (23). Cf. also Peter Canning, "How the Fable Becomes a World," in Rickels, *Looking After Nietzsche*, 175–93. Canning notes in particular the myth-making instinct identified by Nietzsche and renders Nietzsche's own story as the acting out of "mytho-logoi," that is, stories about pure thought embedded in scenes and events (191).

grapevine that has lovingly entwined itself around the tree and now proves inviting to the pilgrim with its ripe fruit (*Za* 275–76). This tree is perhaps a sign that the Tree of Life and the Tree of Knowledge of Good and Evil have merged into a single crooked and knotty one. As such, it would signify that knowledge is acquired through life experiences themselves. Bent and distorted, the tree mirrors the naturally crooked path through life, a path that has been circuitous for a long, long time. The grapevine grown one with the tree symbolizes the soul's embracing the earth as its only guide (on the soul as vine, see *Za* 222–23). That proved to be the seduction to Zarathustra's "final sin" (*Za* 327).[38]

And what is that final sin? His melancholy surrender to pity for the suffering of the higher man who goes alone, ignored, even reviled. "Once the sin against God was the greatest sin," Zarathustra knew all too well. But God died, and "to sin against the earth is now the most dreadful thing" ("Zarathustra's Prologue" #3; *Za* 13). It is an onerous burden. But he has now seen the error of his ways and is resolved never again to lend an ear to the leaden whisperings of his "melancholy devil" (*Za* 296). In the end, Zarathustra is awakened from his slumber and drawn from his cave of inward contemplation to a new day (like Faust emerging from his musty study). Himself luminous and strong like the morning sun, the prophet issues forth with resolute and light step to his own Easter Sunday stroll in celebration of life. The earth and sun have him again. Is it any wonder that the philosopher deemed this novel of ideas to be the premier book of all time, the new Bible? Indeed, he predicted in a letter of 26 November 1888 to Paul Deussen that it would be read like the Bible.[39]

While Zarathustra has seemingly overcome his impish spirit of gravity at the end of his narrative, the dwarf returns in yet another guise seventy years later in Günter Grass's *The Tin Drum*. Using what we have learned from Nietzsche's strategies of iteration and perspectival shifts in the naming of chaos,[40] we are better positioned to appreciate earlier mappings of reality such as Goethe's and also later ones such as Grass's as attempts to get at a common taproot, to explain and interpret the terrible basic text of *homo natura* by playing on and with myth and science.

---

38 In this metaphor of vine and tree there is also an echo of the principles of the vertical and spiral tendencies that Goethe perceived as fundamental to growth in nature. But here the spiral vitality of the vine is achieved at the cost of the almost barren Tree of Knowledge of Good and Evil.

39 Nietzsche: "mein Zarathustra [...] das erste Buch aller Jahrtausende, die Bibel der Zukunft [...] mein Zarathustra wird wie die Bibel gelesen werden"(cited by Colli and Montinari in "Chronik zu Nietzsches Leben," *KSA* 15:188).

40 The principle of iteration in Nietzsche's work seeks to disclose the common taproot of all phenomena and expose the fundamental unity of all existence. Nietzsche's tendency to discuss phenomena within the "frame of constantly recurring or just slightly altered formulations" drawn from his own works (Pütz 1988: 24) is part of that iteration. So too is Nietzsche's practice of borrowing passages from others (e.g., Pascal, Dostoyevsky, Goethe, Emerson, Baudelaire). See Colli and Montinari, *KSA* 8.2: "Vorbemerkung," vii–viii.

Chapter 7
The Tin Drum – Myth and Reality, or The Eternal Return

> Der Mensch ist ein *rhythmen-bildendes Geschöpf.* Er legt alles Geschehen in diese Rhythmen hinein, es ist eine Art, sich der 'Eindrücke' zu bemächtigen.
>
> – Friedrich Nietzsche,
> *Nachgelassene Fragmente 1882–1884*

1. Planting Grass

Günter Grass (1927–) is arguably the best-known contemporary German writer in North America. There he is celebrated as a world-class novelist, although at home in Germany, where he has become one of the most dominant writers since Thomas Mann, Grass is also known as a painter, sculptor, and erstwhile playwright. On both sides of the Atlantic, his bestseller first novel, *Die Blechtrommel* (The Tin Drum, 1959), made his name a household word. Awarded a prize by the prestigious postwar writers association Gruppe 47 even before its publication in 1959, the novel rapidly earned other honors for its author, ultimately leading to the Nobel Prize for Literature in 1999. In France in 1961 upon publication of the French translation, the novel won the prize for the best foreign book. Within the first year of publication in North America in 1963, some 400,000 copies in Ralph Manheim's translation were sold; the book remained on the *New York Times* bestseller list for three months. Having earned widespread praise for its perceived affinities with the work of Dante, Rabelais, Grimmelshausen, Bunyan, Swift, Sterne, Voltaire, Goethe, Melville, Proust, Thomas Mann, Joyce, Beckett, Faulkner, Camus, Dos Passos, Kafka, Döblin, Ionesco, Nabokov, and Heller, the novel continues to be a mainstay in college classrooms despite its bulky size, dense prose, rich allusions, and blasphemous message – or perhaps precisely because of all these factors. The early acclaim for Grass's inaugural effort ensured the author's longterm visibility, far outweighing the protests against the novel's presumed undermining of the human spirit. Unlike most German or Austrian writers, Grass has been reviewed frequently in the *New York Times* and other leading reviewing organs. He was even selected for the cover story of *Time* Magazine in 1970.[1] All this plants him at the

1 On Grass's North American reception, see Patrick O'Neill, "A Different Drummer: The American Reception of Günter Grass," in *The Fortunes of German Writers in America: Studies in Literary Reception*, ed. by Wolfgang Elfe, James Hardin, and Gunther Holst (Columbia, SC: U of South Carolina Press, 1992), 277–85. On the genesis and first reception of the novel in Germany, see

center of the literary world, even when cloaked in controversy. His followers and admirers include John Irving and Salman Rushdie.

Grass's *The Tin Drum* occupies a position in literary and historical consciousness comparable to that of Nietzsche's *Thus Spoke Zarathustra* around 1900 and of Goethe's *Faust* one hundred years before that. All three works are part and parcel of world literature, a term coined by Goethe himself. Their similarity resides in their creative interweaving of history and myth into a new seamless fabric of momentous import. Like Goethe's *Faust,* which mirrors the philosophical and historical fabric of the Age of Enlightenment, and Nietzsche's *Zarathustra,* which reacts to the fin-de-siècle mood of the 1880s, Grass's *The Tin Drum* portrays the thoughts, moods, aspirations, and despair in Central Europe following World War II. Yet the novel's recollections do more than capture the spirit of the past. *The Tin Drum* is also similar to Nietzsche's iconoclastic intent in *Zarathustra* and Goethe's revisionist task in *Faust*, drawing upon history to chart a path to the unknown, it weds past and future in an eternal present. In fact, Grass's novel, like Goethe's play, is really more a book for the future in Nietzsche's sense of a philosophy of emergence. The protagonist in each work is a prophet with no disciples and with a message that many do not wish to hear. What these prophets attempt, however, is an integrated view of humanity within its life-worlds. They all contribute to a new Enlightenment. Thus, each can be seen as an attempt at consilience, at representing a new "integral cultural epoch" that began to emerge about three hundred years ago.

Because of this continuity, *The Tin Drum* serves us well in the current exploration of complex dynamics on the large and small scale, as in the Powers of Ten. Because it evokes events of the not-too-distant past, indeed, of continuing events – two devastating world wars, numerous regional conflicts, horrifying acts of genocide, the collapse of entire political systems – *The Tin Drum* remains particularly close to the sensibilities of many contemporary readers. The series of world-shattering events since 1914 have obliterated historical lines of demarcation and obscured traditional norms and values that had dominated since the early modern era. After initially prompting a sense of fragmentation and loss of identity, these violent eruptions of what we can now call the will to power have paradoxically fed into the desire for an integrative view of things. It is the paradox of hope in a

---

Detlev Krumme, *Günter Grass. Die Blechtrommel* (Munich: Carl Hanser Verlag, 1986), 19–32. German press reaction 1959–63 is reflected in the collection *Die Blechtrommel: Attraktion und Ärgernis. Ein Kapitel deutscher Literaturkritik*, ed. by Franz Josef Görtz (Darmstadt and Neuwied: Hermann Luchterhand, 1984). Claudia Mayer-Iswandy, *Günter Grass* (Munich: Deutscher Taschenbuch Verlag, 2002), 79–89, provides a precise and engaging account. Grass explains his own work in a series of radio interviews with Harro Zimmermann published as *Vom Abenteuer der Aufklärung: Werkstattgespräche* (Göttingen: Steidl Verlag, 1999).

hopeless situation, the promise of renewed life and meaning inherent in the phoenix's ashes. "As long as man hopes," the narrator Oskar Matzerath tells us in *The Tin Drum*, "he will go on turning out hopeful finales."[2]

The Tin Drum is full of the paradoxes and grotesqueness of an anchorless era, not unlike the picaresque novel, in which tradition the narrative stands. Whereas paradox refers to unexpected developments, that is, to results diametrically opposed to anticipated results, the grotesque in its earliest Renaissance etymological meaning of *grottesco* connotes something playfully gay and carelessly fantastic. In the eighteenth century, the focus shifted more explicitly to the complex and contradictory, arousing a feeling of surprise and terror as the known world breaks asunder. With that, its affinity with the paradoxical began to emerge. In the twentieth century, the grotesque came to designate the absence of a definable and appropriate affect: the viewer is in no way instructed how to interpret the picture. The unmasking of our world as chaotic and absurd, perhaps even demonic, gave rise to a feeling of alienation. Thus, the grotesque also refers to something ominous and disconnected in the face of a familiar world turned upside down. We might be tempted to draw an analogy between the grotesque as disconnectedness and disconnected Julia sets. The Julia set, one of several fractal sets that have come to epitomize strange attractors, is "the basin of attraction at the point of infinity, the set of initial conditions that move towards it under iteration."[3] Those qualities of the absurd and the unnerving that we experience as we move farther away from or into a space certainly mark Grass's text, wherein the laws of statistics, symmetry, and proportion are called into question and the realm of inanimate things is no longer separate from those of plants, animals, and human beings. We are not even

2 Günter Grass, *The Tin Drum*, trans. by Ralph Manheim (New York: Vintage International, 1989), "Faith, Hope, Love," 204. Hereafter cited as *TD*. References in the following will generally be to the English translation rather than to the German in order to reach the broadest possible audience. Only when the German offers additional nuance will it be included. German references are to Günter Grass, *Die Blechtrommel: Roman*, 12th ed. (Munich: Deutscher Taschenbuch Verlag, 2002). The dtv edition is identical to Günter Grass, *Werkausgabe*, vol. 3, ed. by Volker Neuhaus (Göttingen: Steidl Verlag, 1997). Hereafter cited as *BT*. I have assigned numbers to the chapters, although the novel does not have such designations.

3 Ian Stewart, *Does God Play Dice?* (Cambridge, MA: Basil Blackwell, 1989), 234–36. Stewart further explains that the Julia set is the boundary of the basin of attraction of the point at infinity, a complex mapping of $z \to z2 + c$ where c is a constant. "Complex" here means "having several components." There are many kinds of Julia sets, but all fall into two basic categories: the connected and the disconnected; that is, some are all of one piece, some fall apart. If you paint the connected points within the complex plane black and the disconnected ones white, you are delineating the basin of attraction of the point at infinity. Just as fractals reveal a regime of nature not normally accessible to us, so too does the grotesque "open our eyes to patterns that might otherwise be considered formless" (*Dice?* 242). These patterns are constitutive of the texture of reality. The black Julia sets will return later in connection with the Black Wicked Witch.

sure whether Grass's protagonist, Oskar Matzerath, is human. However, he is definitely an outsider.

The outsider figure – long a barometer of despair and renewal in the Western tradition since before Goethe's *Faust* – has carried the message poignantly in the face of an astonishing instrumentalization of reason and the numbing of sensibilities through repeated carnage. From a nigh zero-energy state in 1945 Germany, *The Tin Drum* marked a resurgence of creative activity, albeit one stripped of the naive idealism of former epochs. Astonishingly, however, that creative surge proved to be more than a negative lashing out at a world gone mad; it was simultaneously a positive move toward healing and integration. The novel mirrors in many ways a holistic, integral culture, one that is beyond the binary set of alternatives of the either-or model such as the sacred and the profane, good and evil, the particular and the universal.[4] Grass's ability to synthesize antitheses into a productive whole through "bisociative thought" overcomes the sheer iconoclasm of the novel.[5] The result is a work that endures.

At the heart of *The Tin Drum* seems to be a kind of reductionism. It is, after all, an anti-Bildungsroman. Its protagonist would resist complexification, preferring to keep things simple. While reductionism seen as a general prescription for progress in the sciences came under fire in some quarters in the 1950s, reductionism understood "as a statement of the order of nature" remained a viable variant of the model of inquiry. For example, interest in the genome heated up considerably after James D. Watson and Francis H. C. Crick advanced their model of the double helix in 1952. The genome – denoting a set of chromosomes as a working unit or community of genes and nucleotides – testifies to the movement toward holism (Bohm). Thus, paradoxically, reductionism led to the recognition of a highly compact and complex mechanism at the core of the human coding system. Cooperation and communication at the genetic level seem to be key ingredients in any integral culture. At issue in reductionism, therefore, is not the doing of science but rather our understanding of nature.[6]

The search for the ultimate laws of nature that fascinated Goethe and Nietzsche appear to be a hidden agenda in Grass's inaugural novel, as I intend to argue in the

4 Cf. Johannes von Buttlar, *Gottes Würfel: Schicksal oder Zufall* (Munich: F.A. Herbig, 1992), 94. Saliently, von Buttlar dedicates his study to the biochemist Rupert Sheldrake and the mathematician Roger Penrose and draws heavily on the particle physicist David Bohm. All three represent the move to an integral approach in the sciences.

5 Arthur Koestler, *The Act of Creation* (London: Hutchinson, 1965), 230–31.

6 Steven Weinberg, *Dreams of a Final Theory: The Scientist's Search for the Ultimate Laws of Nature* (New York: Vintage Books, 1993), 53–54. Weinberg explains his disagreement with the evolutionary biologist Ernst Mayr. He also devotes an entire chapter to the place of God in the universe (241–62).

following. Drawing on the analysis of chaos, complexity, and creativity in the first part of this study, I wish to plant Grass squarely within debates old and new on the meaning of life and on the relationship between reductionism and the mythmaking process. We can see his novel as participating in the search for ultimate laws in the mapping of reality. If Goethe saw the hand of God inherent in the operations of nature and if Nietzsche determined that humanity must do away with God for the sake of nature, then Grass seems to combine the two views in a new synthesis of profane materiality and sacred belief. The ground had been prepared by instrumental reason and the loss of tradition. The mind of God, Stephen Hawking once remarked, is inscribed in the laws of nature.[7] Others have also asked about the place of God in the universe, much like Grass asks about His place in the historical events rendered in *The Tin Drum*. Even if one believes that the universe is a pointless system (as Steven Weinberg does), we are nevertheless part of that system. As the philosopher Richard Taylor put it, nature is "a vast machine, feeding on itself, running on and on forever to nothing."[8] By asking daring and impudent questions, we influence the very environment that produced us. Maybe that is why Grass reintroduces magic into his realism. More on that later.

Grass once remarked that behind every one of his novels there lies a philosophical concept. For example, *Aus dem Tagebuch einer Schnecke* (From the Diary of a Snail, 1972) pits Hegel against Schopenhauer.[9] Although Grass did not specify which philosopher he had in mind when planning *The Tin Drum*, his extraordinary monument to postwar Germany, he does clearly state Oskar's determination "to wield a will to power that would have no need of vassals or henchmen" ("der Wille zu einer Macht, die ohne Gefolgschaft auskommen sollte"; *TD* 60; *BT* 70). The allusion is both to Nietzsche's concept of the will to power and to Zarathustra, who has no need for disciples. While Nietzsche is a subtle presence in the novel, references to Goethe are quite specific. For example, Oskar admits that he sometimes envisions himself as Goethe and admires his "world-encompassing feeling for nature." Grass uses the aura of Goethe to temper the elemental drive of Oskar's other mentor, the faith healer Rasputin (*TD* 278). In particular, Grass includes repeated references to Goethe's *Faust*, *Elective Affinities*, and *Theory of Color* (e.g., *TD* 90–91, 278), all three of which are heavily indebted to Goethe's nature studies.[10] In the following, I will suggest that Nietzsche as well as Goethe

---

7 Cf. Stephen Hawking, *Black Holes and Baby Universes and Other Essays* (New York: Bantam Books, 1993), 137, 173.

8 Richard Taylor, *Good and Evil* (Amherst, NY: Prometheus Books, 2000), 326.

9 Interview with Günter Grass, *Women's Wear Daily* (Friday, September 21, 1973), 18. See also Volker Neuhaus, *Erläuterungen und Dokumente: Günter Grass, Die Blechtrommel* (Stuttgart: Reclam, 1997), 32.

10 Direct references to Goethe and to *Faust* in Grass's novel abound. Oskar learns to read by using

served as the conscious philosophical inspiration for Grass's novel.[11] Of course, it also contains references to other authors such as Dante, Cervantes, Shakespeare, and Laurence Sterne, but they reflect more localized themes and motifs. In particular, the positive and negative dimensions of the will to power as the total economy of life will loom large. Grass integrates in a single grotesque, childlike dwarf the positive and negative expressions of the Nietzschean will to power as expressed not only by Nietzsche but also *avant la lettre* by Goethe, who observed those processes in nature. In pursuing this course, I depart from the usual focus on *The Tin Drum* as continuing the literary tradition of the picaresque novel while simultaneously offering my own explanation of why one can see in this work a melancholy attempt at enlightenment.[12] In its own unique way, it too is a novel of the universe.

Goethe's novel on chemical reactions and human behavior, *Elective Affinities* (1809) (*BT* 112, 115, 362; *TD* 90, 93, 278); sees himself in the role of Faust descending to or returning from the Mothers (*BT* 118, 771; *TD* 95, 583); evokes the concluding verses of *Faust II* regarding "das Unzulängliche" (*BT* 272), echos Iphigenie's longing for home in *Iphigenie in Tauris* (*BT* 134–135); and refers to *Torquato Tasso* (*BT* 571).

11 In his valuable study of the reception of Nietzsche in twentieth-century German literature, *Nietzsche und die Kunst* (Tübingen: Francke, 1993), Theo Meyer mentions Grass just once, claiming that contemporary authors such as Heinrich Böll, Günter Grass, Martin Walser, Uwe Johnson and Hans M. Enzensberger have displayed little interest in Nietzsche (335-36). Meyer even suggests that such classic Nietzschean qualities as "der elitäre Individualismus, das Pathos des Lebens und die Apotheose der Kunst" have lost their meaning for Grass, even though Meyer does recognize the centrality of the creative impulse for *Die Blechtrommel* (336). My analysis of *The Tin Drum* is a corrective to Meyer's misleading contention. Peter Heßelmann, in his review of Gerhart Hoffmeister's (ed.) *Der moderne deutsche Schelmenroman: Interpretationen* (Amsterdam: Rodopi, 1986), remarks that researchers should take serious note of Laurence Rickels's essay in the volume on Günter Grass's *Die Blechtrommel*. Rickels's piece is deserving of attention not so much because Rickels places the novel between the Bildungsroman and *Schelmenroman* but because he sees the novel as a "rigoroser Nietzscheroman," in which Oskar appears as "die radikalste Nietzscherezeption in der deutschen Literatur" (Rickels 114). See Peter Heßelmann's review in *Heine-Jahrbuch* 29 (1990): 218–20; here 219.

12 Wilfried van der Will, *Picaro Heute: Metamorphosen des Schelms bei Thomas Mann, Döblin, Brecht, Grass* (Stuttgart, 1969), 69. Yet that tradition is by definition concerned with real parameters of the sociopolitical and physical contexts of life. Other writers who have selected gnomes as a filter for their views include John Irving in *Simon Birch* and Ursula Haegi in *Stones from the River*. Harro Zimmermann concludes that Oskar is no mere picaresque carryover but owes his existence to "einem hintersinnigen Aufklärungsexperiment." See Harro Zimmermann, "Das Licht der Melancholie: Günter Grass und die Aufklärung oder Ein deutsches Mißverständnis," in Grass and Zimmermann, *Vom Abenteuer der Aufklärung*, 287–330; here 288.

2. Reality and Modern Myth Making: Science and Fiction

In *The Tin Trum*, Grass grapples with the turbulent history of the years 1899–1956. Adopting a Polish-German perspective, he directs his gaze toward the center from the margins. He plays with history, transforming personal experiences into universal constants. (He does much the same thing in one of his more recent works, *My Century* [1999]). For this reason, we can readily assign to *The Tin Drum*, with its creative rhythms, innovative style, linguistic conceits, and resonant mythologems, a role as mythologically large and as philosophically profound as Goethe's own monumental *Faust* or as critical of its own era as Nietzsche's *Thus Spoke Zarathustra*. Reworking his personal experiences and reminiscences into a universal tale of existentialist angst, Grass transformed the first two drafts of the novel (which date back to 1952) into a "mythology of history."[13] From a chaos of events he constructed a tale with an inner structure that coalesces around "cosmic seeds" of metaphorical meaning. These "Keimmetaphern" (Neuhaus, *Erläuterungen* 84) act like strange attractors. Similar to Gerald Holton's themata, Richard Dawkins's memes, or Edward O. Wilson's nodes-as-memes, the metaphorical conceits such as the gnome, the hunchback, the grandmother's skirts, the tin drum, and the escalator reveal a deeper lying structuring principle. Wilson's suggestion for redefining the meme as "the node of semantic memory" awaiting activation is especially pertinent because it highlights the interactive process in communication between the individual instance and the universal law.[14] The concept of reality in *The Tin Drum* has been expanded to include the realm of the imagination, the alternation between the empirical and the imaginable. That is why the novel is often cited as an example of magical realism. The interweaving of fact and fiction, reality and myth is continued in many of Grass's other works, where characters and scenes from *The Tin Drum* recur like so many reflectaphors.[15] It is as if the characters and motifs have taken on a life of their own in the recurring vortices of

---

13 The term "Mythologie der Geschichte" derives from the romantic poet Novalis (Friedrich von Hardenberg, 1772–1801). On Novalis's conceptualization of the integration of memory, history, and imagination, see Laurie Ruth Johnson, *The Art of Recollection in Jena Romanticism: Memory, History, Fiction, and Fragmentation in Texts by Friedrich Schlegel and Novalis* (Tübingen: Niemeyer, 2002), 103–41. Novalis's thesis that "memory is indispensable for the construction of a system that transcends the merely subjective" (140) is similar to Grass's own use of memory and history as the space of the productive reworking of experiences into a consciousness-raising "mythic" whole.

14 Edward O. Wilson, *Consilience: The Unity of Knowledge* (New York: Alfred Knopf, 1998), 136.

15 For instance, Oskar has cameo roles in *Katz und Maus* (1961), *Hundejahre* (1963), *Der Butt* (1977), and *Die Rättin* (1986). In the last, Oskar is a media mogul and about to celebrate his sixtieth birthday.

Grass's mind. With its large cast of characters and multilayered text, the novel cannot be addressed fully in these pages. To be dealt with effectively, the text must be analyzed selectively. Special care will be given to tracing continuities with *Faust* and *Zarathustra*.

While Goethe was a poet-scientist intimately in touch with scientific developments of his day and Nietzsche had seriously considered a life of science, Günter Grass's exposure to scientific paradigms and debates is less distinctly profiled. Yet his novel mirrors scientific knowledge, however indirectly. The few conscious references to medical science in diagnosing Oskar's condition or to "scientific and pseudoscientific" explanations of Oskar's ability to shatter glass with his voice (presumably caused by cosmic rays and sunspots) are hardly detailed (*TD* 105). In this regard, an observation by John L. Casti seems fitting: "Experiencing the world ultimately comes down to the recognition of boundaries: self/nonself, before/after, inside/outside, subject/object and so forth."[16] Observing boundaries is at the very heart of Grass's opus. What Casti then says about the inability of instrumental reason to calculate mathematically and geometrically the operations of nature is directly related to the attempts of the book's narrator/protagonist, Oskar Matzerath to explain reality:

> And so it is in mathematics as well, where we're continually called upon to make distinctions between categories – stable/unstable, computable/incomputable, linear/nonlinear, real/complex – distinctions involving the identification of boundaries of especially important figures by giving them names like circles, triangles, squares, and polygons. But when it comes to using boundaries to describe the natural world, these simple geographical shapes fail completely. (*Complexification* 230)

As we shall see, geometry and the magic of numbers are employed throughout *The Tin Drum* as a means, however tentative, of mapping reality. Nietzsche contended that the shapes and forms of reality that we assign to objects and that seem so real to us do not exist at all. We simplify things for ourselves to explain complex events through analogies and figures that *we* create.[17] The boundary between the perceiving subject and the perceived object is clearly blurred.

More directly to the point is Grass's response to having won the Nobel Prize for

---

16 John L. Casti, *Complexification: Explaining a Paradoxical World Through the Science of Surprise* (New York: HarperCollins, 1994), 230.

17 Nietzsche writes: "Die Gestalten und Formen, die wir sehen und in denen wir die Dinge zu haben glauben, sind all nicht vorhanden. Wir vereinfachen uns und verbinden irgend welche 'Eindrücke' durch Figuren, die *wir* schaffen." Friedrich Nietzsche, *Sämtliche Werke*, Kritische Studienausgabe, ed. by Giorgio Colli and Mazzino Montinari, 15 vols. (Munich: Deutscher Taschenbuch Verlag, 1988), *Nachgelassene Fragmente 1882–1884*, 10:651 [Winter 1883–84]. Hereafter cited as *KSA* by volume and page number.

Literature in 1999. Passed over in previous years, he finally won well-deserved recognition for his early "revolutionary" accomplishments in the Danzig trilogy: *The Tin Drum*, *Cat and Mouse*, *Dog Years*. His acceptance speech was published in German and English in the *Publications of the Modern Language Association* (*PMLA*) under the title "'To Be Continued ...' / 'Fortsetzung folgt ...'"[18] His title plays on the nineteenth-century practice of serializing a novel over many issues of a weekly or monthly magazine (as did, e.g., Dickens, Zola, Fontane, Tolstoy) and also reverberates with the open ending of *The Tin Drum*. Grass ostensibly uses the reference to underscore his own drive to write, a drive he describes as Sisyphean. Citing his fellow Nobel laureate Albert Camus, he speaks of the endeavor to tell the story of humankind with its struggles and tribulations (war, hunger, injustice). Even more promisingly, Grass cites the 1953 discovery of the double helix by Watson and Crick (also Nobel laureates) that revolutionized gene theory and the possibility for manipulation, eventually leading to the cloning of plants and animals and ultimately to stem cell research. The popularization of the double helix model in the 1950s coincided with the genesis of *The Tin Drum*. Grass specifically points to his novel, *Die Rättin*, for which he coined the term "Watsoncricks" in deference to Watson and Crick. "Watsoncricks" are the increasingly dominant hybrid of rats and humans ("Rattenmenschen") in the novel. Additionally, Grass makes reference to the big bang theory and to the concept of order emerging out of chaos ("To Be Continued" 301). Later, he also alludes to the splitting of the atom (308).

All of this reveals Grass's awareness of developments in the sciences. To tell his story of human life, Grass states that he seeks a distant vantage point (in myth, the past, from outside the whirl of events), which he found early on in the picaresque novel (305, 307). Always interested in subversive writing as a way of affecting things as they are, Grass implicitly sees himself as contributing to the ongoing project of the European Enlightenment (308). He has always wondered how "subversive writing" can function like dynamite yet retain its literary quality. Here one cannot help but think of Nietzsche's self-characterization in *Ecce homo* as dynamite and his writing as explosives (*KSA* 6:365). At the end of his acceptance speech, Grass returns to the notion of gene manipulation when he wonders whether the rumors are true that a new breed of genetically cloned humans is destined to ensure the continuance of human history (309). These late reflections by one of the most celebrated writers at the beginning of a new millennium close the circle of reflection on the Sisyphean task represented by *Faust*, *Zarathustra*, and *The Tin Drum*. Rolling that stone up the hill constitutes the very meaning of life (Taylor 2000: 328), for Grass thinks of the unending task not as mere frustration but rather as challenge and persistence. Grass's *The Tin Drum* is also a book about good and

---

18 Günter Grass, "To Be Continued ... Fortsetzung folgt," *PMLA* 115.3 (May 2000): 292–309.

evil and the responsibility that humanity must bear for its actions or omissions. It is also about seeking purpose in a life that seems to have been deprived of all meaning by catastrophic events. In the wake of a devastating era, the task was undoubtedly Sisyphean.[19]

This chapter, then, focuses on the mythologizing of reality via the tools of science, the forces of tradition, and the creative imagination. It is a paradoxical combination that requires a redefinition of thought as an interpenetrating process inclusive of emotion, intellect, reflex, and artifact all rolled into "*one unbroken field of mutually informing thought*."[20] It is fully in keeping with the integral culture that has begun to emerge since the Age of Reason and empirical science. In recounting some of the most painful experiences in the modern history of humankind, *The Tin Drum* recharts reality along mythical patterns that reach back to ancient times. While the remapping of phenomena is aimed at the myriad historical events that constitute the fabric of human existence, the novel also anticipates – albeit unconsciously – contemporary strides in chaos and complexity theory. Even though scientific inquiry is not the overt focus of *The Tin Drum*, there are, for instance, striking echoes of the DNA coding mechanisms in the novel's deep structure. As the philosopher Richard Taylor asserted, man is not the measure of all things because we – moral being and all – are the way we are as a consequence of numerous acts of nature (Taylor 191). We will view *The Tin Drum*, then, not simply as a willful reordering of reality, but as partaking in autopoietic processes that operate outside as well as within a human system of thought. Subject and object can be seen as two sides of the same coin.

In a 1997 retrospective of the genesis of the novel, Grass explains that the immediate catalyst for the work was the death of his mother, Helene Grass, in 1954. He had always wanted to prove something to her, so he set about erecting a monument that could not be overlooked.[21] The very first sketch of the eventual protagonist Oskar – before he was even called Oskar Matzerath – dates from 1952 in a no longer existent poem entitled "Der Säulenheiliger" (The Holy Man of the Pillar). The hero is an existentialist protesting the small-mindedness of bourgeois society. Not unlike Kafka's hunger artist or Nietzsche's Zarathustra, the column sitter has all the characteristics of the outsider who views things from above. Dissatisfied with the end result because the point of reference was too static and after having observed a three-year old child beating a drum in a crowded café,

19 During a radio interview for the Westdeutscher Rundfunk in 1973, Grass recounted the difficulties in writing the novel. The report is reprinted in Neuhaus, *Erläuterungen*, 58–70.

20 David Bohm, *Thought as a System* (London & New York: Routledge, 1994), xi, 4–6.

21 Günter Grass, "Rückblick auf die Blechtrommel – oder Der Autor als fragwürdiger Zeuge: Ein Versuch in eigener Sache," in Grass, *Der Autor als fragwürdiger Zeuge*, ed. by Daniela Hermes (Munich: Deutscher Taschenbuch Verlag, 1997), 102–114; here103.

Grass hit upon the idea of critiquing his era through the eyes of the diminutive Oskar Matzerath. Oskar had the double advantage of being removed from the action while remaining mobile within it. Grass suggests viewing Oskar as a saintly pole sitter turned topsy turvy ("ein umgepolter Säulenheiliger"; "Rückblick" 106). Strikingly, The German word "umpolen" connotes more than a stepping down from the column; it suggests a reversal of the pole as well. Thus, instead of pointing up and away from the surface of existence, it points deep down into its roots. Oskar himself, like Zarathustra, moves down from the heights to mingle with the people in the valleys. The saint also becomes a sinner. I suggest that we view Oskar as the Nietzschean free spirit who observes humanity from above, from below, and from all around. From these early sketches, then, we can see how Grass intermingled fact and fiction, reality and myth from the outset.

That unity of opposites can be explained on the one hand by the Nietzschean concept of the will to power and on the other by the science of chaos and complexity. Let us first consider the emplacement of history, and then ask who Oskar really is before we consider the relevance of Nietzsche's will to power and of chaos theory for Grass's novel. Then we will analyze the significance of numbers and of non-Euclidean geometry for mapping reality in the novel. Finally, we will conclude with speculation on parallels between DNA coding and the structure of the novel as a living organism.

3. Plotting (His)story: Who's Oskar and What's He Doing Here?

At the beginning of his narrative, Oskar Matzerath explains that his own story is embedded in a larger history of family and world events, remarking, "no one ought to tell the story of his life who hasn't the patience to say a word or two about at least half of his grandparents before plunging into his own existence" ("niemand sollte sein Leben beschreiben, der nicht die Geduld aufbringt, vor dem Datieren der eigenen Existenz wenigstens die Hälfte seiner Großeltern zu gedenken"; *TD* 17–18; *BT 12*). While it is impossible to recount in succinct fashion the details of events that shape the action of *The Tin Drum*, with its three books, forty-six chapters, and some 700 pages, a brief plot summary can still serve as a useful orientation and prelude to an examination of more specific details. The novel recounts the events of twentieth-century Central Europe leading up to the Great War, the interwar period, the atrocities of *Kristallnacht* and the Holocaust, World War II, the aftermath of Germany's defeat, concluding with the incipient economic miracle of the 1950s and the Germans' confrontation with collective guilt and atonement.[22] The personal

22 On the role of history in the novel, see Volker Neuhaus, *Günter Grass: Die Blechtrommel. Inter-*

lives of the numerous characters encountered are drawn against those world-altering events, which themselves are placed within the history of earlier invasions of Poland and the city of Danzig. Moreover, every large human event is balanced by a personalized view of ordinary people (e.g., *TD* 384). Thus, Oskar states unequivocally that the battle of Stalingrad and the entire eastern campaign meant less to him than his amorous interest in the greengrocer's wife, Lina Greff, or in his soon-to-be stepmother, Maria Truczinski (*TD* 305, 318). Of primary concern to him during the infamous *Kristallnacht*, when the Jewish toy store owner Sigismund Markus commits suicide to avoid persecution by the Brown Shirts, is how he is to procure his drums in the future. The momentous fall of the Polish post office to the Germans is marked by playing a game of skat with his uncle Jan Bronski and another resistance fighter. Moreover, the human perspective – whether public or private – is integrated into the larger animate and inanimate universe, ranging from the constellation of the stars, to the rhythms of nature, the interplay of a severed horse's head and consuming eels, the migratory habits of ants, the fabled nine lives of cats, and the curse of the wooden figurehead of Niobe through hundreds of years. The chronology of events is not strictly adhered to, in part because of the narrator's idiosyncratic perspective and in part because Grass rejected "the absurd straightjacket of chronology" ("Rückblick" 108).

At the center of the story is Oskar Matzerath, who decides at birth not to join the adult cycle of guilt, atonement, and development (*Bildung*). He stops his biological growth and spends most of his time observing events from the fringes of society as a perpetual three-year-old child measuring only three feet high. His outsider role is variously expressed as that of an uncommunicative child, a handicapped person, a gang leader, a funky performing artist, and a live-alone bachelor. His perspectives are always off-center: from within closets; from atop bell towers and stages; from under rostrums, tables, skirts, and the Eiffel Tower; from within Schuh's Onion Cellar; and ultimately from a hospital bed in an asylum for the mentally ill. Many of these – especially the last – might be considered an ersatz womb. It is from here that he narrates the contorted events in a tortured chronology. Yet try as he might, Oskar is incapable of extricating himself fully from the turbulent flow of historical and natural events.

A fall down the cellar stairs provides to the adult world an obvious medical explanation for his lack of development. At age twenty-one, he resumes his growth with a second willful fall, this time into the grave of his alleged father, Alfred Matzerath. Again, the adult world attributes Oskar's changed condition to presumed injuries sustained in the fall caused by a stone thrown by Oskar's stepbrother and presumed son, Kurt. Oskar's renewed growth coincides with the

---

pretation (Munich: R. Oldenbourg Verlag, 1982), 53–62; also Krumme. *Günter Grass*, 103–22.

fall of the Nazi regime, fevered visions of an eternal return, reminiscences of the Treblinka concentration camp by his care giver and Holocaust survivor Mariusz Fajngold (*TD* 412–14), the casting aside of his beloved drum, and the acceptance of adult responsibility for Maria and Kurt. (Oskar's falls are distinct variations of Adam and Eve's fall from grace.) A period of life apart from the drum begins in June 1945 at the end of Book 2 and continues for four years until 1949. During his flight from the East Prussian city of Danzig (renamed Gdansk) to the Western city of Cologne, then Düsseldorf, he eventually grows to four 4 feet 2 inches (123 centimeters) tall. Oskar acts responsibly by taking up work first as a stone cutter and then as an artist's model, and – after returning to the drum – eventually makes a comfortable living as a drummer.[23] During this period, Oskar takes a third "plunge," this time deciding to ask Maria to marry him (she declines). Aided by his other talent to engrave (or shatter) glass with his voice alone, Oskar has assumed celebrity status by novel's end. People come to him, so Oskar reveals in the opening pages of the narrative, "to get to know themselves" (*TD* 16)

Oskar narrates from memory the entire action of the novel while committed to a hospital bed after claiming responsibility for the murder of Dorothea Köngetter, a nurse who was part of a love triangle involving a doctor and fellow nurse. This, by the way, is the third instance of Oskar accepting responsibility for the death of another (the other two instances involved his presumptive fathers, Alfred Matzerath and his uncle Jan Bronski). The claim of responsibility for his mother's suicide is more tenuous. The actual writing down of the events is accomplished with the help of Oskar's beloved tin drums, which must be replaced with regularity as they wear out. But who is Oskar really? Before examining individual instances of myth making in the novel, we need to answer this question.

Of course, we cannot simply abstract Oskar Matzerath from his environment. We can start by saying that he is a talented musician with unusual powers to control the actions of others while remaining apart. The original child model for Oskar was rapidly transformed into a magical character who took on a life of his own, evolving into a powerful twentieth-century mythologem of creative iconoclasm. In the first pages of the novel, Oskar states unmistakably that, far from being part of a nameless mass without heroes, he is a hero and an individual (*TD* 17). Indeed, he is one of those "clair-audient infants whose mental development is completed at birth" ("Ich gehörte zu den hellhörigen Säuglingen, deren geistige Entwicklung schon bei der Geburt abgeschlossen ist"; *TD* 47; *BT* 52). While he

23 During the trip itself (June–August 1945), Oskar grew to 4 feet 1 inch but adds another inch during the three days needed to narrate the episode of his growth for a total of 123 centimeters (*TD* 428–29). The growth during the narration of the historical event underscores the "timelessness" of the event, as will be argued in the following.

considers himself to be a gnome ("der Gnom"; *TD* 171; *BT* 219) and his existence a mistake, his fate is inescapable ("irrtümliche Geburt," "unabänderlich"; *TD* 503; *BT* 662). Of course, adults do not understand him, his lack of growth, or his insistence on communicating through his drum. To them he appears retarded and deficient; he is a cross to bear. At times he seems to be "a vicious midget, a crazy gnome" ("Giftzwerg," "übergeschnappter Gnom"; *TD* 290; *BT* 378). Later, aspiring artists see in him "the shattered image of man, an accusation, timeless yet expressing the madness of our century" ("das zerstörte Bild eines Menschen anklagend, herausfordernd, zeitlos und dennoch den Wahnsinn unseres Jahrhunderts ausdrückend"; *TD* 463; *BT* 606–607).

A few people – his dwarfish mentor Master Bebra, the somnambulist midget and girlfriend Roswitha Raguna, the soldier-turned-artist Corporal Lankes, the jazz musician Egon Münster aka Klepp – see past the surface play, recognizing what lies at Oskar's core. For example, Roswitha takes fright at the deep-seated tension she perceives between the divine and the diabolical elements in his genius (*TD* 172). Lankes apprehends his elemental drive to orchestrate movement and orders him to take up the drum again, remarking: "I have seen through you" ("Ich habe dich erkannt!" *TD* 473; *BT* 621). They realize that Oskar is first and foremost a drummer, that he is incomplete without the instrument that alone of all objects makes him complete (*TD* 473).[24] Without his drum, Oskar tells us at one point, he always feels exposed and defenseless ("der Bloßgestellte"; *TD* 281; *BT* 366). Indeed, the drum is a sign that he is "a little demigod whose business it was to harmonize chaos and intoxicate reason" ("ein kleiner, das Chaos harmonisierender, die Vernunft in Rauschzustände versetzender Halbgott"; *TD* 323; *BT* 423). This positive self-assessment is balanced by a negative one when he muses that Goethe, whom he so admired, would have condemned him "as an incarnation of anti-nature" ("die leibhaftige Unnatur"; *TD* 91; *BT* 102).

Given all this, he wonders whether the reader is even willing to accept him as a human being (*TD* 259; *BT* 335). He is hero and anti-hero all rolled into one and can be seen as a representative of the new genius, one who is consonant with nature, not an exception to the norm. In this capacity, he keeps directing the reader's attention back to humanity itself. Grass claimed in 1969: "I am opposed to any objective that leads beyond the human being itself."[25] Why then should Oskar Matzerath, in whom he invested so much creative energy, function any differently? Paradoxically – or perhaps not so paradoxically – Oskar realizes fully the creative

---

24 Grass originally considered calling his novel "Oskar der Trommler" or "Der Trommler," placing the emphasis on Oskar himself rather than his instrument. Grass, "Rückblick," 107.

25 Grass, "Unser Grundübel ist der Idealismus," in *Der Autor als fragwürdiger Zeuge*: "Ich bin – um es schlicht zu sagen – gegen jede Zielsetzung, die über den Menschen hinausweist" (68).

energy that flows through his veins and the forces of nature, even as he seeks to extricate himself from that flow and to negate its power. Though as he refuses to grow, his penis exercises its own independent will, reaching messianic proportions. We will return to this point later.

Yet other dimensions of Oskar's being need to be explored first. They lead us further away from the actual little boy playing his drum in the midst of a crowd. Most obvious is his name. Why Oskar? Why Matzerath? Oskar is an unusual given name, but a significant one; for example, it was American military code for "infinity"during World War II. Furthermore, the "O" recalls the endless circle and the wedding ring as a sign of undying fidelity, again implying infinity. We learn that Oskar becomes a stonecutter's apprentice – a profession, like drumming that leaves its mark on the surface. Oskar confesses a special fondness for inscripting the letter "O" because of its fine regularity and endlessness (*TD* 444; *BT* 546). And while riding the streetcar on the outskirts of Düsseldorf, he picks up on the recurrent, cyclic rhythm of the metal wheels striking the joints in the steel rails. Near Gerresheim in a Schrebergarten, Oskar invokes on his drum the rhythms of the charging Polish calvary in an effort to save Viktor Weluhn, who is about to be executed by two former Nazis for his role as a Polish defender during the battle for the Danzig Polish post office fifteen years earlier on September 1, 1939. Gottfried Vittlar remarks that Oskar's playing created a strange yet familiar rhythm that evoked not only Poland's immediate past but also its thousand-year history of repartitioning: "Over and over again the letter O took form: lost, not yet lost, Poland is not yet lost!" (*TD* 574; *BT* 713). The connotations of eternal return are underscored further when we consider that "OM" is the symbol of the essence and interconnection of reality in Yoga. In the Roman alphabet "M" stands for the number 1000, signifying our ability to approximate the infinite (at least in ancient days), while 'M' in sign language signifies the number 3, that is, the reintegration of the wholeness of the 1 lost in the dialectical opposition of the 2.

And "Matzerath"? Oskar's surname recalls the name of the village from which Jesus hailed: Nazareth. Indeed, Oskar presents himself at various times in the narrative, most notably at its conclusion, as Jesus. In the chapters "The Imitation of Christ" and "A Christmas Play" of Book 2, for example, he appears as an anti-Jesus. From his earliest visits to church with his mother, Oskar compares himself with Jesus, viewing him as a rival (see the chapter "No Wonder"). At the very least, as Oskar tells us, he "was not cut out to be a follower of Christ; for one thing, he has no aptitude for enlisting disciples" ("weil es mir unüberwindliche Schwierigkeiten bereitet, Jünger zu sammeln"; *TD* 360; *BT* 472).

In the narrative, Oskar appears masked variously as the mythical Hermes, Dionysus, Maui, Vulcan, Pluto, and Odysseus. In each instance, the individual clashes with larger cosmological forces. But we can also see him as a variation of the willful Faust, the hunchbacked dwarf Narses, and Shakespeare's fool, Yorick. Thus, Oskar Matzerath invokes characters on different levels of mythological significance. Yet the function of myth in the novel is not designed to lead the reader into a timeless realm divorced from historical reality; rather, it underscores the continuing presence of ordering principles deep below the surface play of conscious existence. The return of the trickster mythologem (Hermes), for instance, suggests a parallel between masks, tricks, lies, deception, and unpredictability. These we have come to associate with Nietzsche's concept of the falsification of all life, of his belief that every profound spirit needs a mask and that "around every profound spirit a mask is continually growing, thanks to the constantly false, that is to say *shallow*, interpretation of every word he speaks, every step he takes, every sign of life he gives" (*BGE* #40). Placed in this light, *The Tin Drum*, does not address exclusively a postwar generation of Germans plagued by collective guilt and social disruption. Translated in over twenty languages, the novel appears as fresh and vital today as it did in 1959.[26] No more easily finished with Oskar than with Faust or Zarathustra, who continue to haunt him long after his encounter with them, the reader is left animated and unsettled.[27]

4. OSKAR: NIETZSCHEAN GNOME OR GOETHEAN EARTH SPIRIT?

An excursus on the etymological connotations of the term "gnome" ("Gnom") used to describe the protagonist Oskar Matzerath proves illuminating in arguing the interconnectivity of Oskar as a mythologem and a product of nature. Tellingly, Oskar explains his relationship to his mother by specifically drawing attention to his gnomic nature: "To her I was never anything but a gnome. She would have got rid of the gnome if she had been able to." Moreover, people explain her death by blaming it on Oskar: "The gnome drummed her into her grave. Because of Oskar she didn't want to live any more; he killed her" ("Herbert Truczinski's Back," *TD* 171; *BT* 204). If we lend credibility to Oskar's exaggerated sense of responsibility for his mother's suicide, we can assign deeper meaning to the denotations and connotations of the preferred term "gnome" to characterize Oskar Matzerath. "Gnomic" is thus to be understood as "small in size" as well as "wise opinion." "Gnome" is etymologically derived from Greek *γνώμων* (gnōmōn) and is related to Greek *γνώμη* (gnōmē). *Γνώμων* (gnōmōn) designates an interpreter or judge, that

26 *"Die Blechtrommel" – Attraktion und Ärgernis*, 23; Jürgen Manthey, "'Die Blechtrommel' wiedergelesen," *Text + Kritik* 1, 6th ed. (1988): 24–36.

27 Cf. a review of the novel in the *Darmstädter Echo* (October 16, 1969) signed "gh." In *'Die Blechtrommel" – Attraktion und Ärgernis*, 45.

is, one who knows. The term "gnōmōn" also refers to the index of the sundial. Thus, one level of meaning underscores the prescience and deep insight of the gnome, while another level of meaning indicates that the gnome is also connected to the revolutions of the sun and the dimension of time resulting from that motion. Furthermore, *γνώμων* is related to Latin *norma*, that is a rule or guide of life. *Γνώμη* signifies mind, thought, or judgment. However, it also has a secondary meaning, namely, that of will or purpose. All of these meanings are discernible in Oskar's characterization while riding the escalator (the final dominant metaphor in the novel), reminiscent of Faust returning from the Mothers, and simultaneously of a pseudo Christ figure now constrained at narrative's end to gather disciples. Moreover, *γνώ* is the root of *γιγνώςκειν* (gignōskein), which means "to know." And of course the reader is informed in the opening chapter that people visit Oskar in order to get to know themselves better.

The German word "der Gnom" is also directly derivative of the Latin "gnomus." The late-medieval scientist and sorcerer, Paracelsus (ca. 1493–1541) adopted the word "gnomus" in his *De Nymphis* as a synonym for "pygmaeus," explaining that the "gnomus" inhabits the earth as a fundamental element. Actually, Paracelsus asserts that " chaos" is its proper element and state. The "gnomus" moves through chaos like a fish in water, a bird in the air, and an animal on land. In essence, then, "gnomus" signifies "inhabitant of the earth."[28] More narrowly, the term is synonymous with "dwarf" and "kobold." In this latter sense, gnome is encountered in Goethe's *Faust* as one of the four elementary spirits in pansophy (*Faust I*, V, line 1276).

Two other associations of gnome are significant. The German word "das Genom" is derivative of the Greek *γένος* (genus), which signifies descendant or race. However, in contemporary German the term designates the simple chromosome pair in a cell that constitutes the cell's hereditary traits, while "genom(e) refers to a haploid set of chromosomes, that is, to the sum total of the genes in such a set."[29] This connection will be explored a bit later in the argument.

When we combine all of these associations of "gnome," we end up with an illuminating view of Oskar as a representation of the deep structure of existence: (1) he is a grotesque yet wondrous being who nonetheless is rooted in the earth itself; (2) he communicates his thoughts, judgments, and opinions about his origins and history at large as messianic messages; (3) he does this by replicating the rhythms of life through his drum, which is made of all natural materials and whose shape (round) and color (serrated red and white) prove highly emblematic; and (4) as a diminutive being with childlike qualities of innocence, he conveys a closeness

28 *Oxford English Dictionary*, 6:614.
29 *Der große Duden*, vol. 3; *Oxford English Dictionary*, 6:445

to the origins of life in a simpler form. His goal, as he repeatedly states, is to return to an undifferentiated state in the womb. In effect, he seeks to reverse the chromosomal production that produced his particular being. This is, of course, a vain effort; it is like trying to reverse complexity. Yet his size, his multifaceted roles, and his unusual perspectives from below, above, behind, within, and outside point us in the direction of an elemental inner structure at work in the novel. Although the step will surely strike some readers as daring because there is not explicit reference to the phenomenon, I wish to argue that the gnome Oskar represents the eternal return of a coevolutionary universe. In sum, he is a variation of Nietzsche's dwarf – Zarathustra's spirit of gravity – whose downward pull prompts Zarathustra's reactive, upward drive. Moreover, Oskar is a variation of the "fine structure constant" in Goethe's *Faust*; that is, the Earth Spirit, who works "in the hum of the loom of time / Weaving the living raiment of godhead sublime" (lines 508–09).

5. The Art of Drumming: Of Mothers and Moths

The anchoring of human birthing in the wider forces of nature seems to support such an interpretation. Seminal in this regard is chapter 3, "Wide Skirts," in which the conception of Oskar's mother, Agnes Koljaiczek in the Kashubian potato fields is recounted. Enshrouded in a light drizzle, sitting at a small fire in the middle of a flat landscape with a broad horizon punctuated by phallic-like telegraph poles that portend the imminent emergence of Joseph Koljaiczek's own rigid member, Anna Koljaiczek munches on roasted potatoes. The reader's attention is focused in spiral-like manner, moving from the horizons, where grayish-brown earth blends imperceptibly with a grayish sky, to Anna Koljaiczek.[30] Eventually, the eye is directed specifically at her skirts, which welcome the arsonist Joseph Koljaiczek into their warm folds as he seeks to hide from the hotly pursuing gendarmes. While Anna sits immovably like a mountain, tending her fire, uniting the four elements (earth, water, air, fire), chewing with a circular motion, rolling her eyes to heaven, and curtly answering the questioning police, interspersed with utterances of the

30 Colors abound in the novel. White, brown, and blue are first encountered (the hospital bed and nurse's uniform are white; Bruno, the ward attendant, has brown eyes; Oskar's eyes are blue), then gray (sky, moth). Later, white and red alternate. Gray is Grass's favorite color (see Mayer-Iswandy), perhaps because of its primordial quality: the mixed state before verdant green. But it is also associated with potatoes, the earth, and Agnes's eyes (*TD* 54). White is the reflection of the full color spectrum discernible by the human eye and connotes innocence. Brown is warm with human qualities (*TD* 58). Red intimates passion, love, and violence (cf. esp. *TD* 156f., 226 for various associations).

names of the saints, Joseph allows his piston to do its work under the cover of the wide skirts. The whole scene, in fact, is enshrouded in smoke, gray skies, and dampness as within an even wider skirt harboring procreative activity. "All was as still as on the first day of Creation or the last," we are specifically told, indicating eternal feedback loops between beginnings and endings, between alpha and omega ("Still war es wie am ersten Tag oder am letzten"; *TD* 21–22; *BT* 18). When the police depart, Joseph emerges, having done his work, and Anna raises herself up as if she were rooted to the earth. The description of the scene is striking for its salient allusions to Gaea, the Earth Mother:

> The smoke of the slowly dying fire enveloped my grandmother like a spacious fifth skirt, so that she too with her four skirts, her sighs, and her holy names, was under a skirt. Only when the uniforms had become staggering dots, vanishing in the dusk, between the telegraph poles, did my grandmother arise, slowly and painfully as though she had struck root and now, drawing earth and fibers along with her, were tearing herself out of the ground. (*TD* 24)

> [Der Rauch des langsam sterbenden Feuers hüllte meine Großmutter gleich einem fünften und so geräumigen Rock ein, daß sie sich in ihren vier Röcken, mit Seufzern und heiligen Vornamen, ähnlich dem Koljaiczek, unterm Rock befand. Erst als die Uniformen nur noch wippende, langsam im Abend zwischen Telegrafenstangen versaufende Punkte waren, erhob sich meine Großmutter so mühsam, als hätte sie Wurzeln geschlagen und unterbräche nun, Fäden und Erdreich mitziehend, das gerade begonnene Wachstum.] (*BT* 21)

Given the mythological significance of Oskar's grandmother as Mother Earth – whose children were the first creatures to have the appearance of life with the shattering strength of earthquake, volcano, and hurricane – Oskar's own connection to the broader forces of life are clearly manifest.[31] In tales about these early creatures, they do not seem to be really alive but rather to belong to a world where as yet there was no life, only tremendous movements of irresistible forces lifting up the mountains and scooping out the seas, as if on the first day of creation or the last.

Not surprisingly, Oskar's own birth (and that of his alleged son, Kurt) is situated within the entire framework of movement on the micro and macro scales.[32] Clairvoyant at birth, Oskar weighs the prospects of life offered him by his parents.

31 Edith Hamilton, *Mythology: Timeless Tales of Gods and Heroes*, 23rd printing (New York: New American Library, 1963), 64–65. Cf. Walter Jahnke and Klaus Lindemann, *Günter Grass: Die Blechtrommel – Acht Kapitel zur Erschließung des Romans* (Paderborn: Ferdinand Schöningh, 1993), 18–20. The authors also point out Biblical allusions – to *Moses I*, for example.

32 Jahnke and Lindemann analyze this chapter in detail (*Günter Grass: Die Blechtrommel* 30–40). My focus on chaos theory and Nietzsche allows me to draw some different conclusions, above all not seeing a transformation from chaos to culture. Jahnke and Lindemann understand chaos naively.

Thinking ahead, Alfred Matzerath pronounces Oskar's destiny to succeed him in the family business; reacting more emotionally and immediately, Agnes promises him a tin drum when he turns three. Though listening to the conversation, Oskar is also aware that a single gray moth is filling the room and everything in it with "quivering motion" ("mit zuckender Bewegung"), a rapid play of light and shadow produced by its fluttering back and forth between two bare 60-watt light bulbs. More striking than the interplay of light and dark, however, is the sound accompanying the quivering motion as the moth darts back and forth, banging against the light sources. Oskar speaks of a dialogue between moth and bulb, designating it the moth's last confession in search of the absolution that only light bulbs confer. That "chattering away" of the moth, "as if it had no time for future colloquies," "no further occasion for sin and folly," Oskar characterizes simply as drumming, as rhythmic undulations omnipresent in nature. The entire, classic passage reads:

> the moth chattered away as if in haste to unburden itself of its knowledge, as though it had no time for future colloquies with sources of light, as though this dialogue were its last confession; and as though, after the kind of absolution that light bulbs confer, there would be no further occasion for sin or folly. Today Oskar says simply: The moth drummed. I have heard rabbits, foxes and dormice drumming. Frogs can drum up a storm. Woodpeckers are said to drum worms out of their hiding places. And men beat on basins, tin pans, bass drums, and kettledrums. (*TD*, "Moth and Light Bulb" 47–48)

> [Der Falter schnatterte, als hätte er es eilig, sein Wissen los zu werden, als käme ihm nicht mehr Zeit zu für spätere Plauderstunden mit Lichtquellen, als wäre das Zwiegespräch zwischen Falter und Glühbirne in jedem Fall des Falters letzte Beichte und nach jener Art von Absolution, die Glühbirnen austeilen, keine Gelegenheit mehr für Sünde und Schwärmerei. Heute sagt Oskar schlicht: Der Falter trommelte. Ich habe Kaninchen, Füchse und Siebenschläfer trommeln hören. Frösche können ein Unwetter zusammentrommeln. Dem Specht sagt man nach, daß er Würmer aus ihren Gehäusen trommelt. Schließlich schlägt der Mensch auf Pauken, Becken, Kessel und Trommeln.] (*BT*, "Falter und Glühbirne" 53).

Later we learn that Oskar drums on flesh during the sex act (*TD* 280, 286), on coffin lids, on Herbert Truczinski's back, on the wooden Niobe, on anything that resonates. The entire narrative is drummed up from the depths of his memory on a percussion instrument. Yet the whole array of drumming throughout has its origin in the "disciplined passion" and "orgy of drumming carried on by that moth at the hour of my birth" (and its death, we might add) ("Trommelorgie"; *TD* 48; *BT* 53). But for the prospect of the tin drum held out by his mother, Oskar would have expressed more forcefully his desire to return to the womb (*TD* 49). In fact, drumming is his way of imitating the moth, his "master" ("Meister"; *TD* 48; *BT* 54). He will drum until he can no longer move.

The pervasiveness of the drumming motif is transparent. Yet it, too, is framed by a cosmic perspective. Oskar's horoscope is sketched with references to the sun being in the sign of Virgo, a reference no doubt to the light of his insight and clairvoyance and to his purity as newborn and untainted. Mercury, we are told, made him critical, Uranus, ingenious, Venus imparted a love of comfort, while Mars caused him to be ambitious. Libra gave him sensitivity, Neptune, caution, and Saturn cast doubt on his origins (*TD* 48). All the while, a late summer storm was brewing in the distance, causing much agitation and movement. As if to draw the reader's attention to the connections between the moth, the ominous weather, and their cosmic significance, Oskar queries: "But who sent the moth and allowed it [...] to make me fall in love with the drum?" (*TD* 48). The answer is indirect. It is provided by the narrative's tendency to turn in on itself like a snake coiled tightly. Metaphorically, it is expressed by Oskar's search for the way back to the womb, where the fetus can be curled in on itself.

Oskar is the incarnation of the rhythmic principle cited by Nietzsche in the quotation at the masthead: "The human being is a *creature of rhythms*, constituting all events as rhythmic phenomena. It is his way of exercising power over sensations" ("Der Mensch ist ein *rhythmen-bildendes Geschöpf*. Er legt alles Geschehen in diese Rhythmen hinein, es ist eine Art, sich der 'Eindrücke' zu bemächtigen").[33] The original creature of rhythms was Proteurhythmos of ancient myth, the harmonizer of agonistic forces in the universe and reconciler of Apollonian order and Dionysian frenzy. Proteurhythmos is the name of a deity derived from cultic traditions of the Attic Iobakchen known from inscriptions dating from the second century AD. The exact identity of the deity is unknown but he (or she) has been variously identified as the leader in a rhythmic procession; as being synonymous with the musician Orpheus, who retrieved Eurydice from Hades; as designating the rhythmic principle in the cosmos itself; or as a companion to Dionysus, who set the tone for the dances. Regardless of which function we ascribe to Proteurhythmos, the common thread is the orchestration of movement through rhythm. She occupies a position between Apollo and Dionysus and has a direct impact on what it means to be human.[34] This very connection Grass draws in chapter 7, "Rasputin and the Alphabet," which details Oskar's early education. Not wishing to stake everything on the harmony and rational clarity associated with Goethe or on the Dionysian

33 Friedrich Nietzsche, *Nachgelassene Fragmente 1882–1884*, *KSA* 10:651 [Winter 1883–84]. My translation.

34 On the cosmic implications of the mythologem see "Proteurhythmos," *Paulys Realencyclopädie der klassischen Altertumswissenschaft*, newly ed. by Georg Wissowa, Wilhelm Kroll and Karl Mittelhaus (Stuttgart: Alfred Druckenmüller Verlag, 1957), vol. 21, part 1, cols. 939–40. See also Erhard M. Friedrichsmeyer, "Aspects of Myth, Parody, and Obscenity in Grass's *Die Blechtrommel* and *Katz und Maus*," *The Germanic Review* 40.3 (1965): 240–49; here 242–44.

ecstasy and instinctual excesses of the primitive Russian monk Grigori Rasputin (1871–1916), Oskar fluctuates between them. In the process of negotiating their "conflicting harmony," he rejects the body-defying idealism of Schiller. "The conflicting harmony between these two was to shape or influence my whole life," Oskar confesses, "at least what life I have tried to live apart from my drum" ("Dieser Doppelbegriff sollte mein Leben, zumindest jenes Leben, welches abseits meiner Trommel zu führen ich mir anmaßte, festlegen und beeinflussen"; *TD* 90; *BT* 111–12). The translation of "Doppelbegriff" as "conflicting harmony" obscures the resonance of Grass's term with Nietzsche's notion of the double will ("doppelter Wille") in *Thus Spoke Zarathustra*, in which the prophet speaks of his rising and falling, his desire for the overman and attraction to the common man.[35]

From Rasputin, he took the elemental drive, from Goethe, the tempering power of a feeling for nature (*TD* 278; *BT* 361). (His life as a drummer is marked by independence from having to choose between the one or the other ordering force, for as Proteurhythmos Oskar is an ordering power in his own right.) When later preparing to join Master Bebra's theatrical troupe, Oskar considers whether he should take along his one-volume library consisting of Rasputin and Goethe. Carrying on negotiations with "his two gods," Dionysus and Apollo, in the chapter "Bebra's Theater at the Front" of Book 2, Oskar confides: "If Apollo strove for harmony and Dionysus for drunkenness and chaos, Oskar was a little demigod whose business it was to harmonize chaos and intoxicate reason" ("Wenn Apollo die Harmonie, Dionysos Rausch und Chaos anstrebte, war Oskar ein kleiner, das Chaos harmonisierender, die Vernunft in Rauschzustände versetzender Halbgott"; *TD* 323; *BT* 423). Indeed, he went right on comparing Goethe with Rasputin "or, when [he had] had enough of the cyclic and endless alternation of dark and radiant, took refuge in historical studies" (*TD* 161; *BT* 169).

As if on cue, Goethe and Rasputin recur in Oskar's fevered vision of God as a carousel owner. The image of the rotating disk seems perfect for picking up on the iterations of the earth as it revolves on its axis, driven by forces of attraction and repulsion. With four thousand screaming children riding on fire engines and hollowed-out animals round and round, the movement of the merry-go-round keeps returning everyone to the same point – the point where the gold ring hangs and God our Father in Heaven stands, putting more coins in the operator box against the

---

35 Friedrich Nietzsche contends in *Also Sprach Zarathustra*: "Der Abhang, wo der Blick *hinunter* stürzt und die Hand *hinauf* greift. Da schwindelt dem Herzen vor seinem doppelten Willen. Ach, Freunde, errathet ihr wohl auch meines Herzens doppelten Willen? Das, das ist *mein* Abhang und meine Gefahr, dass mein Blick in die Höhe stürzt, und dass meine Hand sich halten und stützen möchte – an der Tiefe! An den Menschen klammert sich mein Wille, mit Ketten binde ich mich an den Menschen, weil es mich hinauf reisst zum Übermenschen: denn dahin will mein anderer Wille" (*KSA* 4:183).

protests of the children, who have had enough. Each time that the riders return to where God takes the measure of things, he appears alternately as Rasputin, tipsy and laughing with glee, and as Goethe, sober and refined. The alternation continues relentlessly. No one gets the gold ring. Oskar interprets this diurnal exercise as "a bit of madness with Rasputin and a bit of rationality with Goethe. The extremists with Rasputin, the forces of order with Goethe" (*TD* 412). With a little imagination, we can read the vision as a metaphor for the eternal return. The point of reference defined by the gold ring and God-the-carousel-owner would be a Poincaré section, a point of measurement. The alternating visages of light and dark, Goethe and Rasputin, good and evil, positive and negative might represent the forces of attraction and repulsion that cause so much movement. In his fevered state, Oskar is not an orchestrator of that motion but rather is subject to it. The children's desire to stop the merry-go-round and get off is symbolic of Oskar's aim to get back to the umbilical cord, to return to the womb where he was not subject to the whims of Apollo and Dionysus. The geometric shape of the round disk on which the children sit not only symbolizes the earth's surface but also portends the oblong, rounded shape of the escalator, the final dominant metaphor in the novel. It, too, is symbolic of the eternal return.

A critical turning point in the recognition of Oskar's role as stimulator of regulated movement (and thus inherently related to all this motion) occurs in the aforementioned chapter labeled "Madonna 49" when the artist Lankes (nicknamed Raskolnikov because of his obsession with guilt and atonement like Dostoyevsky's protagonist in *Crime and Punishment*) recognizes that Oskar needs a drum to complete the portrait of Ulla and Oskar as Madonna and Child. The Apollonian order and harmony of Goethe lie dormant in Oskar as the repressed complement to the Dionysian turbulence represented by Rasputin (*TD* 463). "Take the drum," Raskolnikov commands Oskar. "I have seen through you." Oskar's protests are to no avail, for "nothing is ended, everything returns, guilt, atonement, more guilt." Subsequently, Lankes and his students render Oskar as Jesus the drummer, sitting in the nude lap of the modern reincarnation of the original Madonna, the lanky and beautiful Ulla. This scene gathers together key components of the new gospel. Rhythmical drumming, the perverted message of Christian salvation, and the eternal return obviously underlie the external accoutrements of the novel. Raskolnikov intuitively recognizes what Oskar knew all along during his life with the drum: in this world every Rasputin draws a Goethe in his wake and vice versa. Life with the drum is one of conflicting harmony, of an existence beyond good and evil. Life without it is a false dichotomy of alternatives: either/or, good/evil. The rhythms caused by this essential tension have a transformative value. The shapes they conjure up are more asymmetrical than symmetrical (as, for example, in the shift from the disk to the flattened circle); unbending symmetry is cause for suspicion. Oskar makes this point with regard to the rectangular Nazi rostrum (and church altars), which symbolizes rigid ideologies of whatever ilk (*TD* 118–19). The actual shape of reality is fractal, non-Euclidean. When he awakens Klepp from his slumber to the rhythms of life, it is through the rhythmic retelling of his own life from the moth on. And Klepp, even more so than Lankes, prompts Oskar to take up the drum for real again. Klepp touches off a spark in him, so that all of the drums Oskar ever played and laid to rest are resurrected, their resonance filling his whole being (*TD* 506).[36] There are, in essence, no antitheses in nature. Nothing is past; everything is present and future. There is only *Vergegenkunft*. The recurring rhythms of existence make that clear.

In the final analysis, these rhythms are an expression of the will to power; and will to power is associated with life in general.[37] Through Oskar's drums, the will to power assumes various shapes, such as grandmother Koljaiczek's skirts, the scarred back of his friend Herbert Truczinski, greengrocer Greff's drumming machine, the serpentine Lucy Rennwand, nurse Dorothea's ring finger, and even the seductive wooden figurehead, Niobe. In the arts as well as in the sciences, an Ariadne thread is discernible: it is the rhythmic pulsations of organic and inorganic material, a rhythmic beating that forms the foundation of existence and shapes its forms. Art (like the hitech differential microwave radiometer) makes the pulsations audible, discernible (Koestler, *Act* 311–12). Art (like the creation of matter) manifests itself most prominently in the boundary crossings of two or more matrices, each of which is imbued with its own meaning and form. Together they give rise to new forms through a process of repetition, elimination, and assimilation.[38]

Moreover, things have memory, we are told, a better memory than the human kind. Reflecting upon his experiences with Herbert in the Maritime Museum, the showcase of past human actions, Oskar comes to understand that memory is embedded in everything from carpets to wallpaper, kitchen chairs, coat hangers, ashtrays, and wooden replicas of people, such as Niobe. Not God, but each and everyone of these objects registers events and bears witness to human acts (*TD* 192). The German original reads:

---

36 Grass: "Die tausend Bleche, die ich zum Schrott geworfen hatte, und das eine Blech, das auf dem Friedhof Saspe begraben lag, sie standen auf, erstanden aufs neue, feierten heil und ganz Auferstehung, ließen sich hören, füllten mich aus" (*BT* 666).

37 This is the thrust of the chapter "Von der Selbst-Überwindung" in Part 2 of Nietzsche's *Zarathustra* (*KSA* 4:146–49).

38 George Smoot and Keay Davidson draw attention to the importance of "border areas" at the subatomic level when they cite Alfvén's theory that the interaction of opposites causes the universe to expand: "At the boundaries between regions of matter and antimatter, the two mix and annihilate each other; the resulting heat and pressure at the boundary would separate the main bodies of matter and antimatter." It is a process of eternal creation. See Smoot and Davidson, *Wrinkles of Time* (New York: William Morrow, 1993), 99.

> Heute weiß ich, daß alles zuguckt, daß nichts unbesehen bleibt, daß selbst Tapeten ein besseres Gedächtnis als die Menschen haben. Es ist nicht etwa der liebe Gott, der alles sieht! Ein Küchenstuhl, Kleiderbügel, halbvoller Aschenbecher oder das hölzerne Abbild einer Frau, genannt Niobe, reichen aus, um jeder Tat den unvergeßlichen Zeugen liefern zu können. (*BT* 247)

We may forget, but things remember. Instances of other objects that register human deeds abound in the text: drumsticks, ring fingers, body organs, eels, patent leather belts, skat cards, skirts, fiber rugs, onions, concrete bunkers, combs, coffins, scars, cartridge cases, Kashubian potato fields, 60-watt light bulbs, etc. You can drum their memories out of them if you find the correct resonance (that is, adopt the right attitude – see chapter 2). Things serve as so many memory chips in the total economy of life. It is especially fitting, then, that tin, a cheap and readily available material drawn from the earth itself, serves as the medium of memory for Oskar while also functioning as the ordering principle of life. It is an all-natural product, like the simple wooden flute that the jazz musician Klepp plays in accompaniment to Oskar's renewed life with the drum (*TD* 507, *BT* 667). Abstracted from rational reasoning, the drum simultaneously symbolizes the human conscience and the medium of reconciliation between violence and innocence, chaos and order. In this sense, the drum is both receiver and transmitter, with Oskar its energy source. Far from being an anti-palingeneticist, Oskar reconnects and makes whole again.

6. Sex unto Death

The quivering motion described in chapter 3, "Moth and Light Bulb," or the revolutions of the merry-go-round in chapter 33, "Disinfectant," represent much purposive movement. But it was still without specific content. The theme of general (com)motion is transferred from the moth to the one part of Oskar's anatomy that did grow. His penis; specifically referred to as a "third drumstick"(*TD* 280; *BT* 363), it grows to messianic proportions (*TD* 61; *BT* 71). The theme of sexuality and movement is picked up dramatically in the graphic breakwater scene at Neufahrwasser. There we witness Alfred Matzerath help a longshoreman fish a decapitated horse's head out of the water. Phallic-like eels squirm in and out of its orifices, causing Agnes, who is pregnant, to feel nauseous and lose her breakfast. Lest the intimate connection between the function of eels in the decomposition of matter and the creative function of the phallus in the total economy of life be lost on the reader, the narrator draws special attention to the eels and the long illicit affair between Agnes and her cousin Jan Bronski. First, there is the report about the woman who attempted to take her pleasure with an eel only to have it bite into her and refuse to let go (*TD* 152; *BT* 194). It had to be surgically removed in the hospital, after which the woman could not bear any children.[39] Following the episode with the horse's head, Agnes and Alfred argue over the eels, which Alfred is preparing for their Good Friday meal. Agnes retires in tears to the bedroom, flinging herself on the bed beneath the print of the repentant Mary Magdalene, like herself the perfect blend of harlot and Madonna. There Jan seeks her out. Using his middle finger to distract her and satisfy her deepest urges, Jan is able to help Agnes compose herself (*TD* 158; *BT* 202). Jan's finger here mirrors the phallic quality of the eel. Oskar observes the entire action from his hiding place within the "womb" of his mother's clothes closet, close to her white nurse's uniform accentuated by the redness of the Red Cross button. The interplay of the whiteness of innocence and the redness of passion and caring mirrors the harlot-Madonna act insinuated by the picture of Mary Magdalene (a perfect reflectaphor) and being played out anew on the connubial bed.

The reader is prepared for this interconnection of sex, life, and death when she reads that the eels are placed in a bag of salt in order to clear them of slime and prepare them for smoking. It is an unpleasant form of death with a powerful metaphorical message: "For when eels are in salt, they can't help wriggling and they wriggle until they are dead, leaving their slime in the salt" (*TD* 151; *BT* 194). By implication, human beings are placed on this earth and are motivated to move relentlessly until they leave their slime in the salt of the earth and die. Alfred and the longshoreman feel it is right to prepare the eels for smoking in this way, even though the procedure is forbidden. They justify their actions by stating that the eels "crawl into the horse's head ... and into human corpses, too" (*TD* 152; *BT* 194). Thus, it seems fitting to let them wriggle to their deaths. Only gradually does it dawn on the reader that the eels are a metaphor for "sex unto death" as it is subsequently played out in this chapter and the next, "Tapered at the Foot End," in which the connection between sex and violence is recounted through the scars on Herbert Truczinski's back. The association is later continued in the ring finger motif of chapter 44, "The Ring Finger," in connection with the disastrous love triangle involving nurse Dorothea. The dog Lux discovers the finger and brings it to Oskar that fateful day in the "garden of Eden" outside Düsseldorf. Oskar's own

---

39 It would be a stretch to see in this interlude a veiled parallel to the parable of the shepherd boy and the snake in Nietzsche's *Thus Spoke Zarathustra*, in which Zarathustra exhorts the boy to bite off the snake's head and thereby save himself. However, the eel episode does lead Agnes to confront her inescapable fate – even as the boy faced his – and "bite the bullet" in the chapter "Tapered at the Foot End." In a striking parallel to the story of the eel biting into the woman at the end of "Special Communiqués," Oskar's bites into Maria's private parts in anger and desperation and holds fast (*TD* 291).

infatuation with nurses is caught up in the matrix of sexual attraction and rejection. Tossing eels into a sack of salt is thus an allegory of people being born into an existence that makes them struggle on earth until they are dead.

After the bedroom episode, Agnes, only superficially placated by Jan's adept finger, begins to eat fish and in such great quantities that she poisons herself. She seems "possessed by some mysterious demon" or, as Alfred says, "like somebody was making you" do it (*TD* 160; *BT* 205). The men are distraught, not knowing what to think. But Oskar knows, for he realizes that his mother has forgotten neither the breakwater nor the horse's head. He knows that "[e]very organ in her body stored up the bitter memory of that Good Friday excursion and for fear that it be repeated, her organs saw to it that my mama, who was quite in agreement with them, should die" ("Ihre Organe erinnerten sich schmerzhaft überdeutlich an den Karfreitagsspaziergang und ließen, aus Angst vor einer Wiederholung des Spaziergangs, meine Mama, die mit ihren Organen einer Meinung war, sterben"; *TD* 161; *BT* 207). Agnes was looking for a way out. Indeed, Oskar surmises that his mother had been searching for years for a way out of the interminable love triangle (Alfred–Agnes–Jan) with the men figuratively drumming her into her grave. "Fish" becomes a stand-in for "eel" and thus a phallic symbol.[40] Later, in Book 3 in the chapter entitled "In the Clothes Cupboard," which parallels this earlier scene in self-similar if not selfsame ways, Oskar recalls that his mother ate so much fish because she "was sick of eels and sick of life, especially of men, perhaps also of Oskar" (*TD* 496; *BT* 652). Sitting in nurse Dorothea's closet surrounded by her white uniforms, Oskar contemplates a patent leather belt, which he likens to the eels on the breakwater. All the while masturbating. The one thing he cannot do without, he confides are "smoked eels; whatever the price, I can't live without them" (*TD* 496; *BT* 652). Here the implication is that he, like his mother, cannot do without sex. Thus, the connotations of "Good Friday Fare" as sex unto death loom large as one of the major messages of the novel. The old " myth" of Christ's death and resurrection is retold as the tale of the eternal return of sexual reproduction and destruction, of love and violence.

Later, as his mother's coffin is being lowered into the ground in "Tapered at the Foot End," Oskar feels the urge to mount that fish-shaped container and ride it and his mother's womb back into the bowels of the earth. There drumming until he could drum no longer, he and his mother would give over their flesh to the worms for recycling. In these worms we might want to see a reflectaphor of the eel motif.

40 Women are treated primarily as sex objects in *The Tin Drum*, generally standing in contrast to Gretchen and the *mater gloriosa* in *Faust* as symbolic of the essentially asexual "Eternal Feminine." For a detailed examination of Grass's attitude toward questions of sex and gender in his oeuvre, see Claudia Mayer-Iswandy, *"Vom Glück der Zwitter." Geschlechterrolle und Geschlechterverhältnis bei Günter Grass* (Frankfurt a. M.: Peter Lang, 1990), esp. 96–131, 146–54.

The urge echoes his response to his failure to get the little baby Jesus to drum in the Church of the Sacred Heart on Holy Thursday. Oskar takes it so hard because Jesus was his "spit and image" right down to his "watering can" (*TD* 141; *BT* 180). Because of Jesus's failure to drum, Oskar considers himself to be the "realer Jesus" ("eher ist Oskar ein echter Jesus als der"; *TD* 143; *BT* 182). While Jesus will go down into the grave, Oskar concludes, "I shall keep on drumming and drumming, but never again experience any desire for a miracle" ("Schluß mit ihm ... der mir gleicht und doch falsch ist, der ins Grab muß, während ich weitertrommeln und weitertrommeln, aber nach keinem Wunder mehr Verlangen zeigen werde"; *TD* 145–46; *BT* 186). Conflating the image of Jesus descending into the grave and of his own continuous drumming, Oskar would accompany his mother back into the earth. Agnes's being pregnant when she takes her life underscores her desire to cut short the endless cycle of sex, reproduction, and recycling. The image of Oskar sitting on top of his mother's coffin and drumming beneath the earth lends weight to his function as the reincarnation of Proteurhythmos. (Later in the narrative, he senses the same urge to climb up on Mother Truczinski's coffin at her funeral.) As the "realer Jesus," Oskar offers no redemption from the endless cycle; he "turned his back on the crucified athlete," devoting his attention instead to the eternal child theme ("auch dem Turner am Kreuz"; *TD* 140; *BT* 179). Perhaps that is why the German title of the chapter, "Verjüngung zum Fußende," intimates rejuvenation, an association lost in translation.

Yet there is a certain paradox in Oskar's rivalry with Jesus. It is spelled out at the beginning of "Good Friday Fare." The disappointment in Jesus's failure to drum meant that Oskar has the drum to himself. No rival to fear. However, the paradox extends further, for Oskar has no power over the sacred: he is incapable of shattering church windows with his voice, although all "profane" glass succumbs to his power. He is "at home neither in the sacred nor the profane but dwell[s] on the fringes" (*TD* 146; *BT* 187). Oskar's position between the realms of the sacred and the profane is revealing of his deeper significance; that is, he is neither saint nor devil, neither savior nor destroyer. He is part and parcel of life but is not absolutely identifiable with any one part. In a sense he is like Mephisto, who is part of the Whole and, through his opposition to the Something and advocacy of Nothingness, ensures that the dialectic of existence continues. A large part of that effect derives from Oskar's synthesizing of the positive and negative forces of existence: energy/matter, dark energy/dark matter, light/reason and dark/instinct, good/ordered movement and evil/sudden eruption.[41] Master Bebra, Oskar's tutor in the

41 We should remember that Oskar is powerfully attracted to Roswitha Raguna, who acts as a reflectaphor of the basic operative principle in the novel. Her given name, Roswitha, literally means "red and white," a reference to passion/violence on the one hand and innocence on the

ways of the world, remarks that Oskar's genius contains both divine and diabolical elements, that he is marked by "a certain immoderation, a certain explosiveness" ("jäh ausbrechende Maßlosigkeit"; *TD* 172; *BT* 205). And of course Oskar not only heals the pain of others through his drumming as, for instance, in the Onion Cellar. But he also tempts others to crime by cutting convenient holes in store windows for passers-by to avail themselves of exposed goods. Oskar as Tempter; Oskar as Jesus.

The penultimate chapter in the novel, "The Last Streetcar, or Adoration of a Preserving Jar," picks up on the motif of the divine and diabolic in salient manner. In it Oskar narrates his encounter with Gottfried Vittlar, who later denounces him to the police for the murder of nurse Dorothea Köngetter. Gottfried (whose name connotes "peace of God") is lying in the crook of an apple tree in his mother's garden, observing Oskar with his rental dog, Lux. The dog, whose Latin name means "light" and resonates with Lucifer, the name of the fallen archangel, finds nurse Dorothea's ring finger and brings it to Oskar, "tempting" him to take it. Accepting the disembodied finger as a mythic sign, Oskar places the ring in a preserving jar and establishes it as the centerpiece of a shrine set up in Dorothea's former boarding room. Pointedly, Vittlar alludes to his own role of Snake and Tempter in the Garden of Eden. Vittlar, who is described as being "long, willowy, vivacious, collapsible" (that is, like a serpent, even though Oskar says "angel"), becomes friends with the drummer precisely because of Oskar's "particular variety of evil, that drumming of his, which resolved evil into its rhythmical components" (*TD* 562–66; *BT* 743–48). Refusing to turn the finger in as evidence in a murder case, Oskar claims it as his own, explaining that just such a finger had been prophesied on the occasion of his birth – "in code to be sure, the word actually employed being 'drumstick.'"[42] The associations Oskar draws summarize succinctly violent dimensions of the narrative: the finger-length scars on Herbert Truczinski's back and the cartridge case from Saspe cemetery (referring to Jan Bronski's execution). Vittlar acknowledges that a discerning person could not help but see the logic of symbolic progression: "drumstick, scar, cartridge case, ring finger" (*TD* 568). Thus, the drumstick is the source of everything that follows, not just of violence. The rhythms it evokes represent Oskar's particular variety of evil, namely, the movement inherent in existence. In this movement resides that which we know as evil since Adam and Eve's fall from grace and the need to ensure their existence by the sweat of their brow. This is not "evil" in a traditional Catholic

other. Then, too, Roswitha is timeless, an old lady of ninety or a young women of eighteen with smooth yet wrinkled skin (*TD* 171). Thus, she unifies in her person the opposites, much like the trick picture of the young-old woman cited in chapter 2 (fig. 2.7). (we can also see in the colors an allusion to the national colors of Poland.)

42 *TD* 567–68; *BT* 750: "wenn auch verschlüsselt durch das Wort Trommelstock."

sense, but it is in the modern sense of chaos and complexity (see chapter 4). Through his drumming Oskar has gotten to the bottom of things. Or perhaps we should rather say that Oskar has gotten back to the beginning of things.

Herbert Truczinski's back is one of the primary texts for deciphering the varieties of evil Vittlar speaks of. Although not quite achieving the status of grandmother Koljaiczek's four potato-colored skirts – the " eternal womanly" that draws Oskar forever onward – the large, round, scarred back nonetheless looms large as a semiotic sign in the novel, assuming mythic proportions. The numerous scars are always in motion, each wound haing its own particular variety of violent movement to tell. By being permitted to touch the scars, Oskar launches the narrative process of interconnectivity stored in Herbert's body, concluding each tale with the ritualistic phrase "and that's the scar." The scars prove to be highly significant to Oskar, who places them in the same category as "the secret parts of a few women and young girls, my own pecker, the plaster watering can of the boy Jesus, and the ring finger" (*TD* 178; *BT* 229). Whenever Oskar wished later to recall Herbert's back, he would drum, contemplating nurse Dorothea's ring finger. In this manner he would conjure up "the symbols on Herbert's back" ("die Zeichen auf Herberts Rücken"; *TD* 178; *BT* 229), transporting himself to the violence behind the welts, the undulations of aroused reproductive organs, the ring finger, the drumstick, and ultimately the umbilical cord, for "my umbilical cord [...] promised me successively drumsticks, Herbert's scars," and everything else that followed from birth (*TD* 178). Indeed, Oskar admits quite openly, the whole purpose of reading the script of Herbert's scars was to get back to the umbilical chord, back to the womb (*TD* 179; *BT* 229). Like a blind man he reads that script again and again (*TD* 196; *BT* 252). Ultimately, Herbert impales himself on a double-sided ax in a vain effort to mount the wooden figurehead Niobe, the seducer and destroyer of men, the queen of Thebes, who had been punished by Apollo and Artemis for raising herself up too high. Thus, for Herbert too we can speak of a dynamic of "sex unto death." In his case, however, the emphasis is on the violence of life.

A further variation on that theme is provided by the greengrocer and scout master Albrecht Greff, whose homosexual love for a youth drives him to commit suicide in an elaborate drumming machine. That is the subject of chapter 25, "165 lbs."("75 Kilo"), in Book 2 . It draws special attention to the unity of the drumming motif, mythological creation, procreation in the potato fields, the guilt of transgression, and expiation and confession through self-annihilation. While the immediate cause of Greff's elaborate suicide is the summons for immoral behavior (as a scout master he engaged in a homosexual relationship with a minor, Horst Donath), the elaborateness of the mechanism by which he takes his life emphatically underscores the interconnectedness of sexuality, drumming, and the need for balance. Because of the extraordinary machine Greff had constructed to end his life, Oskar comes to regard suicide as one of the noble forms of death (*TD* 317; *BT* 415).

After the death of Horst Donath on the front, Albrecht Greff begins to go downhill, neglecting his appearance, ignoring his business, becoming more and more of a crank, and investing all his time in inventing noise machines that ring and howl. One of these "music machines" in particular attracted Oskar's attention: a drumming machine activated by weights and balances and involving potatoes. The machine and its operation are described in significant detail worthy of citation:

> A wooden framework, inside it a pair of scales, evenly balanced with potatoes; when a potato was removed from one pan, the scales were thrown off balance and released a lever which set off the drumming mechanism installed on top of the frame. There followed a rolling as of kettledrums, a booming and clanking, basins struck together, a gong rang out, and the end of it all was a tinkling, transitory, tragically cacophonous finale. (*TD* 310)

> [In ein hölzernes Gerüst hängte er zwei ins Gleichgewicht gebrachte, mit Kartoffeln gefüllte Schalen, nahm sodann eine Kartoffel aus der linken Schale: die Waage schlug aus und löste eine Sperre, die den auf dem Gerüst installierten Trommelmechanismus freigab: das wirbelte, bumste, knatterte, scharrte, Becken schlugen zusammen, der Gong dröhnte, und alles zusammen fand ein endliches schepperndes, tragisch mißtönendes Finale.] (*BT* 405–406).

Oskar's response is simple: "The machine appealed to me" ("Mir gefiel die Maschine"; *TD* 310; *BT* 406). As well it might, given the drumming effect that transforms ordered balanced into tragic cacophony. The rhythms that are created mirror in a different medium the script of Herbert's massive round back, which is constantly in motion. Like those scars, the drumming machine takes on deep meaning for Oskar who even suspects that the greengrocer has built the drumming machine specifically for him, the gnomic drummer. But no, the machine is intended for Greff himself, as becomes clear on an October day in 1942 when Greff hangs himself, his 75 kilo weight (minus 100 grams) neatly balanced by potatoes in the scaffolding constructed to augment the drumming machine itself.

At the sight of the grocer hanging by his neck, Oskar experiences a tingling feeling that invades every part of his body, converging on his sex organ, moving up his spine, through his hump, and lodging in his neck, where it chokes and stabs him. Oskar feels this sensation not only then, but afterwards whenever anyone speaks of hanging anything ("saß mir abermals ... im Nacken, verengte sich dort – es sticht und würgt Oskar heutzutage noch"; *TD* 315; *BT* 412). An explicit connection is thus made between Greff's suicide, the drumming that drove him to it, and the piston-like action of the penis (Joseph Koljaiczek's penis is referred to as a piston in the potato field where Oskar's mother was conceived [*TD* 24; *BT* 21]).[43]

43 It also recalls the choking induced by the snake that crawled into the shepherd boy's throat in

Initially shocked at the sight, Oskar quickly grows accustomed to the hanging man as being entirely natural. Greff's death is described as "a well-balanced" death, for he had weighted himself to the ounce.

The entire scene verges "on the sublime" (*TD* 316; *BT* 413), with the sublimity underscored by the geometry of the setting. Greff and his counterweight hang within a frame. The four corners are paralleled by four whitewashed crossbeams and the interior of the frame is illuminated by four light bulbs painted white to accentuate the hanging human and the inert potatoes. On the four main beams supporting the scaffolding are four little pictures: one of Baden-Powell, founder of the World Scout Movement; another of St. George, the dragon slayer; yet another of Michelangelo's homoerotic head of David; and a fourth of the handsome boy, Horst Donath. The solemnity of the scene is evoked by the brilliant white light bulbs focusing attention on Greff, the whiteness of the scaffolding, the flowers strewn about in homage to Greff's "heroes," and the precise calculations evident everywhere. The surprise comes when Greff's body is taken down from his "cross." The ordered symmetry and rational clarity inherent in the earthly number four that is recurrent in the scene (various right angles, four-sided geometric structures in the scaffolding, four pictures, the summons torn into four pieces, the age of Horst Donath in the photograph estimated at 4x4) comes undone when Greff's body is lowered. The release of chaos is more than merely metaphorical – it is virtual. Grass writes:

> No sooner had they lifted him than the potato baskets making a counterweight fell with a crash, releasing a mechanism similar to that of the drumming machine, housed on top of the scaffolding but discreetly sheathed in plywood. While down below potatoes rolled over the platform or fell directly to the concrete floor, up above, clappers pounded upon tin, wood, bronze, and glass, an orchestra of drums was unleashed: Albrecht Greff's grand finale. (*TD* 317)
>
> [Kaum jedoch, daß sie den Händler gelüpft hatten, fielen und stürzten die das Gegengewicht bildenden Kartoffelkörbe: Ähnlich wie bei der Trommelmaschine begann ein freigewordener Mechanismus zu arbeiten, den Greff geschickt oberhalb des Gerüstes mit Sperrholz verkleidet hatte. Während unten die Kartoffeln übers und vom Podest auf den Betonboden polterten, schlug es oben auf Blech, Holz, Bronze, Glas, hämmerte oben ein entfesseltes Trommelorchester Albrecht Greffs großes Finale.] (*BT* 415)

The organized din of Greff's drumming machine and of his final removal from the frame of his life fascinates Oskar yet proves to be difficult for him to emulate. The very fact that the potatoes released by Greff (beyond the grave, so to speak) represent a "windfall" to the ambulance drivers is noteworthy. In a time of scarce

---

Zarathustra. The snake, of course, symbolizes the inevitability of the life cycle that leads deeper into life, guilt, death, and the eternal return. It all began with the serpent in the Garden of Eden.

produce, the greengrocer distributes in death life-sustaining *pommes de terre* to the living. The interconnection of life and death, drumming and potatoes – all of which are held together in a delicate balance – underscores the essentiality of that balance for an ordered existence, whose fragility is equally manifest. There is much purposive movement, here even when it is chaotic.

Lucy Rennwand also represents much purposive movement, though it is associated with triangular shapes rather than rectangular ones. The metaphorical reflections upon her significance are integrated in the fabric of historical events and punctuated by mythical allusions. The framework for Lucy and the purposive movement associated with her is provided by the trial of the Dusters' and the fall of Danzig narrated in chapter 31 of the novel in Book 2, "The Ant Trail" (*TD* 382–95, *BT* 502–18). The ant trail is a direct reference to the mundaneness of the events witnessed, suggesting that human tragedy is anchored in the everyday processes of nature. The actual plot developments accentuated in this chapter are twofold: first, the trial of the teenage gang called the Dusters and, second, the fall of Danzig to the Russians in January 1945. The latter is intimately connected to the death of Alfred Matzerath, who chokes on his Nazi Party pin, and to the rape of Lina Greff. The opening and closing frames of these very real and historical events are simultaneously mundane and mythical.

The first half of the chapter is devoted to a rendition of the actual trial of the Dusters via the allegory of a thirty-foot diving board. Lucy Rennwand, "the witness and virgin temptress," lures the Dusters one by one to take the fatal leap into an empty swimming pool (*TD* 385, *BT* 506). Only Oskar, whom Lucy addresses as "sweet Jesus," does not jump. Standing on the edge of the diving board high above the proceedings and suspended between heaven and earth, Oskar has a vision of all the disparate and intermingled activities of humankind at the very moment he is tempted to leap. By taking the plunge he would acknowledge his guilt and responsibility for the deeds of the Dusters whose leader he has been. Oskar explains:

> at my feet I saw not only Europe but the whole world. Americans and Japanese were doing a torch dance on the island of Luzon, dancing so hard that slant-eyes and round-eyes alike lost the buttons off their uniforms. But at the very same moment a tailor in Stockholm was sewing buttons on a handsome suit of evening clothes. Mountbatten was feeding Burmese elephants shells of every caliber. A widow in Lima was teaching her parrot to say "Caramba." In the middle of the Pacific two enormous aircraft carriers, done up to look like Gothic cathedrals, stood face to face, sent up their planes, and simultaneously sank one another. The planes had no place to land, they hovered helplessly and quite allegorically like angels in mid-air, using up their fuel with a terrible din. (*TD* 384)

> [da lag mir die Welt zu Füßen und nicht nur Europa. Da tanzten Amerikaner und Japaner einen Fackeltanz auf der Insel Luzon. Da verloren Schlitzäugige und Rundäugige Knöpfe an ihren Mon-

> turen. Da gab es aber in Stockholm einen Schneider, der nähte zum selben Zeitpunkt Knöpfe an einen dezent gestreiften Abendanzug. Da fütterte Mountbatten die Elefanten Burmas mit Geschossen aller Kaliber. Da lehrte gleichzeitig eine Witwe in Lima ihren Papagei das Wörtchen "Caramba" nachsprechen. Da schwammen mitten im Pazifik zwei mächtige, wie gotische Kathedralen verzierte Flugzeugträger aufeinander zu, ließen ihre Flugzeuge starten und versenkten sich gegenseitig. Die Flugzeuge aber konnten nicht mehr landen, hingen hilflos und rein allegorisch gleich Engeln in der Luft und verbrauchten brummend ihren Brennstoff.] (*BT* 505)

The description goes on to include mundane private acts and historical military actions in other parts of the world. "Inevitably," we are informed, "the thread of events wound itself into loops and knots which became known as the fabric of history" ("So blieb es nicht aus, daß der Faden des Zeitgeschehens, der vorne noch hungrig war, Schlingen schlug und Geschichte machte, hinten schon zur Historie gestrickt wurde"; *TD* 385; *BT* 505). The loops and knots of thread are reminiscent not only of the activities of the three fates (Clotho, Lachesis, Atropos) but also of the string figures that Bruno, Oskar's keeper in the mental hospital, is fond of making and that are largely based on the characters in Oskar's narration. Unfortunately, the English translation does not capture the salient nexus of future and past events in the German formulation.

All of this movement seems due to the virgin temptress, Lucy Rennwand. The name "Lucy" is of course a reference to "Lucifer," while "Rennwand" intimates running up against a wall. Taking the leap from the diving board balanced between air and firmament is tantamount to plunging into the contingencies of existence and incurring guilt. Oskar consciously refuses to accept the challenge to open himself up to guilt and failure – to be what Nietzsche had labeled a tempter and attempter – and reverts to the role of the innocent three-year-old to extricate himself from the fabric of history and guilt. Oskar refers to the metaphorically framed trial as the second trial of Jesus, pointing forward to the ring finger trial to determine who murdered nurse Dorothea. That last trial styled as the "third trial of Jesus" (*TD* 385; *BT* 506), concludes with a determination of Oskar's innocence in the nurse's murder and signals his imminent release from the asylum.

But to return to "The Ant Trail," the second half of the chapter narrates the circumstances of Alfred Matzerath's demise. Huddled in the Matzerath's cellar, the family and close friends are discovered by the invading Russian soldiers. As "three of the rectangular uniforms" turn their attention to Lina Greff, orderly and calmly having their way with her, Oskar espies some ants marching in military style from the winter potatoes to a sugar sack. Oskar notes specifically that the "purposeful industry" of the ants, which he has been using as a standard to measure historical events, remains undisturbed by the human activities above them.[44] When Alfred

44 *TD* 393. The German is more evocative of what that purposeful industry is designed to connote:

tries to swallow the Nazi Party pin Oskar has slipped back into his hand, the soldiers jump up expectantly, ordering him to stand still. Oskar had opened the clasp of the pin so that it lodges firmly in Alfred's throat. Gasping for air, dancing agitatedly, and thrashing wildly about with his arms, Alfred Matzerath is hurried to his death by a machine-gun burst. When he crashes to the floor across their "highway," the ants, undeterred by this occurrence, soon find a new path and detour (*TD* 394–95; *BT* 518). The juxtaposition of these two events – human and insect – underscores the integrated naturalness of human violence. It is all part of a pattern; it is all in the motion from order to disruption back again to an ordered state, an insight that is supported in numerous ways throughout the narrative. It begins with the early remark that Grandma Koljaiczek's four skirts never lost their potato color "despite the most violent military, political, and historical upheavals" (*TD* 416; *BT* 547). And it continues in the later metaphor of life as a merry-go-round that keeps on turning round and round, carrying its riders past the heavenly father, the merry-go-round owner, who alternately appears as the mad Rasputin and the rational Goethe (*TD* 412; *BT* 542). The cycle of life continues for Oskar and Maria and even Lina Greff after the fall of their world. Out of the chaos of destruction arises new order.

7. The Black Wicked Witch

The chapter "The Ant Trail" contains one of the first emphatic references to Oskar's innermost fear – actually, his nightmare. It is of Lucy Rennwand, the skinny teenager who is neither ugly nor pretty; androgynous, she is "always biting men." He fears that one day she "will turn up in the shape of the wicked witch" and for the last time bid Oskar to take the plunge from the diving board (*TD* 386). The image of a serpentine individual biting men recalls the mythical serpent in the Garden of Eden and, more immediately, the eel with which the woman was taking her pleasure when it bit firmly and held fast. Oskar's worst nightmare is realized metaphorically in the final chapter, 46, "Thirty," when the trial for the murder of nurse Dorothea is drawing to a close. Oskar is about to be exonerated, released from his safe haven, and forced back into the muddy stream of life. There he will have to accept himself as he is.

The constant switching from "Oskar" to "I" by the narrator in the novel is

---

"Mich und meine Trommel nahm jemand vom Beton weg auf den Arm und hinderte mich somit, weiterhin und vergleichsweise die Ameisen zu beobachten und an ihrem Fleiß das Zeitgeschehen zu messen" (*BT* 516). The reference to "Zeitgeschehen" connects the ant trail sequence to the mingling of myth and history in narrating the Dusters' trial at the beginning of the chapter.

indicative of Oskar's inability to shed all masks and to accept himself as he really is: Oskar the hunchback with the past of a three-year-old drummer. Yet he is not merely a three-year-old drummer, nor an inmate in a mental institution, nor the responsible adult German citizen of the late 1940s and 1950s. His essence as an individual, like the variety of evil his drumming represents, is not characterized by any particular role he assumes but is the total sum of all these roles taken together. This is the ultimate truth that Oskar must face: he is not one but many. While Oskar consistently refuses to recognize that mere existence entails action and thus responsibility, the Black Wicked Witch is symbolic of the specter of action and responsibility that forever hovers behind, near, and finally before him. She is the "sweetness" of sugar for the ants, the strange attractor of (com)motion for everyone and everything. Evil resides, then, in the motion itself so that evolution makes evil in a postmodern sense unavoidable (cf. Baudrillard, Rötzer). Symbolic of that postmodern sense is the Black Wicked Witch. Perhaps she can also be viewed as a consequence of the denial of the doctrine of sufficient reason. Because humans cannot be sure of the contingency of their actions, they have no assurance that the world and their very own existence in it are predictable. The Black Wicked Witch, then, is a metaphor for the absurdity of life with its hallmark characteristic of predictable unpredictability. Alone in the universe, man is forced to accept responsibility for his every action, even if that action is ultimately beyond his control. Hence, the Witch also symbolizes human fear of the unknown. Moreover, she is analogous to Goethe's Care, who blinds Faust by virtue of all the encumbering big and little experiences of life. Ultimately, like the spirit of gravity, they weigh heavily and prepare one for death. Like the script on Herbert Truczinski's back, Care leaves her mark with every fold of existence.

Riding the escalator in his eternally present memory of how he landed in the asylum from which he is now to be released, Oskar is possessed alternately by anticipation and dread. Actually, he feels quite at home on that escalator despite his terror and fear of the Witch. He reflects upon its mechanical structure as "a gentle, easygoing contrivance" that could lead either to his grandmother Anna Koljaiczek or to the Witch at the top, for they are complementary opposites like Goethe and Rasputin (*TD* 586; *BT* 775). He could step off this contrivance as either a three-year-old child or a man of sixty. As he ascends from the depths of the earth, from his asylum, from behind the mask of the *puer aeternus* to the surface where life is played out as a dangerous game that none can win, Oskar celebrates his thirtieth birthday. All possibilities are open to him on this momentous occasion as he imagines himself on the escalator, wondering whether it is "high, steep, and symbolic enough" to conclude his recollections (*TD* 583; *BT* 771). Can one speak of it as having a "first step" (*TD* 583; *BT* 771)? Actually, it does not because the step keeps reappearing. It follows, then, that it does not have a last step either, rising from the deep structures below at a 45 degree angle to the surface to change direction and receding once again at a 45 degree angle into the depths. Growing older and growing younger are wrapped up in the same cycle, as are having lofty feelings aroused and knowledge enriched. The two 45 degree inclines form two sides of a triangle, the base of which is firmly planted in the earth. That is why Oskar feels at home on the escalator (*TD* 586).[45]

"I shall call in the Black Witch and consult her," Oskar affirms, "and then tomorrow morning I shall be able to tell Bruno my keeper what mode of existence the thirty-year-old Oskar is planning to carry on in the shadow of a bugaboo which, though getting blacker and blacker, is the same old friend that used to frighten me on the cellar stairs." The Witch was there, always there in the shadows: moaning in the stove, squeaking in tune with the door, in the smoke rising from the chimneys, in the foghorns of ships, in the eels, behind the church altar, in the bag with the four bludgeoned tomcats, at the site of Jan Bronski's execution, in the special communiqués from the front, in the potatoes tumbling down from Greff's music machine, lying inside the coffin tapered at the foot end. "She had always been there," Oskar states, "even in the woodruff fizz powder, bubbling so green and innocent; she was in clothes cupboards [...] she borrowed Lucy Rennwand's triangular fox face." Indeed, the Black Witch was even lurking in the shadows as he watched the ants. Oskar knows now: "[I]t's *her* shadow that has multiplied and is following the sweetness." As the novel ends, she is coming ever closer (*TD* 587–89; *BT* 777–79). Unfortunately, the original German connotations of this sinister figure are lost, for in German she is not a witch; she is a cook ("die schwarze Köchin"), whom Oskar first gets to know when he is forced to eat some repulsive brick soup concocted by the local children. That, in turn, leads to his shunning the company of other children. The fact that she is a cook is significant for it allows her to affect our entire physical being. In this connection we are compelled to recall that Nietzsche rooted the human psyche in the body, specifically in the stomach.

45 To be sure, Oskar does wish for some changes to make himself feel even more at home. For example, he wishes that all those persons who had framed his questionable existence were riding the elevator with him rather than the strangers surrounding him. Yet in his own mind, they are all there already. His ultimate goal is to re-enter the "cave" of his grandmother's skirts. Like Zarathustra, Oskar too seeks the safe haven removed from the real world. The passage reads in in full: "Ich fühlte mich auf der Rolltreppe wie zu Hause, hätte mich glücklich geschätzt, trotz Angst und Kinderschreck, wenn es mit mir nicht wildfremde Menschen, sondern meine lebenden und toten Freunde und Verwandten hinaufgetragen hätte [...] – alle die da meine fragwürdige Existenz einrahmten, die da an meiner Existenz scheiterten – oben jedoch, wo der Rolltreppe die Luft ausging, wünschte ich mir an Stelle der Kriminalbeamten das Gegenteil der schrecklichen Schwarzen Köchin: Meine Großmutter Anna Koljaiczek sollte dort wie ein Berg ruhen und mich und mein Gefolge nach glücklicher Auffahrt unter die Röcke, in den Berg hineinnehmen" (*BT* 776).

We are what we eat.

For most of his life, Oskar had not feared the Witch. But ever since he wanted to be frightened when he fled the Interpol police to feign guilt for nurse Dorothea's murder, she has "crawled under [his] skin" (*TD* 581; *BT* 769). There she has remained to the present day. Since the Witch can assume many forms, she can stand metaphorically for the forms and shapes of reality itself:

> Sometimes, for instance, it is the name " Goethe" that sets me screaming and hiding under the bedclothes. From childhood on I have done my best to study the poet prince, and still his Olympian calm gives me the creeps. Even now, when, no longer luminous and classical but disguised as a black witch more sinister by far than any Rasputin, he peers through the bars of my bed and asks me, on the occasion of my thirtieth birthday: "Where's the Witch, black as pitch?" – I am scared stiff. (*TD* 581)

> [So kann es das Wörtchen Goethe sein, das mich aufschreien und ängstlich unter die Bettdecke flüchten läßt. So sehr ich auch von Jugend an den Dichterfürsten studierte, seine olympische Ruhe ist mir schon immer unheimlich gewesen. Und wenn er heute verkleidet, schwarz und als Köchin, nicht mehr licht und klassisch, sondern die Finsternis eines Rasputin überbietend, vor meinem Gitterbett steht und mich anläßlich meines dreißigsten Geburtstages fragt: "Ist die Schwarze Köchin da?", fürchte ich mich sehr.] (*BT* 769)

The Witch represents the wholeness of existence with its seduction to action, be it the stimulus sex, fame, violence, or classical ideals of order and harmony. Hence, it might be best to see her as a modern version of Care from Goethe's *Faust*; the wear and tear of living ultimately force Faust to slow down (entropy?). In terms of chaos and fractals, she is the pervasive, strange attractor in the novel similar to the Julia set, that "basin of attraction at the point of infinity, the set of initial conditions that move towards it under iteration" (Stewart, *Dice?* 236). She represents the interconnectedness of all things, the organizing principle of movement located deep within the structure of reality. By painting the connected points within the complex plane black, as Stewart has suggested, we can identify the basin toward which everything in its sphere is moving (*Dice?* 242). "Die schwarze Köchin" (or Black Wicked Witch) is perhaps black because of this connectedness. Just as the color black reveals the absence of reflected light (because it has taken hold and won't let go, like the eel), so has the Witch taken hold and shapes the texture of reality. On the other hand, white, the color to which Oskar is powerfully drawn, is the reflection of all light. In terms of Julia sets, moreover, white is "disconnected" and falls apart. Applying these notions of connectedness (black, guilt) and disconnectedness (white, innocence) as hermeneutic tools to Grass's text makes sense. Certainly, the grotesqueness of the narrative opens our eyes to patterns that might otherwise be considered formless.

8. Escalator Thoughts, or The Terrible Basic Text
Homo Natura

Grass seems to have made the attempt to reintegrate humankind back into nature. Beneath the "worthy verbal pomp" of all human discourse about life and its meaning scribbled from time immemorial, there lies what Nietzsche labeled in *Beyond Good and Evil* "that eternal basic text *homo natura*" (*BGE* #230). Like Nietzsche, Grass wanted to get back to that original text. The escalator ride is the appropriate time to ask the fundamental questions of life, to reconsider everything. Oskar dwells for a considerable time on his "escalator thoughts" ("Rolltreppeneinfall"): "Where are you from? Where are you going? Who are you? What is your real name? What are you after?" (*TD* 584; *BT* 773). Even earlier Oskar had acknowledged that he "liked to get to the bottom of things" ("Oskar, der allen Dingen auf den Grund gehen mußte"; *TD* 266; *BT* 345). Nietzsche sought the basic text against the backdrop of the idealism and materialism of the nineteenth century, Grass against the background of total devastation. Moreover, Grass's *The Tin Drum*, with the all pervasive Black Wicked Witch, reads like a measured response to Nietzsche's concluding call to confront humankind as it is, without any blinders, without any idealism. Nietzsche writes in *Beyond Good and Evil*:

> For to translate man back into nature; to master the many vain and fanciful interpretations and secondary meanings which have been hitherto scribbled and daubed over that eternal basic text *homo natura*; to confront man henceforth with man in the way in which, hardened by the discipline of silence, man today confronts the *rest* of nature, with the dauntless Oedipus eyes and stopped-up Odysseus ears, deaf to the siren songs of old metaphysical bird-catchers who have all too long been piping to him "you are more! You are higher! You are of a different origin!"– that may be a strange and extravagant task but it is a *task* – who would deny that? Why did we choose it, this extravagant task? Or to ask the question differently: "why knowledge at all?"(*BGE* #230)

> [Den Menschen nämlich zurückübersetzen in die Natur; über die vielen eitlen und schwärmerischen Deutungen und Nebensinne Herr werden, welche bisher über jenen ewigen Grundtext homo natura gekritzelt und gemalt wurden; machen, dass der Mensch fürderhin vor dem Menschen steht, wie er heute schon, hart geworden in der Zucht der Wissenschaft, vor der *anderen* Natur steht, mit unerschrocknen Oedipus-Augen und verklebten Odysseus-Ohren, taub gegen die Lockweisen alter metaphysischer Vogelfänger, welche ihm allzulange zugeflötet haben: "du bist mehr! Du bist höher! Du bist anderer Herkunft!" – das mag eine seltsame und tolle Aufgabe sein, aber es ist eine *Aufgabe* – wer wollte das leugnen! Warum wir sie wählten, diese tolle Aufgabe? Oder anders gefragt: "warum überhaupt Erkenntniss?"] (*KSA* 5:169)

The Tin Drum offers an answer to Nietzsche's "why knowledge at all?" We seek it and it is imposed upon us *because that is the way life is.* Oskar's ultimate objective from the moment of his birth is to return to the womb, to deny the reality of existence and the need to collect experience and gain knowledge. He does not wish to be separate from the oneness of pure potentiality. He does not seek to be the tabula rasa in need of inscriptions for meaning. The fear of individuation and loss of connectivity with the unity of being returns like a refrain throughout, occurring especially at strategic moments in the action. Oskar's reluctance to accept responsibility for his life is synonymous with the will to noncreation, a negation of the life-giving processes inherent in nature itself, not just in the species, humankind. The impossibility of returning to the womb, however, leaves Oskar with no choice but to impart meaning through his drum and to affirm life's impulses. Indeed, the wise Roswitha admonishes him: "Accustom yourself to your own existence that your heart may find peace and Satan be discomfited" (*TD* 173). Drumming reveals itself in *The Tin Drum* as Grass's answer to the Nietzschean question: What is the basic text of *homo natura*?

In *Zarathustra* and *Beyond Good and Evil* (aphorism #230), Nietzsche urges his readers to confront humanity in a scientific and objective manner: we must see humankind as a product of nature, abstracted from all idealizing tendencies. We need to view humans as part of the whole of nature, he claims. We must learn "to master the many vain and fanciful interpretations and secondary meanings which have been hitherto scribbled and daubed over that eternal basic text homo natura" (*BGE* #230). This "strange and extravagant task," as he calls it, amounts to freeing humanity from all the myth making of the past (cf. *BGE* #21). We can read *The Tin Drum* as just such an attempt to get to the bottom of things, as an attempt to decipher the ultimate text. Heaven knows that the narrative is strange and extravagant! Perhaps it must be so because "man is the animal whose nature has not been fixed" and because chance, "the law of absurdity in the total economy of mankind," is not computable (*BGE* #62). To make matters worse, Grass, like Nietzsche, foregrounds the nature of the genuine philosopher as one who "lives unphilosophically and 'unwisely,' above all imprudently, and feels the duty of a hundred attempts and temptations of life – he risks himself constantly, he plays the wicked game" (*BGE* #203). This wicked game constitutes the interactions in *The Tin Drum*. Their inscriptions are left everywhere, their memories preserved by all kinds of objects.

Even this ambiguity bears striking resemblance to Nietzsche's thinking; for example, Nietzsche contends that every profound thinker is more afraid of being understood than of being misunderstood (*BGE* #290). All in all, however, aphorism #230 in *Beyond Good and Evil* provides a concise summary of those core concepts within Nietzsche's system of thought that could very well have served as the source of inspiration for the figure of Oskar Matzerath. As previously noted, Grass indicated in a review of 1972 that he always has a philosopher or philosophy in mind when he composes one of his books, either to show that the thinker is wrong or that he is right. The iconoclastic nature of *The Tin Drum*, with its growing sense of the existential dilemma of humanity, reflects the qualities of Nietzsche's problematic free spirit, who is attracted to life yet prefers to exist on the fringes of society. These impulses in the novel include:

- the mixing of Apollonian and Dionysian forces in Oskar;
- Oskar's aloofness from, yet involvement in, the processes of life;
- his continual denial yet acceptance of responsibility for his actions;
- his urge to withdraw from existence altogether;
- his simultaneous baroque exuberance in the delight that the things of existence provide (belts, eels, uniforms, fingers, Niobe, etc.);
- his sense of superiority over the "herd"; and
- his going over and going under.

Oskar emerges, then, as an exemplification of Nietzsche's will to power, which lauds mastery of self and surroundings. Nietzsche explains it as follows:

> That commanding something which the people call "spirit" wants to be master within itself and around itself and to feel itself master; out of multiplicity it has the will to simplicity, a will which binds together and tames, which is imperious and domineering. In this its needs and capacities are the same as those which physiologists posit for everything that lives, grows, and multiplies. The poser of the spirit to appropriate what is foreign to it is revealed in a strong inclination to assimilate the new to the old, to simplify the complex, to overlook or repel what is wholly contradictory: just as it arbitrarily emphasizes, extracts and falsifies to suit itself certain traits and lines in what is foreign to it, in every piece of "external world." (*BGE* #230)
>
> [Das befehlerische Etwas, das vom Volke "der Geist" genannt wird, will in sich und um sich herum Herr sein und sich als Herrn fühlen: es hat den Willen aus der Vielheit zur Einfachheit, einen zusammenschnürenden, bändigenden, herschsüchtigen und wirklich herrschaftlichen Willen. Seine Bedürfnisse und Vermögen sind hierin die selben, wie sie die Physiologen für Alles, was lebt, wächst und sich vermehrt, aufstellen. Die Kraft des Geistes, Fremdes sich anzueignen, offenbart sich in einem starken Hange, das Neue dem Alten anzuähnlichen, das Mannichfaltige zu vereinfachen, das gänzlich Widersprechende zu übersehen oder wegzustossen: ebenso wie er bestimmte Züge und Linien am Fremden, an jedem Stück "Aussenwelt" willkürlich stärker unterstreicht, heraushebt, sich zurecht fälscht.] (*KSA* 5:167)

This clear and precise statement of the essential tension between the growth process of assimilating and separating recurs in even more emphatic fashion in his posthumous *Will to Power* (aphorism #619), in which Nietzsche expands upon the concept of energy precisely as the "will to power."[46] Finding evidence of this

46 Friedrich Nietzsche, *The Will to Power*, trans. by Walter Kaufmann and R. J. Hollingdale (New

phenomenon throughout organic nature, Nietzsche concludes: "There is nothing for it: one is obliged to understand all motion, all 'appearances,' all 'laws' only as symptoms of an inner event and to employ man as an analogy to this end. In the case of an animal, it is possible to trace all its drives to the will to power; likewise all the functions of organic life to this one source" (#619). Moreover, as argued in chapter 3 of this study, the will to power extends even into inorganic nature.

Oskar's desire to expand and appropriate with the purpose of controlling is manifest in his rivalry with Jesus to determine who is the "realer Jesus." Oskar considers himself the "realer" Jesus because he drums, because he is in tune with the rhythmic undulations and stochastic disruptions of order, because he affirms life over any hope for a harmonious afterlife. Oskar's desire to control is manifest, furthermore, in his claim of responsibility for various deaths. He also asserts that he is Kurt's father. Finally, Oskar regulates his own biological growth, echoing Faust's emphatic "But I will!" (*TD* 409; *BT* 538). This and every other decision is critical to regulating his life and the lives of those around him. Yet once thrown into the "muddy stream" of life, as we know from Goethe's *Faust*, Hesse's *Steppenwolf*, and Nietzsche's *Beyond Good and Evil*, the guilt-laden contingency of existence is ultimately unavoidable and beyond individual control. The final chapter of *The Tin Drum* makes all this clear in summarizing fashion. Oskar's imminent release from the asylum is tantamount to a final "fall," a seduction to action and an acceptance of life.

Grass's profane use of sacred motifs and mythologems attests to the syncratic thrust of Oskar's spirit rather than to its divisiveness. Much like Nietzsche's own view of things, Grass's iconoclasm leads to growth, to a rejuvenation of ancient beliefs, not to nihilistic despair. As Nietzsche states: "[The spirit's] intention in all this [appropriation] is the incorporation of new 'experiences,' the arrangement of new things within old divisions – growth, that is to say; more precisely, the *feeling* of growth, the feeling of increased power" (*BGE* #230). Oskar feels his growth throughout, even before his physical growth resumes. The final chapter of the novel, "Thirty," focuses on the need for renewed growth, for change, for living life actively as saliently represented by the pervasive Black Wicked Witch and the escalator. The latter is a dominant symbol of the eternal return, of the self-similar iteration forever folding into itself, reaching into the depths of inner being and

---

York: Random House, 1967), aphorism #619, 332–33. Kaufmann believes that the second section of Book 3, "The Will to Power in Nature," has few or no close parallels to Nietzsche's published books (*WP* 332n). However, a close reading of *Beyond Good and Evil* reveals otherwise. Nietzsche's rejection of a mechanistic interpretation of the world in *Will to Power* is clearly in evidence in *Beyond Good and Evil* and *Zarathustra*, which date from the same years as the aphorisms in the section on the mechanistic view of the world.

lifting forms, shapes, and figures to the surface. (Here one is tempted to see a situation analogous to Goethe's realm of the Mothers.)

That will – expressed as and stimulated by the Witch – is, of course, not simply a straightforward and direct process; it is also self-denying and circuitous. In the human spirit there coexist contradictory, antithetical drives, Nietzsche notes. On the one hand, there is the drive to expand and to assimilate, that is, an exuberant affirmation of life in its fullness. On the other hand, there is the denial of the will to expand, that is, a withdrawal from life, a negating of life forces. Nietzsche contends:

> This same will is served by an apparently antithetical drive of the spirit, a sudden decision for ignorance, for arbitrary shutting-out, a closing of the windows, an inner denial of this or that thing, a refusal to let it approach, a kind of defensive posture against much that can be known, a contentment with the dark, with the closed horizon, an acceptance and approval of ignorance. (*BGE* #230)
>
> [Diesem selben Willen dient ein scheinbar entgegengesetzter Trieb des Geistes, ein plötzlich herausbrechender Entschluss zur Unwissenheit, zur willkürlichen Abschliessung, ein Zumachen seiner Fenster, ein inneres Neinsagen zu diesem oder jenem Dinge, ein Nicht-heran-kommen-lassen, eine Art Vertheidigungs-Zustand gegen vieles Wissbare, eine Zufriedenheit mit dem Dunkel, mit dem abschliessenden Horizonte, ein Ja-sagen und Gut-heissen der Unwissenheit.] (*KSA* 5:167–68)

We see Oskar closing out the world again and again, whether under the table, in the clothes cupboard, in his attic retreat, or in the asylum. Like Zarathustra and Nietzsche's "free, *very* free spirits," Oskar Matzerath is also a "hermit and marmot" who withdraws periodically to his citadel (*BGE* #230).

Other similarities between Nietzsche's concepts of vitalism and the genuine free spirit and Grass's characterization of Oskar Matzerath include (1) the will to deception, (2) the delight in ambiguity, (3) the love of the mask, and (4) life on the surface. Consequently, the will to power is also the "will to appearance, to simplification, to the mask, to the cloak, in short to the superficial – for every surface is a cloak – is *counteracted* by that sublime inclination in the man of knowledge which takes a profound, many-sided and thorough view of things and *will* take such a view" ("*Diesem* Willen zum Schein, zur Vereinfachung, zur Maske, zum Mantel, kurz zur Oberfläche – denn jede Oberfläche ist ein Mantel – wirkt jener sublime Hang des Erkennenden *entgegen*, der die Dinge tief, vielfach, gründlich nimmt und nehmen *will*"; *BGE* 161; *KSA* 5:168). This art of surface play explains the predominance of things as witnesses to historical events, the multifaceted experiences of life inscribed as scars on Herbert Truczinski's back, and the eternal rising of the individual steps of the escalator. Moving from the depths of deep structure unseen by the inquiring eye to the appearance of dazzling surface play, the steps, after a fleeting moment of "existence," recedes again into the depths. All this clarifies why objects serve so well as symbols, why a tin drum is the appropriate source of memory, why an escalator can signify the eternal return. The mind of God *is* in the laws of nature.

9. Metaphysical Geometry: The Shapes of Reality

Shapes and numbers – in particular, triangles and rectangles and the numbers three and four – abound in *The Tin Drum*, recurring with a vengeance in the final chapter. Their frequent occurrence prompts the question: *Why*. Given Grass's own background as a sculptor and painter, the presence of geometrical shapes is not all that astonishing. Lines, curves, and interstices are a way of organizing matter, of finding the right coordinates for determining the relationships within an image, for focusing attention on significant detail (cf. chapter 2 of this study). In an art catalogue, accompanying an exhibit of his works in Stockholm in 1979, Grass openly acknowledged that, for him, graphic arts and story telling exist in a mutually beneficial relationship to one another. He even characterized himself as "ein schreibender Zeichner" (a scribbling graphic artist).[47] But more is involved than just a reflection upon artistic technique and perspective in rendering the relationships among objects in space. A deeper meaning becomes discernible in Grass's conception, one that is related to Edward O. Wilson's definition of meme as "the node of semantic memory." Defined as a nodal point of reciprocal relations, the meme experiences activation only through an interactive communication process between the observer and the observed. (That interactive process, in turn, resonates with Goethe's concept of the relationship between subject and object.)

For example, Oskar uses photographic images of the past in chapter 4, "The Photograph Album," to jog his memory. He likens his family photo album to a "family cemetery," valuing it as a treasure that makes everything clear to him by according meaning to images that point beyond the people and scenes depicted. Consisting of 120 pages with four, six, or sometimes only two photos mounted symmetrically per page, the album is consistently "governed by the right angle" ("rechtwinklig, sorgfältig verteilt"; *TD* 49; *BT* 56). It is important to note that Oskar narrates the content of the pictures by regenerating their rhythms on his drum. Although he has not experienced them all directly, he accesses their inner essence in his capacity as a timeless demigod. The snapshots are likened to the eye of God making observations of earthly dealings from afar. And Oskar plays the

47 Grass, "Bin ich nun Schreiber oder Zeichner?" in *Der Autor als fragwürdiger Zeuge*, 121–23; here 123.

seer, preferring to dwell on the crooked and complex, what he calls the "tortuous and labyrinthine" ("Liebe zum Labyrinthischen"; *TD* 50; *BT* 56). Nevertheless, he is eager to move from the "photomaton man" ("Kabinenmensch") on the page to the originals (*TD* 50; *BT* 57). This is not unlike Faust's desire to move from the phantasmagoria of Helena to the real person. Likewise, we might see Oskar's querying of the "shadows" on the page as being somewhat analogous to Faust's descent to the Mothers in his quest to conjure up the past. Indeed, like Paris and Helena, all those captured in the photos are so many shades of Hades who continue to dwell in the half-life of memory. Like Faust, Oskar needs a key, but his key is not the phallus. Rather, it is geometry and the magic of numbers.

Contemplating a group picture of his mother Agnes and his two presumptive fathers, Alfred Matzerath and Jan Bronski, Oskar is compelled to "plot the constellation of this triumvirate" that gave him life. In the rectangular photograph of a balcony scene, with Agnes seated and the two men standing behind her, Oskar senses a "dimly visible three-cornered constellation" within the double rectangle of photograph and balcony (*TD* 55; *BT* 64). Engaging in a bit of "metaphysical geometry," Oskar starts with the angle between her neck and shoulder (roughly equaling 90 degrees) and draws a triangle on the photograph, spinning out projections, deducing similarities among the angles, and seeking an explanation for them outside the triangle of the threesome itself, for Oskar needed "a point of departure," "a point of view," "a point of contact" from which to judge the meaning of this triumvirate. He finds that vantage point in the foliage, that is, outside the purely human realm. Significantly, Agnes, the "harmonious blend of Madonna and harlot," gives "the full value of man" (*TD* 55).[48] The image is characterized as "their triangular felicity" (*TD* 56; *BT* 65). Other pictures portray the three protagonists of his early childhood forming a triangle (*TD* 57; *BT* 66). In particular, there is the snapshot of them playing skat (a three-handed card game) with Agnes showing the queen of hearts for the camera to see. The allusion to her own role as queen of their hearts needs no elucidation. Moreover, as Oskar notes, the traditional love triangle in dramatic plays is much preferable to being dialogued to death. The "tense peace" ("spannungsreichen Frieden") of the triumvirate is much preferable to that (*TD* 57; *BT* 66). The allusion to dialogue recalls the large gray moth's colloquy with the two 60-watt bulbs.

---

48 The passage in German reads: "Eine Zeitlang war ich dumm genug, mit einem Schulzirkel, den Bruno mir kaufen mußte, mit Lineal und Dreieck die Konstellation dieses Triumvirates – denn Mama ersetzte vollwertig einen Mann – ausmessen zu wollen. Halsneigungswinkel, ein Dreieck mit ungleichen Schenkeln, es kam zu Parallelverschiebungen, zur gewaltsam herbeigeführten Deckungsgleichkeit, zu Zirkelschlägen, die sich bedeutungsvoll außerhalb, also im Grünzeug der Kletterbohnen trafen und einen Punkt ergaben, weil ich einen Punkt suchte, punktgläubig, punktsüchtig, Anhaltspunkt, Ausgangspunkt, wenn nicht sogar den Standpunkt erstrebte" (*BT* 64).

The triangle motif reappears in connection with Oskar's sexual liaison with Maria. He speaks of her pubic "hairy triangle," which at first frightens then powerfully attracts him, causing his third drumstick to grow (*TD* 268–69; *BT* 348–49). In a manner harking back to the geometric metaphysics of "The Photograph Album," Oskar considers buying a compass and tracing a circle around Maria and himself and then sketching out angles to give the measure to their relationship. Starting with the angle of inclination of her neck while she is reading or sewing or tinkering with the radio, he could inscribe lines and angles from within that circle in an effort to find a point of reference outside their world (cf. *TD* 280; *BT* 364). Cogently, Maria's relationship to Oskar and Alfred parallels that of the earlier "triumvirate": whether Alfred Matzerath or Oskar is the father of Kurt remains unsettled. Later, Ulla's pubic hair is described as a small triangle (*TD* 471; *BT* 618). And then of course there is Lucy Rennwand's triangular fox face, reminiscent of satanic sexuality. Luring young men to their downfall, she offers "her triangle" and whispers sweetly, "Jump!" (*TD* 385; *BT* 506). While the reference to her "triangle" is earlier explained as the triangular shape of her face (*TD* 383; *BT* 503), the sexual connotation of her triangular private parts is part of the allure.

When Oskar later works as an artist's model, the young artists "abstract" him, render him as a "cube," transforming his private parts into a priapus: "two cubes of like size, surmounted by an elongated rectangular block" (*TD* 467; *BT* 613). Here more obviously than in previous instances, the geometric shapes of Cubism intimate a deep structure lurking behind the humps, testicles, and other fractal shapes of appearance. The hump itself comes across as a deformed cube. With the predominance of two contiguous lines, four sides, four corners, and six sides in the cube, those efforts are not unrelated to Oskar's calculations of the family photo album, where he finds two, four, or six rectangles per page.

The triumvirate that determines Oskar's entire existence can be plotted as two triangles conjoined into one rectangle with an iteration of Agnes and of Oskar. While the four corners of the rectangle can be labeled "Agnes," "Oskar," "Alfred," and "Jan," the two constitutive triangles would be Agnes–Alfred–Oskar and Agnes–Jan–Oskar, whereby the Agnes–Oskar line forms the common axis between them. Viewing things in this manner, we can better fathom Oskar's statement that his two presumptive fathers give full value to Agnes, although they are only indirectly connected to one another via either Agnes or their son. After her death, in fact, the two men have little in common and grow increasingly estranged. Thus, the nervous dialectic established between Agnes and Alfred, the industrious German fascist, and Jan, the sensitive Kashubian dreamer, constitutes the full meaning of the relationships. Those relationships can be diagrammed as follows (fig. 7.1):

Figure. 7.1: Presumptive Fathers

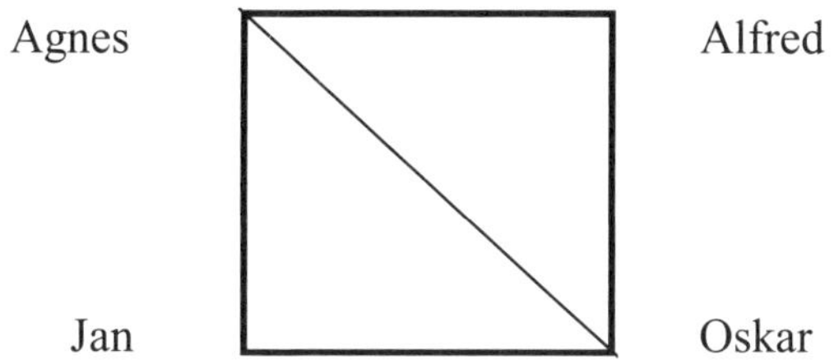

The photo album is, indeed, a treasure trove, for it consists of numerous 90 degree and 45° angles projecting out into three- and four-cornered constellations. Considering that two or four or six (out of which one can create a cube) rectangular pictures are posted per page and that the whole binder contains 120 pages, these numbers seem significant. If we add up the sum of the angles in each of the triangles in figure 7.1, the result is 180 degrees per triangle (two 45 degree angles + one 90 degree angle). If we consider, moreover, that each triangle represents a family, mother–father–child, the entire rectangle is composed of two families sharing the same mother and the same child. Weighing further the fact that Oskar regards himself as the "realer Jesus" and describes his mother as the perfect union of harlot and Madonna, we can easily deduce two "holy families" in the sketch.[49]

But the value of the analogies does not end there. There is magic in the symbols and in the numbers – or, if you will, in the angles – for Oskar has found the point of vantage outside the image of his mother and two fathers that gives fuller meaning to their constellation. The triumvirate is already an elaboration of the original diumvirate exposed in the mythically loaded first chapter of the novel, where the numbers four (four skirts, four potatoes, four persons) and two (two policemen, Anna and Joseph Koljaiczek) dominate the scene near the village of Viereck (= four corners). The line of erect telegraph poles and the stout chimney at the brick works (phallic symbols) accentuate the landscape enshrouded in the mist of creation where Uranus enfolds Gaea. From the interaction of the 2 within the earthly 4 (four elements, four geographical directions, four sensate qualities, four limbs of the human body), a family of 3 emerges, for the union between Anna and Joseph produces Agnes (who, like Oskar, prefers hiding under tables and in closets to full exposure). It is the first "Holy Family" alluded to in the novel (cf. *TD* 25; *BT* 23). Anna, by the way, was the name of Jesus's grandmother according to the proto-evangelist Jacob.[50] Thus, from the beginning the numbers 2 – 4 – 3 are

49 Later, Oskar poses with Ulla in a successful modern rendering of "Madonna with [Deformed] Child" (*TD* 472; *BT* 619).

50 Jahnke and Lindemann, *Günter Grass: Die Blechtrommel*, 18.

intertwined in their sacred and profane meanings and are repeated in various ways throughout the entire narrative.

Figure. 7.2: Four Elements (http://www.sacredspiral.com/Database/symbol/eletri.html)

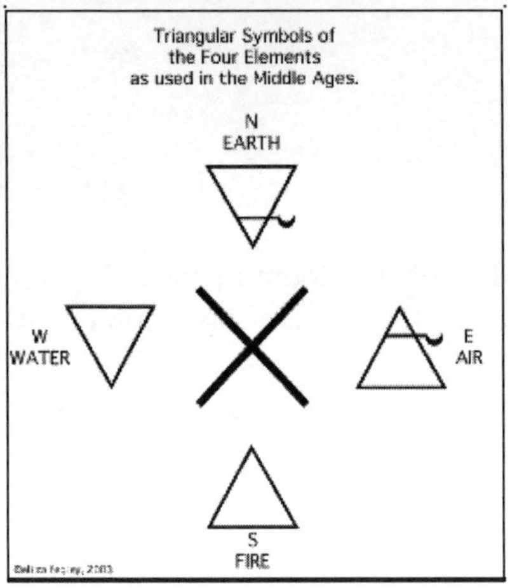

Oskar himself refers to his family as the "Holy Family," but in keeping with Grass's parodic tendencies, this modern "Holy Family" is not identical to the divine 3 of the original Jesus – Mary – Joseph. Rather, the new "Holy Family" resists the transcendent meaning of the 3 to remain firmly embedded in the 4. The 3 evolves from and returns to the 4; that is, it is anchored in the earthly realm of fire–water–earth–air. Notably, alchemists used triangles to symbolize the four elements (see fig. 7.2). The triangle with the point facing up, and without the line drawn through it, represented fire (Δ); it was chosen as a symbol of eighteenth-century Enlightenment (cf. Georg Lichtenberg), the sign of light and illumination in freemasonry. Significant, by the way, is the fact that the triangle Oskar deduces of his triumvirate has the point facing down (because she is sitting, they standing). The resultant sign, with the line drawn through it, is that of the earth (🜃). The significance of that orientation for defining the gnomic Oskar requires no special elaboration. The two 60-watt light bulbs of Oskar's birth are perhaps a play on his precociously enlightened state from the outset. More significant, however, is the fact that the two light bulbs produce in total 120 watts. Only together do they impart full meaning to the moth, just as Alfred and Jan together accord full value to Agnes.

How so, the reader might ask? Let us recall that Oskar's name and its various associations with circles connote infinity, the sign for which derives from two contiguous circles. If we felt venturesome, we could move the two bulbs closer together so that they would be touching one another. Viewed from below, that is, from Oskar's perspective, they would form the sign for infinity (∞). Furthermore, we could recall that Oskar's mother was born in late July 1900. Unfortunately, Manheim's translation does not capture the full import of these dates because Grass actually writes: "Ende des Jahres nullnull" (*BT* 19). The "nullnull" transcribes as 00, connoting the contiguous circles intimated by the two bulbs. Because Oskar takes the moth as his master and because the moth seeks out the light emitted by the two 60-watt light bulbs until it dies, we are tempted to see in this interaction of bulb and moth repeated over generations a dialectic with metaphysical significance.

If we superimpose the equal-sided love triangle of his mother's life onto the circle of Oskar's own existence, that added value becomes further manifest (fig. 7.3).

Figure 7.3: Geometric Magic

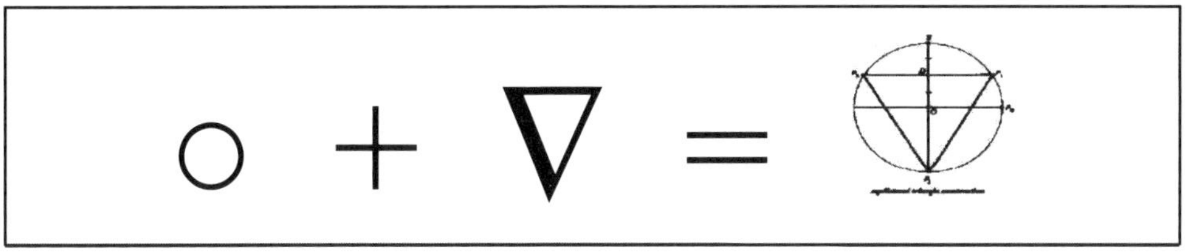

The points of the triangle divide the circumference of the circle into three equal segments, each containing 120 degrees of the total circumference of the circle. Of course, the three angles of the triangle amount to just half of the circle's 360 degrees. Only when both contiguous alignments of Oskar's modern "Holy Family" are taken together as two contiguous triangles forming a rectangle is the "full value" given to his mother and, by association, to himself. In a sense, then, Oskar actually is the "realer Jesus" because he forms an integral part of the two triangles that together result in the full 360 degrees of the endless circle. But wait: the two triangles form a rectangle, not a circle. True. Yet both shapes contain 360 degrees (fig.7.1).

We have seen in earlier in this study how Henri Poincaré overcame the limitations of Euclidean geometry by introducing the innovative concept of topology. Poincaré developed his ideas in response to Swedish King Oscar II's prize-essay question of 1887: "Is the universe stable?" (Would it be going too far to associate Oskar Matzerath's name with King Oscar of Sweden, whose question revolutionized mathematical calculations of celestial movement? Perhaps.) Beginning in the 1960s, Poincaré's treatise was rediscovered and impacted upon the emergent science of chaos. In his *Does God Play Dice?* Ian Stewart explains quite tellingly for the present argument that topology is a geometry of infinitely mutable shapes. Angles, areas, and shape morph easily into one another: "A square, for example, can be continuously deformed into a circle, a circle into a triangle, a triangle into a parallelogram. All of the geometrical shapes that we are taught so assiduously as children: to a topologist, they are one" (Stewart 63). The only restriction in these transformations is that the line must not be cut or broken. Given the self-similarity of the geographical shapes according to topology, we no longer wonder at the major role that shapes, angles, and numbers play in the geographical and temporal reconfigurations of *The Tin Drum*. It is a novel of the universe in which Euclidean geometry is an inadequate tool for fathoming relationships and surface phenomena. For all their diversity, the latter emanate from a deep structure of similarity, from what mathematicians since ancient times have called the Divine Proportion and that is derivative of Fibonacci sequences. This ratio-constant throughout nature is the number phi (1.618), which can be found in both animate and inanimate nature. Like Dan Brown's *The Da Vinci Code* (2003), Grass's *The Tin Drum* discloses codes hidden in plain view. In stressing how the book remaps reality, I go far beyond its usual signification as coming to terms with Germany's fascist past, the process known as *Vergangenheitsbewältigung*.

Archetypical properties of topology are connectedness and knottedness. The defining concept involves the continuity of infinitesimal transformations across a range of scales of space and time. As a postmodern variation on the figure of Homunculus in Goethe's *Faust* (Oskar is also a clairvoyant "small man," that is, a homunculus), Oskar, like his predecessor, must go through multifarious transformations in the process of life. Here we cannot help but think of the art students' attempts to render Oskar in Cubist fashion and of Bruno's string figures. Oskar is dissatisfied with the Cubist rendering of his essence (sexuality), which he feels misses the point, but he admires Bruno's art of modeling string figures on the human actors in his story. The linear string is pressed into angular and curved continuous forms. In a very special sense, the rhythmic variations of Oskar's own drumming belong in the same category, for the drumming reconstitutes not only the shapes and spaces but also the essential movement of life. The metamorphoses of form recall the growth and decomposition cycles of organic matter, their alternation between diastole and systole.

A major difference between Grass's use of topology and the mathematician's approach is that Grass's protagonist cannot reverse the order. While the topologist concentrates on those properties of shapes that remain unchanged under reversible continuous transformations (meaning that the undoing of the transformation must also be continuous), Oskar seeks to avoid the transformations of life. But that proves to be an impossibility. Once born into the flow of life, one must learn to swim. There is no going back to the stasis of nonbirth; there is only movement and emergence, every moment a new gateway. Evolution leads to ever greater complexity, although based on some "simple" operations. According to his theory of things at the time (i.e., 1944), Oskar envisions a perfect family life inside his grandmother Koljaiczek, joined there by all his ancestors. Paradoxically, he sees life as a moving forward to the origins (*TD* 349; *BT* 459). Perhaps that is the reason why, in plotting the triangulated constellation of his mother and two fathers, Oskar finds a point of reference in the foliage outside their immediate relationships. He is seeking a point of origin. Similarly, he begins the narrative of his existence by moving far back in time to the conception of his mother in the potato field. Referencing human meaning in organic nature does, indeed, provide a "metaphysics of geometry."[51] It also draws heavily on myth.

Fractals, the best-known aesthetic computer-generated byproduct of the science of chaos, are also grounded in the triangle. If we superimpose the symbols for earth (🜃) and fire (Δ), we end up with the core of fractal geometry: ✡. The six-pointed star becomes the basis for all kinds of nonlinear shapes, although it is composed of straight lines joined at 60 degrees to one another (at least in the basic unit). Again, the total sum of both triangles is 360 degrees. Strikingly, the figure is twelve-sided; the twelve tribes of Israel, the twelve apostles, the twelve months in the calendar are interrelated and not accidental. The 12 contains the 1 (wholeness) and the 2 (dividedness) and, when added together, connote the infinite cycle of thesis – observation – experimentation in the pursuit of knowledge. This is the accretionary way of doing science since Copernicus. The process is normally diagrammed as a triangle with observation serving as the point of connection between thesis and experimentation (fig. 7.4).

Figure 7.4: Accumulating Knowledge
(John L. Casti, *Complexification* 1994:14)

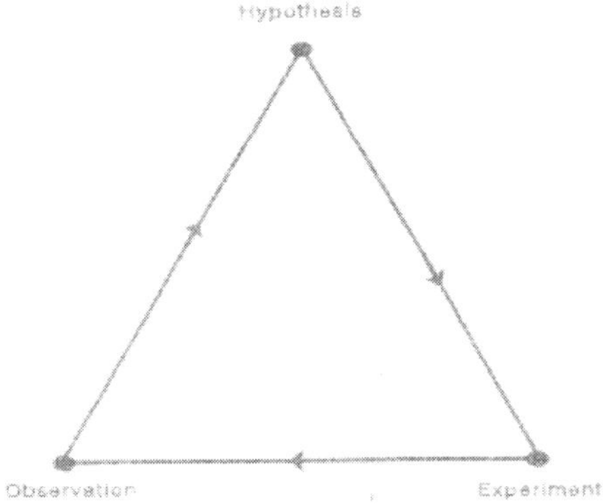

Before leaving the issue of numbers, we need to return to the number 4 one more time. Critics agree that chapter 1, "The Wide Skirt," is crucial to the mythological import of the novel. Until now I have emphasized the four skirts that the grandmother wears in rhythmically alternating fashion. Actually, a fifth skirt is thrown into the mix. Anna Koljaiczek always kept one clean skirt in reserve. Each of the skirts is worn for a day next to her skin, alternating outward each morning. The system of exchange was strictly regulated and every fifth Friday (fifth day of the week) one of the skirts was washed, hung out to dry on Saturday, and inaugurated into the next cycle at Sunday mass, as if to accentuate the eternal recurrence (*TD* 18–19). In interpreting the meaning of the fifth skirt, we might be tempted to liken it to the quintessence that holds the earthly 4 together. But we do not have to go that far, even though quintessence in the postmodern era is situated within the cycle of change itself.

51 To be sure, the original German does not contain the phrase "metaphysics of geometry," which is Manheim's translation of "dillettantische Messerei" (*BT* 64). The choice is fitting even if the context of Grass's term points to everything being grounded in the earth.

10. THE GRAMMAR OF BIOLOGY

Although some readers might consider the next step in my argument to be extraordinary, I beg forbearance. Grass's outrageous mixing of myth and reality in his novel invites similar bold moves. The metaphorical quality of Grass's writing is grounded in the twenty-six signs of the alphabet that he ingeniously inscribes and reinscribes in multifarious configurations on a piece of paper to invoke the shapes of reality. There is a grammar at work here comparable to the human genome in its simplicity and complexity. In the following, I offer the kind of thought experiment pointedly advocated by Goethe in *Faust* and Nietzsche in *Zarathustra*. In turn, both of *their* moves were philosophically anticipated by the principle of the plenitude of possibilities: whatever *can* be thought, *will* be thought (see the explorations in chapter 2). In looking for a "metaphysical" reference, Oskar directs us back to operative nature itself, Spinoza's *natura naturans*.

The late-twentieth-century science of genetics has taught us to decipher the script that marks each one of us at our most basic chromosomal level. What happens on the cellular scale of our bodies determines our outward appearance and the external transformations we undergo. Granted, Grass makes only passing reference to genetics in *The Tin Drum*, waiting until much later in his career to make pointed allusions to the science of biological coding. Nonetheless, we cannot help but wonder at the structural affinity of the novel to a deep lying impetus toward communication and communities.[52] That the novel has a tripartite large outer shell is easily explained in terms of the normal partitioning of a narrative into beginning–middle–end. Striking about this novel, however, is the fact that it begins where it ends: in the asylum. Every narrated event is viewed from that vantage point, in other words, from outside the flow of events themselves. The final chapter of the novel brings us back to the present time of the opening lines of the work. Moreover, it is not a conclusion to the action in the sense that Oskar is about to be released from the asylum to take up his life anew. What he envisions there belongs to the future (and, in fact, occurs in *Die Rättin*, where Oskar is sixty). To be sure, the novel narrates past time, but past and future come together in what Grass later was to call "Vergegenkunft." The coinage itself is a combination of "*Ver*gangenheit" (past), "*Gegen*wart" (present), and "Zu*kunft*" (future).[53]

The overall impression is of continuous, mythical present time, of palingenesis.

---

52 The author Andrew Solomon, "The Closing of the American Book," *New York Times*, 10 July 2004, A29, considers "the rearrangement of 26 shapes on a piece of paper" to be on a par with nature's "complete genetic code made up of four bases" in humans.

53 Grass, "Schreiben nach Auschwitz. Frankfurter Poetik-Vorlesung" (1990), in Grass, *Der Autor als fragwürdiger Zeuge*, 195–222; here 215

Why is that? Because, I suggest, the structure of time and space in the novel bears an uncanny resemblance to the function of the genetic code. It, too, is always past, present, and future. The gnome Oskar, who is rooted in the earth, is not immediately evocative of the genome. A subtle, perhaps too subtle, sign of his symbolic value is the alternating pattern on his drum, which is composed of two large circular surfaces (two "Os") bound together by a band of alternating red and white interlocking triangles (ΔVΔVΔVΔV). In light of our previous explorations, this simple design might connote that the ring of eternity is serrated and marked by reciprocating values.

Then, too, the total number of chapters in the book is forty-six. How is that evocative of the genome? Forty-six is, of course, the total number of chromosomes in the twenty-three pairs contained in the nucleus of a cell. Far-fetched? Perhaps. But why does Grass make such an emphatic point of using the number 23 as Oskar traces his immediate ancestry? For instance, Oskar remarks that the photograph of his mother's nursing class clustered around an army doctor in the Great War depicts 23 nurses, including Agnes, while another picture – taken a few years later – renders Agnes at age 23, presumably just before her pregnancy (*TD* 53–54; *BT* 62). A few lines later we read that Agnes, like her cousin Jan Bronski, stems from the same potato fields as Anna Koljaiczek (*TD* 55; *BT* 63). The sequencing of events is perfectly clear: from the potato field, where Agnes's genetic code was constructed, we move to the family photo album, where Oskar is compelled to seek "and actually find mathematical and, preposterously enough, cosmic references in it," that is, in his ancestral past (*TD* 55).[54] Incredible? Maybe. Yet myth and reality have proven to be quite surprising. So let us return to the chromosomes.

We recall that chromosomes, which control the manufacturing of proteins, consist of two, long, twisted strands of deoxyribonucleic acid (DNA) and protein, the code-bearing material from parent to offspring being DNA. Moving further into the molecular structure, we detect the gene that determines physical characteristics. Genes, in turn, are composed of thousands of nucleotides, the smallest genetic unit. The nucleotides are themselves composed of four nitrogenous bases: adenine (A), cytosine (C), guanine (G), and thymine (T), whereby A combines only with T, C only with G. The sequence of three (there's that number again) of these bases constitute a unit of genetic information, "in that each sequence of three bases codes for one of the twenty different amino acids that go to make up the proteins that control the characteristics of a cell."[55] That information is transcribed to the

54 The entire passage reads: "Was hieß mich mathematische und, lächerlich genug, kosmische Bezüge auf diesem Viereck suchen und wenn man will, sogar finden?" (*BT* 64).

55 E. B. Uvarov and Alan Isaacs, *The Penguin Dictionary of Science*, 7th edition (New York: Penguin Books, 1993), 182.

cytoplasm of the cell via messenger ribonucleic acid. Perhaps this is purely coincidental: 4 nitrogenous bases combine into preset pairs (2) and then form a sequence of 3 pairs (= 6 bases). That combination of 2, 3, and 4 yields the all-important coded information that is combined with other coded information resulting from the iterative process of A combining with C, G with T. Even before the bacteriologist Oswald T. Avery discovered in 1943 that a core substance drawn from one kind of bacteria could induce transformations in similar bacteria, physicist Erwin Schrödinger engaged in speculations about physical aspects of the living cell that proved momentous for deciphering the DNA text. The introduction of just two ciphers organized into groups of four, he mused, allows for thirty different variations of the base line. If one adds a third cipher and allows for groups of ten, the number of possible variations rises exponentially to 29,524 different "letters." The proximity of Schrödinger's mathematical picture to the actual sequence of three of the four base pairs in DNA coding is quite striking.[56] A quarter century later, the chemist Erwin Chargaff cited Avery's discovery as the moment of his own revolutionary insight into the "grammar of biology," with its sequence of three base pairs. That complementarity became a cornerstone of Watson and Crick's model of the double helix (Blumenberg, "Der genetische Code" 380–82).

These repetitive numbers and combinations also mark the deep structure of *The Tin Drum* with its 46 chapters, the predominance of the number 4, the constant splitting and pairing off of the 2, and repeated references to 3, all bound together in an endlessly self-replicating screwlike movement. About 3 billion nucleotides make up the human genome, and the human body holds about 10 trillion cells, the structure and function of which are determined by the large molecules, proteins. Human DNA was thought to be divided into about 100,000 clusters of genes, but it may be only 30,000 to 40,000. Yet like any other complex system – including transmission of the code – what really counts is not so much how each part functions independently but rather how each part is interconnected with and codetermines everything else. We recall Poincaré's frustration in judging whether the universe was stable or not because of the difficulty in calculating the interactions of a "simple" three-body system in 1887. How much more complex is the coordination of enzymes, proteins, and cells in the human body!

The final chapter of the novel, "Thirty," directs attention to the interconnectivity of the content and characters of the preceding forty-five installments, while emphasizing simultaneously the openness and potential instability of this apparently lockstep process over the long term. We might be tempted to compare

56 Erwin Schrödinger, *What is Life? The Physical Aspects of the Living Cell* (Cambridge: Cambridge University Press, 1944). Cited by Hans Blumenberg, "Der genetische Code und seine Leser," in Blumenberg, *Die Lesbarkeit der Welt* (Frankfurt a.M.: Suhrkamp, 1986), 372–409; here 372–78.

the dynamic of the novel's structure to events on both the macroscopic and microscopic scale. After all, the narrative is framed by the reality that exists outside its own specific sphere. Thus, an analogy might be drawn to the regulation of the galactic system in which all of this movement is ultimately embedded. The periodic centers of order represented by the motion of the sun, of other star groups, "and of the galaxy in the local group of galaxies" are similarly threatened with devolution into chaos over the long-time scale (Hawking 1993:144). All of the past events that have shaped Oskar's existence at the same time open up possibilities for the future. What that future holds is not entirely predictable, although the conditions and sequences are known. It is not unthinkable, I suggest, to see in the self-similarity of events narrated on the large and small scale in this monumental novel an analogy to human actions grounded more specifically in what we know to be small-scale DNA coding. Having evolved over the past four million years or so, DNA too has a long-term time scale. Four bases in combinations of two and sequences of three characterize how things work both for the fictional world of the novel (with its penchant for the numbers 2, 3, and 4) and for the human reality outside it.

The biology of grammar outlined here takes us beyond the usual interpretation of the final chapter in the novel. "Thirty" designates not only Oskar's biological age but also alludes to his mythological lineage. At age thirty, Christ began his messianic career, fulfilling an ancient prophecy, on the one hand, and on the other calling the people to a rebirth, to an affirmation of and responsibility for their individual acts in realizing a divine plan. Similarly, at the end of the nineteenth century, Nietzsche reclaimed Zoroaster from the mythic past and transformed him into a secular version of Christ, into Zarathustra. Unlike Christ, however, Zarathustra expected to draw very few disciples in his wake, for he suspected that there were too few strong-backed individuals, willing to bear his message of constant self-renewal. In contrast to Christ's followers, Zarathustra's disciples could not look forward to redemption from the vale of tears on earth. While drawing upon the mythic figures of Christ and Zarathustra in rendering his own protagonist in *The Tin Drum*, Grass takes the secularization process a step further. He locates human action squarely within an ecology of the whole, stressing in particular the biological basis of behavior. Oskar Matzerath is a reluctant messiah. He prefers to exist on the margins, does not want to descend from his "mountain," shuns full integration in life, and distances himself as far as possible from accepting responsibility for his life and his effect on others. But the framework of modern, interactive existence on the micro, macro, and meso scales does not allow splendid isolation. Consequently, with its new "grammar," *The Tin Drum* (here, in particular, its final chapter) invokes the full range of semantic associations within both spheres of the sacred and the profane.

11. SUMMING UP: ON BEING CREATIVE

As we now know, chaos is the scientific method that deals with the whole. With the goal of describing a system from its *behavior* as a whole, it is therefore bound up with motion and positionality. Chaos signifies an indeterminate collective, autocatalytic function of nature and thus stands in sharp contrast to the traditional notion of genius, which connotes self-willed determination and individuation. Both are, nonetheless, expressive of the creative impulse. What that creative content is, however, is not a matter of common agreement. Earlier chapters in this study offer a working definition of creativity as a function of a highly complex holomovement. In simplified terms, creativity is a function of chaos, that is, of fractal nonlinearity, which can take on ordered "shape" through positive feedback loops. Just as easily, of course, ordered constellations can disintegrate into stochastic states via negative feedback loops. Consequently, iteration and self-similarity are forming principles in the emergence of periodic centers of order that are called forth by so-called strange attractors. The genius can be seen as operating like such a strange attractor in that it lies in a middle state between complete randomness and a fixed point or a limit cycle. The fixed point with a dimension of 0 and the limit cycle (a simple closed curve) with a dimension of 1 are examples of classical attractors, and their numbers (0 and 1) are the "*geometric dimension* of the attractor" (Casti, *Complexification* 101). But the strange attractor lies somewhere else, that is, beyond the classical geometric dimension, which weights each point on the trajectory equally regardless of how often it is visited. If points on the trajectory moving in on its attractor (its point of rest) are plotted and the statistical correlation between these sample values computed, we end up with a number called a "correlation dimension," a relative or "fragmented" state compared to the dimensions 0 and 1. This is because the correlation number weights the points on the trajectory according to how often they are visited by the movement. "A telltale sign of chaos," Casti concludes, "is when the correlation dimension turns out to have a noninteger value much greater than 1"(Casti 101).

Thus, chaos and creativity can be defined as a highly complex kind of order that leads to surprising results because they have a noninteger value and are not predictable. Scientifically speaking, nonetheless, chaos is only the appearance of total randomness, not the real thing (von Buttlar 108; Casti 88). Originality and creativity emerge not through structured planning and the setting of predetermined goals, "but rather as a by-product of a mind that is coming to a more nearly normal order of operation" (Bohm, *On Creativity* 26). This definition obviously contrasts with the traditional concept of genius as the individualized attempt at controlling life forces. In the new scheme of things, the productive energy for constituting new forms and insights remains a constitutive part of the genius but is not limited to the extraordinary individual. In the early eighteenth century, J. J. Breitinger had pointed out the inherent connection between the creative forces in nature and the creative forces in the artist. The production of the new is labeled "creative" (see chapters 2 and 3). With the Sturm-und-Drang writers in the 1770s (e.g., J. M. R. Lenz, young Goethe), the self-willed quality of the creative artist rose to the fore. Beginning with them, the emphasis was on the messianic powers of liberation from predetermined patterns. Spontaneity, eccentricity, vitality, and constant disruption became hallmarks of originality and creative genius.[57]

Günter Grass has succeeded in combining both the self-willed genius of Sturm-und-Drang ilk – perhaps more familiar to us now in the garb of Nietzsche's free spirit – and the autocatalytic operations of the creative universe. In any event, nonlinear processes, which quickly evolve into highly complex and unpredictable events with noninteger values, lie at the heart of creativity in nature.[58] With its frequent play on geometric patterns, its chromatic displays, and its continuous disregard for customary time lines, *The Tin Drum* can be viewed as an ongoing creative act; it mirrors the trajectories of nonlinear natural phenomena. Grass's goal is to animate the reader to much purposive movement by means of the chaotic events filtered through his text and its narrative time. That narrative springs back and forth in an eternal present of conflated memory and anticipation.

In this sense, the mythmaking side of the novel functions within the framework of creativity, complexity, and chaos. The mythologems create a basis for communal identity and provide a hermeneutical tool for making sense out of the myriad phenomena to which humans are exposed.[59] In other words, they are so many strange attractors. The dominant strange attractor in *The Tin Drum* is the Black Wicked Witch, a kind of black hole, forcing movement into "a region of space-time from which it is not possible to escape to infinity" (Hawking 1993: 103). As argued

---

57 See Jochen Schmidt, *Die Geschichte des Genie-Gedankens 1750–1945*, 2 vols. (Darmstadt: Wissenschaftliche Buchgesellschaft, 1985), 1:110–19.

58 Reinhard Breuer and Günter Haaf, "Ein ordentliches Chaos," *Geo-Wissen: Chaos + Kreativität* (Hamburg: Gruner + Jahr AG and Co, 1990): 32–60; here 58; cf. also 28–29. See Casti, *Complexification*, 307 et passim.

59 Glenn A. Guidry, "Theoretical Reflections on the Ideological and Social Implications of Mythic Form in Grass' *Die Blechtrommel*," *Monatshefte* 83.2 (1991): 127–46; here 134. The mythological dimensions of the novel have been frequently analyzed. See, e.g., Edward Diller, *A Mythic Journey. Günter Grass' Tin Drum* (Lexington: University of Kentucky Press, 1974); Friedrichsmeyer, "Aspects of Myth," 241–49; David Roberts, "Aspects of Psychology and Mythology in *Die Blechtrommel*: A Study of the Symbolic Function of the 'Hero' Oskar," in *Grass: Kritik Thesen Analysen*, ed. by Manfred Jurgensen (Francke: Bern 1973). Dieter Wrobel, *Postmodernes Chaos – Chaotische Postmoderne: Eine Studie zu Analogien zwischen Chaostheorie und deutschsprachiger Prose der Postmoderne* (Bielefeld: Aisthesis Verlag, 1997), focuses on novel production after 1980. Consequently, Grass does not figure in his analysis at all.

in chapter 4 of this study, evil is inherent in movement. Thus, the Witch is the most appropriate symbol of evil in our recharted era, for she causes disequilibrium and change, counteracting established, contented order. In place of reassuring infinity, the Witch suggests disconnectedness. The German designation of her as "die schwarze Köchin" nevertheless underscores her intimate connection to the material world and to our bodies, which process it.

Connectivity is the bane of existence. That interconnectedness is perhaps the true significance of greengrocer Greff's intricately orchestrated drumming machine. Precisely that embeddedness Oskar fears, for connectedness implies responsibility, guilt, and atonement. It entails an eternal return of Care. The creative thrust of the novel resides in Grass's ability to devise memorable images and signs of self-willed acts caught in a vortex of uncontrolled events. No one can forget the gnome or his drumming. Without a doubt, we can conclude with Kurt Lothar Tank that "this dwarf is a goliath of the spirit and imagination."[60] Indeed, Oskar is a creature of rhythms, a microcosm, seeking to exercise power over the pulsating phenomena of life (see Fig. 7.5). In his realm, myth and reality converge. His presence is in no way limited to this one novel: Oskar reverberates throughout Grass's oeuvre. In the tale of the messianic Oskar Matzerath, we can see a response to the quintessential Nietzschean query posited in *Ecce homo* (*KSA* 6:293): How does one become what one is? Hence, Oskar is a consummate human being after all. Indeed, there are even signs that he is the emergent ideal free spirit who sometimes reluctantly, sometimes exuberantly plays the dangerous game of life.

Figure 7.5: The Microcosm
(Friedrich Schotus, *Margareta Philosophica* http://www.prs.org/gallery-astr.htm)

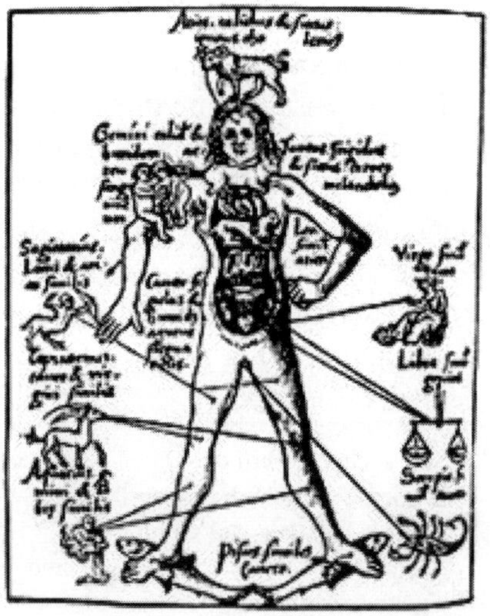

60 Kurt Lothar Tank, "Der Blechtrommler schrieb Memoiren," in Görtz, *Die Blechtrommel. Attraktion und Ärgernis*, 39–42; here 41. Arthur Koestler, "Wurzeln des Zufalls," in Koestler, *Die Wurzeln des Zufalls* (Frankfurt a.M.: Suhrkamp, 1972), argued for the new values of synthesis, symbiosis, periodicity, and affinity, all of which are manifest in Oskar and his world.

Epilogue
Emergence, Horizons, Continuance

> The eye is the first circle; the horizon which it forms is the second; and throughout nature this primary figure is repeated without end.
>
> – R. W. Emerson, "Circles" (1841)

> Das Auge hat sein Dasein dem Licht zu danken. Aus gleichgültigen tierischen Hülfsorganen ruft sich das Licht ein Organ hervor, das seinesgleichen werde, und so bildet sich das Auge am Lichte fürs Licht, damit das innere Licht dem äußeren entgegentrete.
>
> – J. W. von Goethe, *Zur Farbenlehre* (1808)

This investigation into the nexus of science and the humanities as a kind of "third culture" has been about encirclements. Each encirclement was intended to reverberate with inscriptions along a scale of size extending from the nano to the meso and macro, that is, from the quintessentially small (orbits of electrons around the nucleus) to the large (orbits of the planets around the sun) to the vastly large (the Milky Way orbiting toward a black hole). A theory of everything (or TOE) aspires to explain how these movements are related to one another despite their differences in scale. My thesis is that their interconnection occurs according to a deep structure and extends to the human domain (meso scale). In order to assess the lines of attraction, I employed several strategies to encircle the phenomenon of similarity from different angles. Those strategies include a review of seminal moments in the history of science such as, for instance, heliocentrism replacing the Ptolemaic system as the truer map of our reality and the introduction of nonlinear dynamics with its reassessment of the complex nature of causality as a more accurate picture of what happens in our environment.

Other strategies include the dislodging of binary models of exclusionary opposition between good and evil as undertaken by Nietzsche with his radical re-evaluation of values based on lines of mutual contingency. Key with regard to the ethical remapping of the human world has been the association of evil with the body and with the physical presence of the earth since the mythological fall of Adam and Eve from a state of naiveté. Finally, the tactics involved analysis of literary interpretations of what makes this world tick and of how we fit into it. Because humankind is more than a mechanical extension of the environment that sustains its life, a consideration of human consciousness and ethics was unavoidable. Metaphor and analogy, used both internally as well as externally, proved essential to the various discourses. They are equally integral to a rethinking of the map of reality. Goethe long ago recognized that the line separating fact from theory is thin and porous when he conjectured that the ultimate goal of empirical inquiry would be to grasp that everything in the realm of fact is already theory.[1]

Efforts to get to the bottom of things, to see more deeply into the inner operations underlying surface phenomena, led to a re-evaluation of the nature of perception and of imitation. Necessarily, the horizon widened to include a reassessment of the nature of creativity within a redrawn chart of the centrality of motion in the world as we know it. The net was cast broadly – too broadly, some readers will undoubtedly conclude. In our age, which still favors disciplinary stringency and purity despite all the talk about the need for interdisciplinarity, many readers will be nonplused by the inclusion of Cusanus, Leibniz, Kant, Goethe, Grass, Nietzsche, Roger Penrose, David Bohm, Ian Stewart, John Casti, George Smoot, Jean Baudrillard, Edward O. Wilson, and a slew of others in a single study about chaos, creativity, and accountability in understanding the place of humankind within its empirical environment. What do these thinkers have to do with one another? They do not represent the same disciplines, not even cognate disciplines. I have endeavored in the preceding pages to respond to that anticipated objection, and I cite Ralph Waldo Emerson and Goethe at the masthead of this parting commentary to redraw the perceived lines of communication. It is all about horizons, about perceiving what presents itself on those horizons, and about the inevitable intrusion of the perceiving eye into the reality being explored.

The expanding circles Emerson speaks of radiate out from the eye as if the I were the center of the universe, as if it were encircling everything. And in a certain sense the perceiving subject *is* the center of her universe, even though we know all too well just how deeply decentered the human subject has become pursuant to the revolutionary insights into natural operations in which the real action takes place at the margins of existence. At the same time we realize that most likely our universe began with an expansionary omnidirectional impulse outward from an original nodal point. Along the expansionary tracts, new nodal points of energy concentration formed, providing new localized seeds of attraction and cooperative interaction. Why not see each human being as comprising such a localized center of activity, each communicating with other localized centers of energy emission and all inhabiting a basin of attraction within an ultimate framework that continues to expand in all directions? Leibniz laid the foundation for such a view with his theory of monads around 1700. Ontogeny and phylogeny would then emerge as codeterminate. Moreover, the history of each organism and species would necessarily include the history of its life-worlds. The interaction of the perceiving subject and the perceived world is a dialectic facilitated by

---

1 Johann Wolfgang von Goethe, *Maxims and Reflections*, trans. by Douglas Miller (New York: Suhrkamp Publishers, 1988), 307.

the eye/I itself as, for example, in Goethe's notion of the eye as the meeting place of inner and outer light sources. An ecological approach to examining the specific instance seemed best.

To accept the premise of a common deep structure moderating all this movement away from and toward some center requires a willingness to see things in new ways. But then, that is a classic definition of creativity. We would have to put thinking aside, or at least engage in bisociative thinking as Arthur Koestler urged, or accept the value of meditative thinking ("das besinnliche Denken") alongside calculative thinking ("das rechnende Denken"), as Martin Heidegger prompted.[2] Both Koestler and Heidegger were reacting to reductionism in science and to the instrumentalization of reason in other disciplines. Calculative thinking is practical, concerned with solving our problems of everyday life; it counts on definite results and aims at enhancing our comfort level. It is the scientific, dominant kind of thought in our own technological era. By contrast, meditative thinking is ethereal; it only indirectly affects immediate everyday business and is not necessarily focused on creature comforts. By nature the human being is a divided creature. On one level she is practical, that is, concerned with solving daily challenges in the pursuit of happiness and ease. On another level, humanity is also meditative; it looks beyond the pleasure principle asks what we are doing here. In the short run, these tendencies would appear to be opposed, but in the long run they prove to be intimately related, feeding off one another. The distinguishing quality of humans is the fact that we are thinking creatures, what Kant called *Vernunftwesen*. This meditative ability, Heidegger argued, offers salvation from the dangers of the constricting technological ethos upon which we have become ever more dependent. The modern world of mass media and mass entertainment constricts by seducing us via its comforting repetition and ease to think in set patterns, to count on conditions that are given.

By contrast, meditative thinking lures us away from the tried and true. "Meditative thinking demands of us not to cling one-sidedly to a single idea," Heidegger remarked, "nor to run down a one-track course of ideas. Meditative thinking demands of us that we engage ourselves with what at first sight does not go together at all" (Heidegger 22; trans. 53). In order to open ourselves up to this other way of thinking, we must "release" ourselves to that which might present itself on the horizon and be ready to accept the unfamiliar. We must be attentive to nature and open to its mysteries.[3]

---

2 Arthur Koestler, "Bisociation in Creation," in *The Creativity Question*, ed. by Albert Rothenberg and Carl R. Hausman (Durham, NC: Duke University Press, 1976), 108–113; Martin Heidegger, *Gelassenheit* (Stuttgart: Neske, 1977), 12–13. The English is cited according to Martin Heidegger, *Discourse on Thinking*, trans. by John M. Anderson and E. Hans Freund (New York: Harper and Row, 1966), 46.

3 Albert Rothenberg addresses related issues in his *The Emerging Goddess: The Creative Process in Art, Science, and other Fields* (Chicago: University of Chicago Press, 1979), 345-80. Rothenberg

Mystery Heidegger specifically defined as "that which shows itself and at the same time withdraws." The allusion would appear to be to that which is not entirely dependent upon human will, is not merely a human construct, is ephemeral, and is marked by the phenomenon of emergence. The comportment or attitude that enables us to remain open to the hidden meaning he called "openness to the mystery" (Heidegger 23–24; trans. 54–55). This relaxed attitude of mind is necessary to counteract the ossifying tendency to think only in accustomed patterns. Essentially, the meditative mode is a creative attitude. Releasement has nothing to do with thinking, if we conceive of the latter in the traditional sense of *re-presenting* something (Heidegger 34; trans. 62). In order to learn to think in a nontraditional sense, that is, in a meditative sense, we must go beyond what we already know. We must be open to surprise and look past the appearance of objects. We must pass over the scope of the familiar and safe and venture out into a new "open region [...] in which everything returns to itself" (Heidegger 38; trans. 65). In that open region we find ontological unity in diversity. There we find interconnectivity.

Ultimately, Heidegger defined this alternative mode of thinking as a "coming-into-the-nearness of distance" (43, 70; trans. 68, 89) or as a "going toward" (69; trans. 88). This ability to move toward a goal that one has *not* predetermined makes it *possible* to see new things. It also helps us to see familiar things in new ways. It makes it possible to be creative. It opens us up to multiple attunements, as Koestler put it.[4] Both the releasement toward things on the horizon and an openness to the mystery of nature "flourish only through persistent, courageous thinking" ("gedeihen nur aus einem unablässigen herzhaften Denken"; Heidegger 24; trans. 56). Meditative thinking does not depend upon a rejection of calculative thinking. Yet if the latter were left to itself, it would make the practice of the former much more difficult, if not impossible. The spirit of competition must make way for a spirit of cooperation. The separateness and the interrelatedness of the two must be properly understood. The thinkers encountered in this study's attempt to trace the shifting lines of reality are distinguished by their ability to think outside the box. That, too, is part and parcel of the Enlightenment.[5]

At the outset of this study of revolutions real and imaginary, I said that it was about the Enlightenment and its legacy. To be sure, space is devoted to precursors of the epoch (Spinoza) as well as to some of its practitioners (Leibniz, Breitinger, Kant),

---

speaks of "Janusian Thinking" when Koestler would say bisociative thinking (138–206).

4 Arthur Koestler, *The Act of Creation* (London: Hutchinson, 1966), 642–46.

5 On this point, see Max Horkheimer, *Eclipse of Reason* (New York: Oxford University Press, 1947), 187. Theodor W. Adorno breaks a lance for the same cause. See his *Erziehung zur Mündigkeit: Vorträge und Gespräche mit Hellmut Becker 1959-1969*, ed. by Gerd Kadelbach (Frankfurt a.M.: Suhrkamp, 1971). His eye is directed at failures in the educational system to teach critical thinking (see esp. 133–47). Of course, there is the "cult book" by Max Horkheimer and Theodor W. Adorno: *Dialektik der Aufklärung: Philosophische Fragmente* (Frankfurt a.M.: Fischer Verlag, 1988).

especially German representatives. But the restricted view is due only to practical reasons of space because this book is not primarily about the eighteenth century. More important than the actual historical epoch itself are the ways in which the mind of the Enlightenment, its dominant mode of thought and attitude toward empirical reality and toward the inquiring subject, have played out over the past 250 years. In a sense, then, this book is about the New Enlightenment. There have been various incarnations of the movement, ranging from Goethe's *Faust* in the quest for understanding to Nietzsche's iconoclastic philosophy of the future to Günter Grass's revitalization of myth in the face of horrendous disaster to Edward O. Wilson's essay on a unity of knowledge. Indeed, these endeavors have been characterized as attempts to renew the Enlightenment, to extend it. One thing that these four very different thinkers have in common with seekers of truth through the ages is that they ask daring, even impudent and foolhardy questions. Like Copernicus or Galileo or Kant or Poincaré, they have revolutionized the way we draw the empirical and moral maps of our lives. Their daring thoughts reshaped the very terrain that produced us. Against that terrain Heidegger (and Horkheimer) directed his commentaries on the uses and abuses of reason. That thrust provided my point of departure in the above: revolutions virtual and real. Revolutions have in fact served as a major leitmotif on this heuristic journey.

A major influence on my thinking has been Nietzsche, with his rejection of small-mindedness and his call to re-evaluate all received values. I have long considered him to be an heir to the Enlightenment, seeing in his philosophy a mirror of essential enlightened attitudes. Initially, my concern was with his summons to go beyond the traditional concepts of good and evil in understanding what it means to be human. Gradually, I recognized that his exhortation was rooted in a larger network of interconnections. The framework of interconnectivity necessitated a larger theoretical framework. That is where chaos and complexity theory come in. They offer ways of getting at the region of inclusiveness cited by Heidegger but without the aura of mysticism haunting the philosopher. In myths around the world, chaos appears as the unnameable, that is, that which has no specific form or specialized function. Moreover, we have seen that in modern dynamic systems, chaos has come to designate a more specific state marked by sensitivity to initial conditions, aperiodic fluctuation, apparently random solutions, turbulence, dynamic equilibrium, intermittence. Yet for all its indeterminate qualities, chaos is a system. Paul Davies' anti-reductionist map of reality, *The Cosmic Blueprint* (1987), concludes with a clear nod to the uncertainty principle as an analogue to the gaps and spacings that mark all phases of existence. The hope expressed here is that new scientific theories will fill in the gaps left by the inadequacies of reductionist thinking, thus fleshing out the map. In particular, Davies looks to "theories that concern the collective and organizational properties of complex systems" and eschews any appeal to mystical or transcendent principles to supply us with better understanding. To achieve that end, "new approaches to research and the new ways of looking at complexity in nature" are needed.[6] The paradigm shift invoked has produced new perspectives on the interconnection of matter and spirit, of geometric forms such as the Cantor set, of Mandelbrot's gingerbread man, and of topological transformations.

Nietzsche proved indefatigable in his efforts to name the undefined chaos, resorting to myth, metaphor, and above all perspective, the basic condition of life, to attain his goal. Jean Baudrillard, whose points of orientation are Nietzsche and modern science, affirms the value of metaphor when he remarks that while the modern science of chaos is heavily indebted to metaphorical language, chaos is nonetheless more than merely metaphorical, for the tropes are directly applicable to systems beyond the natural sciences.[7] They are for Baudrillard, as Brian Ward avers in his study of the literary appropriation of chaos theory, "not only descriptive metaphors but [function] as prescriptive indicators of social trends and conditions."[8] We have seen that metaphor, image, and parable played a seminal role as so many memes in organizing Nietzsche's thinking on the meaning of life. The recognition of the value of metaphor as an organizing strategy and the key to the interpretive act has led critics to see Nietzsche in a new light in recent years. The title of my own investigation into these matters draws attention to Nietzsche's seminal role in my thinking by listing his medial role after the main title and the multivalent levels of interest. Despite its almost baroque quality, the title nonetheless does not tell the whole story. Evil, for example, is not highlighted.

Evil has, of course, various guises; one that appears to be more inclusive is Zarathustra's "evil spirit of magic and deception" that demands that "we must be different" (*Za* 302). Of primary importance here is the allusion to the philosopher's fundamental conviction that all statements about reality – whether scientific, philosophical, or literary – are essentially lies; that is, that they are interpretations rather than the thing itself. Consequently, the connotations of evil in the aftermath of Eden had to be explored. In doing so, I emphasized complexity and creativity, thereby diverging from such attempts to define evil as Susan Neiman's *Evil in Modern Thought*.[9] What others consider evil is for Zarathustra "man's best strength" (*Za* 288). Granting that these are delicate and distant matters, such a definition of evil easily leads to confusion for those who do not understand the underlying meaning or who believe that such a position amounts to a dismissal of accountability for the evil we do.

A serendipitous example of such a facile reading is John Leo's article in *U.S. News*

6 Paul Davies, *The Cosmic Blueprint* (London: Unwin Hyman Ltd., 1987), 203.

7 Jean Baudrillard, *The Transparency of Evil: Essays on Extreme Phenomena,* trans. by James Benedict (London: Verso, 1993), 42, 100.

8 Brian Ward, "The Literary Appropriation of Chaos Theory," Ph.D. diss. University of Western Australia, Nedlands, Western Australia, 1998, 39.

9 Susan Neiman, *Evil in Modern Thought: An Alternative History of Philosophy* (Princeton: Princeton University Press, 2004), see especially 206-227. She does not consider chaos or complexity theory.

and World Report, "Professors Who See No Evil," in which he decries supposedly rampant moral relativism on American college campuses as an evil and seeks to lay the blame for all ills in American society at the feet of those who endeavor to impart critical thinking skills to the young. Drawing on clichés, innuendo, half-truths, and nonsequiturs, Leo concludes that professors teach that "standards don't exist and moral debate is a personal violation and a sham."[10] Based on my own experience of teaching college students from around the nation, I can find no truth in that claim. No one I know claims that ethical standards are *simply* a matter of personal choice. By its very definition, ethics involves interaction with others and with the environment. Consideration of others and reflection on the impact one's actions are likely to have on a life-world are a sine qua non. John Leo is convinced that his perspective is true; I suspect he would dismiss mine as being false. Critical debate is aimed at bringing these two diametrically opposed truths into proximity to one another, to explore why one believes what one believes, to understand what motivates us to reject someone else's truth in favor of our own. Precisely to teach that exercise of reason is the urgent task of the humanities today. Literature still matters in the twenty-first century, Mark Roche argues in his timely new book about literature as a repository of human values.[11] We may never be able to eradicate prejudice or live without a belief in some transcendental truth, but we can strive to counteract *blind* prejudice and *unquestioned* belief. We all need truth, Nietzsche taught. Yet we need to understand why we choose certain truths over others. In a nutshell, that question informs this present inquiry into the ways our perspectives have changed in the wake of the Copernican Revolution. We are all spinning on the surface of the earth, hurtling around the sun, and being dragged toward a black hole without our having anything to say about it. None of us stands on truly firm ground – a message not everyone wants to hear. No wonder that we hang on to belief and Truth so tenaciously. They provide a safe haven. It is more comfortable in the cave (Plato, Faust, Zarathustra) or the womb (Grass) than being exposed to the

---

10 John Leo, "Professors who see no evil," *U.S. News and World Report*, July 22, 2002, p. 14.

11 Mark William Roche, *Why Literature Matters in the 21st Century* (New Haven, CT: Yale University Press, 2004). While I agree with Roche's essential premise, my own approach to literature as a repository of human values does not require a guarantor of ethical values external to the universe we inhabit. An interrogation of our differences (which would take us too far afield here) would reveal common ground for assigning to Schiller's concept of play a pivot role in judging the intrinsic value of literature in our technologically driven age. Common ground can also be found in the notion of literature as a counterweight to instrumental reason, as a vehicle for expanding our intellectual horizons and for stretching our cultural sensibilities. Finally, Roche and I both believe that a purely anthropocentric approach to nature, with an insistence on manipulation, misses the point. For both of us, nature, with its creative processes, transcends the merely human but for me humankind is acting out nature's law in a particular manner. Integral to nature's way are many of the same qualities Roche cites for the value of literature; for example, self-transcendence, balance, vitality, and connectionism (see Roche, 205–37).

(four) elements. On the other hand, Of course, it is difficult to see new patterns if we do not leave the cave. If we do not evolve, if we do not emerge from the womb, if we do not peek over the horizon, there is no continuance, no renewal. We ossify.

Like Nietzsche many of the other innovative thinkers examined in the preceding pages directed their minds and their messages toward the few contemporaries who might understand. They looked to the distant future and relied on the long run for a measured assessment of their findings and conclusions (cf. *Za* 289). On the final page of *Ecce homo*, Nietzsche presents himself as the philosopher who wishes to be no prophet in the traditional sense of gathering disciples. In turn, he characterizes his *Übermensch* in Darwinian terms as the one who should evolve, survive, and prosper. Naturally, the common man responds negatively to anyone who steps outside the bounds. The herd mentality labels those strong enough to break from the pack as evil ("der Böse"). Yet it is precisely "the evil one" who gives promise of the future, who has not turned his back on life ("den jassagenden [...] den zukunftsgewissen, zukunftverbürgenden Menschen"; *KSA* 6:374). He (or she) is the one who acknowledges our earth-reality ("Erden-Realität") as the only world ("die einzige Welt") of any significance to humankind (*KSA* 6:374). And it is precisely Zarathustra who has dared to conceive reality as it truly is (*KSA* 6:370).

The three literary works examined in this study form a trilogy of critical assessments at seminal nodal points in the playing out of historical events over a two-hundred-year period of accelerated change. Faust, Zarathustra, and Oskar are anti-Christs, prophets of a new breed of independents. Their purpose is not to set themselves up as icons and be revered but rather to provoke and make uncomfortable. Each in his own way also seeks to be or to avoid becoming what he has been destined to become. Faust was unaware of the metaphysical overlay orchestrating his movement. But no matter. Even if he had known, he would not have cared, and it would not have made a difference. Zarathustra is at pains to speak in riddles so that any disciples will be self-selected and inclined to make their own judgments. Oskar does his best to avoid his destiny, but nature keeps drawing him back to his origins, inducing him to accept his participation (willed or not) in the forces of existence.

We have come a long way from the starting point in the pre-Enlightenment period when Truth was rooted in something other than the world that humans inhabit. In these works, the earth with its inner Spirit emerges as the strange attractor of human questing after Truth and meaning. It is like the magnet Goethe cites as an *Urphänomen* in his *Maximen und Reflexionen* to describe that which requires no explanation and for which we have no need of a name (#19). In his *Theory of Color,* he also explains that the *Urphänomen* designates the complex reality of natural phenomena that require no transcendental explanation (#175). To be sure, it is not a message that is likely to attract a mass audience. The message is too discomfiting. It is easier and safer by far to observe the Sabbath with like-minded believers. Yet the quixotic loners portrayed in these monumental "novels of the universe" exude an energy and vibrancy that reinvigorate the soul by encouraging the reader to ask impudent questions of oneself and about what it means to be human. All three of the protagonists teach by word and example to go beyond good and evil in the traditional meaning of the terms. And what is it, then, that one finds beyond good and evil? It is the creative urge – the act of bringing into existence something that existed only as a possibility, an idea, a dream, a suspicion, a fear. The shift in perspective from the created to the creating moment foregrounds emergence as the chief value and the most valued phenomenon within this system of being. Goethe makes that point emphatically in the metaphorically rich finale of *Faust II.* Nietzsche espouses this view decisively in his philosophical novel and repeats it succinctly in the final section of *Ecce homo*": Warum ich ein Schicksal bin" (why I am destiny). Grass creates the fearsome image of the Black Wicked Witch (better, "die schwarze Köchin") in the final chapter of *The Tin Drum* to make his point about the ineluctable need to act in the process of becoming what one is.

What these humanists have outlined in mythological form, scientists have delineated and tried to quantify since Copernicus. Each group has concluded that the "Erden-Realität" is our only real world. It all seems magically inspired. When we then introduce human consciousness into the mix, myth and reality appear so tightly bound to one another that they actually end up defining each other. Hence, the process of mapping reality has progressed in unexpected ways in the wake of the Copernican Revolution. The two cultures of science and the humanities are only superficially opposed. In reality they are grounded via deep structures in a third culture of integration. Those deep structures, which appear on the surface as memes (Dawkins), themata (Holton), motifs (Daemmrich), reflectaphors (Briggs), and strange attractors (Stewart), are accessed through the neural functions of the perceiving subject.

For his part, Edward O. Wilson is daring enough to propose a direct link between cultural archetypes and nodes of semantic memory. Semantic memory – unlike episodic memory, which recalls direct sense perceptions – invokes meaning by connecting objects and ideas to other objects and ideas. In other words, semantic memory operates according to analogy or symbolic thought. Adapting Richard Dawkins's term "meme" from *The Selfish Gene* (1976), Wilson suggests that memes are natural, discrete elements of culture. He sees them as corresponding to nodes, or reference points, in the brain. The nodes are encoded to recognize the cultural memes. Thus, he proposes the concept of the "node-as-meme."[12] The node – or reference point – is not conceived of as a spatially isolated center but rather as existing in a complex circuit of numerous nerve cells distributed over large, overlapping areas of the brain. The individual node is networked with other nodes, and they all cooperate in their identification efforts (136). It is a neat, albeit essentially binary, system of correspondence between the abstract and

12 Edward O. Wilson, *Consilience: The Unity of Knowledge* (New York: Alfred A. Knopf, 1998), 136.

physical worlds. Wilson's conception of how nodes-as-memes function bears obvious similarity to operations at the subatomic and microbiological levels with their essential tensions. Roger Penrose offers an even more refined view of the connectionism uniting the physical universe and human consciousness with his concept of brain plasticity. Here a binary approach is replaced by a system of multiple, changing contacts. Essential in all of the above, however, is the insistence on community and communication in the exchange of information. The nodal point is analogous to Nietzsche's gateway, where opposites meet.

A theory of creativity based on strategies of dynamic interaction in a world in flux with relative values offers a model for the nature of the creative act in the artist. Such a model cannot stop at the traditional notion of the inspired poet or artist with her or his special qualities of genius. Because of the genius's interaction within fields of mutual tension, it does not seem appropriate to differentiate rigorously among the creative person, the created product, and the creative process. The traditional emphasis on the uniqueness of originality and the nature of imitation has emerged as problematic. The need to ward off the natural tendency toward disequilibrium in movement throughout the human and physical universe amounts to the need constantly to seek balance within a field of tension. That effort is at the heart of the dance.

What we call genius is part of this system of communicative interaction. What sets the genius apart from ordinary people is her attunement to the inner operations of the natural world rather than solely to its impressive surface phenomena. The genius exhibits sensitivity to movement and analogies where others see only repetition. Genius does what nature does, only in tune with the full implications of what imitating nature entails. The jester in Nietzsche's *Thus Spoke Zarathustra*, therefore, is more like nature because of his light step. The first stirrings of a modern revitalized view of mimesis as more closely aligned with autopoiesis date from Breitinger's reflections in the early eighteenth century. Goethe's maxim that one cooperates with nature even when one seems to contradict it captures that more encompassing sense of autopoiesis with its emphasis on the economy of the whole rather than on the individualized part. Astute in its summary judgment a century later is Nietzsche's comment in *Menschliches, allzu Menschliches* (Human, All Too Human) whereby he questions our insistence on viewing the artist and the exceptional individual as being essentially different from the rest of us or separate from the productivity of nature itself. The philosopher notes that the so-called genius proceeds in a logical manner. First, she "learns how to lay bricks then how to build." She is constantly on the lookout for (new) material for the construction and is always putting something of herself into the artifice. Perhaps these bricks are carried to Babel, as Koestler mused. Yet it is not wasted activity. Nietzsche concludes: "Every activity of man is amazingly complicated, not only that of the genius: but none is a 'miracle.' – Whence, then, the belief that genius exists only in the artist, orator and philosopher? That only they have 'intuition'? (Whereby they are supposed to possess a kind of miraculous eyeglass with which they can see directly into 'the essence of the thing'!)" (*Human, All Too Human* #162).

Everyday events – space, time, society, labor, climate, food, locomotion, animals, recurring forces of nature – can teach us important lessons if we are willing to listen. "Every property of matter is a school for the understanding," Emerson had asserted long before Nietzsche, " – its solidity or resistance, its inertia, its extension, its figure, its divisibility. The understanding adds, divides, combines, measures, and finds nutriment and room for its activity in this worthy scene. Meantime, Reason transfers all these lessons into its own world of thought, by perceiving the analogy that marries Matter and Mind."[13] The artist does not create in a vacuum, does not call into existence something that had not previously existed. On the contrary, he simply discloses through shifts of attention what has always existed as a "negative presence," whose potential has gone untapped because of the strictures of habit that cause temporary blindness. It is an eternal game of making things manifest through constructive and deconstructive strategies. The aesthetic experience, however, is marked by an additional element lacking in purely natural phenomena; it is reconstitutive and illuminative. The aesthetic experience stimulates change by means of an accompanying emotional catharsis.[14] In the foregoing chapters I have endeavored to show how matter is wed to mind. The reader will of course judge whether the attempt has been successful. Undoubtedly, she will find room for her own interpretation; hopefully, even find a golden nugget treasure.

Although I followed a particular logic in arranging the chapters in the order in which they are presented here, the reader is free to peruse them in any way he chooses. Obviously, I hope he reads these pages with some profit via new insights and some old ones decked out differently and unexpectedly. In any case, I encourage the reader to consider that complex systems are marked by interconnections that become evident only after some probing. The preceding chapters build on one another, engage in a whole series of feedback loops, and combine discourses on various levels. The greatest benefit and the keenest awareness of an innovative approach to the study of literature, of philosophy, and of the history and philosophy of science will result if the reader is prepared to read this book as a coded sequence. The bases of structural formation recombine again and again. Sometimes attention is drawn to their operations explicitly; sometimes the processes are left unspoken.

The explorations of the questions in the foregoing pages have fascinated me for a long period of time: What role does literature play in a world dominated by

---

13 R. W. Emerson, "Nature" (1836), in Emerson, *Selected Writings*, ed. by Brooks Atkinson (New York: Random House, 1950), 20. A modern variation of this theme is found in Wilson, *Consilience*, 64.

14 Koestler, *The Act of Creation*, 335, 383. Moreover, Koestler sees a clear parallel between the genesis of art forms and the history of scientific paradigm shifts: "Most of the general considerations in the chapter on 'The Evolution of Ideas' (224–54) equally apply to the evolution of art" (335).

instrumental reason? Where do good and evil fit into the new scheme of things radically transformed by catastrophic historical events and – perhaps even more dramatically – a world radically repositioned by sense-extending instruments such as the scanning tunneling microscope, the atomic force microscope, the Hubble Space Telescope, and the differential microwave radiometer? The first two allow us to "see" the double helix of our inner coding machine, while the last two tell us where we have come from. These instruments have forever changed the way we see inner and outer space, even if most of us will never come into direct contact with any of these sight extenders.

Those instruments came about because somebody envisioned their use, their promise. The ability to imagine the barely conceivable has long been the forte of artists and writers. Now we know – thanks to people like Gerald Holton, Thomas Kuhn, Hans Blumenberg, and David Bohm – that it is also characteristic of pioneering science in its efforts to decode the Book of Nature, making that which is illegible legible.[15] In this manner, the creative imagination has lured into existence worlds that could not be read, let alone verified, by human instrumentation. The chasm that once seemed to separate the two cultures of science and the humanities has diminished, if not disappeared. The methodologies still differ and the way we formulate our questions is still divergent, but the role of imagination and metaphor is common to both our endeavors. Central has been the concept of the horizon. If there is anything that we should have learned from these explorations, it is that creativity is consonant with seeing something new. It does not matter whether that which is perceived to be new is actually new or not. It might have been there all along, and we were simply not able to let it appear before our eyes.

Has postmodernism robbed us of the ability to believe in something of enduring value? No, I think not. The result of the dialectic between the modernist urge to control and the postmodernist fragmentation of universals is the insight that the goal is not the ultimate objective; the path toward the goal is. Throughout this study, Nietzsche's concept of life as a dangerous game ("ein schlimmes Spiel") that all must play has loomed large, from Faust to Oskar Matzerath. Variations of the theme underscore the value of living life fully, not simply through excessive exuberance, but moderated through the conservation of energy in the total economy of life. The goal, however, so these writers insist, should not be suburban sameness or urban conformity, even though we value the stability they represent. Rather, the goal should be the light-footed balancing act of the high-wire artist who overcomes fear to take delight in the challenges of completing the trek across the entire expanse of the treacherous void. Heidegger conceived of existence (*Da-sein*) as a beginning, as a "still is," as long as it

15 Symptomatic is Hans Blumenberg's intriguing study of readability as a metaphor for deciphering the world in the pursuit of knowledge over millennia, *Die Lesbarkeit der Welt*, 2nd ed. (Frankfurt a.M.: Suhrkamp, 1989).

remains dedicated to the inchoative moment.[16] He also saw it as resulting from cooperation between the willing subject and the willing earth.[17] In this scheme of things, truth (rather than absolute Truth) is an explosive happening rather than an unquestioned given. Mere soporific existence is a betrayal of being as the happening of truth. What the writers examined here seem to agree on is that the meaning of life emanates from within us; it is not bestowed from without. While the physical world we inhabit can run on autopilot, they suggest, our individual balancing acts demand wakefulness. Only then do we participate fully in re-creation and thereby realize the purpose of our *Da-sein*. To live thusly would be tantamount to engaging in a "life-long love affair" with life itself.[18] None of this works without continuance.

---

16 Martin Heidegger, "The Rectorate 1933/34: Facts and Thoughts," trans. by Karsten Harries, *Review of Metaphysics* 29 (1975–76): 473.

17 That is the central thesis of Ernst Fuhrmann's *Was die Erde Will: Eine Biosophie* (Munich: Matthes and Seitz Verlag, 1986).

18 John Lachs, *In Love with Life* (Nashville, TN: Vanderbilt University Press, 1998), 49.

Bibliography

A. PRIMARY LITERATURE

Emerson, Ralph Waldo. *Selected Writings*. Ed. by Brooks Atkinson. New York: Random House, 1950.

Fichte, Johann Gottlieb. *Die Bestimmung des Menschen*. Repr. of original edition of 1800. Berlin: Vossische Buchhandlung, Ed. Theodor Ballauff and Ignaz Klein. Stuttgart: Reclam,1981.

Goethe, Johann Wolfgang von. *Sämtliche Werke*. Frankfurter Ausgabe. Ed. by Friedmar Apel, Hendrik Birus et al. 40 Vols. Frankfurt a.M: Deutscher Klassiker Verlag, 1985–99.

______. *Werke*. Sophienausgabe. Ed. In Commission for Grandduchess Sophie of Saxony. 6 Divisions. 133 Vols. in 143 Parts. Weimar: Hermann Böhlau, 1887–1919.

______. *Werke*. Hamburger Ausgabe. Ed. by Eric Trunz. 14 Vols. Munich: Hanser, 1968.

______. *Faust. Texte*. Ed. by Albrecht Schöne. Darmstadt: Wissenschaftliche Buchgesellschaft, 1999. This edition is identical to J. w. von Goethe, *Sämtliche Werke*. Frankfurter Ausgabe. Ed. by Friedmar Apel et al. 40 Vols. Frankfurt a. M.: Deutscher Klassiker Verlag, 1985–99. Vol. 7/1 (1994).

______. *Faust. Part One and Part Two*. Trans. with an Introduction and Notes by Charles E. Passage. Fourteenth Printing. New York: MacMillan Publishing Co., 1987.

______. *Scientific Studies*. Ed. and trans. by Douglas Miller. New York: Suhrkamp Publishers, 1988.

Grass, Günter. *Der Autor als fragwürdiger Zeuge* Ed. by Daniela Hermes. Munich: Deutscher Taschenbuch Verlag, 1997.

______. "Rückblick auf die Blechtrommel – oder Der Autor als fragwürdiger Zeuge. Ein Versuch in eigener Sache," In: Grass, *Der Autor als fragwürdiger Zeuge* (1997). 102–114.

______. *The Tin Drum*. Trans. by Ralph Manheim . New York: Vintage International, 1989.

______. "To Be Continued ... Fortsetzung folgt." *PMLA* 115.3 (May 2000): 292–309.

______ and Harro Zimmermann. *Vom Abenteuer der Aufklärung. Werkstattgespräche*. Göttingen: Steidl Verlag, 1999.

______. *Werkasugabe in zehn Bänden*. Ed. by Volker Neuhaus. Darmstadt and Neuwied: Luchterhand, 1987.

______. *Women's Wear Daily*. Friday, September 21, 1973, p.18.

Leibniz, Gottfried Wilhelm. *Monadologie*. Trans. by Herrmann Glockner. Stuttgart: Reclam, 1954.

______. *Philosophical Writings*. Ed. by G. H. R. Parkinson. Trans. by Mary Morris

and G. H. R. Parkinson. The Everyman Library. London: J. M. Dent, 1997.
Nietzsche, Friedrich. *The Complete Works of Friedrich Nietzsche*. Ed. by Oscar Levy. 18 Vols. New York: Russell and Russell, 1964.
______. *The Gay Science*. Trans. by Walter Kaufmann. New York: Vintage, 1974.
______. *Human, All Too Human*. Trans. by R. J. Hollingdale with an Introduction by Richard Schacht. Cambridge: Cambridge University Press, 1996.
______. *Thus Spoke Zarathustra: A Book for All and None* (1886). Trans. and with a Preface by Walter Kaufmann. New York: New American Library, 1995.
______. *Sämtliche Werke. Kritische Studienausgabe*. Ed. by Giorgio Colli and Mazzino Montinari. 15 Vols. Munich: Deutscher Taschenbuch Verlag, 1988.
______. *Werke und Briefe. Historisch-Kritische Gesamtausgabe*. Ed. by H. J. Mette and Karl Schlechta. 23 Vols. Munich: Musarion, 1933–40.
______. *Gesammelte Werke*. Musarionausgabe. 22 Vols. Munich: Musarion Verlag, 1922–27.
Schiller, Friedrich. "Über Anmut und Würde." In: Schiller. *Werke. Nationalausgabe*. 43 Vols. Ed. by Julius Petersen, Benno von Wiese, Helmut Koopmann et al. Weimar: Hermann Böhlaus Nachfolger, 1940–.
______. *Werke in drei Bänden*. Ed. by Gerhart Fricke and Herbert G. Göpfert. Munich: Hanser, 1966.
Schlegel, August Wilhelm, and Friedrich Schlegel. *Athenaeum. Eine Zeitschrift 1798–1800*. Reinbek bei Hamburg: Rowohlt, 1969.
______. "Athenäums-Fragmente." In: *Kritische und theoretische Schriften*. Ed. by Andreas Huyssen. Stuttgart: Reclam, 1978.
Schlegel, Friedrich. "Fragmente." *Athenäum. Eine Zeitschrift*. 3 Vols. Ed. by August Wilhelm and Friedrich Schlegel. Berlin: Vieweg, 1798, and Heinrich Frölich, 1799–1800. Repr. Darmstadt: Wissenschaftliche Buchgesellschaft, 1992.
[Spiess, Johann.]. *Historia von D. Johann Fausten. Neudruck des Faust-Buches von 1587*. Ed. with an Introduction by Hans Henning. Halle/Salle: Verlag Sprache und Literatur, 1963.
Wieland, Christoph Martin. *Werke*. Ed. by Fritz Martini and Hans Werner Seiffert. 5 Vols. Munich: Hanser, 1964–68.

B. SECONDARY LITERATURE

http://brint.com/Systems.htm
http://en.wikipedia.org/wiki/Main_Page
http://lbc.nimh.nih.gov/images/brain.jpg
http://marymt.edu/~psychol/brain.html
http://www.msnbc.com–MSNBCInteractive–MicrosoftInternet
http://www.med.harvard.edu/AANLIB/home.html
http://www.powersoften.com
http://www.societyforchaostheory.org/links/html
http://www.uws.edu.au/vip/dimitrov/Studying-Complexity.htm

Adorno, Theodor W. *Erziehung zur Mündigkeit. Vorträge und Gespräche mit Hellmut Becker 1959–1969*. Ed. by Gerd Kadelbach. Frankfurt a. M..: Suhrkamp, 1971.

Alford, C. Fred. *What Evil Means to Us*. Ithaca and London: Cornell University Press, 1997.

Amrine, Frederick (ed.). *Goethe in the History of Science*. 2 Vols. New York: Peter Lang, 1996.

______. *Literature and Science as Modes of Expression*. Dordrecht / Boston / London: Kluwer Academic Publishers, 1989.

Andreas-Grisebach, Manon. *Eine Ethik für die Natur*. Zurich: Ammann Verlag, 1991.

Ansell-Pearson, Keith and Howard Caygill (eds.). *The Fate of the New Nietzsche*. Aldershot: Avebury, 1993.

Arendt, Hannah. *Eichmann in Jerusalem: A Report on the Banality of Evil*. New York: Viking Press, 1965.

Aschheim, Steven E. *The Nietzsche Legacy in Germany 1890–1990*. Berkeley: University of California Press, 1992.

Auxter, Thomas. *Kant's Moral Teleology*. Macon, GA: Mercer University Press, 1982.

Barzun, Jacques. Science: *The Glorious Entertainment*. New York: Harper and Row, 1964.

Baudrillard, Jean. *The Transparency of Evil: Essays on Extreme Phenomena*. Trans. by James Benedict. London and New York: Verso, 1993.

Baumann, Gerhart. "Goethe: Schriften zur Kunst – Vermittlungen einer Poetik." In: *Ein unteilbares Ganzes. Goethe: Kunst und Wissenschaft*. Ed. by Günter Schnitzler and Gottfried Schramm. Freiburg i.B.: Rombach Verlag, 1997. 89–116.

Beiser, Frederick C. "Kant's Intellectual Development 1747–1781." In: *The Cambridge Companion to Kant*. Ed. by Paul Guyer. New York: Cambridge University Press, 1992.

Bell, Matthew. *Goethe's Naturalistic Anthropology: Man and Other Plants*. Oxford: Clarendon Press, 1994.

Bennett, Benjamin. *Goethe's Theory of Poetry: Faust and the Regeneration of Language* (Ithaca and London: Cornell University Press, 1986.

Berger, John. *Ways of Seeing*. London: Penguin, 1972.

Birnbacher, Dieter. "'Natur' als Maßstab menschlichen Handelns." *Zeitschrift für philosophische Forschung* 45 (1991): 60–76.

Birus, Henrik. "Nietzsche's Hermeneutical Considerations." In: *Nietzsche: Literature and Values*. Ed. by Volker Dürr, Reinhold Grimm, and Kathy Harms. *Monatshefte*. Occasional Volumes. No. 6. Madison: University of Wisconsin Press, 1988. 66–80.

Bloom, Howard. *The Lucifer Principle: A Scientific Expedition into the Forces of History*. New York: The Atlantic Monthly Press, 1995.

Blumenberg, Hans. *The Genesis of the Copernican World*. Trans. by Robert M. Wallace. Cambridge MA: MIT University Press, 1987.

______. "Der genetische Code und seine Leser." In: H. Blumenberg. *Die Lesbarkeit der Welt* (1986). 372–409.

______. *Lebenszeit und Weltzeit*. Frankfurt a. M.: Suhrkamp, 1986.

______. *Die Lesbarkeit der Welt*. 2nd Ed. Frankfurt a.M.: Suhrkamp, 1987.

______. "'Nachahmung der Literatur.' Zur Vorgeschichte der Idee des schöpferischen Menschen." In: H. Blumenberg. *Wirklichkeiten in denen wir leben*. Stuttgart: Reclam, 1981. 55–103.

Bodmer, Johann Jakob and Johann Jakob Breitinger. *Schriften zur Literatur*. Ed. Volker Meid. Stuttgart: Reclam, 1980.

Bohm, David. *On Creativity*. Ed. by Lee Nichol. London and New York: Routledge,1998.

______. *Science, Order, and Creativity*. New York: Bantam Books, 1987, 2000[2].

______. *Thought as a System*. London and New York: Routledge, 1994.

______. *Unfolding Meaning: A Weekend of Dialogue with David Bohm*. London: Routledge and Kegan Paul, 1985.

______. *Wholeness and the Implicate Order*. London: Routledge and Kegan Paul, 1980.

______ and F. David Peat. *Science, Order, and Creativity: A Dramatic New Look at the Creative Roots of Science and Life*. Toronto and New York: Bantam Books, 1987.

______ and B. J. Hiley. *The Undivided Universe*. London: Routledge, 1993.

Böhm, Peter. "Energie–Kreativität–Gott." *Perspektiven der Philosophie* 17 (1991): 37–75.

Bonting, Sjoerd L. *Chaos Theology: A Revised Creation Theology*. St. Paul University Research Series: Faith and Science. Novalis: Toronto, 2002.

Bountis, T. (ed.). *Chaotic Dynamics. Theory and Practice*. NATO Advanced Science Institutes Series 298. New York, London: Plenum P, 1992.

Boyle, Nicholas. *Goethe: The Poet and his Age*. Vols. 1 and 2. Oxford: Clarendon P, 1991,2000.

Brann, Eva T. H. "The Canon Defended." *Philosophy and Literature* 17.2 (1993): 193–218.

Braun, Theodore E. D. and John A. McCarthy (eds.). *Disrupted Patterns: On Chaos and Order in the Enlightenment*. Amsterdam and Atlanta: Rodopi, 2000.

Breitinger, Johann Jakob. *Critische Abhandlung von der Natur, den Absichten und dem Gebrauche der Gleichnisse*. Faksimiledruck nach der Ausgabe von 1740. Stuttgart: Metzler, 1967.

______. *Critische Dichtkunst*. Faksimiledruck nach der Ausgabe von 1740. 2 Vols. Stuttgart: Metzler, 1967

Breuer, Dieter. "Mephisto als Theologe." *Goethe-Jahrbuch* 109 (1992): 91–100.

Breuer, Reinhard and Günter Haaf. "Ein ordentliches Chaos." *Geo-Wissen: Chaos + Kreativität*. Hamburg: Gruner + Jahr AG and Co, 1990, 32–60.

Briggs, John. *Fire in the Crucible*. New York: St. Martins Press, 1988.

______. "Reflectaphors: The (Implicate) Universe as a Work of Art." In: *Quantum Implications*. Ed. David Peat and Basil Hiley. London: Routledge and Kegan Paul, 1987. 414–36.

______ and F. David Peat (ed.). *Die Entdeckung des Chaos. Eine Reise durch die Chaos-Theorie*. Trans. from English by Carl Carius with the aid of Peter Kafka. Second edition. Munich: Hanser, 1993.

______ and F. David Peat. *Turbulent Mirror: An Illustrated Guide to Chaos Theory and the Science of Wholeness*. New York: Harper and Row, 1989.

Brown, Jane K. *Goethe's Faust: The German Tragedy*. Ithaca, NY: Cornell University Press, 1986.

Brügge, Peter. "Kult um das Chaos: Aberglaube oder Welterklärung?" *Der Spiegel* 39 (1993): 156–64; 40 (1993): 232–41; 41 (1993): 240–52.

Buber, Martin. *Images of Good and Evil*. Trans. from the German by Michael Bullock. London: Routledge and Kegan Paul, 1952.

Bucke, Richard M. *Kosmisches Bewußtsein*. Frankfurt a.M.: Insel, 1993.

Busch, Thomas. *Die Affirmation des Chaos. Zur Überwindung des Nihilismus in der Metaphysik Friedrich Nietzsches*. Dissertations. Philosophy Series. Vol. 6. St. Ottilien: EOS Verlag Erzabteil St. Ottilien, 1989.

Buttlar, Johannes von. *Gotteswürfel. Schicksal oder Zufall*. Munich: Herbig, 1992.

Cambel, Ali Bulent. *Applied Chaos Theory: A Paradigm for Complexity*. Boston: Academic P, 1993.

Cain, William E. "Canons, Critics, Theorists, Classrooms." *Philosophy and Literature* 17.2 (1993): 302–14.

Canning, Peter. "How the Fable Becomes a World." In: *Looking After Nietzsche*. Ed. by Laurence A. Rickels. Albany: State University of New York Press, 1990. 175–93.

Cassirer, Ernst. *Philosophie der symbolischen Formen*. Part III: *Phänomenologie der Erkenntnis*. Tenth edition. Darmstadt: Wissenschaftliche Buchgesellschaft, 1994.

______. *The Philosophy of the Enlightenment*. Trans. by Fritz C. A. Koelnn and James P. Pettegrove. Boston: Beacon P, 1955.

Casti, John L. *Complexification: Explaining a Paradoxical World Through the Science of Surprise*. New York: HarperCollins, 1994.

Chaos und Kreativität. Geo-Wissen. Ed. Günter Haaf. Hamburg: Verlag Gruner und Jahr AG and Co, 1990.

Chaos and Quantum Chaos. Proceedings of the Eighth Chris Engelbrecht Summer School on Theoretical Physics Held at Blydepoort, Eastern Transvaal South Africa, 13–24 January 1992. Berlin: Springer, 1993.

Cilliers, Paul. *Complexity and Postmodernism: Understanding Complex Systems*. London and New York: Routledge, 1998.

Cohen, Jack and Ian Stewart. *The Collapse of Chaos: Discovering Simplicity in a Complex World*. New York: Penguin Books, 1994.

Collingwood, R. G. "Art and Craft." *The Philosophy of the Visual Arts*. Ed.. V. Philip Alperson. New York: Oxford University Press, 1992. S.381–92. Previously published in R. G. Collingwood. *The Principles of Art*. New York: Oxford University Press, 1938. 15–41, 109–11, 121–22.

Cottrell, Alan P. "The Resurrection of Thinking and the Redemption of Faust: Goethe's New Scientific Attitude." *Goethe's Way of Science: A Phenomenology of Nature*. Ed. by David Seamon and Arthur Zajonc. Albany: State University of New York Press, 1998. 255–75.

Copjec, Joan (ed.). *Radical Evil*. London and New York: Verso, 1996.

Cues, Nikolaus von. *Die Kunst der Vermutung. Auswahl aus den Schriften*. Ed. by Hans Blumenberg. Bremen: Carl Schünemann, 1957.

Coveney, Peter and Roger Highfield. *Frontiers of Complexity: The Search for Order in a Chaotic World*. New York: Fawcett Columbine, 1995.

Cramer, Friedrich. *Chaos und Ordnung*. Frankfurt/M: Insel, 1993.

Daemmrich, Horst S. and Ingrid. *Themes and Motifs in Western Literature: A Handbook*. Tübingen: Francke, 1987.

Davies, Paul. *Are We Alone? Philosophical Implications of the Discovery of Extraterrestrial Life*. New York: Basic Books, 1995.

______. *Cosmic Blueprint*. London: Unwin Hyman Ltd., 1987.

______. *Prinzip Chaos. Die neue Ordnung des Kosmos*. Munich: Goldmann, 1990.

______ and J. R. Brown (eds.). *The Ghost in the Atom*. Cambridge: Cambridge University Press, 1986.

______ and John Gribbin. *The Matter Myth: Dramatic Discoveries that Challenge our Understanding of Physical Reality*. New York, London etc.: Simon and Shuster, 1992.

Del Caro, Adrian. *Nietzsche contra Nietzsche: Creativity and the Anti-Romantic* Baton Rouge:. Louisiana State University Press, 1989.

______. *Dionysian Aesthetics: The Role of Destruction in Creation as Reflected in the Life and Works of Friedrich Nietzsche.* Frankfurt a.M: Peter Lang, 1981.

Deleuze, Gilles. *The Fold: Leibniz and the Baroque.* Trans. by Tom Conley. Minneapolis: U of Minnesota P, 1993.

______. "Pensée nomade." In: *Nietzsche – Aujourd'hui?* 2 Vols. Paris: Centre Culturel Internationale Cérisy-la-Salle, 1973. 1: 159–74.

______. *Spinoza: Philosophie pratique.* Second, expanded edittion. Paris: les Éditions de Minuit, 1981.

de Stael, Anne Louise Germaine. *De l'Allemagne.* Frankfurt a.M.: Insel Verlag, 1985.

Diller, Edward. *A Mythic Journey. Günter Grass' Tin Drum.* Lexington: U of Kentucky P, 1974.

Döblin, Alfred ."Der Wille zur Macht als Erkenntnis bei Friedrich Nietzsche" (1902). In: *Nietzsche und die deutsche Literatur.* Ed. by Bruno Hillebrand. 2 Vols. Munich: Deutscher Taschenbuch Verlag, 1978. 1: 315–30.

______. "Zu Nietzsches Morallehre" (1903). In: *Nietzsche und die deutsche Literatur.* Ed. by Bruno Hillebrand. 2 Vols. Munich: Deutscher Taschenbuch Verlag, 1978. 1: 331–58.

Donat, Sebastian and Hendrik Birus. *Goethe. Ein letztes Universalgenie?* Göttingen: Wallstein, 1999.

Drazin, P.G. *Nonlinear Systems.* Cambridge: Cambridge University Press, 1992.

Duff, William. *An Essay on Original Genius and its Various Modes of Exertion in Philosophy and the Fine Arts, Particularly Poetry.* Ed. by John L. Mahoney. London, 1767; repr. Gainesville FL: Scholars' Facsimiles and Reprints, 1964.

Eagleton, Terry. *The Ideology of the Aesthetic.* Oxford: Basil Blackwell, 1990.

Eco, Umberto. "The Poetics of the Open Work." In: *Role of the Reader* (1984). 47–66.

______. *The Role of the Reader. Explorations in the Semiotics of Texts.* Bloomington: Indiana University Press, 1984.

Eibl, Karl. *Das monumentale Ich – Wege zu Goethes Faust.* Frankfurt a. M. and Leipzig: Insel Verlag, 2000.

Einem, Herbert von. *Beiträge zu Goethes Kunstauffassung.* Hambrug: Schröder, 1956.

Ersch, J. S. and J. G. Gruber (eds.). *Allgemeine Encyclopädie der Wissenschaften und Künste in alphabetischer Folge.* Part 6l: *Cea bis Chiny.* Leipzig: Johann Friedrich Gleditsch, 1827.

Esslin, Martin. "Goethe's *Faust*: Pre-Modern, Post-Modern, Proto-Postmodern." In: *Interpreting Goethe's Faust Today.* Ed. by Jane K. Brown, Meredith Lee, and Thomas P. Saine. Columbus SC: Camden House, 1994. 219–227.

Fink, Karl J. "Immagini virtuali nella scienza di Goethe." Goethe Scienziato. A cura di Guilio Giorello e Agnese Grieco. Turino: Giolio Einaudi editore, 1998. 171–93.

Fleischer, Margot. *Der 'Sinn der Erde' und die Entzauberung des Übermenschen: Eine Auseinandersetzung mit Nietzsche*. Darmstadt: Wissenschaftliche Buchgesellschaft, 1993.

Fox, Matthew and Rupert Sheldrake. *Natural Grace: Dialogues on Creation, Darkness, and the Soul in Spirituality and Science*. New York: Doubleday, 1996.

Frenzel, Elizabeth. *Stoff- Motiv- und Symbolforschung*. Stuttgart: Metzler, 1963.

Friedrich, Theodor and Lothar J. Scheithauer. *Kommentar zu Goethes Faust*. 3. Auflage. Stuttgart: Reclam, 1994.

Friedrichsmeyer, Erhard M. "Aspects of Myth, Parody, and Obscenity in Grass's *Die Blechtrommel* and *Katz und Maus*. *The Germanic Review* 40.3 (1965): 240–50.

Fröhlich, J. et al (ed.). *New Symmetry Principles in Quantum Field Theory*. NATO Advanced Science Institutes Series 295. New York, London: Plenum P, 1989.

Fuchs, Albert. "Mephistopheles" (1968). In: Werner Keller (ed.). *Aufsätze zu Goethes "Faust I."* Darmstadt: Wissenschaftliche Buchgesellschaft, 1974. 348–61.

______. "Die 'Mütter'. Eine Mephistopheles-Phantasmagorie." In: A. Fuchs, *Goethe-Studien*. Berlin, 1968. 64–81.

Fuhrmann, Ernst. *Was die Erde Will. Eine Biosophie*. Munich: Matthes and Seitz Verlag, 1986.

Fulton, James Street. "Creativity and Openness."*Rice University Studies* 61.3 (Summer 1975): 1–12.

Gaier, Ulrich. *Goethes Faust-Dichtungen. Ein Kommentar*. 2 Vols. Stuttgart: Reclam, 1989.

______. *Goethes Faust-Dichtungen. Ein Kommentar. Urfaust*. Second edition. Stuttgart: Reclam, 1990.

______. *Magie: Goethes Analyse moderner Verhaltensformen im Faust*. Konstanz: Universitätsverlag, 1999.

Gebhard, Walter. "Erkennen und Entsetzen. Zur Tradition der Chaos-Annahmen im Denken Nietzsches." In: *Friedrich Nietzsche. Strukturen der Negativität*. Ed. by Walter Gebhard. *Bayreuther Beiträge zur Literaturwissenschaft* 5. Frankfurt a.M.: Peter Lang, 1984. 13–47.

Gegenfurtner, Karl R. *Gehirn und Wahrnehmung*. Second ed. Frankfurt a.M.: Fischer Taschenbuch Verlag, 2004.

Gleick, James. *Chaos: Making a New Science*. New York: Penguin, 1987.

______. *Chaos – Die Ordnung des Universum. Vorstoß in Grenzbereiche der modernen Physik*. Trans. from English by Peter Prange. Munich: Knaur, 1990.

Görtz, Franz Josef (ed.). *'Die Blechtrommel'– Attraktion und Ärgernis. Ein Kapitel deutscher Literaturkritik*. Darmstadt and Hermann Neuwied: Luchterhand, 1984.

Goiccoiccea, David. "The Bad and the Evil in Augustine and Nietzsche." In: *The Problem of Evil: An Intercultural Exploration*, ed. by Sandra A. Wawrytko. Amsterdam and Atlanta: Rodopi, 2000. 53–60.

Greene, Brian. *The Elegant Universe: Superstrings, Hidden Dimensions, and the Quest for the Ultimate Theory.* Vintage Books: New York, 2000.

Grimminger, Rolf. *Die Ordnung, das Chaos und die Kunst.* Frankfurt a.M.: Suhrkamp, 1986.

Grolle, Johann. "Hatte Gott eine Wahl?" *Der Spiegel* 6 (1993): 182–88.

Gross, Paul R., Norman Levitt, Martin W. Lewis (eds.). *The Flight from Science and Reason.* New York: The New York Academy of Sciences distributed by The Johns Hopkins University Press, 1996.

______ and Norman Levitt. *Higher Superstition: The Academic Left and Its Quarrels with Science.* Baltimore and London: Johns Hopkins University Press, 1998².

Großes vollständiges Universal-Lexikon aller Wissenschaften und Künste, welche bißhero durch menschlichen Verstand und Witz erfunden und verbessert worden, Bd. 5: C–Ch. Halle and Leipzig: Johann Heinrich Zedler, 1733.

Grünzweig, Walter. "Computer und Kreativität. Postmodernismus, Fraktale Geometrie und John Updike." In: *Medien und Maschinen. Literatur im technischen Zeitalter.* Ed. by Theo Elm und Hans H. Hiebel. Freiburg: Rombach Verlag, 1991. 168–77.

Grumach, Ernst. "Prolog und Epilog im Faustplan von 1797" (1952/53). In: Werner Keller (ed.). *Aufsätze zu Goethes "Faust I."* Darmstadt: Wissenschaftliche Buchgesellschaft, 1974. 310–26.

Guidry, Glenn A. "Theoretical Reflections on the Ideological and Social Implications of Mythic Form in Grass' *Die Blechtrommel.*" *Monatshefte* 83.2 (1991): 127–46.

Guthke, Karl S. *The Last Frontier: Imagining Other Worlds from the Copernican Revolution to Modern Science Fiction.* Trans. by Helen Atkins. Ithaca, NY: Cornell University Press,1990.

Gutting, Gary (ed.). *Paradigms and Revolutions: Appraisals and Applications of Thomas Kuhn's Philosophy of Science.* Notre Dame, IN: University of Notre Dame Press, 1980.

Habermas, Jürgen. "Life-Forms, Morality and the Task of the Philosopher." In: J. Habermas. *Autonomy and Solidarity. Interviews.* Ed. by Peter Drews. London and New York: Verso, 1990. 191–216.

Habermeier, Steffi. "Science, Gender, Text: Eine Untersuchung zum Beispiel der Diskursivierung der Chaosforschung in literarischen und nichtliterarischen Texten." Diss. Munich 1995.

Hall, Nina (ed.). *The New Scientist Guide to Chaos.* London: Penguin, 1992.

Hamilton, Edith. *Mythology: Timeless Tales of Gods and Heroes,* 23rd printing. New York: New American Library, 1963.

Hänsel, Ludwig. *Goethe. Chaos und Kosmos – Vier Versuche.* Vienna: Thomas Morus Presse im Verlag Herder, 1949.

Hayles, N. Katheryn (ed.). *Chaos and Order.* Chicago: University of Chicago Press, 1991.

______. *Chaos Bound.* Ithaca, NY: Cornell University Press, 1990.

______ *The Cosmic Web: Scientific Field Models and Literary Strategies in the Twentieth Century*. Ithaca, NY: Cornell University Press, 1984.

Hawking, Stephen. *Black Holes and Baby Universes and Other Essays*. New York: Bantam Books, 1993.

Hederich, Benjamin. *Gründliches mythologisches Lexicon.* Ed. by Johann Joachim Schwabe. Leipzig 1770. Photomechanical Reproduction. Darmstadt: Wissenschaftliche Buchgesellschaft, 1986.

Heidegger, Martin. *Discourse on Thinking*. Trans. by John M. Anderson and E. Hans Freund. New York: Harper and Row, 1966.

______. *Gelassenheit*. Stuttgart: Neske, 1977.

______. "The Rectorate 1933/34: Facts and Thoughts." Trans. by Karsten Harries. *Review of Metaphysics* 29 (1975–76): 473.

Heinrichs, Norbert. "Scientia Magica" (1970). In: *Aufsätze zu Goethes "Faust I."* Ed. by Werner Keller. Darmstadt: Wissenschaftliche Buchgesellschaft, 1974. 607–24.

Heßelmann, Peter. Review of *Der moderne deutsche Schelmenroman. Interpretationen.* Ed. by Gerhart Hoffmeister. Amsterdam: Rodopi,1986. In *Heine-Jahrbuch* 29 (1990): 218–220.

Higgins, Kathleen Marie. *Nietzsche's Zarathustra*. Philadelphia: Temple University Press, 1987.

______. "Reading *Zarathustra*." *Reading Nietzsche*. Ed. by Robert C. Solomon and Kathleen Higgins. New York and Oxford: Oxford University Press, 1988. 132–51.

Hölder, Helmut. "Goethe als Geologe." *Goethe-Jahrbuch* 111 (1994): 231–45.

Hoffmann, Nigel. "The Unity of Science and Art: Goethean Phenomenology as a New Ecological Discipline." In: *Goethe's Way of Science* (1998). Ed. by F. Amrine. 129–75.

Hoffmann, Ulrich. "Mephistopheles: 'Ich bin ein Teil des Teils, der anfangs alles war.'" *Goethe-Jahrbuch* 109 (1992): 57–60.

Holland, John H. *Hidden Order: How Adaptation Builds Complexity*. Reading, MA: Helix Books / Addison-Wesley Publishing Co., 1995.

Holton, Gerald (ed.). *Science and Culture. A Study of Cohesive and Disjunctive Forces*. Cambridge MA: Houghton Mifflin, 1965.

_______. *The Scientific Imagination: Case Studies*. Cambridge: Cambridge University Press, 1978.

______. *Thematic Origins of Scientific Thought: Kepler to Einstein*. Cambridge MA: Harvard University Press, 1973.

Holub, Robert C. *Friedrich Nietzsche*. TWAS 857. New York: Twayne Publishers, 1995.

Horkheimer, Max and Theodor W. Adorno. *Dialektik der Aufklärung. Philosophische Fragmente.* Frankfurt a.M.: Fischer Verlag, 1988.

Max Horkheimer, *Eclipse of Reason*. New York: Oxford University Press, 1947.

Horn, Susanne. "Bergrat Johann Carl Wilhelm Voigt (1752–1821): Beiträge zur Geognosie und Mineralogie." In: Andrea Heinz (ed.). *"Der teutsche Merkur" – die erste deutsche Kulturzeitschrift?* Heidelberg: Universitätsverlag Winter, 2003. 199–214

Iser, Wolfgang. *Der Akt des Lesens*. UTB636. Munich: Fink, 1976.

Jahn, Robert G. and Brenda J. Dunne. *Margins of Reality: The Role of Consciousness in the Physical World*. San Diego, New York, London: Harcourt Brace Jovanovich, 1987.

Jahnke, Walter and Klaus Lindemann. *Günter Grass: Die Blechtrommel – Acht Kapitel zur Erschließung des Romans*. Paderborn: Ferdinand Schöningh, 1993.

Jantz, Harold. *The Mothers in Faust: The Myth of Time and Creativity*. Baltimore: The Johns Hopkins University Press, 1968.

James, William. *The Varieties of Religious Experience*. Cambridge, MA: Harvard University Press, 1985.

Jasper, Willi. *Faust und die Deutschen*. Berlin: Rowohlt, 1998.

Jeßing, Benedikt. *Johann Wolfgang Goethe*. SM 288. Stuttgart: J. B. Metzler, 1995.

______. Bernd Lutz and Inge Wild (eds.). *Metzler Goethe Lexikon*. Mit 150 Abbildungen. Stuttgart and Weimar: J. B. Metzler, 1999.

Johnson, E. A. "Does God Play Dice? Divine Providence and Chance."*Theological Studies* 57.1 (March 1996): 3–16.

Johnson, Laurie Ruth. *The Art of Recollection in Jena Romanticism: Memory, History, Fiction, and Fragmentation in Texts by Friedrich Schlegel and Novalis*. Tübingen: Niemeyer, 2002.

______. "Bringing Chaos into the System: The Aesthetic Authority of Disorder in Friedrich Schlegel's Philosophy." In: *Disrupted Patterns: On Chaos and Order in the Enlightenment*. Ed. by Theodore E. D. Braun and John A. McCarthy. Amsterdam and Atlanta: Rodopi, 2002. 119–33.

Kanitscheider, Bernulf. *Von der mechanistischen Welt zum kreativen Universum. Zu einem neuen philosophischen Verständnis der Natur*. Darmstadt: Wissenschaftliche Buchgesellschaft, 1993.

Kant, Immanuel. "Dialektik der ästhetischen Urteilskraft." In: *Werke in zehn Bänden*. Ed. by Wilhelm Weischedel. 5th ed. Darmstadt: Wissenschaftliche Buchgesellschaft, 1983. 8: 441–61.

______. *Kritik der ästhetischen Urteilskraft. Werke in zehn Bänden*. Ed. by Wilhelm Weischedel. Darmstadt: Wissenschaftliche Buchgesellschaft, 1983. 8: 173–465.

Kauffman, Stuart. *At Home in the Universe: The Search for Laws of Self-Organization and Complexity*. New York: Oxford University Press, 1995.

Keller, Evelyn Fox. *A Feeling for the Organism: The Life and Work of Barbara McClintock*. New York: W. H. Freeman and Co., 1983.

______. *Reflections on Gender and Science*. New Haven and London: Yale University Press, 1985.

Kellert, Stephen H. "Science and Literature and Philosophy: The Case of Chaos Theory and Deconstruction." *Configurations* 4.2 (1996): 215–32.

Kelly, Joseph F. *The Problem of Evil in the Western Tradition: From the Book of Job to Modern Genetics*. Collegeville MN: The Liturgical P, 2002.

Kerner, Charlotte. "Hab Chaos im Herzen." In *Geo-Wissen: Chaos + Kreativität*. Ed. by Günter Haaf. Hamburg: Verlag Gruner + Jahr AG and Co., 1990. 139–42.

Knapp, G. P. "Stoff–Motiv–Idee." In: *Grundzüge der Literatur- und Sprachwissenschaft*. Ed. by Heinz Ludwig Arnold and Volker Sinemus. Vol. 1: *Literaturwissenschaft*. Munich: Deutscher Taschenbuch Verlag, 1978.

Köster, P. "Nietzsches Beschwörung des Chaos." *Tübinger Theologische Quartalschrift* 153 (1973): 132–63.

Koestler, Arthur. *The Act of Creation*. London, Hutchinson, 1966.

______. "Bisociation in Creation." Albert Rothenberg and Carl R. Hausman (eds.). *The Creativity Question*. Durham, NC: Duke University Press, 1976. 108–113.

______. *Bricks to Babel*. New York: Random House, 1980.

______. *Der göttliche Funke*. 1968.

______. *Diesseits von Gut und Böse*. Berne, Munich, Vienna: Scherz, 1965.

______. *Die Wurzeln des Zufalls*. Suhrkamp Taschenbuch 181. Frankfurt a. M.: Suhrkamp, 1972

______. *Drinkers of Infinity: Essays 1955–1967*. London: Hutchinson, 1968.

______. *Janus: A Summing Up*. New York: Random House, 1978.

______ and J. R. Smythies (eds.). *Beyond Reductionism. New Perspectives in the Life Sciences*. The Alpach Symposium 1968. London: Hutchinson, 1969.

Kofman, Sarah. *Nietzsche and Metaphor*. Trans. by Duncan Large. Stanford, CA: Stanford University Press, 1993.

Kondylis, Panajotis *Die Aufklärung im Rahmen des neuzeitlichen Rationalismus*. Munich: Deutscher Taschenbuch Verlag, 1986.

Kowalik, Jill Anne. *The Poetics of Historical Perspectivism*. Chapel Hill, NC: University of North Carolina Press, 1992.

Koyré, Alexandre. *From the Closed World to the Infinite Universe*. New York: Harper, 1958; repr. Johns Hopkins University Press, 1994.

Krause, Jürgen. *"Märtyrer" und "Prophet". Studien zum Nietzsche-Kult in der bildenden Kunst der Jahrhundertwende*. Berlin and New York: Walter de Gruyter, 1984.

Krumme, Detlev. *Günter Grass. Die Blechtrommel*. Munich: Carl Hanser Verlag, 1986. 19–32.

Küppers, Bernd-Olaf. "Wenn das Ganze mehr ist als die Summe seiner Teile." *Geo-Wissen. Chaos + Kreativität*. Hamburg: Gruner + Jahr AG and Co., 1990. 28–31.

Kuhn, Thomas S. *The Essential Tension. Selected Studies in Scientific Tradition and Change*. Chicago: University of Chicago Press, 1977.

______. "The Natural and the Human Sciences." In: *The Interpretive Turn: Philosophy, Science, Culture*. Ed. by David R. Hiley, James F. Bohman, and Richard Shusterman. Ithaca: Cornell University Press, 1991. 17–24.

______. *The Structure of Scientific Revolutions*. 2nd ed. Chicago: University of Chicago Press, 1970.

Lachs, John. *In Love with Life*. Nashville: Vanderbilt University Press, 1998.

Leo, John. "Professors who see no evil." *U.S. News and World Report*. July 22, 2002. p. 14.

Leshan, Lawrence and Henry Margenau. *Einstein's Space and Van Gogh's Sky: Physical Reality and Beyond*. New York: Macmillan Publishing Co., 1982.

Levine, Peter. *Nietzsche and the Modern Crisis of the Humanities*. Albany: State University of New York Press, 1995.

Liss, Tony M. and Paul L. Tipton. "The Discovery of the Top Quark." *Scientific American* (Sept. 1997): 54–59.

Löw, Erwin von. *Strukturen in Goethes Faust. Graphische Darstellungen*. Augsburg: Guido Pressler, 1982.

Loistl, Otto and Iro Betz. *Chaostheorie. Zur Theorie nichtlinearer dynamischer Systeme*. Munich: R. Oldenbourg Verlag, 1993.

Love, Glen A. "Ecocritism and Science: Toward Consilience?" *New Literary History* 30 (1999): 561–576.

Lovejoy, Arthur O. *The Great Chain of Being: A Study in the History of an Idea*. New York: Harper and Row, 1960.

Lovin, Keith. "Free Will and Moral Evil." *Rice University Studies* 61.3 (Summer 1975): 45–58.

Lungstrum, Janet. "Self-Constructs of Impermanence: Kafka, Nietzsche and Creativity." *Seminar* 27.2 (May 1991): 102–120.

MacIntyre, Alasdair. *After Virtue: A Study in Moral Theory*. South Bend IN: Notre Dame University Press, 1981.

Mandelbrot, Benoît. *The Fractal Geometry of Nature*. San Francisco: W. H. Freeman, 1982.

Manthey, Jürgen. "'Die Blechtrommel' wiedergelesen." In: *Text + Kritik* 1. 6th ed. (1988): 24–36.

Martin, Günther ."Goethes Wolkenlehre im Atomzeitalter." *Goethe-Jahrbuch* 109 (1992): 199–206.

Mason, Eudo C. *Goethe's Faust: Its Genesis and Purport*. Berkeley and Los Angeles: University of California Press, 1967.

Maxwell, Donald R. *Science or Literature? The Divergent Cultures of Discovery and Creation*. New York: Peter Lang Publishing, 2000.

Mayer-Iswandy, Claudia. *Günter Grass*. dtv portrait. Munich: Deutscher Taschenbuch Verlag, 2002.

______. *"Vom Glück der Zwitter." Geschlechterrolle und Geschlechterverhältnis bei Günter Grass*. Frankfurt a. M.: Peter Lang, 1990.

McCarthy, John A. "Beyond a Philosophy of Alternatives: Chaos, Cosmology and the Eighteenth Century." In: *Disrupted Patterns: Chaos and Order in the Enlightenment*. Ed. by T. E. D. Braun and John A. McCarthy. Amsterdam and Atlanta: Rodopi, 2000. 21–36.

______. "Chaos: Motif, Theme, or Theory?" In: *Thematics Reconsidered: Essays in Honor of Horst S. Daemmrich*. Ed. by Frank Trommler. Amsterdam and Atlanta: Rodopi, 1995. 133–43.

______. "'A Chain of Utmost Potency": On the Agon and the Creative Impulse." *Agonistics: Arenas of Creative Contest*. Ed. by Janet Lungstrum and Elizabeth Sauer. Albany: State University of New York Press, 1997. 199–225

______. "Crisis Consciousness: An Enlightenment Legacy from Kant to Bloom." In: *Crisis and Culture in Post-Enlightenment Germany*. Essays in Honor of Peter Heller. Ed. by Hans Schulte and David Richards. New York: Lanham, 1993. 42–72.

______. "Criticism and Experience: Philosophy and Literature in the German Enlightenment." In: *Philosophy and German Literature, 1700–1990*. Cambridge: Cambridge University Press, 2002. 13–56.

______. "Emerson, Goethe und die Deutschen." *Goethe Yearbook of North America* 8 (1994): 179–93.

______. "Enlightenment Today or Movement at the Borders." *Transactions of the Ninth International Congress on the Enlightenment I–III*. Ed. by Werner Schneiders. Oxford: The Voltaire Foundation, 1996. I:173–86. (= *Studies on Voltaire and the Eighteenth Century* 346–348, 346:173–86).

______. "Nietzsche-Rezeption in der deutschen Literatur, 1880–1918." In: *Hansers Sozialgeschichte der deutschen Literatur*. Vol. 7: *Naturalismus, Fin de siècle, Expressionismus (1890–1918)*. Ed. York-Gothart Mix. Munich: Hanser, 2000. 192–206.

______. "The 'Pregnant Point': Goethe on Complexity, Interdisciplinarity, and Emergence." In: *Goethe, Chaos, and Complexity*. Ed. by Herbert Rowland. Amsterdam and New York: Rodopi, 2002. 17–31.

______. "Strategien der Schöpfung. Paradigmenwechsel der Kreativität in Natur und Kunst." *Paragrana. Internationale Zeitschrift für Historische Anthropologie* 4.2 (1995): 261–79.

McCauley, J. L. *Chaos, Dynamics and Fractals: An Algorithmic Approach to Deterministic Chaos*. New York: Cambridge University Press, 1991.

Mechsner, Franz. "Im Anfang war der Hyperzyklus." In *Geo-Wissen: Chaos +*

Kreativität. Ed. by Günter Haaf. Hamburg: Gruner and Jahr AG, 1990. 72–86.
Meyer, Theo. *Nietzsche und die Kunst.* Tübingen: Francke, 1993.
Miller, A. I. *Imagery in Scientific Thought: Creating 20th-Century Physics*. Boston: Birkhäuser, 1984.
Morfill, Gregor and Herbert Scheingraber. *Chaos ist überall ... und es funktioniert. Eine neue Weltsicht*. Frankfurt a.M.: Ullstein, 1991.
Medio, Alfredo. *Chaotic Dynamics: Theory and Application to Economics*. New York: Cambridge University Press, 1992.
Mesh-hadi, Nabil. *Die Einschätzung der Alchemie in Faust-Deutungen* . Frankfurt a.M.: Peter Lang, 1979.
Meyer, Hermann. *Diese sehr ernsten Scherze. Eine Studie zu Faust II*. Lothar Stiehm Verlag: Heidelberg, 1970.
Molnár, Géza von. "Hidden in Plain View: Another Look at Goethe's *Faust*." *Eighteenth-Century Studies* 35.3 (2002): 469–96.
Moore, Gregory. *Nietzsche, Biology and Metaphor*. Cambridge: Cambridge University Press, 2002.
Moses, Alastair. *Nietzsche's Philosophy of Nature and Cosmology*. New York: Peter Lang, 1990.
Müller-Sievers, Helmut. *Self-Generation: Biology, Philosophy, and Literature Around 1800*. Stanford, CA: Stanford University Press, 1997.
Munzel, G. Felicitas. *Kant's Conception of Moral Character: The 'Critical' Link of Morality, Anthropology and Reflective Judgment*. Chicago: University of Chicago Press, 1999.
Murray, Penelope (ed.). *Genius: The History of an Idea*. Oxford: Blackwell, 1989.
Nakamua, Katsuhiro. *Quantum Chaos: A New Paradigm of Nonlinear Dynamics*. New York: Cambridge University Press, 1992.
Nehamas, Alexander. *Nietzsche: Life as Literature*. Cambridge: Harvard University Press, 1985.
Neubauer, John. "Goethe and the Language of Science." Elinor S. Shaffer (ed.). *The Third Culture: Literature and Science*. Berlin and New York: Walter de Gruyter, 1998. 51–65.
Neubauer, Wolfgang. *Das tragische Prisma des Irrtums. Überlegungen zur Lösung des 'Hexen-Einmal-Eins' und zu Mephistos 'Vaterschaft' in Goethes 'Faust.'* Konstanz: Hartung-Gorre Verlag, 1986.
Volker Neuhaus, Günter Grass. *Die Blechtrommel. Interpretation*. Munich: R. Oldenbourg Verlag, 1982.
Newman, James R. (ed.). *The World of Mathematics*. New York: Simon and Schuster, 1956.
Noé-Rumberg, Dorothea-Michaela. *Naturgesetze als Dichtungsprinzipien. Goethes verborgene Poetik im Spiegel seiner Dichtungen*. Freiburg: Rombach Verlag 1993.

Oehler, Richard. *Nietzsche-Register*. Stuttgart: Alfred Kröner Verlag, 1965.

O'Neill, Patrick. "A Different Drummer: The American Reception of Günter Grass." *The Fortunes of German Writers in America: Studies in Literary Reception*. Ed. by Wolfgang Elfe, James Hardin, and Gunther Holst. Columbia SC: U of South Carolina P, 1992. 277–85.

Oppenheimer, Paul. *Evil and the Demonic: A new Theory of Monstrous Behavior*. New York: New York University Press, 1996.

Osten, Manfred. "Die evolutionäre Reise – Zur Modernität des Goetheschen Homunculus,." *Goethe-Jahrbuch* 120 (2003): 216–227.

Ott, Edward. *Chaos in Dynamical Systems*. Cambridge: Cambridge University Press, 1993.

Overbye, Dennis. "String Theory, at 20, Explains It All (or Not)." In *New York Times*, Tuesday, December 7, 2004. Section D: "Science Times." Pp. 1, 4.

"Papal Message." In: Robert Russell et al. (eds.), *John Paul II on Science and Religion: Reflections on the New View from Rome*. Vatican City: Vatican Observatory, 1990. M 1–14.

Partenheimer, Maren Beuck. "Die Tragweite Goethes in der Naturwissenschaft: Hermann von Helmholtz, Ernst Haeckel, Werner Heisenberg, Carl Friedrich von Weizsäcker." Diss. U of Utah 1987.

Paulys Realencyclopädie der klassischer Altertumswissenschaft. New edition by Georg Wissowa, Wilhelm Kroll and Karl Mittelhaus. Stuttgart: Alfred Druckenmüller Verlag, 1957. Vol. 21, Part 1, Cols. 939–40.

Peat, F. David. *The Blackwinged Night: Creativity in Nature and Mind*. Perseus Books, 2000.

______. *The Philosopher's Stone: Chaos, Synchronicity, and the Hidden Order of the World*. New York: Bantam Books, 1992.

______. *Seven Lessons of Chaos: Timeless Wisdom from the Science of Change*. New York: Harper Collins Publishers, Inc., 1999.

Peitgen, Heinz-Otto, Hartmut Jürgens, Dietmar Saupe (eds). *Bausteine des Chaos. Fraktale*. Berlin and Stuttgart: Springer-Verlag / Klett-Cotta, 1992.

Peitgen, Heinz-Otto and P. H. Richter. *The Beauty of Fractals*. Berlin: Springer-Verlag, 1982.

Penrose, Roger. *Shadows of the Mind: A Search for the Missing Science of Consciousness*. Oxford: Oxford University Press, 1994.

Pettey, John Carson. *Nietzsche's Philosophical and Narrative Styles*. New York: Peter Lang, 1992

Phillips, Dana. "Ecocriticism, Literary Theory, and the Truth of Ecology." *New Literary History* 30 (1999): 577–602.

Pleines, Jürgen-Eckhardt. "Das Dilemma der Ethik." *Philosophische Rundschau* 38 (1991): 48–82.

Plotnitsky, Arkady. *Complementarity: Anti-Epistemology After Bohr and Derrida*. Durham, NC: Duke University Press, 1994.

______. *In the Shadow of Hegel: Complementarity, History, and the Unconscious*. Gainesville: University Press of Florida, 1993.

______ and Barbara Herrnstein Smith. *Mathematics, Science, and Post-Classical Theory*. A Special Issue of *South Atlantic Quarterly* 94.2 (1995).

______. *Reconfigurations: Critical Theory and General Economy*. Gainesville: University Press of Florida, 1993.

Poincaré, Henri. *La Valeur de la Science*. Paris: Ernest Flammarion, 1905.

Polet, Jean-Claude. *Mythe de Création et Création Poétique*. Conférences et Travaux 6. Louvain-la-Neuve: Centre d'Histoire des Religions, 1984.

Popper, Karl R. *Objective Knowledge: An Evolutionary Approach*. Oxford: Clarendon Press, 1972.

______. *The Open Universe: An Argument for Indeterminism*. 2nd ed. Totowa NJ: Rowman and Littlefield, 1982.

Potter, Elizabeth F. "Synthesis and Consciousness." *Rice University Studies* 61.3 (Summer 1975): 59–66.

Prigogine, Ilya and Isabelle Stengers. *Order out of Chaos: Man's New Dialogue with Nature*. New York: Bantam Books, 1984.

The Problem of Evil: An Intercultural Exploration. Ed. by Sandra A. Wawrytko. Amsterdam and Atlanta: Rodopi, 2000.

Prokhoris, Sabine. *The Witch's Kitchen. Freud, Faust, and the Transference*. Trans. by G. M. Goshgarian. Ithaca and London: Cornell University Press, 1995.

"Proteurhythmos." In: *Paulys Realencyclopädie der klassischer Altertumswissenschaft*. New Edition by Georg Wissowa, Wilhelm Kroll, and Karl Mittelhaus. Stuttgart: Alfred Druckenmüller Verlag, 1957. Vol. 21, Part 1, Cols. 939–40.

Pütz, Peter. *Friedrich Nietzsche*. Stuttgart: Meztler, 1967.

______. "Nietzsche: Art and Intellectual Inquiry." *Nietzsche: Imagery and Thought*. Ed. by Malcolm Pasley. Berkeley: University of California Press, 1978. 1–32;

______. "The Problem of Force in Nietzsche and His Critics." In: *Nietzsche: Literature and Values*. Ed. by Volker Dürr, Reinhold Grimm, and Kathy Harms. *Monatshefte* Occasional Volumes No. 6. Madison: University of Wisconsin Press, 1988. 14–28.

Reahard, Julie A. *"Aus einem unbekannten Zentrum, zu einer nicht erkennbaren Grenze": Chaos Theory, Hermeneutics and Goethe's Die Wahlverwandtschaften*. Amsterdam and Atlanta: Rodopi, 1997.

Rennie, Nicholas. "Between Pascal and Mallarmé: Faust's Speculative Moment." *Comparative Literature* 52.4 (fall 2000): 269–90

Rescher, Nicholas. *G. W. Leibniz's Monadology. An Edition for Students*. Pittsburgh: U of Pittsburgh P, 1991.

Rickels, Laurence A. (ed.). *Looking After Nietzsche*. Albany: State University of New

York Press, 1990.

Ritter, Harry. "Science and the Imagination of Thought of Schiller and Marx." In: *The Quest for the New Science: Language and Thought in Eighteenth-Century Science*. Ed. by Karl J. Fink and James W. Marchand. Carbondale IL: Southern Illinois University Press, 1979. 28–40.

Roberts, David. "Aspects of Psychology and Mythology in *Die Blechtrommel*. A Study of the Symbolic Function of the 'Hero' Oskar." In: *Grass. Kritik Thesen Analysen*. Ed. by Manfred Jurgensen. Bern 1973.

Roche, Mark William. *Why Literature Matters in the 21st Century*. New Haven, CT: Yale University Press, 2004.

Rolston, Holmes, III. *Genes, Genesis, and God: Values and their Origins in Natural and Human History*. Cambridge: Cambridge University Press, 1999.

Ronell, Avital. "Namely, Eckermann." In: *Looking after Nietzsche*. Ed. by Laurence A. Rickels. Albany: State University of New York Press, 1990. 233–57.

Rosen, Stanley. *The Mask of Enlightenment: Nietzsche's Zarathustra*. New York: Cambridge University Press, 1995.

Rötzer, Florian. "Das Böse ist überall." *Süddeutsche Zeitung*, Nr. 107 (May 11, 1993), 11.

Rothenberg, Albert and Carl R. Hausman (eds.). *The Creativity Question*. Durham, NC: Duke University Press, 1976.

______. *The Emerging Goddess: The Creative Process in Art, Science, and other Fields*. Chicago: University of Chicago Press, 1979.

Rouse, Joseph. "Interpretation in Natural and Human Science." In: *The Interpretive Turn: Philosophy, Science, Culture.* Ed. David R. Hiley, James F. Bohman, and Richard Shusterman. Ithaca and London: Cornell University Press, 1991. 42–56

Rowland, Herbert (ed.). *Goethe, Chaos, and Complexity*. IFAVL 55. Amsterdam and New York, 2001.

Runco, Mark A. and Robert S. Albert. Eds. *Theories of Creativity*. Newbury Park CA: Sage Publications, 1990.

Russell, Jeffrey Burton. *The Prince of Darkness: Radical Evil and the Power of Good in History.* Ithaca, NY: Cornell University Press, 1988.

Sallis, John. *Spacings – Of Reason and Imagination in Texts of Kant, Fichte, Hegel*. Chicago: University of Chicago Press, 1987.

Salm, Peter. *The Poem as Plant: A Biological View of Goethe's Faust*. Cleveland and London: The Press of Case Western Reserve U, 1971.

Schieren, Jost. *Anschauende Urteilskraft. Methodische und philosophische Grundlagen von Goethes naturwissenschaftlichem Erkennen*. Düsseldorf and Bonn: Parerga Verlag, 1998.

Schmidt, Jochen *Goethes Faust. Grundlagen – Werk – Wirkung*. Munich 1999.

______. *Die Geschichte des Genie-Gedanken*. 2 Vols. Darmstadt: Wissenschaftliche

Buchgesellschaft, 1985.
Schmithals, Walter. "Die ethische Forderung." *Philosophische Rundschau* 38 (1991): 131–42.
Schneewind, J. B. *The Invention of Autonomy: A History of Modern Moral Philosophy*. Cambridge: Cambridge University Press, 1998.
Schneiders,Werner. *Deutsche Philosophie im 20. Jahrhundert*. Beck'sche Reihe 1259. Munich: C. H. Beck, 1998.
______. *Wieviel Philosophie braucht der Mensch? Eine Minimalphilosophie*. Munich: C. H. Beck, 2000.
Schnitzler, Günter and Gottfried Schramm (eds.). *Ein unteilbares Ganzes. Goethe: Kunst und Wissenschaft*. Freiburg i.B.: Rombach Verlag, 1997.
Schöne, Albrecht. *Fausts Himmelfahrt. Zur letzten Szene der Tragödie*. Munich: Carl Friedrich von Siemens Stiftung, 1994.
______. *Kommentare. Johann Wolfgang von Goethe – Faust*. 4. Auflage, Lizenzausgabe für die Wissenschaftliche Buchgesellschaft Darmstadt. Frankfurt a.M.: Deutscher Klassiker Verlag, 1999. [same as FA 7/2]
______. "... wie Teufel die Natur betrachten." *Goethe-Jahrbuch* 111 (1994): 141–50.
Schrift, Alan D. *Nietzsche and the Question of Interpretation: Between Hermeneutics and Deconstruction*. New York: Routledge, 1990.
Schrödinger, Erwin. *What is Life? The Physical Aspects of the Living Cell*. Cambridge: Cambridge University Press, 1944.
Schulz, Gerhard. "Chaos und Ordnung in Goethes Verständnis von Kunst und Geschichte." *Goethe-Jahrbuch* 110 (1993): 173–83.
Shusterman, Ronald. "Ravens and Writing-Desks: Sokal and the Two Cultures." *Philosophy and Literature* 22 (1998): 119–35.
Seamon, David and Arthur Zajonc (eds.). *Goethe's Way of Science: A Phenomenology of Nature*. Albany: State University of New York Press,1998.
Secker, Wilfried. *"Wiederholte Spiegelungen." Die klassische Kunstauffassung Goethes und Wilhelm von Humboldts*. Frankfurt a.M.: Peter Lang, 1985.
Seidlin, Oskar. "Das Etwas und das Nichts. Versuch einer Neuinterpretation"(1944). In: Werner Keller (ed.). *Aufsätze zu Goethes "Faust I."* 362–68.
Sens, Eberhard (ed.). *Am Fluß des Heraklit. Neue Kosmologische Perspektiven*. Frankfurt/M: Insel, 1993.
Seyhan, Azade. *Representation and its Discontents: The Critical Legacy of German Romanticism*. Berkeley: University of California Press, 1992.
Shaffer, Elinor S. (ed.). *The Third Culture: Literature and Science*. Berlin and New York: Walter de Gruyter, 1998.
Shapiro, Gary. *Nietzschean Narratives*. Bloomington and Indianapolis: Indiana University Press, 1989.
Shusterman, Richard. "Beneath Interpretation." *The Interpretive Turn: Philosophy,*

Science, Culture. Ed. by David R. Hiley, James F. Bohman, and Richard Shusterman. Ithaca, NY: Cornell University Press, 1991. 102–28.

Sloterdijk, Peter. *Kopernikanische Mobilmachung und ptolemäische Abrüstung*. Frankfurt a.M.: Suhrkamp, 1987.

Smith, Gudmund J. W. and Ingegerd M. Carlsson. *The Creative Process: A Functional Model Based on Empirical Studies from Early Childhood to Middle Age*. Madison CT: International Universities P, 1990.

Smoot, George and Keay Davidson. *Wrinkles in Time*. New York: William Morrow, 1993.

Stafford, Barbara Maria. "Revealing Technologies / Magical Domains." Barbara Maria Stafford and Frances Terpak. In: *Devices of Wonder From the World in a Box to Images on the Screen*. Catalogue of an Exhibition held at the J. Paul Getty Museum from Nov. 13, 2001 through Feb. 3, 2002. Los Angeles: Getty Research Institute, 2001.

Steer, A. G. "Goethe and Science." In: *Approaches to Teaching Goethe's Faust*. Ed. by Douglas J. McMillan. New York: The Modern Language Association of America, 1987. 55–65.

Steiner, George. "Life-Lines." In: *Extraterratorial: Papers on Literature and the Language Revolution*. New York: Atheneum, 1976. 172–96.

______. *Real Presences*. Chicago: University of Chicago Press, 1989.

Steiner, Jacob. "Die letzte Szene von Goethes *Faust*." *Études Germaniques* 38.1 (1983): 147–55.

Steiner, Rudolf. *Geisteswissenschaftliche Erläuterungen zu Goethes Faust.* Band I: *Faust der strebende Mensch*. Freiburg i. Br.: Novalis Verlag, 1955.

Steinmann, Martin. "A Half Century of Critical Torpor." *Philosophy and Literature* 17.2 (1993): 219–33.

Stewart, Ian. *Spielt Gott Roulette? Chaos in der Mathematik.* Trans. from the English by Gisela Menzel. Basel, Boston, Berlin: Birkhäuser, 1990.

Stewart, Ian. *Does God Play Dice? The Mathematics of Chaos*. Cambridge MA: Basil Blackwell, 1989.

Stolnitz, Jerome. "The Aesthetic Attitude." *The Philosophy of the Visual Arts*. Ed. by Philip Alperson. New York: Oxford University Press, 1992. 7–14.

______. *Aesthetics and the Philosophy of Art Criticism*. Boston: Houghton Mifflin, 1960.

Neiman, Susan. *Evil in Modern Thought: An Alternative History of Philosophy*. Princeton: Princeton University Press, 2004.

Talbot, Michael, *The Holographic Universe*. New York: Harper Collins Publishers, 1992.

Tank, Kurt Lothar."Der Blechtrommler schrieb Memoiren." In: Franz Josef Görtz (ed.). *Die Blechtrommel. Attraktion und Ärgernis* (1984). 39–42.

Tanner, Michael. "Nietzsche on Genius." In: *Genius: The History of an Idea*. Ed. by Penelope Murray. Oxford: Basil Blackwell, 1989. 128–40.

Tantillo, Astrida Orle. *The Will to Create: Goethe's Philosophy of Nature*. Pittsburgh: U of Pittsburgh P, 2002.

Taylor, Richard. *Good and Evil*. Amherst, NY: Prometheus Books, 1999.

Thomas, Owen (ed.). *God's Activity in the World: The Contemporary Problem*. Chico CA: Scholars, 1983.

______. "Recent Thoughts on Divine Agency." In: *Divine Action*. Ed. by Brian Hebblethwaite and Edward Henderson. Edinburgh: T. and T. Clark, 1991. 35–50.

Trousson, Raymond. *Thèmes et mythes: Questions de méthode*. Bruxelles: Éditions de l'Université de Bruxelles, 1981.

Tsonis, Anastasios A. *Chaos: From Theory to Applications*. New York, London: Plenum P, 1992.

Turnheim, Georg. *Chaos und Management. Denkanstoß und Methoden für das Management im Chaos*. 2., neu bearbeitete Auflage. Vienna: Manz, 1993.

Uvarov, E. B. and Alan Isaacs. *The Penguin Dictionary of Science*. 7th edition. New York: Penguin Books, 1993.

Ulfers, Friedrich and Mark Daniel Cohen. "Friedrich Nietzsche as a Bridge from 19th-Century Atomistic Science to Process Philosophy." West Virginia University Philological Papers (fall 2002).

van der Will, Wilfried. *Picaro Heute. Metamorphosen des Schelms bei Thomas Mann, Döblin, Brecht, Grass*. Stuttgart, 1969.

Vazsonyi, Nicolas. "Searching for 'The Order of Things.' Does Goethe's *Faust II* Suffer from the 'Fatal Conceit'?" *Monatshefte* 88 (1996): 83–94.

van Peer, Willie. "Sense and Nonsense of Chaos Theory in Literary Studies." In: *The Third Culture: Literature and Science*. Ed. by Elinor S. Shaffer. Berlin: Walter de Gruyter, 1998. 40–48.

Waite, Geoff. *Nietzsche's Corps'e: Aesthetics, Politics, Prophecy, or, The Spectacular Technoculture of Everyday Life*. Durham, NC: Duke University Press, 1996.

Waldrop, M. Mitchell. *Complexity: The Emerging Science at the Edge of Order and Chaos*. New York: Simon and Schuster, 1992.

Wallas, Graham. *The Art of Thought*. New York: Harcourt, Brace, and Co., 1926.

Walls, Laur Dassow. "The Anatomy of Truth: Emerson's Poetic Science." *Configurations* 5.3 (fall 1997): 425–61.

Ward, Brian. "The Literary Appropriation of Chaos Theory." Diss. The University of Western Australia. Nedlands, Western Australia, 1998.

Ward, Keith. *God, Chance and Necessity*. Oxford: Oneworld Publications, 1996.

Watson, Lyall. *Dark Nature: A Natural History of Evil*. New York: HarperCollins, 1995.

Weidhorn, Manfred. "Evil." In: *Dictionary of Literary Themes and Motifs A-J*. Ed. by

Jean-Charles Seigneuret. New York: Greenwood P, 1988.

Weingart, Peter and Sabine Maasen. "The Order of Meaning: The Career of Chaos as Metaphor." *Configurations* 5.3 (fall 1997): 463–520.

Weisstein, Ulrich. *Comparative Literature and Literary Theory: Survey and Introduction*. Bloomington IN: Indiana University Press, 1973.

Weizsäcker, Carl Friedrich von. *Die Einheit der Natur. Studien*. Munich: Hanser, 1971.

______. "Einige Begriffe aus Goethes Naturwissenschaft." In: Johann Wolfgang von Goethe. *Werke*. Hamburger Ausgabe. 14 Vols. 14th ed. Ed. by Erich Trunz. Munich: Deutscher Taschenbuch Verlag, 1989. 13:539–55.

Wheaton, Bruce R. *The Tiger and the Shark: Empirical Roots of Wave-Particle Dualism*. Cambridge: Cambridge University Press, 1983.

Wieland-Burston, Joanne. *Chaos and Order in the World of the Psyche*. London and New York: Routledge, 1992.

Wilson, Edward O. *Biophilia*. Cambridge MA: Harvard University Press, 1984.

______ and Stephen R. Kellert (eds.), *The Biophilia Hypothesis*. New York: Island Press / Shearwater Books, 1993.

______. *Consilience: The Unity of Knowledge*. New York: Alfred A. Knopf, 1998.

Witzenmann, Herbert. "Goethes Idee des Experiments und die moderne Naturwissenschaft." *Goethes universalästhetischer Impuls. Die Vereinigung der platonischen und aristotelischen Geistesströmung*. Dornach: G. Spicker, 1987. 45–69.

Woolf, Harry (ed.). *Science as a Cultural Force*. Baltimore: The Johns Hopkins University Press, 1964.

Wyder, Margrit. *Goethes Naturmodell. Die Scala Naturae und ihre Transformationen*. Weimar: Böhlau 1998.

Young, Julian. *Nietzsche's Philosophy of Art*. Cambridge: Cambridge University Press, 1992.

Zabka, Thomas. "Dialektik des Bösen. Warum es in Goethes 'Walpurgisnacht' keinen Satan gibt." *Deutsche Vierteljahresschrift für Literaturwissenschaft und Geistesgeschichte* 72.2 (1998): 201–226.

Zee, Anthony. *Magische Symmetrie*. Trans. from English. Frankfurt/M: Insel, 1993.

Zeller, Robert. *Astrologie und Zahlenmystik. Die arabischen Punkte im Horoskop*. Trans. from English. Munich: Hugendubel, 1989.

Zeitler, Herbert and Wolfgang Neidhardt. *Fraktale und Chaos. Ein Einführung*. 2nd ed. Darmstadt: Wissenschaftliche Buchgesellschaft, 1994.

Ziman, John M. *Prometheus Bound: Science in a Dynamic Steady State*. Cambridge: Cambridge University Press, 1994.

Zimmermann, Harro. "Das Licht der Melancholie. Günter Grass und die Aufklärung oder Ein deutsches Mißverständnis." In: Günter Grass and H. Zimmermann. *Vom Abenteuer der Aufklärung* (1999). 287–330.

Zimmermann, Volker. "'Den Menschenstoff gemächlich komponieren': Vom Homunkulus zur Gentechnik." *Faust. Annäherung an einen Mythos*. Hrsg. Von Frank Möbus, Friederike Schmidt-Möbus, Gerd Unverfehrt. Göttingen: Wallstein Verlag, 1995. 343–56.

Zoller, Robert. *Astrologie und Zahlenmystik. Die arabischen Punkte im Horoskop*. Trans. from English by Clemens Wilhelm. Munich: Hugendubel, 1989.

Index